MW01102024

O.D. SKELTON

A Portrait of Canadian Ambition

O.D. Skelton

A Portrait of Canadian Ambition

NORMAN HILLMER

UNIVERSITY OF TORONTO PRESS
Toronto Buffalo London

Library and Archives Canada Cataloguing in Publication

Hillmer, Norman, 1942–, author
O.D. Skelton : a portrait of Canadian ambition / Norman Hillmer.

Includes bibliographical references and index.
ISBN 978-0-8020-0534-2 (bound)

1. Skelton, Oscar D. (Oscar Douglas), 1878–1941.   2. Political consultants –
Canada – Biography.   3. Statesmen – Canada – Biography.   4. Canada – Officials
and employees – Biography.   5. Canada – Foreign relations – 1918–1945.
6. International relations – History – 20th century.   I. Title.

FC541.S54H55 2015   327.710092   C2015-900220-6

University of Toronto Press acknowledges the financial assistance to its
publishing program of the Canada Council for the Arts and the Ontario Arts
Council, an agency of the Government of Ontario.

   Canada Council   Conseil des Arts
        for the Arts   du Canada

University of Toronto Press acknowledges the financial support of the
Government of Canada through the Canada Book Fund for its publishing
activities.

This book has been published with the help of a grant from the Federation
for the Humanities and Social Sciences, through the Awards to Scholarly
Publications Program, using funds provided by the Social Sciences and
Humanities Research Council.

For the Hillmers and the Whitneys

Contents

Preface

For a long time, I thought that O.D. Skelton's life was less interesting than his ideas. I was wrong. He was fiercely patriotic, determined in his youth not to squander his birthright and yet he almost did just that, twice, seeking out a career in the Indian Civil Service and soon after signing an application for American citizenship. His ambition for a life out of the ordinary had tempted him away from his roots, as Canadian ambition has a habit of doing. Once settled on Canada, the intensely private man pushed himself into the public arena, first as an activist professor at Queen's University and then as the head of Canada's Department of External Affairs from 1925 to 1941. He was a vociferous critic of British imperialism, but not of the British Empire. He worried about how pressures from the world outside complicated the lives of Canadians and yet was anxious to promote international cooperation – he acted vigorously on both of these impulses. He admired the United States and sought to North Americanize Canadian policies, but had no doubt that his country's future belonged to it alone. He applauded Canada's contribution to the First World War, but became one of the government's great detractors by the conflict's end. He worked against Canada's participation in the Second World War, only to embrace it a year later. He was a principled public servant, but also a Liberal partisan who blurred the distinctions between his duty to the state and his allegiance to a political party.

Skelton was all of this and more, not a contradictory man, but driven, complex, and ambitious for his country and himself. The biographer's challenge is to explain a lifetime of shifts of mind and mood, without explaining them away.

I am grateful, for grants that facilitated my research, to the Social Sciences and Humanities Research Council of Canada, the Champlain Society, the Marston LaFrance Research Fellowship, and the Faculty of Arts and Social Sciences and the Centre for Security and Defence Studies at Carleton University. The Carleton Department of History, led most recently by Dominique Marshall and James Miller, is a model of how a university department should work. The book was completed at the School of Social Science, Institute for Advanced Study, in Princeton. I am indebted to Joan W. Scott and the Institute for their hospitality and the example of intellectual rigour that they set.

An army of supporters lent their expertise, found documents, advised me on what to say and how to say it, and gently (and sometimes not so gently) asked "How's Oscar coming along?" I thank Ryan Barker, Andrew Burtch, Kevin Caldwell, Janice Cavell, Adam Chapnick, Alexander Comber, Tim Cook, Terry Crowley, Grant Dawson, Colette Derworiz, Lisa Dillon, Greg Donaghy, Carter Elwood, David Farr, Malcolm Ferguson, John Glendinning, Trista Grant-Waddell, Charlotte Gray, Charles Gunning, John Hilliker, Stephen Hoogenraad, Phillip Hughes, William Johnston, William Kaplan, Jordan Kerr, Jon Keyes, Philippe Lagassé, Claude LeBlanc, Lorna Lloyd, Jennifer Macdonald, Daniel Macfarlane, Roy MacLaren, Michael Manulak, Andrei Marinescu, James Marsh, David McIntyre, Mark Moher, Erin Mooney, Richard Newport, Dean F. Oliver, Galen Perras, Vincent Rigby, Patricia Roy, Michael Ryan, Roger Sarty, Angelika Sauer, Ryan Shackleton, Craig Smillie, Andrew Sopko, Kevin Spooner, Boris Stipernitz, Gerald Tulchinsky, and Ian Wereley.

The entire manuscript was read by Stephen Azzi, David Banoub, Sandra Campbell, David Dilks, J.L. Granatstein, Duncan McDowall, H. Blair Neatby, and three anonymous reviewers. Each of them had a positive influence on the refinement of my ideas and my understanding of the subject. Jack Granatstein was at my side from the beginning to the end of the project: he is an extraordinary friend and colleague. Blair Neatby gave me a valuable collection of papers that he compiled as the official biographer of Mackenzie King. Theresa LeBane did research that contributed greatly to my analysis of Skelton's early years. At the University of Toronto Press, Len Husband put his vast experience, deft editorial touch, and abundance of common sense at my disposal. Curtis Fahey was the book's copy editor, an inadequate term for the imaginative work that he does for his authors. Megan Sproule-Jones meticulously prepared the index and Lisa Jemison sped the book to publication. This is also an opportunity to acknowledge all that I have learned from, and owe to,

Robert Bothwell, Ian M. Drummond, John English, Anne Trowell Hill-mer, J. Elliott MacGuigan, S.J., Nicholas Mansergh, and Charles P. Stacey.

Members of the Skelton and Menzies family were always available and encouraging, notably Arthur Menzies, Kenneth Menzies, Norah Menzies, Sheila Skelton Menzies, and Alexandra Skelton. Over the years, I also had the good fortune of getting to know Skelton by getting to know his contemporaries. I remember fondly Sir Harry Batterbee, Jean Chapdelaine, Lord Garner, James Gibson, H.L. Keenleyside, Malcolm MacDonald, Paul Martin Sr, L.B. Pearson, J.W. Pickersgill, Maurice Pope, Escott Reid, and Benjamin Rogers. There was, too, Charles Ritchie, the most delightful lunch partner anyone could have.

My research was done all over Canada and in Australia, England, France, Ireland, New Zealand, Russia, Scotland, and the United States. Archivists and librarians are historians' indispensable allies. Paul Banfield and the resourceful staff of the Queen's University Archives were particularly important to the writing of a book about a Queen's man. I also want to recognize Terry Cook, Paulette Dozois, Maureen Hoogenraad, Paul Marsden, Gabrielle Nishiguchi, and Glenn Wright. They contributed mightily to the reputation that Library and Archives Canada once had as the best national archives in the world. I hope that the new leadership at LAC will restore that lustre.

My life, and the life of this book, has been made brighter by the companionship and counsel of Suzanne Evans and Alan Cumyn, Kathy Giles and Hector Mackenzie, Deborah Gorham, Elizabeth Hay and Mark Fried, Marcia Pfotenhauer, and Barbara Uteck and Graham Fraser. Nor would there be a book at all without the skill and professionalism of Isaac Cristoveanu, Ronald Gerridzen, Susan Humphrey-Murto, Elizabeth Pringle, Thomas Shaw-Stiffel, and Susan Wilkinson.

I dedicate the book to my families – the Hillmers and the Whitneys. At the age of sixteen in 1922, my father began at Queen's University as a student of political science and economics, just as the Skelton era was winding down. He gave me my first glimpse of Dean Skelton – head down, purpose clear, rushing across the campus in beaten-up clothes and an ancient academic gown. My mother and father, Monica and George, were educators by profession and incomparable parents to my brother Robert, sister Jane, and me. Bob died at a too early age, but his immense heart and personality left an indelible impression on me and everyone around him. Jane lived a long and caring life as a nurse and mother. Their children – Beth, Judy, Robert, Suzanne, and Jennifer – have children of their own. I cherish them all. My son, Michael, his wife, Melinda, and their children, Sydney, Alexander, and Lauren, are the source of indescribable joy and pride. Susan Whitney, my wife and partner in all things, has given me a second family, and they in turn have given me a second home. To Nancy, Bill, Jim, Doug, and the rest of the Whitneys, I express my deep appreciation, and to Susan my unending love and my gratitude for all she has done for this book and for me.

I write this preface on the date of my mother's birth, looking out on Lake Huron from Southampton, my father's hometown, where our family inhabits multiple cottages (and now the old railway station) in the midst of over a century of memories.

NH
Southampton, Ontario
4 August 2014

O.D. SKELTON

A Portrait of Canadian Ambition

Introduction

He was quiet, at first glance easily overlooked. When, at the age of thirty, he took up the John A. Macdonald chair in political economy at Queen's University in 1908, contemporaries noted a conscious professorial restraint. He seemed a man apart – contained, solitary, abrupt even, not readily looking a person in the eye. He moved awkwardly and spoke hesitantly. His teaching was strong on content but faltering in delivery. As middle age approached, and he embarked on another career, his youthful clutch of sandy hair and his angular face began to disappear. His scrutinizing eyes were covered by ever thicker glasses. He slumped a little, in a self-deprecating way, making him seem shorter than his medium height. His uniform, even in the heat of summer, was a heavy tweed suit, often with a vest, accompanied by stiff white shirts, dark ties, and serviceable shoes. As Canada's deputy foreign minister, some thought Canada's deputy prime minister, he specialized in silent gestures, burying his increasing profile and content in the shadows, in fact preferring the shadows. He blended in with prosaic Ottawa, a sombre embryo of national government that had the look and smell of the lumber town from which it was emerging.[1]

Oscar Skelton's lack of ready charm was deceptive. He had a sharp wit followed by a shy smile. He enjoyed film, music, theatre, and dining out with good food and good company. He prospered in the classroom, enjoying his students and helping them to learn and progress. He was a good university politician who took on the hierarchies, rivalries, and intellectual rhythms of the academy – so much so that he was for years the person thought most likely to be the next principal of Queen's. One of the reasons he decided to go into government work was so that he could travel and meet people. He relaxed best in his own company

and joked that he was unfit for human consumption, but he was not the
loner that he was sometimes thought to be. He took getting to know, as
the men of his Department of External Affairs discovered when their
august boss turned out to have an affectionate and funny side.

Skelton was most comfortable when he wrote. In letters to his family and colleagues, he could best convey his emotions and enthusiasms.
He was a generous, sympathetic, eloquent correspondent. He cajoled
and flattered when it suited him, dispensing the compliments that move
careers forward. His fountain pen flashed across the page, often making
two or three words into one, his thoughts and ideas exploding. He composed his frequent books and articles that way, quickly and without inhi-
bition. One Queen's principal remembered that to listen to "his rather
hesitating speech" was to have "no idea of the singleness of his mind or
the rapidity with which he could get on to paper."[2]

On paper, alone at the small writing desks he kept at home and in the
office, engaging Canadians on the issues that were important to him
and, he thought, to them – he was in his element then. He wrote stylishly
in lucid prose, unencumbered by jargon, lightened by humour, memo-
rably full of robust turns of phrase. It was all the easier because he knew
what he thought and believed it. While he was a graduate student at the
University of Chicago, away from his wife Isabel, he wrote to her of his
"strong convictions on many subjects that are likely to excite controversy
in Canadian life." What appeared to him "most attractive in the future
is the chance of taking part in the discussions that are to mould Canada's future, to stand for a liberal progressiveness, against corporation or
Imperialist or sectarian interests."[3]

Isabel Skelton upbraided her husband for his presumption. He did
not yet have the professional rank or status to take on the world. "If one
waits till one has standing before expressing an unpopular opinion," he
replied, "God preserve me from the standing such a jellyfish would give.
Possibly one's life would be simpler & smoother if one kept quiet on all
controversial questions till one had a standing – by which time the habit
of acquiescence & cautious timeserving would be so ingrained as to be
a fetter impossible to break." He admitted that "I'm a queer mixture of
over confidence in my opinions & lack of confidence in myself."[4]

The young Skelton thought he could see signs of a better balance:
more humility about his opinions and more confidence in himself. He
succeeded with himself, but not with his opinions. His intellectual confidence – over-confidence is not too strong a word – remained intact
over a long career as a scholar and civil servant. He was always certain

that his way was the right way, and he could be stubborn, inflexible, and intolerant of what others said or thought. A surer sense of self overcame his social awkwardness, developing with time and determination, as he put his inhibitions aside and set out quite consciously to become a public man. He did so in pursuit of immense appetites and ambitions, wanting Canada to get ahead, and to get himself ahead at the same time.

Skelton took risks. As an activist professor, he was unafraid of the unpopular, never missing an opportunity to promote his causes on the public platform. Appointed to the civil service as an outspoken Liberal and a supporter of Mackenzie King, he quit his job at Queen's, brought his family to Ottawa, and bought a too-expensive house on the verge of an election that threatened to bring the Conservative Party to power and end his time in the capital city before it began. A cautious man would have been more cautious. In the Department of External Affairs, which he headed from 1925 to 1941, he advanced independent Canadian institutions and points of view that were ahead of his time, ahead of public opinion, and ahead of where his prime ministers wanted to go. He became the consummate government insider, the confidant of politicians of all stripes, and the undisputed master of the public service.

Knowing his limitations and wanting to shape as well as teach about politics and government, Skelton pursued his ideals and advanced his ideas through others. He became a practised courtier, sniffing out where power lurked and developing a knack for making himself useful. He was self-interested, but not cynical. He found nobility in those who thrust themselves into public life, absorbing the hard blows and looking optimistically beyond the mudslinging. Theodore Roosevelt, the early-twentieth-century United States president, captured the sentiment with his energetic declaration that it was not the critics who counted but those who placed themselves "in the arena," and so set lofty goals, gave their all for worthwhile causes, and knew the great enthusiasms of commitment. The speech struck a chord with Skelton, who often repeated its phrases to family, friends, and colleagues. "In the arena" defined what he admired and what he wanted for himself.[5]

Skelton chose his allies wisely. First it was Adam Shortt, a Queen's professor of political economy with a similar background, personality, and outlook on Canada and the world. Shortt made Skelton's academic career: he supported Skelton's application to the doctoral program at the University of Chicago and brought him back to Queen's as a fellow, and then a lecturer, and ultimately as Shortt's successor in the Macdonald chair. Their relationship was facilitated by Skelton's chatty letters from the United States seeking advice and energetically exploring their mutual interests. Skelton became a younger version of his professor, connecting scholarly expertise to the formulation of public policy in a way common to transatlantic progressive thinking at the time. As students of political and economic affairs, of the questions that the two scholars thought were most crucial to a young country coming of age, they saw themselves as part of the "select, active minority" that would fashion Canadian life and opinion. Their lecturing and writing was designed not just to advance academic knowledge but, more important, to make a difference in the working out of the people's business. That logic led them to take a direct role in government.[6]

After Adam Shortt came Sir Wilfrid Laurier and Mackenzie King. Skelton attached himself to them, as he had attached himself to Shortt. Skelton had been a Laurier Liberal since he could remember. He worked for the Laurier government and for King, its labour minister, in 1910 and during the election campaign of 1911. That election ended the fifteen-year Liberal grip on power and put Laurier in the mood for a sympathetic biographer. Enter Skelton, working on a small book of Canadian history centring on the Laurier years. Skelton interviewed Laurier as part of the research for the project and they got along: within a year Skelton had been named the former prime minister's official biographer. He revered Laurier, but when the old man died in 1919, making way for Mackenzie King to become the Liberal leader, Skelton immediately began to manufacture a role for himself in the coming government of his new chief. He offered King advice, compliments, and encouragement, while King opened up an avenue to big events.

From Queen's and the Macdonald chair, Skelton had marked himself out as someone to be noticed. His first book, *Socialism: A Critical Analysis*, published in the United States in 1911, was widely read and praised. Vladimir Lenin, the Russian revolutionary, wrote Skelton to say that his indictment of socialism was the finest ever mounted by a scholar from the bourgeois camp. The story of that letter got around, probably because Skelton got it around. He had credibility because he also took on the excesses of capitalism, arguing for its reform and regulation and drawing attention to conditions of poverty and economic injustice. At the same time, he vigorously promoted clean government and a modernized civil service. Implicitly in his academic work and explicitly in his frequent commentaries on public affairs, he aimed at a better and fairer country for all Canadians.

   The First World War had a dramatic impact on Skelton and his reputation. At the outset of the war, convinced that "honor and freedom and
democracy" were in the balance, he supported the British Empire and
subscribed to an all-out national effort to defeat the enemy. Though he
was sympathetic to the scepticism that francophone Quebecers developed towards the war, he worried that they were a people in isolation,
"merely Canadien," when they ought to embrace the whole country. But,
as English Canada bore down on French Quebec, demanding that it participate more fully in the war, Skelton's position changed. He thought
now what he might have been expected to think in the beginning, that
Canada had entered the war for the wrong reason – because of the
"racial sympathy with England" that he had always deprecated. His stand
alongside Wilfrid Laurier against compulsory military service was deeply
unpopular. Skelton's father all but called him a traitor. Some wealthy
and therefore influential Queen's alumni plotted to have him fired. He
angrily fought back and survived.[7]
   After the Laurier biography was published in 1922, the memories of
conscription were rekindled. The heat was sufficient that Skelton took
refuge in a contract for a book of British political science. He was not,
however, prepared to step away from debating the great international
and domestic issues that beset Canada. He regretted that he had not
gone into politics or journalism, where he could have made more of a
difference, and told his detractors at Queen's that the wartime conscription controversy had made him all the more determined to speak out
about where Canada was going and where it ought to go.
   The conscription furore was a reminder of Skelton's contentious ideas
about the British Empire. He was a campaigner for what he called "out
and out independence" and the ending of virtually every tie with Great
Britain. As he knew well, however, Canadians preferred what they had,
a combination of the imperial and the self-governing. "Autonomy" was
the popular description for the contradictory national condition, part
free and part not: it was used to suggest various degrees (depending on
the circumstances, the speaker, and the partisan tilt) of breathing room,
while the country remained all the while tucked warmly inside the British womb. The autonomy gambit had all the elasticity in the world, and
it carried none of the political hazard of a declaration of independence.
That was how the disloyal Americans had begun their revolution against
Britain. Canadians were different. They knew instinctively that independence was not right for them – not yet, perhaps never.[8]

On the delicate matter of independence, Skelton was more careful than he was on other issues, but what he had to say was seen as bad enough. He plumped for an empire that would remain an empire while transforming itself into an association of equal states, each with its own foreign policies and security institutions. Canada's imperially minded saw through the tactic. The journalist Sir John Willison put Skelton on the short list of the country's most dangerous men, intent on taking Britain and the empire away from Canadians. "He had a strong and lasting suspicion of British policy and an unchanging coldness towards Great Britain," added Vincent Massey, a long-time colleague and adversary. "In other words, to put it bluntly, but I feel not unfairly, he was anti-British."[9]

Such contemporary views of Skelton were understandable. He had gone off to London as a young man to try out for the Indian Civil Service (ICS) and returned empty-handed. Did that not explain his animus towards the British and their empire? Like Mackenzie King, he had lived, worked, and studied in the United States, further grounds for suspicion. He and his Department of External Affairs presided over a time when Canadians questioned their connection to the old empire. There were many stories, told by close observers like Vincent Massey, of the hard face that Skelton turned against the British.

The charges that Skelton was anti-empire and anti-British became the orthodoxy. Soon after his death, scholars went on the attack. The historian J.M.S. Careless wrote derisively that Skelton had fought to snatch "pure young Canada" from the clutches of a British lion that was fearsome no longer, having "become rather a straw-stuffed beast." Donald Creighton of the University of Toronto fulminated against the "simple-minded" Liberal nationalist doctrine of Skelton and his friends, which had been used as a club against a proud empire that had sustained Canada in fact and in spirit. Canadians, said Creighton, had possessed a recognized position and considerable authority in the British imperial system. By the time that Skelton and Mackenzie King were finished, almost all that was left was the empire of the United States, where Canada was a bit player, with no influence or standing. Similar interpretations have persisted, usually (but not always) without the sarcasm. In 2013, when Canada's British heritage was again being celebrated in some Canadian circles, an essay about Skelton in a conservative journal was titled "Mackenzie King's Anglophobe-in-Chief."[10]

Skelton was very suspicious of the power of British and Canadian imperialists to sway opinion and certainly anxious that Canada stand on its own at home and abroad. Yet he praised the British Empire as "the

most extraordinary political organization of this or any other time." It
was true, he acknowledged, that a great part of the empire had been won
by force and was held by force, not by free will or affection. The record
of imperial rule was full of bad motives and serious missteps. Colonial
grievances had a justified fire and focus. But, writing after the First World
War that he said had justified it and demonstrated its worth, Skelton
declared that the empire had brought peace and harmony to one-fourth
of the world and served as a model for institutions such as the League
of Nations. In the two great imperial dependencies, Egypt and India,
Britain had "much to its credit, in law and order established, justice rendered, material prosperity assured." At the heart of the empire, he maintained, British policy in Ireland was the most flawed and misguided. But
even there, the responsibility lay with one slice of opinion among people
who had been unwilling to unfasten their hold on the nearby island; on
the other side of the debate was a much larger number willing to be flexible in the granting of some form of self-government, "a section larger
than would have been found in almost any other country under similar
conditions." The British had passed on to Canada a responsible political culture, more responsible than what could be found in the United
States. They were "good compatriots," with "a repute for fair play, for
devotion to liberty, and for ordered progress that any country may well
seek to share."[11]

Skelton had a particular enthusiasm for Ireland, the homeland of
his ancestors, who were Protestants from Ulster in the northeast of the
island. His father and grandfather were members of the Orange Order,
fervently dedicated to Britain and the Protestant cause in Ireland and
implacably opposed to the Catholic Church. Oscar Skelton dramatically
went the other way, supporting an independent and unified Ireland
where Catholics would be in the majority. The argument he made for
Ireland was similar to the one that he set out for Canada. Ireland, in fact,
met the qualifications for an autonomous existence even more than Canada. By all the measures – of history, ethnicity, economic self-sufficiency,
geographical unity and distinctiveness, and consciousness of difference –
the whole of Ireland, the Protestant north as well as the Catholic south,
was entitled to form a national unit. The British resisted at their peril.
They risked their reputation for sympathy with causes of liberty, distraction from their adversaries in Europe, and a contagion of discontent in
the other "non-free" parts of the empire. They were damaging the good
relations between the empire and the United States, on which the peace
of the world greatly depended, since there were millions of people of

Irish descent living in the United States whose sympathies were with Ireland's aspirations. It was too soon, Skelton reasoned, for complete Irish independence. The solution was a wide freedom of manoeuvre under a common monarch, precisely the relationship that Canada was hammering out within the British Empire.

At the end of 1921, he received a public letter from P.C. Macnee, an Ontario lawyer and Queen's graduate, questioning Skelton's remarks in the *Queen's Quarterly* about Ireland's grievances and his claim that the only appropriate response was a granting of "full and free equality." Exactly what were those grievances, Macnee asked, and why was it that they were not shared by Scotland and Wales? Skelton replied that Ireland was a more distinct entity, separated from England by a gulf of geography, religion, and social difference. It had been atrociously misgoverned in earlier days, encouraging a vigorous Irish nationality that confronted the empire and demanded change. That had come, to the credit of the British, but "good government can never take the place of self-government."

The advances that London was prepared to make were never going to be enough to satisfy the Irish temper. A moderate regime of home rule would have done the trick in the 1890s; more self-government would have sufficed in 1914. The First World War, and the Allies' rhetoric that they were fighting for the smaller peoples, raised the stakes higher. The bitter Anglo-Irish armed conflict ended, Skelton thought, the only way it could, in the peace settlement that brought the Irish Free State into being. Skelton was bitterly disappointed that the new Ireland did not include Ulster, where his grandfathers had been born. He concluded his reply to Macnee, published in a small Ontario newspaper, with (for him) an extraordinarily personal statement: "I write as a Canadian of three generations standing, every drop of whose blood is Ulster and Protestant, and I may say 90 per cent Orange. That has, however, not prevented me from coming to sympathize very strongly with the Irish demand for self-government." Once he had the chance, Skelton forged a strong bond with Irish leaders and worked, often conspiratorially, with them at imperial meetings to loosen remaining imperial ties.[12]

Skelton's Irish sensibility helped to explain the burning resentment that he felt when outsiders told Canadians their business. That was a common enough feeling among Canadian nationalists, who distinguished between a worthwhile British Empire and the imperialists who distorted its meaning, and between sturdy British folk and English elites, with their titles, Oxbridge accents, and certainty that they knew what was best. It was made worse because there were imperialist Canadians, apparently willing to subordinate their own country to Mother Britain. Skelton shared his fears and insecurities with Mackenzie King, as they shared so much, but where they differed was fundamental. Skelton favoured "ultimate independence." He put that to King only once directly and retreated when he met violent opposition, realizing that it was best to work stealthily for his ends. King saw Canada as a proud "Britain of the West." Skelton did not wish his country to be an echo of anyone else's country.[13]

Skelton's anti-imperialism was not extreme, at least not until near the end of his life, when he was very ill and certain that his ambitions for a Canada independent of the British Empire were doomed. A careful follower of the comings and goings of the politics of Great Britain, he took inspiration from the apostle of transatlantic liberalism and four-time British prime minister, William Ewart Gladstone, who in an early speech set out his political vision – "The equality of the weak with the strong; the principles of brotherhood among nations, and of their sacred independence." In the foreign as in the domestic, Gladstone taught and Skelton believed, the lust to dominate was evil. Self-government had to supplant imperial rule, and international cooperation must take the place of arrogant national pride and the denial of freedom. Laurier, King, and U.S. President Woodrow Wilson, a Skelton favourite, were all convinced anti-imperialists and devoted Gladstonians.[14]

C.P. Stacey, the eminent international historian, maintained that Skelton wanted to replace British influences in his country with those from the United States. It is a natural enough argument, and the literature of Canadian-American relations frequently identifies Skelton as having taken the "American" viewpoint in his thought and action. This is true to the extent that he believed that strengthened ties with the United States and the development of a North American way of thinking in Canada could offset the sometimes suffocating British connection. Skelton, however, rejected the idea that Canada must be American if it could not or would not be British. When asked to consider whether Canada's future belonged with the United Kingdom or the United States, he wondered why it did not occur to more people that "the future of Canada might perhaps lie with Canada." He knew the United States well, and admired its optimistic and entrepreneurial instincts, but he was a critic of America's runaway capitalism, readily corruptible politicians, too-powerful courts, and habit of indulging in wild swings of rhetoric and emotion. He celebrated Canada's British system of government and the balance that it achieved between the executive and Parliament. Canadians moved more slowly but also more responsibly. They needed to work closely with Americans, "but we do not think it necessary to sacrifice our nationhood to do so."[15]

Skelton was among the first Canadian intellectuals to have developed an expertise in international affairs. By early in the 1920s, he realized that an independent foreign policy based on strictly national interests was the arena in which he could make his greatest contribution. It had become, he told himself, "my chief interest, almost my religion." On that issue alone he was an original, with a "distinctive viewpoint" and the capacity and responsibility to give "advice to my countrymen." Six weeks after Mackenzie King became prime minister in late 1921, Skelton delivered an address to the Ottawa branch of the Canadian Club in which he exposed, and exaggerated, the threat posed to the country's fragile autonomy by the British Empire and its powerful agents. His thoughts about the urgent need for a separate and distinct Canadian international policy had been developing for a long time. They also happened to be the thoughts of the prime minister, who was in the audience. Judging him after the talk to be just the right man with just the right point of view, King began to think of Skelton as the next permanent head of the Department of External Affairs. That, surely, was the professor's intention. Years later, Isabel Skelton wrote in her scrapbook that it was the Canada Club speech "which really brought Oscar to Ottawa." Years earlier, when External Affairs was being created by Wilfrid Laurier, Skelton had told Adam Shortt that the post of under-secretary in the department promised to be "a mighty desirable billet for somebody."[16]

King invited Skelton to accompany him to the Imperial Conference of 1923, where the "expert adviser" seized much more than his advertised role. Skelton vigorously prepared the Canadian case and entered the London meetings brimming with the confidence – much more than the prime minister was feeling – of a man who knew exactly what he thought and wanted to accomplish. He saw imperial conferences as international poker games and acted on that premise, negotiating with the toughness of a riverboat gambler. A British colleague, the influential Sir Maurice Hankey, appealed to him to compromise. Skelton replied that he had no intention of doing so. When the conference was all but over, he reported home to Isabel, exhausted but exultant and bursting with self-importance. "I have at times been about as popular with the Imperialists here as a skunk at a tea party: I am quite sure they would have been ready to pay a good many thousand pounds if I had been at home." He had never been more fulfilled. "O.D. feels a missionary call," his wife wrote in her diary, hoping that he would not listen to King's increasingly loud offers of employment in Ottawa.[17]

There was a great deal of saying no at the Imperial Conference of 1923, and there can be no doubt that resistance to British designs, real and apparent, was a large measure of Skelton's international strategy. First the negative, he would have said, and then the positive. The top priority had to be given to escaping from the trap of British imperialism and European militarism. The strengthening of the Department of External Affairs and the establishment of an independent diplomatic presence in the world were means to that end. So too was the distancing of Canada from the Old World through the building up of strong links with the United States. Once independent, Canada could take on heavier international burdens. Skelton granted that, in the years between the two world wars, many Canadians were in a mood to isolate themselves from the world, but that was understandable while the country grew and matured. He saw the Canadian-American relationship, the League of Nations, and the British Commonwealth that was growing out of the British Empire as beginnings in the establishment of a new international order marked by peaceful collaboration, with Canada taking a modest but committed place in the society of nations.

Knitting together all of Skelton's convictions was an ardent Canadian nationalism. Chest-thumping, crude self-flattery, a complacent contentment with material progress, a barren prejudice against other countries or races – they were all easy. Much harder was to ensure that the Canadian spirit had a positive content, so that a way of life and achievement in civilization could be developed that was not an imitation of New York or London. Canada, he believed, had been given trusteeship of a half-continent of the world's geography, the last frontier of human experience. Its citizens had a responsibility to seize "the great aim of welding our country into one" and to carve out a distinctive contribution to "the common pool of mankind's experiment in the art of living."[18] Canadians had to know that their future would be better than their colonial past, and that their destiny was for them alone to decide.

1
Going Away and Coming Home, 1878–1908

In June 1901 Oscar Skelton travelled to England to write the examinations for the Indian Civil Service. He had to hurry. He was about to turn twenty-three, the age limit for ICS candidates. A brief time in Oxford followed, which perhaps involved employing one of the crammers who prepared young men for the gruelling test to come and perhaps finding short-term employment of his own – perhaps both. And then to London, where the exams took up almost all of a dry and sunny English August. From a wide variety of possibilities, Skelton chose to write the papers that tested his knowledge of Greek, Latin, and German language and literature, Roman, Greek, English, modern, and economic history, and political economy and political science. He excelled only in English composition and political science; in each of the other subjects, even the classical languages that had been his majors at university, he struggled. The examinations were exacting. Almost all of his rivals struggled as well.[1]

The ICS was a risk taker's first big risk. The odds were steep against him. Three-quarters of the candidates came from Oxford and Cambridge, great universities that helped plan the rigorous ICS process and trained their students accordingly. Almost none of the applicants, five or fewer, were from outside Great Britain. Skelton was admittedly at loose ends. He had found post-graduate work in the classics at the University of Chicago unsatisfying, and his university romance with Isabel Murphy, which had been felt more on his side than on hers, had not ended in marriage as he wished. But if the ICS was an escape, it was on a breathtaking scale. He had next to no money and no one to champion his cause – and no Canadian, it was said, had ever passed the ICS examinations. Yet, when the results were posted, Skelton was among the successful ICS applicants. He ranked just 55th of the 57 who made the grade, but he was on the final list when so many were not.[2]

"There is no Service like it in the world" – so Lord Dufferin, a Canadian governor general of the 1870s and a viceroy of India of the 1880s – described the ICS and its men. "For ingenuity, courage, right judgement, disinterested devotion to duty, endurance, open-heartedness, and, at the same time, loyalty to one another and their chiefs, they are, to my knowledge, superior to any other class of Englishmen. They are absolutely free from any taint of venality or corruption." This was too much praise, but it caught the romantic view of the ICS that was in the ether as Skelton grew up. He read a lot of Rudyard Kipling, whose popularity was at its height when Oscar was in his teens. What he took from the celebrated author's stories of the British Empire in India were lessons of manliness, adventure, and a world larger than anything Canada had to offer. Kipling highlighted the virtues that Dufferin praised. Daydreaming in one of his Ontario schoolrooms, Skelton might have conjured up a Kiplingesque vision of "the typical young district officer in the I.C.S., dispensing justice and upholding the majesty of his Queen, perhaps sitting on a camp chair in the open air in front of a collapsible desk."[3]

During the summer after his graduation from Queen's, Skelton gobbled up Kipling. After reading *Soldiers Three*, he recorded in his writing book that "Terrence is a strong bighearted wild Irishman, with a weakness for wine and women, but clearheaded & true-hearted ingenious in device & daring in action." Kipling had seized the truth. There was more morality in this swearing and drinking soldier "than in a dozen mealy mouthed fair faced hypocrites who have none of his vices but none of his manly virtues." Skelton liked the pace, the simplicity, and, most of all, the exhilaration of Kipling's imaginative world. But he had more depth and intelligence than to view India solely through a lens that he knew to be "fantastical," or to describe it, from the perspective of Kipling's Miss Agnes Laiter, as "divided equally between jungle, tigers, cobras, cholera, and sepoys." He understood the hardships the Indian people were facing and gave a dollar – a lot of money on his tightly managed budget – to a famine-relief fund in early 1900.[4]

The examinations conquered, the next steps on the ICS ladder were a medical test, studies in Indian law, history, and language, an exercise to demonstrate that he could ride a horse, and one year of probation. These were straightforward enough, or so it appeared, but Skelton was concealing something. He was suffering from a recurrent hernia in his groin that he knew would require attention before he undertook the strenuous work of an ICS officer. H.H. DePew, his Chicago doctor, had advised Skelton to undergo an operation to correct the condition, with an estimate of one month's recovery time. Why he had gone this far in the process without addressing the problem is a mystery, but it may have been nothing more than a sunny optimism that something good was bound to turn up, a characteristic he inherited from his always buoyant father. But nothing had turned up, and the difficulty of finding a London surgeon to correct the problem and the expense of the operation now apparently were insurmountable obstacles. Without even taking the medical examination, Skelton withdrew his name from further consideration for the ICS and the other civil-service positions for which he had qualified. Offered a job in the British War Office nevertheless, he refused that as well. It was only India that interested him, although it is doubtful that he would have found there what he thought Kipling promised. He returned home immediately.[5]

The Skelton family would have been pleased, and perhaps quite surprised, by their young man's voyage to London. They were Northern Irish Protestants and staunchly imperial. Oscar's father, Jeremiah, was a vigorous supporter of the Conservative Party, whose pro-Empire sentiments may not have been as strong as his but certainly were stronger, in his eyes, than those of the governing Liberals. Oscar attended meetings of the Orangeville young Conservatives at the end of high school, where it was the liveliness of the debates that seems to have attracted him.[6] He was soon striking out on a path distinctly different from that of his father: separating Canadian from imperial patriotism, scolding the empire, and latching on to the Liberal Party. He was doing all of that when he made his application to the ICS. Kipling was part of the explanation, but so too was an ambition that turn-of-the-twentieth-century Ontario could not accommodate.

Jeremiah Skelton was restless and entrepreneurial and never a complete success in business. He met Elizabeth Jane Hall when they were both teaching primary school in Caledon, Ontario, near the prosperous Hall farm and not far from Toronto. They were married in 1873. Four years later, Jeremiah (Jerry, as he was known) moved his family to nearby Orangeville, joining his brother in the partnership of a dry-goods store: advertisements for "Skelton Bros" became a fixture in the Orangeville *Sun*. In 1883 Jerry began commuting the short distance by train to Shelburne to manage a second store, soon moving his family and home there. A fire destroyed the Shelburne enterprise in 1888. He rebounded with "Skelton & Co.," but that venture was bankrupt within a matter of months. Jerry went back to teaching, briefly in Pembroke in eastern Ontario, and in 1890 he took a public school principal's job in Tilbury Centre, a small town of less than two hundred families, a third of whom were French-speaking and Catholic. After two years, he moved to a teacher position in Cornwall, a mill town on the St Lawrence River, larger than the places they had lived earlier but, like Tilbury, with a mixed population and many francophones. He stayed there for more than a decade before his appointment in 1904 as secretary-treasurer and accountant at the Cornwall Paper Manufacturing Company in close-by Mille Roches. Sometime between 1906 and 1908, he opened the Maple Leaf Cash Grocery in Toronto, another short-lived project. He became a sales representative for the Hoover Vacuum Company in 1910 and later the Toronto district manager. He worked into his seventies.[7]

Wherever Jeremiah Skelton found himself, he took a lively part in civic, religious, and political affairs. In Shelburne, he was variously a town councillor, secretary of the Board of Trade, critic for the Literary Institute, vice-president of the Conservative Association, choir leader at Knox Presbyterian Church, and trustee of the school board and instrumental in the establishment of the local high school. In Cornwall it was the Loyal Orange Lodge, the Ancient Order of United Workmen, the Cornwall Public Library, and the Stormont Teachers' Association, which he served as president. Jerry was outgoing, well liked, respected, and wore the British Empire on his sleeve. He expounded a combination of imperial and Anglo-Canadian patriotism in the classroom and to his colleagues, and his Empire Day displays drew favourable notice. In January 1900, "in his usual excellent style" said the Cornwall *Freeholder*, he recited a Kipling poem, "The Absent Minded Beggar," to an Order of Workmen meeting that raised $11 for the family of a Cornwall boy who was leaving to fight in the South African War.[8]

The second of four Skelton children and the only boy, Oscar was born in Orangeville on 13 July 1878. The family, extending to the grandparents who lived nearby and were visited often, was loving and closely knit, the more so because Jeremiah was constantly on the move. By the time Oscar was thirteen, his father had relocated three times and they had lived in four different southern Ontario centres. Oscar remembered himself as a youngster who hung back, but he made an impression as a strong student and "a social companion and a ready helper" in the Shelburne primary school that he attended from the age of six. When Jeremiah announced that he was taking the family to Tilbury Centre, Oscar's Shelburne classmates gave eleven-year-old "Kitty" (as he was affectionately

but inexplicably nicknamed) a going-away present of a writing desk that
he kept all his life, along with a testimonial from the school expressing
the hope that he would "be spared many years to follow that career of
usefulness for which your ... talents and youthful inclinations promise
so brightly." That was the moral path that the Skelton-Halls – Oscar's
Irish-born grandparents on both sides and his Canadian-born parents –
carved out for themselves and that Jeremiah taught and lived. When his
son went into the Department of External Affairs in the mid-1920s, Jeremiah congratulated him in exactly those terms, saying that the position
would "open up a great field of usefulness."[9]

Although aware enough of his academic ability to send him away to
Orangeville to attend its well-regarded high school, Jeremiah had given
little thought to university for Oscar until the family learned that one
of his classmates had been admitted to the University of Toronto. Oscar
wrote the entrance exams for Toronto and Queen's in 1896 and won
scholarships for both. The money offered by Toronto was better, but
Kingston and Queen's were closer to home in Cornwall and the university specialized in students from eastern Ontario. He arrived at Queen's
at the age of eighteen. He had nothing to put down under "Intended
Profession" when he filled out the University Register, but he was from
the start a disciplined ("When your work lacks system, little can be done")
and industrious student with a gift for clear and decisive thought. Latin
and English were his major subjects. He graduated three years later with
first-class honours in both and the university medal in Latin. After brief
work as a teacher at the Cornwall Commercial College and three months
as a purser on a steamship that plied the St Lawrence and upper Great
Lakes, Oscar returned to Queen's for the academic year of 1899–1900 to
follow up on his studies in Greek and carried off the university medal as
well as another prize in that subject.[10]

In the summer of 1898 Oscar had travelled with a friend to Europe and
begun two journals. One was a critical analysis and sophisticated summary of his reading; the other was a personal diary, composed entirely
in Latin for several months to prepare him for his final Latin examination, and turning into English for notes on his busy social life, on the
world outside Canada, and on a carefully regimented existence that he
complained was not nearly systematic enough. The writing book was
an exercise in self-improvement: even the light fiction of Mark Twain,
Kipling, and W.A. Fraser's *The Eye of a God and Other Tales of East and West*
was taken seriously. Skelton's selection of books ranged into *The Ana-
lects of Confucius*, *Fabian Essays in Socialism*, and *Primitive Man* by Edward

Clodd, "a brief but comprehensive outline of what the new science of anthropology has revealed of our early ancestors, from pre-human days till the dawn of our present civilization. It is written from the correct standpoint – Clodd's religious sentiments are orthodox (= my doxy) – and give a good bird's eye view of our origin."[11]

Oscar's remarks about Clodd hinted that he was rejecting his family's religion – indeed, all religion. He attended church services, and gave to the collection plate, but he did so to please his parents and particularly for his mother. He wrote of a morning in June 1899 that "I played the hypocrite by going to the preparatory services in St. John's. Mr. Mastie preached an orthodox old-fashioned sermon on Heaven, full of far fetched allegories and wonderful interpretations. The utter rot of it made me feel like getting up and honestly leaving, but regard for mother's feelings restrained me. – Is the hypocrisy justified?" He openly discussed his secular views with the deeply religious Jeremiah. At his request, Oscar read "the work of a Christian Socialist who tries to deduce socialism from the Bible and seems to think that once thus deduced it must forthwith be accepted. He tries to make out that Christianity will produce Socialism and further that it is the only force that can. I gave a good many anti-religious arguments against it, and spoke out freely on the value of the ethical as opposed to the dogmatic element in religion." Commenting on some family friends who had not complimented him on his academic success, Oscar concluded that it was not jealousy: "The real reason I have no doubt is their pious horror at my shocking (ir-) religious principles."[12]

Skelton liked to go against the current. In February 1899, at the Queen's Political Science and Debating Club, he argued the case against Imperial Federation, the idea that Canada and the other self-governing colonies of the empire ought to come together in a new and close cooperative arrangement. It was a popular cause at Queen's, but he and his partner won the debate. Convocation week that year, when Oscar was the valedictorian and was given the university medal in Latin, demonstrated that his performance at the Debating Club was not play-acting. He refused to remove his hat when "God Save the Queen" was sung. "I like a fool or otherwise kept on my hat while all the others took theirs off. Can't they sing The Maple Leaf or anything but God Save the Queen!" About the Canadian-American boundary dispute over the Alaska-British Columbia border that was in the news, he sniffed that the "blooming Yankees are waxing even more impudent every day." The mendacious American press campaign was "evidently meant as the first step in a commercial war, by which they hope to coerce Canada and get our lumber and fisheries and canals and nickel and everything else free." Its result was "to make Canadians more and more patriotic and more Anti-American."[13]

Skelton joined clubs and societies, took part in debates, and attended sporting events and dances. His diary talked a good deal about friendships, which he cultivated and valued. With much self-consciousness, it recorded dates and near-dates with young women, along with his ratings of them, with 6½ mysteriously the maximum score. When Ida MacDougall let him know that she would dance "if the right people asked her," Oscar stepped back: "My Kingdom then for an educated foot, but alack the chance had to go unimproved." He had a passing romance with someone he identified only as Edna. They parted awkwardly. She attempted to keep up the friendship, sending a gift here and a parcel there. Oscar debated the repercussions of writing back to her. On the one side there was good manners, on the other was the possibility that Edna would think him more interested than he was. "Safety or Courtesy, which?" He chose safety. Ida and Edna had a way to go before they approached 6½.[14]

Oscar had already found his ideal – Isabel Murphy, who shared his Irish roots and was a triple threat: "modest unaffected winsome." In his diary, he sometimes wrote as if he was speaking to her: "What a day it was, and to think it was only an ordinary mortal like McGee I had to talk with, and not you, my goddess queen." At home in Cornwall in 1899, he concocted an elaborate plan for a casual encounter with Isabel, who was spending her summer on the family farm in Antrim, Ontario. "This morning I had a glorious inspiration, Bella. If I can manage to get a bike some way I intend taking a trip up West, via Renfrew County ... but how am I to see you? I had thought of having my wheel break down in front of your place ... But this morning the glorious idea came to me. Why not just happen along at Church-time in the morning, go into the English Church there, meet Isabel and if fortune is favourable be invited home? Whew!" It was an enterprising idea, and surely only an idea, since the bike ride from Cornwall to Antrim would have been more than 150 kilometres.

In June of that year, after painting his boat green, he had pondered an appropriate name for the craft. "With green inside and a certain name outside: It'll be Irish enough I hope. Of course I intend to ask advice as to what name to put. Whether I'll take it or not is another question. Think of going out for a couple of hours every day with my own – 'Isabel'!" Six days later, he wrote, "Today the boat was finished at last, and the question is, what to call it? Of course there is only one name under heaven worthy – Isabel, but equally of course I don't want to suggest that too openly." He bought twenty cents of paint and lettered "Isabel" on the boat, but lost his nerve, rubbing the name away with turpentine, another expense recorded in his obsessive accounting of everything he spent. The next month he changed his mind again. Sixty-four cents later, he was ready to paint Isabel's name on the side of his boat.[15]

A lot of dreaming was going on, but Skelton was a worker. In his diary he implored "my Isabel" to "help me by your inspiring presence, tho it be but presence to the eye of faith," and he summoned up his belief in systematic planning. A practical thought followed: he would marry Isabel. She said no; the when and why are unclear, but her decision may have had something to do with her natural restraint and his, in the matter of Isabel, lack of it. Yet he did not give up easily. He carried on with his studies at Queen's and, we can surmise, kept in contact with her. Once his Greek was firmly in place alongside his Latin, he applied successfully to enter the doctoral program in those subjects at the recently established University of Chicago. The Cornwall *Freeholder* reported on 28 September 1900 that Skelton was leaving for Chicago with his elder sister Emma, who had accepted a "good position" there as a stenographer. Oscar received high marks at the university but had no enthusiasm for his courses. He came home after a single term and departed on his Indian Civil Service adventure. It too began and ended quickly.[16]

Emma Skelton worked for the Booklovers Library in Chicago, moved on to lead the Milwaukee branch, and was brought into the head office in Philadelphia.[17] Without any other immediate prospects, Oscar decided to join her at Booklovers. The transition to the United States was seamless. He had been a student at the University of Chicago, taking easily to a big American city. In his teenage years, he rowed his little boat from Cornwall on the St Lawrence River to northern New York. The border was easily breached. It hardly seemed a border at all.

Booklovers, offering books for rent and home delivery, was headquartered at 1323 Walnut Street in downtown Philadelphia. Oscar's boss, Seymour Eaton, founded the business in early 1900, pitching it as an exclusive club for the wealthy and cultured. Membership was by invitation only; subscriptions were limited. Skelton's job, like Emma's, was in the Booklovers editorial department, mired in the barrage of paperwork and advertising that pushed the enterprise forward. He seldom saw the energetic Eaton, whose photographs depicted a handsome arch-salesman, as slick as oil and with a hint of danger about him. He was

bustling his way towards an empire of companies, including food and
drug stores and a network of over fifty rental libraries in the United
States and Canada and extending as far as London and Paris – a pioneering version of international retailing.[18]

Skelton enjoyed Philadelphia. The work at Walnut Street was congenial enough. He liked what he did, despite his complaint that "the
chariot wheels" of printer's deadlines wore on him. The pay was fine,
and there was the promise of more money and a promotion. His sister
was nearby, and he didn't need a lot of people in his life anyway. Booklovers was temporary, just a resting place between ambitions. India was
gone and forgotten. The new dream (which he said was really "my first
ambition") was a doctorate, no longer in classics but in political economy, following along after Adam Shortt, who had fired Oscar's interest
when he audited two of the professor's courses during his Greek year at
Queen's. He assured Shortt that he was spending his nights and weekends "reading up history, especially American, and some pol-science
and sociology, especially works with a statistical, laboratory flavour
which will, I hope, counteract my tendency to 'glittering generalities.'"
Skelton had a disarming way with his own weaknesses, and the generalities were perhaps not an entirely bad thing. Shortt told him that "I
trust that in all your future studies you may neither be carried away on
the wings of windy theories nor buried in mere excavation mounds
of details." The "living realities of humanity" ought to be his guiding
light.[19]

Skelton applied to pursue doctoral studies in political science at
Columbia University for the fall of 1902, telling Shortt in an offhand way
that "as the chance for a scholarship there is rather slim I think I shall
apply to Harvard as well; it'll only cost a postage stamp." Skelton again
emphasized to Shortt how much he would have gained had he taken
more courses with him during his undergraduate days. "I wish more and
more I'd have taken more work with you." What he knew of political
economy was "rather too flimsy and chaotic to make a good foundation for graduate work. However that's the penalty I pay for not knowing
what I wanted to do in time." Strong letters of recommendation came
from Shortt and George M. Grant, the principal of Queen's University,
a powerful inspirational influence leading students in the direction of
a productive life. Shortt declared Skelton to possess "a mind at once
of refinement and power," and Grant wrote that "Mr. Oscar Skelton's
record at Queen's shows that he is not only a first-rate classical scholar
but a clear and vigorous thinker. He is one of that exceptional class which

should be encouraged and aided to undertake post-graduate work." Not yet, though. Skelton's applications were unsuccessful.[20]

His correspondence with Shortt gave Skelton an outlet for his views on Canadian politics. "I'd like some light from you on the question," Skelton asked about the "imperialist flood ... running high all thro' the Empire" in 1902, even though he already knew what the anti-imperialist professor's answers would be. "Every time I pick up a Canadian paper now and read the enthusiastically British speeches or editorials," Skelton declared, "I wonder where I'm at and fainthearted fears trouble me that perhaps after all the ideal I've always cherished, Canadian independence, is fated to be only an ideal." He rejected utterly the politicians and publicists who thought that they could build up Canada's participation in the empire by means of high tariffs giving a preference to Britain and loud talk that was sure to set one group of Canadians against another. He requested that Shortt excuse his outburst, "but I feel so at sea here, neither able to sympathise with present Canadian sentiment nor to forget Canada and barter my birthright."[21]

Skelton was telling Shortt what he wanted to hear, but his letter was heartfelt and written to a fellow believer. For Shortt, the British Empire got in the way of the facts. Geography was what mattered. Canada was a North American state, Canadians and Americans having far more in common than the peoples of Canada itself. The line separating Canada and the United States was permeable, but that did not mean that Canada was an impossibility. Shortt believed the contrary: the United States, so similar to Canada, had survived and thrived – why not Canada too? Skelton agreed. His fierce and instinctive nationalism and British Empire-scepticism was influenced by what he described to Shortt as the North American "current of destiny." The United States might sometimes be a rival, as in the Alaska boundary dispute, but the continent was where Canada's "lasting community of interest" lay, not with "Australia or Timbuctoo, or whatever other part of the map a Jingoistic spree may chance to paint red."[22]

In January 1903 Eaton began *Booklovers Magazine*, appointing himself as the editor and Skelton as an assistant editor. The New York *Times* greeted the twenty-five cent publication as "a new thing in the magazine line." The covers were striking; the use of colour images was generous. As the magazine evolved, personality sketches, portraits, illustrations, and cartoons accompanied poetry ("A Spring Poem") and short stories ("Whatsoever a Woman Soweth"), as well as articles on art ("Photographic Portraiture – The New American School"), politics ("Radicalism

Captures the Democratic Party"), international affairs ("If Japan Should Win"), literature ("Mark Twain – Made in America"), science ("The Romance of Scientific Pioneering"), and business ("How a Newspaper Syndicate Works, by an Ex-Syndicator"). Packed at the front and back were advertisements for rail travel to play tennis in California or for the Armour Company's New American Girl Art Calendar. *Booklovers Magazine* was, of course, a vehicle for the Booklovers Library: there were lists of "all the good new books published in America," available to order through Seymour Eaton.[23]

Skelton became impatient. He had grown tired of Philadelphia boarding houses, having already moved eight times in a little over two years. He was homesick for Canada and his family, and Isabel Murphy was giving him hope of a future together. In early 1904 Oscar wrote to William Lawson Grant, the son of the Queen's principal, "presuming on a London morning's acquaintance and our common Queen's-ship," to inquire about teaching positions at Toronto schools, particularly "summer vacancies" and those "which do not require going thro the purgatory of pedagogy." He would regret giving up the thoroughly satisfactory work and prospects in Philadelphia, "but the reunion of the family and my incurable Canadianism offer compensations." Grant provided him with detailed information and also alerted Skelton to his own intention to quit St Andrew's College, an exclusive Presbyterian boys' boarding school that had been established in 1899 just outside Toronto. Skelton replied that "I need hardly say that the St Andrews position would suit me to perfection, for a few years at least." Asking for specifics, he wanted to know the duties of a "residence master" and "to what extent is he tied to the young hopefuls?" He also wondered whether the "unmarried qualification" was essential: "I am of course still in single blessedness but hope not to be after another year."[24]

The Canadian teaching possibilities did not materialize, and Skelton hedged his bets by considering American citizenship. In fact, he went further, signing a document in May 1904 at the Philadelphia Courthouse that it was "his intention to become a Citizen of the United States, and to renounce forever all allegiance and fidelity to any Foreign Prince, Protectorate, State or Sovereignty whatever, and particularly to the King of Gt. Britain & Ireland of whom he is now a subject." He then hesitated, folded up the paper, and took it home, where it remained.[25] The bartering of his birthright, even if it was not quite bartered, seems to contradict the "incurable Canadianism" that he boasted about to Grant and Shortt.

The explanation lies in a letter that he had written earlier in the year to Grant as they reviewed their mutual restlessness: "Canada's a great country, Heaven bless it, but at present it's chiefly for the farmer and the shopkeeper." In another generation, there'd be "more culture & leisure" and therefore "opportunities for the writer and the teacher. At present their scope is limited and their reward chiefly the missionary's." In England, said Skelton, gifts and training like Grant's would have led to a half-dozen possibilities, whether in journalism, public life, or university work – but not in Canada. Skelton concluded with the hope that "whatever work you finally decide on, you will not give up writing. Canada has had a fair crop of poets of second hand inspiration & her full share of novelists, but of men who can write on literary or national subjects with applied culture and sane perspectives very few."[26] Skelton wanted Canada, but he was not sure that Canada could give him the life that he wanted.

His application for American citizenship undoubtedly had something to do with Isabel Murphy and the likelihood that he would be bringing her to live with him permanently in the United States. Oscar had never stopped being convinced that Isabel was the only person who was right for him, but he had been turned down once and so he moved warily. The negotiation went well. In June 1904 he was ready to propose for a second time, having taken the precaution that she would accept. "Sweet Mistress Isabel Murphy," he began a letter that was almost overwhelming in its release of pent-up emotion, "will you marry me?" He spoke beautifully of the dreams and plans that they shared and of "seeing all double, each through the other's eyes." There were also practicalities, because he wasn't just a hopeless romantic. He was gathering cash and had requested a raise in pay. And he added what she already knew, that their engagement would have to be brief because *Booklovers* was offering him a lengthy working honeymoon in Europe, to begin in August. They would have "the glories of English country, the amazement of London, the delights of Paris" and the opportunity to "get acquainted with new peoples & lands, and incidentally with each other, which they say is the purpose of honeymoons." Oscar's mother received the news coldly. She knew Isabel enough to like her, but "I shall be greatly disappointed if I am not gaining another daughter instead of losing my boy. For you know dear Oscar I have only one boy and he is very very dear to me."[27]

They married on a Tuesday, 16 August 1904, at Isabel's family home in Antrim. All three of Oscar's sisters were in attendance. Isabel's sister, Edith, was maid of honour, and George Dolan, a friend from Cornwall, was Oscar's best man. With such short notice, only two of their friends from Kingston could get to the wedding. Leaving almost immediately, the bride and groom caught the train to Montreal and boarded the Canadian Pacific liner *Lake Champlain* the next day for Liverpool and five months in England and on the continent. They returned in January, Oscar effusing to the Cornwall *Standard* that he had seen "no country during his tour that he likes better than Canada, and none so intelligent, industrious and prosperous as Canadians are."[28]

Not knowing that *Booklovers* was failing, Oscar went back to Philadelphia alone to get back to work and establish their new home. At the end of March 1905, he wrote to Isabel that "the end of letter writing days is coming fast, fast, when we'll no longer have to depend on pen & pen, & on 400 mile telepathy for communication. Yet I'll be sorry when they stop coming." He told her about the talk of trouble at the magazine and that he did not believe it, but within days the whole Eaton enterprise came crashing down. The last issue of the *Booklovers Magazine* was published in June.[29]

Skelton was unemployed, but not for long. While visiting his parents at the end of the summer, he heard from the University of Chicago, which was hunting for a press officer with "magazine experience," "a feeling for style," and good judgment about "the temper of the newspapers" – as well as willingness to combine that work with graduate studies. Skelton would have preferred Columbia or Harvard, but the arrangement suggested by Chicago meant that he could enter its doctoral program in political economy and earn enough to keep him and Isabel afloat. They arrived in Chicago in October 1905. Oscar said that he and Isabel enjoyed "life in a flat immensely: it is infinitely above a boarding house." They had already discussed starting a family. He thought one girl and two boys "much the best combination" of children, but told her that "it's your affair: settle it as you please." Their first child, Douglas Alexander (known as "Sandy"), was born the following July after a difficult pregnancy.[30]

The Skeltons' married life quickly settled into a routine. He was constantly busy and preoccupied, while she was consigned to the apartment and the baby. Having a considerable intellect and literary ambitions of her own, Isabel had no desire to end up in "greasy domesticity" as "a pitiful example of a woman who gives up her own work and washes dishes instead." Oscar commiserated, in theory. Perhaps thinking of his sister Emma, he thought how different and "free, happy, independent" a woman's life could be compared to the "hemmed-in possibilities" of a century before. Yet he assumed, and told her so, that Isabel was doing what mothers in her circumstances had to do.[31] Meanwhile, he galloped off in a dizzying number of directions – taking his diet of courses; acting as the university's media man in an era that saw the birth of public relations; publishing journalistic pieces and trying his hand at fiction and literary criticism, usually under a pseudonym (he used his mother's surname) and almost always unsuccessfully; breaking into major academic writing with an article in the *Journal of Political Economy*; and keeping in close touch with Queen's, to the extent that, courtesy of Adam Shortt, he took up a fellowship there in 1906 and a lectureship the next year, both requiring his presence in Kingston for months on end.

Two of his University of Chicago professors, Thorstein Veblen and J. Laurence Laughlin, made a lasting impression on Skelton. He took three courses from Veblen, the author of *The Theory of the Leisure Class*, celebrated and reviled for never having met an economic orthodoxy that he liked. His iconoclasm, teaching methods, and way with words appealed to Skelton, and so too the democratic liberalism that characterized Veblen's thought. He was never an intellectual follower of the great man, however, and had little interest in theoretical economics. Veblen left Chicago for Stanford University in 1906, a loss that Skelton feared would be "irreparable" to the university. When Veblen returned to Chicago for a visit, Skelton was drawn again to "the same soft drawling voice, the square low forehead with the hair parted in the centre, the same exterior whiskers, & internally also the same detached irony, the same droll originality." Laughlin was the long-time head of the political economy department, "a not-very-big sharp-looking energetic steel-trap type of man." Resolutely in the economists' mainstream, he lacked Veblen's flair, but Laughlin was an influential figure in the profession and willing to throw some of his clout in Skelton's direction. In a "Labour and Capital" class, Skelton and Laughlin wrangled over "the obtuse mathematical and marginal utility theorizings now in fashion," but the professor "was so tickled with my criticisms that he quite forgave my heresies on other points." Both Laughlin and Veblen taught Skelton courses on socialism, and in April 1907 their student announced that he was changing his thesis topic from economic history to "The Case against Socialism," the title of Laughlin's seminar.[32]

He was a keen student of American politics, doling out praise or censure with equal vigour and self-assurance. In 1907, writing from Chicago for the *Queen's Quarterly* audience, he marvelled at Americans' optimism and their confidence in themselves and their country, giving rise to the widespread belief that there was no ill in society that could not be rooted out. Skelton identified himself with the insurgent democracy of the progressive movement, which combatted concentrations of economic and political power and sought, in his approving words, "a better social order for the average man." Later on, when the Progressive Party was organized to fight the presidential election of 1912, he interpreted it as a response to unchecked business interests, indiscriminate immigration and urban lawlessness (he linked the two), the disappearance of free western land, and a rigid U.S. constitution resistant to change. He forecast that the support of the celebrated reformer Jane Addams, "the world's foremost woman," would win the party a hundred thousand votes, but he was disdainful of its leadership under former president Theodore Roosevelt. Skelton favoured the winner of the presidency that year, Woodrow Wilson, who had the right views on the issues, approached them constructively, and was "the most flexible of opportunists," a high compliment from the persistently pragmatic Skelton. As for Roosevelt, he specialized only in "incurable egotism" and "personal faithlessness." It was evident to the young Canadian that, if the United States did not adopt term limits, it would have "to chloroform its ex-Presidents."[33]

Skelton dealt confidently with the opportunities that came his way as a graduate student. Wondering if he might not want an appointment at one of "the larger universities," Laughlin offered Skelton a position at the University of Chicago at the end of 1907. He declined. Despite the rosy picture of his Chicago prospects that Laughlin painted, Oscar complained to Isabel that the courses he was being offered were not very interesting. Queen's was better, at least in the short term, and if it was in his best interest he would still be able to get back to Chicago "in a year or two probably." Shortt pushed Skelton to choose Canada: he could have a greater impact in his own country. Skelton assured Shortt that he did not want to have to fall back on "an American situation," at the same time making it clear that he was aiming high – at "a Canadian professional chair ... in Queen's, or in Toronto or McGill, or elsewhere in the civilized regions of Canada." He went so far as to suggest that there were greener pastures for Shortt outside Queen's that he might like to consider. Only when Shortt decided to leave Queen's to become a civil service commissioner in Ottawa, arranging for Skelton to take over the Macdonald professorship in political economy, was the seal set on the resolve to go back home for good.[34]

Skelton was uneasy as he prepared to defend his doctoral dissertation in 1908. The Macdonald position, due to begin in September, made success imperative. He had taken on a new subject only a year and a half before, and had dashed off the thesis – a "hasty summer's effort," he acknowledged – while enmeshed in his many other commitments. Laughlin, his supervisor, was away from the university and unavailable to help with the final drafts. Robert Hoxie, a labour expert in the political economy department, stepped in to help; they worked together over many days to get the manuscript ready for examination. Even so, the final product was flawed and obviously rushed. The prose style sometimes stumbled, the organization was scrappy, and there was the Skelton tendency to sweep cavalierly over complex issues. The readers of the thesis, no known copy of which still exists, couldn't miss the candidate's evident ability but were bound to conclude that he was capable of much more.[35]

Staying with her family in Antrim, Isabel knew Oscar's shortcomings, as well as the stakes. She encouraged him with long letters that he said put him "in as good trim as a week's vacation." Yet she fretted as her husband headed to his examination on a searing August morning. She felt "sore & blue & distressed," Isabel admitted later, knowing that Laughlin and other Skelton champions at the university were absent, and that there were subjects that he had not had the time to review. Hours passed, and her concerns mounted: "I was so miserable." Then, finally, she heard from him. It had been an intense and difficult exam, but in the end Oscar had been awarded his doctorate with high honours – magna cum laude, in the language of American universities. "Such good news! My dearest, dearest boy you did splendidly," Isabel exulted. "My own clever, brilliant boy you have no idea how proud & happy I am. I stepped into another world at half-past-five yesterday evening." Off she rushed to Chicago, where the two painted the town "a mild red for the next ten days."[36]

On the long train rides that returned him to Canada and Queen's in August 1908, Skelton might have reflected on India and the United States and the travels that had taken him so far and were bringing him back to a small place in Ontario, close to where he had begun. He might have thought about the family and country that he had not wanted to leave but was willing to leave all the same. Or he might have concentrated only on the career of usefulness that lay ahead and on the great dreams and ambitions that continued to drive him.

2
Citizen Entrepreneur, 1908–14

Skelton returned to Canada in late August 1908, this time to stay. Queen's was small and parochial, but it had successfully emerged from a prolonged financial crisis. Taking over the John A. Macdonald professorship, with its salary of $2,000 a year, Skelton had the security he longed for. He had his country as well. There was no need to "put patriotism in my pocket book & hie southward."[1] He saw Adam Shortt, the man who had made Oscar's academic career, off to the civil service in Ottawa. He would miss Shortt, but not too much. Goodbyes were easier for Oscar than for Isabel, who was losing her great friend Elizabeth, Adam's wife.

The Skeltons rented the Shortt house and took charge for the year of Muriel, the Shortt's daughter, who was still in high school. In the fall Isabel became pregnant. She gave birth the following July to Herbert Hall Skelton, her second son. Herbert, it turned out, was his brother Sandy's opposite – patient and taciturn of temperament, not adept at small talk, an outsider observing life with a quiet amusement. He seemed to go out of his way to avoid the drive for excellence that characterized the rest of the family.[2]

When Queen's installed Skelton as the Macdonald professor at the autumn convocation, a proud father arranged publicity for his son. From his latest venture, the Maple Leaf Cash Grocery, Jeremiah Skelton used his contacts at the Toronto *News* to have an article appear about Oscar's progress from Queen's student to Queen's professor. He wrote the article himself and pushed Oscar to send a photograph showing him in his academic gown to accompany the piece. In their letters, the two talked politics, the subject that paradoxically bound them tightly together and separated them. Jeremiah did not hide his outrage at the tactics of the Liberal government during the just-completed 1908 federal election, when his Conservatives had been beaten for the fourth time by Sir Wilfrid Laurier. The elder Skelton had a clear recollection of every campaign since Confederation, "yet I know of none where there were so many attempts to purchase constituencies with public money." "You see," he wrote to the Kingston Skeltons, "what it is to be under a corrupt and immoral government." On his way to being convinced of Laurier's political sainthood, Oscar saw no such thing, but across the party divide both father and son fervently sought "a different tone in public life."[3]

In his two prior years at Queen's, Skelton had established himself as a committed teacher. As the Macdonald professor, however, he had more autonomy in the choosing of courses. He lectured on economics but his specialty was political science, and in particular constitutional and international law, comparative government, and political theory. The basic documents were the staples of liberal democracy. John Stuart Mill's *On Liberty* was his favourite book and he admired Walter Bagehot's *The English Constitution*. He folded into his teaching contemporary authors such as the English polymath H.G. Wells, the American journalist Walter Lippman, and socialist thinkers and writers Sidney and Beatrice Webb. Their work was not required reading, but Skelton wanted his students to be aware of fresh and challenging points of view, and to measure the unconventional against established ideas.[4]

Skelton confronted immediate Canadian issues in the classroom, whatever was current and controversial. This was his practical bent in action: events shaped his thinking, not abstractions. One student was seventeen-year-old J.B. Stirling, who became a successful engineer and the chancellor of Queen's in the 1960s. Stirling "enjoyed Skelton's lectures which were not on my curriculum but I took them because he was reputed to be one who related his subject to everyday affairs rather than giving a text book lecture." He alternated courses that dealt with the public agenda. One year it was national preoccupations, the next it would be Canada in the British Empire. In the Canadian course he looked at bilingual schools, immigration, trade and tariffs, Senate and electoral reform, and provincial rights. Recalled another of his early students, W.A. Mackintosh, "There were no text-books: there was no expounding of masters. Both student and teacher ranged widely in a joint exploration which was limited only by the bounds of the problems. The discipline was the discipline of the quest for knowledge. The subjects changed from year to year for they were never dead issues." Skelton's strong views were apparent, but the admiring Mackintosh insisted that his professor never bounced over the line into advocacy. Lectures ended with choices, not answers, Mackintosh claimed, although Skelton knew what he thought the answers should be.[5]

Skelton had worked hard on his public speaking. He was, however, never fluent or easy in front of a crowd. He entered the lecture room inconspicuously, "hair askew, the coat rumpled, the kind eyes blinking behind the thick glasses, and the routine beginning: 'Well, as we were noting last day,' and five minutes before the end of the hour: 'Well, to sum up.'" He compensated for his unobtrusiveness with substance, self-deprecation, and a compassionate interest in his students. "His mouth was sensitive and mobile," Mackintosh remembered, "now pursing in considered judgement, now diffidently smiling at his own comic para-phrase of a well-known quotation, or encouragingly at an inarticulate student."[6]

He was affectionately called OD, or Skelly, and had a youthful energy that appealed to students. Immediately after his arrival at Queen's, they elected him as their representative at the political science and debating club, and it was not long before they chose him as the honorary presi-dent of the Alma Mater Society, an unusual distinction for a new mem-ber of faculty. Skelton gave the young his respect and expected the same integrity and high standards from them as he expected of himself. He experimented with ways to motivate his classes by discouraging mindless note taking and trying to replace lectures with seminars. Stories circu-lated around campus of exchanges between distressed students or fac-ulty and the whimsical professor. When a complaint came that someone had been told to go to hell, Skelton advised: "Well, don't go!"[7]

The vehicle for his robust opinions was close at hand. The *Queen's Quarterly* had been established in the 1890s as a forum of ideas for Queen's alumni but one also consciously designed (in the words of its founder, Queen's Principal G.M. Grant) as a "medium through which the best thought in Canada can find its way into every home." The jour-nal had a regular "Current Events" column, drawing attention to politi-cal and economic issues in a lively and often provocative way. Skelton made substantial contributions to it every year from the time he became a Queen's fellow in 1907 until 1921, when he began to edge away from the university in the direction of the public service. He was also a fre-quent member of the journal's editorial committee. The *Quarterly* had only 750 subscribers, but its reach was wide. Skelton became known.[8]

Shortly after taking up the Macdonald chair, Skelton submitted his doctoral thesis on socialism for a $1,000 "economic prize" given by the Chicago men's clothing firm Hart Schaffner and Marx. The thesis

had been written quickly, but he had the inside track for the award, as
he undoubtedly knew. His University of Chicago supervisor, Laurence
Laughlin, was the chief judge and had added socialism as one of the topics for which the award could be given that year.[9]

In January 1909 Laughlin wrote a matter-of-fact note to Skelton to say
that he had won the competition. A cheque for $1,000 was enclosed, two-
thirds of the amount Oscar had earned for his first full year of teaching
at Queen's in 1907–8. A few days later came official notification from
Hart Schaffner and Marx, along with the company's patronizing congratulation: "The fact that Canada has walked off with the first prize does not
lessen the importance of your paper in our minds. We are aware that you
were a Chicago student, and a much broader view is that good thoughts
are pearls whether they emanate from Canada or elsewhere."[10]

Publication of the manuscript was a possibility that went with the
award, and that too was up to the sympathetic Laughlin. He urged Skelton to revise the thesis rapidly as a book, but not so quickly that quality
would suffer: "Do not let it go to press before you have made it a finished
product, on which you are willing to stake your reputation. I am very
anxious that you should make a ten-strike with this book." Skelton was
not good at one thing at a time and not good at saying no to yet more
commitments. He had a restless disposition and was already expressing
interest in doing public-policy research work on contract for the federal
government. Still, he began to carve out time to make his socialism study
less narrowly about Marx and Marxism and more accessible to readers
beyond the academic community. His new research included a return
to Chicago after the 1910 Queen's academic year was over to attend the
national convention of the American Socialist Party, where his negative
view of the movement was reinforced. The "opportunists and the impos-
sibilists, the crafty politicians and the simple doctrinaire, Jew and Gentile
have been hammering away," he wrote to Isabel, disdain that he would
never have expressed about a meeting of the Liberal Party.[11]

Two weeks after Chicago, Skelton was on Canada's west coast as a member of a commission charged with finding a permanent site for the just-
established University of British Columbia. The little group began with
Victoria, taking up residence in the elegant Empress Hotel. Oscar told
Isabel that he had never "had quite so lovely a view of life … surrounded
by tourists & residents who pour out money like water, motoring about
country roads, consorting with Cabinet ministers & judges & millionaires, – well one's ideas expand rapidly." He was ambivalent, thinking
that a return to a university professor's straitened existence would be

hard to swallow but decrying at the same time the "selfish snobbery" of Victoria's elite. He felt a twinge as he imagined what socialists would make of the wealth and privilege he was observing, and enjoying, all around him. But it was only a twinge. The "sublimely self-confident, self-centred" socialists had no lessons to teach him.[12]

The University of British Columbia commission moved on to Vancouver. Skelton found the city "crude, boastful, sprawling" and "tiresome with its eternal talk of real estate." Nevertheless, it was "one of the most interesting I was ever in, & bound to be more so." He was impressed by the "system & grit" of the presenters of the city's case, especially when it was contrasted with the blithe Victorians. The commission quickly came to the conclusion that Vancouver was where the university must be based. For form's sake, however, the search went on for another two or three weeks, and the commissioners did their best "to look wise & non-committal and judicial." The work brought out Skelton's ambition, which was not difficult to bring out. If he were fifteen years older, he imagined that he would be putting in an application to become the first president of the University of British Columbia.[13]

In spite of Laughlin's urgings that he concentrate on the socialism book to the exclusion of everything else, Skelton could not take his eyes away from Canadian politics. What he derisively called "the Imperialist school" enjoyed a revival in 1909–10, as Germany's big gun navy threatened Britain and Canada was expected to help in the defence of the Motherland – expected, as Skelton saw it, by imperialism's champions and their enablers, British and Canadian. They wanted an immediate cash contribution to the British navy. He wanted a Canadian navy that might, at the discretion of the Ottawa Parliament, merge with imperial forces if a crisis of sufficient magnitude arose. The Canadian Naval Service, established by the Laurier government in 1910, pleased Skelton because he believed that self-defence was the only stance consistent with national self-respect. A Canadian navy might be a poor thing compared to a great imperial fleet supported by colonial cash. It might have to accept lessened strategic efficiency as the price of autonomy. But a home navy would be Canada's own, and more than worth it for that. The country was moving in its own direction, determined not to be governed from Britain or to accept protection at British expense.[14]

Skelton elaborated on the theme in an emotional *Queen's Quarterly* piece. A nation worthy of the name, he insisted, did not hire another nation to defend it. Only colonies meekly accepted what seemed right not to them but to those far away. Skelton rejected the proposition that all Britain's wars were automatically Canada's wars. If Britain were assailed by Germany, "Canada would strain every nerve in aid." But what if the British were the ones doing the assailing? "A recollection of the process by which the British Empire has expanded from 120,000 square miles to 12,000,000 might suggest that she has had at least her share of attacking." And if Britain were fighting France across the English Channel? Would it be responsible for Canada's leadership to intervene, risking a clash between French and English Canadians at home?[15]

The *Quarterly* article came to the attention of the Tory premier of Ontario, Sir James Whitney. He expressed his outrage to P.D. Ross, the owner of a Conservative newspaper, the Ottawa *Journal.* Whitney denounced Skelton as a member of a cabal of parochial, negative empire-doubters who "without a blush" refused to help the Mother Country, failing to understand "that we should certainly do something in return for the benefits we receive as part of the Empire." With a sigh, Ross echoed Whitney's sentiment: "Some university professors are very disheartening at times."[16]

Whitney saw that his adversary was more dangerous than he let on. For all his strong convictions and insistence on expressing them, Skelton cloaked his project in clever language. He spoke of healthy trends towards "national development," "a sturdy national spirit," and "an aggressive confidence in our ability ourselves to play whatever role fate may assign." However, since few Canadians contemplated a future without Britain by their side every step of the way, Skelton did not explicitly make the case for independence from Britain. He muddied the issue by referring to "a new imperial consciousness" in the country and by claiming that Canadians had evolved into "national imperialists," an ambiguous term that suggested Canada could have the best of both its worlds.[17] Whitney did not believe that. Neither did Skelton.

Skelton was clear about what he was against if not what he was for. His target was the notion that Canada and the other dominions of the empire could merge with Mother Britain to become a new international force. The idea was being promoted by an empire-wide movement romantically called the Round Table, recalling the legend of King Arthur, his courageous knights, and their battle for all that was good in the world. Skelton rejected all schemes for reorganizing the empire on political, economic, or military lines. They added up to a reinforced centralization of power in London and the end, or at best the sharing, of hard-won Canadian liberties. He pointed out that the empire was without coherence, scattered all over the world, the parts ignorant of and having nothing in common with one another. Devising a quiz to prove his point, Skelton told readers of the *Queen's Quarterly* what he wanted to ask after-dinner orators who talked of the empire as if it were a tightly connected family. The questions would be simple. "What slang is current in Johannesburg today?" Or, "Name six statesmen in Australia – politicians will do."[18]

Skelton sniffed another anti-nationalist plot in 1911, in the form of organized opposition to the trade agreement reached between Canada and the United States early that year. He could sympathize with the nervous distrust of closer ties with the United States that persisted in many quarters, an echo of earlier times when fears that the Americans were out to gobble up their northern neighbour had real meaning. But Canada was strong now, he maintained, vibrant both in its economy and in its national spirit. There was no reason to refuse better access to a market of ninety million English-speaking customers at Canada's door. The reciprocal trade deal was limited in scope, confined mostly to natural products. The Laurier government's negotiators had got the better of the bargain. The farmer, the fisher, and the miner would all benefit, while the manufacturer remained protected behind Canada's high tariff wall.[19]

Yet professional imperialists, Skelton's contemptuous description, denounced the agreement. They claimed that it was national suicide, the sundering of the vital link to Britain and the softening up of Canada for eventual annexation to the United States. Skelton agreed that trade reciprocity would increase the distance between Canada and Britain, a healthy development from his standpoint, but he ridiculed the idea that "when a Canadian farmer sells a bag of potatoes to a New Yorker he throws in his country to boot." And, he added, Rudyard Kipling sold books in the American market but not his loyalty to king and country.[20]

Skelton regularly advertised himself to Mackenzie King, the ambitious minister of labour, and his deputy, F.A. Acland, a colleague from the *Booklovers* days in Philadelphia. He had done a small study for them in 1910 on the eight-hour workday, giving evidence on the subject to a House of Commons committee and enjoying "politics as it is played" in Ottawa, even though the Opposition at first fastened on his participation rather than the issue itself, accusing the professor of acting as the labour minister's mouthpiece. Now King brought Skelton to Ottawa to bolster the case for the trade agreement, which was encountering dogged resistance in Parliament and outside. Renting a room with food thrown in at a dollar a day, he was away from Isabel, who was not happy about it, for much of the summer of 1911. He worked closely with Robert H.

Coats, the labour department's chief statistician, on a report that set out the market conditions on both sides of the Canadian-American border. "Like a hen on ice," Skelton reported, Acland drove his charges to have the document ready for the beginning of a new parliamentary session on 18 July.[21]

They didn't quite make the deadline, but by then it did not matter. The debate had gone beyond the dry data that Skelton had dug out and shaped into dozens of statistical tables demonstrating the economic advantages of reciprocity. The pact's opponents, shouting that nation and empire were in peril, were on to the profitable field, as Skelton judged it in a letter to Mackenzie King, "of political prejudice and bumcombe loyalty where the demagogue has freer scope, and can't so readily be brought up against concrete facts." When Parliament returned, he gave a briefing to Finance Minister W.S. Fielding designed to help him fend off questions from the Conservatives in Parliament, but the minister botched the opportunity, making matters worse. The Laurier Liberals were floundering. The prime minister, seizing an opportunity to regain the momentum, called an election that he thought he would win. He had led the country for fifteen years of unchallenged dominance. The Canadian people would listen to him.[22]

Skelton stayed on in Ottawa to turn his research into Liberal campaign literature. His employment at the Department of Labour had been carried out on a confidential basis, and he was anxious that it remain that way, especially since he had become a plaything of the Conservatives in Parliament when he worked for King the previous year. He told Mackenzie King that he had taken a strong public stand in defence of reciprocity in American, British, and Canadian publications. However, he did not want "to be open to the criticism of preparing campaign material while in the pay of the public preparing official statistics." He also informed the minister that he had no intention of charging the taxpayer for Sunday and overtime work that was not part of his contract. When King disagreed and paid him anyway, OD returned the cheque. He was not ungrateful, he assured King, and he was being paid less than he had been for any work he had undertaken since his time at *Booklovers*, but he wanted to avoid "even the shadow of reproach."[23] This was the careful Skelton, the upright Skelton, but not so upright that he was unwilling to blur, on the quiet, the distinction between government responsibilities and Liberal Party partisanship. It was a lifelong failing.

As the election campaign evolved, Skelton realized that even the magnificent Laurier was struggling. In Quebec, his political base, he was pilloried by francophone nationalists, led by Henri Bourassa, for conspiring with imperialists to create a navy that would drag Canada into Britain's wars. In English Canada, where the prime minister was regarded as not having been imperialist enough on the naval issue, Skelton could see that the trade agreement was the dominant issue. Manufacturing, banking, and railway interests lined up against it, fearing that their livelihoods would be on the block in the further Canadian-American trade negotiations that were bound to follow the 1911 agreement. Money flowed, underwriting a massive advertising blitz. Anti-reciprocity groups formed. Prominent Liberals defected. The British-born were mobilized under the banner of the Canadian National League. American politicians, President William Howard Taft included, made statements suggesting that freer trade would hasten the day when Canada would become part of the United States. "The flag was waved," Skelton admitted, and Canadians "voted against any entangling alliance."[24] Robert Borden's Conservatives won with ease, piling up a forty-six-seat edge over Laurier's troops.

Skelton had sensed trouble with about two weeks remaining in the campaign. When defeat came, though, he was surprised by its scale, particularly in Ontario, where the Conservatives all but swept the Liberals away, leaving them with only a handful of members of Parliament. Oscar wrote immediately to Mackenzie King, who had lost both his cabinet and his parliamentary seat, saying that it was a shame that their fellow citizens had to sacrifice economic advantage in order to prove their loyalty to Canada and Britain, and that unscrupulous interests with unlimited funds could pervert national sentiment to serve their own base ends. But governments, he consoled his political friend, could not last forever. The swing of the pendulum would have come in a year or two anyway. As for King's future, whatever the arena, there was "no limit."[25]

Skelton was philosophical about the election result. He was pleased by the debate generated by the trade issue, ending, he hoped, the unwholesome political stagnation of recent Canadian political life. He had sympathy with the feelings that motivated sincere voters on the other side. They were nationalists too, even if their nationalism had led them to a different conclusion. He expressed pride in the robust self-reliance underlying the anti-reciprocity vote and the willingness to put ideals above pocketbook, and hoped that "the demonstration of national spirit will not be lost on American prophets of manifest destiny." Retaining his sense of humour and proportion, he remarked that he and his anti-imperialist friends had indulged in the gentle art of twisting the British lion's tail in earlier days. In doing so, they had provided a model for the plucking of the American eagle's feathers in the memorable election of 1911.[26]

"Canada and the United States are quits," was Skelton's quite different opening salvo to an American audience after the election. This was theatre, designed for dramatic effect, and the opposite of his core belief about Canada's ultimate destiny as a North American state. He did not think for a minute that the end of reciprocity spelled the end of North Americanism. The steady drumbeat of social, economic, and diplomatic cooperation between Canada and the United States would continue. Trade unions, missionary movements, and professional baseball teams operated as if there was no border. Canadians and Americans read the same magazines, attended the same plays, ate the same breakfast food, used the same slang. Canada and the United States, moreover, had announced the establishment of a binational International Joint Commission to oversee shared boundary waters and with a mandate that allowed any problem whatsoever to be submitted to it. Skelton enthused that "serious friction between the two democracies which halve the continent will henceforth be almost as inconceivable as a clash in arms between Alberta and Saskatchewan or New York and New Jersey." North America was an example to Europe of common sense in international relations.[27]

He told Isabel that he would return from his trade work in Ottawa free for "husbandly duties." What he really returned to was his normal heavy schedule of academic and government work. "Grinding away" was his way of life – churning out a multitude of publications, preparing lectures and courses, and hatching bright ideas to advance his causes and himself. He loved his wife deeply. He said the right things to her, sometimes very passionate things, particularly on birthdays and on the monthly anniversaries of their wedding, and he meant them. Nevertheless, he was always preoccupied, rushing on the next meeting or possibility, usually oblivious to Isabel's need to be something more than a wife and mother. He was impatient with causes that smacked of women's rights. Once, he mused, women quietly bore heavy burdens and were subject to their lords and masters, but no longer; modern women had been given all but equal privileges, and yet they seemed to feel it necessary to proclaim their grievances from the housetops.[28] Isabel fought for the space to grow and be creative. He would sympathize and hire one of a series of maids to help her, but the division of labour was clear in the Skelton household. She had the day-to-day responsibility for the care of home and family. He was the hunter and gatherer.

Earlier in 1911, despite the commitments that pulled him in several directions, Skelton had his revised thesis published by Houghton Mifflin of New York and Boston. The title captured the theme: *Socialism: A Critical Analysis.* Professor Laughlin had predicted that the book would make Skelton's reputation. It did, in spades. *Socialism* was an academic monograph, destined for the university reading lists on which it would sit for years, but it was widely noticed and praised for its accessibility, stylishness, and balance. The book resonated with intellectuals and educated readers because it caught a moment when capitalism was generating staggering profits but also staggering excesses. Socialism, the antithesis of private enterprise, was on the rise as an ideological counterforce and a potent social and political movement. Edward Peace, a prominent British Fabian socialist, concluded that Skelton conveyed socialism's attack on competitive capitalism so vividly that "one might mistake him for being a socialist himself."[29]

A legend grew of the book's link to Vladimir Lenin, the Russian revolutionary leader. The story that had increasing currency as the years passed was that Lenin, while in exile in Switzerland early on in the First World War, wrote a letter to Skelton congratulating him on the best response to socialism by a bourgeois scholar, and that the revolutionary leader, at his dying request, was buried in his public tomb with *Socialism* at his side.[30] The first story was true, the second pure fantasy, but both became part of Skelton's growing reputation as someone with influence that went far beyond Canada. He had the glamour of large ideas and large events on his side, and enjoyed, in his quiet way, the celebrity.

Socialists thought Skelton sympathetic because he shared their anger at what capitalism could get up to. *Socialism* scarcely mentioned Canada, but his other writings of the period emphasized the tight grip that the country's privileged had on the national economy: the highly centralized banking system; the close interweaving of financial interests; the rapid consolidation of industrial enterprises; the aggressive club of manufacturers; and the domination of politics and transport by the big three railways. These were the barons of industrialism who had distorted and bludgeoned reciprocity, a noble attempt to spread the wealth. In his 1913 *General Economic History of Canada*, begun as he was finishing the socialism book, Skelton excoriated the buccaneers who had made millions from mergers, the promoters of fraudulent companies, the land speculators growing rich overnight, the holders of unregulated public-service monopolies, and the owners of protected industries whose profits did not filter through to the common people. He concluded that they did more to bring honest wealth into disrepute than any socialist orator ever could.[31]

Skelton took socialism seriously, unusual for a Canadian at the time. Unbridled capitalism had made the emergence of its opposite inevitable, he argued, warning in a business publication that "every tax-dodging millionaire, every city slum, every instance of shady high finance or of overworked and underpaid employees, is a potent argument for socialism." The disparate bands of dreamers and conspirators of early socialism, Skelton believed, had evolved into a force to be reckoned with, the most remarkable international movement in world history. He was disgusted by the rich and those on the right who employed the socialist bogey as a device to scare the public or deflect attention from their own deficiencies. Socialism, after all, was "a word with a definite and ascertainable meaning," with adherents who had principles and deserved respect.[32]

But Skelton rejected socialism. It painted too bleak a picture, concentrating on the few failures rather than the many successes of the competitive order. Socialists were right to criticize the dangerous and unwholesome tendencies of free-for-all private enterprise but wrong to concentrate on those alone. The capitalist system had survived and prospered through a judicious combination of individualism and social control. The harrowing socialist picture of a factory wage-slave cowering under the lash of a tyrannical industrial entrepreneur, forced into long hours, low wages, bad working conditions, and dreary monotony, lacked perspective and proportion. The reality was that employers were more enlightened than ever, trade unions defended workers' rights, insurance programs to cover personal calamities were coming into view, and the state-as-referee was increasingly willing to intervene in the marketplace. Capitalism was open, dynamic, able to adapt.[33]

More than that, and more important, Skelton claimed that socialism contradicted human nature, while capitalism made the most of peoples' "ceaseless striving for betterment." The discipline of the competitive struggle developed the industry, thrift, insight, and initiative that compelled success. Skelton was poetic, and sincere, in emphasizing that "making a living is not living": "life's choicest gifts, love and honor and consecration to other's service, the glory of the sunset and the peace of the midnight stars are goods not bought with a price." But the good life was not enough. Progress lay in discontent. People, and societies, advanced or they stagnated. Every step forward opened new horizons; achievement persistently lagged behind conception.[34]

Skelton's perspective on life as a series of challenges to be overcome, seen as a daily investigation of character, fit with his own capitalist instincts. He was constantly on the prowl for writing, teaching, and government work not only to supplement the family's income but also to expand his horizons and his credentials. Giving up their rental of the Shortt house, the Skeltons bought three properties in quick succession, each an improvement on the last; they ended in 1916 by building their own home at 138 Albert Street, near Queen's. They called it Chateau-de-Lys, because it was both grand and heavily mortgaged – leased, not owned.[35] Material evidence of having made it in the world was not of great importance to Isabel, but to Oscar it was. He was not entirely a self-made man, up from nowhere, but he liked to think of himself that way.

His upwardly mobile ambitions did not interfere with OD's zeal for social justice. He viewed his world not as it was but as it could be. His articles in the *Queen's Quarterly* were aimed at economic democracy and political reform. He floated ideas for investigation into and regulation of the mammoth companies that honeycombed industry; a federal income tax to put the burden of national expenditure on the wealthy, where it ought to be; a comprehensive workman's compensation regime and old age pensions; a rearrangement of the tariffs that pressed heavily on primary producers; proportional representation in the House of Commons to ensure that the voice of minorities was heard; transparency of political campaign contributions, to monitor the big money that had sabotaged reciprocity; and improvements in the civil service, directed at recruiting the best people into government and rewarding them with cash and kudos.[36]

Skelton kept his optimism in check. He worked within what he called "our existing order," with an eye to the sensible. He wanted to abolish the Senate, "the entrenchment of wealth and privilege," but inertia, tradition, and constitutional obstacles seemed likely to make it impossible to do away with Parliament's upper chamber, the members of which were appointed by the prime minister alone. He opposed changes, such as the election of senators, that would make the institution stronger and more effective. It was relatively harmless as it was. "So, hands off the Senate! If we cannot end them, do not let us mend them."[37]

Skelton's Canada was a white Canada. He was wary of Asians, and for that matter blacks and Jews, hewing closely to the attitudes of most Canadians at the time. Commenting on "our Asiatic problem" in one of his first "Current Events" articles in the *Queen's Quarterly*, at a time of heightened concern about Japanese and Chinese immigration, he wrote that "almost any brand of white man, in the second generation at least, when put through the national digester, the public school, may make a good Canadian. But the Oriental, our equal though he is, or it may be our superior, remains alien to the end of time, inscrutable, unassimilated, loyal only to his kin and his homeland, as dangerous by his virtues as by his vices."[38]

"Oriental" included the men and women of India, the place where he would have been serving as an officer of the British Empire had fate taken him in a different direction. That, however, did not soften his attitudes to "Hindoos," as Skelton and Canadians called East Indian immigrants even though most of them were of the Sikh rather than the Hindu religion. In early 1914, when the freighter *Komagata Maru* arrived at Vancouver hoping to land 376 East Indians for settlement in British Columbia, Skelton saw the attempt as an unwanted invasion and yet another argument against the notion of the empire as a single unit, one and indivisible – because, if that was accepted, all of the empire's citizens had the right to pass from one part to another. Canada was Britain's partner, not its subject, and "must be kept a white country." The *Komagata Maru* was turned away from the British Columbia shore, perhaps, Skelton felt, demonstrating the truth of his argument that Canadian autonomy was the only basis on which the imperial connection could continue.[39] His views about Asian immigration changed, at least so far as the Japanese and Chinese were concerned: by the 1920s, he was complaining to the prime minister about the severe restrictions that were being placed on immigrants from the Pacific Ocean region.

Skelton might have seen the *Komagata Maru* incident as proof of the soundness of his position regarding Canadian autonomy, but Canada's imperialists still had the upper hand, particularly under a Conservative administration in Ottawa. Prime Minister Sir Robert Borden might not be an all-out empire man, but with a push from his political allies in English Canada he could tack in that direction. After Borden's victory in the reciprocity election, the naval issue was back in play, subtly at first but then with a vengeance. Early on in the term of the new government, Skelton complained that Laurier's Canadian navy was receding from view. The momentum was building again for a direct contribution of ships to Britain's Royal Navy. Canada was about to join in the "mad Dreadnought folly" that it had avoided under the Liberals.[40]

While OD conceded that something would be done to help the British, he asked which cause the Dreadnoughts were going to serve – that of a centralized British Empire or of an alliance of autonomous states?

He knew what he preferred, but, under the cover of assisting a belea-guered Britain, the imperialists were pushing their dreams of a federated empire controlled from London. In the days of colonial dependence, the empire had served a purpose. It saved Canada from dependence on the United States, giving time "for the development of a nationalism which stands in the way of all proposals for merging our national identity in any larger whole." But Canada had grown up. The ties of empire, or at least the Anglo-Canadian part of it, had loosened. Centralizing the empire again made no sense. Imperial federation was an out-of-date concept, unworkable and impossible in fact. Instead, Canadians had before them the possibility of working out "still further the mechanism of an empire that is not an empire, to build up fleets and departments of external affairs in each allied state, and to use and extend the means of consultation between these centres."[41]

"True Skeltonism" was Isabel's way of describing her husband's way of arranging his arguments. He established two extremes, ultra-nationalism and ultra-imperialism, and seemed to rule them both out. The first, sepa-ration from Britain, he brushed aside as not currently relevant, because Canadians continued to cling to their empire. He discarded the sec-ond option, ultra-imperialism, by caricaturing it, claiming that it could only lead to the coercion of Canada in an empire controlled entirely by the British. Skelton used imperial consolidation to undermine a sub-tler imperialism, characterized by Canadians' passionate commitment to Britain. His pretense was of moderation. Apparently he was in the centre, but behind the mask he was the ultra-nationalist, a word that he thought "is really too good to be abandoned to the provincialists of Quebec."[42]

The Canadian League, an organization claiming a non-partisan approach to the Canadian naval predicament and a sturdy national defence, sought to expropriate Skelton's growing reputation by bringing him onto its executive board. The invitation came from Arthur Hawkes, an English journalist who had immigrated to Canada in 1905 and had been a masterful propagandist for the Conservative cause during the election of 1911, making an effective case that Canadians had a stark choice between "remaining in the orbit of the Empire" and "gravitating to the lesser glories" of the American republic. Skelton's suspicions were natural enough when Hawkes approached. In a series of letters from mid-1912 to late 1913, however, Hawkes persuasively advertised himself to Skelton as a fellow nationalist and possibly even a fellow Liberal. Skel-ton was tempted by Hawkes's appeals and the league's promotion of "an intelligent devotion to the country and its institutions," but there was enough about the group and the people it attracted to keep him wary. He resisted suggestions that he arrange a league meeting in Kingston, angering Hawkes's impatient co-organizer, John A. Cooper. When Cooper sarcastically returned OD's hefty donation of $25 to the cause, saying that it was no substitute for a real contribution to the league's work, Skelton's brief dalliance with the organization ended abruptly.[43]

The Borden government presented Parliament with the Naval Aid Bill, a proposal that Canadians contribute $35 million, one-quarter of the government's annual expenditure, to the British Royal Navy for the building of three Dreadnought battleships. It was an imperial emergency, Borden and the British maintained. Skelton retorted that there was "no vital peril." Britain was keeping pace with Germany in the construction of new ships, and the Germans in turn were threatened by a resurgent France on one side and a massive Russia on the other. The intent of the first lord of the Admiralty, Winston Churchill, was clear to Skelton. An atmosphere of crisis was allowing Churchill to contemplate an even bigger British navy, entirely at his command. If the empire was to be remade as one unified entity, Skelton scoffed in the spring of 1913, "there is a modest gentleman in the Admiralty quite prepared to become that One."[44]

There were other pressures, unofficial pressures, that made it difficult to resist Britain's bidding. Skelton listed the London organizations that flooded Canadian newspapers with propaganda, the social temptations brought to bear on visitors to London, and the quiet missionary tours of Canada undertaken by "serious young men predestined to save the Empire." Some of what came from these quarters, he acknowledged, was grounded in goodwill and common interest. Britain's needs merited respectful consideration, but not awestruck acquiescence. Those days, if they ever existed, were gone. Canadians must absorb whatever information came their way, assess it carefully, and make up their own minds. They might get it wrong, "but that is our privilege and our responsibility."[45]

Skelton accused the government of underestimating the capacity of Canadians to develop their own national institutions. If Canada was to have its own navy, a real navy, there was admittedly a lot to learn about naval organization and shipbuilding, but the Borden Conservatives had forgotten the pluck and resolve of John A. Macdonald's Conservatives and "their courageous faith in their country, a faith held through dark days." Old John A. had made a unifying marvel of the transcontinental Canadian Pacific Railway (CPR), defying the pessimism of critics who predicted that it would not earn the grease for its wheels. The railway became synonymous with the nation "not only because we were materialists but because we were idealists. We were determined that in spite of geography and diplomacy, in spite of Rocky Mountains and Lake Superior wildernesses, Laurentian plateaus and Maine intrusions, this Canada should be made one and independent." Skelton cautioned Borden and his party to "never bet against Canada."[46]

The Conservative bill to aid the British navy failed in the Liberal-controlled Senate, and the government was left with nothing to fall back on except the all-but-defunct Canadian navy. For Skelton, the naval issue had never been a choice between militarism and anti-militarism, but between sponging and independence, and between militarism at someone else's expense and a modest but necessary military spending at Canada's expense. He was disgusted by the billions spent around the world on armaments, causing the march of social progress to slacken, slums to fester, schools to remain unbuilt, and the fundamentals of unemployment to continue unaddressed. In a small gesture of defiance, he vigorously opposed the establishment of a military training scheme at Queen's in late 1913, while applauding the recent advances in the cause of world peace and the forms and institutions of international solidarity that were taking shape at the Hague Conference and elsewhere.[47] Perhaps his Canadian navy would never have to go to war.

He knew better. Canada was a stout member of the British Empire, tied unshakeably to the shifting kaleidoscope of European alliances that was driving an unceasing growth of weapons and nervous prophesies of an Armageddon at the centre of the world. Skelton saw inevitability in the frantic race of arms. Great powers felt compelled to out-build and out-manoeuvre their rivals, a pattern that fed on itself and was repeated over and over again. With no nation daring to step aside, he did not doubt that a still madder waste of money and men lay ahead.[48]

Six years into his time as the Macdonald chair of political economy, Skelton had established himself as a forceful man of ideas at Queen's and beyond. Breezily confident in his worth and ability, he was a citizen entrepreneur – intent on changing the way Canadians saw themselves and their country and simultaneously pushing his own career and prospects forward. His ambitions for himself and his country overwhelmed any of his natural reticence. He was in the thick of things – young, cocky, fashioning a reputation for controversy, and delighting in his success. And then the world exploded.

3
War and Sir Wilfrid, 1914–19

It happened as Skelton feared it would. Governments armed. Great powers manoeuvred. Alliances formed. Europe was a powder keg, vulnerable to the spark of an incident. At the end of June 1914, a member of the Austrian royal family was assassinated in the streets of Sarajevo. Nations and empires, one after another, implicated themselves, or became implicated, in the chain of events that followed. The guns sounded in August. The British Empire and half the world went to war.

Canada paraded to the front at Britain's side. Years later, it seemed to Oscar Skelton that the First World War put an intolerable strain on the unfinished patchwork of national unity, but that was not the mood as he observed it in the summer of 1914. French and English Canada alike – Montreal, Quebec City, Toronto, and Vancouver – greeted the conflict with enthusiasm. The government of Sir Robert Borden pledged that Canada would make every effort and sacrifice "necessary to ensure the integrity and maintain the honour of our Empire." Sir Wilfrid Laurier, on behalf of the parliamentary Opposition, assured Canadians that "we raise no question, we take no exception, we offer no criticism, and we shall offer no criticism so long as there is danger."[1]

OD was among those who cheered. In a conflict that pitted the British Empire, France, and Russia against Germany, Austria-Hungary, and the Ottoman Empire, he made it clear that Canadians could not be neutral observers, and neither could he. The choice was obvious and the cause wholly just: "Here and now no man with unwarped vision can question on what side lies honor and freedom and democracy." The enemy alone had caused the war and the enemy must be crushed; only a decisive and lasting victory could preserve international justice and Europe's political freedoms. Canada would fight alongside Britain, whose leaders had done all they could to avoid war.[2]

Zeal for a British war far away was not unusual among English Canadians, but it was unusual for Skelton. He put to one side his habitual suspicion of imperial motives, his demands for more autonomy from Britain, and his insistence that the raw national interest had to be at the core of all Canadian thinking and action. In explaining the British decision to enter the war, or the reluctance of the United States to become a belligerent, he declared that governments and peoples did not go to war simply for justice or humanity. Abstract and benevolent attitudes might be present, and they could help to validate action and unify the public, but some direct interest had to be at stake. The British were fighting for nothing less than their self-preservation, while for the Americans no clear and present danger presented itself.[3]

Canada, however, was in the war despite its interests, not because of them. Skelton believed in the destiny of geography; Canada's real interests lay close by. Canadians were part of North America, a distinctive region far away from disorder and hatred, and so peaceful in its international relationships that Canada and the United States would no more go to war than Ontario would fight Quebec or New Hampshire would fight New York. The "ideas that drive men on," in combination with a favourable mix of shared purposes, were turning North America into a community of peoples. The contrast with Europe, contaminated with militarism and Darwinism, was striking.[4] Canada ought to remain aloof from the First World War, as the United States was doing, if self-interest was the issue. But it was not.

Nor, apparently, was it the tie to the Old Country that was taking Canada to Britain's side. Laurier made the case for the defence of a threatened Motherland, but Skelton did not. He tossed aside what he termed the "vivid home memories and sympathies" of the British half of the Canadian population. Instead he justified his, and his country's, commitment to the war on the basis of what was right and responsible. "This war is our war," he declared for the readership of an English journal, "our part in it is not, as in the Boer War, a testimonial of affection for the Mother Country, but a realization of our own duty and of the cause at stake."[5]

With Canadian soldiers soon involved in intense fighting on a Western Front that extended from the North Sea to the French-Swiss border, Skelton spoke of a deepening determination to ensure the world's freedom and to see the war through to the end. He observed the widespread support for Canada's war effort – the volunteers flocking to the colours; the khaki uniforms filling the streets; the eruption of fund-raising to support military families; and the explosion of knitting to keep the troops abroad warm with socks, mitts, and scarves. He expressed Canadian pride in the grit and steadiness of the troops in withering battles and Canadian sorrow at the loss of sons and husbands "from our own town and country" who had sacrificed themselves in the common cause. Battlefields with names like Ypres, where Canada lost six thousand soldiers, were being etched in the national memory. Canada "is moved as never before in its history," Skelton wrote.[6] Queen's mounted its own military units, including a medical unit, but there is no indication that Skelton, then thirty-six years old, thought of enlisting, or that he was reproached, then or later, for not signing up.

Skelton waged his war as a Laurier Liberal. He had been that ever since he could remember, and he underlined the fact during the summer of 1914 by agreeing to become Sir Wilfrid's official biographer. Discussions between the two men had begun the previous year, as Skelton researched a little book in the Chronicles of Canada series, *The Day of Sir Wilfrid Laurier*, a political survey of the country's progress from a colony to a free nation centring on the former prime minister – history, not biography, as Skelton planned it, but with plenty of admiring biography nevertheless. From their first meeting over dinner at Sir Wilfrid's Sandy Hill home on Laurier Street in Ottawa, when Skelton struggled to stifle yawns after a long day, he was convinced that Laurier was frank in his recollections and judgments on people and politics. Making up his notes of their conversations, as he did after each session, Skelton was never inclined to doubt what he had been told.[7] His subject's honesty and decency shone as OD honed his life of Laurier.

In spite of Laurier's efforts to put him at ease, a distance remained between the two men, which Skelton thought was appropriate. With Sir Wilfrid, Oscar told Isabel, "one can never forget you are talking to a Prime Minister or ex-Prime Minister." When OD hosted Sir Robert Borden at a meeting of the Canadian Political Science Association (CPSA), he couldn't help comparing him to the Liberal leader. Borden was nice, but ordinary, too easy to be with. Laurier was extraordinary, formidable, impossible to forget.[8]

Before and after the onset of the war, Skelton visited the Lauriers at their family home in Arthabaska, cradled in the green hills of Quebec's Eastern Townships, a part of the country that reminded him of the geography north of Kingston. Trips to Arthabaska became less frequent as

the war pressed in on Laurier, and the summer of 1914 was the last
time that the former prime minister had an opportunity to be there for
an extended period. Skelton remembered his sleepy hot summer days
with the Lauriers affectionately: the idyllic village with a great church
and grand court buildings; the rambling square brick homestead; the
conversations in the deep, wild garden shaded by copious trees; the big
meals with an endless supply of wild strawberries; the evenings of game
playing and conversation with friends and neighbours; the "perfect and
spontaneous hospitality." Skelton spoke to the bilingual Lauriers in
English but, at his own insistence, stumbled along in his halting French
with the rest of the household. "I am forgetting how to speak English
here," he reported to the family, "though not altogether replacing it
with French."[9]

When Skelton was with Laurier, Isabel and the children were an after-
thought. Letters home became perfunctory, ending often with a dutiful
"yours ever" or "your own husband." On his wife's birthday in the summer of 1914, he chose to be with Laurier in Arthabaska rather than with
her in Kingston. His birthday letter from Quebec was addressed to the
whole family, including his mother, not to Isabel alone, and it spent time
instructing her about how to handle his academic affairs while he was
away. On the same day, he sent a postcard to Sandy, then eight years old,
telling him that he was expected to be taking care of the house and his
little brother as well as "giving your Mother a Happy Birthday." Oscar was
aware of how much trouble his two young "gorillas" could be, but all that
Isabel usually got was the unsympathetic hope that she was finding ways
of keeping the boys outdoors "to lessen the disturbance."[10]

Once the draft manuscript of *The Day of Sir Wilfrid Laurier* was complete, Skelton sent it to the Liberal leader for comments and corrections.
Laurier was just out of hospital after an agonizing illness, but he replied
promptly, systematically marking up the manuscript in red and blue –
red for major points, and blue for smaller criticisms. Skelton replied that
he "should have been gladder if it could have been possible to avoid
errors altogether. I mean errors of fact: errors of opinion I am afraid will
be charged against it by our good Tory friends, without number." Laurier
found the work sympathetic, fair, and thorough: "I think you have presented a complete & impartial review of the period in which I lived." He
might well think that. The book, published in the summer of 1916, was
entirely favourable: Laurier was portrayed as the principled, balanced,
and courageous paragon of national and imperial politics, opportunistic
as to means but never to ends. The Vancouver *Sun* got the point: Sir

Wilfrid was fortunate to have such a sympathetic interpreter of his life and politics.[11]

By the time that *The Day of Sir Wilfrid* appeared, the war no longer brought Canadians and their politicians together. As the bloody stalemate on the Western front continued, casualties mounted, and recruiting slackened, the question of compulsory military enlistment – conscription, as it was known – slid towards the top of the political agenda, uniting Skelton and Laurier but dividing the country. Skelton noted that 350,000 men had volunteered for the military by mid-1916, but critics set that against the Borden government's goal of 500,000 men. The demand for some form of obligatory military service was growing.

The volunteer system had not failed, Skelton contended. Recruiting had fallen off when the initial waves of the eager and the British born had dried up, but thousands of men were still joining up every month and Canadian factories and farms were contributing mightily to the war effort, themselves requiring large outputs of manpower. There were rising cries that certain parts of the country were not pulling their weight, but enlistment rates across the country, OD insisted, varied for perfectly good reasons. Quebec and the Maritime provinces were falling short of their government-assigned enlistment quotas, he acknowledged, but they had a smaller proportion of British-born citizens, city dwellers, and men of military age than Ontario and the west. What would be demanded next? Comparisons of the contributions of Presbyterians and Christian Scientists? Of red-haired and black-haired men, or tall men and short? Equality of sacrifice was an ideal impossible to achieve. The quest for uniformity obscured all the things that Canada and Canadians were doing well as they adjusted to the new war order.[12]

At bottom, Skelton knew that complaints about recruiting were really complaints about Quebec. The French-speaking province was not doing its part, it was being said more and more loudly. Skelton's response was that it was unsurprising, inevitable even, that French Canadians were enlisting in much smaller proportions than English Canadians. Quebec was predominantly rural, far from recruiters' appeals, and isolated from the Old World. There were not many British-born, and scant "racial sympathy, the personal relations with the United Kingdom which have counted so largely in taking tens of thousands from the English-speaking provinces overseas." There wasn't a bond with France either; that link had been broken more than one hundred and fifty years ago.[13]

At this point in his reasoning, Skelton stopped his sympathetic understanding and became one of Quebec's critics. If Quebec was not British or French, it was not yet Canadian. On the one hand, it was more colonial, more passive, than English Canada, willing to have an imperial power dominate its world and do its fighting. On the other hand, it was aggressively provincial, so many of its people preferring to be "merely Canadien." Skelton could sympathize with the elements of French Canadian nationalism that sought to escape from Britain's heavy hand, but he deplored "the exaggerated sense of provincial and racial separateness, the desire to keep Quebec apart and exclusive" that was "full of danger to national unity and achievement." Henri Bourassa, Quebec's nationalist-in-chief who was leading a highly effective anti-war campaign, was the target of Skelton's scorn for undermining the war effort, tearing at the national fabric, and vilifying Laurier as a traitor to his people. OD took attacks on Sir Wilfrid personally. The old man's enemies were also his.[14]

Skelton rejected Bourassa's accusation that English Canada was persecuting the country's francophones, while knowing how effectively the claim played in Quebec. The evidence for Quebec nationalists lay in Regulation 17, an Ontario edict that restricted the teaching of French in the province's schools, allowing Bourassa to point out that francophones were being asked for their cooperation abroad when they were denied simple justice at home. How easy that made it to rant – OD's word – about an English Canada that was unworthy of a war it claimed to be fighting for freedom and democracy, or that the real danger to French language and civilization lay across the Quebec-Ontario border, not across the sea.[15]

Skelton maintained that Bourassa was a zealot, out of the mainstream on Regulation 17, as on so much else. Fortunately, he argued, most English- and French-speaking Ontarians, and their leaders, wanted adequate training in English for every child in the province, while providing as much French education as was practicable and consistent with progress in English – a precise lawyer's phrasing that permitted Skelton to justify substantial limits on the teaching of the French language. The French had come to the shores of America before the English; they had agreed to join in the founding of a federation; their cooperation was vital if Canada was to survive and prosper and stay together. Their language deserved respect, but too many obstacles already divided the country. The majority of Canadians spoke English, which was the language of economic opportunity, not simply in Canada, but in North America. More important, without the widest possible knowledge and use of English, common Canadian action, purpose, and consciousness were impossible.[16]

Skelton wanted Quebec more in Canada and more in the war. That impulse made him flirt with the Bonne Entente movement, which sought to bring French and English Canada back to the unity of 1914 and encourage francophone Quebecers to engage more actively in the war. Bonne Entente was led by Arthur Hawkes, who was anxious to heal French-English wounds, and John M. Godfrey, intent on persuading Quebec to do "her fair share in this war." Packed with Liberals, the movement was initially inspired by Sir Wilfrid Laurier, who used the notion of an entente to describe an understanding that he hoped would develop and "extinguish the prejudices that pull us apart." Laurier, however, resisted the unsubtle Godfrey's appeal to join in bringing Quebec "into line with the other Provinces of Canada."[17]

Skelton departed from Laurier on Bonne Entente, although with reservations. The movement originated in Toronto, where conscription was popular and Laurier was increasingly not, even among members of his own party. The presence of Godfrey was not reassuring, but Skelton had come to know and admire Hawkes, who demonstrated a knowledge of and sympathy with Quebec and expressed a desire for "a better mutual understanding between the races." He signed onto the movement cautiously, a rare intellectual in a Bonne Entente fraternity from the business and legal communities of Ontario and Quebec – patriots all, no doubt, worried by the angry words that were passing between English and French Canadians, but also by what the rift was doing to their bottom line.[18]

Skelton was part of a forty-eight-person Bonne Entente delegation from English Canada that descended on Montreal in October 1916, full of trepidation. National unity seemed so fragile that there was danger in the air: one of the visitors recalled they would all have run home if someone had let off a firecracker in the Windsor railway station. Instead, one hundred and fifty smiling Quebecers greeted them and dispensed frantic hospitality, topped off by a Club Saint-Denis banquet with the rich food that OD adored. The tourists, most of them knowing nothing of Quebec, tramped around the province on a tight schedule of visits to factories, schools, and hospitals. Everywhere there were speeches, but few in French and even fewer confronting the problems that divided Canadians. OD nevertheless formed a positive impression of the trip, and Louis St Laurent, a young Quebec City lawyer, formed a positive (and lasting) impression of him. Skelton believed that all shades of Quebec opinion had been exposed. His Entente colleagues seemed to him "a very solid and wide awake lot" who "came home a little more enlightened though not in all cases more sympathetic." A return visit of Quebec businessmen to Toronto at the beginning of 1917, Skelton remembered, "was more of a dinner and oratory affair, but as such very successful."[19]

Anodyne words of goodwill could not keep Bonne Entente together indefinitely. The war was lasting longer than anyone but a rare prophet had forecast, Skelton observed: "The going became harder, the strain greater, tempers sharper." The drain of years of enlistment and the growth of industry were making it difficult to find men, who were coming into the army at a few thousand a month, compared to almost 34,000 in early 1916. Three Western Front battles that year – Saint-Eloi, Mount Sorrel, and the Somme – left more than 35,000 Canadian troops killed or wounded. Godfrey began to push Bonne Entente in the direction of "aggressive measures for hastening the successful issue of the war" and to marginalize French Canada. Skelton realized, a bit late, that conscription had been Godfrey's "special purpose" all along. He would have quit Bonne Entente but there was no need. The tiny group disintegrated as the conscriptionist chorus grew irresistibly loud in 1917.[20]

Although he had never really been away, Skelton came energetically to Laurier's side in the fight against conscription. Their aversion to the practice began with core principles drawn from the Anglo-Canadian tradition of William Ewart Gladstone and Edward Blake, Laurier's predecessor as leader of the Liberal Party. When Skelton looked at Sir Wilfrid, he saw himself: a liberal democrat by temperament and training, an unrepentant believer in human rights and self-determination, hating absolutism (and absolutes) and damning compulsion except as a very last resort. It was dangerous, they believed, to give governments too much power; worship of the state, as the Germans were proving, was a contagious disease. Canadians and Britons were fighting against "the Prussian spirit of ruthless oppression of all individual liberties." To give in to conscription would violate the freedoms that were "the glory and justification of the British people in this war." Not doubting "our present imperial and international responsibilities," Skelton and Laurier were fierce advocates for the war, but they opposed conscription just as fiercely.[21]

The controversy over conscription returned Skelton to views about Canada's relationship with the British Empire that he had held since his student days. On 19 March 1917 he told W.L. Grant, who was in England and encountering among overseas Canadians bitter feelings towards Quebec, that he could not find any justification for such emotions, "in view of the plain fact that we went into the war wholly from racial sympathy with England." The idea that the empire was making Canadians do something that was against their interests was trademark Skelton, but he had said nothing of the kind since August 1914. He predicted to Grant that the conscription issue would likely "lead to some precipitation of the discussion about imperial relations & perhaps matters will hereafter be put on a self-respecting national basis whereby we will act as a nation, not as an echo, and we can find room for every national element in our action." He began publicly to complain that Canada did not control the conduct of a war run from London, and to call for "sturdy Canadianism" and "the feeling of responsibility that follows in its wake."[22]

In May 1917 Prime Minister Borden told his cabinet that he was determined to introduce conscription. Skelton urged Laurier not to accept it until an election or referendum had been held. Borden offered Laurier participation in a coalition government that would enforce compulsory military service after an election. The Liberal leader refused, but not all of his party followed him, allowing Borden to form a Union government made up of his Conservatives joined by conscriptionist English Canadian Liberals. Laurier was condemned roundly for his decision, Skelton told Grant, but "I think he was quite correct in his view that if he were to support conscription now it would simply mean handing over a solid Quebec to Bourassa and to still greater extremists." Skelton had little doubt that Borden himself "was absolutely sincere in his desire to strengthen the Canadian forces in what seemed the only adequate way." The lesser lights of the prime minister's party were, however, a different matter: they were out to isolate Quebec from the rest of Canada. Skelton tried to reassure Laurier that Quebec was not alone in opposing conscription, "though elsewhere the minority is less outspoken."[23]

Privately and in the *Queen's Quarterly*, Skelton acknowledged that the supporters of conscription had some plausible arguments on their side. In the abstract, he admitted, compulsory service "was the fairest solution of our military tasks." It aimed at equality of sacrifice and a more efficient organization of resources. Skelton praised the Military Service Act, which put conscription into effect, as reasonable and balanced. Arranging for the minimum of dislocation to industry, for tribunals to deal with a wide range of exemptions from military service, and for those men who had the fewest family ties and obligations to be the first to be called up, the legislation was in line with the best British and Canadian parliamentary traditions.

Yet, systematically making his case, Skelton argued that the Conservative government had not proved that compulsory service was necessary,
or that Canadians were not doing their full part in the war. With its population of eight million, Canada had raised a volunteer armed force of
400,000 soldiers; before the war, an optimistic forecast would have been
100,000 men at most. The United States, which had entered the war on
the Allied side in April 1917, would have to enlist over 6,500,000 men to
match Canada's record. None of the other British dominions had developed war-manufacturing industries on a scale anything like Canada's
and the country's farmers were contributing mightily to the common
cause, requiring a massive commitment of men who were not available
to the armed forces.[24]

Most important of all, from the Skelton point of view, conscription
ignored a central fact of Canadian political life: Quebec's difference
from the rest of Canada, and its right to be different. Had Borden and his
colleagues handled Quebec more sympathetically from August 1914 on,
putting more effort into understanding its special place in the national
bargain, unity might have been salvaged. That had not happened, and
Quebec was unalterably opposed to conscription. Skelton did not think
that the additional military strength that might result from compulsion
would outweigh the danger to the country itself. Events proved him
right. Conscription delivered 24,132 soldiers to France, but, as he predicted, its imposition substantially set back the great cause of national
unity to which Laurier had devoted his political career.[25]

The Military Service Act had a legislative companion that Skelton
abhorred more than conscription itself. The Wartime Elections Act was
designed to prepare the way for a federal election on the government's
terms, stacking the deck against Laurier. Likely opponents of the government, such as Canadian citizens born in enemy countries or conscientious objectors, were stripped of the vote; female relatives of soldiers
overseas were at the same time given the franchise in the expectation
that they would opt for conscription to support their men in harm's
way. A distinct breach of national faith, Skelton termed it, unworthy of a
country that professed to be fighting a war for democracy and reminiscent of the way enemy governments prolonged their grip on power. The
excuse given that ends justified means, that any measure was warranted
that would prevent the victory of the "traitorous and disastrous" Laurier,
"added insolence to highway robbery."[26]

Skelton wrote to Sir Wilfrid often during that bitter conscription
summer and autumn, which culminated in a divisive election called by

Borden for December 1917. The Liberal leader was encouraged to fight on and to see silver threads in the very black clouds "in our sky," while OD tried to do the same. He had hoped that he might do something that "would count" when a Toronto newspaper approached him over the summer to do work in an editorial capacity, but the publication's views on conscription were too far removed from his to make the arrangement possible. He confided to Laurier that he often regretted that he had chosen to become a scholar rather than taking up "some career which would have made it possible to go into politics at such a juncture."[27]

Laurier asked what ought to be in the Liberal election manifesto. The reply came back quickly, with the clarity in which Skelton specialized. Liberals must emphasize that "we are all in the war to the finish," but "we want the war to be Germany's finish, not Canada's." National unity had been put in jeopardy, and the country diminished in its capacity to prosecute the war, by a bungling and partisan Borden government. The prime minister had forced conscription on Canadians, suddenly, without consultation, and against his repeated assurances that he would do no such thing. During the election of 1911, Skelton continued, Borden had conspired with Bourassa to tell Quebec that it was no part of its duty to fight in Britain's wars; the government was reaping the whirlwind that its leader had unleashed, and blaming Quebecers for thinking what they had been taught to think. Nor had there been a thoughtful audit of the full range of national resources that the country had available for the war effort. It was not soldiers alone that were needed. "To make our weight tell," Canada should aim at "more food, more supplies, more ships, and of all the necessaries that Canada can supply better than almost any other of the belligerents."[28]

Skelton advised Laurier to hit hard at Borden's failure to bring economic policies in line with social justice. The government had piled up debt for future generations to pay and allowed the cost of living to soar, while a few businesses and their proprietors reaped obscene war profits. A tax on income had been introduced earlier in 1917, but it had come late and was too easy on the rich. The farmers, who were getting a raw deal both in the east and in the west, needed relief in the form of lower tariffs. When Laurier issued his election letter to Canadians in early November 1917, Skelton's ideas were all there, if only a few of his words. Laurier wrote his own prose.

Skelton tried to be optimistic about the Liberals' election prospects, especially in his cheerleading letters to Laurier, who was told that he was still the titan of Canadian politics, surrounded by loyal followers.

Even with the defection of key Liberal leaders in the western provinces, OD assured his leader that the chances of victory were more than even. The people would put up a "good fight" in a struggle that would vindicate national unity and national independence, the central political principles for which Laurier and Skelton stood and without which the country had no hope. The new Liberal Party would be positioned "to take a pretty radical stand on the question of imperial relations – a question that the next parliament will largely decide, no matter on what it is elected."[29]

Jeremiah Skelton was a better judge of the national mood. He wrote to his son "lovingly," but his indictment of Oscar's Liberals was harsh. The elder Skelton's universe imagined little else but righteous conscription and the perfidy of Quebec. Father reminded son that the Union government had the backing of the premiers, the preachers, and the professional class. All that was left for Laurier were the slackers who refused to enlist in the armed forces, the Germans and the pro-Germans, Bourassa's *nationalistes*, and discredited Liberals, Oscar presumably among them. Laurier was a disgrace. With a wave of his hand, he could have prevented anti-conscription riots in Kitchener and Quebec City, but instead he had tacitly encouraged them. A true man, "a manly man," would have done otherwise.[30]

Jeremiah rightly expected a big Unionist victory. He was very close to the mark in his prediction of the seats that would be won in the various regions of country except in the west, where the extent of the Unionist sweep surprised him, as it did his son. In the most divisive election Canada had seen, English Canada went one way, Quebec the other. Laurier was met on the campaign trail by cries of "traitor" that brought tears to his eyes. Outside Quebec he won only twenty seats. When he drafted the final pages of his biography of Laurier, Skelton remembered the election as bringing the country to the very edge of the precipice. He thought that unimaginable if Laurier or John A. Macdonald had been in charge.[31]

The election over, the Liberals crushed, Skelton communicated first not with his father but with Laurier. The result was disastrous, he allowed himself to admit to the man he admired most, splitting the country absolutely on French-English lines. A generation would be required to reassemble what the fanatics had destroyed in the bat of an eye. Yet the struggle had been wonderful. The other side had all the cards, and played them with flag-waving ruthlessness, but Laurier had met the challenge with "courage and persistence and the glamour and prestige that you enjoy so widely." Of course, Laurier must do everything he could to prevent trouble in Quebec, but no one should be allowed to forget the unscrupulous means that English Canadians had used to have their way. "People in Ontario who expect reconciliation to come by Quebec returning in sackcloth and ashes to beg forgiveness need to be shown that there must be advances from both sides, an attempt in both provinces not in one alone, at greater understanding & sympathy."[32]

The divisive election put Skelton's standing at Queen's on trial. He had been elected to the Royal Society of Canada the year before, and his reputation on the campus as an established scholar and progressive intellectual was immense. Presenting his strong views gently and with humour, "Skelly" was popular with his students. Everyone knew that he was a committed Liberal. So too was the just-appointed principal of the university, R. Bruce Taylor, a severe-faced Presbyterian minister who had been with Skelton on the Bonne Entente trip to Quebec. But Skelton was on the opposite side of the conscription debate from Taylor and the majority of the faculty and students – and, as he himself conceded, most of the country too. As 1918 began, two wealthy and influential Queen's alumni tried to force Skelton's resignation. One was the Winnipeg businessman James A. Richardson, the father of one of Skelton's students; the other was Walter Douglas, a prominent mining executive in the United States and the son of the Queen's chancellor, who was the university's chief benefactor. Taylor turned the protests away, even though the junior Douglas threatened (unsuccessfully, as it turned out) to scuttle a substantial donation from his father. Taking a brave stand in an angry time, Taylor asserted that "I have made up my mind that I would stand for liberty of utterance for every honest opinion. Queen's is going to be a place of freedom as long as I have anything to do with it."[33]

OD was grudgingly pleased by the firmness with which his adversaries had been dispatched. It was good to have "a man at the head of Queen's," even though the principal's position had been "the only one that could be expected." Skelton had opposed Taylor's appointment because he lacked a scholarly reputation and administrative experience. He was "second-rate," in no way exceptional. A university that wanted to be distinguished ought to have a distinguished chief executive. Despite Taylor's defence of Skelton at a crucial moment, the two men spent the next years at loggerheads on a wide range of university issues. Skelton wanted Queen's to do more research into and teaching of social and economic subjects and public policy. Taylor's "backwoods preacher" mentality got in the way.[34]

Skelton was not prepared to let the attempt to bring him down pass without a forceful response. Hitting back at the "heresy-hunters," he exploded in a letter of six densely packed handwritten pages addressed to G.Y. Chown, the secretary of the Queen's Board of Trustees, and through Chown to the board.[35] Unrepentant and at the same time on the defensive, Skelton insisted that he had not misused his position during the election campaign. He had privately discussed the election with a few senior students who solicited his views, but he was adamant that he had "religiously abstained" from any classroom discussion. When some of the young women in his politics class, about to vote for the first time, asked if he would take an hour to canvass the issues, he replied that he could not, "since in my opinion a member of the staff should not use the class room to air his own election views." Skelton did not wish to be forgiven on the grounds of academic freedom for something he hadn't done.

Academic freedom was nevertheless a vital principle, one that had to be maintained and defended. When, Skelton explained to Chown, he had arrived at Queen's ten years before, he realized that a professor who taught economics and politics could not avoid airing controversial problems. He did not wish to. Serious engagement with contemporary national debate was part of the way he taught. He did tell Chown, however, that the university could reasonably expect him to refrain from one-sided or partisan discussion.

There was a professional duty that Skelton felt even more keenly, to take his learning to the Canadian public. He conceded that it was a delicate business, to be done in a moderate and reasoned way, after careful and scholarly scrutiny of the subject and taking account of the fact that a university had crucial relationships with the public and government. Keeping a balance between freedoms he insisted on and the best interests of an institution that did not exist in a vacuum was a challenge that left him "intellectually cross-eyed" and thinking that he could operate more independently and effectively in a job outside Queen's. He acknowledged that his "truth" might simply be his pet version of it, but he came to his opinions honestly and with a training and experience that made him "more familiar than the average man with issues that come before the public." He had the citizen's right, and the scholar's responsibility, "to endeavor to make his views prevail."

Skelton ended his long letter to Chown as he began it, truculently. The conduct of his detractors was an "intolerable impertinence," and Richardson's views on political issues "were about as valuable as those of his scrubwoman." As for the criticisms of his conscription stand by George Callender, a Queen's professor of Greek who had immigrated to Canada ten years before and escaped its borders every chance he got, OD wondered whether it wasn't "slightly presumptuous" for a newcomer "to attempt to dictate to those of us whose ancestors have been here three or four generations what Canadian patriotism means." And wasn't a man whose life work was the study of political and economic questions at least as well qualified to speak about them as someone who taught Greek for a living? Skelton boasted that he did not need the university. There had not been a single year since 1908 that he had not received at least one offer to go elsewhere, and always at a much better salary – twice his Queen's pay or more. He was not therefore "under the temptation to submit to dictation because of fear of losing my job."

The country's conscription crisis, and the crisis it caused for Skelton, made him perversely determined "to do a good bit more in public" and "to discuss Canadian issues a good deal more freely in the future than in the past." His immediate preoccupation, however, was the war, which turned against the Allies in the spring of 1918. In March, when the Germans smashed the British Expeditionary Force and advanced their lines deep into France, Skelton wrote Laurier about the "most disturbing" progress of the enemy. The Russian Revolution of 1917 had sidelined Britain and France's principal ally, freeing half a million German soldiers from the eastern front for the attack to the west. Germany's offensives continued into June, causing Skelton to lament again to Laurier about how badly the war was going. At the same time, he casually reported some household news. His baby daughter, Sheila, had been born on 5 June.[36]

Skelton confronted the war's black turn resolutely. The Germans had captured men, supplies, and territory, but Paris remained in Allied hands and the will of the Allies had not been broken. Germany's brutal and immoral conduct of the war justified retaliation in kind – war was not "a pink tea," he warned *Queen's Quarterly* readers – and made an unconditional Allied victory more than ever indispensable. The avalanche of American troops pouring into France was beginning to make a difference. "A year ago," Skelton said to Laurier, "I thought the entrance of the Americans into the war was chiefly of value to themselves; now we see it is the only thing that saves us from an inconclusive peace or worse." The president of the United States, Woodrow Wilson, was emerging as the global exponent of a principled, sane, and tough liberalism, an international version of Wilfrid Laurier.[37]

Suddenly, or so it seemed to Skelton, the war came to an end. After a three-month Allied counter-offensive, with the Canadian Corps at the sharp end of the fighting, Germany surrendered on 11 November 1918. Kaiser Wilhelm abdicated his throne and Germany's war partners, the Turkish and Austro-Hungarian empires, fell by the wayside, soon to dissolve. OD exulted to Sir Wilfrid: "It is almost impossible to realize that the long struggle is over, and over so well. The Allies have a clean sheet whereon to write whatever future for the world they will."[38]

Skelton had been thinking seriously about the post-war global order. He informed Laurier that he had been working with the Canadian Council of Agriculture in devising a manifesto for farmers' political action. He attached the suggestions that he had sent to Norman Lambert, his contact at the council, beginning with a plea for the elimination of balance-of-power thinking, secret diplomacy, mad armaments spending, universal military service, and exclusive combinations of states. Picking up on a line of thought that he had frequently tried out in the past, he counselled that "we must build up a League of Nations, in order to restrain outlaw powers, to safeguard small nations, to permit orderly expansion and change, and give the world security for the immense task of rebuilding that must be faced." The remodelled international system should include international courts and a regime of sanctions "to prevent or punish wanton breach of the peoples' peace."[39]

Skelton's support of the farmers came naturally. Grounding his ideas in the conviction that agriculture was a vital part of Canadian social, economic, and political development, past and future, he had been consistently critical of national policies that emphasized the cities at the expense of the country. He marked sections of his attempt at a farmers' platform to show Laurier how many of the ideas, and how much of the phrasing, had been taken up by Lambert. Skelton told Lambert, however, to keep his role in the dark, because it would damn the document "to have it known that a professor had had anything to do with it." OD expected that little of what he had written would survive scrutiny when council members met, but he was wrong. His ideas and frequently his words became the United Farmers' platform in 1919 and was in turn put forward to Canadians as the agenda of the Progressive Party in the election of 1921.[40]

The Farmers' platform was a precise reflection of Skelton's agenda for a reformed Canada. It, and he, called for the democratization of agriculture, industry, economic organization, government, politics, and education, the embracing of better farming and farm-marketing methods, a direct voice for workers in the determination of hours, wages, and shop conditions, more opportunities for women in the workplace and politics, transparent election campaign contributions and expenditures, a greater role for individual members of Parliament and a reduction in the power of the executive, health and unemployment insurance, and the abolition of knighthoods and peerages imported from Great Britain. Skelton's aim was "to make our country in reality a land of freedom and equal opportunity, a land where every man and woman among us will have a fair chance to share in the decencies and comforts and the possibilities of development that hitherto have been restricted to the few."[41]

Skelton repeatedly stressed the transformative and contradictory impact of the war. It threw precedents and institutions into the melting pot. It frazzled nerves and generated a desperate and reckless temper. It damned Great Power politics, with its exclusive alliances, incessant intrigues, and perpetual instability. It broke old habits of industry and gave rise to vague promises of a new heaven on earth. It put the premium on force and accustomed people to the coercion of minorities and the worship of the state. It left the impression, through the expenditures of billions of government dollars, that society's resources were infinite. It unleashed revolutions and nationalisms, caused bankruptcy and famine, toppled governments of long standing, and refashioned the moral, economic, and intellectual universe. It was giving birth to a League of Nations that could be a channel for lofty aspirations of world peace and justice, but that also might become a tool in the hands of governments and selfish interests seeking prestige and loot.[42]

The war had torn Canada and its world up by the roots, destroying much of the established order. Labour had been divided from employer, west from east, urban from rural, francophones from the rest of the country – and soon, as their post-discharge gratuities inevitably ran out, returning soldiers would be another element of discord. There was danger everywhere of social cleavage and class conflict.

Even Skelton's farmers were not immune from the narrow impulse to organize for exclusively class ends. It was true beyond question, he wrote, that "for forty years the country has followed the policy of building up industrial at the expense of agricultural interests and made the economic privilege of the protected manufacturer a sacred and patriotic dogma." Nevertheless, "two class dogmas do not make a right, and rule by single clean-cut classes or by unstable and log-rolling combinations of classes is not in the country's interest." A government of and by farmers just for farmers would be next to no improvement over a government by lawyers on behalf of manufacturers. Skelton insisted, however, that this was not the spirit or the aim of the agrarian groups' "biggest men," who wanted not a farmer's brigade but a broad and democratic people's movement seeking no favours for anyone and refusing to give any. He was hopeful that the farmers would add to, not subtract from, national unity, and that "in time its main stream will flow in the channel of a genuinely liberal and progressive citizenship." Skelton was marking out a vital centre of national politics and citizenship. The cure for excessive class interests lay in a "spirit of moderation, a sense of solidarity, a feeling of common Canadianism and common brotherhood." The way forward was to sweep away class privileges and devise concrete methods of reconciling class interests.[43]

Skelton condemned the extreme left and the extreme right. As a student of socialism, he followed its chaotic course in revolutionary Russia with anxiety and disgust. The propagandists might deny it, and might think that they saw in the Russian experiment a model for a better way of capitalism, but there was a necessary connection between effort and reward. Once that combination was discarded, incentive disintegrated and the harsh disciplines of bureaucracy and bayonets came crashing down. "Ruthless repression of free speech, forced labour, compulsory military service, 'preferential feeding,' a huge bureaucracy saddled on the peoples' backs, spying, terrorism and ceaseless propaganda, these are the policies of socialism in practice in Russia." Yet it was a mistake for the Allies to send armed forces to Russia, as they did in 1918–19, in an effort to crush the revolution. The evidence was mounting that the invasion from outside was only strengthening the regime inside, as anyone versed in elementary human psychology could have warned. Left to its own devices, the infant regime would have to change direction or collapse; however, if brought down by foreigners, socialism would become a martyred cause, the victim of a bourgeois assault. Class wars, moreover, were infectious. If Canadians did not want one at home, they ought not to indulge in one abroad.[44]

The numerous Canadian strikes in the immediate aftermath of the First World War – the product of wartime inflation – were demonstrations of a radical labour unrest that Skelton imagined would have been impossible before 1914. The "limousine class" of the rich and the privileged saw a communist conspiracy in motion, but Skelton responded that the gang of thugs who shrieked for the overthrow of organized society and propagandized "for freedom as they have it in Russia" were few in numbers and supporters. He did not approve of the tactic of the general strike, employed in Winnipeg and Vancouver and aimed at shutting down the life of an entire city. He did, however, sympathize with the bulk of the strikers, particularly in their demand for collective bargaining, since "no economic policy is less open to question." An ardent defender of the free market, he still thought that organized labour deserved a public recognition of its rights and an appreciation of the seriousness and complexity of its dissatisfaction. No little band of fanatics could be permitted to force a revolutionary dictatorship on the majority of citizens, but the government could produce no certain evidence that that had been the strikers' plan or intent. What was more, when the disturbances ceased, the politicians abandoned the labour question that Canada faced in common with the rest of the world, making no effort to understand what precisely had happened and gone wrong, or how the social gulf could be healed.[45]

In Skelton's frame of reference, the workers were less to be feared than the bosses. Faced with a challenge from the left to capitalism, terrified plutocrats and hysterical officials ruthlessly put down the general strike in Winnipeg, imprisoned ideas and dissent, tromped on free speech, prohibited books, and censored foreign news. The communist parties in Soviet Russia and North America, evolving out of Marxian socialism and the Bolshevik Revolution in Russia, had a good friend in the panicky despotism of capitalists and conservatives. They would do more to create class warfare "than a generation of Socialist propaganda, more to strengthen the Communist party than thousands of soap-box orators." Never had there been more need to emphasize liberty of thought, speech, education, and the press as the cornerstones of democracy. The capacity and willingness to discuss, the opportunity to convince others peacefully of a point of view that was not their own, was "the only workable alternative to the machine gun from above and dynamite from below." Anarchists could not be tolerated at either end of society. Socialism as an idea, and at its root, was erroneous, "most of us believe," but the citizens of a democracy had the right to employ legitimate means to make their arguments and attempt to have them prevail.

Canada was saved from the worst radicalisms by superior national psychology and culture – superior, at least, to that of the United States. The virus of anti-socialism and anti-communism had not infected Canadians as it had Americans because of "our more responsible political machinery, our more slow-going temperament, our greater immunity from waves of '100 per cent' emotionalism." These happy advantages were inheritances from Great Britain. Class was more deeply entrenched in the Old Country, but there was calm assurance in the British approach to serious problems, and a willingness to build bridges over divergences of ideology and opinion. Great Britain was an exemplar of freedom and tolerance, at least so far as its internal affairs were concerned. And, more often than some people might think, in its empire as well. The achievements of this "most extraordinary political organization" were not to be deprecated, particularly after the acid test of a successful war had proved the empire's worth, adaptability, and right to exist.[46]

Independence was still a way off, but it was coming. Canada was no longer too weak to stand alone, and it had survived, grown, and prospered even during the recent disturbing years for "many a smaller power." The war had stimulated national consciousness at home and advanced the international understanding and recognition of Canada's status as a nation. Among the greater tasks and opportunities of the peace would be "the effort to enable Canada to take its full share in the work of the world."[47]

By war's end, the first volume of the Laurier biography was close to completion. Skelton's subject was his constant collaborator. Since their first encounter five years before, Sir Wilfrid had dispensed his considerable charm in the younger man's direction. The easy-going politician set aside time for interviews and visits; sent warm handwritten notes and offers, sometimes accepted, to pay Skelton's expenses; provided confidential documents and allowed him to take boxes of personal papers away to his Kingston attic; and put OD up in accommodation that made him gush to Isabel that "I'll be getting spoiled for common houses." Skelton gave Laurier the first three chapters for comments at the end of the summer of 1918, and sought out the documents covering the former prime minister's period in office, which was to be at the heart of the second volume. These papers were turned over and taken home to Kingston the next year.[48]

At the beginning of February 1919, Laurier asked Skelton to write a pamphlet "in order to counteract the anti-French campaign which has been going on in the English-speaking provinces for some years." The suggestion appealed to Skelton. "There is no room for question as to the unscrupulous character of the campaign, or as to its success. After poisoning Ontario, the bigots are doing their best to induce the same result in the western provinces. I feel that no work more truly patriotic could be conceived than an attempt to expose some of the misrepresentations, and let the plain unadorned facts speak for themselves." It was an emergency, there was no doubt, but the project would have to wait.

The university's faculty was understaffed, and Skelton's tiny political and economic science department particularly so with the departure of Clifford Clark for a temporary stint at the Department of Labour in Ottawa. Clark had not been replaced. Skelton was "swamped with work, and in fact have never been so busy or so tired." He announced to the other members of the executive of the Canadian Political Science Association that he would give up his position as secretary-treasurer "on account of pressure of college & other work."[49]

The booklet to combat anti-French prejudice was never written. Buoyed by the end of the Great War, Laurier had rallied back from illness with plans for a great national convention of the Liberal Party. But he was a frail seventy-seven years old. Not quite two weeks after asking for Skelton's help, he suffered a severe cerebral hemorrhage and partial paralysis. He died the next day, on 17 February 1919.[50]

Skelton was a cool, even frosty, observer of the human cavalcade, but Laurier's death affected him deeply. He was among the "sorrowing pilgrims," his description of the Canadians who flocked to Ottawa to pay their respects to a man whose life was interwoven into their lives. Laurier had shared with the first prime minister, John A. Macdonald, the sympathetic understanding of people, the passion for a unified country, and the flexible adaptability of a great party and national leader. Most of all, Skelton remembered from their dozens of times together, it was Laurier's "courtliness, tolerance, and breadth of view" that was so striking and memorable.[51]

Skelton felt the heavy weight of Laurier's legacy. There was more urgency now, a country to build – and, after conscription, a country to rebuild. Accused himself of letting down his country during the war, Skelton never again questioned Quebec's loyalty to Canada, instead shaping his biography of Sir Wilfrid into an explicit defence of national unity and an implicit plea for national reconciliation. In the meantime, the caravan moved on: the irreplaceable man would have to be replaced. If Laurier's vision of a single Canada was to be preserved, OD was sure who the next leader of the Liberal Party must be.

4
Courting Mr King, 1919–22

The 1919 Liberal national convention made the choice Skelton hoped for, narrowly electing Mackenzie King as the party's leader. The two men had an association that went back to the Laurier government, and earlier in the year Skelton had favourably reviewed King's just-published *Industry and Humanity*, an appeal for a more harmonious partnership between management and labour that underlined the similarity of their ideas about the industrial workplace. King, so OD wanted to believe, was in the Skelton mould: "a clear-cut progressive" who followed "the old individualist programme of free trade, freedom of speech and action, a free nation in a peace-seeking empire."[1]

Sending congratulations to the new Liberal chief on the convention's "very happy result," Skelton assured King that everyone who knew him would have hope for a vigorous Liberal Party. He was no admirer of large-scale American-style political conventions, with brass bands and brave speeches "as guides to sober decision," but he declared that "democracy has once more been justified by its fruits." The "old crowd," he purred, would be slow to forgive King for "the crime of being young and taking the business of statesmanship seriously," but "your election is a significant proof of the widespread feeling that training and special capacity and not mere glad-handing are needed in our politics."[2]

This was a nice way of accentuating the positive, an acknowledgment that King might have clear purpose, manifold qualifications, and a grasp of public issues, but he had none of the flair or humanity of Wilfrid Laurier. Nor had King yet demonstrated the consistent and clearly conceived body of principles that marked out a real leader. His problems were daunting. In the party as in the country, there were sectional antagonisms and racial tensions left over from the First World War. The discontent of the farmers was particularly worrying, because they seemed disposed to hive off from the Liberal Party and run candidates on their own. Nevertheless, Skelton was confident that King would "more than rise to the great occasion" and pledged himself to following King's career "with the warmest good wishes." King responded that he would look towards Skelton for advice in dealing with the economic and social problems that promised to be of ever greater significance in national politics. He said nothing of British Empire dilemmas or foreign problems more generally – such issues, for King apparently, were much less pressing. Skelton should visit if he found himself in Ottawa.[3] He began to do that, and their exchanges of views and letters accumulated as time went on.

Skelton was named dean of arts at Queen's just after the Liberal convention, good evidence that the wartime conscription controversy had not permanently damaged his standing in the university. Probably at his instigation, the university gave King an honorary degree in the fall of 1919. After the ceremony, OD repeated his concerns about the political influence of the farmers. The United Farmers of Ontario had won the recent provincial election, and farmer power seemed determined to go its own way on the federal scene as well. Skelton was troubled by the disintegration of the two-party system that had been fundamental to the stability of national politics. He hoped that farmer demands would be accommodated in a new Liberal Party – a broader, more responsive, and reform-minded coalition.[4]

A federal election, Skelton urged in his *Queen's Quarterly* column, was owed to Canadians. It was wrong for the Borden Union government to use a war majority to maintain power in peacetime. Coalitions were artificial combinations that in normal times bred "deadlock, intrigue, a mere canceling of principles." The war over, the government had deteriorated into a crumbling wreck, the tool of the big interests and "the most unpopular government in Canadian annals." Thoroughly worn out, Borden tried to resign as party leader and prime minister in December 1919, but his colleagues would not let him go, and he carried on grimly for another six months. Once he was gone, the professor's appraisal was generous. Borden was another of the men willing to chance the public arena, animated by an elevated purpose and sincere patriotism. His government's legislative and administrative record compared favourably with that of previous administrations. The deeply rooted discontent at war's end was debilitating: it would have defeated "a cabinet of archangels with a parliamentary following of cherubim and seraphim."[5]

The good and prudent Borden was succeeded by the Unionists' dark prince, Arthur Meighen, the architect of conscription and the jailer of the leaders of the 1919 general strike in Winnipeg. Meighen was anathema to Skelton, who thought of the Conservative leader as a Canadian version of Lenin, the leader of the new communist state in Russia. OD agreed that the two men shared reputations as smart, able, industrious, and honest men, but that masked the fact that they were destroyers of freedom. The passage of Meighen's 1917 Wartime Elections Act, loading the electoral dice to ensure the victory of the Unionists, was not very different from Lenin's Soviet organization, which excluded everyone from participation in the Russian government except his fanatical backers. There was more to be said for the tough Meighen policy on the Winnipeg strike, since many Canadians shared his apprehension that a Russian-like revolution was in the offing and were prepared to support what was necessary to prevent it. However, Skelton wrote in the *Queen's Quarterly*, that did not justify Meighen's tactics during the Winnipeg strike: "the hysterical exaggeration, the lack of adequate inquiry into the real facts, the midnight arrests, the attempt to deny a public trial to some of the men accused" and "for that matter the antiquated interpretation of the law which makes a sympathetic strike a seditious conspiracy." Lenin took refuge in class warfare and Meighen in a superior patriotism. Their blunt instruments and undemocratic methods were the same, as was their conviction that they had a monopoly not simply on the truth "but the whole truth." Taking his cue from Skelton, Mackenzie King publicly alluded to the similarities between the prime minister of Canada and the ruler of revolutionary Russia, incendiary language at a time of widespread fear that foreign ideas and influences were infiltrating Canadian minds and hearts.[6]

Skelton was anxious to continue Laurier's work in reuniting the Liberal Party, still split after the bruising wartime battle over conscription. He chided his friend Charles Murphy, an MP for the Ontario riding of Russell and a former Laurier cabinet minister, for his intransigent stand against allowing pro-conscriptionist sinners to return home to Liberalism. "If only men who have been always 100% Liberals are ... to be admitted, I'm afraid the membership of the party will be as scant as it will be select," OD wrote to his fellow Irishman. "I quite grant you that it is one thing to welcome men back to the fold, and another to give them immediately posts of power & confidence. But why not let them at least earn their spurs, without being hopelessly damned for ever for deserting in 1917?" On another issue, this time agreeing with Murphy, Skelton added that a national Liberal Party fund ought to be established to help underwrite campaign expenses, as well as "to make individual Liberals feel they had a stake in the party & convince the public that the Liberal party was not relying on patronage & subsidy sources."[7]

A federal election was set for the end of 1921. Midway through the autumn campaign, Skelton explored its dynamics in a liberal American periodical, the *New Republic*. The government was old and tired, he reported, but Meighen was (at forty-seven, the same age as King and five years older than OD) young and purposeful. Acting more like the leader of the Opposition than a prime minister, Skelton wrote, the intellectually keen and eloquent Meighen was on the attack, employing high tariffs and the danger of revolutionary change as his crude weapons. Calling his party the Conservatives again, the prime minister declared war on the farmers' movement, running in the election under the Progressive banner, "as a reckless and selfish class organization, seeking to impose its will regardless of justice or national necessities." He targeted both the Progressives and the Liberals as economic wreckers who menaced the country's industry, unity, and independent existence with their demands for lower tariffs on imports into a still-developing Canada. Skelton was convinced that even unsophisticated voters would reject the idea that protectionism created progress and prosperity and that freer trade meant stagnation and unemployment. The National Policy's tariffs had sheltered Canadian industry for forty years. It was time to try another course, moderately. Skelton informed his American audience that the majority of Liberals favoured a careful and gradual downward trajectory in tariff rates, and possibly a renewal of attempts to conclude a freer trade agreement with the Americans like that of 1911.[8]

In the confusing state of post-war Canadian politics, with irksome Progressive and Labour candidates on the scene, Skelton imagined it possible that the Liberals would lose their relevance. That was happening to his brother Liberals in Britain and Europe, crushed from above by the right and from below by the left. He wrote to King at the end of the campaign to repeat his hope that an accommodation or, even better, a true meeting of minds could be reached with the farmers, so that a sound basis for a vibrant Liberal movement could be established and "a new and genuine Liberalism will be continued under your guidance and inspiration."[9]

Skelton insisted that he was "very hopeful" of a good election outcome, but he was less convinced than King of an outright Liberal victory and more committed to an alliance with the Progressives. Although the

Meighen campaign had gone well for a while, pulling the Conservatives out of the deep slough in which they were mired when Parliament was dissolved, it seemed probable that most of the seats in House of Commons would go to the Liberals and Progressives. Yet a clear majority for the Liberals, OD told King, "hardly seems likely." They were dominant in Quebec and the Maritimes, but the Progressives were strong in Ontario and on the prairies; the two parties were competing against each other in too many constituencies, with the inevitable result that Meighen would sometimes win in a three-cornered contest. Just as they had in 1911, the Conservatives were cooperating with *nationaliste* forces in Quebec, which might cut into Liberal strength there. And all of Canada's women were entitled to vote for the first time in a federal election, a reform for which Isabel Skelton had campaigned, adding further to the uncertainty of the outcome.[10]

The Liberals won but fell short of a majority, winning 116 out of the available 245 seats in the December 1921 election. In his letters over the previous two years to King, who had not cut an impressive figure as leader of the Opposition, Skelton had been uniformly complimentary, unearthing something positive in every negative. Writing two days after the election, he again overdid the praise. King had "swept" the dominion, although he had done no such thing. The victory in the country and in his riding had been "magnificent." With fifty seats to the Progressives' sixty-four, Meighen had been utterly defeated. "I had not dared to hope for as much," OD enthused. "I shall not venture to add to the advice with which you must be deluged. I can only say that I congratulate you and congratulate Canada. You face a hard task, but I am fully confident that you will carry it through to complete success."[11]

Quebec gave all of its sixty-five seats to the Liberals. Skelton was pleased for the short term, because, as went Quebec, so went his party's fortunes at a moment when Meighen had to be beaten for the good of the country. That the province had voted as a bloc, wrote OD in the *Queen's Quarterly*, "should not surprise anyone who happens to remember that there was an election in Canada in 1917 in which the majority of the English-speaking people of Ontario and the West combined to impose upon Quebec the policy of conscription." The memory was understandably sharp, and racial feeling was intense: it was inevitable "that the preservation of the position and standing of the French element in our population should assume first place in the thought and policy of Quebec." He had observed, however, encouraging hints of harmony and reconciliation in the province and outside. Race, language, and religious differences were natural in "this land of many stocks," but with a growth of Canadian national sentiment, and a reprieve from war and the crises of empire, the fault lines of cleavage and group organization would fade. The solid Quebec of the present would become the differentiated Quebec of the future, with healthy consequences for the "common Canadianism" that was Skelton's hope.[12]

Six weeks after the election, and hard on the heels of the publication of his Laurier biography, Skelton travelled to Ottawa to address a Canadian Club luncheon meeting on the subject of "Canada and Foreign Policy." In front of (the Ottawa *Citizen* reported) "an unusually large gathering, which included Premier King and other members of the government," Skelton described himself as an outsider who had come to the capital with an educating mission to get his subject the public attention it merited. He proceeded from the premise that foreign affairs were an imperative of nationhood, an extension of domestic self-government, because a line could not be drawn between issues at home and issues abroad. Claiming that there was nothing very mysterious about foreign policy, he likened it to the day-to-day routine of coping with neighbours. Canada had been doing diplomacy for a long time, extending its control in the field and building up a machinery to carry out its responsibilities in the form of a minister of external affairs with a small (but effective, he stipulated, probably without meaning it) department at his disposal. Thus, the Canada of early 1922 legislated tariffs, secured trading arrangements with other countries, controlled immigration and emigration, and administered military forces, "nearly all the matters ordinarily dealt with under the head of foreign policy." Nation building in foreign affairs had proceeded steadily over decades, and under both political parties. It was an almost continuous process, growing out of "a certain definitely Canadian, as distinct from Liberal or Conservative viewpoint on these matters."[13]

But no longer, Skelton warned. The British were mounting a revolution, "very quietly, very casually, apparently, without any authority or any ratification by the Canadian parliament or the Canadian people, and with very little discussion." The intent was nothing less than to reverse the emphatic progress towards self-government over two generations and return to the bad old days when there was a uniform imperial foreign policy run by London for the British and only for them. A unified empire would require the Canadian government to make out a series of blank cheques payable on demand to the British foreign minister and intended to underwrite the empire's worldwide commitments. "It means that we are to ignore all the differences of interests, all the differences of situation, all the differences of sentiment, all the internal complexities, and to set up what in the long run, even it were tried, would prove to be a hopelessly impracticable unity where there really is diversity."[14]

"Even if it were tried" was a telling phrase. Apart from a couple of official speeches and some words buried in the communiqué of the 1921 Imperial Conference, Skelton had no evidence to justify his sweeping rhetoric about revolutions and reversals. As his description of the march forward of Canadian autonomy demonstrated, he believed that British-dominion relations had on the whole developed positively and that Canadians could now opt out of major empire decisions if they had the will to do so. The country was not yet free, and there would be always be danger as long as it was not. Nevertheless, the urgency of his message to the Canadian Club was entirely of his own making. A short while before, he had had no pressing concerns about the direction of events, praising Arthur Meighen's nationalist stance at the recent Imperial Conference. But now the King Liberals, the heirs to Laurier, were in power, and the prime minister and other ministers were seated in front of him. It was too good a chance to miss. He exaggerated the imperialist threat to make his case for self-government in external affairs. "In all matters of foreign relationship," he demanded of his Liberal friends, "the stand that Canada is to take must be decided in Canada by Canada's elected representatives – by men responsible to the people of Canada."[15]

Autonomy, Skelton was quick to add, did not mean isolation from the international community and its problems and opportunities. Canada was a long way away from most other countries, but the last few years had shown that it was part of an interdependent world "and must be of it." Even if they simply acted according to the principle of enlightened self-interest, Canadians had obligations and interests that bound them to "the society of mankind." That was particularly true of Canadian membership in the British Empire, "the most wonderful experiment in political relations that has ever been attempted ... absolutely unique, unparalleled, unprecedented, in its structure and relationship." There ought to be cooperation with the other states of the empire for the common good, as well as participation "in measures, particularly constructive measures, particularly measures that do not tangle us for ten, twenty or forty years, for the amelioration of the conditions in the world around us." Canada's influence should not be exaggerated. With a population of only eight million people and little experience of international institutions, Canada was small and decidedly junior. "We are not born to set all the world's difficulties aright in the next two or three years. We have a few at home that will tax the ablest of our statesmen. Let us take our part, but let it be a modest part, and at the same time an intelligent part."[16]

Skelton's lecture argued for the democratization of Canadian foreign policy. External affairs ought not to be the preserve of the few. Even in a country as liberal and democratic as Great Britain, there had not been a sufficiently wide parliamentary and popular consideration of foreign policy. Secret diplomacy had contributed to the headlong rush to war in 1914. If they were going to take on a more independent global role, Canadians needed to expect more of themselves and their politicians. Members of Parliament had a responsibility to familiarize themselves with foreign issues and to air them in debate and perhaps in a new House of Commons committee dedicated to the subject. Canadians had to become much better informed, not about the specifics of some passing dispute between faraway countries, but about the broad lines of world events and the way the country fitted into the complex equation of international life. Good citizenship demanded serious study and an awareness that travellers to another country, and everyone who came in contact with a foreigner, was an ambassador for Canada. "Each action of ours, each foolish and slighting word or each sensible and sympathetic word, goes to build up a fund of prejudice or a fund of good-will in other countries, and it is that fund of prejudice or that fund of good-will that is the texture out of which foreign policy in the last issue is made."[17]

The Canadian Club address, and a similar one given in Toronto to the same organization a week later at the King Edward Hotel, was the subject of several newspaper stories, not all of them favourable. The press fastened on the professor's remarks about Sir Robert Borden. The former prime minister, then at the Disarmament Conference in Washington, had done excellent work for Canadian self-government in foreign affairs, Skelton had declared, "apart from a few aberrations in the way of Imperial cabinets and so on," a reference to Borden's First World War experiments in closer empire cooperation that prompted laughter from the heavily Liberal Ottawa crowd. Yet, in Skelton's reckoning, Borden's mission to Washington was "a slur upon the dominions' post-war status." He (and the Meighen government that had dispatched him) had consented to be part of the British team, rather than to sit for Canada, going back on the precedent of separate national representation that Borden himself had established at the Paris Peace Conference.[18]

The Ottawa *Citizen* contradicted Skelton. The plain fact was that Borden represented Canada at the Disarmament Conference, not Great

Britain or the empire. The newspaper's editorial noted in a friendly way the surprising error of "such an authority on Canadian political development as Professor Skelton," but the cross-town Ottawa *Journal* used the mistake to mount an assault on the scholar and his dangerous ideas. Under the heading "Shall We Balkanize the Empire?" the *Journal* maintained that the British and Arthur Meighen had reversed nothing and changed nothing; their only aim, at the 1921 Imperial Conference and elsewhere, was fruitful cooperation between the self-governing states of "the greatest league of nations that the world has seen – the British Commonwealth." The alternative was to let Canada's "bigoted autonomists" and "narrow separatists" have their way. His professorial spectacles askew, Skelton was the real revolutionary, wanting to divide the empire into watertight compartments and precipitate its "swift and certain sundering."[19]

There was one aspect of the Skelton lecture that was indisputable, the *Journal* editorial sarcastically concluded. He had urged his listeners "to study foreign policy, and – we say this without desire to give offence – he illustrated the need, by a series of misconceptions on his own part, remarkable in a Canadian of acknowledged ability and erudition." To Isabel, her family pride stung, the criticism made sense if she considered the source. She identified the piece as the partisan twaddle of the *Journal's* Grattan O'Leary, a staunch Conservative who had been Meighen's private secretary during the 1921 Imperial Conference and who subsequently spent a career justifying the former prime minister's life and works.[20]

The Canadian Club speeches amplified Skelton's profile as a spokesman for Liberal nationalism and pushed him closer to Mackenzie King. The prime minister, who doubled as secretary of state for external affairs, had inherited a Department of External Affairs that he characterized as a "Tory hive," populated by Sir Joseph Pope, who had been private secretary to John A. Macdonald, and the empire-minded Nova Scotian Loring Christie, for the past decade the foreign policy adviser to Conservative prime ministers Borden and Meighen. King told Skelton after his Ottawa talk that he might be wanted one day as the successor to Pope, the under-secretary and permanent head of External Affairs. "Skelton's address would make an excellent foundation for Canadian policy on External Affairs, and Skelton himself would make an excellent man for that department," King wrote in his diary that night. "He certainly has the knowledge & the right point of view."[21] The knowledge, the point

of view – and the ability to dress King's ideas up and trot them forth for
public consumption.

The years immediately after the war were the busiest and most productive of Skelton's career as a public academic. He wrote quickly, and often,
finishing off a history of Canada for the United States market, publishing
thick biographies of Wilfrid Laurier and A.T. Galt, and co-authoring a
history of a pioneering national institution, the Canadian Bank of Commerce. He dispatched articles to the *Queen's Quarterly*, the *Grain Growers'
Guide*, the *Journal of the Canadian Bankers' Association*, and a variety of
magazines and newspapers. Skelton also edited the Canadian Bankers'
Association journal, was back on the executive of the struggling Canadian Political Science Association, and served on editorial committees for
the *Queen's Quarterly*. This was in addition to his obligations as Queen's
dean of arts and head of the political economy department under an (he
thought) imperfect principal, full-time administrative work that he combined with his teaching. He gave guest addresses at the hint of an invitation, often on a very small stage like that provided by women's groups
or Rotary Clubs, but sometimes on occasions that required considerable
thought and preparation, as in his series of addresses in the first Queen's
Chancellor's Lectureship, where he spoke in the autumn of 1922 on race,
religion, and business in world politics, remarking on the role of oil and
the rise of Islam as contemporary forces in international relations.[22]

As the son of a man who held many jobs and often struggled, money
was always on OD's mind. He was determined to have the good things he
wanted for himself and his young family, among them the fashionable
house he had built at 138 Albert Street in Kingston. Extra cash was the
particular motivation of his work for the bankers; many other academics
performed similar services. Since 1915 Skelton had been earning $500
a year for the courses he arranged at Queen's for the bankers' association, and he was paid for his work on their journal and his participation
in the Canadian Bank of Commerce history. He gave up the position
of university director of banking when he became dean for a five-year
period, but the dean's work added $500 to his professor's pay of $3,500.
He lived constantly beyond his means, asking for advances on his salary at Queen's and taking out bank loans at the Kingston branch of the
Merchants Bank.[23]

Skelton was compensated by Galt's son to write *The Life and Times of
Sir Alexander Tilloch Galt*, and the younger Galt (no longer young) paid
for the book's printing by Oxford University Press. The product of the

most extensive historical research that OD ever undertook, there was as much "times" in the volume as there was "life," which Skelton thought was necessary because so little of the context of Galt's Canadian life had yet been exposed. This made for a big book of almost six hundred pages, and often a dull one as Skelton plodded through the minutiae of railways policy or trade negotiations. He did not really get inside Galt, or apparently want to. As a later critic assessed the book, "propriety seemed to restrain Skelton from probing beneath the surface to discover what motivated this dynamic, volatile, infectiously enthusiastic person."[24] A mercurial man, that is, so different from OD, which might have been part of the problem.

The Galt biography was solid and stolid stuff, and its author was the first to agree that it was "weak in the lack of personal touch." The book was nevertheless admired in the tiny academic community of the time for its thoroughness and industry. What shone most brightly was Galt's nation making – the Province of Canada's finance minister, who issued a declaration of independence from Britain with his pioneering 1859 tariff; the father of Confederation, present at the creation of Canada; and the country's first diplomat, who brought "the new power among the nations" before the world. A recurring theme in Skelton's writings was the indissoluble link between politics and commerce and the manner in which economic measures such as the Galt Tariff and a stable banking system contributed to the growth of Canadian autonomy.[25]

The *Life and Letters of Sir Wilfrid Laurier*, which Skelton was pushing frantically through to the end at the same time as he was finishing the proofs of *Galt*, was a more personal project. He made his commitment to Laurier clear from the outset, in the preface to the two volumes, when he described his subject as "a moving orator, a skilled parliamentarian, a courageous party leader, and a faithful servant of his country" and "the finest and simplest gentleman, the noblest and most unselfish man, it has ever been my good fortune to know." The journalist Grant Dexter later used the last of those same words to describe Skelton himself.[26]

The Laurier-Skelton perspective on things national and international was similar, but not perfectly so. The account in the *Life and Letters* of Canadian encounters with the British Empire as the nineteenth century became the twentieth reflected the predilections of the purposeful young man OD had been back then and the nationalist missionary he had become. Skelton's main target, because he was convinced that it was the main threat to Canadian unity and independence, was the "frank and arrogant gospel" of a narrowly racial imperialism that excluded anyone who could not be transformed into an Englishman, "while the lesser breeds of Africa and Asia must accept the rule of their trustees for all time." Yet the flood tide of imperialism had swept away doubts about a Canadian contribution to the South African War in 1899. Laurier capitulated, Skelton believed, in part because he had empire sympathies himself. No amount of pressure from the manipulating elite of England, *Life and Letters* acknowledged, would have had any effect had Canadians not met Britain halfway over South Africa.[27] He never stopped believing that an incorrigible English imperialism could count on its Canadian accomplices – even, in this case, his beloved Laurier.

Unlike *Galt*, a fat and footnoted doorstop of a book about a politician and a time scarcely remembered, the Laurier biography made something of an international impression. A British edition, issued by the Humphrey Milford imprint for Oxford University Press in 1922, caught the attention of several newspapers, including the Manchester *Guardian* and *The Times* of London, as well as serious periodicals of the stamp of the *Spectator* and *Statesman*. The commentary, employing phrases such as "highly interesting" or "very skillful," was usually restrained. The *Guardian* rightly concluded that Skelton was "an austere biographer in that he shuns the personal and intimate, and scorns the 'good story.' But he has a vigorous and polished style, and on occasion a dry humour." The *Times Literary Supplement* added that Skelton had "given to the world a comprehensive life of Laurier on a monumental scale, thoroughly well informed and manifestly the result of long and patient research." However, there was far too much dreary background and not enough of the foreground, where "a true measure of the personal charm and power of the great French-Canadian Prime Minister" ought to have been captured and conveyed. The narrative was also marred by "a manifest political bias."[28]

The biography was serialized in the *Century Magazine*, a popular U.S. monthly, beginning in October 1919. Three years later, the complete volumes were published in New York by the magazine's parent company. The reviews in the United States were many fewer than in Britain and much less polite. The *Nation*, on the left of American politics, deployed a Canadian, V.L.O. Chittick, who was teaching university students in the United States, to examine the biography. From the perspective of that "genuine lover of democracy," Skelton had revealed a shameful Canada, awash in public immorality, religious conflict, economic distrust, and sectional hatred. OD's Laurier was a good man, but the biographer had failed to justify him, documenting nothing much more than the life of an opportunist politician sailing with the breezes of the moment. Writing dismissively in the *New Republic*, the prominent historian Charles Beard wondered what Laurier secrets lay hidden below a surface that Skelton had not begun to penetrate. A "plain, prosaic account of a plain, prosaic man" was the best the author could do. Isabel did not paste that review into her scrapbook.[29]

The Canadian edition of *Life and Letters* caused a minor sensation, beginning with news stories detailing Skelton's occasional revelations about Laurier's personal life. The publisher, S.B Gundy, brought the two books out together in an $8 boxed set in the late fall of 1921, in time for "the most important Canadian publication of the decade" to be advertised as the ideal Christmas present. The Laurier biography was either the splendidly readable "romance of a rapidly developing nationhood" or the shoddy and prejudiced work of "a poor historian" who had "shown himself to be wholly unfitted for the task allotted to him, however distinguished he may be in other lines of literary achievement." One of the toughest critics was J.W. Dafoe, the editor of the *Manitoba Free Press*, a committed Liberal but still smarting over his break with Laurier (and so implicitly with Skelton) over French-language issues and conscription during the First World War. In a series of articles that became a small book, Dafoe set out to correct "the official version" of Laurier's performance, as executed by Skelton, "a thorough-going partisan."[30]

The most perceptive assessment of the biography came from Arthur Hawkes, who had been Skelton's brief but sympathetic colleague in the Canadian League and in the Bonne Entente movement. For Hawkes, *Life and Letters* was the result of OD's "honorable enthusiasm" for Laurier and for Canada. Skelton was one of those brainy youngsters who had tried the United States, returning cheerfully to Kingston "because he was a Canadian first and wanted to be a Canadian last and all the time." He had experience away from college halls, but he demonstrated the conscious restraint of the professor. The Laurier biography was "a splendid statue being moved on Skeltonian wheels. Everything is clear, and clear cut." The statue was "fine on its wheels," but "it might have had a little more body and blood and bones."[31]

As a hectic 1922 winter term wound down, Skelton planned a workaholic's summer vacation. Working with his secretary until almost midnight the day before his departure, he set out for Quebec City and on to England by ship in early June to fill personnel gaps in the arts and commerce programs at Queen's and, as he told Mackenzie King, to study post-war social and political conditions in Britain and on the continent of Europe.[32] For six weeks he hurried from his base at the Canadian

High Commission in London to Glasgow, Edinburgh, Leeds, Sheffield, Manchester, Birmingham, Oxford, and Cambridge, visiting their universities, drawing comparisons with his own, and searching out recruits in accounting, history, and English. His Queen's arts faculty seemed to him as good as all its British counterparts, and he felt that the university's commerce courses had the potential to be easily better than about half of its rivals in England and Scotland. He spent extra time at the colleges in the Midlands and the industrial north, because they were more like Queen's in their organization and spirit and represented a broadening of the highway of British education. The architecture of the new universities was presentable enough, although he thought they lacked the charm of the Cambridge Backs or the High Street of Oxford. The students were keen and self-reliant. When a professor complained that the well-to-do continued to send their sons to Oxbridge colleges, and that his charges were too much from the lower middle class, OD replied that Canada was saved from that fate because "we were all lower middle class."[33]

After an extensive canvass of professors and private practitioners in the field, and interviews with eighteen candidates, Skelton settled on two accountancy appointments. Always stingy, he drove a hard bargain on salaries and transport to Queen's. Arts men were more difficult to secure. He reported back to Principal Bruce Taylor that it was impossible to get established teachers to consider the move, especially since Queen's wages were simply not competitive, a complaint he repeatedly made during his time as dean of arts. Great Britain could also offer "a full and interesting life," which OD implied was richer than anything his country could give, though "I couldn't imagine wanting to move from Canada to England myself." He could find no one suitable for a history job and repeated to Taylor his suggestion that Sir Robert Borden be invited to give a series of lectures on the subject. For the post in English, he discovered one possibility. He told the principal, however, that he favoured a Canadian candidate, who had "the exuberance of a very imaginative mind" and was "a real man in every way." In his assessments of potential British colleagues, he favoured congenial young scholars who had the capacity to grow and develop intellectually, and who were readily detachable from their surroundings and could easily adapt to Canadian ways. He sought character, energy, industry. He valued "distinct individuality," "a very clear orderly mind," "a good deal of initiative," and "a good quiet teacher." He deplored the self-absorbed and those who were "quite too dilettante."[34] In short, he looked for himself.

Returning after many years to a country he admired, Skelton first noticed the gaudy surface of post-war Britain. Lumbering buses crowded the city streets and roared through the countryside from Land's End at the foot of England to the Scottish Highlands. There were more motorcycles than ever, making a huge racket. Twelve-horsepower cars, slung low to the ground, had multiplied, their prices slashed to ward off the invasion of competition from Canada and the United States. Huge office buildings had risen up, equipped with flashy transatlantic technology, and there was an inexorable if cautious trend towards the skyscrapers that he had observed in big American cities. Sport was popular, drinking prevalent but less common than before the war, and betting an obsession. Lowbrow news and advertising cluttered the ancient landscape: one of the newspapers had unleashed a "new terror," a skywriting airplane that blared demands for cheaper beer or some politician's head. The music hall had lost some of its shine, and motion pictures, with American films dominating, had a tight hold on the public.[35]

Skelton ate up several newspapers a day. The London press, he concluded, had diminished in personality and moral force. Only the *Times*, the *Telegraph*, the *Morning Post*, and in a pinch the *Daily News* made a serious effort at news and editorial content, and none of the London papers took on the world sufficiently for his taste. The advertiser ruled in an atmosphere of intense competition, gimmicks, and commercialization. Millionaire amateur proprietors (the Canadian Lord Beaverbrook was one) meddled, their personal ambitions at the ready and their newspapers rudderless, simply "all things to all men, and all women, and all office boys." Canada was almost impossible to find in the papers, an omission that was understandable since the country was a "fringe" but that also ran against the rhetoric about how much the empire mattered to the British. The press was a crucial ingredient in the Skelton formula for democracy, citizenship, and nation building; newspapers shared "with the school and the church the great and unending task of public education, the mission of interpreting and guiding its time." Yet the better Canadian papers had a more balanced coverage of British, American, and European events than could be found in those of the imperial capital. He observed that smaller countries were perhaps less provincial than the bigger ones.[36]

The war had altered Britain, but not its people, who remained calm and patient, moderate of temper, respectful of tradition, and capable of rational compromise. This managed to be true in spite of masses of debt and unemployment, bitter class divisions, the notable and shameful gap between rich and poor, a decided gender imbalance after so many men had failed to return home from the 1914–18 conflict, and a hardening of opposition nearly everywhere against established ways. Skelton remarked that, alone among the great European states, Britain was "exempt not only from revolution, but from a revolutionary movement of serious import." There were no mobs, no riots, no disorder. "Not one capitalist has been hanged to a lamp-post, while many continue to be elevated to the House of Lords." Poor workers looked instead to the unions, cooperative societies, education, and sometimes to emigration. Or they turned to the church or to gambling, two expedients that Skelton thought were not an answer to anything. Organized religion had lost its old power, and betting was a corrosive influence on character that threatened Britain more than economic evils, or even "the problem of drink."[37]

At the end of July, Oscar joined Isabel and Sandy, who were already at Bembridge, on the Isle of Wight in the English Channel. At sixteen, Sandy was handsome, bright, and a dominant athlete, thoroughly spoiled by busy and admiring parents who could not control him; his charisma burst out in photographs of a drab-looking family. The Skeltons had heard of a small, secluded, and educationally innovative school at Bembridge, where they hoped their son's wildness could be tamed and his enthusiasms focused. A visit to the school sealed the decision to leave Sandy there for the final year of his secondary school education. Isabel managed to relax on the island, watching the boats and listening to music, but not Oscar, who could not stay still, even though the place was "delightfully restful, and I'd like to stay for a while."[38]

A while on the Isle of Wight turned out to be only a day, and a day during which Skelton wrote a nine-page letter to Principal Taylor about Queen's matters. Europe was next on the itinerary, he told Taylor, but that would have to be "a hasty flight" and a journey to the Soviet Union would have to be scrapped, since the prime minister had asked him to represent Canada at an international historical conference in Brazil, starting in September. Skelton had probably planted the seed for that invitation by lobbying Mackenzie King earlier in the year to send scholars to academic meetings in Latin America. After all, the prime minister was informed by his ever more regular correspondent, Canadians were part of the American continent. If they could go east to Genoa or Geneva, they should also go south to Latin America. Skelton warned Taylor that Clifford Clark would have to do some of OD's autumn teaching while he was in Brazil. His young colleague would get a box of cigars as thanks for holding the fort, but cheap German cigars would do since Clark did not smoke.[39]

The Skeltons, with Sandy in tow, spent early August on the continent, moving from the Isle of Wight across to Paris and on to Germany, Czecho-slovakia, and Austria. Europe was drab and depressed, its currencies so wildly inflated that one of OD's lasting memories was that men had taken to carrying large compartmented wallets to accommodate the cash that was needed to get by day to day. Isabel wrote of their time in Vienna that the people she saw on the streets were "past starvation point." Oscar was less gloomy, but only a bit: the city was "no longer starving," but it was "shabby, listless, hopeless." Time was short, however, and impressions were superficial. They rushed quickly in and out of Vienna, and Berlin, Dresden, and Prague as well, encountering and reinforcing the stereo-types they carried with them all their lives: happy and artistic Austrians, thorough and humourless Germans, and cautious and practical Czechs. Much of the excursion was spent on packed trains and in negotiating a path across the countless frontiers of central Europe. Skelton wearily recalled running the gauntlet of time-consuming passport checks, labo-rious money exchanges, visa and customs obstacles, and sceptical border guards.[40]

What a contrast it was with North America, Skelton told readers of the Toronto *Globe* and other Liberal newspapers in a series of articles about his summer trip that were published later in 1922. At home there was so much space and freedom of movement: a single Canadian province could hold a dozen European countries. Everyone on the continent was jumbled together, packed close and yet remaining distinct, each group stamped with its own brand of race and religion, and each country iso-lated from its neighbour behind walls of soldiers, misunderstandings, and economic barriers. Greed and fear, the two roots of extreme nation-alism, were planted deep in the soil. Memories of glories past or wrongs inflicted bore the compound interest of centuries-old hate. Kings or capitalists or the devil or whoever had caused the First World War had let loose further, and incalculable, passions. The fighting was over, but it was only the latest war, and probably not the last. The scramble was still on for freedom or for dominance, for "a foothold in crowded lands" and for "coal, or oil, or strategic boundaries."[41]

OD, who had dabbled in journalism while he was at *Booklovers* and the University of Chicago and liked the company of newsmen, had an eye for the sharp phrase and the big picture.[42] He wrote swiftly, clearly, and evocatively, but he had the weaknesses of the craft, which did not completely leave him when he became a professional foreign-policy analyst. His hard judgments about Europe and Europeans, slickly delivered, came after a visit of only two weeks. They reflected what he already believed more than what he had seen or studied.

Skelton managed to inveigle the prime minister into adding Isabel to the Canadian contingent for the International Congress of the History of America in Brazil. They returned to England in mid-August, left Sandy at Bembridge, and travelled north to Liverpool to rendezvous with the *Desna*, a ship of the Royal Mail Steam Packet Company bound for Rio de Janeiro via Spain. The two-week voyage gave them some rest and allowed OD to work on his newspaper articles, an assignment he had taken to help pay for the expensive family vacation to England and Europe. They arrived in Brazil on 2 September. In the year marking the one hundredth anniversary of Brazilian independence, Oscar steeled himself for the obligatory cocktail parties, dances, and receptions, along with a visit to the immense British warships *Hood* and *Repulse*, anchored in Rio's harbour. He detested diplomatic pretense and empty formality, joking that he was going to have a uniform "drawn up on Brazilian lines with plenty of gold braid and plumes and bright colours, and assigned to the Dean of Arts when he gets home: and that the said Dean will wear it on all important occasions."[43]

Representation abroad had its virtues. Skelton informed the prime minister and his friends in the Canadian Bankers' Association that Brazil was Canada's "great southern counterpart," a country like their own in the way it had evolved and the challenges it faced, and unlike their own in the lessons of racial tolerance it could offer to the exploitative "white man" to the north. He picked up on Brazil's growing economic power and drew attention to the substantial opportunities for development to be found there. The British and especially the Americans had a major presence in Rio and elsewhere, but Canada had no official standing and no one to assist the creative Canadian colony of business people and companies resident there. OD's trip credentials had to be awkwardly obtained from the British, not directly through Ottawa, a lesson in the practical advantages that would flow from Canada's control of its own international existence.[44]

As Skelton sailed from Rio to Halifax, and as his articles from the European tour appeared across the country, Mackenzie King was dealing with his first major foreign-policy crisis. Colonial Secretary Winston

Churchill, a member of the Lloyd George government that was clinging to power, issued a call to Ottawa in mid-September 1922 for a contingent of troops to bail out British soldiers pinned down by Turkish nationalist forces at Chanak, near Asia's narrow and strategically vital Dardanelles Strait. From the Skelton standpoint, Churchill was the caricature of the brash and bumptious John Bull imperialist, already celebrated for his overseas follies and determined to use Canada as a public convenience. To the fledgling Prime Minister King, nothing could have been more unwelcome to his minority government than an emotional appeal from Mother Britain, especially when Churchill made his request known to the newspapers before King got the information himself.

King temporized, declaring that the people would decide through their Parliament, a tactic that became a favourite. The September crisis passed in October, proving King's delaying instincts correct. Back in the dean's office at Queen's, Skelton wrote effusively to his leader: "You have made history. Never again will a Canadian government be stampeded against its better judgment into giving blank cheques to British diplomacy, now that your government has set this example of firm and self-respecting deliberation. My sincerest congratulations on a great stroke for Canada."[45]

The prose was overcooked. King had not been firm but flabby, aware that the British had supporters in his cabinet, in Arthur Meighen's Conservative Party, and in the country, and that a large cohort of Quebec MPs wanted to keep the rest of the world at arm's length. The prime minister had refused to take a stand one way or another. He delayed, that was all, which is what he did best. The congratulatory note to King was one of a number of letters of praise written to the prime minister during 1922 in the exaggerated way that was Skelton's habit when dealing with figures of authority, particularly those who had something that he wanted. Letters to Principal Taylor, with whom OD had a rocky relationship, proceed in a similar vein, employing honeyed language and sometimes the same phrases that he used in his correspondence with the prime minister. "Great strokes" were not reserved for King alone.[46] Skelton had few words in person, but in his written communications he could be downright unctuous. Like awkward people everywhere, Oscar could express his purposes more easily from a distance than he could face to face.

After Chanak, never again? Skelton did not believe that for a minute. The Middle Eastern crisis was clear evidence that excessive demands would speed across the Atlantic again and again, finding fertile ground in Canada, until his country extricated itself from the comfortable cocoon of the British Empire. His campaign for an intelligent and intelligible national policy in the world apart from the British Empire was becoming his chief interest, "almost my religion."[47] Identifying himself with Mackenzie King, courting him relentlessly, Skelton edged closer to the political arena.

5
Amen, Downing Street, 1923

Skelton began the summer of 1923 in Ann Arbor, at the University of Michigan. A trip south to lecture on politics and government, he told himself, was "an interesting variation in a university teacher's life,"[1] but his motives ran deeper. He was searching for new directions after a bruising year. His mother had died the previous December, the Laurier biography was dredging up old controversies, and he felt overworked and underappreciated at Queen's. Michigan was therapeutic. In a short time his natural optimism returned, and before the summer was out, an opportunity presented itself that he had been preparing for all of his adult life.

OD came to Michigan without Isabel and the three children. He soaked in prosperous, manicured Ann Arbor, explored the rolling countryside around the town, and inspected the well-maintained homes and gardens. Ann Arbor had an "other side" – Skelton went there too – but not one that was as prominent as Kingston's, and not one that disturbed his sense of the order and peacefulness of his temporary home. Joining an Ann Arbor professors' discussion and dining group called the Apostles, he meticulously made an inventory of the members with their names, disciplines, and affiliations. He placed himself precisely on the list, exactly at the centre of his summer community. Skelton revelled in the Apostles' discussion of issues high and low and was not surprised by the rampant gossip and the tearing down of campus administrators, the standard fare of university life.[2]

Skelton's undergraduate course in comparative government was mostly populated by passive University of Michigan students preoccupied by grades, but there was also a graduate group in post-1830 English political theory where he was excited by some good brains and intimations that he was a worthwhile teacher. John Stuart Mill's classical liberal individualism struck a chord with the graduates as it had with Skelton when he was at a similar stage of his studies. On the whole, his students seemed to him not so well prepared as those at Queen's – more alert perhaps, but often superficially so. They consumed contemporary American writers such as Sinclair Lewis and Sherwood Anderson, not the British literary canon of Pope and Woodsworth. Those interested in ideas were apt to be readers not of Karl Marx but of H.L. Mencken, the cigar-wielding iconoclast of United States journalism. OD recorded these fashions without comment, but he clearly deplored them, even though he was a regular reader of Mencken's pyrotechnical broadsides against corruption, mediocrity, and pretension.[3]

A Western Union telegram from Mackenzie King interrupted a restful Ann Arbor Sunday in early July. It asked Skelton to be the government's "expert adviser" for the Imperial Conference scheduled to begin in October, as a drafter of policy documents in Ottawa and a consultant for the meetings themselves in England. In King's roundabout language, Skelton was informed that the cabinet agreed with the prime minister "that this opportunity might have far reaching consequences of first importance to yourself and are in hearty accord with myself in hoping that you might find it possible so to arrange your plans as to accompany other ministers and myself in capacity mentioned." Since Skelton would need to spend at least two months examining and preparing materials, he must begin very soon.[4]

In his mind's eye, Skelton had attended all the great colonial and imperial conferences since the late nineteenth century. His biography of Laurier recreated the romance and attraction and danger of travel to the Mother Country – the lavish banquets, royal garden parties and country house weekends, Mansion House and Lincoln's Inn, Windsor Castle and Buckingham Palace, the gallery of the House of Commons and the naval review at Spithead, "with its impressive five miles of towering battleships, darting destroyers, snaky submarines and hovering aeroplanes." These were the heady times when the blank cheques of imperial enthusiasm and loyalty were signed by awestruck colonials. Sooner or later, London would expect to cash them in full.[5]

He replied at once to King's invitation: the prospect of Imperial Conference employment was a "tremendous honour" that "appeals to me very greatly." Skelton agreed to meet with the prime minister the following weekend in Ottawa, while he thought through the difficulties. His contract at the University of Michigan had a way to go, and he was expected back at Queen's for the fall session. The government offer meant that he would again be away from home for weeks and even months. During the Michigan summer, time with the family was restricted to two weekends in Kingston and a road trip in their ramshackle Ford to meet Sandy's ship at Montreal, as he returned from his year in England. The seventeen year old had done well in his Isle of Wight school, but he remained, in his father's words, "pretty irresponsible and visionary still" and full of "the same cocksure arguments on every serious question under the sun." Isabel later reproached Oscar and herself "over our not putting first things first" at a formative time in their tempestuous son's life.[6]

Skelton would go to London, no matter what. Over many years, he had been preparing the case for the prosecution against an overbearing 10 Downing Street, the home and office of the British prime minister and the pivot of imperial power. He saw that a chance had come "to utilize this study, to apply these ideas, at the heart of affairs, not indirectly by creating a public opinion but directly as a member of a London delegation and a participant in discussions of the Prime Ministers of the Empire." As he explained to his wife in a letter that did not ask for her reaction to another extended absence, "I need hardly say there are few jobs in one's life equal to this opportunity. It's going to be an epochmaking Conference." If he could be at the centre of great events, "it will be worth five years of ordinary life." There would be someone on the spot to stiffen Mackenzie King's all too flexible backbone when the imperialists came calling.[7]

OD needed a change, or at least a change of pace. He worked as hard as ever, and no one would have noticed, but his usually steady existence was in flux. At the end of 1922, he had watched his mother pass away in the Skelton house on Moore Street in Toronto. If she had lived until Christmas day, it would have been Elizabeth Skelton's seventy-third birthday. Next to Isabel, she was the most significant person in Oscar's life, clear-minded, unselfish, "pure gold through and through," as he wrote in a heartfelt letter to Sandy hours after her death. The biography of Sir Wilfrid Laurier, published just before she started to become very ill, was dedicated to her, one indication of the singular place she had in his heart; none of his other books says anything personal about family or friends. Only his mother could reconcile the quietly emotional element of his personality with its relentlessly practical core. He moved on after her death, piling commitment upon commitment, but he was more on his own than ever.[8]

The publication of the Laurier volumes administered a further emotional battering. They were generally well received, but the publicity that surrounded them was intense, bringing back memories of the divisive conscription crisis of 1917, when Skelton had been accused of having backed one section of the population against the interests of all Canadians, betraying the national interest and Mother Britain. Stung by the criticism, he moved away from Canadian politics as a subject for his scholarship; in early 1923 he signed a contract with a New York publisher to write a book about British government.[9]

Was he distancing himself from Queen's as well? His term as dean of arts at Queen's was coming to an end. He was frustrated by a balky administration that had again and again rejected his advice about the future course of the university and strategies for individual departments, including his own. Added to that was his sadness over the departure of Clifford Clark, the colleague he valued most, who had left Kingston for a lucrative business career in Chicago. Clark wrote to OD that his greatest regret "was not in leaving Canada or Queen's, but in leaving you. My best friends express something of my regard for you when they prophesied that I would not leave Queen's because I could not leave Skelton." Clark went anyway and without finishing the academic year. With Clark gone and economist W.A. Mackintosh ill, Skelton had to shoulder staggering departmental responsibilities merely (as Clark guiltily put it) to "survive the session in some sort of way."[10]

OD might have been sniffing around for a University of Michigan appointment as a way out of Queen's. In Ann Arbor he observed a once fine institution rising again and a capable faculty that was advancing in quality and numbers. In his graduate class, he put "much more preparation & of myself into class than in ordinary Queen's work" and was "rewarded by distinct aliveness." If offered a job in the United States, he would have had to choose – love of Canada, or the opportunity and escape that the United States might offer.[11]

King's Imperial Conference overture offered a much better possibility, carrying an official stamp of approval at a time when he needed to know that he was valued. His relationship with the prime minister had intensified over the eighteen months since the Canadian Club address in January 1922. King solicited the professor's help with parliamentary debates and foreign policy, while OD used his privileged access to the country's highest office to push his own agenda forward – in pursuit one day of a tougher line on dealings with the British Empire or on another day advocating a revamped Dominion Bureau of Statistics to make for "greater

efficiency in administration at home and greater prestige abroad." When
King had his first dinner party in the remodelled Laurier House, the
home in Ottawa's Sandy Hill that Lady Laurier had left to him in her will,
his guests were Skelton and Andrew Haydon, the Liberal Party's chief
fixer and a Queen's alumnus. Isabel wrote excitedly to Sandy after her
husband's report on the evening to say that Daddy and the prime minister had talked almost until midnight. The subject was perhaps foreign
policy, since King had told OD that he was hoping to turn his views on
the subject to "some advantage."[12]

A fatigued Skelton arrived in Ottawa four days after he received King's
1923 Imperial Conference invitation. They met at Kingsmere, the prime
minister's Quebec retreat outside the capital, in the quiet and beauty
of the Gatineau Hills that Skelton loved. A deal was struck. He would
come to Ottawa as soon as someone could be found to take his classes
at Michigan, a problem solved by giving an Ann Arbor colleague $175
of Skelton's $850 summer stipend to complete the lectures in compara-
tive government. King proposed a $30–$40 honorarium per day plus
expenses and arranged for accommodation in the apartment of his
friends, the Pattesons, at the Roxborough Apartments at the corner of
Elgin Street and Laurier Avenue, a short walk from Parliament Hill, at
the cost of $75 a month. Another $65 bought thirty days of meals in the
Roxborough dining room.[13]

As the minister in charge of the Department of External Affairs, King
was thinking beyond the Imperial Conference. Permanent employment
for Skelton in External Affairs had been on King's mind since OD's
Canadian Club speech. At their Kingsmere meeting, the prime minister made Skelton a firm promise to elevate him to under-secretary,
the top civil-service position in the department, as soon as Sir Joseph
Pope could be persuaded to retire. Pope had reigned as a constitutional
monarch over the tiny office since its inception in 1909, but the power
in the department over many years had been Loring Christie, the legal
adviser and policy wizard who was close to prime ministers Borden
and Meighen. King had inherited Christie but was uncomfortable with
him personally and professionally, and relations between the two were
fraught. Squeezed out of the policy process, such as it was in King's
chaotic first months in office, Christie resigned from the department
in May 1923. King proposed to replace Christie with Skelton, appointing him as "technical adviser" while they waited for Pope to leave.
When confronted with a concrete offer along these lines, Skelton was
non-committal.[14]

For now there was more than enough to think about. With the conference only eight weeks away, work in Ottawa began on 30 July. The newly minted expert adviser had a mountain of tasks to do, while King was continually rushed off his feet, with little opportunity or willingness to get down to the hard business of thinking policy through. Fearing that he was not up to the physical, emotional, and intellectual burden of the conference, King confessed to Skelton that he was "filled with terror" by the pressure that was building as he contemplated his first major imperial gathering. Skelton observed the prime minister working himself into a "blue funk" over the conference, which would "make or break him." Skelton took that as a sign of how necessary he was.[15]

He was given Sir Robert Borden's former office in the Privy Council wing of the East Block of the Parliament Buildings – "very magnificent and very quiet," a perfect combination, thought Skelton. Within a little over a week, he had a twenty-four-page memorandum dealing with organizational matters, foreign policy, defence, and various other questions ready for the cabinet. Taking account of his impressive beginning and the sacrifices Skelton had to make to come to Ottawa, King asked ministers to approve a per diem of $50 in addition to the payment of OD's travelling and living expenses. The order-in-council that authorized his appointment as a special adviser to the government for the Imperial Conference and the Imperial Economic Conference, which was scheduled for the same time in London, gave as much attention to his expertise on economic questions as it did to his "great deal of study" on the organization of the British Empire.[16]

Ottawa's political and bureaucratic community was small, and it did not take long before Skelton had formed a strong impression of the good, the bad, and the indifferent. In the first category was the postmaster general, Charles Murphy, "stoutly Canada first," and a group of Quebec cabinet ministers, including Ernest Lapointe and Raoul Dandurand, who were "opposed to any cooperation whatever" with the empire. Less helpful was Justice Minister Sir Lomer Gouin, the senior francophone in cabinet, who had been named to the Imperial Conference delegation and was "more ready to compromise" with the British. The enemy was the finance minister and King's chief opponent in the 1919 leadership race, W.S. Fielding: "stiff, growingly autocratic, hopelessly colonial on inter-imperial questions, shakes & threatens stroke of apoplexy when nationalist views put forward." Fortunately, at least for OD, the elderly but still influential Fielding had been left out of the conference delegation and he was absent when Skelton's memos flooded cabinet, which approved them unanimously. In the Department of External Affairs (and in the rest of the public service), Skelton discovered competence and goodwill but not much initiative or breadth of either compass or knowledge. Of Joseph Pope he wrote: "perfect Civil Servant, polished ... prepared to subordinate own views to those of temporary political chief, not now very vigorous & not at all in touch with intimate affairs of office which are in hands of P.M."[17]

The "preliminary notes" memorandum that Skelton prepared in the first week of August sounded all his familiar themes about the dangers of galloping imperial consolidation and the importance of Canada's control of its own affairs. He warned that the pressures at the conference would be intense. The Australian prime minister, Stanley Bruce, wanted a concerted empire foreign policy. His South African counterpart, General Jan Smuts, was rumoured to see the conference as a launching pad for his dreams of international cooperation. The British foreign secretary, Lord Curzon, "will repeat his bland assurance that the Empire's foreign policy is and must be one and he must be that one." The demand for an imperial naval policy was likely to be even more insistent, Skelton was certain, and he devoted more than half of his memorandum to that concern. A single strategy would be urged by the British, each dominion to undertake definite and substantial responsibilities. Canada might be asked to share in the construction of the new naval base at faraway Singapore, or at least to endorse the scheme.[18]

Skelton elaborated on the naval question in a separate brief. He claimed that under the London plan the Admiralty, the British navy department, was "to be the central controlling authority, outlining policy, and fitting the various local units into a mosaic." He did not point out a less convenient fact, that it was up to each dominion to decide the extent of its involvement in the mix. Skelton was not against defence spending, even while preferring international reconciliation through the League of Nations, but it must be "a natural outgrowth of our own conditions and on the full and undivided responsibility of our government." OD wanted to see, he added in a personal aside to King, "a decent Canadian navy, perhaps beginning with shore defences, & air development." This was uncongenial advice. The King government had savaged the defence budget and reduced the navy to bare bones.[19]

OD, convinced that he was a procrastinator, drove himself hard. Once the preliminary overview memorandum was written and approved by cabinet, hundreds more pages poured forth during the rest of August and into September, first on such subjects as the economic, financial,

and commercial position of the country, immigration, and capital investment, and then on more specifically British-Canadian questions relating
to constitutional matters, defence, and tariffs. Even to the self-critical
Skelton, progress in the end seemed "pretty fair." He drafted fluently
on big sheets of paper in longhand with a fountain pen, often throwing
together words in his haste but eventually turning piles of neat text over
to the typist. He consulted experts and interested parties whenever possible in the limited time available to him, operating outside the ambit of
the Department of External Affairs, where he discovered few resources.
His memoranda, clear-minded in conception and organization, were
executed in the clean, understated, jargon-less prose of his books and
articles. Always the academic, he could not resist the temptation to quote
at length and include footnotes and references. There was, on the surface, scholarly balance, because he began to evolve the technique, which
became a Skelton trademark, of systematically listing the pros and cons
of an issue or argument. He made it abundantly clear, however, just
where the advantages – and his truth – lay, leading his readers where he
wanted them to go.[20]

The centerpiece of his efforts, the memorandum into which he put the
most of himself, was "Canada and the Control of Foreign Policy," which
repeated the warnings of his recent speeches and writings. A revolution
was under way, he reiterated, reversing the trend towards dominion self-
government in external affairs and pulling Canada towards a future in
which London and its empire partners would share all authority and
thus share all responsibility. The control was illusory. Canada would be
forced "in advance to an endorsement of courses of action of which it
knows little and of which it may not approve, or in which it may have
little direct concern." Yet the responsibility was unquestionable. There
were bound to be more Chanaks in the future, more expectations that
the dominions would participate in what was becoming, under the new
practice, an institutionalized commitment to the empire.[21]

Skelton insisted that the empire's centre of gravity had to remain in
each self-governing state. If the dominions were "committed to action
only by their own parliaments and peoples, they will have real influence
and responsible control." Decentralization did not preclude close relationships within the empire, nor would it destroy the institution. With
national autonomy, a future for the empire was more likely, not less.
"That is the principle on which this Empire has been maintained, that
is its unique and distinctive contribution to the world, that is the principle which has been tested in fire of late years and not found wanting.

It cannot now be abandoned." As Skelton put it, a bit too cleverly, in his notes for the prime minister's opening conference speech, "irksome pledges do not bind; a peoples' enthusiasm cannot be requisitioned. Imperialists should learn to have faith in the Empire."[22]

Canadians had more than enough problems of their own. They could not afford to be diverted by foreign adventures and imperial dreams. In addition to the perennial issue of national unity, Skelton identified the complications of war-weariness, heavy taxation, and the depression of trade, along with the prosperity of and proximity of the United States, which acted as a magnet drawing Canadian emigrants southward. The American aloofness from Europe was seductive, and to seem to be different, to impose burdens and commitments arising out of the British connection, was to risk losing people to the friendly neighbour to the south. Canada's persistent need was "to build up the Dominion, with this power of attraction ever present at her side," a problem that Britain and the other dominions did not have to face.[23]

Skelton claimed the moral high ground in the great contest set to unfold at the Imperial Conference. With the one exception of their discriminatory policies towards Asian immigration, his argument ran, Canadians were a good people with the right instincts about the world. They had given unstintingly to the empire's cause in the First World War and owed no obligations to Britain or the empire. The debts in fact all ran the other way. Canada had been a distinct imperial asset, never a liability. Skelton told the cabinet that Canada "has never yet involved any other part of the Empire in trouble; no British soldier has ever fired a shot, no Australian parliament ever voted a shilling, in any war entered upon by Canada or on Canada's behalf, whereas there are a few important entries on the other side of the Empire war ledger. There is no indication that it will be different in the future."[24]

Predisposed in that direction, King accepted without reservation Skelton's conclusions about Britain's designs on Canada. The prime minister enthused in his diary that he had "read a splendidly prepared brief by Skelton on Foreign Policy, with every line of which I am in hearty and entire accord. He has an unusually clear mind & brain, his work is excellent." It was clear that the "whole purpose of the Conference is a centralizing imperial policy, first re foreign policy to be made in London & next for control of Navy & distribution of cost of upkeep among outlying dominions." King was incensed when he read Skelton's memo on naval policy, purporting to expose the scope of the plan that the Admiralty was dispensing to the dominions. It was an "outrageous interference with the autonomy & self-government of the dominions." The imperialists "will break up the Empire yet."[25]

Skelton's analysis of imperial relations was sweeping, exaggerated, and lacking in subtlety, and it rested on a selective interpretation of recent history. He argued that the common empire theory was a British conspiracy contradicting the natural flow of steadily expanding Canadian autonomy, never admitting that the concept had been actively promoted by the Conservative prime ministers who had preceded Mackenzie King. Their aim had been to enhance Canada's international standing through the assumption of grand responsibilities. Skelton fulminated that an attempt was under way to reverse the order of events when the claim could as easily have been made about him. Nor would empire cooperation in the big questions of foreign affairs have stripped away all the powers of self-government that Canada had acquired over two generations. Skelton had to know that it was misleading to argue that cooperative empire policies would bring about a state of affairs where South Africa could determine whether Canada would join with the United States in the building of a St Lawrence seaway or Canadians might be able to dictate Australia's trade policy.[26]

Skelton's detractors were apt to scoff that he was fighting unnecessary and misguided battles. National autonomy was already won; the cooperative empire idea was yesterday's solution, no longer relevant to a new age; a great empire was being undermined for no good reason. Skelton could not have known, as we know now, that in the 1920s Downing Street and the Foreign Office in London were running away from common empire ideas as fast as he and King were. He did know, however, that Lord Curzon continued to assert that he spoke and acted not for Britain alone but for an entire empire, Canada included. Skelton had reason to be concerned as long as the British treated Canada as a department of their government – and as long as Britain's leaders, abetted by many Canadians, refused to draw a clear distinction between the interests of the two states.[27]

King and Skelton, along with a good part of the Canadian Imperial Conference delegation and assorted journalists, sailed on the Canadian Pacific liner *Montcalm* to Liverpool in late September. On the river between Montreal and Quebec, in cold and rainy weather, Skelton dashed off his quarterly "March of Events" article for the *Journal of the Canadian Bankers' Association*. Once delivered of his deadline, he had a pleasant ride through the Gulf of St Lawrence and the Straits of Belle Isle. The sea then turned rough and the ship by turns rolled, pitched, and corkscrewed. Quickly, Oscar told Isabel, "our company vanished. About one in ten turned out for meals on Monday and about one in twenty on Tuesday. The storm went down Wednesday night & most of the passengers have now straggled back to deck & dining room." Skelton was a good sailor and a big eater. He had "one queerish qualm Monday night while sitting in the smoking-room," but a glass of champagne made him feel normal again, and he downed all available food and drink. Little work got done. "The prime minister wasn't in shape, the rest of us haven't done much beyond casual reading and a good deal of conversation."[28]

J.W. Dafoe of the *Manitoba Free Press* was a *Montcalm* companion, not inadvertently. His presence at the Imperial Conference had been arranged by his autonomist boss, Clifford Sifton, to ensure that the prime minister gave nothing away to Downing Street and by King to ensure some favourable press. Dafoe was instructed to keep an eye on Skelton, since Sifton doubted the professor's intellectual credentials and his patriotism in light of OD's record on wartime conscription. Added to the mix was Dafoe's criticism of the Laurier biography and Skelton's opinion that that the newspaper editor had a "seemingly incurable prejudice against the French Canadian."[29]

OD displayed unexpected political skills. He avoided discussion of Dafoe's frontal attacks on the Laurier volumes and concentrated on the imperial issue, where he identified the common ground between them. He showed the newsman the briefs he had prepared for the conference and they had several good talks, including one in King's cabin before, Skelton wrote home, "the ocean, as an imperialist agency, intervened." A "rougher Westerner" was Oscar's conclusion after their exchanges, but also "level-headed & right on the Imperial issue." They were "almost absolutely at one." If help was needed to fight off the British in London, Dafoe would be "a very useful reinforcement." Dafoe's impression was similarly positive. Skelton was "soundly Canadian in every respect and advanced."[30]

Skelton and Dafoe spent time on the *Montcalm* with a young British Columbia Rhodes Scholar, Norman Robertson, on his way to Balliol College, Oxford. Robertson enjoyed the company of Dafoe, but not that of Skelton, who was "extremely dull and if he isn't saturated clean through with dullness then he was also rather discourteous." This was a common enough first impression of Skelton, who was commonly branded austere and uncaring. It was easy to mistake his self-containment and social awkwardness for disinterest or rudeness or worse. The two men were much more alike – intellectual, reserved, introverted even – than Robertson thought at the time, although he would acknowledge it later when he became one of Skelton's foreign-service recruits and his successor in 1941.[31]

Reflecting on his shipboard alliance with Dafoe, Skelton recalled a lengthy article written the year before by Sir John Willison, who was on the other side of the imperial debate. Willison had identified a mounting attack on Canada's connection to the British Empire, pointing an accusing finger at Skelton, Dafoe, Sifton, and J.S. Ewart as the four greatest menaces to Canadian imperialism. Oscar wrote proudly to his wife that two of Willison's dangerous men were at King's side on the *Montcalm* to carry the fight to England "and of the other two, I had a conference with Ewart in Ottawa & Dafoe had two days with Sifton at his country place near Gananoque. However, this is not for publication – though our good Tory friends will discover it soon enough." Beginning his journalistic career as a Laurier Liberal and a nationalist, Willison had transformed himself into a Conservative imperialist. The Skeltons hosted him at Queen's from time to time, and the two men were working together to resuscitate the Canadian Political Science Association. Willison, however, privately warned colleagues about OD's "domineering" presence in the CPSA, and he publicly sneered at the "aggressive Nationalist, in all of whose references to the Empire there is the flavour of vinegar."[32]

British hospitality was flamboyantly in evidence as soon as the *Montcalm* arrived in Liverpool. A welcoming party at dockside was followed by another at Euston Station in London. The connection between the two was by rail in a "semi-royal" carriage, "something like what we would call a private car here," OD told Isabel. "All the luggage was looked after at both ends, no trouble, no pay, not even tips." Then on to the "impressively subdued" Ritz Hotel, which would be home for the next seven weeks: "a large seven or eight story hotel at the west end of Piccadilly, just overlooking Green Park & opposite the Duke of Wellington's town place. It is not as new as some of the other mammoth places, but solid and substantial in structure & appointments." The Canadian delegation was assigned the bulk of the first upstairs floor and some of the floor above, with three rooms fitted out for offices. Skelton shared a huge suite next door to the prime minister with Dominion Archivist and Mackenzie King favourite Arthur G. Doughty, who had been on the Brazil trip and acted as the Canadians' unofficial social secretary at the Imperial Conference. They each had bathrooms as large as the Skeltons' Kingston dining room, and there were countless waiters, valets, and chambermaids. The prime minister, used to such things, took no notice of the spectacle that greeted them, but, for OD, London and Piccadilly and the Ritz were "a pretty overwhelming combination."[33]

The Good Life paled. Host Britain was paying the bills, tweaking Skelton's nationalist conscience. The Ritz was a rich person's place. The cuisine was "unexcellable," but the prices too extravagant. Oscar preferred plain meals, simply and quickly delivered. He usually ate in his room to save time – "service too long" – and to avoid the conspicuous consumption of the hotel's dining rooms, which he contrasted with the poverty that he saw in the streets of London. The "much waste apparent," he assured Isabel, "is not in our party, which is pretty abstemious on whole, but in the general public which dines here." Guests, though, "must not for present be critics."[34]

With the conference scheduled to begin early on Monday of the next week, the Canadian delegates only had the weekend to rest and unpack. Skelton took the first night off, asking eight of his companions from the *Montcalm* to dinner and the theatre. They began with oysters, consommé, sole, pheasant, sorbets, and champagne at the Ritz, moved on to the Aldwych Theatre in the Strand for a slapstick farce, "Tons of Money," and finished with supper and a bottle of Chablis at a nearby restaurant. OD wrote resignedly in his diary that he arrived "home to bed with ... £70 gone." That was seven days' pay, but his "sense of duty" had been fulfilled. At the end of the conference he took the Canadian newsmen and their wives out for a similar evening. They came cheaper, even though the night included a play starring Sybil Thorndike, who "quite warrants her repute as the greatest living mistress of tragedy & emotion, on the English-speaking stage at least." The right thing had been again done, but this time it cost £14 – some seventy Canadian dollars.[35]

On a hot Saturday, Skelton went to work. He met with the master bureaucrat, Sir Maurice Hankey, the secretary of the British cabinet who was to watch over their delegation and lead the conference secretariat: "extraordinarily efficient, good organizer, smooth manipulator, apparently anxious to avoid friction, everything ready to sign on the dotted line." King wanted Skelton to attend all the meetings and to act as secretary to the Canadian delegation for the main Imperial Conference. Hankey's approval for that was required, and he quickly gave it. Arrangements were also made to receive the "sacred Foreign Office key" so that Skelton could get into the red leather boxes of confidential dispatches.[36]

In a morning coat and a battered top hat that Doughty said would pass in a crowd, Skelton attended the opening session of the Imperial Conference in the Cabinet Office at 10 Downing Street on 1 October 1923.

He was more impressed by surroundings that dripped with history than by the largely ceremonial first day's proceedings. King and his adviser were ushered down a long hall, lined with busts of former prime ministers, "into the Sanctum Sanctorum: a room about 15' x 25', high ceiling, white and gilded pillars & Corinthian capitals, lined with sombre bookcases of statutes." Over the fireplace was a portrait of Sir Robert Walpole, the longest-serving British leader. Just outside the windows was a "pleasant little garden, green grass on west, gay flower borders on north."[37]

British Prime Minister Stanley Baldwin and his colleagues and officials were lined up on one side of a long table covered with green baize. There were about thirty of them, outnumbering everyone else in the room. Dominion ministers were on the opposite side and the secretaries and advisers gathered behind their delegations, within whispering distance of their charges. Directly across from Skelton was the legendary Curzon, a former viceroy of India, and, behind him, his Foreign Office secretary, Robert Vansittart. OD liked Baldwin, "not a man of great intellect or initiative, but fair, honourable, level-headed," and was impressed by Lord Curzon, "who spoke little but has personality & distinction as well as obvious intellect." The other members of the British cabinet were not up to much, "quite stupid the lot, or average at best." Among the dominion leaders, the South African Smuts stood out: "keen as a razor, quick, of wide vision, & wide sympathies, essentially sound on imperial matters ... speaks well, conversationally." From New Zealand, always dismissed by Skelton as the most colonial of colonies, William Massey was "a bumptious bore, & of small bore at that." The exotic Maharajah of Alwar, representing the princes of India, was gloriously arrayed in a puce velvet outfit topped off by a green turban with large diamond star. Completing the portrait was the secretary of the Indian delegation, L.F. Rushbrook Williams, who had been a history instructor at Queen's before the war. OD wrote Isabel that he was thrilled "to have a seat myself in that room where so many great decisions had been taken, & to see at close range the men who now rule the British Empire."[38]

The main conference was slow to get moving, spending most of the rest of the first week on organizing itself. Every other day was given over to the economic conference, which began to plow its way through the complexities of commercial travellers' samples, trade catalogues, patents, and customs-valuation certificates. Even though he had been absolved of the secretary's job on this side of the delegation's work, it was clear that Skelton's role in the economic conference would be substantial and time-consuming, even if mostly routine. The lavish meals and receptions, with their great displays of "jewels and ugly women," were also in train. While enjoying the parade of fine architecture, art, food, and wine, Skelton saw a transparent British attempt to catch naive colonials in the imperial web. At his first big dinner, given by the London Chamber of Commerce at the Mansion House, he endured the speech making by rating speakers on length and effectiveness, approving most of brevity and "pithiness." The New Zealander – "prosy, 23" – received the professor's poorest grade. As the conference wore on, he escaped from his social duties as quickly as he could.[39]

With a touch of hubris, OD informed Isabel that "I find that my 'reputation' has preceded me here: I am regarded as very dangerous by the ultra-imperialists." Some of his reputation came from George Glazebrook, a Canadian member of the empire-promoting group, the Round Table, who on the eve of the conference warned a well-connected counterpart in the United Kingdom that the prime minister had chosen as his chief adviser "a narrow-minded, extreme autonomist, whose time has been spent in hack writing and who is nervously jealous of what he suspects as English 'superiority.' I don't think King could have made a very much worse selection of a man to take over." The Round Table's journal, some of it written by Canadians, had articles in September 1923 questioning whether Canada had "a real national life" and insisting that the foreign policy of the self-governing empire "must be one."[40] Skelton returned the Round Tablers' scorn. Colonialism seemed to him the lowest form of imperialism.

Skelton was drawn to the uncompromising nationalists like himself – to Dafoe, whom he frequently consulted, and to Canada's chief official statistician, R.H. Coats, a tenacious defender of national freedoms at the conference. Long sympathetic to the cause of Irish independence, Skelton also allied himself with the delegates from the Irish Free State, the newest of the dominions. He built links especially with Kevin O'Higgins and Desmond FitzGerald, who sat at the conference table across from the men who had jailed them during the armed struggle to escape Britain's grasp. The Irish nationalist movement had split over the 1921 treaty with Great Britain, which brought a stop to Anglo-Irish hostilities and gave the Free State the status of a dominion within the empire rather than outright independence. O'Higgins, FitzGerald, and their colleagues had agreed to the treaty and were denounced as traitors during the civil war that raged in 1922–3. That second bloody Irish conflict ended in April 1923 with a victory for the pro-treaty forces of O'Higgins and FitzGerald, but Skelton understood how precarious their position was.[41]

Skelton thought O'Higgins the ablest of the Irish at the Imperial Conference, with FitzGerald a close second. He also liked the politician-professor John McNeil, "a queer combination of the gentle scholar & the shrewd man of action" – something, perhaps, of what OD was becoming. His closest collaborator was FitzGerald, the Free State minister for foreign affairs, who acted as the chief Irish delegate while O'Higgins shuttled back and forth between London and Dublin. Skelton took FitzGerald to see Mackenzie King. The three agreed that their countries had a great deal in common and ought to cooperate wherever possible. Yet the Irish navigated their way at the conference carefully. They were content to work for their ends through King and Skelton, who described to Isabel the "close alliance" with the Irish, "with myself as go between."[42]

Skelton had great hopes for South African Prime Minister Smuts, but he proved an enigma. The general who had been a Boer hero of the South African War and a member of the British War Cabinet during the First World War was a less straightforward and more unpredictable commodity than the Irish, acting the autonomist in public but playing the "imperialist game in private" and speaking of "we" or "our" as if he were an Englishman – "not dishonest, merely subtle, opportunist, balancing." There was no doubting the prestige or influence of the celebrated warrior-statesman, and he showered praise on Skelton from the beginning, telling him that the Laurier biography was the "guiding star" in South African politics and inviting him to an intimate lunch on his own at the luxurious Savoy Hotel.[43]

On Friday, 5 October, the hard business of the conference began with the British foreign secretary's lengthy and much-anticipated address on foreign affairs. Skelton was impressed by Lord Curzon's "masterly performance, lucid, persuasive, magisterial, ordered," and delivered mostly from memory. An autocratic aristocrat who spoke "as one with authority," Curzon, and others like him, had forgotten nothing and learned nothing, continuing blandly to assume that Downing Street and the Foreign Office were all that really mattered in empire diplomacy. Later in the day, there was an English public-servant version of the same thinking when Hankey visited Skelton to promote his scheme for an empire secretariat of dominion public servants headed by a British official – himself. Canadian Loring Christie, working under Conservative prime ministers, had been keen on this kind of bureaucratic imperialism, which was meant to develop permanency and form "a bulwark for the British Empire." Skelton recorded in his diary that he "of course" was "not prepared to accept any such game," although he agreed to take charge for one day a week of the conference's secretarial work, "convinced it will be purely formal."[44]

Skelton spent the weekend concocting a reply to the foreign secretary's address for the prime minister's debut imperial conference speech. He had pecked away at this earlier, laying out some preliminary points, but now, under pressure and needing to inject both length and substance, he resorted to the ancient speechwriter's trick of plagiarizing himself. An extra copy of "Canada and the Control of Foreign Policy" was cut up and large chunks pasted into the new text. The overall tone was politer, with bows in the direction of imperial loyalty, but the thrust was pure Skelton. Canada had the right to as much control over its foreign policy as it had achieved in the realm of domestic affairs. It had as much right to complete self-government as Britain itself.[45]

While Skelton sweated, Mackenzie King spent a lazy Sunday with friends in the country, arriving back at the Ritz just after midnight. He was in the habit of extensively revising what was written for him, but it was too late to make a substantial dent in what had been already prepared. Although he had given his adviser a general outline of his wishes in the morning, he knew that he had taken a risk in not putting the whole day aside for the speech. However, he found Skelton's work "splendid from every point of view." His confidence had not been misplaced: "I feel I am as far ahead as if I had attempted to do the work myself." The next day, Skelton sat in the cabinet room at 10 Downing Street "and had the pleasure of hearing the Prime Minister of Canada read verbatim a long statement of Canada's position as to the control of foreign policy which I had written & which wasn't a mild one by any means." This was understandable exaggeration. King read Skelton's text, but he edited along the way and made several impromptu additions. In the most striking of his personal embellishments, King pledged that Canada would respond wholeheartedly to "a great and clear call of duty" if a major war threatened Britain.[46] The prime minister was predisposed to cast around for a synthesis of imperial obligations and national prerogatives, exactly the kind of balancing act that OD had noted and so disliked in General Smuts.

Even with assurances of future cooperation, the speech was an unmistakable declaration of a more independent Canadian tack in foreign policy. Skelton recalled that the faces of British ministers were grim as Canadian heresies were "calmly & at length proclaimed in Downing Street itself." A red-faced Curzon shifted uncomfortably in his seat. Prime Minister Baldwin screwed up his eyes and madly scribbled on the pad in front of him. Others looked "hurt" or "surprised," while the empire-minded Australians and New Zealanders were in shock. It was a "notable day," Skelton enthused, "in the history of Canadian self government and incidentally my own." King complimented OD publicly at the meeting, and the British began to think it best to avoid Skelton and go directly to King, who was seen as accommodating or weak or both. This dismayed Skelton, but it also pleased him.[47]

Skelton had often written about the lure of the empire, a seductive force that was felt most deeply when Canadians visited the imperial capital. He had felt it himself when he came there twenty years before to write the Indian Civil Service exams, and Mackenzie King was feeling it now. The first lord of the Admiralty, Leo Amery, saw the Canadian prime minister "certainly coming on in the Imperial atmosphere": it was "great fun to hear Mackenzie King roll the word 'Empire' from his lips every second sentence." OD discerned the same weakness when he pushed the nationalist line too hard with the prime minister, an incident that he described in detail in his diary and never forgot. Insisting that Canada was British through and through and demonstrating that he was too, King swung into a "quite imperialist strain," declaring that he "would fight himself for England against France," a reference to the poor state of relations between the two countries. There was "quite a wrangle for a time" before Skelton backed off, identifying the major difference between the two men: "I defend ultimate independence, which he opposes."[48] It was the first time that the two had argued, and the last time Skelton raised Canadian independence directly with the prime minister.

"Ultimate independence" was a form of words meant to soften the blow. Skelton wanted independence sooner not later, and he saw it as his mission to speed the process along. In post–First World War articles in the *Grain Growers' Guide* that were assembled into a pamphlet and distributed by the Canadian Council of Agriculture, he had allowed himself to dream of a "charter of Canadian nationhood and freedom," accompanied by a systematic attack on the remaining irritants of colonial subordination, some symbolic but some very real, and even about a monarch who might in future be chopped up, speaking for different states with different voices.[49] But all that, it was clear by the 1923 conference if it had not been earlier, was a bridge too far for Skelton's prime minister.

Skelton was working long hours seven days a week. He prepared briefs and speeches, arranged for the daily Canadian side of the story to get out to the media, and carried out substantial organizational work, both for his own delegation and for the conference secretariat, as well as attending most of the plenary meetings of both conferences and innumerable committees. And there was further pressure, which was self-inflicted. He had come to believe in his own indispensability. Only he, it seemed, was fully up to what was needed.[50]

Skelton complained bitterly about an indifferent Canadian ministerial team. Once his central message about self-government had been delivered to the conference, he set himself the task of keeping "Mr. King and his colleagues up to the mark & to prevent anything being slipped over on us at later meetings." He was gaining respect for the prime minister, although he would still not plan his time and was "absolutely uncertain" what he would do next. Justice Minister Gouin and Railways Minister G.P. Graham were incompetent and unwilling to stand firm for principle. They were distinctly "not the type of ministers Canada needs whether in Ottawa or in London." Political office ought to be "an opportunity of doing something, not a reward for party services." Smuts asked Skelton why he looked so serious, as if the weight of the empire was on his mind. Graham interjected that it was the strain of keeping Canadian ministers under control, causing the smug professor to think to himself that there was "more truth than poetry" in the remark.[51]

One negotiation went surprisingly well, hardly seeming like a negotiation at all. At the treaty committee, Skelton and King were astonished when Britain conceded, without a fight, the dominions' right to negotiate, sign, and ratify their own bilateral international agreements. OD pronounced this the "chief constitutional development of the Conference, & all our way." He was convinced, however, that imperial defence was the real kernel of Britain's centralist strategy. King's pronouncements on the subject followed his adviser's memoranda closely, and Admiralty minister Amery's pitch to make his plans public, a transparent attempt to appeal to Canadians over the head of the government, was killed. Skelton wanted to go further, downgrading the traditional conference resolution on defence to a simple statement of topics covered in the various discussions. King told him that a resolution was unavoidable but a clause asserting the ultimate control of the dominion Parliaments would turn the exercise Canada's way. Though he was anxious to have a private discussion with Smuts, Skelton included King in his lunch with the South African leader, where the three discussed the British wording. The original draft was eviscerated and the emphasis placed on local responsibility for national defence.[52]

Finding Skelton at the Cabinet Office, Hankey asked if they could discuss another conference resolution, this time on air forces, that would promote extensive cooperation in peacetime and mutual assistance should the necessity arise. Skelton refused to bargain. Hankey pleaded that Canada had made formidable gains at the conference; his ministers had to have some victories to show their electorate. OD replied that it was "not our Conference." He and Canada were not required to compromise. When he next saw his prime minister, Skelton suggested that Hankey's wording on air forces be condensed and folded into the general defence resolution. This was done, the final draft bearing Skelton's unmistakable stamp: it was for the parliaments of the several parts of the empire, on the recommendations of their governments, to decide the nature and extent of any action they might wish to take.[53]

There was more conflict over the resolution on external affairs, with Skelton again in the midst of it. On 5 November, in a secret session with all the prime ministers present, Curzon read out a statement he wanted to place onto the conference record that failed to take adequate account of what Canada had been saying about its desire for a distinct foreign policy and seemed to implicate the dominions in British foreign policy in the Middle East. King objected but was alone in doing so, and he had to fight "like a bear in a pit" simply to hold out until he could secure an adjournment. The prime minister scurried straight to Skelton, who had warned that something like this might be attempted. It did not take him long to pronounce Curzon's wording, even if it were watered down, "absolutely impossible to accept." The prime minister went off to dinner – "as usual," Skelton sighed – leaving OD to create an alternative, despite a dinner engagement of his own at the Brooks Club, a short distance from the Ritz. Oscar wasn't going to miss out on Brooks, celebrated as "the most exclusive Club in London" and boasting a 150-year old betting book that the historian in him very much wanted to see. He enjoyed the evening, "but shadow of foreign affairs tangle rather spoiled full appreciation."[54]

Skelton was up the next morning at daybreak. He met at length with Dafoe and King before the prime minister's departure to receive an honorary degree at Oxford University. King and Skelton had drafted four new paragraphs, two each. King's paragraphs, Dafoe wrote in his diary, were "a jumble of words," but "Skelton's contribution was a perfectly clear declaration that it was desirable and necessary that the Dominions should attend to their own foreign affairs recognizing their powers to confer together for the formulation of common policies where this was in their interests." On his own authority, Skelton decided to jettison the King paragraphs and substitute a single paragraph of his own stipulating that imperial conferences were occasions not for the fixing of policy but for an interchange of information and views. No viewpoints expressed could be regarded as imposing any obligation upon any of the self-governing dominions. Dafoe concluded that Skelton had wide knowledge and a very alert mind. He was "evidently a little quicker on the uptake than King."[55]

Skelton went to Hankey, who told him that the foreign secretary would not contemplate any further additions to or subtractions from his draft. The premiers of Australia and South Africa would not budge either. Again raising the big concessions already granted, the cabinet secretary proposed that Skelton see Curzon himself. OD preferred to let Hankey make the approach. Two hours later, Hankey was back, unhappy. Curzon was adamant, and he had Smuts's backing. Hankey had "quite a talk" with Skelton, saying that the British were mystified about just where Canada stood. Borden had asked for a share in empire foreign policy during the First World War, and the Canadian government had agreed to a uniform policy and common responsibility at the Imperial Conference of 1921. Now King was repudiating this already established policy. Skelton gave his well-rehearsed reply: it was Borden and his gang, not King and the Liberals, who were out of step with half a century of Canadian history. He added that any system of imperial consultation involving a measure of joint control was unworkable anyway. Even while the present meeting was under way, Curzon had sent communications to several countries in the name of the conference without the knowledge, consent, or authority of dominion representatives.[56]

For Skelton and Dafoe, there was only one recourse. If their prime minister could not get his way, he would have to let the others sign the conference report and enter an explicit "reservation" that nothing in the document bound Canada without the express consent of its government and Parliament. Furthermore, no obligations would be assumed beyond those of immediate and direct Canadian interest. King was reluctant, but another day brought only minor concessions from the British, and by then even Hankey was urging King to pursue the Skelton-Dafoe line in order to jolt Curzon into some flexibility. King produced a draft – Hankey called it "poisonous" – and Smuts, fearful of a document that would make him seem less nationalist than the Canadians, helped to bring the foreign secretary around. Skelton's effort of the previous day, much boiled down but with his essentials, was incorporated into the final report. His words became the meeting report's best known: "This conference is a conference of representatives of the several Governments of the Empire; its views and conclusions on Foreign Policy ... are necessarily subject to the action of the Governments and Parliaments of the various portions of the Empire." Hankey was convinced that the conference had been dominated by officials like him and Skelton, not the politicians.

Dafoe told Skelton that he had earned his pay "each second these days," while Smuts exclaimed: "You should be satisfied – certainly this is Canada's Conference."[57]

The parallel meetings of the Imperial Economic Conference were poking along unproductively. As the principal adviser to the economic delegation, Skelton warned King to be vigilant about the country's fiscal freedom and to steer clear "absolutely and entirely" from any central board for economic cooperation. There was little cause for concern. Imperial visionaries like the irrepressible Leo Amery, who were activists in promoting imperial economic development through migration reforms and tariff changes, were having a tough time finding support in the empire and within the British government. London had no clear or dramatic economic plan for the conference it had called. In the event, the British offered nothing substantive in the way of migration initiatives or tariff cuts.[58]

The conference did agree to set up an Imperial Economic Committee, but Canada dissented from the decision, robbing even this modest achievement of much of its weight. Skelton believed that the committee was simply another variant of the endless schemes for establishing a central imperial government in the British capital: "Parliament or council or secretariat, it matters not, so long as the machinery of control can somehow be established in London." Canada would be committed to a "central review of every important economic activity of our government, and would for example give good ground for intervention if we proposed a reciprocity arrangement with the U.S." This was nonsense. The committee was to have advisory powers only. On this and other matters, Skelton had difficulty in getting Graham to follow the script that had been prepared for him, but the important points got made. Empire economic bodies ought to be formed only if and when a specific need arose. Canada would never seek advice on fiscal policy from such an institution, or be subject to its directives.[59]

When the meetings were not yet half over in mid-October, OD was already telling Isabel that he was "getting fed up on this jamboree." That remark was mostly manufactured for home consumption. Skelton had been away since the summer, first in Michigan and now with this lengthy voyage to a place too far away to get back to Kingston in case of an emergency. He was sensitive enough to be aware of the distance between them, and his family responsibilities. He showered affection on Isabel from afar, remembering their special days and sending "a raft of kisses for my beloved." His wife managed the household and the in-laws in his absence, writing regularly to keep him current on family news. Sheila, now five years old, inquired "when Daddy would visit us again."[60]

As the conference wound down, Skelton paid more attention to theatre and the shopping that had already produced two suits and his first handmade pair of shoes. He began a punishing travel schedule that took him to Sandy's old school in Bembridge, to Newcastle in the north of England, where he preached the "gospel of Canadian autonomy," and to Scotland and recently partitioned Ireland. Dublin, the capital of the new Irish Free State, was banged up and rebuilding after the civil war – "the recent unpleasantness," OD genteelly termed it. He did research in the Irish National Library for a book on Thomas D'Arcy McGee that Isabel was writing, went to the Abbey Theatre, and visited with Desmond FitzGerald, who quoted poetry by the mile and fascinated Oscar with tales of his freedom fighting against the British. FitzGerald's wife was an Ulster Protestant and more fervently nationalist than he was. She told Skelton that she threatened to throw FitzGerald out of the house when she discovered that he had been presented to King George V at Buckingham Place during the empire conference.[61]

The trip reinforced Skelton's Irishness. He saw danger, romance, and fulfilment in the struggle of "this small people" for national liberation. He went north to Castleblaney in Ulster, the home of his ancestors, but he could locate none of his relatives. He spent long enough in Belfast to draw an emphatic contrast with Dublin. The impression left by the southern capital was "one of attractive society, delightful talkers, distinct initiative and achievement in literature," while Belfast had a "hard, hustling, efficient American look." Moving back towards London by boat and train via Scotland, he visited Glasgow, Edinburgh, and Newcastle. Along the way, and at Oxford University and the London School of Economics, he searched for candidates for employment at Queen's, a common pattern of recruitment at the university until decades after Skelton's time. It was a generally disappointing exercise. "Stodgy and solid, if not stolid," was one appraisal, a judgment often made about him.[62]

After two months away from home, Skelton sailed from Liverpool near the end of November, when the Atlantic Ocean was not at its most hospitable. Many of the Canadians from the Imperial Conference were on board, Mackenzie King included. OD again withstood bad weather better than most of the Canadian party, reading a good deal, taking long walks with the prime minister, "manfully" dressing formally for dinner each night, and writing up an extensive diary based on conference date books and papers – by far the most careful record he ever kept, a mark of the meeting's importance in his life. The ship arrived at Halifax Harbour in a thick blanket of fog six and a half days later. From there he travelled by train to Montreal in a painfully slow thirty hours, getting to Kingston on the day the Queen's University Golden Gaels beat the Regina Roughriders 54–0 to win a second consecutive Grey Cup as Canada's national football champion.[63]

Some of Skelton's conclusions about his first experience in imperial negotiation were not predictable. The conference generated a goodwill and mutual respect that he did not expect. He described the farewell meeting as a "love-feast" and "as a matter of fact I think we all appreciated each other more because of the scrapping." He had acquired a "high respect" for the diligence of British ministers and the ability of their chief civil servants: "a tradition of efficiency, culture & responsibility which Canada needs to develop ... badly." In that spirit, he thought of the defeated British minister, Curzon, who "certainly was an impressive figure." His arrogance was repellent, but "I felt a good deal of sympathy for him in his disappointment, and when we learn of the physical difficulties which hampered him from boyhood, it perhaps explains still further some of his idiosyncracies."[64]

Skelton told Mackenzie King that he was "very gratified" by his reception in London. King in turn relayed the news to Burgon Bickersteth, the warden of Hart House at the University of Toronto and one of the prime minister's favourite young men. Bickersteth was a transplanted son of the British establishment and very wary of Skelton, whom he saw as the centre of a negative little group that wanted to separate Canada from the empire. Bickersteth had heard what was widely rumoured, that Skelton's "veiled hostility" towards Britain was the result of the snub he received when he had been refused entry into the Indian Civil Service two decades ago. Now, Bickersteth hoped, those bad memories had been replaced by the warmth of the British welcome at the Imperial Conference. Perhaps Skelton would change his mind about the empire's value and importance.[65]

Yet unsuspected sympathies and second thoughts did not diminish Skelton's suspicions of empire motives or his satisfaction at what he had accomplished at the London conference. He was pleased that Canada had forcefully asserted its right to full self-government and that the imperialists in London regarded him as a dangerous adversary. "Amen, Downing Street," he jotted in his diary: "feel as if we have its measure."[66] The future was uncertain, but the 1923 Imperial Conference had belonged to Canada and to him.

6
The Decision, 1924–5

At the beginning of 1924, Mackenzie King held a dinner at his home for Oscar Skelton and J.S. Ewart, the two main contenders for the prime minister's foreign-policy heart. King judged Ewart to be "better informed than any one in Canada on foreign affairs," but he regarded the crusading Ottawa lawyer as too strident and extreme. Ewart was for complete independence from Britain, King recorded in his diary that night, and "I am not." He preferred Skelton, whose benign temperament was a stark contrast to Ewart's explosions. OD had displayed his own beliefs about an independent Canada during the 1923 Imperial Conference, but only momentarily. He quickly retreated when he encountered King's steadfast opposition, allowing the politician to think that he might have won the scholar over. What King saw in Skelton, at any rate, was not available in Ewart. OD was a solid and undemanding colleague, with an appetite for the daily grind of government and a flexible willingness to subordinate himself to the imperatives of raw politics. Still to be decided, though, was whether Skelton would take up King's offer of permanent employment in Ottawa, made again on the voyage home from the recent conference in London.[1]

Skelton and Ewart had known each other for over a decade, and the professor was in the habit of inviting Ewart to talk to his Queen's students. But there was rivalry. Ewart, then in his seventies, was the aging lion of the nationalist movement, while Skelton was its coming voice. Skelton found Ewart inflexible and prejudiced, especially towards francophone Canadians; Ewart thought Skelton hurried and imprecise. It was imprecision that Ewart, like a stern teacher, had drawn to OD's attention immediately after his hasty remarks about the country's status at the Washington Conference during the Canadian Club speech in January

1922. They followed up that verbal exchange with letters, where Skelton was firm and respectful while Ewart lectured and split legal hairs in a tedious way that irritated the younger man. Ewart ended by saying that there was really little difference between their views. What was important was that "the good work" continue.[2]

The good work was Canadian independence. Both men put the emphasis on the national interest as the paramount consideration in the making of foreign policy. They liked to pile up the evidence to illustrate that Mother Britain was no different from other countries. British leaders acted in their interests, and Canada had to do the same, without regard to the emotional ties that linked the two countries. Geography ought to protect and insulate and teach. The history of Europe was not North America's history. Canada could not make France love the Germans or the Serbs love the Italians or the Turks love the British. All Canadians could and must do was to decide their own future and make their own destiny. Since early in the century, Ewart had been writing pamphlets and books arguing that the "strong strivings of strenuous manhood" demanded a kingdom of Canada separate from Britain. Skelton was influenced by him, but how much? OD was not generous about his intellectual debts.[3]

For the first six months of 1924, with Department of External Affairs chief Sir Joseph Pope ailing and irrelevant, Skelton and Ewart functioned as King's unofficial foreign-policy team. Ewart had the advantage of proximity: his home was only a short walk from Laurier House, King's residence in central Ottawa. Skelton was two hundred kilometres away in Kingston, and pressed by administrative and teaching duties, but he was coming to Ottawa more frequently and kept in regular touch with the prime minister by mail and telegram. He had something to say about a treaty of peace with Turkey and an inter-Allied reparations conference, two pieces of unfinished business left over from the 1919 Paris extravaganza that ended the First World War. Concerned that the British were implicating Canada in decisions made by London in the name of the entire British Empire, Skelton nevertheless warned King that he might have to swallow some imperial diplomacy in order to obtain the international benefits that accompanied it. It was all very well to stand aloof from the British negotiation of the 1923 Treaty of Lausanne, and to deny any responsibility for it, but some way would have to be found to end "this war of ours" with Turkey and to secure the economic privileges that were part of the peace arrangement. Ewart was able to find a form of words to satisfy King that Canada could escape from a state of war with

Turkey while shielding itself from further commitments under the treaty. Skelton's part in the Lausanne affair was not an important one. The government had done its best, he told an academic colleague, but it would probably not be possible "to secure a wholly satisfactory outcome in any such problem, owing to the ambiguous and contradictory character of our present international status."[4]

Skelton gave King advice freely and frankly, whether it was solicited or not. Picking up on a debate in the House of Commons, he urged the prime minister to clarify his position on the British North America Act. The BNA Act, the written part of the Canadian constitution, was a British law; the power to change it resided in London. Canada could request an amendment of the act, but the final decision was the prerogative of the members of a British Parliament that still called itself "imperial." There was no doubt that the British would pass any amendment that had the unanimous approval of the federal government and all the provinces. If, however, there was less than unanimity in Canada, and only a majority of governments were in favour of a change, no one knew what the British Parliament would do. Canadians, Skelton told King, must work out an amending process for altering the constitution that would guarantee religious and racial minorities ample protection "without insisting upon a degree of unanimity for general amendment purposes which would make our constitution more rigid than that of the Medes and the Persians and the Chinese to boot." Once an agreed amending formula was in place, the BNA Act could come home as a Canadian act of Parliament. Canada would have its own constitution rather than someone else's.[5]

Skelton understood King's caution. Opinion in Quebec, suspicious of anything that smacked of a realignment of federal-provincial relations, and the lack of a pressing issue as a catalyst for change were significant obstacles, but sooner or later the issue of the constitution would have to be faced squarely. The British web extended into every aspect of Canadian life, not always to the country's detriment, but the complications of allegiance to traditional ties and the sheer complexity of the imperial system made it difficult to bridge the gap between Canada's vague status and the stature it needed and deserved. For Skelton and Canadian nationalists like him, each advance in autonomy revealed another problem to be solved and reinforced their understanding of the distance to be travelled before Canada was free.

Skelton had to choose between the university and the public service. He told Isabel and university officials that he preferred Queen's, but he was drawn to Ottawa more and more. In early April 1924, King dispatched Andrew Haydon, who had recently become a member of the Senate of Canada, to convince Skelton that his future lay in the civil service. Haydon was persuasive and OD attentive, but he told the prime minister that he needed more time: "I appreciate both the honor of the proposal and your kindness in giving me a little longer to think it over. I have so many roots here that I hesitate to tear them up, but I realize also the very great opportunities the Ottawa appointment would hold." King read that as a positive sign.[6]

Isabel was betting on Queen's, and praying that she was right. She was unenthused about a disruption of her comfortable existence – a move away from the alumnae association and her work with women at the university; from St James Church and her bridge and dramatic clubs; from the Frontenac Club, where she and Oscar went often; and from the Queen's varsity hockey and football games and student dances that both of them attended. Her biography of Thomas D'Arcy McGee was chugging along, with OD the rigorous editor and critic. He told her that she used too much quotation and poetry, and that her writing was diffuse and undistinguished: "Oscar at work on McGee for me & knocks conceit out of me." The children were divided about the possibility of life in Ottawa. Sandy, always adventurous, saw wider horizons there. Herbert, always diffident, feared that he would lose his friends. Sheila was too busy acquiring her first permanent teeth to record her opinion.[7]

The year before, King had promised the deputy minister job to Skelton when Pope left, but the under-secretary wanted to stay on active service until April 1925 and then take a one-year paid leave of absence. The prime minister was loath to push a man of Pope's age and seniority too hard. He did promise Skelton, however, that he would speak with the sixty-nine-year-old about the date of his retirement. This King did, very gently, suggesting that Pope write the prime minister a letter about his intentions. This can only have annoyed Skelton. "I am still thinking over the question of Kingston vs. Ottawa," he wrote to King. "I have never found such difficulty in making a decision (so far as the decision rests with me), and I could not say at this moment which opportunity has the greater appeal." He realized that he would have to reach a definite conclusion very soon, "and shall probably take a day off in order to think it out, so as to be prepared when you write finally as to the way matters stand." Those last few words amounted to a little of Skelton's own pushing: it was time for King to make up his mind.[8]

The way matters stood was that Pope would go, but not yet, and not at a time that fit the prime minister's timetable. King could not, or rather would not, ask the under-secretary to leave, but he wanted Skelton in Ottawa as soon as possible – and permanently. King's wooing of the professor continued, but on Pope's terms, not Skelton's. OD stayed at Laurier House in mid-May to discuss the matter. He wrote home after his host had gone to bed: "Mr. King's biggest asset is his ability to sleep," Oscar marvelled to Isabel, since he never got enough rest. The two men talked about External Affairs over Scotch, cheese, and biscuits, making the prospect of Ottawa "appear more attractive in some ways & less so in others," perhaps since it seemed that the top position in the department would not be vacant for another two long years. King telephoned Kingston on 9 June saying that he was going to include money in the Department of External Affairs budget to create an External Affairs "advisorship." "O.D. feels a missionary call to work," his wife wrote in her diary after the call, adding, hopefully, "but w'd rather be here."[9]

Perhaps not knowing of King's offer, or thinking it was inadequate, Haydon intervened on the 11th in the hope "that no slip should occur in the endeavor to secure the services of Dr. Skelton at the present time." The senator drew the prime minister's attention to the fact that the auditor general earned $15,000 a year, the commissioner of the Royal Canadian Mounted Police (RCMP) $12,500, the chief electoral officer $12,000, and several deputy ministers $8,000. "I have only to add that surely the Prime Minister with the questions that he has to deal with ought to be in a position to pay some fairly decent salary to a man who is worth while." This was more the case because "Dr. Skelton's presence would serve to organize your whole Department, including your secretariat." Skelton himself would never say these things, Haydon was sure: "He is just the opposite of one who would seek to advance his own cause."[10]

Skelton totted up the advantages and disadvantages of External Affairs just as if he were writing one of his foreign-policy briefs. The pros and cons seemed of roughly equal weight. A good salary, which would solve the Skelton family's financial concerns, was one of the benefits, and it was far from the only positive consideration. Life in Ottawa held out "the possibility of doing something effective & on a big scale for the country & particularly of defining and nailing down the imperial and international status which so long I have had in mind." There was also "the prospect of finding congenial friends" and "the opportunity of travel & of meeting eminent men." Naively, and demonstrating his bias in favour of Ottawa, he reckoned that he might have more leisure for research and writing than was possible at Queen's. Nor had he liked the trend of events at the university. He disagreed with major recent decisions and appointments and had little faith in the principal's leadership. When he got to Isabel as a consideration, he demonstrated his insensitivity – or obliviousness. He judged that External Affairs would probably make no great difference for her, "except that she has more friends in Kingston & a quieter life there." As for Sandy, his favourite child was bound to benefit from Ottawa's bigger canvas. He was isolated in Kingston, "with his impulses and desire to do things differently from other people."[11]

There were drawbacks. He had a good life, security, and plenty of fulfilment already. He would be losing the academic's freedom to roam from issue to issue and to speak out at will. King's hold on power was tenuous. There could be no mistaking the political nature of his appointment or the likelihood that a Conservative prime minister would not want him to stay at External Affairs. No doubt he thought of all the pejoratives he had tossed in the direction of Arthur Meighen, who had a good chance of winning the next election. He had also seen enough of Ottawa to realize that he would have to contend with a highly artificial social life and intense bureaucratic rivalries. Queen's had been his home for fifteen years. He felt a "deep interest & responsibility" there, and he would miss "the constant opportunity of developing youngsters of promise & helping them to count for something hereafter; the friends in the university; the possibility of doing more in the future." It was "extremely difficult to decide, with so many factors to consider, and so many facets and uncertainties."[12]

He compromised. After a delegation of Queen's trustees from the Kingston area suggested it, he wrote to Principal Bruce Taylor requesting a fifteen-month leave of absence. It was possible, he said, that his interest in the Department of External Affairs would grow and he might stay on, "but certainly, as I see it at present, I do not want to go into Government service permanently, and expect to be ready to take up teaching again after that measure of experience of the other way of life." The Board of Trustees accepted his resignation as dean of arts, since his five-year term was coming to an end anyway. Taylor knew his man. He told the trustees that he eagerly hoped that Skelton would return, but that they must understand that he was going to "a position for which his whole training has singularly fitted him." The expedient of a leave from the university resolved the dilemma, for the time being at any rate, and postponed the day when a final decision would have to be made. Maybe, when Skelton explored the mysteries of the capital further, a return to the university would look very attractive. "Queen's would certainly be a hard place to forget," Skelton assured the principal, who expected all along that he would lose his professor to the "tangled new world" of the public service.[13]

Skelton informed the prime minister's private secretary on 18 June that he was willing to accept the temporary position of counsellor at the Department of External Affairs, with the possibility "of staying on further."[14] His appointment dating from 15 July 1924, he was to earn $5,000 a year, only a small increase of $500 over what he was earning as a professor and dean of arts at Queen's.[15] About to breach the compulsory retirement age of seventy, Pope was reappointed for one year.[16] The Toronto *Globe* and the Ottawa *Citizen* welcomed the Skelton appointment, the *Globe* extolling his virtues as "a scholar and man of action" and predicting that he would stay on to succeed Pope.[17] Skelton's academic colleagues were not so sure. The University of Toronto historian George M. Wrong, sympathetic to OD's nationalism, wondered if he would want to stay at External Affairs. "You have been so long your own master, so long been free to say and do things on your own free judgement, that I suspect you will find the restraints of a government post irksome." Perhaps not, though, and "you are, as it seems to me, admirably qualified for the work."[18] After Skelton became under-secretary of state for external affairs, one of the first young recruits to his department was Wrong's smart and combative son, Hume, who prepared for his first posting in Washington by reading the Laurier biography.[19]

The family agreed that Oscar would come to Ottawa alone and return to Kingston on weekends. Tiny Sheila was given charge of the garden, and Skelton warned Sandy, about to enter his second year at Queen's, that much was to be expected of him as he approached his eighteenth birthday. He would have to help take care of the house in his father's absence, to say nothing of his university responsibilities. "It will be a year that will count a great deal in your character & your capacity for leadership and I can only hope that whenever difficulties arise you will take time to think what your judgment & your honour advise, and, wherever possible, to talk things over with your Mother, fully and frankly. We are hoping great things of you, Sandy."[20]

Skelton reached Ottawa on the morning of 17 July 1924 full of enthusiasm and promising himself that he would record daily notes in a small green book – "a new chapter, & so new resolutions as to keeping of diaries, to say nothing of more important matters." But, over what became a long career in the capital, he was so preoccupied by the business of government that his diary entries seldom stretched over more than a few days each year: within a short while, he was noting that the 1924 diary had suffered "a quick and prolonged gap." He split his first days in Ottawa between long sessions at the House of Commons and the comfortable Laurier House, where King insisted he stay until lodging was arranged. With the help of the prime ministerial chauffeur and his Cadillac limousine, Skelton found a room at Mrs Gray's boarding house on Maclaren Street for $20 a month with an extra 25 or 30 cents for breakfast. Lunch or dinner might be with the assorted guests, who included a Nova Scotia MP, at 480 Maclaren or at the parliamentary restaurant, the Russell Cafeteria, the Belmont Pharmacy, the Gem and Elegant cafés on Bank Street, or Murphy-Gamble, the Sparks Street department store. He entertained or was entertained often. A notable guest during the first month in Ottawa was the once and future British prime minister Stanley Baldwin, an acquaintance from the 1923 Imperial Conference, who was given lunch in the Rideau Room of Murphy-Gamble and dinner at the Wayside Inn at Britannia Bay. Skelton had liked Baldwin from the start. He was unpretentious, a quality OD admired in people, politicians most of all, since they were the least likely to lack self-importance.[21]

OD was an instant insider, meeting cabinet ministers by the carload, gossiping with the supremely well-connected Haydon at the snooty Rideau Club, receiving personal intimacies from King about the rich and famous men he had known in the United States during the First World War, and meriting a disapproving look from Conservative leader Meighen. Skelton cultivated newspaper correspondents and enjoyed their company. He already knew John Bassett of the Montreal *Gazette*, another member of the parliamentary press corps, from the Imperial Conference. Skelton had approved of him from the time, on board the *Montcalm*, that he discovered that Bassett's family came from the same part of Ireland as the Skelton clan. They planned a trip together to their native Ulster. OD also became and stayed friendly with the "quick" and "very decent" Grant Dexter of the *Manitoba Free Press*, whom he met for the first time in August 1924. "He liked newspapermen because, at heart, he loved journalism," Dexter recalled. "He would look up at you with a kindly, shy smile, push up his spectacles which were forever getting down low on his nose. 'Well,' he would ask, 'what is the news?'"[22]

At External Affairs Skelton took up residence in Loring Christie's former office, number 269, in the East Block of the Parliament Buildings, a large space overlooking Wellington Street. His desk had belonged to Sir Robert Borden, someone he respected. Next door, in 271, two departmental stenographers were at his disposal, soon joined by twenty-eight-year-old Marjorie McKenzie from Queen's, installed as his secretary on a temporary certificate from Adam Shortt's Civil Service Commission. The small senior staff had all been with the department since 1909, the first year of operations. Sir Joseph Pope, bearing the interloper no ill will, flitted by from time to time, a "feeble, curious, courteous" figure in the twilight. The assistant under-secretary, W.H. Walker, struck Skelton as "formal, no initiative, friendly." F.M. Baker, the chief clerk, was close to retirement himself but "breezy & helpful," while accountant Agnes McCloskey was "very efficient & alert." The entire Ottawa establishment of External Affairs numbered around two dozen. The department's new counsellor was already thinking about a substantial increase in those numbers.[23]

Skelton was in Ottawa only a few days when Senator Raoul Dandurand, who had been named as a delegate to the autumn 1924 League of Nations Assembly meeting, requested the services of a knowledgeable secretary who could accompany the Canadian team to Switzerland. Noting Loring Christie's indispensability as a helpmate to the Conservative government and Skelton's just-announced appointment, the senator asked if King could spare his adviser for the month of September. The prime minister replied that "no one could fill the bill quite so well as our friend Skelton" and added that OD would be on hand to travel from Geneva to London to represent the country if a projected meeting on British Empire constitutional relations was called. Skelton regretted another absence from home and a trip away from External Affairs so soon after his appointment, but he too thought it would be advantageous to have a first taste of the League and that, as he said, made it unanimous. He had not asked Isabel. She gave no hint of anger and he none of guilt as they prepared him for another overseas voyage, his third in three years. King considered it "a loss to me to have him go just when retained but quite advisable – He has been no end of help and his coming into the department has eased my mind & burden quite beyond words. If I had had him from the start it would have meant everything."[24]

On the way to meet the CPR liner *Minnedosa*, Skelton stopped in Montreal to check on the progress of Léon Mercier-Gouin's translation of the Laurier biography. Gouin, the son of Sir Lomer, had little progress to report and all the usual excuses to offer. The conversation became one about the prospects of the Liberal Party in Quebec, and there was enough good news on that front for Skelton to take something positive away from the encounter. He also saw Frank Smith, a former colleague from *Booklovers Magazine* in Philadelphia. Now the head of a large American advertising agency, Smith had a Canadian project in mind and, he assumed, a friend who could help him reach the prime minister. Skelton was polite but firm: he could do nothing in the furthering of his friend's scheme because his job was confined to external affairs.[25] His role in government was going to extend well beyond foreign policy, but he was not about to peddle influence in the way Smith wanted.

Skelton was becoming a student of transatlantic voyages, which he regarded as minor sociological experiments. The year before, on the way to the Imperial Conference, he had worked hard at examining and dissecting the ship's company and describing it to Isabel. Despite his shyness, he was intensely curious, enjoyed fresh encounters, and was willing to seek out new acquaintances. But the *Minnedosa* lacked the dynamic of the earlier voyage, partly because of Skelton's lack of fluency in French. He could read the language with ease but spoke it only occasionally: he was halting enough of speech even in English. Almost half of the passengers in first class were French-speaking, and he rarely spoke a word to them – "their English is negligible & my French not at hand." He occupied his time reading, listening to the orchestra, or watching the third-class passengers below, "an English conception of Heaven looking down on Hell," although he said that he would gladly have brought a good many of the people he saw below up top with him. The first officer's dining table was congenial. The seating included Ralph Campney, a recent Queen's graduate hired by King for his office on Skelton's recommendation, who was accompanying OD to Geneva as a private secretary. His eating companions received passing grades on the grounds of intellect, experience, and manners, except for "an Amurrican," who was evidently in the clothing business and displayed his wares to the tune of sporting one or two new suits a day. Combining two of the stereotypes of the age, Skelton thought him "absolutely incredible in the perfection of his rendering of the provincial boasting Yankee of stage fame." He was not Jewish, Skelton concluded, but a very close approximation.[26]

OD brought himself up to date with British, Irish, and American periodicals, while also poring through novels, serious and otherwise, detective stories, and French sociologist André Siegfried's study *l'Angleterre*, which had been recommended by Senator Dandurand. Thinking of his own book on British politics that had been promised to an American publisher, he found the Siegfried work admirable in its comprehensiveness, orderliness, and clarity. It did "not accuse the Englishman of looking after his own interest in foreign policy – it simply shows how each section of the people conceives and follows its interest, taking the generalization for granted." Canvassing publications on League of Nations

affairs, including verbatim reports of previous meetings, he saw that
a command of French was essential at the League, where English was
a secondary language, and that it was helpful to have continuity in a
country's representation at League meetings, which had been lacking
in the Canadian case. The year before, Canada's delegation had nearly
succeeded in an attempt to water down Article X of the League's core
document, the Covenant, which committed signatories to the defence of
the territorial integrity of all League members. Canada's attack on the
League had been a big news story in Europe, but the Canadian people
and their Parliament were scarcely aware of it. How out of touch, Skelton
thought, North Americans (and even the British) were with events on
the continent.[27]

Once the ship reached the French port of Cherbourg, Skelton went
by train to Paris and on to Geneva. The Swiss capital was bustling with
excitement and anticipation – and people. Its promoters believed passionately that the League, with Britain and France in the lead, was poised
to come into its own as a force for peace and a parliament of the world.
The fifth meeting of the Assembly attracted high-level representatives
from almost every member nation, among them the premiers or foreign
ministers of twenty-one European countries. Tourists had been forced
out of their accommodation to make space for delegates, officials, and
journalists; even hotel corridors were pressed into service to make space
for the unfortunate visitors who had not made careful arrangements
long in advance. Punctilious about taking care of his own well-being,
Dandurand had a good suite at the massive Hôtel de la Paix, but Skelton
was at first relegated to a small double room with no bath that also had
to house Campney. He did not complain. The room was clean, comfortable, and cheap.[28]

The Assembly opened business on 1 September in the Salle de Refor-
mation, a poorly ventilated, unimposing hall. Spectators crowded in on
the delegates and their advisers from the side and back. Skelton wrote
home that it was a great international achievement "to bring together
in one room representatives of practically every nation on earth, brown
& black & white, Europe & America & Asia," although how much more
it was than an elaborate talk shop remained to be seen. His duty was to
manage the two Canadian chief delegates, Dandurand and Defence Minister E.M. Macdonald, and to serve on the second (technical) and fourth
(finance) committees of the Assembly. Dandurand proved "a mighty
likable & kindly chap," while OD considered Macdonald a nonentity
whose one constructive suggestion was to hire a car for the delegation's

weekend jaunts around the lakes and through the mountains of Switzerland. Lining the two politicians up with the "right" point of view, Skelton lamented to Isabel, "isn't always easy."[29]

The committee work was steady and detailed, with meetings usually occupying six to eight hours a day. It took time to digest the parcels of literature hurled at the delegates by the League Secretariat, and not much seemed to be happening, but the personalities could be spectacular, the problems interesting, and the amount of heat generated on apparently innocuous subjects surprising. OD quickly discovered "twenty things in which we were not doing anything right at Ottawa," and he resolved that he would get the government more interested in the League. Walter Riddell, a former Ontario deputy minister of labour working at the International Labour Organization (ILO) in Geneva, was extremely hospitable to Skelton, providing dinners and drives, and the two men got better acquainted on a Sunday-long trek up nearby Mont Joli, where OD "found a dozen muscles & lost two knees on the way down." He supported, and might have been behind, the appointment of Riddell as permanent Canadian advisory officer at the League in 1925.[30]

Believing that character was as important as circumstance in international politics, Skelton assessed each member of the cavalcade of speakers at the plenary sessions of the Assembly. Édouard Herriot, the pipe-smoking Radical premier of France, was clearly "the biggest man there," a "solid, cattle-drover looking type, but able, sincere & with a very interesting mixture of idealism & practicality." Despite his unprepossessing appearance, Edvard Beneš from Czechoslovakia qualified as "astute & logical" and "the most active & best-informed expert in foreign affairs in Europe." Four of every five delegates spoke French, and Skelton's facility in the language improved over the four weeks: "A good deal depends on the clearness of the speaker, of course," he wrote Isabel. "I could follow every word of Herriot, but only half of Benes – and a good deal depends on the ventilation of the hall & whether I'm awake or asleep."[31]

Skelton grumbled that the long finger of British imperialism stretched even to Geneva, the one place where Canadian independence was supposed to be established beyond question. That, after all, had been the point of the country's entry into the League in 1919. Nevertheless, the British held their seat in Geneva in the name of the "British Empire," which, as far as the international community knew, included Canada and made its separate representation at the League superfluous. A tangible example of the empire's phenomenal staying power came on the third day of Assembly business, as the agenda plodded its way through minorities questions and heard Japanese gratitude for the outpouring of international support during the previous year's devastating earthquake. At 11:00 in the morning word came from the United Kingdom camp of a meeting of the British Empire delegation (Skelton underlined the British use of the singular twice in his diary) called for noon, while the Assembly was still sitting. The teams from the dominions stood at the appointed hour, one by one in the full sight of everyone, and filed out of the room from their different parts of the hall. It was as bitter a blow to Canada's ambition to act as an individual at the League as Skelton could imagine: "It was so evident & concrete an illustration of the British Empire as one unit that it may well be that it undid in the eyes of many European states much of the good of the past three years." He was furious to be led out of the Assembly hall by Dandurand, suspecting that the British had orchestrated the mass exodus to demonstrate that the dominions were still their creatures.[32]

No sooner had the empire delegation meeting begun than the British prime minister, Ramsay MacDonald, announced that he had rejected the draft treaty of mutual assistance, the League's 1923 attempt to strengthen collective security, partly because the dominions would not accept it. OD questioned the chronology. The British had made up their minds before Canada did, he believed, and simply sought a pretext for a stand they were making in their own interest. MacDonald held to his story that the dominions had been an important ingredient in the decision, replying sweetly that his government knew Canada's position in advance because it could be guessed from previous attitudes. Skelton detested the way that the Australians and New Zealanders "kowtowed" to MacDonald as "our prime minister." Only the Irish, represented by his ally from the Imperial Conference, Desmond FitzGerald, could really be counted upon to support Skelton's insistence on dominion rights.[33]

Although he disapproved of empire discussions in principle, Skelton had to admit that being "summoned into the presence of the great" could be valuable in obtaining inside information on what he called the "many gorgeous plans for disarmament & security" that were being hatched in various committees under the strong hand of Beneš. By the end of September there was a single plan and document, the Protocol of Geneva, which Oscar praised as "a courageous and well-coordinated attempt to outlaw war" linking together for the first time "the three indispensable factors of arbitration, security, disarmament." The establishment of more machinery and more penalties to punish aggressors, however, did not go to the root of the problem. If future conflict was truly to be prevented, "we must try to remove or lessen the causes of wars and to create an international atmosphere in which a peaceful settlement may be reached." Instead of trying to stiffen the Covenant, "we should continue, as Canada has tried to do in the past, to make it more flexible." Then the United States would be more likely to become a member of the League of Nations. Without the Americans, the League could never succeed.[34]

The Protocol was welcomed by Assembly delegates in early October. Only Canada expressed doubts and hesitations, with Dandurand stipulating that Canada was a producer not a consumer of security and subject to different rules than other League members. "We live in a fireproof house, far from inflammable materials," he declared, in a memorable phrase that sounded more like Skelton than Dandurand, who favoured the Protocol and almost certainly had to be talked out of putting it in a more positive light. There is no direct evidence that OD drafted the speech and he did not claim credit for it, but all of his central arguments and rhetoric were there. The Protocol offered security to Europe but promised nothing to Canadians except the possibility that more of them would have to die if the League failed to prevent war. Canada was a peaceable kingdom, heavily indebted from the First World War and living happily alongside a United States that had stayed aloof from the League. This view was blinkered, but no more than that of other countries. When it found its way to the capitals of Europe, the Protocol quietly died.[35]

Word came from the British that the constitutional conference planned for London had been cancelled, but King asked Skelton to stay on in Switzerland to represent the country at the governing body of the International Labour Organization from 8 to 12 October. He enjoyed that responsibility more than any part of the League proceedings, probably because he had to take on a much more active role in explaining Canadian policies on matters such as immigration. Between the League and ILO meetings, he used his spare time for a quick train trip to Venice, "incomparably the most interesting" of all the cities he had ever seen. He and Campney came out of the dingy Venice train station "into fairyland" – the Grand Canal with black gondolas; the brilliant Piazza of St Mark and the narrow, jumbled streets that surrounded it; and the Doge's Palace and its innumerable sisters and brothers. It was ridiculous, he wrote to Isabel, to come to a place like that for only twenty-seven hours, "but we have seen enough to understand something of its charm. I had read so much about it that I had been rather blase, but it

exceeds my highest expectations. I feel that I have been making a trip as
an advance agent, preparing for the next trip we take together."[36]

He had been away from Canada for almost six weeks, with nearly a
month to go. Isabel was more cut off from Oscar than when he was in
Ottawa, because he could not get home quickly. She wrote him letters
detailing household problems and he regularly dispatched rational,
well-meaning advice. He was thoughtful of her family when he was far
away, purchasing gifts and inquiring about their health. Understanding that Isabel was rushing to finish the McGee book, he returned a
chapter that she sent him almost immediately with his comments and
encouragement. Sandy caused more heartburn, this time because of his
absorption in sports to the exclusion of his academic work at Queen's. "I
wouldn't worry," Oscar mused, "it's a passing craze & an inevitable one;
he is proud & ambitious & wants to be first in anything he tries – the
discipline will be good on the whole, & later his interest in books will
revive." OD assembled a surrogate family of his own in Geneva, including Campney and Nan Saunders, a family friend employed in the League
library. He tried to throw the two young people together, hoping they
might become interested in one another, but the spark was missing.[37]

Skelton returned home through Paris and London with a short trip
to Ireland squeezed in. The first piece of Ottawa business was to ensure
that the Geneva Protocol would never become Canadian policy. That was
not difficult. He also warned King that something had to be done about
the British government's insistence that it spoke for the entire empire at
the League. His overall impression of the institution, however, was not
unfavourable. The League had an efficient Secretariat and the meetings
he had attended were marked by a high seriousness and earnestness of
purpose. The institution was doing splendid and fundamental work in
bringing together peoples in common causes, gradually building up "a
reserve of tolerant world's council." When King remarked that Canada's
contribution to Geneva seemed to him excessive, and asked Skelton to
report on the question, the reply came back carefully but unmistakably
on the side of the League, which he pointed out was receiving from Canada only about 1 per cent a year of the annual amount the country spent
on the war effort during 1914–18.[38]

Pope had decided to go on 1 April, or had it decided for him. In
early February, having been told that Skelton would be his successor,
Pope called to wish the younger man well and to ask if they could discuss
future personnel questions. Skelton responded that, in his own case, he
was leaning towards Ottawa but had as yet made no final determination.

The rumours of an impending announcement were gaining momentum, and on 7 March Toronto and Kingston newspapers reported the "expectation" that Skelton would leave Queen's for External Affairs in such similar language that it was a sure sign of a leak, probably from King himself to encourage a final end to the affair. Commenting that "some of the newspapers have been busy deciding the matter for me," OD's letter of 10 March to Principal Taylor of Queen's made it official that he was leaving Kingston for good. "It has been the most difficult decision I have ever had to make," he told Taylor. There was work left to do at the university and "I feel sure that I could never anywhere else develop friendships and associations that would mean so much." He would have cause to regret his decision, but "I feel that I would probably have regretted it more if I had declined this opportunity which has come to me of taking a direct part in helping to shape Canada's external relations in this formative period." External Affairs was too big a chance to turn away from, and Skelton later admitted that he had taken the counsellor position "preparatory to taking over the position of under-secretary." The next day he wrote to the prime minister, formally accepting the position of deputy minister for external affairs. "So that's that at last," said OD, the decision finally made. The hunt for an Ottawa house began.[39]

OD received his baptism as under-secretary-designate at his first Government House dinner. He arrived punctually, a habit of long standing. After checking his coat, he ambled admiringly through long corridors, drinking in the pictures on the walls and the amplitude of servants, until he got in sight of his destination, the reception room, where the governor general and his wife would soon appear. Mild panic set in when he noticed that the man ahead of him had gloves on, causing a rapid retracing of steps to the dressing room to retrieve the pair that he had recently bought but left with his coat. On the way, he spotted the patrician MP Herbert Marler, stylish and impeccably mannered – and without gloves. OD changed his mind again, and was relieved to discover that almost all of the guests waiting for their excellencies were gloveless as well. No sooner was this minor social dilemma solved when he encountered another, looking down to see that he had forgotten to take off his rubbers, which completely covered his patent leather evening shoes. He debated another flight back in the direction of the cloakroom but decided that, because the rubbers were brand new and as shiny as his shoes, he would "go ahead & be the first & only person who attended a Govt House dinner in rubbers. So I did, & think I got away with it; everybody was thinking about what he or she wore and not about others."[40]

Oscar's proud father wrote to "congratulate the Country on your appointment." It would offer many more opportunities for a contribution to Canada than even becoming the principal of Queen's. Jeremiah's great regret was that his late wife could not join in the celebration: they both knew how much it would have meant to her. He was not finding it easy to make a living or cope with life after his Elizabeth's death. His preoccupied son sympathized, but Isabel was the one who kept in closest touch with Jeremiah.[41]

On 31 March 1925, a cool, sunny spring day, the governor general signed an order-in-council elevating Skelton to the position of under-secretary of external affairs at $8,000 a year, more than the prime minister earned. With obvious satisfaction and pride, OD copied out the document for his wife, who remained in Kingston, and recreated for her the moment when "I went in to the office of the Clerk of the Privy Council & solemnly swore to be faithful & true to His Majesty his heirs & successors & swore also to carry out the duties & keep the secrets of my office – the oath of allegiance & the oath of office as they are called & signed the book in which all the Privy Councillors, ministers & occasionally a Deputy Minister record their signatures." That night Isabel wrote reassuringly and unselfishly from Kingston. "Congratulations & best wishes to you, my own beloved, for the new work & life you enter upon tomorrow. I do hope we shall always look back on it as the opening day of a very happy & right choice in your life." At the bottom she added: "Love & Kisses dearest – & best – beloved – my thoughts will be with you all tomorrow – make it as easy as you can for Sir Joseph – I know you will do this. Again, Love & Kisses. Your own Isabel."[42]

There was also sadness and some resentment as Isabel contemplated further months alone and then a wrenching move away from Kingston. Her letter of congratulation to her husband described the difficulty of handling Sandy and his headstrong friends – "if you were here it would be different" – and she wrote about "the life you enter upon" and "the right choice in your life" rather than using "we" and "our." Oscar was not quick to notice what his wife needed when it conflicted with what he wanted. His life and his choices consistently came first in their relationship, and his priorities were the central and constant preoccupation of the household. He was the patriarch, often a stern one, of their home on Albert Street in Kingston, sometimes using it like a hotel. Isabel became used to packing his bags for his frequent absences, and he was unhappy that she was not with him in Ottawa to help with the transition to External Affairs. If it had been up to her, they would have stayed in

Kingston. She published her very positive biography of McGee in March 1925, a significant milestone in her career as an historian but one inevitably overshadowed by Oscar's simultaneous appointment to External Affairs.[43]

Yet their marriage was strong and stable. They were affectionate partners, touching, hugging, fiercely protective, inhabiting their correspondence with a loving playfulness that was sustained over their four decades together. Isabel found Oscar's patience and generosity, inside the house and out, almost saintly, and he supported her literary ambitions with research, drafting ideas, warm encouragement, and blunt editorial commentary. OD cheered the good reviews of the McGee biography and derided the bad, while using his connections to get the volume noticed and promote sales. He wrote the advertising copy for the book and publicized it in the speech that he wrote for Mackenzie King to deliver at a banquet celebrating the centenary of McGee's birth, held just after the book's publication. Deeply interested in all the family's concerns – Sheila's cold ("blow one nostril at a time," he advised), Sandy's Spanish, Herbert's writing – he craved all the news from Isabel when he was away. Two letters arrived from her as he assumed his responsibilities on 1 April, one of them her note of congratulation sent the previous day. He responded immediately that her good wishes were "very welcome & very dear." He ended with "Good night dearest mine, & a hundred kisses on this new day, Your own Oscar."[44]

As his wife had asked, Skelton did his best to be understanding of Sir Joseph Pope's pain on his final day at the office, and he put considerable effort into finding appropriate gifts to mark the occasion. He did not go to the under-secretary's office on 1 April until noon out of deference to Pope. He found the master bureaucrat lovingly surveying his filing cabinets, chairs, and bookshelves, as an old general might inspect his troops for the last time. They shook hands three or four times and Pope went out, finally leaving Skelton alone to contemplate the mammoth office on the southwest corner of the East Block of the Parliament Buildings, with a direct view of the green lawn in front of the House of Commons. It had been Sir John Macdonald's room when he was prime minister, and the first cabinet held its meetings there. "So it's a very historic spot I'm sitting in just now."[45]

The Liberal *Manitoba Free Press* of John Dafoe welcomed "an event of considerate importance in government circles." Skelton was an experienced hand, which was just as well, because the work of the department was bound to increase in volume and significance as it developed "from a branch of the Prime Minister's office, dealing largely with our relations with Great Britain and the other Dominions, into a department of foreign affairs dealing with all the world." The government's journalistic enemies were friendly to Skelton personally but not to his views or the implications of his permanent arrival so near the seat of power. The London *Free Press* acknowledged that Skelton was an outstanding Canadian, but anyone anxious for cooperation between the motherland and the overseas dominions was bound to be disturbed. "Dr. Skelton belongs to the school of extreme autonomists, who imagine that there is a continual plot to deprive Canada of her rights and privileges." The Ottawa *Journal* lauded Skelton as a person of integrity and an acute student of international affairs. "His conceptions of Canada's world status may be the wrong conceptions, his advice the wrong advice; but his character and intelligence at least ensure that our methods of dealing with London will be free of that boorishness and lack of dignity – which too often characterized them when this Government first took office."[46]

He began his new employment at a quick pace, and it was only a matter of weeks before a crisis arose. Until then, the question of Canada's Arctic sovereignty had been handled mainly by the Department of the Interior, which since 1922 had sent out regular ship patrols to the northern archipelago. In the spring of 1925, the matter took on urgency because of plans by the Americans Donald Baxter Macmillan and Richard E. Byrd to make a base on Ellesmere Island and explore by airplane west into the last remaining unmapped portion of the Arctic. On 23 April an interdepartmental body, the Northern Advisory Board, was established to deal with the situation. The first meeting was held the next day. Chairing the board was the deputy minister of the interior, W.W. Cory, but Skelton quickly established a dominant position. Under his leadership, Canada's claim to all the northern islands was proclaimed through statements in the House of Commons and at a press conference held by the minister of the interior, Charles Stewart. In June diplomatic correspondence with Washington on the subject was initiated.

Mackenzie King – to the despair of civil servants from both External Affairs and the Department of the Interior – had previously meddled in Arctic matters on the advice of the unscrupulous but charismatic Vilhjalmur Stefansson. Such was King's confidence in Skelton, however, that from this point on he left Arctic policy to the bureaucrats. The threat from Macmillan and Byrd fizzled out when their airplanes performed poorly and their expedition had to be cut short. More significantly for the Canadian legal case, the U.S. State Department did not protest against

Ottawa's claims of ownership over the entire northern archipelago. Five years later, Skelton and his colleagues on the Northern Advisory Board successfully secured Norway's recognition of Canadian sovereignty over the islands discovered by Norwegian explorer Otto Sverdrup during his 1898–1902 expedition. The last uncertainty hanging over Canada's title was thus removed.[47]

As the Arctic drama unfolded in the early summer of 1925, Skelton settled into a routine of obsessively long working days that he never abandoned. Arriving early in the morning at the East Block, he would stay until late at night, working on weekends and holidays as well. "I spent the day in the office," he told Isabel on 20 May. "I didn't go to the garden party at Rideau Hall this afternoon." The next day would be a holiday for the civil service, but not for him: "I'll be in the office in the morning." Two weeks later, he wrote: "Today, tempted to go to the races – not tempted to go to the Garden Party, but compromised on a solid day's work in the office." His compulsion to overdo things was reinforced by fussy perfectionism and reluctance to delegate responsibility. In family matters too, during long absences he liked to remain in control of the most minute social particulars, down to whether or when Isabel would have a party at home or the hours of the day that his wife and children took the train.[48]

Skelton realized that he was being inundated by an ever-increasing weight of diplomatic and administrative detail. Perspective and planning suffered. Some of this he considered inevitable, and even desirable in the short term, but only some of it. The office routine was greater and more absorbing than he had anticipated before coming to Ottawa, "or even when I sat at the Counsellor's detached seat." Perhaps "some work I attract – or grasp; perhaps I take too long to decide many matters; at any rate I sit at my desk all day with little chance for the broader work of such a department, much less for any outside reading. It is well, for the present, as it is essential that I should get to know all that is going on (officially, that is) in the office, but I must not let myself get swamped by it." For the first time in a long career of lecture giving and speechmaking, he wrote out an address in full beforehand, simply because the press of everyday business did not allow him the luxury of assimilating the material so that it could be delivered only with a few notes.[49]

He understood the importance, real and symbolic, of the French language in Canada's government, and his Geneva experience had revealed how pivotal knowledge of French was to the practice of international diplomacy. Wanting to acquire better skills, he engaged a teacher,

Mademoiselle Gautier, for evening lessons, but he made little progress. He had no time to study between sessions and he was usually too tired at night to be very alert. Nor did he take any concrete steps to advance the use of French in his new department. Francophone officers would get their small share of the jobs, but the language of Skelton's Department of External Affairs was English.[50]

Still boarding at 480 Maclaren Street, he continued to go out a good deal, often for lunch or dinner. Supper with the Labour politician J.S. Woodsworth was an exciting prospect and had the advantage that a dinner jacket was certain not to be required dress – "that's one place I'm sure of." Evenings with colleagues or old friends like the Shortts were apt to inspire a heavy air of obligation, palpable weariness, or even a hint of academic snobbery. One night, "feeling that I wouldn't do much else," he decided to call on the Shortts, where he met a doctor from the Civic Hospital and endured what he called a "vigorous hammer chorus" of complaints about that institution's internecine rivalries and management failures. He reported that he liked the doctor, "tho he's a curiously ill-read man, with very chaotic and half-baked ideas on most subjects outside of medicine."[51]

Long walks cleared his head. One took him, after working all Saturday in the office, across the interprovincial bridge to neighbouring Hull "in a vain effort to find a decent restaurant." He compromised on "a medium clean-35 cent dinner" and then moved to "a cafe, a quart bottle of Dow's beer, & a survey of the scene." The experience was not uplifting. The crowds of drinkers were "not prepossessing": he saw "a good deal of quarrelling & staggering & foul language" and the "curious freeing of inhibitions under the sway of alcohol." Hull was "a God-forsaken hole, shoddy, dirty, dilapidated," a city of "low-grade industries, cheaply-paid roustabouts with large families, poor buildings & streets & little community pride; its eating as bad as its drinking." Adding to the problem was the influence of the Catholic Church and "the easy going French Canadian temper which probably shows to better advantage in country than in city; so whether the beer drinking crowds are cause or effect I'll not try to say."[52]

OD worked the next morning and after lunch took a stroll to look at a house in Rockcliffe Park, which he thought magnificent in the spring, particularly in the way the park opened on the Ottawa and the Gatineau rivers and the hills beyond. It was a striking contrast "with the squalor & misery of Hull the day before." Going past Ashbury College a few blocks to Fairview Avenue, he discovered a house for sale near McKay Lake. It seemed a good value for $12,000, and the spot was quiet, attractive, and only a few minutes from the public school and the streetcar. While the mosquitoes were a major drawback, he had found the area where he wanted to live.[53]

King had a wide conception of his new charge's participation in government, and it was inevitable from the start that Skelton's ambit and influence would extend beyond the Department of External Affairs. King saw the department, not as a separate and distinct unit of government, but as an extension of himself and of the prime minister's office – and therefore as a legitimate resource when he trolled for policy and logistical support. Skelton's office was next door to the prime minister's, and OD was an authority on domestic issues, a ready, available, and always willing source of wisdom and sympathy. He became, in fact if not in name, the deputy minister to the prime minister, responsible for an array of domestic duties that included the giving of political advice. Skelton told a prospective employee that the prime minister's office "was an extraordinarily difficult mechanism, work of all kinds from all quarters at all hours; a man to be of aid to the P.M. must be on tap at any time."[54]

No less than King, Skelton overrode the barrier between the world of politics and his formal obligations as under-secretary. It would not have occurred to him to refuse a request to write a partisan speech or question the secondment of one of his employees to the prime minister's office. He was a party man, rejoicing when life went well for Liberals and downcast when they did not. When Saskatchewan Premier C.A. Dunning won a massive victory in June 1925 on the same day that King walloped the Conservatives on the tariff issue in the House of Commons, Skelton wrote that "all told it was a great day for Liberalism or at least for the Liberal party."[55]

Inheriting Jeremiah's passion for politics as the lifeblood of democracy, OD had moved easily in such Liberal circles for a long time. He admired and studied its practitioners. He respected the slashing rhetorical style of the speeches of Conservative leader Meighen, although he decried his parliamentary tactics, carried out by "hopelessly asinine" obstructionist MPs like Sir Henry Drayton. King, Skelton concluded, was badly out-manoeuvring the Opposition, but the prime minister was clearly out of sorts and unhappy with his colleagues, many of whom he characterized as "barnacles rather than fighters." King was "unsystematic & procrastinating in getting down to work, but hardworking & with a strong intellectual grasp when he does get to it."[56]

Skelton was willing to turn himself over completely to Mackenzie King. The bachelor prime minister, who had no anchored home life of his own, expected complete devotion from all his employees, pacing himself with great skill but driving his subordinates hard and tending to forget that they had lives outside of the office. King made huge demands on Skelton's time and energy – "he had a dozen things ready to fire at me, all needing attention instanter if not sooner" – and OD always responded by putting duty first and family second. Skelton's devotion to King added to the close relationship that already existed between the two men. The prime minister had the perfect obsessive employee, one bonded to him by shared goals and their Liberal lineage. Sir Wilfrid Laurier, King assured himself, "would have been genuinely pleased with this relationship of Skelton and myself in our present positions."[57]

In the realm of foreign affairs, King had the expectation that Skelton would improve the government's capacity to make independent decisions. The deputy responded that he needed the money and people to forge a true foreign office. The Department of External Affairs that he had inherited from Pope had 101 employees but only a meagre three at officer-level positions, one of them Skelton himself. There were offices of one kind or another in London, Paris, Washington, and Geneva but as yet not a single diplomatic mission to give autonomous policy intelligence, distinguish Canada from Britain abroad, and proclaim Canada's growing international status. Almost everything the government learned about the world outside Canada came from Britain, a fact that irritated King but incensed Skelton, who believed that Canada's representation in Washington, which consisted of a journalist and an almost forgotten agent residing in the British Embassy, was especially inadequate because of the importance of the United States to Canadians. Without sufficient bureaucratic resources, Skelton warned King after his first months as under-secretary, it was "absolutely impossible even with 7 day weeks and 16-hour days to secure the independent and exact knowledge of external affairs which is now desirable." The prime minister was sympathetic but unwilling to act, apart from agreeing to fill the vacant counsellor post with Jean Désy. King feared that his hold on Parliament was not strong enough: there would be criticisms of excessive expenditure and disloyalty to Britain. Skelton was told to wait. King claimed that he did not even have the personnel to serve all his needs as prime minister.[58]

Skelton did what he could, beginning with his own office. With Pope's departure, he joked that his first priority was to supervise the removal of the "immemorial dust (some of pre-Confederation vintage, which should go to the Archives)." He inherited the two private secretaries who had taken practically all Pope's dictation; one of them combined the advantages of being the daughter of a senator and the niece of Liberal Party titan Sir Clifford Sifton. Skelton was insistent on retaining Marjorie McKenzie, but he wanted to hurt no one and accommodate the career aspirations of all. He took the liberal way: "I keep Miss McKenzie to do most of my filing & looking up data & the other girls for dictating." Before long, McKenzie, who had a Queen's master's degree and became almost a member of the Skelton family, dominated proceedings, controlling the flow of information to the under-secretary, watching over his confidential records, and drafting materials for his signature.[59]

McKenzie was fiercely loyal to him, and he to her. He refused to certify a promotion for one of his secretaries despite cabinet approval– "that I'll not do until I'm sure what chance there is for promoting Miss McKenzie – who is now getting 1320 + 180 bonus or 1500, which is her maximum unless promoted into a new class." When McKenzie, her mother, and OD found themselves on the same train shortly after he became under-secretary, he insisted on travelling with them in second class, though his position entitled him to a first-class seat. They were comfortable enough together to discuss McKenzie's fear that she had a malignant growth. With apparent expertise, OD dispensed advice based on information gathered at his medical evening at the Shortts.[60]

In July 1925, as the summer of Skelton's first year as under-secretary was beginning, he had conquered most of the challenges, small and large, that External Affairs was likely to present.[61] His future in Ottawa was nevertheless precarious, hanging on the thread of a federal election that could not be far off. He was Mackenzie King's man, a prominent adversary of Arthur Meighen and a rejuvenated Conservative Party. If the prime minister were defeated, his top adviser seemed very likely to be fired or frozen out by another government. But Skelton avoided negative thoughts. The family was about to join him in the making of a new Ottawa home. He was watching the flowers bloom, and looking forward to a garden of his own.

7

You Ought to be
Prime Minister, 1925–6

The weekly Montreal *Standard* took a dim view of OD's close relationship with the prime minister. In two "Talking It over with Ozzy" stories by H.F. Gadsby published in 1925, Skelton's position in the government was described as a sinecure that required little more than unthinking devotion to the Liberal cause and allowed plenty of leisure for the faithful retainer to pack on the flesh at the taxpayer's expense. "You will be mine near-valet," Gadsby has King saying, "a sort of gentlemen's gentlemen to my business mind, always on hand with honorable precedents, modern instances, apt analogies and pertinent facts. I don't keep a dog and do my own barking. I don't pay a professor and do my own plugging." The *Standard's* Ozzy was full of political gossip, inside jokes, and obsequious reassurance for the prime minister. When the subject of an upcoming election was raised, Ozzy promised King that the government's record made the Liberals unbeatable. They were sure to win. For Ozzy's sake, they must win: "If you get in my job goes on. The heroic role for you, sir, but what I'm looking out for is the breakfast roll." "You look like one," King replied. "You fat little rascal!"[1]

Skelton was a public property now, he understood that. He had been in the arena of controversy a long time, and savagely attacked for his ideas and his allegiances, but the *Standard* article was disturbing because it was so deeply personal, not least in the references to his "well-padded" appearance. Although not the bloated figure in the cartoon that accompanied the story, he no longer had what his old friend Arthur Hawkes had described as the "fair crown and chiseled face" of his youth. At forty-seven, he was eating and smoking more than he should, and putting on weight. Apart from his intermittent walks, he took no regular exercise, and his obsessive work schedule led to frequent bouts of "feeling fagged & all in."[2]

Back in Kingston, Isabel was offended by Gadsby's assault, and even more by a Queen's colleague who sneeringly drew it to her attention. Oscar was not there to reassure her, but she tried not to complain about the consequences of their increasingly visible life. Feeling the strain of his frequent absences and her heavy family responsibilities, she suffered from debilitating headaches that required a doctor's attention. Her husband's choice to stay in Ottawa added to the pressures, since there was no one to help her prepare their Kingston home for sale and get the family ready for the move. When she joined OD in August 1925 to hunt for an Ottawa house, moreover, she promptly encountered a decision already made. He was now determined to live in Rockcliffe, where he had set his sights on 459 Buena Vista Drive, with its extensive grounds, six bedrooms, maid's quarters, and library. Isabel would have been quite content with a smaller home on Echo Drive in Ottawa South, near the Rideau Canal. She worried that the bigger property would take all her energy just to keep it up, leaving no time for anything else and certainly not for the historical writing that gave her fulfilment. Against her wishes, Oscar pushed ahead with an offer of $18,000 on Buena Vista. He calculated that the value of the Kingston house was $15,500, with a little over $5,000 left to be paid on its mortgage; that meant he would have a down payment of about $10,000 for the Buena Vista purchase, with a manageable mortgage of $8,000 – exactly his yearly salary at External Affairs.[3]

Skelton was used to getting his own way in the marriage. "All such things he feels he wants," Isabel wrote in her diary, "bulk far more with Oscar than with me & he feels hurt & irritated with me if I oppose him." Determined to have the home he wanted despite her misgivings, he resorted to accusing her of having lowbrow tastes. She could have countered that the Rockcliffe house was far more than they needed, and that what he really wanted was to show that he had arrived in the world. Instead, Isabel tiptoed around him, unwilling to confront the situation or even to mention it, and anxious above all to "keep main end in view that the two of us must be happy & one in Ottawa." On the surface they remained "quite ordinary & friends," and she tried to make herself attractive to him, wearing pink and mauve pyjamas she thought he would like. With the "confounded houses between us," she went back to Kingston, "too sore to move & too worried to sleep."[4]

The $18,000 bid on Buena Vista was turned back, and another $1,000 was added to it. While he waited for a response, Oscar received word

that his father was ill. He hurried to Toronto to be with Jeremiah, who
had suffered a stroke. Returning to Ottawa with a bad cold, blue and
depressed, he was cheered by the news that his improved offer on the
Rockcliffe house had been accepted. Isabel expressed her relief that the
matter was finally settled. She was perturbed about leaving the headstrong Sandy at Queen's and about the burden of social duties that went
with OD's position as the country's diplomatic chief, but she resolved
to "now have 'strength & grace' to do what I know will make for happiness in the new home." With her husband immersed in the intricacies
of trade, immigration, and European security, she coordinated a major
renovation of 459 Buena Vista, named "Edgehill" because it was built on
a gentle incline.[5]

The Skeltons settled into their Rockcliffe life. Isabel and Oscar were
together again, after a two-year period when they had lived mostly in
separate cities. There was no sign that the rift over the purchase of Edgehill persisted. She remained committed to her literary career, and he to
speeding it along whenever he could; he noted, without any disapproval,
the late nights she put in on her various projects. Second son Herbert,
fifteen years old, had been installed in Rockcliffe's high-tone private
school, Ashbury College. When he badly injured his back in a hockey
game at Montreal, and that was compounded by the flu, Oscar took to
sleeping at Herbert's side to make sure that he was comfortable. "Feeling
a little stupid," OD recorded in his diary, "because not sleeping well with
Herbert as a partner." Breezy Sandy, out of reach at Queen's, informed
his parents that he had taken up boxing without consulting them, as
he had promised. His father lectured him "perhaps over strongly" on
the need for more "intellectual activity & for absolute straightforward-
ness," but then wondered if he had overreacted. Sandy was generous
and self-sacrificing and had sympathy for the underdog, characteristics
his father admired intensely, "but his lawyerlike capacity for making out
a case leads him to suppress & conceal things a franker boy would avow."[6]

The large property on Buena Vista gave Skelton a home base. He was
occasionally able to extract himself from the office in the late afternoon
to "cultiver mon jardin"; walks from Rockcliffe to various "outskirts,"
as the squire of Edgehill phrased it, provided "more exercise & peace
than anything else." In the library of the dark-wooded and heavily wall-
papered house, he read constantly, often late into the night, and with
the most catholic of tastes – adventures and mysteries but also current
fiction and contemporary affairs, such as Percy Mark's *The Plastic Age* – "a
sensational picture of U.S. college life, sex-ridden, athlete & fraternity

obsessed, weak faculties, but on the whole making something out of the chaos & superficiality of the undergraduate life." He contrasted Canadian literature with the country's art after a visit to the National Gallery. He liked the English portrait painters most of all, but his attention was also attracted to the modern landscapes of the Group of Seven "with their crude blotches & deep browns & blue snows, effective added distance in many cases, less imitative & amateurish than Canadian letters but less finished."[7]

In taking on the big Rockcliffe house, Skelton seemed oblivious to the coming federal election. As Gadsby had declared in the *Standard*, "Premier King's Skelton" could not survive if the prime minister could not. A careful man would have kept the Kingston house and rented accommodation in Ottawa until it was clear that Mackenzie King had extended his hold on government. But that is not what Skelton did, because he was much more of a gambler than his timid exterior suggested. He had appeared uncertain about taking the position at External Affairs, but there had never been any doubt what he would decide. He was where he wanted to be, making a difference and making a mark for himself. The house, the job, Canadian independence – they were worth the risk. If a roadblock presented itself, Queen's would always be there. He kept up on the politics of the university with former colleagues; they wanted him on the Board of Trustees, to which he was elected in 1926, and they never lost hope that they could bring him back as principal.[8]

King called the election for 29 October, and from the beginning the campaign stumbled. Skelton attributed the problem to the public's anti-government mood, as well as to King's lacklustre record and his blandly middle-of-the-road policies. The leader of the Opposition, Arthur Meighen, was "more definite but no more constructive," with his fetish for high tariffs as a solution to the country's ills. In Skelton's analysis, the Conservative chief was buoyed by strong sentiment for trade protectionism in the country and a brilliant press campaign supported by the manufacturers, the Canadian Pacific Railway, and the Bank of Montreal. Corporate Canada's arguments had more punch, "perhaps because not restrained by any considerations of truth." On election eve, King was predicting a clear majority of seats, but OD was more realistic. The Liberals were vulnerable and the outcome very uncertain. He attempted a forecast, writing out a detailed province-by-province breakdown of seats that gave the Liberals 107, the Conservatives 96, the Progressives 40, and Labour 2. King could not win outright, and neither could Meighen. "Tomorrow the fate of governments if not of Canada is to be decided."[9]

Election Day was a Thursday. Skelton did not vote, even though he was on the register both in Kingston and in Ottawa – why is unclear, but perhaps he was simply too busy to leave the office. He stayed in the East Block of the Parliament Buildings after work to monitor the results with the prime minister. The returns from eastern Canada came in first, giving the Conservatives a big lead, and then from Ontario, where they won almost everywhere, all but wiping out the Progressives and reducing the Liberals to a handful of seats. Quebec, even more loyal to King than expected, brightened the picture for a while, but the west (Liberal Premier Dunning's Saskatchewan excepted) went solidly Tory. Skelton's guess had been pretty accurate, except that the Liberals fared worse in Ontario than he had estimated. Meighen was very close to an overall majority, and half the cabinet, the prime minister included, had been defeated in their own ridings. King had a bad cold and was wounded by the loss of this North York constituency, but he stayed calm, saying goodnight to Skelton "with nothing more than we'll see what things look like tomorrow." OD departed King's office by taxi at 3:00 in the morning, pondering a gloomy night and an uncertain future, with "prophets at a discount."[10]

After a brief rest, Skelton returned to the office to find a "very subdued air about the office, apprehension & gossip in all the corridors," particularly among those who had been appointed by King "and so going out with the government if it goes, as seems to be assumed generally." Ross Munro, the former Toronto *Globe* reporter who had been part of the prime minister's election staff, thought that King should go gracefully, and suggested that Skelton should give him that advice, like a Dutch uncle. OD declined, "not being his uncle, & adding that if I had any advice to give I'd prefer to wait until the full returns were in & I had slept over them." At that moment, he did not think that King should resign, unless a clear Conservative majority was apparent. In the afternoon, Oscar retreated to his garden and "thus put all questions of politicians' fates – & my own – out of sight." He had been warned to take precautions for the next night, his first Rockcliffe Halloween, when herds of little pranksters would be out looking for some fun. He removed the front gates to his property, locking them away, but he found on Sunday morning that he had not been cautious enough. His garden had been plundered.[11]

The next day, the election returns were still not final but the prognosis was more promising for the Liberals than it had seemed on the 29th. They would get at least 100 seats to the Conservatives' 117, with the anti-Tory Progressives, now almost exclusively a western party, at around two dozen members and holding the balance of power. The Conservative press was pushing hard for King's resignation on the grounds that he had lost, and not narrowly so, but this simply served to harden Skelton's position: "It therefore begins to be quite clear that this is precisely what the Government should not do." On his own initiative, he worked up a memorandum urging King to stay on and fight, stating that he could not find any precedent for a government's resignation before the opening of Parliament when no opposing party or likely combination of parties had a clear majority. The government must call Parliament into session immediately and put forward a positive administrative and legislative program, abandoning, as Skelton put it in his diary, King's "wobbling" and "dodging," which had taken "the heart out of the Liberals everywhere."[12]

Working over the weekend to flesh out his strategies for keeping the Liberals in power, Skelton recommended tax reduction and cuts in every government department. Vigorous administration, a tight grip on the levers of the bureaucracy, was always "good politics as well as good Canadianism." On the tariff, King must move to lower rates using the expedient of the Tariff Advisory Board to substitute science for politics in the making of policy. Specific cases and industries, such as motorcars, ought to be targeted with an eye to the education of public opinion, which had been bombarded for decades with protectionist propaganda. There was no satisfying the business classes, and the government ought not to try. The election had shown clearly that the manufacturers were out to smash the Liberal Party. "They will not favor it even if it adopts a policy of moderate protection: they will take all they can get from a Liberal moderate protection government, and then at election time move heaven and earth and hades to put in the party which is out-and-out protectionist."[13]

Skelton had his latest advice typed up first thing Monday morning, the 2nd of November, and sought a meeting with the prime minister. It did not come easily. King had a heavy schedule and continued to feel unwell – worse, he complained, because he had been given the wrong medicine by his new English butler. Since there was no opportunity for a talk between a meeting of cabinet and an audience with Governor General Lord Byng, the prime minister suggested that Skelton accompany him on the drive to see Byng. OD did not want to attract any attention to himself, but there seemed no other way to get his views across directly. He was more circumspect in person than he had been in his latest memorandum, but left no doubt that King and the Liberals ought to stay on, "provided they could get & keep a majority" in the House of Commons. As they approached Byng's residence, Skelton grew more and more edgy. He tried to escape from the car at the gate to Rideau Hall, but King insisted he go further, and so they swept up the drive in the full view of the governor general and his aides-de-camp. "Drive Dr. Skelton home," the prime minister bellowed to the driver, removing any doubt that might have lingered about the adviser's identity.[14]

Skelton was reinforcing the view of the cabinet that Mackenzie King should not resign. The prime minister's own instincts were to stay in office, which he had the right to do. In the practice of British parliamentary government, prime ministers in King's circumstances could either resign or wait for Parliament to decide whom it would back. King believed that he could continue to govern with the support of the Progressives and the two Labour MPs; together with the small parties, the Liberals would control the House of Commons. Meighen might have won the most seats, the logic proceeded, but he would be unable to win over the small parties and thus command the confidence of Parliament. Byng thought differently, arguing that King ought to step aside and allow Meighen to form a government, or at least to try. The election had demonstrated a clear movement to the Conservatives and away from the Liberals. In the name of what was fair, Byng asked King to give way to the Conservatives.[15]

King informed the governor general that he wanted the people's representatives in Parliament to decide the government's fate. The next day, however, Skelton was astounded to learn that King was having second thoughts. If he resigned right away, the prime minister reasoned that he would win great public acclaim. Then, he told Skelton, the Liberals and Progressives could combine their votes in the House of Commons when the moment was right to bring Meighen down. Byng would have no choice but to give King a chance to govern and, if need be, to grant a dissolution of Parliament and an immediate election. King's ministers did not like what they were hearing – OD wrote in his diary that they "were ready to throw the P.M. out of the window" – and neither did Skelton. The subterfuge seemed to him ill-advised and ultimately futile. He surmised that it could be explained only by King's illness and the assault of the Conservative press.[16]

Skelton moved to staunch the bleeding. He prepared another memorandum advising King that the government in power when Parliament met would have the advantage. If King allowed the Conservatives in, Meighen was likely to get the support of enough independent MPs to stave off a Liberal motion of non-confidence in the government. Even if Meighen did lose such a vote, the governor general would probably grant the Conservatives a dissolution rather than sending for King. Government revenues, in addition, were on the rise and deficits were falling: "Whichever party is in power in the spring may have the kudos of reducing taxation and the national debt." There were two paths that were equally likely to damage Liberal Party morale – to abandon ship if there was still a fighting chance, or to carry on without strong determination. The most hopeful course, Skelton repeated, would be to meet Parliament and "put through a definite, vigorous and not overloaded, programme." He added what he privately called "some taffy," an appeal to King's giant ego: "If any leader can snatch victory out of these difficulties he will win a prestige that will ensure power for 20 years. For such a task, the Prime Minister, with his courage, address, and personal popularity, and given the position of strategic advantage, is pre-eminently qualified." The memorandum came to Laurier House with a short note pleading that Skelton's role be kept quiet, since "every group, even a Cabinet, contains some men who are not always discreet."[17]

Though he gnawed on the idea, there was never much chance that King would resign. Skelton knew this by the morning of 4 November, when he was asked to be available for the vetting of a press release that announced the government's intention to remain in office and meet Parliament as soon as possible. He was embarrassed when the governor general's secretary arrived at the East Block, "not losing sight of fact that here again I was at the P.M.'s right-hand," and once more when King asked him to Laurier House for lunch and they saw a man outside watching them and taking notes. King and Skelton worked through the draft text of the announcement, shortening and cleaning it up, and removing the impression that there had been any disagreement with the governor general about what was proper and necessary. That accomplished, they rushed to an afternoon meeting of cabinet, where Skelton once more encountered astonishment, this time from a Liberal minister, that he and King seemed inseparable. At night OD waited in his office in case he was required for last-minute amendments to the statement, which eventually went out to the newspapers just before midnight. Because he had not backed up his earlier constitutional arguments with careful research, he searched the precedents in the days that followed, using his assistant Marjorie McKenzie to look up British and Canadian election results going back to the 1860s. King thought the resulting memorandum was "absolutely conclusive" in showing that he had acted correctly. He made sure the governor general had a copy.[18]

Skelton had more than stepped over the line separating a public servant from a political adviser. He had obliterated it. What was more, he had implicated his most trusted External Affairs aide in his work to extend the government's life. It was natural enough for Skelton to behave that way. He had been giving political advice, solicited and unsolicited, for many years, but he now had an official responsibility that forbade such activity, or put severe limitations on it. His shyness about any kind of publicity, expressed time and again, reflected his retiring personality, but it also demonstrated that he knew he was compromising his position as the head of a government department. Skelton justified his conduct by telling himself that he was saving the Liberal government and by extension the country. Had he not intervened, he reasoned, King would have capitulated and Canada would have fallen into the hands of the dangerous Conservatives. That comment was an exaggeration of his influence. He was only one of several voices, including King's own, that were telling the prime minister not to surrender office.

Even before these election-related pressures descended on him, Skelton had been "feeling seedy for some time, not digesting properly & with frequent gas gulpings also diarrhea." At last he gave in and consulted his doctor, R.S. Stevens, who gave him a full physical, concentrating on his blood pressure and heart. Finding nothing wrong, the doctor made arrangements for further tests. Skelton was told to prepare for them with two cups of tea and two slices of plain toast, after which his stomach's contents were pumped out and sent for analysis. He returned home, "slowly," and had a square meal. The results were ready in three days. The chief trouble was diagnosed as a deficiency of hydrochloric acid, preventing the complete digestion of food. Stevens prescribed twenty drops of hydrochlorine before each meal, as well as "less work & worry," more exercise, and a diet with much less fat.[19]

OD embarked on the Stevens regimen immediately but desperately needed a holiday. Since he could be away only for a few days and was overdue on a payment of mortgage interest, he could not go far or spend much. Nor could he take Isabel, who was immersed in editorial work on a Queen's alumni publication. He found a cozy inn in Quebec's Gatineau region, a short train ride north of Ottawa, and explored the struggling one-street town of Wakefield, with its "mixed storekeeping, railway, retired farmer & decayed gentlefolk population," and "the typical rounded remains of the Laurentian hills." The weather was all rain and cloud, and he was cold and wet by the evenings. He searched out a pair of felt bedroom slippers and raced through a stack of crime books and Low's *Governance of England*. He was soon feeling better, which was just as well. The diet was difficult to maintain, and the prime minister was complaining about his absence.[20]

Returning to the office, Skelton buckled down to a thorough analysis of a major initiative in European security affairs that had implications for Canada. In mid-October of 1925, a series of international agreements had been reached at the Locarno Conference in Switzerland. The most important of these was the Treaty of Mutual Guarantee, or Rhine Security Pact, under which France, Belgium, and Germany undertook to accept and maintain the Rhine River boundaries set out at the Paris Peace Conference, and to submit all their disputes to arbitration. Great Britain guaranteed these undertakings. There was no doubting the magnitude of the achievement, which gave Germany international respectability and brought it into the League of Nations; the German, French, and British foreign ministers were awarded the Nobel Peace Prize for their part in the negotiation of Locarno.

On the face of it, this was a purely British and European affair. The European nations promised not to fight, and Great Britain pledged to fight anybody who did. Skelton judged the first wholly commendable, but the second was worrying. The bonds with the Old Country were strong, and many still argued that the empire remained an international monolith, so that British wars had a habit of becoming Canadian wars. Worse, the British wanted Canada to sign onto Locarno. Describing himself as "dead opposed to their Downing Street wishes," Skelton warned that adherence to the treaty automatically involved Canada in every conflict that might break out in Western Europe, the cockpit of the First World War and sure to be the cockpit of the second, when it came. Canada would be underwriting an agreement that might lessen the overall danger of conflict but ensured participation in any war that did eventually arise. Canada had long asserted the right to determine the extent of its involvement in a British war, but Skelton cautioned that Locarno was different. Stripped down to its essentials, it was a pact for certain war in the future, from which Canada could not escape with a claim of limited liability or the supremacy of the national parliament.[21]

Skelton advised a congratulatory note to the British government, accompanied by a simple statement that Canada did not consider it necessary to guarantee the settlement reached at Locarno. The recommendation was buttressed by one of the under-secretary's ample memoranda, displaying the advantages of signing the treaty at the start and demolishing them at the end. He claimed that Locarno carried with it fresh and heavy responsibilities that made sense for Britain, so close to France and Belgium, but not for Canada, which was separated from Europe "by 3000 miles of sea and incalculable differences in culture, in problems, in outlook." Not one country on the continent of Europe would lift a finger to help if the United States were to attack Canada. The security of Canadians lay in their own reasonableness, the decency of the United States, and the steady development of common standards of conduct and points of view with the friendly neighbour to the south. Europeans ought to take a lesson from peaceful North America.[22]

The memorandum was sent to King on New Year's Day, 1926, with a copy to Ernest Lapointe, Skelton's autonomist ally. The prime minister was exultant. At a meeting of ministers on the afternoon of 6 January, he read the thirty-page brief word for word, reporting back to his deputy that his colleagues "were tremendously impressed, swallowed it with popping eyes and fine appreciation." The cabinet agreed to tell the British that Canada would assume no more responsibilities for European security than it already had. Skelton was asked to compose a telegram to that effect. He did so the next morning with the help of Marjorie McKenzie and the newest member of the Department of External Affairs, Jean Désy. King declared the result a "splendid stroke," adding, "Skelton, you ought to be Prime Minister, not I." OD said nothing to King in response. However, his ego and ambition led him straight to his diary, where he recorded the compliment and his agreement with it.[23]

Jeremiah Skelton visited Edgehill for several weeks in January and February of 1926. "He is much feebler & slower than two years ago," wrote a subdued Oscar, "can walk better than I expected after his stroke, but has difficulties on a hill or stairs, & finds it difficult to get up out of the chair." They went to see Dr Stevens, who found Jeremiah's blood pressure high, urging leisure and some changes in diet if another stroke or kidney trouble was to be avoided. But the old verve was there. He was up each morning at 6:30 for his tea, keenly interested in the world and in politics; during this stay, he was in the House of Commons gallery virtually every day, his son frequently at his side. OD's elder sister, Bea, concerned him too. Two or three times a year she lamented her bleak existence and the lack of any understanding or assistance from the family. OD did not know what to say or do, beyond suggesting a change of scene, a diversion to Europe perhaps. He offered to help pay the costs of the trip, but she wanted his company, not his money.[24]

Oscar and Isabel attended the opening of Parliament on 8 January 1926. OD was proud of his wife's intricately beaded dress and even prouder that she waded into the crowd when he had to leave her: she dreaded it, he noted in his diary, "not knowing anyone, but went thro it all right." Remaining deeply implicated in the political work of the government, he had written the first draft of the Speech from the Throne, laying out the government's parliamentary agenda for the months ahead. He worked and reworked the text right up until the last minute, adding details of his own, but he was not pleased with the final product, which had had many hands on it besides his own: "On the whole, it is a jejune document, no man's style or thought united it – a pretty fair programme as programmes go, but nothing to rouse enthusiasm."[25]

Once MPs trooped back into the House of Commons after the Throne Speech in the Senate chamber, Ernest Lapointe (leading the Liberals in the House in King's absence) asked for an instantaneous vote of confidence approving the government's actions since the election. Skelton had advised against the tactic, since he thought it better not to require of the smaller parties "a positive, tho mild, expression of support of the gov't." King, however, was tired of hearing Meighen's charge that he was usurping office, and wanted the matter settled. Skelton "still demurred, but did not press it." When Lapointe made his case in a major speech to the Commons that evening, with Oscar and Jeremiah looking on from the visitor's gallery, the justice minister used two of the constitutional briefs that OD had prepared for King, making the case that the Liberals had every right to carry on in government. Skelton had sent them to Lapointe only as suggestions and was both astonished and pleased when he read them verbatim as part of his remarks. Afterwards, Oscar introduced his father to Lapointe and other ministers. Arthur Meighen passed by, glancing up and then quickly down as Lapointe launched into loud thanks for Skelton's assistance with the speech.[26] So much for OD's neutrality, if anyone in Ottawa believed it had ever existed.

The support of the Progressive and Labour MPs was crucial to the government's survival. Skelton helped in the wooing of J.S. Woodsworth and fellow Labourite A.A. Heaps with promises of legislation on old age pensions and assistance to the unemployed. He drafted a letter to Woodsworth for the prime minister's signature, interpreting cabinet discussion but adding his own refinements about consultation with the provinces and cautioning against permanent decisions that might be regretted later. He warned that the government was going too far, much farther than was needed, and that a written commitment to Woodsworth

ought not to be part of any arrangement because it would be made public at once and regarded as a transparent bribe to a caucus populated by
only two members. If a private understanding could be reached, and a
pronouncement made in the House of Commons, "that would appear
a more normal procedure." An accommodation with Woodsworth was
struck, and announced by Lapointe in the House, giving King Labour
support in return for a commitment to bring forward pension legislation and consider the sharing of emergency relief for the unemployed
with the provinces. Woodsworth insisted on having it all in writing, and
Skelton worried that the resulting document was "dangerously vague."[27]

Senator Andrew Haydon seemed to Skelton to have soured on King.
The two Queen's men reviewed Haydon's complaints about their leader's disturbing lack of decisiveness and practicality, as well as his reliance
on dreams, coincidences, and the spirit world for guidance and reassurance. They agreed, however, that any change in the leadership of the
party would be disastrous. Skelton admired King's resilience, stamina,
and ability to weather crises despite doubts and insecurities. Yet OD also
listed King's shortcomings: his tendency to indulge in "weakly sentimental sympathies" and be "vague on facts" and "led away by a phrase," thinking "in speech headlines." The adviser watched his chief carefully, trying
to harden his resolve and ensure that he drove ahead with a reforming
agenda, while reassuring him of continuing help "if I wasn't dragged into
publicity." So much was riding on King's success – the Liberal Party, the
government, Skelton's own future, but most of all the future of Canada
itself. The "country is safe," he wrote after the government won an early
February confidence vote in the House of Commons with the solid support of the Progressives and Labour. A few days later, the prime minister
won a by-election in Prince Albert and returned to head the Liberals in
the House of Commons.[28]

King was relatively secure until June 1926, when revelations of widespread corruption in the federal Customs Department undermined
Progressive and Labour support for the Liberals. The prime minister's
makeshift majority in the House of Commons dissolved, and MPs
moved to censure the government. The only sure way to avoid defeat in
the Commons was to ask the governor general to dissolve Parliament,
precipitating a sudden election. This was the course King decided on,
with Skelton feeding Laurier House with arguments and precedents to
support the case that the governor general could not refuse a request
for dissolution and arguing that Lord Byng's only recourse was "to
take the advice of ministers upon whom the electors could wreak

vengeance if they so desired." Cabinet members agreed entirely with OD's briefing, which King read aloud to them. Skelton saw the prime minister on his way to the governor general's on 26 June, advising him to push Byng hard if he had to. King wanted him available outside a cabinet session that night, but Skelton "did not think it prudent to go down as newspaper men galore would be hanging around," and he "couldn't add anything at the moment" anyway. The next day he wrote down further points to support the case "that the only safe rule for the G.G. to follow in order to avoid criticism was to throw the responsibility wholly on the PM."[29]

Lord Byng refused King's advice, and the King-Byng crisis burst into the open. The governor general maintained that the Conservatives, the largest party, should be given a chance to govern, and he was determined to give them that opportunity. After urging Byng to reconsider, King resigned and Meighen agreed to take his place. "Pandemonium & intense excitement," Skelton recorded in his diary, "thus ends, for the time being at least, the W.L.M.K. government." A downcast OD helped with the prime ministerial letter of resignation, and he and Haydon commiserated with King, telling him that they could not "conceive how his Ex could have refused a dissolution." Skelton pondered the line-up at the Imperial Conference scheduled for London in the fall. Under Meighen, Canada would join the empire-minded countries, Britain, Australia, and New Zealand, to defeat the forward-looking Irish and South Africans. There would be no Imperial Conference for Skelton, and "a Tory triumph," along with "all the loss of influence & comfort a reversal involves."[30]

Skelton was a blatant partisan, never more than in the last six months. His position at External Affairs was an order-in-council appointment, subject to the "pleasure" of the new prime minister. Meighen nevertheless greeted Skelton with "rather surprising geniality," causing the under-secretary to wonder a little guiltily whether it was "surprising to my conscience or to my preconceived idea of his temperament." But just as Skelton was beginning to brief his leader on external affairs issues and prepare him for the 1926 Imperial Conference, and only a few hours after OD had thought that the Conservatives seemed firmly in the saddle, they were defeated on a razor-thin House of Commons vote of non-confidence in the government. The luckless and unsubtle Meighen had only been in office for three days. Governor General Byng gave Meighen the dissolution of Parliament that he had refused King, and Canada was plunged into another general election. Meighen remained prime minister, but he was away from Ottawa most of the time, campaigning for his political life. [31]

Skelton scrupulously avoided contact with Mackenzie King during the election campaign, but he kept in close touch with Liberal operatives like Ralph Campney. He was pleased to see the campaign going well, with the argument that Arthur Meighen had illegitimately taken power providing "a coat of constitutional whitewash" to cover the Liberal customs debacle. Yet OD was hearing disturbing gossip about the procrastinations and superstitions of "my old chief." When Campney and his colleagues informed him that a Kingston fortune teller, Rachel Bleaney, was coming to the Liberal leader's home to interpret one of King's dreams, Skelton exclaimed, "Ye Gods – what folly & infantile superstition: folly in itself & in the danger of being laughed out of the country & of politics for ever if the Conservatives ever learn of it." A few hours later, he clucked: "Rarely was there a clearer contrast between the man as he is or as he appears to his intimates (no man being a hero to his own secretary or his deputy) and the man as he appears to the mob than in the fact that after the sorceress interview W.L.M.K., on leaving for the West, was met at Laurier House by a crowd of several thousands in motor & foot parade, & escorted triumphantly to the station as a hero & struggler for constitutional liberty."[32]

With Meighen usually absent from Parliament Hill, Skelton was getting home by 5 o'clock. He did research for his socialism and English government books and planned a short holiday with his sister Bea. There was more time to be active in the huge garden at Edgehill, which seldom got the personal attention he thought it deserved. In July, Isabel and Oscar exchanged birthday gifts before she and the two younger children departed for the west to visit her brother in Kamloops, using railway passes that came with OD's government position of under-secretary. On the ninth, Isabel's forty-ninth birthday, he wrote: "She given to more introspection than I & so more regretting her 49 years & wishing for 34 again." His turn came four days later, after the family had left: "Birthday: but with my usual optimism & ability to put unpleasant things in the proper background, I have not had any worries over obtaining what would a score of years ago have seemed the patriarchal & effete age of 48."[33] That rare moment of introspection says so much about Skelton's resilience in withstanding the pressures that he had been under since his arrival in Ottawa two years before.

The election was held on 14 September 1926. King had been able to show off an improved economy and an advantageous federal budget, as well as to play the constitutional card, charging with brutal skill that Lord Byng had wrongly refused King's advice and that the Meighen government was a subversion of democracy and the constitution. The Liberals won handily, despite the cloud of scandal, and Mackenzie King quite suddenly had the majority government that had so far eluded him. Skelton spoke of his enthusiasm "about the outcome of the elections and the campaign generally" and his "real pleasure" that the King-Skelton partnership was back in business. He complained about the slipshod ways of the prime minister's office under Meighen and expressed his disgust at "the looseness of much of the work." Personal relations between Skelton and Meighen, however, were never less than cordial during the three-month interregnum. After the Conservative leader's defeat, OD confessed to "a very high regard and sympathy" for Meighen, "even if not agreeing with every policy he proposes. He has courage and decisiveness and the ability to work tremendously, which are certainly great and rare assets among public men."[34]

Three weeks after the election, Skelton boarded a train for Quebec City and the *S.S. Megantic*, en route to London and his second Imperial Conference. His reunion with King had not been held until eleven days after the election, and there was no time to prepare a coherent government agenda on the issues that were likely to face the delegates. The prime minister's greatest interest seemed to be in keeping spending down; he demanded that his team spend $10,000 less on the conference than they had in 1923. This was undoubtedly a reaction to a recent report of the auditor general, which drew attention to the expenses of Canadian delegates to the League of Nations in 1924. Senator Dandurand had spent $3,130 and E.M. Macdonald $5,000, while Skelton had charged only $960. The Ottawa *Journal* commented favourably on "Dr. Skelton, who is a modest man," and acidly on the two politicians.[35]

Skelton held out no great hopes that the 1926 meeting would do anything much for "the Canadian programme" (a phrase he could hardly have used if Meighen was prime minister) of "the completion of responsible self-government." Aside from the accidents of party and personality, imperial conferences drew members of varying international outlook corresponding to differences in history, stages of political and economic development, populations, and neighbourhood relationships. They were poor places for revolutions, or even big advances. They were more apt to register gains already made by the "more progressive Dominions" and help "bring the other members into line." Yet some progress on concrete issues was perhaps possible, and who knew what the British (and others) were capable of if Canada did not resist. "The end of the road may not be reached now – may never be reached for a new trend may open up around the corner – but at least the wrong turnings may be avoided."[36]

The Canadian delegation included Vincent Massey, slated to become Canada's first minister to Washington, Commodore Walter Hose, the head of the navy and a Skelton favourite, and Marjorie McKenzie. The team was headed by Mackenzie King and Ernest Lapointe; Skelton's responsibility, because they were not even scarcely acquainted with the conference agenda, was to get the two down to work on board ship. He failed miserably. Lapointe had begun the voyage ill, a situation made worse by rough seas; King insisted on gossiping and doing correspondence from the start, using McKenzie for dictation and typing, and he soon joined "the sick squad" as well. McKenzie admonished Skelton: "Don't let that man monopolize me, I came to do your work." Yet OD told Isabel, after almost a week on the ocean, that he had not been very ambitious himself, despite his promise to have the Speech from the Throne prepared as well as a number of Imperial Conference documents. "Laziness & the feeling that I was already several laps ahead of my chiefs prevented my doing very much until today, when I got off a few brief memos."[37]

A short encounter with the prime minister, who was sleeping the mornings away, finally achieved a first review of the agenda and a scamper through the various issues it threw up. Not one of the British or Canadian departmental documents had yet been opened, and the time was almost gone. As of the day before arrival in Liverpool, Skelton lamented that "I've still not managed in all this week to get my two chiefs together for a review of Conference matters." Spotting Skelton on the deck of the ship, Lapointe called out to him, "How's our manager coming on with his effort to get us into a Conference?" OD replied he was on the point of resigning the job. "It requires a tremendous belief in one's star or one's secretary," he wrote home, "to go into an Empire Conference in such shape."[38]

The same suite at the Ritz as he had occupied in 1923 was waiting in London, and the same roommate, A.G. Doughty, the chief archivist of Canada – "so unique & so kindly & distinct a personality." Skelton had scarcely arrived when the Irish connection was re-established by Desmond Fitzgerald, the minister of external affairs, who had written beforehand to give a taste of Irish thinking and now improvised "an extremely interesting but exhausting evening" with the delegates from the Free State. Hoping for a collaboration like the one in 1923, Skelton arranged a meeting between the Irish and Canadian chief delegates. Their "fairly satisfactory talk" ended just as two Canadian journalists happened along, and since Skelton did not want them cabling back to Canada that King's first interview was with the Irish, he diverted the newsmen into his suite to shake hands with Doughty. He was congratulating himself on this deft manoeuvre when the British dominions secretary, Leo Amery, arrived on the scene, missing nothing of what had gone on. Fitzgerald laughed as he left: the Ritz "was very badly planned, not having any back exit for disreputable characters."[39]

There was a new member of the disreputables: J.M.B. Hertzog, a Boer War general who had succeeded Jan Smuts as prime minister of South Africa. Skelton met Hertzog at a reception early on, describing him to Isabel as "a mild-looking man for a general, but with obstinate close-set eyes, a good hair-splitter I'd imagine." The South African was the conference's key player, having come with an urgent demand for a public declaration trumpeting the independence of the dominions. Skelton and the Irish did not oppose this approach, but they preferred to pick away at specific concrete inequalities such as British control over merchant shipping, the absence of extraterritorial jurisdiction, and the position of the governor general as an agent of the British government and a channel of communication between the British and dominion governments. This, OD predicted, would "permit further development of the national consciousness and make ready for another advance three years hence."[40]

An abstract definition was open to manipulation and misinterpretation. Skelton worried that it might emphasize unity too much, the British that it would accentuate disunity. When a group of leaders got down to discussing Hertzog's first draft declaration, Lord Balfour, the former British prime minister who chaired the committee (and who specialized, Skelton said, in looking wise), opposed the initiative and smoothly produced his own draft. Soon the South African was discussing not his draft but Balfour's, which had, from Hertzog's vantage point, some dangerous assertions about the empire's interdependence and common obligations. "The British are very clever at this sort of thing," Skelton told a Canadian reporter to whom he was feeding inside information.[41]

Skelton imagined that the wily Balfour was luring Mackenzie King into "a pledge of one Empire & one Crown inter-dependence." The Canadian prime minister expressed his sympathy with some of the South African ideas but was concerned that a declaration of independence, the method by which the Americans had broken away from the Mother Country, "would be disastrous to his own position" in Canada.

It was evident, however, that something had to be done to accommodate Hertzog. The Canadian delegation, with King in the lead, moved
between the two sides and produced its own compromise formulas,
which removed both the notion of independence and suggestions that
the empire was a supra-national state. A form of words emerged: Great
Britain and the dominions were "autonomous communities within the
British Empire, equal in status, in no way subordinate one to another in
any aspect of their domestic or external affairs, though united by a common allegiance to the Crown, and freely associated as members of the
British Commonwealth of Nations."[42]

Skelton was at the margins in the making of the carefully balanced
sentence that quickly became known and repeated and celebrated as
conveying the essence of a new Commonwealth relationship. He could
see its drawbacks, and its value. He wrote to J.W. Dafoe that a general
statement of the Balfour sort left many ambiguities and created some
new ones. "Apparently," he continued, "no two Prime Ministers who
were present gave exactly the same interpretation of the text of the gospel." Yet that was perhaps "one reason why the thing will work."[43]

In the report of his committee's activities, which was eventually embedded in the final conference document, Balfour surrounded the new definition of the Anglo-dominion relationship with several paragraphs of
eloquent prose about the geographical and historical ties and positive
ideals that bound the various parts of the old empire together. But the
admission that the former colonies were the masters of their own destiny was explicit and unmistakable. Specific constitutional reforms of the
kind Skelton and his Irish friends had been advocating would be difficult
to resist now.[44]

OD felt oppressed and exhilarated by his conference responsibilities. "I have never been in such a whirl and strain; I'd like to see the
whole damned Conference under the Atlantic," he observed after only
a few days, sentiments he repeated as the weeks ground on. The meetings were relentless, and the schedule of social "sideshows" punishing,
although taken on with more ease than in 1923, so that he was brought
into relaxed contact with the economist J.M. Keynes, the dramatist
George Bernard Shaw, a former prime minister, Lloyd George, and
even a jovial and "quite human" King George V. The British and the
other delegations were better prepared, and the British infinitely better staffed, and "with that & the lack of any word on Conference matters by the PM, I've had to prepare everything for him." The drafting
of the entire opening address on foreign policy had to be rushed into

a weekend, and there were constant commands for speeches and memoranda on various subjects, all necessary immediately. Skelton represented the government on the conference secretariat and a number of committees and gave considerable time to matters of organization and drafting. The Winnipeg *Free Press* representative at the conference told his editor: "King has spent the bulk of his time here eating with duchesses. Skelton carried the bulk of the load and seems to have the brains."[45]

OD recalled what Smuts had said to him in 1923. "I looked as if I had the whole weight of the British Empire on my shoulders." But the burden now seemed heavier to him than before, "particularly as my bad repute has gone forth this time. The British Ministers & officials all know me, to my surprise, & regard me with intense suspicion, & even more embarrassing is it to find that the disreputables of the Conference ... Hertzog and his colleagues and the Irish Free State people also seem to look to me to do something on their side." He ached for Isabel: "I wish I had you in my arms this hour & could rest my head between my beloved's dear sweet breasts & rest her head on my shoulder by turn, my own & all."[46]

Skelton's digestion gave out again under the intense pressure, causing a visit to Dr Bolton, a bluff Yorkshireman regarded as the leading stomach and intestinal specialist in London. OD thought he did his job well, but not as thoroughly as Stevens earlier in the year. Bolton diagnosed no organic problems but nervous indigestion and sensitivity of the large colon. The prescription was rest, lack of worry, and a diet very close to that recommended in Ottawa. Bolton did not put much stock in the hydrochloric acid that Stevens had prescribed in Ottawa, though it might help "somewhat." None of this added to Skelton's faith in medicine. "As a matter of coincidence," he reported home, "I've been feeling better since."[47]

He could rely on almost no one, and particularly not on the enemies of change. Stanley Bruce, the Australian prime minister, was "as much an Imperialist tom-tom beater as ever and as truculent." J.G. Coates of New Zealand was "very mediocre – in fact most of the new Zealanders are, though pleasanter than the Australians." The Newfoundlanders were "a joke in the Conference." As for Hertzog and King, they were basically sound on the issues, but he did not know whom he silently cursed more often, "my own chief for not giving more time to Conference questions instead of dinners & portrait sittings, or Hertzog, who works all the time & is a very decent but very doctrinaire chap, ready to go off at unexpected tangents." Lapointe and the Irish were "our only sure-fire reliables." Skelton worked closely with Fitzgerald and was in the Irish Free State's rooms nearly every day planning strategy.[48]

With the substance of the Balfour arrangement settled early on, the disreputables were freer than ever to demand progress at what Skelton realized had been transformed into a constitutional conference. Before the meeting, he had recommended that the governor general ought to be a viceroy only, that is, the formal head of the Canadian government and not the representative in Canada of the British government as well. Having had the governor general's men hold up diplomatic papers so that he could not work on them until the last minute, he also wanted to see that office no longer used for communications between Ottawa and London. These changes were easy to achieve. King was in full agreement and prepared to push hard if needed; the issue of the governor general, brought to the fore by the Byng crisis, was the only one that he felt strongly about at the conference. The Irish were on side as well, and the British did not resist.[49]

Skelton looked to the day when Canadians would occupy the position of governor general, but he realized that opinion had probably "not yet crystallized to the extent of insisting on Canadians only, or even Canadians sometimes for this post." He did not favour the appointment of a quasi-diplomatic representative to take over the governor general's work on behalf of the British government because of its potential for "a certain active pressure and intervention which would not make for smooth relations." The first British high commissioner to Canada was nevertheless dispatched from London in 1928.[50]

King had little interest in related constitutional issues, but Skelton seized his opportunities. As the Canadian representative on the treaty procedure subcommittee, which Lapointe chaired, Skelton was in a position to lend strong support to Fitzgerald and Hertzog in rejecting the theory that the empire was a single political unit for the purpose of international accords. Their adversary was the Foreign Office's leading jurist, Sir Cecil Hurst, who (as a New Zealand delegate recalled) was driven from pillar to post, gallantly defending each position as he was forced to retire from it, showing a cooperativeness "that is not common with the Foreign Office." Hurst and Skelton, friendly after their work together in London in 1923 and Geneva in 1924, worked closely in drafting the group's report, much of which was written by Skelton.[51]

In his jousts with Hurst, Skelton displayed a certain subtlety, sympathizing with the Foreign Office's difficulty in presenting a common front and explaining dominion status to the world, but contending that a system giving British plenipotentiaries signing authority that covered the entire empire damaged the cause of imperial unity. Side by side with the evolution of self-government in the dominions and its acknowledgment by foreign countries, he told the treaty subcommittee, there had also been a growing recognition of the greater strength and stability of the British Commonwealth. Foreigners had less expectation that the organization would break apart than twenty or thirty years before. He said that he knew little of the world, but his experience at Geneva the year before had taught him "that there was nothing like being brought up against foreign nations to realize how much we are at one in the standard of looking at things." The question, however, was a wider one: "whether this organization to which we all belong is to be considered one international unit or an association of international units." The only danger to "our unity" lay in the preservation of possible sources of irritation.[52]

This was a clever argument, but Skelton did not believe it. The whole emphasis of his approach to imperial relations was on diversity, not unity. He did not think that there had been anything like sufficient recognition of the dominions' status in the international community. The people who counted were all too likely to conclude, as so many Americans and continental Europeans did, that dominion autonomy was a sham, clearly contradicted by experience at the League of Nations, where the British went out of their way to demonstrate that they were in control.[53]

Skelton and the Irish wanted to clear away all of the other administrative, legislative, and judicial obstacles that stood in the way of complete equality, but the most they could obtain was a promise in the Balfour Report that expert bodies would be set up to study them. That was a good start, and Skelton hoped that someone like Lapointe would be one of the experts, because nationalists could easily imagine reports from these special committees recommending that British supremacy be allowed to continue in many areas on the grounds of convenience and tradition. The forces of reaction were sure to attempt another stand, and it would be important to prepare for the next battle in the course of which the application of the principles set out in the Balfour Report would have to be insisted upon.[54]

But Skelton was delighted. There had been defeats, and anomalies remained, but the report was "really an epoch-making document," the most important pronouncement on the subject of inter-imperial relations yet made, and "90% of it is in the right direction. We didn't get all we wanted," but it was "the direction & not the pace that tells." Preliminary opinions, he wrote home when the conference had finally ended, seemed "divided between the views that it has broken up the Empire, that it has put it at last on a firm foundation, and that it has done nothing at all. Perhaps a judicious combination of the first two is correct."[55]

King jokingly offered to make OD a lord in recognition of his Imperial Conference work. Skelton replied that he would settle for a long family holiday in Europe the following summer. After some shopping in London and stints in Paris and Geneva, he boarded the *White Star Majestic*, the largest ship in the world, at Cherbourg in early December. "Perhaps I'll not be glad to get back. But already I'm planning next summer's trip – a rest not work."[56]

He arrived in New York on 8 December to discover that his father, who had deteriorated badly since his son's visit to Toronto before the Imperial Conference, had died in Toronto from another stroke. They had been very close over the past year as Skelton's career soared and they shared the crisis-ridden politics of the time. For the Conservative Jeremiah, the destruction of Meighen had been a high price to pay for his son's successes, but his pride in Oscar was unstoppable. Skelton knew that his father's health and his natural optimism had been failing, but he was completely unprepared for his death, "particularly," he told the governor general, "as I had been planning to go up to see him a day or two after the landing."[57]

Despite the sadness that struck at the end of the year, Isabel Skelton remembered this period as the most fulfilling and exciting of her husband's life. The King-Byng crisis and the 1926 Imperial Conference put him at the centre of national politics, and with highly satisfying results. His Liberals were firmly in power. The Balfour Report seemed to him Britain's grudging admission that the way to Canadian independence was opening up. Locarno, meanwhile, brought a stability to Europe that was unknown since before the First World War, all at no price to Canada, because the prime minister followed Skelton's advice in refusing to endorse the treaty at the Imperial Conference. As his wife phrased it, Skelton was making the ammunition and Mackenzie King was firing it. It wasn't the same as being prime minister, but it was the next best place to be.[58]

8

Inching towards Independence, 1927–9

OD was safe, his job secure. Mackenzie King was in full control of national politics. The Meighen Tories had been routed. Their threats to autonomy in international affairs, irritating though they remained, receded into the background. External's deputy minister turned his energy, quietly, towards Canadian independence and the transformation of his department into a practical instrument of a foreign policy grounded in interests that were his country's alone. Canada made its first experiments in diplomatic representation in foreign countries and Skelton began to recruit a cadre of first-class young departmental officers. Now, when H.F. Gadsby poked fun at Ozzy Skelton in the Montreal *Standard*, it was not as King's scheming companion in political crime but as the head of an Institute of Diplomats, the learned professor who was teaching "a post-graduate course in savoir faire" for ambassadors-to-be.[1]

Canada's first diplomat, Vincent Massey, did not take well to Skelton's instruction. The two had been friendly enough as political advisers to King after the 1925 election, Skelton discovering in Massey "a good deal of sympathy & respect under the surface differences" between them. Massey seemed open-minded, constructive, and an asset to public life. Yet they were competitors for King's attention, with vastly dissimilar temperaments and much more than surface differences in outlook. Massey was a self-styled aristocrat, a confident member of one of the country's wealthiest families, a haughty patron of the arts; OD was resolutely middle class, without pretense and hating ostentation, a zealous promoter of the meritocracy that he believed had been his making. Content to be wrapped in a British world that he thought protected Canadians and advanced Canadianism, Massey had ambitions for himself and his country that were radically different from Skelton's.[2]

Massey was King's choice as Canada's minister to the United States in 1927, not Skelton's, and from the first moment there was trouble. Massey insisted on three senior diplomats for his Legation staff, with a price tag of $9,000 a year each for salary and living expenses. When he phoned Ottawa to press the matter, Skelton lost his temper. He could see no justification for "a cent above $8,000," although when he cooled down he allowed that, if he "stretched his conscience" and was provided with some good arguments from Washington, he might be willing to support a maximum salary for Massey's assistants of $8,500. Skelton bent, however, agreeing eventually to the higher figure and apologizing to Massey for the fit of temper: "I have been brought up in a thrifty school, and sky high estimates of living needs irritate me."[3] It was vital, OD admitted, "to secure good men and enable them to live decently." Meagre wages meant that only wealthy men could take on such work. "That unduly restricts the choice of men and involves serious political dangers. The state should foot its own bills ... it should provide as much for a rich man as for a poor man."[4] Massey, a very rich man, probably saw those words, which made their way to Washington, as part of Skelton's war against him.

On the heels of that exchange came Massey's proposal to purchase a luxuriously furnished Washington mansion at 1746 Massachusetts Avenue, with a price tag of $500,000, to serve both as a residence and as a place of business. Skelton opposed the idea as extravagantly expensive and politically risky. He suggested instead that the patrician Masseys live in and work out of a hotel until something suitable was found. OD acknowledged that diplomacy was an expensive business. Prestige demanded a good front, especially for a new player on the international scene. Some of the expenditure could be justified on the grounds of national advertising and, just as banks tried to do with their palatial quarters, providing assurances of stability. Long-established traditions and standards could not easily be set aside. Diplomats were dined and wined, "and must retaliate in kind."[5]

Yet necessity was no excuse for extravagance or affectation. Massey, Skelton wrote sardonically, had been dispatched to tell lies for his country, not to give others in the same trade and their wives a good time. With its easy money and heiresses in search of diplomat husbands, Washington was an expensive place to practise the representational art; however, it was not foreigners or society in general that Canada should be trying to impress, but American politicians, who had the clout and were unlikely to be fooled by gold plate flashed by British ambassadors. "Our

jobs in Washington are our own and call for little of that daily hobnob-
bing with other legations which is inevitable in European capitals where
everyone is playing the same game – how to tilt the balance of power a
little more his own way – and is interested in every move and intrigue of
every other representative." In the final analysis, it was the man, not his
house, that counted: "Knowledge of human nature or a sense of humour
will go farther than tapestried walls and elaborate soirees such as some
Latin American legations give."[6]

The prime minister and the cabinet initially ruled out the purchase of
1746 Massachusetts Avenue, "no matter what the consequences may be,"
but they quickly reversed themselves. Massey got his mansion. That did
not change Skelton's view that the purchase had handed ammunition to
the many domestic critics of representation in foreign capitals and seriously prejudiced the Washington experiment "in the eyes of a great part
of the country."[7]

Skelton loathed pomp. Massey adored it. When OD suggested that
Massey's U.S. counterpart, William Phillips, would be welcomed to
Ottawa "quite informally," Massey protested to the prime minister, after
tattling to the United States State Department, that it would be "distinctly unfortunate" if the reception was any less grand or dignified than
the one he had been given in Washington. Skelton responded angrily,
reminding Massey that the suggestion had come from the governor general, not the Department of External Affairs, and that, even if the State
Department was unwilling to trust Ottawa to do right by Phillips, the
under-secretary might have hoped that Massey would take it for granted.
As for the Americans, "personally I wish more of their time might be
given to such questions of diplomatic procedure as remembering that
His Majesty's Government in Canada is not a branch of His Majesty's
Government in Great Britain."[8]

Skelton and Massey also clashed on the giving of British honours and
titles, which the King government had discontinued, and on the wearing of diplomatic uniforms. His tone laced with disdain, Skelton asked
the minister in Washington what ought to be done about the question
of formal dress for Canada's young diplomatic service: "Do you think we
should seek some sartorial genius to devise a new one, or vary the British with some distinctive Canadian feature? Or should we try the frock
coat of the American gentleman, or the overalls of modern democracy?"
Massey replied that British diplomatic uniforms could be easily adapted
with some maple leaves and Canadian buttons. Skelton's own preference
was clear. He favoured the overalls.[9]

Massey took these encounters personally. The two tried to get along, but they brought out the worst in each other and the sniping continued for years, Massey issuing advice on the way diplomacy ought to be done, and Skelton replying with sarcasm. "More talk with Herr Doktor Skelton in a.m.," the Canadian minister in Washington wrote in his diary after two years in the job, revealing his impression of a rigid Germanic taskmaster, insistent on complete control of his charges. Skelton's ability and brilliance were conceded, but Massey thought that OD had no knowledge of diplomatic life, regarded cooperation with anyone at all as a confession of inferiority, and lacked the true scholar's objectivity, notably in his cold-hearted attitude towards the British.[10] Skelton, though, admired much about Great Britain and the British. His objection was to outsiders who thought they knew best what was good for Canada and Canadians.

Massey was allowed the initiative in naming three diplomats to his Washington staff without a competition. In this way Hume Wrong, a Massey family friend and grandson of the former Liberal national leader, Edward Blake, found his way effortlessly into the Department of External Affairs. Wrong was supremely well qualified. For Skelton, his appointment was patronage nevertheless, and acceptable only as an emergency measure in order to get the Washington mission running at a high level of efficiency as quickly as possible. The deputy minister was determined to have a different sort of department and had been studying the diplomatic organization and procedures of other countries. He was able to investigate the British Foreign Office in conversations with Sir Cecil Hurst in London and Geneva. He also learned a good deal about the American diplomatic service during long lunches at the Chateau Laurier Hotel with the likeable Texan Jack Hickerson, who was posted to Ottawa shortly after Skelton became under-secretary in 1925.[11]

Many of the big powers were taking steps to democratize their foreign offices in the 1920s, an impulse that Skelton applauded. He took from the American and British models the principle that diplomacy was a career, to be lived out by professionals who were recruited by a competitive process and promoted on their merits. At the same time, he saw that the United States and the United Kingdom ran diplomatic services that had the stuffy and inbred odour of an exclusive gentleman's club.[12] He was intent on creating an elite corps of his own to build the nation in the world, yet he hoped that his men would take themselves less seriously than their British and American counterparts.

Skelton began comprehensive examinations for entry into the department in 1927, with an emphasis on finding well-educated generalists, flexible and capable enough to take on any challenge that might arise as diplomacy played itself out at home or abroad. Candidates were required to have a university degree or the equivalent, with training in the law, history, political science, or economics particularly favoured, and to possess (according to the job poster) the characteristics of "undoubted integrity; tact; astuteness; keen perception; good judgment; and good address." The first hurdle, a written exam, had four parts: a general essay designed to extract the applicant's view of imperial relations; questions on Canada's role in international affairs; a segment devoted to candidates' area of academic expertise; and a document that the applicant was asked to summarize. Skelton set the papers, marked the results, and usually chaired the board that administered an interview to those who got at least 70 per cent on the overall exam and a pass in each of the four parts. Under the law, he had to give war veterans preference, but he refused to do so until they had satisfied him in the written examination.[13]

Skelton was disappointed by the response to his first competition, which yielded only a few applicants and just two who met the standard: J. Scott Macdonald and D'Arcy McGreer. He redoubled his efforts the next year, advertising nationwide, approaching universities in search of candidates, and obtaining permission to hold exams outside the country in order to interest graduate students living abroad. This time there were sixty candidates, six of whom were brought into the department: L.B. Pearson, Norman Robertson, H.L. Keenleyside, Kenneth Kirkwood, Paul-Émile Renaud, and Keith Crowther.[14]

Skelton personally encouraged Pearson and Robertson, future under-secretaries of the Department of External Affairs, to apply. He had known Robertson since their ocean-crossing in 1923; the Rhodes Scholar had then taken a dislike to Skelton, but they had a more relaxed time together during the summer of 1927. "I must say that I've changed my mind about him," Robertson told his mother in British Columbia. "He really is very nice and undoubtedly able ... a very good sort indeed."[15] Skelton met Pearson, a colleague of Hume Wrong's in the history department at the University of Toronto, at a dinner in Ottawa after the Imperial Conference of 1926. Pearson learned of the deputy's plans for a foreign service governed by ability, where the young Mike (his First World War nickname, which became a Pearson trademark) was assured that he could reasonably look forward "to occupying the highest diplomatic posts without private income or political influence." He wrote the External Affairs examinations in the summer of 1928 and was immediately interviewed, Skelton observing "something curiously loose

jointed in his physical bearing and perhaps to a lesser extent in his men-
tal makeup." Pearson's "distinct capacity and attractive personal qualifications" made up the deficit.[16]

Skelton surrounded himself with his own kind. Five of the six 1928
recruits had graduate degrees from institutions outside Canada and had
taught university courses. Two, Keenleyside and Renaud, had doctorates.
This pattern persisted: more than a third of the staff that Skelton selected
during his years as under-secretary consisted of professionals from the
sphere of education, the vast majority with post-graduate degrees. He
sometimes contradicted the merit principle, naming officers to positions
by order-in-council if some specific or urgent need arose, but that too
reinforced the strong ties with the university world that were developing out of the examination system. In 1929 he chose John E. Read, the
dean of law at Dalhousie University, as departmental legal adviser, putting through the appointment without advertising the position.[17]

Bilingualism was not a requirement for entry into External Affairs, but
Skelton encouraged French representation in the department and by
1930 30 per cent of his officers were francophones. Even so, the Montreal
intellectual newspaper Le Devoir (among others) questioned why there
were "si peu des nôtres dans cette carrière nouvelle" and wondered about
the "perspectives d'avancement" for the few there were. French might be
the language of diplomacy, but English was the language of Skelton's
External Affairs. Although he clearly respected men like Jean Désy, Skelton never seems to have communicated with his francophone officers in
their own language or to have taken concrete steps to promote the use
of French in the department, beyond beefing up the translation services
as business increased. Below the level of under-secretary, there was evidence in the late 1920s of what one British official called "bitterness and
jockeying" between French and English officers and already a tendency
on the part of both language groups to see francophones as most useful
and happiest in posts abroad. Out of sight, however, was out of mind,
and continual service away from headquarters was apt to marginalize
foreign-service officers and impair opportunities for promotion.[18]

Only men could apply for posts at External Affairs, and that remained
the practice throughout Skelton's time there and one that he never questioned. He valued women, however, and three in particular. Each had an
importance belied by her title. OD's assistant, Marjorie McKenzie, was at
the heart of everything, controlling access and the flow of information to
the under-secretary, watching over his confidential records, and drafting
materials for his signature. Competent in French, German, and Spanish,

she demonstrated her ability and determination when she insisted on taking the foreign-service exam in 1930, even though she was not eligible for appointment. She tied for first in tough competition. Accountant Agnes McCloskey, energetic and often acerbic, was in effect the chief administrative officer of the department; she scrutinized the finances and enforced regulations in a manner that many found autocratic and inflexible. Hugh Keenleyside recalled in his memoirs that Skelton "was alternately amused, grateful, or impressed, and he trusted her, although not necessarily her judgement, completely." On her side, the "one sure way of falling into her disfavour was to criticize or fail in respect for or service to Dr. Skelton." Grace Hart, a graduate of Queen's and McGill hired in 1928 to organize the library, completed the group of indispensable women. Although she and her little empire seemed chaotic, they gave the department the professional and independent research function that Skelton realized was a vital component of any modern foreign office.[19]

The powerful McKenzie and McCloskey worked in Skelton's inner office, only a few feet from the under-secretary. The foreign-service officers were relegated to the attic of the East Block, where they walked the corridors in darkness and fought for space with the bats. When Mike Pearson won the first-secretary competition in 1928, at a salary of $3,450 (a modest raise over his university salary), he rushed to Ottawa in response to a message to start work immediately, only to find that there was nothing much to do. His initial job was to prepare routine background for a League of Nations conference on the causes of death, followed by requests for a list of British Empire treaties affecting Canada and materials relating to lighthouses in the Red Sea and international tariffs on cement. Pearson's companion in a cramped and depressing room under the eaves was Keenleyside, assigned in the beginning to reorganizing and filing documents, a task for which he was discovered to have some flair. Their typing was done by a kindly but inefficient secretary on a crank-handled machine that Keenleyside recalled was "even older than herself."[20]

Pearson and Keenleyside were beginners in a frequently unglamorous business, but Skelton's use of them suggested neither urgency nor a systematic use of highly trained minds. External had the unrushed, ramshackle air of a university department, and it was growing without any clear organizational direction. Skelton was no administrator, and no delegator of responsibility. He ran the department the way he ran his family, as a benign dictator sensitive to others but determined to have his own way. When Vincent Massey, who moved on in the 1930s to become Canada's high commissioner in the United Kingdom, requested an increase in the allowances of Léon Mayrand, one of his diplomats, Skelton responded as the stern father: "Mayrand is a good man, but he will have to cut his coat according to his cloth, and will have to learn, what most of us have had to discover, that we cannot do everything we would like to do when we are young."[21]

OD understood his shortcomings as a manager and supervisor, and particularly the way office routine was absorbing so much of "my nights & days."[22] Yet he was too busy and preoccupied to stick to even his rough organization of departmental responsibilities, and his young men were often given work that duplicated one another's. All were directly accountable to the under-secretary, who reviewed every scrap of paper written in the department and every communication to or from the department. The prime minister might interview top candidates during the recruiting process, but he was only dimly aware of them after they were hired. Every memorandum or recommendation he saw came from Skelton. The department *was* Skelton, and he wanted it kept that way.

His employees complained about Skelton's weak commitment to administration and the delegation of responsibility. They found him tight-lipped and tight-fisted, retiring, and even distant. Only Keenleyside of the early recruits believed that they became friends, and he was wrong about that. But almost all of them revered "Dr. Skelton" for his command of language and international affairs, for his immense political influence, and for his generous spirit and high principle. They shared his rock-solid nationalism – Skelton's examinations and interviews were designed to expose that – and his disdain for the showiness and hierarchy of high diplomacy. He gently improved their drafts, suffered their practical jokes with a smile, and tolerated a diversity of views on social, economic, and political questions. Everyone was treated with respect, whatever their rank.[23]

When Keenleyside had been in the department for a few days, Skelton arranged travel for him to Vancouver on business so that he could help his wife with the family's move to Ottawa. A short time later, the under-secretary took his new officer to a Canadian-American smuggling conference, keeping him carefully under control but offering an early taste of raw diplomacy. It was Keenleyside's first intimate glimpse of Skelton – quiet and diffident but also astute, easy to underestimate, and far harder on the Americans than his reputation suggested. He was "at least as strongly opposed to the neo-imperialism of Washington as he was to the remnants of colonialism in London."[24]

If officers wanted substantial responsibility, they had to get it away from headquarters, and most of the seventeen recruits of the late 1920s were quickly assigned outside the country. The establishment of the Legation at Washington in 1927 was followed by an announcement early the next year that Paris and Tokyo would be next. Action in this field was part of Skelton's grand but gradualist scheme of national independence, a natural and logical outgrowth of evolving self-government. As the country grew in population, industrial development, and foreign trade, and as the progress of science increased contact with the world outside, self-respect and self-interest demanded that Canadians begin to make provision for their distinct requirements abroad. Representation in three major capitals was only a start, but it was indispensable in both symbolic and real terms, setting the seal on Canada's international standing and allowing important work to be done on the spot. Washington, Paris, and Tokyo would be all that were possible for now, politically and financially, but these were, for OD, "the most necessary steps." Further expansion could be left for experience and expediency to determine. To those, notably in the Conservative Party, who predicted that Canadian diplomats running amok in foreign capitals would fragment their beloved British Empire, Skelton replied that disintegration had been prophesied at every step forward since responsible government had been achieved in the nineteenth century. The empire, in a favourite phrase, was "still doing business."[25]

For public consumption, Skelton put an eloquent geographical gloss on the decision to locate legations in the United States, France, and Japan. Canada's position was "that of the centre of a sort of world amphitheatre, surrounded as we are, on three sides, by these great powers, our frontiers are completely exposed of necessity. In friendship and goodwill ... lies our security." Each of those states, moreover, had a significant relationship with the United Kingdom. It was Canada's role to foster goodwill between the British Empire and the three big powers where the country would have a resident diplomat.[26]

Skelton's real motives were neither strategic nor imperial. Even if he had wanted to further British Empire or national-defence aims, foreign representation was not the way to achieve them. He saw the diplomacy of a new nation in more concrete and down-to-earth terms, as mostly having to do with the little disputes and opportunities that neighbours shared. It was crucial to have a representative in the United States, which had generated so much of the ordinary business that had come across his desk since he became under-secretary. Various complicated aspects of Canadian-American waterways, for example, consumed an enormous amount of his time, occasioning his trip to Washington and the Oval Office of the White House to visit President Calvin Coolidge, "a stronger man with more individuality than I had imagined," and an article on the St Lawrence Seaway in the American journal, *Foreign Affairs*, written by OD under the pseudonym Henry Lawrence. He noted that, in its first year of operation, the Legation in Washington had helped him deal with specific public questions, including immigration, radio broadcasting, aviation, smuggling, extradition, and fisheries, as well as the more general protection of the interests of Canadian citizens in matters ranging from business enquiries to claims against the U.S. government. Based on the Washington experience, the $80,000 additional cost of the Paris and Tokyo legations was bound to be a good investment.[27]

Paris needed little justification. France, Skelton said, was "one of our Mother Countries," and there was an already existing foundation for representation in the commissioner general of Canada's office, which had been in the French capital in one form or another since 1882. Paris could also function as a European base for trade promotion and a convenient centre for participation at the League of Nations and in various international conferences.[28]

Tokyo was a less obvious diplomatic target, and more difficult to defend, but the project was, as OD put it, a hobby of the prime minister's and so had to be done. To prepare King for the wounds the Opposition would try to inflict in the House of Commons, Skelton pointed out that the Pacific was on the rise as an area of "increasing and decisive importance" in world development and that the commercial possibilities were great, since Canada already exported more to Japan than it did to the United Kingdom when the Laurier government took office for the first time. Moreover, a legation in Tokyo would help, as OD delicately put it, in the "constructive regulation" of the immigration question that had been dividing the two countries for years. This was a controversial political topic, particularly in British Columbia, where there was a long-standing demand for a "white Canada" policy and a complete ban on Japanese immigrants to Canada. Skelton had more liberal views than his colleagues in the public service, many of whom were out-and-out exclusionists. Nevertheless, he was a hard bargainer in the negotiation of an international agreement limiting immigration from Japan on a mutually agreeable basis, a necessary (because it was politically neces-sary in Canada) part of the negotiation for an exchange of diplomatic representatives.[29]

There was a complicating imperial dimension to diplomatic appoint-ments. The British insisted that a formal note accompany all dominion representatives when they presented their credentials, assuring foreign governments that the empire's diplomatic unity remained intact – that is, that the British Foreign Office remained the official voice of all parts of the empire when it came to communications with foreign governments. In the gospel according to Oscar, this was another and entirely predict-able centralist stratagem, an attempt to make the dominions appear to foreign powers as "satellites of the central sun." If the Canadian gov-ernment continued to acquiesce in such dangerous assertions of impe-rial control, "we would find that we had tied our hands for the future and had undertaken that Canada would accept whatever view on any foreign policy might seem good to whatever Conservative or Labour or Liberal Government might be in power in London." At bottom, the Brit-ish believed that Canada must not have any different ideas from theirs.[30]

As preparations were being made to establish the Tokyo Legation in early 1929, Skelton was pleased to find that South Africa and the Irish Free State were also opposed to any reference to imperial unity in Moth-er's note to foreign powers. Sir William Clark, the recently installed Brit-ish high commissioner in Ottawa, reported that Skelton was cabling his own radical suggestions to his sympathetic dominion friends without his prime minister's or the British government's knowledge. Skelton was a good man to work with as a rule, said Clark, but on this topic had "an obsession which makes him secretive and not wholly scrupulous." Coming to similar conclusions, Robert Hadow, Clark's Foreign Office assistant, added that Skelton "has a decided fear of the British attitude towards his country, and a curious lurking preference for the United States, based, I think, chiefly, upon closer contact and a better under-standing of the people of that country." He was a pleasant and cultured companion in leisure hours: "Given dinner and some tolerable wine, or a comfortable chair in his own house, he is generally amenable to rea-son, whereas in the office he seems obsessed with a mixture of suspicion and nationalism which makes him very hard to deal with at times."[31]

In view of Skelton's "obstinacy and power of getting his own way," Clark decided to face the prime minister directly with the clandes-tine telegrams to the Irish Free State and South Africa. Claiming to be "frankly puzzled," King summoned his deputy, who admitted that correspondence suggesting the omission of all reference to diplomatic unity had been dispatched from his office. Skelton vigorously defended the action and the policy upon which it was based, openly challenging his boss in front of Clark. King acknowledged that he had agreed to "a telegram," but he "had not fully realized what Skelton proposed." There was no reason, the British official concluded, to doubt King's sincerity. There was every reason to question the propriety of Skelton's actions. In his diary, the prime minister recorded that the under-secretary had "put one over on me re 'diplomatic unity of Empire' by sending message to Ireland & S. Africa which did not use this phrase or rather sacrificed it." King had no idea that it would "have this effect & he knew I stood solidly for the phrase." It had been "a trying situation in a way as it was first time I had differed from Skelton before another."[32]

Skelton had reason to be upset. He had put his recommendations to King in a considered and explicit form. The prime minister kept the external affairs portfolio firmly in his grasp. Always cautious, he guarded the prerogatives of office jealously, and he was careful to read what went out over his signature. One telegram might have slipped his notice, or been misunderstood, but there were many such communications. No one who had scrutinized the documents on the file, written in Skelton's lucid prose, could mistake their intent.[33] Confronted directly with his government's sins, King played the innocent victim of his civil service, tossing his subordinate overboard without a pang of conscience. He told the story to his diary as he had told it to Clark. By then he was undoubtedly convinced that it had happened that way.

Using King's embarrassment as a weapon, the British were able to cling to their cherished phrase. Yet the dispute over imperial diplomatic unity suggested that Skelton was a bigger danger to Anglo-Canadian relations than even they had imagined. Reading Clark's assessment that the prime minister exercised little authority over his subordinate, high-ranking officials in the Foreign Office fussed about "what we are up against in Dr. Skelton" and "his power over Mr. Mackenzie King." It was all very well for King to talk grandly about imperial unity and cooperation, but those "fair words" would "have to be translated into practice by Dr. Skelton!" The foreign secretary, Sir Austen Chamberlain, lamented that "we should have less difficulty" if King was not so weak. The assistant under-secretary at the Foreign Office, Sir Hubert Montgomery, lamented: "I am afraid Mr. Skelton is, in some respects at any rate, a 'bad man.'" Skelton would have smiled at the reactions of the minister and senior officials to his attempts to confound British designs. He was proudly subversive, out to resist imperialists and their projects small and big. He was more than prepared to be troublesome in making the case for Canadian independence.[34]

Yet King was in full control of Skelton, and OD knew it well, just as he understood that from time to time blame would be laid at his feet when it was expedient to do so. He had observed the tactic before. "I think," he said on a similar occasion, "Mr. K. had made it appear that it was I who imposed the disagreeable details." King's capacity to be insensitive to his staff, or worse, was illustrated by the death of Mrs Moyer, the wife of his private secretary, after a long illness. Skelton remembered her as "one of the most vivid & likeable personalities I have met in Ottawa," and he was proud to act as a pallbearer at her funeral. All that King could think of at that sad time, however, was whether Moyer had been an entirely trustworthy employee. Skelton took Moyer's side in a heated argument with King, writing in his diary that the prime minister was "deplorably self-centred."[35]

King's private view of his deputy, on the other hand, was almost always positive. Their disagreement over diplomatic unity was remarkable because it was so unusual. The prime minister felt at ease with Skelton, trusted him implicitly, and relied on his judgments across the full spectrum of government and political affairs. He was King's sounding board on every imaginable issue, domestic as well as foreign. When a federal-provincial conference met, or talks were under way to grant Manitoba jurisdiction over natural resources, King wanted him there. When the arrangements for the celebrations of the Diamond Jubilee of Confederation pressed in on him, he resorted to his under-secretary of everything for administrative help and speechwriting. When the budget address was being drafted, or appointments made, or the tariff rethought, Skelton was a key adviser. King raised the salaries of a number of deputy ministers to $10,000 a year in 1929, largely so that Skelton's work in making External Affairs into such a useful and powerful department could be recognized. It was his dependability and selflessness, and his ability to produce briefing papers and speeches on demand, that were so striking. He was "a really great man & a true soul."[36]

King turned naturally to his deputy to represent the government abroad and in the United States. Skelton did not mind that a bit, although he did not have diplomatic training, experience, or aptitude. He loved to be on the move, was intensely curious, and embraced fresh experiences. Without really believing it, he said that he was as likely to be made use of by wily foreign diplomats as to be able to contribute anything to their enlightenment. In the late 1920s, Skelton was in the United States frequently, in London three times, and at the League twice. He thought that Canada must begin to face its responsibilities in the world. Europe might be a dangerous and sometimes unsavoury place, but Canada was not an island, isolated from international currents. His country's future was intimately linked to the ancient continent. If it could remain peaceful and prosperous, Canada would as well.[37]

Skelton fit Canada's role at the League of Nations into his framework of cautiously internationalist ideas. When Canada's election to one of the three-year seats on the League Council was broached in the spring of 1927, he gave nearly equal weight to the advantages and disadvantages. He deplored the League's excessive Eurocentrism and worried about the practical difficulties of finding the means to represent national interests on the Council properly, particularly when Geneva was far away and he had few personnel and little money at his disposal. Canada had joined the League, however, and must share in its obligations and opportunities. A successful candidacy had advertising potential for Canada's international status, and the time was right to establish that the British dominions, contributing one-seventh of the League's budget, had a right to a regular seat on the Council. He hoped that his friends in Ireland would put their country's name forward but wondered if the Free State could be elected. If so, that would be "well & better; if not, unlucky" – unlucky for the ambitious Irish, but also perhaps for Skelton and his boss, who would then be forced to make a decision one way or the other. Mackenzie King wanted no part of the Council, where public differences might arise with Britain or France, causing tensions on the home front.[38]

Very soon after dispatching his even-handed memorandum on the subject to the prime minister in early June 1927, Skelton became an active proponent of a run at the Council seat. He learned of the assassination of the Irish minister of justice, Kevin O'Higgins, with whom he had worked at the previous year's Imperial Conference. The tragic murder did not ruffle a restful weekend in Ottawa – was that more of OD's obliviousness? – but he realized it was a scar on the reputation of the fledgling Irish state that made its election to the Council in 1927 even more unlikely. That was followed by a visit from the Foreign Office's legal adviser, Cecil Hurst, on his way to Chicago to give a Harris Foundation lecture. Skelton had refused a similar invitation and the $1,200 fee "because of scruples as to official position," a concern his British colleague clearly did not share. Hurst reassured Skelton that King's fear that Canada might have to run counter to England or France on the League Council, or be forced to support one against the other, was largely unfounded because differences were almost always ironed out behind the scenes, before they became public.[39]

The prime minister still balked. He named Skelton and Senator Raoul Dandurand as Canada's delegates for the September 1927 meeting of the League, but they departed for Geneva with no instructions about what to do when the Council election was held. At the last minute, King decided to give way, not to Skelton, but to the justice minister, Ernest Lapointe, who had been insisting all along that a Council seat would bring with it enormous international and political prestige. "Let Canada again lead dominions," Lapointe declared, and King reluctantly gave in out of respect for his chief francophone minister's position in Quebec and in the Liberal Party. He continued to think that it was a mistake.[40]

Word of King's change of heart reached Skelton on 5 September, a Sunday, just an hour before a gathering of the British Empire delegations at the Hotel Beau-Rivage in Geneva. The British, he noted with some satisfaction, were "obviously taken aback" at the Canadian news. They pledged their support, but the U.K. foreign secretary, Austen Chamberlain, raised the prospect of Anglo-Canadian differences on the Council, precisely King's fear. Chamberlain counselled patience and delay, which only made OD more determined. The Canadians left the meeting and fanned out among the various delegations to make their ambitions known. Skelton drew particular attention to the strong line his country was taking on the need for the rule of law in international relations and compulsory arbitration under the Permanent Court of International Justice, in contrast to the British, whose worldwide interests made them reluctant to submit disputes to the authority of an alien institution. Dandurand's tactics were rougher, blaming the British for having jettisoned the Geneva Protocol and appropriating their good deeds on minority rights, tactics Chamberlain found ungentlemanly and "crooked." The foreign secretary was one of the scrutineers during the balloting, his face hardening as it became clear that Canada would be elected. "The result," Skelton related to King, "aroused a good deal of surprise and much interest, but on the whole comments have been quite favourable."[41]

The election took effect immediately, and the Canadian delegation was plunged into Council affairs and major new duties. From Geneva, Skelton warned the prime minister that both his cabinet and the Department of External Affairs would have to pay considerably more attention to League matters. There ought to be a cabinet minister present at every session, and he hinted that Dandurand, well known at the League but impulsive and pro-French, was not up to the task. For "our own sake and our own safeguarding as much as for the sake of the League," King should come to the next meeting of the Council, and if not him, then Lapointe, who received the same urgent appeal. Knowing that Lapointe was the most sympathetic of King's cabinet ministers to Skeltonian ideas and dreams, OD was more candid with the justice minister than he was with the prime minister. He admitted to Lapointe that he had not completely overcome his doubts about the enterprise, "but once we are in it we will have to try and meet our full responsibilities."[42]

The European trip was partly for the family. Oscar had promised vacations to his wife and sister, and Bea had sailed with him on the Cunard ship *Ascania*. Sandy accompanied them, on his way to Oxford University to begin a Rhodes Scholarship, won after four remarkable years at Queen's as a student of history and economics, president of the student body, intercollegiate debater, and magnificent athlete. His father was not enthusiastic about the Rhodes, preferring a year at Harvard and perhaps Oxford later, but he recognized that the award had immense prestige and represented "a very fine financial legup." In Geneva, Skelton invited two other Rhodes Scholars to lunch. Escott Reid and McGill's Eugene Forsey, who had already been at Oxford for a year, were described as "very bright & likeable fellows," and entirely worthy of Sandy's company, as two "rather crude" Acadia University students apparently were not. Like most who encountered Skelton for the first time, Reid was disappointed, expecting a polished diplomat and finding instead a rumpled and unprepossessing university professor.[43]

Held up in Ottawa with the two other children, Isabel was at last able to join her husband in France, after he had finished at the League and spent a short while in Berlin. That meant abandoning visits to North Africa and Italy, but Paris, with the Louvre and her first experience of fresh figs, was sublime. After a few days, they took the Calais-Dover ferry to England, where the fine dining included Simpson's-In-The-Strand, celebrated for its roast beef, Yorkshire pudding, cabbage, and butter-sodden mashed potatoes. Oscar had become used to living well on his transatlantic trips; Isabel was discovering that she liked it too. Work was close by. OD discussed Canadian consular representation and trade commissioners with British officials and Isabel was in awe as they visited the powerful British cabinet secretary Sir Maurice Hankey's home, Highstead, on the Kent-Surrey border. Hankey's discussion of the preparation of documents for his government's consideration reminded Isabel of her husband's own methods. She could see why they were drawn to each other.[44]

Skelton returned to Europe in 1928. He and Mackenzie King sailed in the *Ile de France*, the modern French ocean liner. "The ship is comfortable of course," OD wrote in one of the wonderfully detailed letters he sent Isabel whenever he was away, "and striking if not Art Nouveau bizarre, in its furnishings and decorations ... Mural paintings, hangings, chandeliers, tables and chairs, are all in startling shapes & colours. Some of it I like very much & some I've come to tolerate, but there are other bits still beyond comprehension." Skelton and King travelled in first class. Skelton's snobbery was exposed by the "outlandish specimens" who "rather terrified" him as he came on board. He was relieved to discover that the worst of them were New York visitors looking over the ship. When they cleared out, the residue was "pretty respectable," including diplomats, moving-picture impresarios, millionaires, vaudeville performers, and department-store buyers, topped off by a Vanderbilt, a Rockefeller, a Rothschild, the American secretary of state, and Dolores del Rio, "who is said to be the most popular movie star in the U.S. after Mary Pickford."[45]

The glittering assembly ate, drank, danced, gambled, gossiped – and dressed for every occasion. "The dresses in the evening are gorgeous," Oscar wrote to Isabel, "excelled in many cases only by the makeup. One damsel at a table beside us has had on a different gown every morning, afternoon, & evening & sometimes an extra one, with complexion to match, each time." Tempted by the splendid food, Skelton succumbed again to overeating. On the second day out, at dinnertime, he tried seven kinds of hors d'oeuvres, fried sole with a heavy sauce, pâté de foie gras, quail, rum babas, and Roquefort cheese. Staggering to his room, he vomited what he had eaten but came right back for more. "I've since adopted a simpler menu," he assured his wife.[46]

Mackenzie King and the U.S. secretary of state, Frank Kellogg, were travelling to Paris for the signature of an international treaty to ban war, popularly known (after its originators) as the Kellogg-Briand Pact. Pointing out that it was an election year in the United States and that the document had no effective enforcement mechanism, Hankey assessed it "a great fraud." OD appeared to share in the widespread international scepticism. After witnessing the signing ceremony at the home of France's foreign ministry, presided over by the French foreign minister, Aristide Briand, Skelton reported home that the "great gesture has been made and another pledging and dedication by the great men. The show at the Quai D'Orsay was quite impressive; the Foreign Office is a magnificent building, a bit too ornate in decoration but lending itself splendidly to such displays," and with Briand and his fellow foreign ministers "looking as if they meant it."[47]

Beneath the cynicism, Skelton supported the treaty.[48] He believed that a solemn promise by all the great states to renounce war as an instrument of national policy opened a new chapter in human history and marked the greatest step towards world peace since the establishment of the League of Nations. Kellogg-Briand, which produced the Nobel Peace Prize for its two originators, branded war as a futile and outworn means of settling international disputes. Skelton told King that "statesmen will not be able to embark on war or in courses leading to war with the levity, the false glamour of glory, the support of tradition of former days. Any government rejecting peaceful means is put on the defensive, brought before the bar of civilised opinion, and if condemned, regarded as an outlaw." From then on, conflict in any part of the world "is a common interest, and aggression will more and more be met not merely by individual self-defence as in the old days, but by cooperative defence, by coordinated action, whether positive or negative, directed against the aggressor."

Skelton acknowledged that the treaty offered no certainties, but he reasoned that it made a declaration of war less likely and created an international norm for the peaceful settlement of disputes. The advanced peoples of the world were determined "to put down war before war puts down civilisation." The First World War had taught that "wars of the future would be wars of peoples, wars in which every perverted ingenuity of science, every resource of industry, would be thrown into a struggle for extermination, in which whole cities would be at the mercy of poison gas and bombs raining from the air, with human suffering and financial burdens incalculable, with the victor losing, and the triumph of right, if the original right did triumph, bought at an impossible cost and incalculable consequences." Even the very general terms of the commitment were helpful: simplicity was essential if opinion leaders wanted to capture public imagination.

Canada, Skelton went on, had nothing to gain from war and less to fear than other states. The treaty offered special advantages to Canadians nevertheless, and there was practically nothing on the debit side of the sheet. In particular, Kellogg-Briand committed the country's southern neighbour irrevocably to a policy of peace and international cooperation. The trajectory would be from a general commitment to outlaw war towards specific means of settlement, and the United States would be forced, because of its leading role in the treaty's negotiation, to take part in the preparation of arbitration and conciliation treaties that would be more far-reaching than it had ever accepted. Furthermore, the treaty strengthened the undefended Canada-United States border, giving an American promise that there would be no attack on Canada by the only power that could mount a successful invasion.

The prime minister cast a pall over the 1928 French trip by treating Oscar as his private secretary, expected to sort and answer correspondence as the national archivist, Arthur G. Doughty, had done at the 1923 and 1926 imperial conferences. Having read of this development in the newspaper, Isabel commiserated: "I hope you will not have to do the Dr. Doughty act for long. It is a good job for A.G.D. but not one you should be wasted upon."[49]

Nothing could completely spoil Paris, the throbbing, prosperous Paris of the late 1920s. Skelton adored its streets, people, architecture, cafés, and bookstores. The French government arranged and paid for accommodation at the Crillon on the Place de la Concorde, one of the best hotels in the city, allowing him to pocket his entire daily allowance and eat at establishments like the exquisite Joseph's, run by Sir Wilfrid Laurier's former butler. Oscar used his extra money to buy two gowns for his wife at Colette's, an exclusive dressmaking establishment. Since he was anything but a choosy shopper, he carried out the whole operation in fifteen minutes. In his own sphere of business, he did further preparation for the exchange of diplomats with France and continued his diplomatic education. He visited the British Embassy and the North American section of the Quai d'Orsay, meeting with its head and with Jean Knight, slated to become the minister to Ottawa later that year. An inspection of the quarters for the new Canadian Legation showed that they passed the crucial thrift test: "not pretentious, but adequate, well laid out and attractively furnished."[50]

Skelton was already weary and still had to shepherd King to Geneva and the League. They arrived at the Hôtel de la Paix, under the majestic mountain, Mont Blanc, and beside Lake Geneva, at the end of August, during the first rain in two months. OD managed to slip out of his responsibilities as a prime ministerial secretary but as a consequence had trouble getting King's attention. His efforts to give King a lesson on League matters failed miserably, as they had on the *Ile de France*, and hours were wasted in the hotel waiting for an audience with the prime minister. When they did speak, it was about King's speech before the Assembly, which Skelton drafted by hand at the last minute on old scraps of notepaper, combining bows to the League and Kellogg-Briand with the habitual bromides about Canadian superiority and North American peacefulness. He knew there was nothing in what he wrote that was particularly new, but it was a forceful speech and King delivered it well, so that Isabel was told that it "made a good impression." The prime minister had worried "himself & everybody else a good bit over it, but is quite happy now, & feels he can depart from Geneva with a good conscience." Skelton preferred politicians who took their work more seriously.[51]

Sandy came to visit, not mentioning that his main ambitions at Oxford had been to enjoy himself, join the boxing, track, and rugby teams, and sail ("the king of sports," he announced to the undoubtedly startled manager of his Rhodes Scholarship) the waters of Europe during long vacations. To his father, he looked disreputable. Oscar cleaned him up and lent him a blue suit so he could be presented to the prime minister and Senator Dandurand. Sandy was about to return home before beginning his second Rhodes year, and Isabel was instructed to have his eyes and teeth checked when he arrived in Ottawa.[52]

Skelton always saw a lot of his Irish colleagues in Geneva, but in 1928 he had an additional reason for talking with them and other British Empire delegations. The expert legal committee promised by the 1926 Imperial Conference report was finally in view. Skelton wanted to know how other countries were preparing and how far they had come. He was relieved to discover that most were no farther ahead than he was. After getting back from the League, he received formal notification that the British would be convening a meeting of the committee the following autumn, in about a year's time. He began to write detailed briefs on the complicated set of problems that required attention and contacted the Irish, promising cooperation and arranging for an exchange of ideas and documentation. He also involved John Ewart, and Dalhousie University's law dean, John Read, had already been hired on contract. Competent though he was as an international lawyer, Skelton judged Read as inadequately nationalist in perspective: "Dean Read has not fully absorbed your views," OD whispered to Ernest Lapointe. "I gathered from incidental conversation that he appreciated the position of the Canadian Government, but apparently not all lawyers are sufficiently free from the shackles of precedent to realize that legal difficulties exist only to be overcome." In the under-secretary's blunt view, "the purpose of our investigation should be to consider how far it is possible to remove every vestige of Imperial legislative supremacy," except for the power of the British Parliament to amend the Canadian constitution, a subject on which the federal government and the provinces were unable to agree.[53]

The constitutional conference met during the late fall of 1929 in London as the Conference on the Operation of Dominion Legislation and Merchant Shipping Legislation – the ODL, delegates were soon calling it. Skelton and Lapointe were the main Canadian protagonists; Read, Ewart, Jean Désy, Marjorie McKenzie, and assorted experts were supporting players. When he arrived in England, Skelton considered his team well-enough prepared, but not as well as Ireland's delegation. He took the initiative in striking an informal alliance with the Irish, and they encouraged him to think of the ODL, which included his initials, as belonging particularly to him and to the ideas they shared about throwing off the chains of British control.[54]

The conference opened on 8 October in the Moses Room at the House of Lords, with its huge mural depicting the biblical handing down of the Tables of the Law. Skelton mused that the atmosphere was very impressive for the first five minutes, but winter was coming and the heating dated "from the time of King Alfred, minus the fireplace that is sometimes associated with his name." The Labour Party had taken power in the United Kingdom earlier in the year. As a result, the eminent socialist, Sidney Webb, now Lord Passfield and secretary of state for the dominions, was the conference chair. That should have been a good sign – Passfield and the evolutionary wing of the party had been champions of imperial decentralization – but he and his government colleagues seemed to Skelton colossally ignorant of contemporary developments in the empire. Identifying him as the author of *Socialism: A Critical Analysis*, Passfield told Skelton that it was the fairest presentation of the subject ever written by a non-socialist, although he had serious reservations about OD's discussions of the movement's drawbacks. It occurred to Skelton that there might be something personal in the remark. Webb-Passfield had probably been hurt by the short shrift Skelton's book gave to his part in the building of English socialism.[55]

The United Kingdom attorney general, Sir William Jowitt, began the ODL meetings with an admonition to the delegates to move very cautiously if they wanted to avoid a violent wrench from which the empire would not readily recover, and the battle was on.[56] The British and Australians were at one pole, arguing that the British parliament must be left with real powers to act as the empire's benevolent legal trustee. At the other end of the spectrum, the South Africans railed against any limitation on the freedom of their elected Parliament to do as it wished;

they were led by F.W. Beyers, described by Skelton as "about the most obstinate Dutchman in history." Canada and the Irish Free State were committed to fundamental change, but said that they were willing to accept compromise in the common interest. Two months of difficult discussions ensued, and at different stages right up to the final day the conference's complete disintegration seemed possible. Not for the first time, the British identified OD as the villain-in-chief, Jowitt telling Lapointe that the Canadian deputy minister was the most extreme nationalist of the bunch. When a British official accused him of wishing to destroy the legal links that unified the British Commonwealth, opening the way for the secession of one or more of its members, Skelton did not deny it. There were certain virtues, he replied coolly, in a grouping of states that would cooperate, or not, on the basis of free association.[57]

Alongside the arduous negotiations, life over the eight weeks in London assumed a pleasant routine. Oscar shared a suite with Désy at the May Fair Hotel in Berkeley Square, only three hundred metres from Piccadilly and close to Green and Hyde parks. The hotel was new and modern, but not as "swanky" (a recurrent Skelton word) or as solidly impressive as the nearby Ritz. He was not bothered, as some of the Canadians were, by the May Fair's elaborately ornamented Italian-villa style. Breakfast – orange juice, a boiled egg, toast, and cocoa – was served in his room, and often lunch and dinner too. The menu was varied and temptingly rich, but after one or two indiscretions he learned (or so he told his wife) to restrict the range and number of his eating experiments. The only exercise was walking, which he liked to do with Marjorie McKenzie or other Canadian colleagues; his sense of direction was not strong, and even after all his experience in London, he would quickly lose his bearings. Theatre nights were common, a light comedy if he had others to please, but a play that was thought-provoking was more to his taste. All these occasions, frothy or disturbing, were dutifully reviewed for Isabel. He was shaken by Sean O'Casey's *The Silver Tassie*, an experimental reflection on the horrors of the First World War: "the scenery by Augustus John, the outré words and the weird chanting make a picture not easily forgotten."[58]

The English countryside looked as beautiful as ever, despite a long drought. One weekend he and Désy were able to get to Salisbury and its cathedral, which stood alone in a great green field, not forced to share the horizon with any other buildings as in other cathedral cities. Salisbury seemed "the essence of England – the most English city I've seen, & the most Cathedral-like – quiet closes and bi-ways, neat & attractive shops, old stone gates as 700 years ago, just such a place as Jane Austen or Anthony Trollope might write about, as they did." Stonehenge was only nine miles away: "It lies, a jumble of huge stones, on a high wind-swept heath, a plain & simple sight, but it moved me strangely – all during the walk I felt as if the spirits of the Britons of 1300 B.C. were about us. The contrast between this crude sun-worship structure, built by skinclad savages with no tools but stone hatchets ... & the magnificent Cathedral built in 1300 A.D. or a little earlier, was very striking." He promised his "sweetheart" at home that he was saving up these sights for their next visit.[59]

Skelton inadvertently precipitated a family crisis when he tried to use the primitive transatlantic telephone service without warning his wife in advance. He made the call but could barely hear what she was saying, and she could pick up nothing at the other end. She assumed that he was sick, and badly enough to warrant an extraordinary effort to contact her. It took several hours before her mind was put at rest. Oscar recognized what a shock this had been for Isabel. All of her three children and Bert, her brother, had been ill over the past few months. Each had recovered, and Bert miraculously so, because he was diagnosed as suffering from an incurable creeping paralysis and had been, OD wrote in his diary, "snatched back from the jaws of death & despair – it is incredible & splendid."[60]

The ODL meetings pivoted around Skelton and Sir Maurice Gwyer, the ablest of the British government's legal minds. They served together on the conference's key committee, drafted much of the final report, and built the coalitions that made ultimate consensus possible. Skelton was apt, as he admitted, to lay down the law from time to time, but he compromised to make a settlement possible, in part because he realized that his side could not press too hard, "as after all it is the British who will have to pass the act granting what we want." Gwyer discovered that the Canadian position was the best deal he could achieve, and OD and his Irish friends helped by convincing the South Africans of the need to retain at least some of the old imperial legal forms and conventions. Sir Maurice was quite resentful, or envious, that a public servant like Skelton was allowed to operate in a major leadership role at the most senior political level. Lapointe allowed him to do so; Mackenzie King, had he been there, would not have. Gwyer and the other British officials had been soaked in the portfolio for two years, but their expertise had to be filtered through Jowitt and Passfield, who made concessions based on a superficial knowledge of the issues. Gwyer suggested that a committee of officials only be struck, so that he could have a greater impact on the outcome. Knowing a tactical advantage when he saw one, Skelton declined the offer.[61]

The ODL was a triumph for Skelton. The final report urged the complete elimination of Britain's legislative authority over the dominions except in certain agreed areas such as the monarchy, and suggested that an act titled the Statute of Westminster be passed in Britain giving formal effect to the delegates' recommendations. None of the participating governments was formally committed to its findings, but the ODL added to the momentum generated by the 1926 Imperial Conference, making it nearly impossible to resist the concrete acknowledgment of the dominions' right to make their own laws. It took a little time, and some more persuasion, but the British Parliament eventually passed the Statute of Westminster; it was signed into law by an unhappy King George V on 11 December 1931.[62]

The Statute of Westminster offered a clear path to legal independence, but it did not make Canada independent. The great document of the Canadian constitution, the British North America Act, could still be amended only by applying to the British Parliament. The Judicial Committee of the Privy Council in London remained the highest court of appeal for Canadian cases. Having no citizenship of their own, Canadians remained British citizens and British subjects. At the end of the Statute's decade, in March and again in September 1939, Minister of Justice Lapointe referred to the long list of laws, agreements, and protocols that bound the two countries tightly together. Britain and Canada, he made clear, were not even then separate sovereignties.[63]

Imperialism, Skelton was convinced, was "of a day now going," but the going was taking its time.[64] The forces of history were on his side. They needed help, of course; history, even trending in the right direction, always needed help. Skelton's work at the Department of External Affairs and at the ODL was part of a deliberate strategy to liberate Canada from its colonial past. The Statute of Westminster, however, could not legislate peoples' minds, and it left a great deal undone, even in the legal realm. The country could only inch towards independence – the idea, even the word, was as yet beyond the realm of Canada's imaginings. He waited impatiently for a shift in Canadians' centre of gravity away from the ancient ties that remained embedded in their understanding of themselves.

9
Life with RB, 1930–3

In January 1930 a delegation from Queen's offered Skelton the job he had once coveted. Maybe he still did. The university's principal, R.B. Taylor, was gone; a replacement was urgently needed. The hiring committee, led by the business tycoon James Richardson, who had tried to have him fired in 1918, was confident that Skelton had all the right qualities to lead the university: strength as an administrator and recruiter of staff, the prestige to "maintain the status of the University as we would like to see it," and the personality to "insure a happy Queen's family." OD's critics fretted about his agnosticism, his reputation for pro-Americanism, and his lack of public punch, but none of this was important, or important enough. Queen's was intent on bringing Skelton home.[1]

The Skeltons had kept in close touch with their university. Their lives remained full of Queen's business, Queen's gossip, Queen's people. OD joined his mentors Adam Shortt and Andrew Haydon on the Board of Trustees in 1926; two years later, Skelton was elected by the students as rector, their representative on the board.[2] A steady stream of former colleagues came through Ottawa, visiting with him in his office at the East Block or in the Rideau Club, and griping about Taylor, who had made abundant enemies as the university's chief executive since 1917.

Skelton agreed with Taylor's detractors that Queen's standing was in decline and that the principal bore a good deal of the responsibility. OD had originally believed Taylor a "second-rate appointment" and saw little to change his mind, quickly forgetting that Taylor had protected him at the most vulnerable time in his Queen's career, when he was under attack for his views on conscription during the First World War. In his decision to leave the university, Skelton gave heavy weight to a series of Taylor leadership errors that dislocated the English department in the early 1920s. The principal repeated the performance after Skelton's departure, mishandling the reorganization of economics and political science, and in the process passing over W.A. Mackintosh for head of department after promising he would get the job. OD commiserated with Mackintosh: "The only explanation I can give is that after the wrecking of the English Department it has been felt that it would be invidious not to wreck the Economics Department also."[3]

Taylor's impending departure was announced in May 1929. Skelton immediately began to hear from admirers urging his candidacy, first a group from Kingston and then colleagues in Ottawa and Toronto. He told them to look elsewhere. W.C. Clark, a former student and political economy department member who left Queen's to become an investment banker in New York, sent a heartfelt note. Skelton had widespread respect and support, Clark insisted, even though he was too much of a political partisan and too little of a churchgoer for some tastes. OD had done his best for the country, the empire, and the Liberals. Now Queen's badly needed saving. The main lines of a foreign policy were laid down at External Affairs, and Ottawa was close enough to Kingston that he could continue to exercise a guiding hand. As the head of an important university, he need not fear that his mission "in shaping public opinion in your direction" would be finished.[4]

Skelton replied at length. He thought it gratifying that so many people had thought of him: "I think I'd rather have the memory that my friends had such confidence in me than the post itself." But was he fit for the position, which was so multisided and difficult to fill that they would soon be remembering Taylor more fondly? A reputable scholar was certainly needed and "possibly my qualifications would pass in these easy-going days." Sympathy with the student body he had, "and interest also in what I take to be the chief task ahead of a Queen's principal for the next ten years – searching incessantly for strong men, men of achievement and men of promise, who will keep up the Queen's tradition of personality and leadership." Ability to manage finances was not so important because there were first-rate business people on the Board of Trustees. A modern university head, however, had to be capable of oratory and inspirational stunts. Neither was of interest to Skelton. He considered himself an only adequate public performer, who spoke best and most easily when he was fortified with alcohol.[5]

OD didn't like change. He explained to Clark that he became completely absorbed in whatever he was doing at the moment. "Perhaps the work I'm in now isn't any more important, but I've put my hand to it, and would find it easier to continue in it than to shift to another field." If he was still at Queen's, and faced with a choice between External Affairs and the principal's office, he probably would stay where he was. "But being in the other groove – or rut – I also feel, why change?" He was happy in Ottawa, and although there were certainly drawbacks at External Affairs, "I'm inclined to think that I can put in the next ten or fifteen years with most satisfaction to myself and most to show for the work, by staying here." Skelton meanwhile told others a somewhat different story: that his health was too precarious for a move and his greatest concern was to build up the Department of External Affairs. The message at bottom was the same: only if there was no one else would he consider the principalship.[6]

When the formal offer came, Skelton was tempted enough to talk the possibility over with the prime minister, who was informed that Isabel was pushing hard for Queen's and that the stress of his work in Ottawa was wearing on Oscar. He did not press Mackenzie King for more salary or recognition, simply saying that he would have a quieter life at the university. His Queen's friends piled on the pressure that night and the next day and had him all but convinced, but after a talk with Senator Haydon and "full reflection," he declined the post once and for all. King and Richardson were told that he would be remaining in Ottawa. The prime minister was very relieved. "Thank heaven," he whispered to his diary."[7]

Whatever the apparent confusion of motive and explanation, Skelton knew his mind. He enjoyed Ottawa, his impressive house and garden, the prestige of a senior government responsibility, the whirl of events. Just back from the ODL conference in London, he was at the height of his influence. He wavered, but only that, because his Queen's suitors were able to appeal to his devotion to the university that had never been far from his thoughts since the age of eighteen – and perhaps because of Isabel. "I may say," he wrote King when the final decision was taken, "that my wife does not think very highly of my judgment in this matter."[8]

The worries about his health were genuine, even though he used them at times to justify both the Kingston and Ottawa sides of the argument. There was an accumulation of long days, the unrelenting press of business, the inability to delegate and set priorities, the overdeveloped sense of responsibility, the rich food, and the relative lack of exercise. His stomach was a persistent problem and recently his eyes had been giving out under the strain so that there were times he simply could not see.[9] Money was not a decisive issue, although he continued to struggle with the mortgage on Edgehill and the expense of educating the children, and the salary that was being offered at Queen's was $2,500 less than he was earning as a deputy minister. Later, when he learned that the hiring committee had agreed to pay substantially more to attract W.H. Fyfe, the man eventually chosen to succeed Taylor, Skelton protested against the amount at a Board of Trustees meeting, not out of any personal pique, but because he thought it was too much money for an underwhelming candidate.[10]

He quickly regretted his decision. He had not expected an election until 1931, nor that the Liberals would lose it. Both assumptions were faulty. With the economy shrinking and international trade barriers mounting, King complacently took Canadians to the polls in the summer of 1930, boasting of a strong record of achievement and vaguely promising more good things to come. R.B. Bennett, Arthur Meighen's successor as Conservative leader, offered hope and dynamism, accompanied by promises of strong action to protect Canadians and teach outsiders like the high-tariff Americans a lesson in economic nationalism. The shift in popular vote was small, but the Tories won a solid majority of seats. Mackenzie King was gone, and probably Skelton too. He would have accepted the university's offer earlier in the year, he told King, had he had any inkling of the election calamity that was coming.[11]

Skelton knew and liked "RB," but they were very different and unlikely to be able to work together. Bennett was emotional, mercurial, confrontational – "fundamentally uncivilized," as the London *Times* Canadian correspondent characterized him, or, in the telling of Conservative newspaper publisher John Bassett, "a most extraordinary combination of brain-power and childishness."[12] Skelton was placid and predictable. Bennett courted anti-Americanism and British Empire fervour. Skelton detested them. Bennett was a vigorous advocate of his party's high-tariff religion; even King's moderate tariff rises of the late 1920s were too much for Skelton. Bennett was opposed to what he thought unnecessary and provocative claims of national autonomy, and to assertions that Canada was Britain's equal when the facts said otherwise. Skelton wanted independence and the institutions of independence as soon as possible. Bennett spoke forcefully about Canada's international commitments to the empire and the League of Nations. Skelton considered the collective-security aspects of them a distraction at best and a trap at worst.

Official Ottawa buzzed about who was in and who was out. There were rumours that Bennett planned "cheerfully" to abolish Skelton's Department of External Affairs and return to the happy days when the British government spoke for Canada abroad and footed all the diplomatic bills. Bennett was subtler than his swashbuckling demeanour suggested, but he did, as he later recalled, intend to rid himself of Skelton within the first forty-eight hours so that he could not "continue his Isolationist activities."[13] The prime minister, however, did not act immediately. His desk was piled high with paper to read, there were more important decisions to make, and he had personally taken on the extra responsibility of minister of finance.

As the new administration settled in, Skelton established a leisurely pace at the office, not arriving until after nine in the morning and often leaving early for his garden. After more than fifteen months away from his diary, he began it again, "perhaps because of a feeling that under present political conditions I'll be less busy doing & have more time for observing." There was time for celebrating his twenty-sixth wedding anniversary, for a first driver's test (he was rated as good but not excellent), for chats about Herbert's decision to shift his career interests away from medicine towards business, and for testing Sheila's cooking and commiserating over the disappearance of her seven kittens. He was far from relaxed, though. The uncertainty was intense, and he was "more tired & washed out than for months." He talked frequently to Vincent Massey, who was being pushed out as high commissioner to London, a post King had given him on the eve of the election. Rumours were everywhere that Skelton would be next to be put under the Conservative guillotine.[14]

Bennett's hostile views, directed at public servants as well as Liberals, were made unmistakeably clear to Skelton. The new prime minister complained that the Liberals had stocked the tiny diplomatic service with their own kind. OD denied it, insisting that most of the posts had been filled through the Civil Service Commission. Bennett snorted that the bureaucracy was no improvement on the Liberal Party, as he had learned during his brief stint in the 1926 Meighen cabinet, when ministers were easily "wangled and set aside" by their advisers.[15] When Skelton suggested that he ought to accompany Bennett to the Imperial Conference coming up in a month's time, RB exploded: "I'm not going to have you monkeying with this business. It is for the Prime Minister's office and not for External Affairs, to run these conferences."[16] Skelton's network at Queen's decided to make it easy for the prime minister by telling him that they wanted OD back in Kingston. The principal's post had been filled, however, and a professor's income was only half that of a deputy minister.

Skelton waited for the axe, but Bennett kept saying to himself and to others, "I'll fire him next week." As soon as the under-secretary arrived at the East Block, the early-rising prime minister would be waiting with a request for information or documents on New Zealand's tough new tariff or the League's fall session. Skelton was anxious to please, either having the answer or rushing to find it. Bennett had someone who would listen to his confidences and outbursts, understood how the bureaucracy operated, and was prepared to put in long days and unrelenting work. Skelton kept his ties with King and the Liberals, and particularly with Andrew Haydon, but transferred his professional loyalties completely to the Conservative leader, the man he called without reservation "my chief" and "my boss." Bennett later recalled his "great mistake." He did not jettison Skelton quickly, "and then I began to find that I couldn't get along without him. He knew everything." OD became so busy that his diary entries petered out once again. Bennett found that it "was difficult to imagine a better public servant than Skelton."[17]

OD was courteous, sympathetic, respectful, even unctuous in the presence of the prime minister, but he gave Bennett his unvarnished views. There was no trimming of policy advice to meet Conservative attitudes or biases. The department's memorandum for the Imperial Conference of 1930 bristled with indignation at Britain's continuing attempts to stifle progress towards Canadian independence and use the empire to restore its old primacy and staunch the contraction of its export trade. Even though he was not at the prime minister's side in London, Skelton was confident that nothing would be done to halt the adoption of the 1929 ODL recommendations. The British had their hopes that Bennett would help them overturn the ODL report, but he did not. Following the course set out in the report Skelton had done so much to mould, the Imperial Conference ended in agreement that the British Parliament would pass the Statute of Westminster, handing the dominions the rest of their legal freedoms except in those areas where they chose not to take them up. The prime minister, OD observed, was transforming himself into as much of a constitutional nationalist as the Irish and Skelton himself. It was worrying, though, that at the same time Bennett remained emotionally wedded to vague notions of British Empire solidarity.[18]

Shortly after the 1930 Imperial Conference, and still in the Conservative government's first six months, the under-secretary put forward a design for the expansion of Canadian diplomatic representation. Bennett readily admitted that he held the title of external affairs minister as part of his constitutional responsibility as prime minister, not because of background, temperament, or expertise. The departmental memorandum therefore assumed nothing. Skelton wanted the boss to know just how vital and basic the department's work was. Diplomacy's objects were to promote international cooperation and defend national interests. Diplomatic representation was widely accepted as a fundamental principle in international law, and an essential attribute of nationhood. Failure to exercise its right to maintain missions abroad threatened a state's present and its future. Great powers understood that. So did thirty-eight countries with a population equal to or smaller than Canada's. Canada was a country on the move in the world and ought to act like one, instead of spreading a meagre contingent of thirteen officers over legations in Washington, Paris, and Tokyo and the League office in Geneva. It should be represented in Germany and Italy, and a strong case could be made for missions in Belgium, Brazil, Argentina, Cuba, Mexico, China, Norway, and Poland.[19] This advice found no fertile ground, nor had it with Mackenzie King, but Bennett did not cut back the size of the Department of External Affairs and let a modest recruiting program proceed.

Bennett was at first reluctant to meet Skelton regularly, and so OD peppered the prime minister with written briefings, tilting the subjects to his interests. By early 1931, however, they were meeting every morning. They were not short sessions. The prime minister talked to – or rather at – Skelton about every conceivable subject. OD watched RB's confidence ebb as the country slid into a catastrophic economic depression that held Canada in its grip for the rest of the 1930s. The wealthy Bennett explained that he had a simpler life in mind, a country home and perhaps a seat in Parliament in his cherished Britain. He had taken over a frail Conservative Party, and ploughed $750,000 of his own money into it, but had never expected to become prime minister of Canada. His was a "remarkable achievement," if he did say so himself.[20]

Bennett dominated his government utterly. OD observed how J.W. Dafoe's *Manitoba Free Press* political cartoonist, Arch Dale, got under Bennett's skin by his depiction of cabinet sessions with the prime minister meeting only various replicas of himself. Bennett claimed that he wanted to consult and use his colleagues but had found them unreliable. In tariff negotiations with Australia, carried out at the beginning of the new regime, he tried to get the help of his trade minister, Harry Stevens, but Stevens made a mess that Bennett and Skelton had to clean up. Skelton, although agreeing that the cabinet was not very impressive, urged the prime minister to let up on his punishing schedule. Bennett took no notice. If he worked himself to death, so be it. Men's whole lives turned on slight twists of chance, and there was nothing to do but accept what fate had to offer. Skelton was inclined to the same view.[21]

Bennett liked to hear advice and contrary points of view. Skelton liked to dispense them. Yet it was hard to alter the prime minister's unshakeable conviction that he knew best. When Stevens suggested that Skelton head a council from labour, industry, and the universities to study unemployment, Bennett rejected "such nonsense." "Do they think I want a lot of long-haired professors telling me what to do? If I can't run this country, I will get out." "He is the darndest man to *teach* anything," Skelton complained. "He always knows something about a subject – I never met a man who knows something about so many things – but he never knows enough & no matter how much I try to enlarge on any particular things – at the end of the interview he will be back to exactly the little & the few facts he had at the beginning." Isabel wrote to her mother that Bennett asked for Oscar "so frequently" but "seemingly wants him only to confirm his own conclusions." OD thought it useful that Bennett felt the need to justify himself "to me & that is quite a brake on him." His wife was less sure: "Poor Oscar – he can't 'teach him' but he flatters himself he is a 'brake' & perhaps he is."[22]

Underlining Isabel's scepticism about his influence, Skelton was excluded from the prime minister's inner circle when Bennett travelled to Washington in early 1931 for discussions with Herbert Hoover, the engineer-president of the United States, who was bewildered by an economic depression that he could not comprehend. OD found life with the prime minister exhausting, and was relieved at the "great peace" that descended after he left town, but it hurt that Bennett, while relying on him for extensive policy and logistical preparations, did not think to bring him along to meet Hoover. Returning a few days later, Bennett railed against the opulence and impracticability of Canada's U.S. Legation and claimed that the staff, although fine as individuals, did not have enough to do. Skelton demurred. His men were busier than the occupants of any other diplomatic post in Washington, except possibly the British Embassy. Bennett filled the position of minister to the United States, vacant since Massey had left it the previous summer, with William Herridge, his confidant, soon to be his brother-in-law. Skelton got along with Herridge, telling Bennett that it was a good appointment. He had not been consulted in advance, but no one else was either.[23]

Neither Skelton nor Bennett drew a line between the work of the prime minister's office and that of the Department of External Affairs, so that the practice of employing the department and its people for all manner of government tasks continued. OD encouraged the habit as a means of underlining the usefulness of his department. Early on, he offered one of his young men as a secretary to the overworked prime minister. Skelton was happy to oblige when Bennett asked him to prepare for a meeting with the provinces to discuss the position of the Canadian constitution under the Statute of Westminster. That request fit with a Skelton area of expertise, but it was the first time that Bennett had relied on External Affairs for a major enterprise. "I never had material worked up in better shape for me than this by you & your men," the prime minister said. "If there were a few more departments like yours the Civil Service would be above all criticism." For the 1932 Dominion-Provincial Conference, Skelton's assistance was again sought. This time the agenda included unemployment insurance and relief for the disadvantaged, far from his department's bailiwick but exactly the sort of subject he had tackled for King.[24]

With his training and background, Skelton was an obvious target for exchanges with the prime minister about the economy. After less than six months of office, Bennett knew the country was in a depression, but OD did not find his explanation of events very sophisticated. Bennett seemed to think that the chief problems were laziness, extravagance, rash speculation, and dishonest promotion. What the country needed was a dose of religion and hard work. That was not likely, Skelton responded, to be a popular public message. Bennett was taking too little account of the underlying causes of the Depression, many of which came from outside the country and were beyond the power of Canadians to control. The prime minister airily promised to make a speech with an analysis along those lines "some day."[25]

An exchange-rate crisis struck in late 1931, and the value of the Canadian dollar fell precipitously. Skelton and Bennett mulled over the problem, OD adding his voice to those calling for a central bank to regulate credit and monetary questions in the national interest. He worried that currency instability might drive the country into the maw of the New York money market or towards Britain's sterling area, with all the implications that had for the "eventual political alignment of Canada." He began to draw Clifford Clark, who had lost his high-paying job in New York and was back teaching at Queen's, into the prime minister's circle as a source of independent expertise. Clark's memoranda for Bennett recommended the monetary autonomy and central bank that Skelton advocated.[26]

The idea of a central bank had been widely favoured at the previous year's annual meeting of the Canadian Political Science Association, where Skelton was unanimously elected president of the recently reconstituted academic society. The band of available Canadian intellectuals was tiny, too much so, Skelton thought. He expressed pleasure at the good turnout at the gathering of young political economists, who would be needed to deal with the difficult problems that Canada was going to face over the next ten to fifteen years. The CPSA executive brimmed with colleagues he had worked with for years: S.A. Cudmore of the Dominion Bureau of Statistics was the association's secretary, and F.A. Knox of Queen's the treasurer; James Richardson, J.W. Dafoe, and W.A. Mackintosh had positions as members of the association's executive committee. Stephen Leacock, famous less as a McGill University economics professor than as an internationally popular writer of whimsical books and stories, was one of the vice-presidents. Skelton did not know him well, but he was on the other side of the debate about the British Empire and OD judged his academic credentials to be pretty insubstantial. After reading Leacock's argument for stronger imperial ties, *Economic Prosperity in the British Empire*, Skelton called it "incredible piffle for an economist supposedly in touch with political realities." He agreed with the common remark that economists considered Leacock a humourist and humourists thought him an economist. What Skelton did not acknowledge was that Leacock was a social critic who had attacked the excesses of industrial capitalism in a manner reminiscent of OD's own early writings.[27]

Skelton's predecessor as president of the CPSA was Adam Shortt, who died in 1931 at the age of seventy-two. He and Skelton were part of a small group that had kept the association alive after it had fallen by the wayside during the First World War, holding executive meetings of what was in effect a paper organization in the 1920s, and the two men were key figures in its revival. Shortt's last years were productive and happy, partly because of League of Nations work that Skelton arranged for him. OD sadly watched over his friend as he ebbed away and gave a lengthy eulogy at the Queen's Convocation, calling him typical of the university "at its best, together with much that was individual, distinctive, the mark of a vigorous personality."[28] No one had done more than Shortt to shape Skelton's academic perspective and professional career.

Skelton's CPSA presidential address dealt head on with the Depression, asking whether it spelled the bankruptcy of capitalism. The depth, range, and seriousness of the crisis could not be denied, he said, nor the serious limitations of the present economic system. For the first time in a great world crisis, the west was confronted, tempted, and taunted by a practical alternative, the daring communist experiment in Russia, which offered "a seeming way of escape, not a bookish Utopia, not a fanatic's dream, but a working model, a going concern." Skelton countered with a ringing defence of the marketplace's superior productive and distributive capacity, and of progress and growth through adaptation, experimentation, and risk. There were "serious weaknesses, as any human system, any system worked by fallible men, must have," but most of the defects could be overcome without abandoning individual initiative supplemented at its weak points by state action within a limited field. He was not about to announce the funeral of capitalism. The patient might be ill, but the organs were sound: "Our democratic, competitive western system will outlast and outgrow any system which relies upon external compulsion as the propelling force."[29]

The presidency of the CPSA was another serious responsibility taken on uncomplainingly, but Skelton was tired, "fagged out," all the time. A ten-day vacation in the Maritimes during September 1931 – loafing, swimming, golfing in a Prince Edward Island cow pasture – took the edge off his fatigue, although only that. Over the next winter, he had a number of close scrapes in his car, once swerving to avoid a streetcar, missing a telephone pole by six inches, and slamming into a snowbank – "a tight squeeze but enough," he recalled. His weak eyes and withering exhaustion probably had as much to do with these near-disasters as the icy, rut-infested roads of early 1930s Ottawa.[30]

In his free hours, he liked to divert himself by reading near the fireplace at Edgehill. Agatha Christie detective stories, with their over-clever plots and unchallenging prose, were a favourite, and he pawed away at research on Greek and Roman socialism for a revised version of his famous first book. There was occasionally a moment for a foreign film, which he preferred to "Hollywood mush," and he was intrigued by a biography of the Scottish poet Robbie Burns and a cynical farce about American journalism, *The Front Page* – "pretty hard boiled & frank if not foul spoken, but vigorous & interesting." The big garden was as much of a passion from spring to autumn as ever, but it got less of the personal touch. He consoled himself that giving the work to the poor constituted something of a personal unemployment-relief project. In 1932 he took a 10 per cent cut in salary, like all civil servants, but he was a plutocrat by Depression standards, so much so that he purchased two fur coats from China for Isabel and Sheila, each costing a staggering $1,499 plus $528 in import tax.[31]

At External Affairs he was no better at sharing authority than the prime minister, not having learned to give up even the most routine files, although he admitted to himself that they would not have "much importance a hundred years from now." Like a conscientious schoolteacher, he was proud of his charges, brought them into the detail of his work, promoted their causes with headmaster Bennett, and protected them from him. Yet he could not overcome his driving need to control his staff, which was reinforced by evidence of their immaturity and inability to produce what was needed. Mike Pearson seemed better at compiling information than distilling it into something useful, while another young officer, H.F. Feaver, had appropriated a copy of Mackenzie King's diary and was showing it around to his Conservative friends. Even legal adviser John Read, for all his experience and intelligence, was seen to lack judgment and analytical ability. There was wistfulness when OD returned to Queen's on a rain-soaked October Saturday in 1931 and observed the beauty and tranquility of the campus in the fall. He wondered again if he had been right to reject the principal's job, but characteristically allowed himself only a minute to consider what might have been.[32]

His anxieties were accelerated by family worries. Taciturn Herbert had none of the interest of the other children in intellectual or academic pursuits for their own sake. He was given standing in third-year commerce at Queen's in 1931 after completing a degree in history and philosophy at Bishop's College. The summer that separated the stints at the two schools was punctuated by research on the Canadian branch plants of American businesses at the Dominion Bureau of Statistics and some late nights of beer and gambling that were reminiscent of his older brother Sandy's student life. OD hoped that Herbert was settling down with the help of his girlfriend Daisy MacCracken, an animated nurse he had met the previous year; but he had further doubts when his son, while travelling home from Bishop's for Christmas, was stopped with some friends by a Quebec policeman for driving too fast and under the influence of alcohol. Oscar paid the fine. In early 1933 he was astounded to discover, only a couple of days before the Ottawa *Citizen* did, that Herbert and Daisy had been secretly married in Ogdensburg, New York, more than a year earlier.[33]

Sandy remained an enigmatic figure – a bit of a wild rogue to some, simply eccentric to those who were more sympathetic. After his second year at Oxford in 1929, a period interrupted by a severe illness and ending with a third-class degree in philosophy, politics, and economics that disappointed his Rhodes Scholarship sponsors, he had married Kathleen

Green, the daughter of a Canadian mother and a prominent St Louis corporation lawyer father – "an improvement over Marion," Oscar dryly noted, "as Marion was over Dolly." Sandy had met Kathleen in Oxford, and Skelton concluded that either she or the university must have had a moderating influence on his son, who "is much less socialist & much less keen to roam the outlying spaces of the earth than he was two or three years ago." Otherwise the university did not seem to have done much to change or improve him, and he had no definite professional goal. Sandy accepted a teaching position in political science at the University of Saskatchewan, which was thrilled to have him. He was much less so, complaining bitterly about the barrenness of the prairies and going off to drink himself senseless for days at a time, a regular pattern since his days at Queen's. Employing his skills as a boxer, he got into a fight with a janitor in the hall not long after he arrived in Saskatoon. The job lasted only for the academic year 1929–30. Skelton mused that no father of Sandy and Herbert could afford to be critical of other people's children.[34]

Sandy became an economist on the staff of the Montreal-based Beauharnois Power Company in 1931, the same year it became known that the company had given favours to Prime Minister Mackenzie King and Senator Andrew Haydon while receiving a late 1920s contract to divert water on the St Lawrence River for a hydroelectric project. The Beauharnois scandal was sensational political theatre, and a humiliation for King and the Liberals. Skelton, who had been very close to St Lawrence River questions in the late 1920s, feared that he would be engulfed in the controversy when auditors discovered that money had gone directly from Haydon's office to Beauharnois to cover Sandy's wages. For a short while OD wondered if a "suspicious & jealous" public "would conclude that my son had got a job as pay for my influence with the King government & that R.B. would feel I had been a Beauharnois sympathizer in his camp." The auditors' review concluded that there was nothing sinister about Sandy's position in the company or the pay that he was receiving, which may have resulted from the innocent desire of Skelton's friends to put some distance between Sandy and a company that was so closely associated with Mackenzie King and the Liberals. Bennett did not raise the matter with Skelton. He may never have known about it.[35]

Skelton loved the children, and they knew it, despite his stern lectures about thrift and responsibility and his frequent absences. He was particularly close to Sheila, who was in her teens, still at home, and displaying the frailties of both families' constitutions, including OD's awful eyes. He taught her German and the house seemed to him lifeless when she was gone. Herbert played football for Queen's as he had at Bishop's. The Queen's *Journal* described him as a "shifty ball carrier," with a reputation for "being a hard tackle and a great broken-field runner." He was not the sparkling athlete his brother had been, but OD watched his progress just as keenly, noting it in his diary when the Associated Press unjustly downgraded one of Herbert's performances and the university magazine got it right. When Sandy's job was threatened by a reorganization of the Beauharnois corporation, his father ignored a raging cold to travel to Montreal by rail on a day ticket, just to spend a few hours with a worried son and daughter-in-law. He was proud of a forceful article against tariffs and in favour of North American free trade that Sandy published in a New York periodical the next month, but the father questioned his son's judgment in drawing attention to himself when his position was in danger.[36]

OD very much wanted Canadian-American freer trade himself, for its own sake and as part of his campaign to extract Canada from Britain's grasp, but he thought that such proposals had little chance of success in the near term. The idea had thrived in the nineteenth century, he thought, because the two countries were comparatively isolated and had not yet become involved in political and economic networks on a global scale. Now the trend was towards higher tariffs, despite the good arguments that could be made against "fiscal isolation." The United States had started it, with its punitive Hawley-Smoot Tariff in 1930. Bennett too was heaping on the trade barriers, which Skelton predicted would result in the establishment of American branch plants in Canada to avoid the high-tariff wall. Even the British had decided to abandon free trade to protect their home market. The world's greatest trading nation had withdrawn into a domestic shell, he wrote to Bill Herridge in Washington, confessing "its inability to compete with its newer rivals even at home or to reorganize an antiquated industrial equipment and a rigid social structure."[37]

There was a move in the direction of economic agreements between the various self-governing parts of the empire – the British Commonwealth, as Skelton and others increasingly called it. At the Imperial Conference of 1930, Bennett invited member countries to discuss trade and economic cooperation at a meeting that he planned for Ottawa. The conference was arranged for the summer of 1932, with OD coordinating arrangements as chair of a large interdepartmental committee. Bennett told him he wanted to hire a University of Toronto professor to help lay the groundwork, saying that Skelton could not possibly object because that was exactly how King had brought OD in for the 1923 Imperial Conference. The under-secretary did object. Things were once very different in the Department of External Affairs, he insisted. It was unnecessary to go outside, because he had well-qualified, highly educated personnel with a command of economics.[38]

This was less truth than territorial imperative. There were very few people in External Affairs or, for that matter, anywhere else in the government with experience or expertise in the area of tariffs and trade agreements. Skelton before long began to involve Clifford Clark as a drafter of briefing papers. Clark was eventually named a special economic adviser to the Canadian delegation and after the conference became deputy minister of the Department of Finance. Skelton was drawing able men to government service outside as well as inside External Affairs. His example of recruiting men of "breadth and flexibility of view" was being emulated in other government departments.[39]

Neither the Ottawa economic conference nor the preparations for it went smoothly. What little Bennett would let out of his own hands went not to his officials but to the Canadian Manufacturers' Association, the natural ally of the high-tariff Conservatives. He insisted on writing the agenda himself. "We are up against the usual difficulty," the British high commissioner wrote home two months before the conference was to begin, "that the Prime Minister would not allow anything to be done until he can handle matters himself." The agenda was put in final form only two weeks in advance of the conference's beginning. As the British were about to sail for Canada, Bennett finally let them have his personal list of requests for concessions, far too late for them to give any intelligent response before the meeting. Isabel reported to her family Oscar's impression that Bennett was tired, irritable, and foul-tempered. "His day is just one succession of quarrels with his own ministers, to say nothing of the Press & the Civil Service."[40]

The conference opened in the blistering heat of an Ottawa summer, not calculated to put participants in the best of moods, and it continued for most of July and August. Skelton was the conference secretary, watching with bemusement as the meeting degenerated into the most bitter and divisive in the long and controversial history of imperial conferences. The Canadian leader was brusque and badly prepared, and contrived to be both domineering and capricious. One member of the British delegation, the combative dominions secretary, Jimmy Thomas, was convinced that Bennett was tapping the British telephones, while the chancellor of the exchequer, Neville Chamberlain, said that their host was a liar who made progress impossible and cried when he did not get his way. Only at the last minute was it possible to pin Bennett down to an agreement, which turned out to be far short of original hopes. Chamberlain, who had been very partial to Canada beforehand, said he never wanted to see the country again.[41]

Skelton was not surprised, but he was sympathetic to Bennett, who put himself and was put under such enormous pressure. Yet OD was not the best judge: he was some distance away from the epicentre of his prime minister's conference explosions. Skelton's role was not his usual one of adviser; he had no formal connection to the Canadian delegation. He sat where Sir Maurice Hankey habitually did as the Imperial Conference's chief administrative officer – keeping track of nine national delegations, coordinating their schedules, answering daily logistical gripes, greasing the path to the final communiqué. This was the first major Imperial Conference held outside England. There was no institutional memory in Ottawa, and Skelton had no experience in stage-managing big events. He muddled through, imagining that he had done his best and that the conference had not gone too badly, or least that the result was more satisfactory than he had at times thought it would turn out to be. But how much better the result could have been, he told his wife, had there not been such a chaotic rush to the finish line, or if RB had taken him into his confidence and allowed him see the agreements beforehand. At the final session, Isabel proudly wrote her mother, she heard the leader of every single delegation praise Skelton by name. One declared he was second to none among the public servants of the world.[42]

At the end of 1932, Skelton was offered a knighthood in recognition of his Ottawa conference services. The instigator, he thought, was Jimmy Thomas in London, but Bennett was a happy collaborator because he wanted to revive the British-style honours system that had been discontinued in Canada after the First World War. OD suspected that he was being lured into an empire trap and used to blunt criticism of the Bennett initiative, to which the prime minister was attracted "partly because of his Tory mentality & partly because of the usefulness of such toys in managing men & playing politics." No doubt recalling Sir Wilfrid Laurier's reception in certain quarters after his knighthood was proclaimed at the end of the nineteenth century, Skelton declined the bauble without the slightest regret. "I was not keen on being made the spearhead for that movement & the joke of all my radical friends, to say nothing of my own dislike for such distinctions both on social & on nationalist grounds." Isabel "did not have my scruples." When RB announced the first New Year's honours list in sixteen years, Skelton suffered some embarrassment when congratulations came from those who thought he was bound to be included and commiseration when they discovered he was not. He was surprised by how little condemnation there was in the capital of the Bennett honours. "Of course Ottawa is hardly a fair sample of the country, as it contains an abnormally high proportion of people on whom the lightning might fall next time."[43]

Skelton decried the unappetizing pattern of economic discrimination against countries outside the empire represented by the twelve bilateral "Ottawa Agreements." The nations of the world were turning in on themselves, and his own country was as bad as all the rest. When Bennett had recently instituted an embargo on most of the imports from the Soviet Union, OD forcefully disagreed. The Bolsheviks were the "enemies of liberty," but that was not sufficient reason for refusing to trade with them. The flourish of a holy war against this or that evil might be emotionally satisfying, but it was damaging to the fabric of international relationships and went against the grain of a cooperative economic order. In the face of provocative American protectionism and fears that Britain's declining world position had occasioned, the Ottawa Agreements were understandable and perhaps even defensible, but they had the regrettable effect of "hardening & perpetuating tariff wars."[44]

The 1932 economic conference raised another concern. The delegates agreed to strike a task force that would meet in London the next year to examine imperial economic boards and agencies. One of these was the Imperial Economic Committee, about which Skelton had been complaining since its creation over his opposition at the 1923 Imperial Conference. He was convinced that the British were going to follow up on the Ottawa conference with a proposal for "a central committee – permanent – in London to handle all economic questions for all the King's dominions." Bennett chose Skelton to represent him at the London meetings, although the prime minister made it clear that he wanted to make any final decisions that might be required. Isabel glumly told her mother that Oscar was anticipating another tough encounter with an empire that was not done yet: "It is not exactly a plum R.B. has given him."[45]

In late January 1933, Skelton assembled two trunks, two suitcases, a hatbox, and an attaché case and departed for the port of New York en route to England. Once he was aboard the gigantic Cunard liner *Aquitania*, his suspicion that the economic task force was not a low-level affair was reinforced when a press photographer representing the Toronto

Star and other Canadian newspapers tried to take his picture. "I declined
to pose," he wrote home. Ample meals, saltwater baths, films, detective
stories, and desultory preparations for "my confounded committee" followed, but he avoided the gambling with "English sportin' gents and New
York Jews," where big sums were wagered "in spite of the Depression."
After a week, the nine hundred passengers and crew arrived in Southampton to bright blue skies that did not last long. At the Waterloo train
station in London, he was greeted by a correspondent from the *Times*
and an impressive group of British officials, including the ceremonial
officer of the Dominions Office, who was shocked that "the Canadian
minister" was wearing an ordinary working man's cap. Skelton playfully
informed Isabel that they had thought "that I was somebody really important." Colonel Georges Vanier, serving at the High Commission in Trafalgar Square, and Mike Pearson, who had been helping out at the League
in Geneva, accompanied their boss to his familiar haunt at the May Fair
Hotel in Piccadilly. Vanier served as Skelton's second-in-command at the
meetings, and Pearson as the Canadian team's secretary.[46]

More evidence of the committee's prominence came with an invitation from the British prime minister to Chequers, his weekend retreat in
the Chiltern Hills about thirty miles from London. Ramsay MacDonald,
the aging Labour leader who had abandoned his party to form a national
government with the Conservatives, "looked tired, preoccupied, & self-
centred as usual," but he was pleasant and gracious, showing off the historic Elizabethan house from basement to attic. Skelton and Pearson
saw an inscription over the garden gate, "Abandon care all ye who enter
here," and OD concluded that it ought to be rewritten to reflect "Ramsay Mac's" betrayal of his socialist principles: "Abandon radicalism all ye
who enter here." The prime minister had been entirely corrupted by the
establishment and by ornaments like Chequers, with its fine antiques
and art. "The English governing classes," her husband assured Isabel,
"certainly know what they are doing."[47]

Skelton was surprised to come under pressure from the British to pre-
side over the task force's work. It made him suspicious, "as it looked
like a move to muzzle me in the Chair, & to make me responsible for
the report." He preferred to leave that role to one of the British delegates, Sir Horace Wilson, the government's chief industrial adviser, or
Sir Fabian Ware, the vice-chair of the Imperial War Graves Commission.
Wilson, who had been an important figure at the 1932 Imperial Conference, was the better of the two from Skelton's standpoint, "as he is not so
ultra-imperialist as Ware & is anathema to R.B., so that I'd be much more

likely to find support in opposing him than in differing from Ware." But Wilson refused the chair and vetoed his bureaucratic adversary Ware, who badly wanted the position. That left the Australian delegate, a dismal prospect since he was certain to be foursquare behind the British in desiring an imperial economic general staff. Skelton consulted with Pearson and Vanier and the other delegations and reluctantly "decided as the lesser evil to take the job. It will mean more work & some difficult corners, but I'll insist that I'll be free to talk as Canada's representative as well as Chairman."[48]

The deliberations of the Imperial Committee on Economic Consultation and Cooperation within the Commonwealth began formally on 14 February. Putting Skelton forward as chair, Ware praised his unsurpassed administrative experience "in the service of the British Empire" and his "strict and honorable impartiality." The Canadian parried that he would be giving up his neutrality from time to time to help his colleagues present distinctive national points of view. He played with the committee's cumbersome title – should they call it the Four C's or the Seven Seas? – but went too far in jokingly introducing Wilson as the next "victim" to give a speech, eliciting a sharp response from him, with the implication that Skelton was being insufficiently serious and constructive.[49]

In the Skelton Committee, as it rapidly became known, OD lined up in now-traditional style beside South Africa and Ireland against the British, Australians, New Zealanders, and representatives of Newfoundland, India, and various colonial governments. The year before, the South Africans and Irish had made it clear at the Ottawa conference that they wanted no part of an imperial economic secretariat, or any similar organ of centralization. So had Bennett's Canadians, but not quite so explicitly, and there were hopes in the British camp that the 1933 meeting would agree to a measure of close economic interaction and the establishment of some form of all-encompassing coordinating agency. Yet the British and their allies found that the "Skelton crowd" were "a complete stumbling block," opposed to centralized imperial institutions and dead set on having their way. A.C.D. Rivett, an Australian close to the scene asked, "What is the matter with Canada? A virus disease of sorts or just sheer cussedness resting on twisted pride?" For Jimmy Thomas, the dominions secretary who had wanted to dispense a knighthood to OD a short time earlier, there was no mystery. Skelton was what was the matter with Canada. After a month of the committee's work, Thomas introduced Skelton at a British government luncheon as an exponent of "Canada first, Canada second, the Empire third, and the rest also rans."[50]

Skelton was generally pleased with the calibre of the members and the secretariat of his committee, although entirely too many of them were inclined to put an "imperial slant" on things. In the first phase of the proceedings, he had to endure testimony from representatives of the flock of boards and institutes under scrutiny, meticulously explaining to "these blooming Colonials" why they ought to be proud to provide the cash for the empire's schemes. He complained that every one of "these confounded imperial organizations, once launched, has given half its time to propaganda and planning to make itself permanent and secure fresh funds." The Empire Marketing Board (EMB), charged with promoting and publicizing the food exports of the colonies and dominions in the British market, had been particularly clever at creating vested interests and had to be eliminated before it took further root. Once it was given £500,000 a year to spend for five years, "the whole British Empire would be so dependent on it that it couldn't be abolished & would be a dominating centralizing force." Yet the EMB had strong support, and Skelton doubted "how far when it comes to the pinch, I'll be able to persuade R.B. to back me up, in alliance with the Irish & the S. Africans."[51]

The South Africans and Irish delegates were to some extent shackled in their opposition to central planning, because they had come to London without a mandate from their governments. Skelton decided that he alone could counter the strong momentum that was developing not simply for the retention of the EMB but also in the direction of a permanent imperial central body. He prepared "a cold douche on distinctly Skeltonian principles of Empire co-operation" and had Vanier read it out to the committee on 20 March, "to preserve my impartiality as Chairman." The speech caused a great "sensation," Oscar reminisced for the family's benefit, knocking "the wind out of most of the delegations & there was quite a strained air as if a corpse had suddenly been found in the room." If Bennett did not back him up, he would have to compromise, but "I'll try it on."[52]

The committee knew now how much it differed, but not yet what it would be possible to agree upon. Meetings grew sharper and more prolonged. Consensus on the tough issues, the EMB continuing to be the toughest, seemed doubtful. At the end of March, Skelton wrote: "It looks at present as if we could agree on about 60 per cent of the field, and as to the rest we will simply have to set out our varying views in the Report to the several Governments and let them decide." Sliding between the delegations, he demonstrated an ability to bring together disparate views and a willingness to compromise, notably on the Imperial Economic

Committee, which he was prepared to keep along with some other imperial remnants – just so long as there was to be no EMB or central economic authority with a roving commission and the inevitable bureaucratic impulse to spend and expand. On 4 April he announced to Isabel "progress toward the Canadian point of view," but it remained "very hard to convert a majority convinced they're right & convinced that when the Governments receive our recommendations ... they'll show themselves more imperialistic."[53]

Everyone understood the importance of unanimity if the report was to have any weight, and the Irish and South African members were putting up roadblocks of their own, making the Skelton position seem not quite so radical. The British gave way, along the lines OD had suggested, and with them their allies. They realized (as the London *Times* grumbled) that "meagre" proposals were "the maximum to which all could agree," with the unfortunate result that "the amount of co-operative effort for the common benefit is to be diminished instead of being increased." Skelton thought it anything but unfortunate, but he praised the "very good spirit in the Committee" and had some sympathy for his defeated colleagues: "Our committee report will be a great disappointment for the imperialists; I didn't think it possible two weeks ago that we could have got the UK, Australia, New Zealand & the Colonies to agree to it; but we stuck to our guns & they had to come to us."[54]

OD had become an accomplished meeting-goer. His letters home from the Skelton Committee were full of the social side of diplomacy, which he carried out generously and strategically, if often reluctantly. His puckish sense of humour made a shy person accessible. Collegiality led to coalition building. He negotiated differences and made the concessions necessary to achieve consensus. There was cunning too. In reporting to Bennett, who might not have liked everything Skelton was up to, he painted a picture of himself and his work that was different from what was actually taking place. He did not admit what he his committee adversaries saw all too readily: that he had been an advocate of "a degree of co-operation even more limited" than the radical Irish and South Africans had been prepared to accept.[55]

He need not have worried about Bennett's attitude towards what he was doing. The prime minister's approval of the Skelton report came readily, and he wanted no part of any suggestion that it could be overturned. When he was in Geneva the following summer, Bennett was approached by Sir Fabian Ware, who predictably saw the report as a "damned packet of death warrants." Bennett's response to Ware's plea that the Canadian government revisit Skelton's work was brief and brutal. Ware and his friends had signed the document; they must live with it. Bennett knew nothing, and wanted to know nothing, of the pros and cons of the issue. At the same time he said how much he loved the empire, delivering a harangue to a meeting of Commonwealth representatives on the need for more imperial cooperation.[56] That was the rhetorical Bennett. He was always more of a Canadian nationalist, and so closer to Skelton's views, than his bluster suggested. The British had discovered that at the 1932 Imperial Conference in Ottawa.

Skelton had adapted himself, and his department, to a combustible prime minister. Bennett returned the favour. RB came to like and admire OD, and implicitly allowed him to persist in his independence campaign. The London trip was the under-secretary's first prolonged absence since the Conservatives had taken office. Bennett wrote from Ottawa in the warmest possible terms to his deputy, gossiping about the time his Liberal friends had been wasting in the House of Commons while he was away, letting him know how much he was missed, and yet encouraging him to enjoy himself "if that is possible for one who works as hard as you do."[57] A letter in that easy and comfortable tone from Mackenzie King was unimaginable.

10
The Moderate Leaguer, 1933–5

In mid-March 1933, Skelton travelled from London to the League of Nations in Geneva, immediately after the international community's condemnation of Japanese aggression in the Chinese province of Manchuria and Adolf Hitler's ruthless consolidation of power in Germany. OD was not anxious to leave his work on the Skelton Committee, because that would prolong his absence from his department and his family. But R.B. Bennett insisted on it. "I thought it well that you should go to Geneva," the prime minister wrote good-naturedly, "for reasons that I fancy are obvious *even* to yourself."[1]

Skelton imagined that he was wanted at the League to demonstrate that the government took seriously the downward spiral of world events. He was sure that there was nothing he or Canada alone could do to reverse the tide, but certain that disaster loomed unless a collective sense of international responsibility took hold, to be followed by collective action. Governments and the people who controlled them had better apply themselves to achieve broad-based solutions to the mammoth economic and geopolitical problems that marked off the dangerous 1930s from the desultory 1920s. Civilization could not endure another great war.[2]

The crisis in the Pacific had erupted after Japanese military forces attacked the Manchurian capital of Mukden in the autumn of 1931. Already with a foothold in Manchuria under treaties of long standing, Japan seized complete control of the whole territory, turning it into the puppet state of Manchukuo. Sensing challenge and opportunity, the League moved against Japan, but just enough to alienate Tokyo without altering Japanese attitudes or behaviour. Skelton deeply regretted the League's inability to restrain Japan, but, like most of Geneva's putative

supporters, he was fearful of the risks that members would have to take
to enforce the peace, especially when the burdens of the institution's
membership were not distributed equally. Although long away from
trouble and safe from attack, Canada would be asked to do more than
its fair share if the League decided to confront an aggressor. Skelton
believed that something had to be done about Tokyo, but nothing too
dramatic or ambitious. The League must learn to mediate disputes, not
imagine that its work was to mete out punishment.[3]

Skelton received his first intelligence about the Manchurian imbroglio
from Hugh Keenleyside of the Department of External Affairs. Skelton
had sent Keenleyside to the Legation in Tokyo to keep an eye on Herbert
Marler, the Canadian minister to Japan, appointed for his wealth, social
standing, and good Liberal Party credentials, not his skill or experience
in international affairs. "Ivory from the neck up," was a common view
of the stiff and stuffy Marler. With the minister absent from Japan, his
young assistant wrote tough but balanced dispatches describing for the
under-secretary the Japanese army's guilt in initiating the emergency
and Tokyo's inability to restore civilian control. When Marler returned
to the Japanese capital, he took a kindlier view. China was an unruly, chaotic pretense of a country that had repeatedly violated Japan's commercial rights in Manchuria and treated Japanese nationals shabbily. Japan
had no territorial ambitions, nor was it seeking to gain something it did
not already own. Its position in China was no different from that of the
United States, which had staked out and now protected its interests in
Latin America. That was what great powers did.[4]

Skelton complimented Marler on "a very vigorous and acute analysis
of the situation" but at the same time admonished him for giving Japan
"rather too clean a bill of health." The Japanese had real grievances
and vital interests in Manchuria, there was no doubt, but "the question
remains whether she did not violate her treaty engagements in the steps
taken to assert her rights. I am inclined to think that she has, and the fact
that other Imperialist powers have taken similar action in the past does
not justify a breach of the higher code of international conduct which
the world has been endeavouring to build up since the Great War." Marler's "beloved Japs," Skelton spit out contemptuously as the crisis wore
on.[5]

Skelton coupled the developing Pacific emergency with the growing
popularity of fascism in Germany. They were both "threatening clouds,"
and it would be "a testing time for the League." Horrified though he was
by what he saw as clear evidence of Japanese lawlessness in Manchuria,

followed up by more of the same in early 1932 at the port of Shanghai a thousand kilometres to the south, he did not support the use of force against Japan. He could not stifle the uncharitable thought that, as they called on all countries to promise assistance in advance should European peace be disturbed, countries like France would not dream of coming to the aid of China or, for that matter, Canada, if they were attacked by a great power. Paris and its friends imagined it "all right if it is our teeth to be put into Germany but not quite so if it's France that has to provide the teeth to bite Japan."[6]

Skelton was "frankly prejudiced" against League of Nations economic and military sanctions, the instruments in the League Covenant for the punishment of aggressors. They were blunt instruments, he thought, likely to be both ineffective and unworkable. Military action against Japan would be "fighting the devil with fire"; he doubted the possibility "of ending war by going to war." As to an economic embargo aimed at the Japanese, it could only with difficulty stop short of conflict. Canada, furthermore, would carry a heavy responsibility for the boycott's enforcement. When members of the League of Nations Society in Canada visited Skelton to discuss the possibility that Geneva ought to "act energetically," he said that translated into "our acting energetically, prohibiting not only our own Canadian trade with Japan but that of the United States." He had no desire to clash with the United States for the sake of the League.[7]

In the League as Skelton conceived it, the first duty of members was to exhaust every possible means of restoring peace through the conciliatory and mediatory measures that had proved their value over time, "before resorting to other methods whose efficacy is untried and whose consequences are incalculable." He was not without hope that the prospect of unanimous and concentrated world disapproval would strengthen the forces for peace in Japan. If the flagrant violation of League principles continued, Canada would have to consider sanctions while knowing that they were best used only to get Japan's attention and that they had next to no public or media support.[8]

To Skelton's "plain man," there might be "no doubt that Japan has made war on China in Manchuria, and that it is as definitely the aggressor as any country can well be." Yet among the governing, in countries where the burden of enforcement would fall, no support could be found for ordering military or even economic penalties under the Covenant. The British, from whom Bennett liked to take advice, were utterly unwilling to engage Japan over Manchuria. Nor would the United States join in an economic blacklist, despite Secretary of State Henry Stimson's demands that the Japanese be confronted by their sins. So it was up to the French and others who boosted sanctions to show their hand first. They were predictably nowhere to be seen. "Every country," Skelton concluded, "has too many troubles of its own today to go knight-erranting; it cannot afford to cut off trade even with sinners."[9]

Skelton and Bennett aired the Far Eastern affair infrequently but with considerable emotion. Both were outraged by Japanese aggression. At the end of January 1932, Skelton told the prime minister that the action at Shanghai placed Tokyo irrevocably in the wrong, stripping away the veneer of Japanese national respectability. Bennett replied that he would condemn their callous brutality in the House of Commons, but Skelton was anxious to contain his superior's indignation. Only restraint would keep Canada out of the international spotlight, which a small power and its leader ought to avoid. Most of the time, OD did succeed in keeping the private prime minister from becoming public, assisted by his overloaded daily schedule and intermittent interest in the details of international issues. Bennett was content to trust his deputy's judgment, so Skelton flattered himself, on the grounds of "my greater experience and knowledge." Behave "as if I was P.M. & had the responsibility," Skelton was told when asked to invent a response to a parliamentary question from J.S. Woodsworth, the pacifist member of Parliament who wanted "do something" against Japan. It did not take long before Bennett let Skelton know his views on the matter, which, OD wrote in his diary, "fortunately coincided largely" with his own.[10]

RB and his political colleagues were an unpredictable commodity. For a special session of the League in late 1932, the government agreed to take the carefully modulated line worked out by Skelton, favouring the constructive rather than the punitive "in the hope of working out a solution which will take account both of Japan's desire to save its face, and of China's political chaos." Two of the prime minister's brash allies, however, had different ideas. Bill Herridge, Canada's diplomat in Washington, told the American secretary of state that the Canadian government wanted to identify itself with the United States in condemning Japanese aggression outright. Meanwhile, cabinet minister C.H. Cahan, dispatched to the League to speak for Ottawa, improvised a strongly anti-Chinese speech in a coordinated effort with the British to head off a bloc of smaller states urging the censure of Japan. Herridge and Cahan were pulling in diametrically opposite directions, neither approved by the administration they represented.[11]

A discomfited Skelton set out to repair the damage. He gently apologized to the Chinese and, receiving the warm thanks of the Japanese minister, did not refuse to accept them, "thinking we had better keep at least one friend for the time being." He expected the Americans to be forgiving, and they were, but had "they not known that we Canadians are simple folk unversed in the ways of diplomatic intrigue, they would have thought that we had double-crossed them."[12]

Much of Skelton's irritation was reserved for Cahan and his collusion with the British, but the under-secretary also directed his unhappiness downward, to Canada's permanent representative at the League, Walter Riddell. "I may observe," he wrote stiffly to Riddell after the Cahan speech, "that the useful custom of consultation between Commonwealth delegates at League Assemblies can hardly be continued if it takes the form of submission 'on approval' of the views of the Canadian Government to the British Secretary of State for Foreign Affairs." Riddell had a responsibility to ensure that Canada's League delegates did not drift away from "the general policies of the government." This was unfair, since Riddell had tried his best with Cahan, who refused to disclose what he was up to or show the text of his remarks to Skelton's employee. Soon thereafter Skelton sought to replace Riddell in Geneva with Hume Wrong, then stationed in the United States.[13] Wrong, tart-tongued but intellectually brilliant, was one of Skelton's boys. Riddell was not.

Cahan gave his unorthodox speech when Bennett was on board ship in the mid-Atlantic. Immediately upon landing in England, the prime minister summoned his colleague for a dressing down. The meeting did not take place as anticipated. Away from Skelton and closely in touch with British officials, Bennett told Cahan that he was pleased with his address and invited him to return to the fray in Geneva at Britain's side. Then Bennett returned to Canada, where OD sat him down for "the most serious discussion he had ever had with the Prime Minister," convincing him that they must return to the moderation and caution of their original position. Minister Cahan was brought home immediately. Bennett defended him briefly in the House of Commons but left Cahan to do most of the talking himself.[14]

Such was Bennett-style foreign policy, well meaning but haphazard, uneven, makeshift, and allowing Cahan and other diplomatic amateurs to make up their own rules as they went along. The prime minister from time to time trumpeted his conviction that League membership brought with it serious obligations that could not be set aside. That belief occasionally, but only occasionally, seized policy, as it did when Bennett agreed to Canadian participation in a League of Nations negotiations committee established in early 1933 to seek solutions to the Manchurian dispute. From London, Skelton counselled against the move, but the committee came to nothing. Last-ditch efforts at a settlement of the Manchurian crisis had already failed. Japan, comparing itself to Christ on the cross, announced its withdrawal from the League.[15]

When OD arrived in Geneva in March 1933, the city was momentarily the capital of Europe, the centre of planning, gossip, and, for some, guarded optimism when resigned gloom had been the mood. The League's Disarmament Conference was opening its second year. Prime Minister Ramsay MacDonald was in Switzerland to put his personal prestige behind a new British formula that Skelton believed had the potential to bring sufficient general agreement on the reduction of weapons to prevent Germany from tearing up the 1919 Treaty of Versailles and France from insisting on enforcement of a tough peace.[16]

MacDonald presented his dramatic proposals to the League Assembly on 16 March, with Skelton only a few feet away. He retailed the common view to Isabel that "Ramsay" was "a tired man, & overdid the evangelical appeal & schoolmastery scolding, but in spots it was eloquent & impressive." The British plan was "not new & is distinctly British in that it involves no British concessions," but it had merits, coming "at an opportune time when everybody is tired of detailed discussions & fearful of the consequences of a breakdown, so there are good chances that something will come of it." Those words, directed at his wife, considerably overemphasized Skelton's enthusiasm for the idea, but he was encouraged by MacDonald's inclusion of a visit to Rome in his itinerary, because that would help to prevent Italy's fascist leader, Benito Mussolini, from "giving too much backing to his crazy imitators in Germany."[17]

OD was out of sorts. His stomach did not travel well. He was fighting a bad attack of diarrhoea with a combination of hydrochloric acid and a morning cocoa. He considered himself simply part of a political show, "eyewash ... designed to make the Canadian public realize Canada is on the disarmament job, even if as a matter of fact we will & can do nothing." His companion on the trip, the Canadian high commissioner to the United Kingdom and a former Ontario premier, Howard Ferguson, was likeable enough but a lightweight, soaking up the whisky and talking too much. Attempts "to suppress him" failed, and Skelton was left with the embarrassing consequences. He scurried from the Council to what was left of the Manchurian issue to sessions on air-power disarmament, but he felt on the periphery, concluding that meetings with the powerful

British were a "quite a farce so far as any real discussion went." "Having nothing to do," he wrote his wife, "we're extremely busy doing it."[18]

The British asked Skelton to underwrite the MacDonald Plan. OD was reluctant because one of its articles stipulated that a breach of the 1928 Pact of Paris would trigger obligatory action under the League Covenant – more commitments for Canada, in other words. London's officials kept up the pressure, and he reluctantly gave in, perhaps because of his deepening anxiety at the terror being orchestrated by Hitler's "reckless gangsters." "Nazi forces are drunk with success and seek victims for suppressed emotions," he wired Bennett at the end of March. "Some of their leaders neurotic and irresponsible, others slowly gaining responsibility but unable to restrain forces they have aroused." Skelton was appalled by Hitler's treatment of Jews and threats that German Judaism would be eradicated if foreign disapproval of the Nazis did not cease. Once back in London, he visited the Foreign Office to make his concerns about the plight of German Jews known, reporting home that attacks on German Jews were "dangerous & disgusting" but the British government was not prepared to intervene.[19]

Skelton's week in Geneva, sandwiched between meetings of the Imperial Committee on Economic Consultation and Co-operation, had been frantic. He rushed from meeting to meeting – from the Air Committee to the Committee of Twenty-Two on Manchuria – and visited with officials at League headquarters, delegates and staff from Britain and France, diplomats from the United States, and "all the Canadians in Geneva." He also spent time with Walter Riddell, talking over administration and personnel problems that the Canadian Advisory Office was encountering. Policy was not discussed because the Canadian position on the League was scant and rested wholly with Bennett and Skelton. Riddell complained about how cramped his office space was; with encouragement, he might be able to find more ample quarters. In response, "Dr. Skelton merely smiled," the diplomat wrote in his diary. OD told Riddell that $3,000 was likely to be provided to bring Norman Robertson on to the Advisory Office staff. He also said that he regarded Robertson as "by far the best authority on economic and financial matters in the Department," adding that the External Affairs entrance exams had shown him to be "quite as competent" as Mike Pearson, usually thought the most impressive of the department's younger officers. Neither man was sent to the Geneva office, although Pearson sometimes came temporarily there from London, where he was posted from 1935 to 1941. Skelton kept Robertson close by in Ottawa.[20]

When he thought about it, Skelton took some of the blame for the poor communication between Ottawa and Canada's office at the League of Nations. He vowed to do better in the future, but he made no changes to his overstuffed daily agenda and did not check his urge to control every aspect of departmental business. The reading and analysis of dispatches from overseas consumed him, and his diplomats complained about the infrequency of his replies and the inadequate numbers of available staff. In Ottawa he had to cope with the demands from the missions in London, Paris, Washington, and Tokyo, along with a smattering of consuls and consuls general representing foreign countries who devoured his time with social duties and visits to the office. The Japanese minister, lobbying hard for Tokyo's point of view, had been a frequent caller during the Manchurian crisis.

OD's schedule was full of compulsory audiences with a high-pressure prime minister, often taking place after a substantial wait; representations from special interests; studying correspondence and dictating replies; and meetings with staff, officials from other departments and agencies, diplomats, and politicians. He rushed lunch, unless it could be used for business. Only infrequently did he have an opportunity to turn to his small second desk, where he wrote position papers and brooded over longer documents; that work usually had to be held for the evenings and weekends. After a grey Friday in January 1934, he scribbled in his diary the bureaucrat's epitaph: "A day of routine, no let up, constant tension, calls, telephones, and at end what accomplished?"[21]

Like Mackenzie King before him, Bennett treated External Affairs as a personal fiefdom. Raids for administrators of commissions or conference secretaries were commonplace. The department had about 140 employees, a number that remained stable in the first half of the 1930s, but a bare handful of these were foreign-service officers at the under-secretary's disposal in Ottawa and most of this small group were of junior rank. Skelton pressed for more men for his department and more posts abroad to reinforce the notion of diplomatic autonomy and diminish the dependence on British sources of information.[22]

Bennett did not always say no. The largest intake of foreign-service officers took place by competition in 1933–4, when four third-secretary positions were filled. The applicants who advanced to the final stage were interviewed in depth by Skelton and his colleagues, Laurent Beaudry and John Read, at the offices of the Public Service Commission. Afterwards, they were brought before the prime minister, where Bennett (with OD fiddling nervously with the blinds in the background) quizzed

"My Goddess Queen": Isabel Murphy at the end of 1897, around the time when she met Oscar Skelton for the first time. The impact from his perspective was immediate, but she took her time. They married in 1904. (The Menzies and Skelton Family)

Booklovers Magazine, where Skelton found a home as an editor while he plotted a more fulfilling career. Cosmopolitan elegance was the magazine's message. Less than a year after this July 1904 issue was published, *Booklovers* and the enterprises surrounding it came crashing down. (*Booklovers Magazine*)

The ambitious John A. Macdonald Professor of Political Economy at Queen's University around 1910, two years into the job, thirty-two years of age, and his eyes looking beyond the university. Though self-contained, Skelton was popular with students because of his keen interest in them, his dry wit, and his engagement with contemporary issues. (Library and Archives Canada, C-26030)

Skelton's Department of Political Economy, Queen's University, c. 1916. He dreams in the centre, a man apart. From the left, Humfrey Michell, W.N. Sage, Skelton, W.C. Clark, W.E. Macpherson. (Queen's University Archives)

Isabel Skelton, standing on the right beside her son Sandy, along with the other Skelton children, Herbert and Sheila, and Isabel's mother, Jeannie Murphy. Sandy stood out. He was smart, athletic, handsome, and a handful. (The Menzies and Skelton Family)

Skelton, at the right, on the porch of Mackenzie King's Gatineau Hills cottage, with the prime minister and his sister, 29 July 1923. The King-Skelton alliance was sealed that summer. (Library and Archives Canada, C-26031)

At the League of Nations in Geneva, Switzerland, 1928: from left to right, Skelton; Philippe Roy, Canada's minister to France; League perennial Senator Raoul Dandurand; Mackenzie King; Charles Dunning, minister of railways and canals; and W.A. Riddell, Canadian advisory officer at the League. Riddell was well intentioned but troublesome. (Library and Archives Canada, C-9055)

Skelton is featured in the Montreal *Standard* in March 1928 as the sophisticated leader of Canada's "Institute of Diplomats." Three years earlier, Arthur Racey's cartoon and the accompanying article by H.F. Gadsby had ridiculed Skelton as an overstuffed acolyte of the prime minister. (Montreal *Standard*)

Departing on the *Empress of Australia*, 1 October 1929, for the Conference
on the Operation of Dominion Legislation and Merchant Shipping Legisla-
tion, left to right: Maurice Ollivier, law clerk of the House of Commons;
H.E.A. Hawken, assistant deputy minister of marine and fisheries; Skelton;
Ernest Lapointe, minister of justice; Halifax lawyer Charles Burchell;
C.P. Plaxton of the Department of Justice; and External Affairs legal adviser
John E. Read. The dapper Lapointe dominates the picture, and, with Skelton
at his elbow, he dominated the conference that drafted the 1931 Statute of
Westminster. (Library and Archives Canada, C-5822)

The celebrated *Winnipeg Free Press* cartoonist Arch Dale depicts Prime Minister
R.B. Bennett at the cabinet table surrounded by fellow Bennetts, January 1931.
The *Free Press* was a resolutely Liberal newspaper, but this was already the common view of how Bennett did business – by himself. Bennett told Skelton how
much he disliked this cartoon. (*Winnipeg Free Press*)

Skelton and a very self-assured L.B. Pearson aboard the *RMS Berengaria*, the flagship of the Cunard line, headed home in the spring of 1933 from the grand success of the Skelton Committee. Skelton loved ocean travel and its rich food, light entertainment, and distance from the world's problems. (Library and Archives Canada, PA-110825)

...both glad to let Skelton run our foreign relations.

Mackenzie King (background, far right) smiles amiably at R.B. Bennett (something they did not do), improbably agreeing that Skelton could run Canada's foreign policy on his own. (Isabel Skelton Scrapbook, Queen's University Archives, undated and unidentified cartoon)

The Hamilton *Spectator* political cartoonist, Ivan Glassco, captures Skelton for the *Canadian Forum*'s January 1935 article, "The Invisible Government." The *Forum* identified a small group of "invisible powers," Skelton notable among them, "who have acted as a continuous advisory body to successive Liberal and Conservative governments." (*Canadian Forum*)

Isabel and Sheila Skelton decked out for presentation to King George VI and Queen Elizabeth at Buckingham Palace, 1 July 1937. It was a world they hated, according to Sheila, whose face revealed her unease. Unlike the others in the Canadian party, Oscar had refused to dress grandly for the recent coronation. (The Menzies and Skelton Family)

Skelton tried his best to discourage Mackenzie King from visiting Hitler in 1937. The prime minister went anyway, gushed over the German leader ("a man of deep sincerity and a genuine patriot"), and returned home with this picture in a silver frame. Hitler's inscription read: "To his Excellency the Canadian Prime Minister, Dr. W.L. Mackenzie King, in kind memory." (Library and Archives Canada C-11452)

Skelton trying to relax in Florida after his 1937 heart attack. The heavy tweed suit cannot have helped. Nor did his companion, Mackenzie King, who expected their vacation to include government work. (Library and Archives Canada, C-71513)

A playful evening on the ocean in the autumn of 1938. Mackenzie King is to the right of the woman in the hat and Skelton two seats away. "No words can express what this country owes to Dr. Skelton," King told the press as they departed, but the two men argued heatedly about the nature of Canada's international responsibilities. (Library and Archives Canada, C-26028)

The American president, seated at the centre, with Mackenzie King on his left, at the signature of the 1938 Canada-United States trade agreement in President Franklin D. Roosevelt's office. Skelton is standing third from the left, his hair matted down by the heavy silk top hat that he wore to the ceremony. (Library and Archives Canada, C-62098)

Canada's top public servant, uncharacteristically well groomed and impeccably tailored. (Library and Archives Canada, C-2089, undated)

the young men collectively for a quarter of an hour and then propelled them from his presence with a loud, disquieting exclamation, "Remember, many are called; few are chosen!" Skelton was astounded to find that the boss, himself a stout believer in the merit principle in public-service hiring, could acutely sum up each of the candidates and assess them "much as we had done after 2 hours examination." Skelton's top-ranked candidates were Léon Mayrand, who had distinctly improved his performance since his unsuccessful application two years before but was "still superficial on any economic question & Francophile on political questions," and Charles Ritchie, "self-possessed, more mature, scholarly but not brilliant."[23] Mayrand and Ritchie were hired and had long careers in External Affairs.

Skelton was convinced that his hiring practices, centring on special examinations followed by rigorous interviewing of the top performers, ensured solid results rooted in merit. He was proud of the process and the employees it produced; their "superiority in general to the men obtained by other Departments through the ordinary Civil Service procedure, has been a matter of comment and envy, and I hope in time of emulation." He was a critic of the public service's overall recruitment practices, which were lamentably weak. There had been "no attempt except in our department to get university men of first rate qualifications."[24]

Skelton was courting Loring Christie, the key foreign-policy architect of the Borden-Meighen era, hoping that he could bring him back into External Affairs. Never trusted or properly employed by King, superseded by Skelton, Christie left Ottawa in the mid-1920s, disillusioned by government service and the course of international affairs. He tried employment in England and ended up at the Beauharnois corporation in Montreal, where he worked with and watched over Sandy Skelton. OD kept in touch with chats and lunches, admiring Christie's restless and independent brilliance, observing the robust nationalism that now characterized his views, and imagining someone of that stature and experience at External. Christie had the right beliefs and would make a wonderful colleague: he was a good "Canada Firster" and a "likable chap."[25]

OD was back at the League of Nations in the fall of 1934, at the side of the prime minister. He soaked up the splendour of the Canadian Pacific's ship *Empress of Britain*, "the last word, or at least … the last sentence, so far as luxury & decoration go," but the prime minister thought it too much, pointedly asking why he had been given such expensive accommodation. Skelton replied with a jest: "It was the best we could do on short notice." RB kept mostly to himself, but they competed for the ship library's collection of detective stories, and the prime minister insisted on buying Skelton a glass of sherry and a bottle of cider to go with his ample lunches and dinners. Little work was accomplished. The voyage took only five days, which "isn't of the usual ocean amplitude," and Skelton felt the need of lots of sleep. He walked a lot and tried to skate around the bores, cultivating instead the "interesting people" and the "notables," including Oxford University's H.A.L. Fisher, who as a youngster had known the poet Alfred Lord Tennyson, and Liberal MP Chubby Power, a politician surely on the rise "if he can keep away from whiskey." The daily cinema was usually diverting, but *Secrets*, with Canadian-born Mary Pickford, was "really the worst film I ever saw, & Mary P. a joke, unable to act beyond a simper & that restrained by the enamel & waterproof paint" on her face.[26]

By the time the two travellers reached Geneva by way of Paris, the prime minister was ill. Oscar reported to Isabel that RB was doctoring himself with some success, "but he is weak & entirely without power to concentrate or interest himself in anything, certainly not in the League, & not much even in the Government of Canada." Skelton was careful with his diet, but he had his usual attack of conference diarrhoea followed by a sick stomach. He had Bennett's chores as well as his own, and it seemed important in the circumstances to stick close to the chief. "I don't want to give the impression the P.M. has been exacting, quite the contrary, but when he was feeling as he was physically & reacting against the League and all its works, I did not feel I could be away anytime he felt like company ... I'm hoping he'll feel better disposed toward it after he recovers his vitality a bit."[27]

Geneva needed all the friends it could get. Following the collapse of the League's World Economic and Monetary Conference, Hitler had abandoned the Disarmament Conference and followed Japan out of the League of Nations. Skelton saw a "Fascist trend" extending from Germany and Italy to Austria, "where it is merely a choice between one brand & another & the usual anti-socialist program is already in swing," and into France, Ireland, and England. The First World War had been fought to make the world safe for democracy, he mused. It had made it less so, leaving behind a ghastly heritage. The new frontiers thrown up by the post-war settling of accounts reverberated with bayonets, tariffs, war debts, and reparation payments, flaming nationalisms, and restless organized minorities. Class antagonisms intensified in highly industrialized settings. The scope of the state's activities was growing, placing a nearly intolerable burden on democratic politicians. Dictatorships were being established everywhere; democracy was openly reviled and rejected.[28]

Democratic institutions required reform if they were to survive. Skelton favoured the delegation of more power to executive bodies, made up, for example, of permanent representatives of economic groups, which would advise parliaments and administer policies determined by them. Adjustments in the "content of democracy" had to be made to ensure equality of economic opportunity in the national but also in the international sphere, "so as to reconcile separately existing nations with the new economic unity which bound the world together." In the final analysis, though, the only alternative to responsible government was irresponsible government. "We may not be good enough to govern ourselves but there is no class or group good enough to govern the rest of us for any length of time."[29]

The major issue at Geneva in the fall of 1934 was the Soviet Union's candidacy for League membership. Bennett and his brother-in-law Bill Herridge were virulently anti-Soviet, and denunciations of communism were good politics in which the prime minister indulged with gusto. Skelton, on the other hand, had opposed Bennett's 1931 embargo on Russian trade and argued for "a more responsible foreign policy" towards the Soviets "if we are to do our bit to bring the world back to sanity." Before the trip, the prime minister reluctantly agreed to support Soviet admission into the League; once in Geneva, the distinguished patient heaved himself out of his sickbed to sign a multinational telegram inviting Moscow to join the struggling institution.[30]

Even then, Skelton realized, Bennett was wavering: "His head was convinced Russia should come in, but his heart wasn't." The question was slated for initial discussion in the Assembly's Sixth Committee on political questions, and as the two men drove from the Hôtel de la Paix to the committee hall, Bennett revealed that he planned to use the occasion to take "a whack at the Rooshians." Skelton told the prime minister flatly that it was not going to be possible. He, not Bennett, was the Canadian member of that committee. Besides, RB had responsibilities elsewhere, as chair of the Economic Committee.[31]

It might be too late to go back on the original decision to support the Soviets, but Bennett ordered Skelton to lambaste their style of government and the extent of Russian propaganda activities in Canada. OD rewrote his speech on the spot to highlight the prime minister's views but "embalmed them in some of my own ideas, so didn't have to stretch my conscience too much." Canada, he informed the Sixth Committee, had "substantial difficulties" with the entrance of Soviet Russia into the League, but the condition of the world made it very desirable. While Skelton knew that his address had been too hastily manufactured, it had gone pretty well and "under all the circumstances I thought I got off very lightly." He constructed for Isabel the picture of "a great audience, & a tense debate, quite the high light of the Assembly. It was quite amusing that on a question the P.M. had so much at heart it should be I who spoke for Canada." An item from the Toronto *Star* celebrating Skelton's "dignified" performance was pasted in the family scrapbook.[32]

On 18 September Skelton attended the League Assembly meeting that overwhelmingly adopted the Sixth Committee's recommendation that the USSR be brought into the League. The well-staged and historic event impressed him mightily, but the democracies' favourite Soviet diplomat, Commissar of Foreign Affairs Maxim Litvinoff, did not. The "chief actor didn't rise to the occasion," Oscar told Isabel. Litvinoff was "a pushing parvenu." Much of what he said in his "broken & guttural" English was simply in bad taste. Skelton got much closer to "Lit" at a Riddell luncheon a few days later and at a meal hosted by the Soviets, replete with the finest caviar, lobster, pheasant, pâté de foie gras, and cordon rouge champagne, to say nothing of buckets of vodka. It was "quite the swankiest lunch I had seen in Geneva" and "quite a striking commentary on proletarian principles & practices." What hypocrites the Russians were.[33]

The Sixth Committee was at the heart of all the major issues that came before the League's Fifteenth Assembly. Skelton had to decide whether to speak up or stay silent. He said nothing about the bloody dispute between Paraguay and Bolivia, "as everything I could have said was better said by others," but on the Polish demand for a universal system of minority-rights guarantees, he "scribbled out some remarks which because brief and not so polite as usual at Geneva made some stir." Not content to reject interference from other countries about the treatment of minorities who had freely chosen to emigrate to Canada, he slammed the Polish proposal and pointed specifically to the inconsistencies in the argument of the speakers who supported it. The limelight was seductive: "If I stay here much longer, I'll be talking as freely as Mr. Woodsworth," the long-winded socialist MP.[34]

A fresh Geneva acquaintance was the Irish prime minister, Éamon de Valéra, who did not come highly recommended. He had displaced Skelton's collaborators in Ireland's Labour Party and promised a separatist departure from their (and Skelton's) strategy of breaking down the British imperial structure from within, piece by piece. OD was afraid that de

Valéra would challenge the British too boldly, and that they would fight back with the club of economic discrimination. To his surprise, Skelton came rather to like de Valéra, a reaction surely influenced by his flattering compliments about OD's performance in the Sixth Committee.[35]

Skelton responded less timidly than usual to what he always called the social struggle, although, with a squeamish stomach and heavy responsibilities, he avoided evening occasions as much as possible. He gave a lunch for the Canadians in Geneva that cost him $140 of his own money in Canadian funds, and wondered whether he ought to offer to pay for part of the expenses incurred by the prime minister for a British Commonwealth dinner that attracted fifty guests. He reported to Isabel that he had had only one genuinely pleasant evening since his arrival, when Jean Désy took him to an Italian marionette show. "It was splendid – humorous in conception & extraordinarily skilful in execution, the highlights being a bullfight and a piano player. I haven't laughed as much in months." Moving homeward via Paris and London, he became ill again, this time with a severe cold that required liberal applications of a doctor's four medicines. While he rested in bed, a Canada-France trade agreement almost went off the rails, with Bennett on a tack of his own and none of the other Canadians able to sway him.[36]

In the months immediately following this latest trip to Europe, OD was optimistic about the League of Nations, viewing the Soviet Union's appearance on the scene as one of a series of events helping to revive the institution's prestige. The world was full of inflammable tinder, he told Bennett in a major appraisal of external affairs prepared in early 1935. Policy makers faced more economic problems, reckless dictators, and powerful weapons than they had on the eve of the First World War. Yet the prognosis was not as serious, in large measure because there was a widespread and resolute anti-war feeling along with "an organization for focusing this sentiment and forcing the statesmen to take decisions after conference rather than in their separate propaganda-ridden capitals." The League was contributing materially to the furtherance of international peace and stability.[37]

According to Skelton's estimate of public opinion, the majority of the Canadian people believed in the League as "an indispensable agency for international conciliation and organization, and, if not always a sufficient protection against one's foes, sometimes a useful protection against one's clamant friends." Canadians expected their country's leadership to take its Geneva duties more seriously and with more continuity of interest than in the past; they supported agencies for the settlement of disputes and the ventilation and removal of grievances; they wanted their leaders to press for genuine disarmament or at least armament limitation. Nevertheless, they would "not be led by the hot gospellers of a managed world or the manoeuvres of European countries to go in for war alliances or for transforming the League itself into a war alliance."[38]

Canadians, Skelton continued, understood that isolation was not possible. Their country was less vulnerable to attack than any other nation of significance in the world, and only the foolhardy would assume front-line responsibility in every international dispute and "throw away our heritage and place ourselves in the precarious position of a Czechoslovakia or a Lithuania." However, no country could escape serious direct or indirect consequences if war came to Europe. Most Canadians, with their reasoned understanding of the value of the British Empire-Commonwealth as a force for moderation and an example of peaceful settlement of differences, were ready to help Great Britain "if believed to be right and in serious trouble." Skelton was tilting his analysis in the direction of a very pro-British prime minister, but he believed in an evolving commonwealth of nations. He was an independentist, but not one like Ireland's de Valera, who ruled out British Commonwealth cooperation on principle and wanted to demolish all links with Britain in a single revolutionary blow.[39]

Skelton's views of the League were similar to those that he described as the "prevalent attitude" among Canadians. He fell into the camp of what he termed the "moderate Leaguer," who emphasized the preventive side of the League's work, insisted on autonomy in judging obligations under the Covenant, recognized the difficulties of Canadian sanctions if the United States remained out of the League, and hoped "to find in League action a reconciliation of our national freedom and our imperial feelings." There was even in Skelton a sympathy with the "moderate imperialists" in the United Kingdom. The British had been the most constructive of the Great Powers in recent days and the chief voice for restraint and stability.[40]

Skelton realized that Canadians had no stomach for fighting Japan during the recent crisis over Manchuria, even though the whole experiment of world organization was in peril. He lamented, however, that divided councils and pro-Japanese sympathy had prevented the League from standing up to aggression. That taught unhealthy lessons to Germany. OD advocated measures "within the range of possible Canadian action" to make clear his country's continuing solidarity with the aggrieved Chinese. Thus, he told Bennett that they ought to support the further non-recognition of Manchukuo, establish a legation in China when possible, revise anti-Asian voting laws in Canada, and change "our offensive immigration exclusion laws in such a way as to save China's face without involving more than a nominal immigration." Canada's paltry defences on the Pacific, facing towards Japan, also needed attention.[41]

Skelton saw the main dangers to peace coming from Japan and Germany, "both nations on the make, cursed with an inferiority complex which compels dangerous swaggering." He was critical of France's unremittingly negative attitude towards Germany and of the Americans' refusal to underwrite a League of Nations designed to control aggression. Russia was a recent convert to the defence of the status quo, and Italy, though as "drunk with the new wine of doctrine and almost as dissatisfied with the war outcome as Germany, has had longer time to sober down and realize the limitations of its economic and military power." Major-General A.G.L. McNaughton, the head of the army, dissented. Reviewing Skelton's commentary, he said: "The impression is left of a more sober Italy which I doubt."[42]

Skelton was conscious of Benito Mussolini's designs on Ethiopia (also known as Abyssinia), an African country whose nineteenth-century defeat of the Italians still struck at their national pride. Yet Ethiopia seemed to OD unlikely to become a major international issue. The Great Powers happily exchanged slices of Africa and were shutting their eyes to Italy's colonialist aspirations. The people of Canada thought little about it. Their own economic problems were sufficient to prevent Ethiopia from being regarded as anything rather than a diversion – "a new color film in which Signor Mussolini struts his usual magnificent role." And if some Canadians did care, or if they came to care, they were apt in Catholic Quebec to back Catholic Italy – not the unfortunate Ethiopians.[43]

Bennett agreed with Skelton that Germany and Japan were much more worrying than Italy, but the prime minister was disturbed by the League's "impotence" in the face of Italian threats on Ethiopia. In August 1935 Bennett told Skelton that he was willing to support economic sanctions against Italy if that country moved against Ethiopia, even if it entailed "the risk of becoming involved in war."[44] OD responded with a memorandum that listed the pros and cons of a tough Canadian stand against aggression. The pros, however, were deliberately weak; the cons were crafted to win the argument. Skelton reiterated that the United States was firmly isolationist, making any action by Canada "doubly difficult," and the Canadian people were themselves "immensely more interested in Alberta than Abyssinia." Canada, moreover, had always supported conciliation and prevention under the League Covenant, never its punitive features. Passions would rise if economic sanctions were invoked, he warned, since "incidents multiply out of embargoes and blockades of this stringent character, and recourse to arms is difficult to avoid."[45]

Skelton's case for discretion was reinforced by Loring Christie, OD's latest External Affairs recruit. He had finally convinced the prime minister that Christie was badly needed in the department. To be sure that he would be acceptable to a new government if Bennett were defeated in an election, Opposition leader King's agreement for the appointment was informally secured as well. Skelton and Christie had once been on opposite sides of the debate about Canada's future: Christie, the imperialist, wanting Canada to become great in a greater British Empire; Skelton, the nationalist, intent on a Canada independent of all but the loosest ties to Britain. Christie had come around to Skelton's point of view, with a vengeance, railing against Canadians who continued to follow Britain meekly, it hardly mattering "a damn what policy London pursues." As for sanctions, that was simply Geneva's word for war.[46]

Bennett took Skelton's advice, sending instructions to Canada's delegation at the League to move cautiously. The prime minister had other things on his mind. RB had called an election. He had to, having governed for a full five years, the maximum possible without returning to the voters. His name was synonymous with the Depression, and he seemed surely headed to a humiliating defeat. At the beginning of 1935 he presented a package of reforms dramatically expanding the government's power to regulate the economy and offering government support to every major economic group. Skelton thought that the Bennett "New Deal," taking its name from President Franklin Roosevelt's popular program in the United States, might attract enough support to bring the Conservatives back from the dead. He had little time for RB's "punk economics" but admired his forcefulness and daring, his desire to control events rather than be controlled by them. When the campaign began, Skelton was pleased that Bennett put Ethiopia in the right perspective. On 6 September, in the first of his election radio addresses, RB pledged not to become embroiled in "any foreign quarrel where the rights of Canadians are not involved."[47]

As Mussolini prepared for war, and Bennett campaigned, the Canadians at Geneva went in a different direction, hoping to deter Italy and restore the reputation of the League of Nations as a serious international institution. Their rallying cry was an 11 September speech to the League Assembly by the British foreign secretary, Sir Samuel Hoare. Delivering his remarks with deliberate force, Hoare captivated his audience with a call "for steady and collective resistance to all acts of unprovoked aggression." Canada's League delegation, led by Howard Ferguson, backed up to the hilt by Walter Riddell, took up the cause with passion. Over the next weeks they gave the impression that their country and its government was a leading supporter of sanctions, even to the extent of making the suggestion that the League move on that front before the fighting began. Sometimes they did not trouble themselves to let Skelton know what they were doing; sometimes they deceived him about their intentions and actions. They were, after all, out to save the world. They did not know that Hoare and the British were more interested in a deal with Mussolini than in making the League work.[48]

There were two Bennetts – the practical politician facing an electorate that wanted nothing to do with international responsibilities, and the emotionally charged League advocate who would occasionally materialize, ready for battle. He could not decide whether he was with his chief foreign-policy adviser, Skelton, or with Ferguson, his political friend. So he went with them both, depending on his mood. After the Hoare speech, buttressed by similar remarks from French Premier Laval, Bennett approved a Skelton telegram to Geneva instructing Ferguson to make no public declaration. But then the prime minister began to fret. Accusing Skelton of abandoning Canada's historic commitment to the League, Bennett drafted a firm statement of support for collective measures to stop the Italians in their tracks. He allowed Skelton to tone down his words, but the intent was unmistakeable. "If he never did anything else in his life he would stand by Laval and Hoare," RB blustered. Ferguson communicated the prime minister's message of support to the League Assembly on 14 September. "Farcical," was Skelton's description of his chief's latest explosion.[49]

Mussolini's troops crossed over the border into Ethiopia on 2 October. The Council, the League's senior body, condemned Italy and passed the matter on to the Assembly for similar treatment. Skelton and Bennett agreed that Canada, with an election imminent and a new Parliament in view, should abstain from any formal Assembly declaration about Italy's aggression. Ferguson was outraged. He telephoned the prime minister and received permission to line Canada up with the vast majority of League members in stipulating that Italy had violated the Covenant. This caused an angry telephone exchange between Bennett and Skelton, who thought that a vote against Italy was a vote for automatic sanctions. RB denied the connection, but said that if there were one, Canada could not evade it: there was "no doubt we signed Covenant; no doubt of Italy's guilt; we must take the consequences." Canada could not and should not try to hornswoggle itself out of League commitments of long standing. Skelton's response was that Canadian governments had made their opposition to a punitive League known since the beginning. It was rewriting history to suggest otherwise.[50]

In doing everything he could to prevent Canadian involvement in the Ethiopian affair, Skelton at least had the virtue of consistency. He had never believed that the League could succeed as a war office or super-state; its work was in mediating disputes and throwing a harsh light on international problems and criminality. He went out of his way to align Canada with thinking in the United States because the two countries shared an interest in keeping their distance from European quarrels. Ethiopia threatened to bring Great Britain onto the European continent once more, and where the British went, some Canadians, with men like Bennett and Ferguson at the head of the pack, were sure to follow. OD did admit, however, that Italy's sin was flagrant, and he did not exclude the imposition of economic (but not military) sanctions to bring Mussolini to see sense.[51]

Bennett was only hours away from a humiliating election defeat. Skelton worried that Mackenzie King might run a complacent campaign, setting out no positive alternative, and relying too much on the unpopularity of the government. That is what he did, and King knew best: it was enough to cry "It's King or Chaos" and wait for election day. The Liberals won 173 of the 245 seats in the House of Commons, the most lopsided election victory a Canadian political leader had ever achieved. Bennett lost 97 seats, leaving his party with only 40 MPs.[52]

OD was not sorry to see Bennett depart the prime minister's office. He could be as "chilly as an Antarctic breeze" to everyone with whom he worked, Skelton included.[53] His violently shifting impulses made him difficult to predict and manage. Working for him was like standing near quicksand: exciting perhaps, but very unsettling. The League of Nations misadventures from Manchuria through Russia to Ethiopia had illustrated how erratically Bennett led Canada, and how misguided and damaging his views on international relations were for the country.

Yet their disagreements did not diminish the fondness Bennett and Skelton felt for one another. Skelton's RB was bursting with life, committed to Canada, and much more of a progressive and reformer than his hidebound reputation suggested. The prime minister's generosity of spirit touched OD. Called to the House of Commons for a night debate on the estimates in early 1934, just as the family was leaving home to watch Sheila act in *She Stoops to Conquer*, Skelton wearily returned downtown, disappointed that he was again going to miss his daughter in one of her school plays. He found the prime minister concerned less about work than that he might have disrupted the Skeltons' plans. Bennett instructed him to return to Isabel, who had been unwell with phlebitis, and tell her that, even if she could not be the wife of Sir Oscar, "she can at least have her husband to go out with her on a Friday evening." Later in the year, Bennett donated his Stearns-Knight automobile and chauffeur for OD's trip to Queen's University to receive an honorary doctor of laws.[54]

Days before the federal election, there was more of Bennett's thoughtfulness. The prime minister arranged a special payment of $2,000 to recognize Skelton's service to the government at a time when his department had been seriously understaffed. Eight other public servants were honoured in a similar way, but OD worried that Bennett would be seen as "taking very good care of his own" in External Affairs, particularly when two other members of the department were also on the list. The bonus received considerable notice in the newspapers, enough to put Isabel in a very bad mood as they set off for a grand government dinner bidding farewell to the governor general, Lord Bessborough. Skelton assured her that $2,000 plus publicity was better than privacy minus $2,000. His wife was a quick convert. "It is a wonderfully splendid boost for us & Oscar didn't ask for it; like all Mr. Bennett's acts it was wholly his own although of course it went through the Auditor-General's hands." The extra money was welcome. Skelton was in debt, struggling to help Herbert and Isabel's family in Peterborough, as well as to pay for Sheila's private school. There was also the matter of the fur coats.[55]

In the three more years that RB remained as leader of the Conservative Party after his election defeat in 1935, Skelton encountered him from time to time in the East Block, at the Rideau Club and Rideau Hall, the governor general's residence, or on Wellington Street as Bennett marched his way from his Chateau Laurier Hotel suite to Parliament Hill. They smiled at one another, remembering their times together both bad and good.[56] Then the wealthy politician and the professorial public servant faded away from one another, back to worlds in which they had almost nothing in common.

11
Fortunate in Our Neighbours, 1935–6

In October 1935 Skelton allowed himself a moment of satisfaction that his Liberals had returned to power and then settled back into his killing routine. With the principalship of Queen's again vacant, he could have had the top job there for the asking, and at double his Ottawa salary with a free residence thrown into the bargain. Instead, he agreed to serve on the committee that would choose a new principal.[1] The university was never far from his mind, but as a place of work sleepy Kingston held little appeal.

Queen's was perhaps not the only possibility. Oscar's mercurial friend, Bill Herridge, had submitted his resignation as Canadian minister to the United States immediately after brother-in-law R.B. Bennett's defeat in the 1935 election. The position of senior diplomatic representative in Washington was available, and the newspapers were full of speculation that Skelton would be sent to the American capital. Such an appointment, the Ottawa *Citizen* said, would help to distinguish party politics from diplomacy, but the newspaper agreed with the Toronto *Star* that Skelton was more needed in the government at home. Still, the *Star* editorialized: "His wide knowledge of international questions, his judicial temperament and his unassailable integrity provide him with some of the most essential qualifications for the Washington post." "They are talking of Dr. O.D. Skelton as Canadian Minister to Washington," enthused the Ottawa *Journal*. "A better man could not be obtained and The Journal would be all for it if it did not interfere with his splendid work as a general foreign adviser."[2]

Mackenzie King was the most selfish of men. He was not about to send his bureaucratic packhorse off to another country. Nor was Skelton fashioned for the hypocrisies of diplomacy. Why would he want to leave Ottawa, asked King: "He has great power where he is," thriving on pressure-packed seven-day weeks at the core of the nation's business. He slaved "day in & day out," but it was not a sacrifice – "he likes the work & the opportunity it affords."[3]

The under-secretary waited until the new prime minister was officially sworn in before he contacted him. "May I express my great pleasure," OD wrote when the time was right, "in being able to work under you again." The goodwill was reciprocated: "It was a great delight to me to be again in association with Skelton," King recorded after they met over lunch. Bennett had been a surprisingly good master, but Skelton and King were comrades whose relationship worked on the level of instinct. There would be none of the swings of emotion and the wild uncertainties of the previous five years. Yet "the tasks facing the new government are tremendous," OD wrote his Queen's friend, the new Liberal MP for Kingston, Norman Rogers. It was a good sign that Rogers and a handful of other young Canadians with "vigor as well as vision" were going into public life, but they would have a tough time dislodging the old guard of politics, which had neither.[4]

On 24 October 1935, the day after King took control of the government, Skelton sent the new prime minister a note on Canada's "outstanding external questions." First on the agenda was a need for a decision about the economic sanctions that the League of Nations planned to impose on Italy in the wake of Mussolini's attack on the kingdom of Ethiopia earlier in the month. Skelton urged caution and, to drive the point home, resuscitated the major memorandum he had written for Bennett on the subject, which was heavily weighted against involvement in the African crisis. The deputy feared the League's fervent backers as much as he feared the imperial centralizers in London. Both resided a long way from Canada, and Canadian interests, and both were busily plotting to inveigle the country into their wars. Skelton knew full well that Canada would sign on to economic sanctions against Italy. He had lost the battle to have the Bennett government remain aloof from the collision between Europeans over issues about which he thought Canadians knew and cared little. However, he wanted King, and the cabinet, to know how close they all could be to a disaster.[5]

With Skelton's brief in front of them, in fact read to them by the prime minister, the cabinet deliberated and disagreed among themselves. The Quebec ministers, led by Ernest Lapointe, the powerhouse Quebec minister who was Skelton's frequent ally in the campaign against overseas entanglements, wanted to follow the under-secretary and "to say and do as little as possible." A knot of English ministers favoured a strong stand short of military sanctions against Italy. In the end, the cabinet agreed to accept the League's recommendations for economic and financial sanctions.[6]

A press release capturing the cabinet's compromise was issued on 29 October, but it was written by Skelton and shot through with qualifications. Successive Canadian governments, he wrote, had opposed the view that the League's central purpose was to guarantee the territorial status quo and to rely on force to establish the peace. The League, furthermore, had been weakened by the absence of the United States, Germany, and Japan, the failures to achieve the disarmament contemplated in the Covenant, and the unwillingness of member states to enforce penalties in the case of aggression taking place some distance from the European scene. The Canadian government was prepared to cooperate fully in economic sanctions in this one instance, but it did not recognize any commitment to follow those with military action, which could not be taken without the permission of Parliament. Nor was the approval of sanctions in any way a precedent for future endeavours. The statement concluded by emphasizing the country's geographic and economic position, the necessity for national unity, and the importance of "common consent" for international policies – all factors that suggested that Canada would only do what it had to do in the world. Skelton could not have been happier. The innocents in the cabinet had been kept in check and some distance had been established between Canada and the League. He told his wife that to have the press statement accepted as he had written it was even sweeter news than the recent election returns.[7]

Then he made a mistake. Skelton sent a cable to Walter Riddell, the chief Canadian delegate to the League, with a summary rather than a full text of the press release, so that the full extent of its negative message was masked. That gave Riddell an opening to claim that he had no understanding of just how hesitant the government was in its support of the League. Instead, Riddell chose to construe the telegram as a "heartening surprise" and promptly jumped into the lead of the anti-Mussolini forces in Geneva. On 1 November he spoke forcefully in the Committee of Eighteen, putting his country on the line for forceful measures and exhorting others to follow. The next day, Riddell entered history – the international "hall of fame," OD later told the diplomat. "Canada," it was widely reported, proposed that the sanctions list be extended to include oil, coal, iron, and steel. Riddell was certain that an embargo on these crucial war-fighting commodities, and on oil in particular, would grind Mussolini's mechanized military machine to a halt.[8]

Skelton was in part to blame for Riddell's improvisational policy making. The under-secretary was not in regular contact with Riddell; the communications that had been sent from headquarters were brief and written on the fly. He had not taken the measure of his man at the League, who had been away from Canada for fifteen years and was completely out of touch with the country he represented. Nor had Skelton picked up on the recent dynamic in the Canadian delegation at Geneva, which had established a pattern of clear support for the League in, Riddell was telling Ottawa, its "supreme test."[9]

All that said, Riddell knew exactly what he was doing. His guidelines in the aftermath of the election were perfectly clear: he was to take no initiative without prior consultation and precise instructions. During the Manchurian crisis, Skelton had warned him to be very careful in the way in which he represented the views of the Canadian government in Geneva. He and Skelton had exchanged letters earlier in 1935 about the importance of acting under "definite instructions from Ottawa." But this time Riddell put the League above his responsibilities to his country. This, in the circumstances, was brave and understandable, but it was not what he had been sent to the League to do. Skelton and King were livid, and now it was their turn to express "much surprise." Riddell was told in what the prime minister regarded as a "pretty sharp despatch" that he had far exceeded his authority.[10]

Part of the problem was that Skelton's priorities did not include a vital League. King had made a rapid completion of a trade agreement with the United States his central election promise. Skelton wanted the same thing, passionately. He had been quietly working in that direction since Bennett began to consider the idea earnestly in 1933, putting aside his earlier doubts and encouraged by the election of Franklin Roosevelt to the presidency. In July of that year, Sandy Skelton had been sent, speaking "personally and unofficially for his father," as an emissary to U.S. Secretary of State Cordell Hull, urging, in the words of a Hull assistant, "the importance of concluding at an early date some form of reciprocal tariff agreement with Canada."[11]

OD must have known that his son had been asked by the well-connected Professor W.Y. Elliott of the Department of Government at Harvard University to develop some detailed materials on Canada-United States trade, Sandy's area of expertise, and that these had been forwarded to the American State Department. "I think that you will find the data exceedingly interesting," the professor wrote to the U.S. under-secretary of state, Bill Phillips, a former American minister to Ottawa, "and it may well be that some of it will present you with a basis for asking for treaty concessions in the approaching negotiations." Phillips passed on these memoranda "by the son of our friend" to Jack Hickerson of the Division of Western European Affairs.[12] Sandy Skelton thus turned up as an unofficial adviser to the Americans in their trade talks with a Canadian team whose most prominent member was his father.

When the Canada-United States negotiations really got under way, the 1935 election was too close for success to be likely; nevertheless, Skelton pressed the Americans hard. He repeatedly made the point that they would be far better off reaching an agreement with the Conservatives than the King Liberals, because the high-tariff moguls in the Canadian Manufacturers' Association would not be critical of a deal reached by *their* government. In early October, fighting a sciatica that laid him up in bed for a few days, OD expressed his "extreme discouragement" to the American minister in Ottawa, Norman Armour, that the Washington government had been unwilling to consider many of the key demands made by Canada. Armour reported home that Skelton "deeply regretted the trend events had taken as he really felt that the list of concessions his Government had been prepared to make to us, had we been able on our part to present a more 'effective' list, would have resulted in a really constructive and worth-while agreement."[13] There was no sign whatsoever that Skelton was holding back, knowing that his Liberals would soon be in power and able to reap the rewards of an undoubted political coup. He was working assiduously for a deal that might have been a powerful last-minute vote getter for the Conservatives.

As soon as the election results were in, Skelton continued the campaign, not waiting for Mackenzie King's approval to assume the role of prime ministerial spokesman. In a meeting on 17 October with Armour, OD said that the Liberals, always a low-tariff party, would surely want to pick up the negotiations where the previous government had left them off. Canada and the United States had reached a "very important crossroads in our relations." If they were able to conclude a commercial agreement sufficiently broad to effect real improvement in the two economies, "then all would be well." If not, how "regrettable" that would be, especially in light of the Ethiopian crisis and the dangers to European peace, which ought to be sending a message to North America about the importance of continental solidarity. "The two nations could either erect a closer political community or they could continue down independent paths marked by a minimum of cooperation, understanding and goodwill."[14]

Skelton continued that, if Canada could not count on its friend in North America, it would be forced back into the arms of the British. They would be ready with commercial offers of their own, but at a price. Canadians would have no choice but to fall in line with the narrow plan, promoted by Neville Chamberlain at the 1932 Ottawa Conference, for "a world-wide British economic Empire whose interests, as progressively developed from London, might soon diverge seriously" from those of the United States. Canada would become a British dominion once again, with its economic interests dominated by London and important secondary industries falling by the wayside. As Armour summarized the conversation, Skelton thought it essential to develop "what he termed 'a North American mind,'" and that this would be difficult if the doors to the United States were closed and Canada was told, to all intents and purposes, that we were not interested or at any rate not able to meet them half way and they better throw in their lot with the British."[15]

One week later, King gave Armour essentially the same message. There were two roads open to Canadians, and the prime minister "wanted to choose 'the American road' if we made it possible for him to do so."[16] Intent on a trade agreement that would establish an anti-tariff momentum for fighting the Depression, King was saying what the Americans wanted to hear. Skelton, however, believed fervently that Canada's only salvation lay in the development of a sturdy North Americanism. That would be an inoculation against the poison of British imperialism.

Skelton told the Americans that there was, from his perspective, little point in a narrow agreement of the kind that they had offered Bennett. They must be more forthcoming on Canada's crucial demands. He was immensely pleased by Mackenzie King's prompt attention to deal making, but he warned the Liberal leader that Canadian-American talks, while promising, were still a considerable distance from producing an agreement. King's plan to travel to Washington immediately in order to make a direct appeal to President Roosevelt could seriously damage Canadian prestige if the prime minister returned empty-handed. King was undeterred and instructed his deputy to accompany him to the American capital. He considered bringing the finance and trade and commerce ministers with him as well, but Skelton convinced him that it was best to have the whole cabinet approve any draft agreement that might result from the trip, so as to spike criticism that King did not have the full backing of his government. "Skelton is a very wise counselor," King confided his diary.[17]

On the morning of 6 November, Skelton attended a cabinet meeting as (in his wife's phrase) the government's "trade expert," again proving his worth by pointing to a couple of potentially dangerous clauses that had escaped the politicians' notice. "You've just saved the country," King said. Leaving the cabinet room to prepare for the train to the United States, OD ran into Bennett, who exclaimed: "I see you are going to Washington with King – well now remember in his present mood Billie King would sign anything to say he had got a treaty so we are all depending on you – on you Skelton to save the country." Inside a few minutes, Isabel told her mother, "both Mr. King & Mr. Bennett had used the identical phrase!"[18]

Isabel packed three suitcases and a hatbox for Oscar, who must have anticipated a long trip. Pretending that they were on vacation to fool the media, he and King took the overnight train to Washington, arriving around noon on the 7th, a day of squalls and downpours. Met by Bill Phillips and a barrage of cameras, they proceeded to the Canadian Legation where they were given lunch and comfortable rooms at the back of the building, overlooking a small courtyard. After lunch at the Legation, temporarily presided over by Hume Wrong as chargé d'affaires, an exhausted King napped while Oscar reviewed the state of the trade discussions with the triumvirate of Canadian officials, Hector McKinnon, Dana Wilgress, and Norman Robertson, who had been appointed by Bennett to represent Canada in the negotiations and were subsequently dispatched by King to Washington on 4 November to renew the battle. They were Ottawa's real trade experts. Skelton worked with them into the night while King dined with an old friend and fellow spiritualist, Julia Grant, the granddaughter of President Ulysses S. Grant.[19]

The next day broke bright and crisp in the American city. At 11 a.m. King and Skelton called on Cordell Hull at the State Department. The two politicians engaged, OD reported, in "a very edifying and elevated conversation." Only later on in the day did Skelton get beyond woolly generality when he examined some of the "sordid details" with State's officials. But it did not yet seem like hard work. "My visit thus far might be classified as a holiday compared with my usual Ottawa routine."[20]

Evening brought an informal dinner at the White House, which Skelton carefully assessed both from the outside and from the inside. He admired it very much. It was "dignified, liveable & definitely American." Franklin Roosevelt was clearly a charmer, "quite self-satisfied & not given to worry evidently." Disabled years before by polio, he walked with the support of a military aide and a cane, travelling up and downstairs by an elevator or a ramp for his wheelchair. He had great difficulty in getting out of his chair, but it seemed not to bother him at all. Eleanor Roosevelt, a prominent public figure in her own right, was a vigorous talker, with a patrician voice that trilled as she warmed to her liberal causes. Their son John, down from Harvard for a couple of days, was a rather wild youth, probably not unlike the boy Sandy had been. All three gave the impression, Skelton perceptively concluded, of being very much their own beings, off on their own tangents, and not much concerned with the others. When the meal was over, and as arranged beforehand, Roosevelt and King slipped off to talk about the trade agreement. OD hoped for an early evening, but Mrs Roosevelt had other plans, summoning the remaining nine guests upstairs for a showing of the Charles Laughton-Clark Gable 1935 extravaganza, *Mutiny on the Bounty,* which was entertaining but lengthy. It was after midnight when Skelton escaped the White House.[21]

By then, the American president and the Canadian prime minister were rushing headlong towards an accord. Fantastic though it seemed, an agreement would be initialled almost instantly, the day after the White House dinner, and unveiled on the 11th of November, the anniversary of the end of the First World War. An Armistice Day announcement was King's idea. Liking such sentimental associations of past and present, he wanted a public demonstration of North American cooperation on 11 November to "have its effect upon the war in Europe and be the forerunner of a new era of peace." Skelton deprecated the linking of a trade deal with memories of the dead, and yet he saw the importance of moving quickly, while the two leaders were, as Roosevelt jauntily put it, in the mood. So OD and his American and Canadian colleagues put in a full Saturday until ten that night, reviewing the colossal mass of technical detail, trading concessions on knotty issues such as the Canadian insistence on a cream concession, and cobbling together a sketchy agreement in principle. McKinnon, Wilgress, and Robertson wrestled with their U.S. counterparts, while Skelton and King were a good team in taking on the people at the State Department. Then, late at night, they all gathered in the secretary of state's apartment for impromptu speeches and a signing of a document by Hull for the United States and King for Canada.[22]

While King took the train back to Ottawa to consult with the cabinet and make his Armistice Day announcement, Skelton remained in

Washington. He had wanted to sneak home himself to deal with Ethiopian sanctions and get his troublesome teeth fixed with some extractions
and new plates, but there was too much to be done in the U.S. capital.
The trade agreement had to be put in its final form and the strategy set
for publicity. He toiled until one or two in the morning all week, telling
Isabel that others occasionally worked until 3 or 4 a.m. before they saw
their beds. "The mechanical checking of the multitudinous details & cal-
culation of alternative devices takes a tremendous amount of time, quite
aside from the many real snags still facing us ... The capitalist statesmen
who sign have little idea of the work to be done (some of the U.S. people
have sat up all night, though they have at least five men at work for one
of ours), but they also had their bit to do & did it well."[23]

King was back later in the week for the formal signing ceremony. He
found Skelton looking exhausted, the result of "working at a very high
pitch." They fought to be the one to congratulate the other first, the
prime minister thanking Skelton warmly for his contribution, "which
had been all-important." At the White House on 15 November, Roosevelt beamed, the entire U.S. cabinet applauded, and Skelton stood in
the background while King and Cordell Hull put their signatures on the
final agreement. OD celebrated by drafting the press release and doing
some light shopping at Brentano's bookstore.[24]

Having a great deal invested in it, Skelton believed that the agreement
was a remarkably good one, achieved despite the obstacles of American
economic nationalism. The ultra-protectionists, who regarded every cut
in the tariff as a loss to the country giving it, would not be happy, nor
would the free traders, who sought nothing less than a bargain as comprehensive as that which had been reached in the abortive Canada-U.S.
trade agreement of 1911. The protesters in the Canadian Manufacturers' Association would howl, and so too would their allies in the Conservative Party. But the deal was the best that could be got, and it was
immensely more than the Bennett government could have mustered.
The 1935 agreement found markets for important Canadian primary
industries and made concessions "of which 90 per cent are for our own
good & which the present party in power was pledged to make anyway."
More than that, it was an alternative to the tariff wars of the early 1930s
and would "prevent the U.K. from thinking we had no place else to go &
gouging us accordingly." All in all, Oscar told Isabel, it was "a fine job."[25]

He took his greatest pleasure from the collegiality of the exercise. The
U.S. side, which included people he knew well, like Phillips and Jack
Hickerson, had been "extremely decent." Hickerson told him that the

president had acted with great courage and had run decided political risks when it would have been easy to give in to "the avalanche of telegrams and lobby protests that have begun to pour in against sacrificing 1/1000 percent of 1 per cent of any U.S. producer's market." His old friend Hickerson had been "our great standby." He could not "have done more for us – while defending all real U.S. interests – if he had been one of ourselves."[26]

Skelton's assessment was quite naive. Roosevelt was gearing up for another run at the presidency, and his negotiators had assured him that the United States was the clear and demonstrable winner in the exchange. To his American government colleagues, Hickerson boasted that the United States had gained "staggering" advantages in the negotiation. The agreement was "so favourable to us" that "it will be recognized generally as a great economic and political asset." In addition, there was more than a hint in American official thinking at the time that Washington had an opportunity to supersede London as the key influence in Canadian affairs. Armour predicted that the trade agreement "would have the long-range effect of bringing Canada not only within our economic but our political orbit," more than offsetting any opposition to the "minor concessions" made to the northern neighbour in the agreement.[27] This was not Skelton's idea of a North American mind.

An enforced vacation was the price Skelton had to pay for the trade agreement. Exhausted, and worried about the antifreeze in his car and Sheila's schooling, he was anxious to get home, but King needed a rest and expected his deputy to come with him. "My personal convenience is a small matter beside the achievement of a really good treaty," was Skelton's resigned explanation. Phillips recommended a hotel named The Cloister, in Sea Island, Georgia, which he guaranteed Skelton would be very comfortable in the off-season, between the summer "when Southerners come and darkies do the waiting and the expensive and exclusive season from December to April when the Northerners come down, with imported waiters." Once the agreement was signed and delivered, Skelton and King set off on the train ride south to the Georgia-Florida border. Looking at the sports listed in the hotel brochure, Skelton thought that croquet would be about his limit.[28]

Even that seemed too strenuous when the time came. For two weeks the two men rested, reminisced, and became reacquainted after the five-year period when they had seldom met. OD wrote home about their long walks on the beach at Sea Island and the stunning scenes in the late afternoon, with "the endless marshes with their waving

reeds before us & behind us a magnificent crimson sunset." There
were meals together, recitations of poetry by the prime minister, and
small outings by car and foot to view the island. Skelton was struck by
Christ Church, which they had spotted as they drove around the island
and to which they returned when King had reassured himself that its
denomination was Episcopalian, not Methodist. The little building
stood in a quiet oak forest populated by huge trees that had two crops
of leaves a year and were always green. The famous English Methodist
preachers John and Charles Wesley had spoken there in the 1730s.
With "tremendous festoons of Spanish moss hanging down in the sun-
light," Skelton wrote, "it was a cross between fairyland and a cathedral." Inside the church, however, the rector quickly broke the charm.
He was a Lee, descended from General Robert E. Lee, the leader of
the south in the American Civil War, "and quite belligerent in his attitude to his small flock."[29]

On his first Sunday in Georgia, Skelton received a cable from Isabel
informing him that their friend, Senator Charles Murphy, was in very bad
health. Later that day, King announced that Murphy had died. When Isabel wrote to him about her attendance at the funeral on behalf of the
family, where she delivered a eulogy, Skelton mused that the Catholic
service "when done in full regalia is certainly impressive if too imper-
sonal for one with Protestant traditions." Oscar and Isabel were bonded
to Murphy by their common Irishness and the admiration they shared
for Thomas D'Arcy McGee. "It is hard to believe that alert, vital figure is
gone," OD wrote of Murphy. "He was a true & kindly friend and a fine
Canadian. Ottawa will be infinitely poorer for his lack." Skelton tried his
best to talk King, who had feuded with Murphy since the 1920s, out of
his negative feelings towards the senator. He failed, but he did not hold
back his own strong views.[30]

Skelton was relaxing, uncharacteristically so. He had been away from
Ottawa long enough that the constant barrage of paper and routine
seemed less important to him. Yet the League of Nations and Ethiopia weighed on him and his prime minister. Riddell's suggestion for
an oil, coal, iron, and steel embargo on Italy had put Canada in the
forefront of the efforts to stop Mussolini, an uncomfortable perch
for a government cautious in the extreme and obsessed by national
unity. Everywhere the plan was being referred to as Canada's. The
national and international press had picked up on the sanctions proposal as a bold insistence by one government upon the enforcement
of wider sanctions. Skelton wrote to headquarters from The Cloister

on 26 November to insist that they rein their man in Geneva in from further excesses: "In view of Riddell's previous unfortunate actions, he must not be allowed to act at his own discretion." The issue was "full of dynamite" for Canada and the world. War would be a catastrophe; a war that could be construed as Canada's fault would be intolerable. The government, Skelton insisted, "was prepared to consider any proposal on its merits, but not to thrust Canada into the commitments and responsibilities implied in initiating and pushing policies for the regulating of a European or Afro-European conflict."[31]

For three weeks, King and Skelton had refrained from any public reference to Riddell's Ethiopia scheme. That changed at the end of November. Ernest Lapointe, acting as external affairs minister while King was away, asked Skelton whether there was anything that could be done to clarify Canada's widely misunderstood position on the oil sanction. The result was a little plot, hatched by the sightseers as they toured Sea Island. Skelton telephoned Lapointe, asking him to arrange an encounter with the press, where he would let it be known that Riddell had been acting on his own in Geneva, without the government's knowledge and without its authorization. King wanted to repudiate not simply Riddell's action but Riddell himself, but Skelton convinced the prime minister that their diplomat had given long service and had acted in good faith. Eventually, Skelton agreed, Riddell ought to be dismissed from the diplomatic corps, but he told the prime minister that it was vital to avoid any impression that the League was weakening its stand against Italian aggression or backing down in the face of Mussolini's threats of a European war. He added later in a private note for the prime minister that there did "not seem to be any reason why Canada should be more zealous in defending the sanctions policy than France, its vigorous and traditional advocate from the beginning, and Britain, its most recent and thorough-going convert."[32]

Skelton made excuses for Riddell while condemning him for his "fool gesture." The prime minister wondered if five years with the hated Bennett had dulled Skelton's outsider's instincts, making him more inclined to protect his officials and less inclined to be on the alert for political danger: "Even Skelton had not seen how far Canada was going in taking the lead at Geneva." His "association with Bennett has made Skelton less sensitive to these dangers ... than he would have been many years ago." Always worried that his public servants might lead him astray, and convinced that he knew best, Mackenzie King resolved to be more vigilant than ever.[33]

Skelton supported the League while denigrating it as an instrument of collective security. He had more of an intellectual and moral commitment to it than King ever did, but neither could tolerate its transformation into an international war office. They need not have worried. Britain and France soon surrendered abjectly to Mussolini with their infamous Hoare-Laval Pact, completely overshadowing Canada's cowardly withdrawal from the field. Skelton had feared that his officer at the League was in cahoots with the British in the pursuit of rigorous sanctions, but this was a misreading of London's pusillanimous policy, which simply annoyed the Italians without deterring them. He at least felt some shame at his part, as he put it, in "cheering up Mussolini." King felt none.[34]

The close relationship that had existed between Skelton and King before 1930 was quickly re-established. On Christmas Eve of 1935, the prime minister sent his deputy a deluxe edition of Norman Rogers's biography of King, which had been issued in time for the election with extensive (and unacknowledged) edits and additions from the Liberal leader himself. Rogers was yet another of the links between King and Skelton. A one-time Queen's professor, he was close to Skelton and a King political protégé; he had been included in the cabinet as minister of labour, which had been King's first portfolio. In the handwritten note accompanying his gift, King wrote to Skelton that the volume "has so many associations with some of the events which have brought me once again into such pleasant relations with yourself, that I shall be grateful if you will accept this copy ... as a sort of souvenir of 1935."[35]

Skelton made his 1936 New Year's rounds of the diplomatic missions and the homes of the governor general and the party leaders, dragging Sandy along after insisting that he substitute "a milder dark suit & attachments" for his green shirt and tie. He observed Bennett in his Chateau Laurier Hotel suite, swamped in defeat and warning OD darkly that the Japanese trade agreement that he was helping King negotiate would be a disaster. Mackenzie King's residence on Laurier Avenue was "jammed as the rising sun ever is." At Rideau Hall, Skelton met the new governor general, Lord Tweedsmuir, who as John Buchan had written racy thrillers of the kind OD admired. His reaction to the vice-regal couple was snobbish: Buchan was a smooth talker, with the widest possible range of "acquaintance anecdotes"; "Lady T" was "rather commonplace." Skelton was probably a bit jealous. He had none of Tweedsmuir's social ease, swallowing public functions as the necessary duty that accompanied his job. Sandy predictably became fed up before his father did.[36] As for Isabel, she had long ago had enough of Ottawa's social life.

Resolving once again to be more faithful to his diary, Oscar identified a lull in foreign developments after the spectacular League crisis of the previous fall. Tired out and sometimes feeling dizzy, he took advantage of the respite to supervise the replacement of a thirty-year-old furnace, read the New York *Times* and *Foreign Affairs*, listen to the radio, and spend time with Sheila, who was suffering from bad headaches and needed help with her history courses. There was also an opportunity to get caught up on his paperwork, including the "chicken feed for the P.M. to sign."[37]

King was proving a trial, whining about the inadequacy of his staff and threatening to resign from the office he had newly won because of sheer exhaustion and fear of attacks from Bennett in the parliamentary session that was about to begin. "Sorry for him, genuinely lost nerve," OD scribbled in the diary, which tailed off after only a few days; "part of his trouble due to his unwillingness to organize or rather to work as part of an organization, and to his preoccupation with personal correspondence with acquaintances the world over whom he should ignore – can't be both P.M. & the world's greatest letter writer." The staffing emergency demonstrated how much Skelton was relied on; the prime minister wrote in his journal that Skelton "is the only one who can really save the situation." OD reassured King that Bennett was no threat while devising solutions to the prime minister's office difficulties. What that meant, in the end, was that External Affairs would have to sacrifice one of Skelton's own young men to the political wars. Hugh Keenleyside, returning to Ottawa after six years in Japan, was chosen as the most available and easily spared victim. He didn't last long as a Mackenzie King aide.[38]

On the evening of the first Friday of the new year, Skelton settled down at home to listen to President Roosevelt's 9 o'clock State of the Union Address. Fully half of it centred on foreign affairs. The president spoke of his policy of ensuring a peaceful and democratic good neighbourhood, which he claimed had spread throughout all of the Americas, from the Arctic to the Antarctic, and which contrasted mightily with "the temper and the purposes of the rulers of many of the great populations in Europe and in Asia." A big war might be coming, but the Americas could only watch and warn, remaining neutral while building their defences and, "through example and all legitimate encouragement and assistance," persuading others to return to the ways of peace and goodwill.[39]

OD thought Roosevelt "a great showman" and the speech "forcefully & clearly developed & enunciated," but he listened with scepticism and concern. He noted that Roosevelt had very pointedly included Canada in his prescription for the Americas, and that he was advancing the case for "North American isolationism" and "even seeking to speak for all." It was not the role of great democracies, Skelton believed, to impose their will on others, and the recent history of Europe had shown that they could not do so even when they tried. Referring to the recent U.S. neutrality law, which forbade the export of war materials to belligerents, he concluded that "other countries who may have to reckon with ultimate eventualities would seem well advised not to count upon action in their interest in affairs which, in the President's words, are 'not of immediate concern' to the U.S." Roosevelt had made it plain, after all, just how unlikely the United States was to help out any country that was the victim of aggression, and that reinforced Skelton's argument that collective security was the futile hope of a few dreamers.[40]

Skelton might have been expected to applaud the speech as furthering his campaign for anti-imperialism and North American solidarity. Instead he interpreted it as an example of interference and over-reaching, a variation on imperialism itself. It was "sentimental folly, a refusal to grow up," not to acknowledge the benefits of the Canadian-American relationship; nevertheless, life alongside a neighbour of overwhelming strength had its drawbacks. Canada must never allow itself to become the tail to the U.S. kite. Emphatically isolationist for the moment, the United States might in years to come swing to a policy of overseas adventure, driven by idealism, profit, or jingoism. Americans would always act to further their own interests, even if that meant direct intervention in Canadian affairs. Nor was a political or military alliance possible or advisable; that would be inconsistent with the country's historical alignment to Britain and the empire. Canada must take up national defence more seriously, so that the coasts would be safe if the government decided to take part in other peoples' wars or, if it decided not to, had to protect Canadians against the infringement of their neutrality.[41] The urgent necessity of a substantial increase in defence spending was becoming a constant in Skelton's thinking, as it was in King's.

The lull in international affairs was just that. On 26 February 1936 young officers of the Japanese army staged a bloody coup, which was in turn ruthlessly put down, moving Japan in the direction of military rule. On 7 March, German troops marched into the Rhineland, which had been demilitarized under Articles 42 and 43 of the 1919 Treaty of Versailles, an understanding reinforced by the Anglo-French-German Locarno Treaty of 1925, which had produced a Nobel Peace Prize for its negotiators. Those international treaties were now shattered; the British and French were rearming. Then, in July, army officers rose up against the legitimately constituted republican government of Spain, sparking a civil war that turned the country into a playground for foreign dictatorships, with the Soviets intervening to aid the government and Hitler and Mussolini rushing to the side of the rebels.

Skelton's personal views about these developments were consistent with his most fundamental beliefs in human freedom and liberal democracy. He loathed Hitlerism and all other forms of authoritarianism. His sympathies were "strongly" with the government forces in Spain. When the Italian consul general in Canada claimed that his country's success in Ethiopia was largely attributable to the work of the engineers and workmen who had the old Roman faculty of road building, Skelton replied caustically that "he should not forget to pay a tribute to the chemists who had produced, and the aviators who had scattered, bombs of mustard gas."[42]

Skelton repeatedly claimed that the international challenge was not one that Canadians could meet by running away. "We are a member of the British Commonwealth, a member of the League, a nation of the American Continent," he wrote in a draft speech for King in May, "and bound by ties of interest and friendship to many other lands." The foreign policy of Great Britain, the country's closest partner, was of necessity taking on a European orientation, with consequences that could "scarcely fail to be of the greatest significance for Canada." A British-led and heavily armed League of Nations, managed in Europe and for Europe, might be on the horizon, drawing Canada into its maw. In the enigmatic Pacific, a Japanese military dictatorship seemed on the rise, with all its implications for neighbouring China and Russia and the intensification of "every other international difficulty." Canadians, moreover, were internationally minded. The newspapers covered global events fully and promptly. Although opinion was not very articulate, Skelton was sure that it was interested and engaged.[43]

Yet he reminded an attentive King that they were thousands of miles away from it all. Canada must not attempt "tasks beyond our interest" or uncritically accept "doctrinaire or interested proposals for international action." When asked by the prime minister to list the obligations arising out of Hitler's takeover of the Rhineland, Skelton argued for the minimum. Versailles was "presumably a treaty to end a war, not a promise to begin another." Locarno guaranteed a demilitarized Rhineland, but it had been signed by Britain, not Canada, which had explicitly opted out of the treaty on Skelton's advice ten years before. The League could act but was unlikely to; if it did, it was not clear in any case that Canada would be committed to go along. For Canada, the only possible real obligation for action against Germany lay in the Commonwealth connection. If Britain went to war on the issue, was Canada at war? The present British Commonwealth relationship was an admirable peacetime arrangement, but the problem of what to do if another great war broke out had not yet been solved or frankly faced. Skelton hoped "that Britain will seek a solution that will avoid war for her, and avert the possibility of wrecking Canada to aid France and Russia in a preventive war against Germany (and possibly Japan and Italy)."[44]

The League of Nations had not moved to impose oil sanctions against Italy, and perhaps Canada had failed the world on the one occasion when its leadership could really have mattered. Skelton waved this criticism away as "an absurd failure ... to understand Canada's importance in the scheme of things." Besides, he repeated in a careful memorandum for King justifying the government's actions and making it clear that Ethiopia was Europe's problem, Canada had not declined to support oil sanctions. The debacle over oil came down to the hesitations and priorities of the Europeans, and had nothing to do with Canada. It was difficult to back people who were backing down.[45]

The prime minister told Parliament on 11 February 1936 that "the whole of Europe might have been aflame today" had the government not repudiated its representative and announced to the world that Walter Riddell had acted on his own. Skelton told King that he had made a mistake to put the matter in such apocalyptic terms.[46] King fell silent on the issue until after Mussolini had completed his rape of Ethiopia. By the late spring, the Ethiopian government and armies had collapsed and Emperor Haile Selassie had fled the country.

On 18 June King spoke again, in a rare major address on foreign policy, and this time he delivered the message the way Skelton had written it for him. Canada was ready to abandon sanctions now that Ethiopia had been subjugated, the prime minister announced, but it had carried out the League's embargo program as faithfully and efficiently as any other country, and more so than some. Riddell's oil proposal had been a "pretentious gesture," coming from the representative of a country that had no special power to deploy or interest at play in the conflict. Nevertheless, the government had been willing to impose oil, coal, and steel sanctions if there had been a general will to support them.[47]

That was the rub. Europe feared not Italy but war on a wide scale, and rightly so. There was no ignoring the fact that economic sanctions could trigger military conflict, since an aggressor might prefer the gamble of a sudden battle to the prospect of slow strangulation. Most League members, however, were unprepared to make the leap from the economic to the military, and to assume the firm commitments beyond the range of their immediate interest that would ensure a plan of universal compulsion. That made their threats hollow. Collective bluffing could not bring collective security.

Most of the rest of the speech was a repackaging of the Skelton conception of the Canadian national interest measured against the claims of collective action. The League of 1936 was not in the position or the mood to dictate peace to the world. Canada's vital and day-to-day relationships, at any rate, were with Great Britain and the United States. The League was necessarily secondary, and it could realistically be for most Canadians only an instrument of prevention and for the peaceful remedy of grievances, rather than a methodology for meting out punishment. European states were apt to think of it as a place to receive but not to give; they should not expect others to accept obligations for their continent's security if they were regularly going to throw overboard their reciprocal responsibilities for the safety of American or Asian states. Canada could have done more at Geneva. It could have been more involved, and stronger in its advocacy of good causes, but it had supported every League movement for disarmament and extending the range and facilities for peaceful international conciliation.

Geography was at the heart of the matter. Skelton, through King, repeated that Canada was a small country, distant from the threat of foreign attack or conquest. It was "fortunate both in our neighbours and our lack of neighbours." This might not have much to do with any special virtue, and instead be an accident of time and place, but Canadians had only to be in a European nation for one day to realize how fortunate their position was, and what folly it would be to throw it away. Yet if geography was an advantage, it was also a burden: "Some countries have too much history," but "we have too much geography." A big, sprawling, regionally oriented half-continent of a country was preoccupied inevitably by the problems of development and unity. Finally, and paradoxically, Canada was tied to an interdependent world, not least because its climate, resources, and economic structure made it dependent on trade. A prolonged war, and even the preparations for war, endangered the economic future and national cohesiveness of Canada. Peace was essential to nation building.

The speech was a powerful statement of government policy, lucidly written and memorable in both words and impact. Always attributed to Mackenzie King, the phrases "fortunate both in our neighbours and our lack of neighbours" and "if some countries have too much history, we have too much geography" have become part of Canadians' understanding of themselves. Skelton's old boss, R.B. Bennett, warmly praised the address in the House of Commons. Encountering Skelton as he left Parliament, Bennett congratulated him on it. When OD pretended not to understand, the former prime minister said that he had instantly recognized the style and the direction of the reasoning. "Oh, Dr. Skelton, I listened to those epigrammatic idiosyncrasies too long not to recognize them."[48]

Members of the League met over the summer, with the Ethiopian debacle and the threats of further serious disturbances to world peace on their minds. King and Skelton saw to it that their representatives at the discussions laid low and said next to nothing. Vincent Massey, the new high commissioner in London, was chosen to speak for Canada, but he felt marginalized and guilty as he watched the tiny Ethiopian emperor plead his dignified case a final time, all to no avail. The League Assembly listened respectfully and promptly abandoned the economic sanctions that had been imposed on Italy the previous fall. There was no point in them, now that Mussolini had his imperial conquest and Britain and France were rushing to his side in hopes that he might be turned against Hitler, an even greater menace. The League needed reinvention, everyone agreed, but they differed fundamentally on whether obligations under the Covenant, the body's founding document, ought to be increased or decreased. Member states were asked to send their ideas for League reform to Geneva for discussion at the September 1936 meeting.[49]

Skelton set to work on a memorandum that eventually came to more than 20,000 words, bringing to bear his encyclopedic knowledge of League procedures and of the politics of two dozen countries with a stake in the League's future. After sixteen years in the life of the League, he concluded, peace was in more jeopardy than at any time since the end of the First World War. Socialists contended that the world's economic and political problems were rooted in the inherent weakness of capitalism, while fascists argued that they were caused by the inherent weakness of democracy. It was the Great War itself, however, which had revolutionized the international system, with the impacts being felt still. The war had sanctioned the habit of violence and established wide familiarity with modern weapons. The spirit of economic nationalism, for Skelton one of the great evils of his time, had been intensified. New assertions of state power over the lives and activities of peoples had risen up, along with new bureaucracies to wield those powers. Colossal burdens of war debt and war reparation broke down the delicately balanced structure of international finance, leading to demoralized currencies, fluctuating exchanges, and shifting prices. The stress and change of conflict weakened the restraining force of custom, turning respectable citizens like German junkers into gangsters.[50]

In Skelton's diagnosis, the distinctive feature of the threat to international peace was that it arose as much from the conflict of class as from national rivalry. Class antagonisms and class sympathies were overflowing national boundaries. Newspapers and radio painted vivid pictures of conditions in other countries, exacerbating resentments and manufacturing longings. An unceasing, audacious, and unscrupulous use of propaganda, especially but not exclusively by the dictatorships, thrust problems and antipathies across borders. The tactics of class warfare, notable in the Nazi murders of Jews, introduced a new fearfulness into the international equation. Capitalists and workers alike acquired a direct interest in the dominance abroad of the regimes with which they sympathized. Much of the debate at the League, accordingly, ran in terms of fascist and anti-fascist sympathy – a problem the founders of that body had not considered and one that made intervention by outside states in European conflicts all the more complicated.

Skelton judged Germany, Italy, and Japan all to have substantial economic problems and grievances, but it was the dynamic and magnifying power of political and psychological factors that made them direct dangers to their neighbours. They suffered from "prestige desires" – "Germany because of defeat in war, Italy because of having to be rescued by her allies in the war and being cheated by them in the peace, Japan because of the necessity of proving her equality with white peoples." The ruling forces in Germany had openly and repeatedly scorned peace, putting their desire for domination forward with specific objectives, from the annexation of Austria perhaps even to the penetration and control of the Ukraine and southeastern Europe. They were deterred from more open challenges on these fronts by the recent Franco-Soviet alliance, uncertainty about Britain's response, and increasing domestic economic strains. Perhaps the Germans really did not want war, if they could secure what they wanted by bluff, bullying, and blackmail. Perhaps time, if there was time, would lessen "this neurotic fanaticism and give fuller play for the many fine qualities of the German people." In Italy, success had swollen Mediterranean ambitions and strengthened the fascist regime. The

early and widespread criticism of the Ethiopian adventure had been
diverted by sanctions into hatred of foreigners and especially Britain.
Mussolini threatened an alliance with Hitler, but he might change his
mind if Germany advanced closer to Italian borders.

The militarists were in full control in Japan, Skelton continued, with
nothing less than complete domination of northeast Asia as their goal,
and possibly the East Indies and Australia beyond. There was no present likelihood that the British, or the Americans, would block Japanese
designs. Nor would the League, "which has forgotten that China or the
Covenant exist, except when an inconvenient Chinese delegate annually
raises their ghosts in an Assembly speech." There were, though, other
factors at work too. China was weak, disunited, and ravaged but was still
moved by an increasing sense of national pride and national bitterness,
and it had found an appropriate leader in the subtle and supple Chiang
Kai-shek. The Soviet Union had a new sense of energy and mission, and
Japan could hardly challenge Russian military and air power in the east
unless the Soviets were held down on the other flank by Germany. In
Japan itself, the financial burdens of militarism were being felt, though
the opposition to it was afraid to let out a peep.

With the threats to peace and the conflict of classes, there were substantial limits to what the League of Nations could do. Skelton was persistent in the thought, however, that the League could still be a positive
force if it could be directed towards the removal of political grievances,
the lessening of economic tension, the reduction of armaments, and an
emphasis on conciliation at an early stage of a crisis. Such endeavours,
and the League's notable social and humanitarian work, lacked "the dramatic and spectacular touch of the plans for world coercion of an aggressor." Critics would say that the League had to be more than a debating
society to be worth $6 million of Canadian taxpayers' money, but the
League's preventive functions "have the advantage of being practicable,
of gradually educating the world to world needs, and establishing a
world procedure, and of holding the League together until changing
conditions may make it more feasible to adopt and put into practice
more ambitious measures." King might be willing to say similar things,
but he was too practical to believe them. Skelton did.

He told the prime minister that the September meeting of the League
would be of extreme importance. It would be difficult for anyone except
him to represent Canada adequately on that occasion in Geneva. King
agreed, asking Skelton to accompany him. As they toured the prime
minister's country estate at Kingsmere, Quebec, on Dominion Day at

the beginning of July 1936, King told his deputy to work out a leisurely schedule for Europe, so that they could really enjoy themselves. "We have both *earned* that much," King said, adding in his diary that Skelton had a "marvelous sense of duty" and "great chivalry." He was "as fine a character as I know," better than his British counterpart, Sir Maurice Hankey, "in what he knows & equal to him in tact – a delightful personality – very modest, exceptionally good judgment & well informed, – a god-send in the truest & fullest meaning of that word." King instructed Skelton to get all the rest he could over the summer in order to be in shape for their trip. A week later, Oscar and Isabel took a week off to drive around the Gaspé peninsula.[51]

When they returned, Skelton completed his mammoth memorandum on League reform. He added several draft paragraphs for King's speech to the Assembly, making the by now familiar case that the League was a failure only when measured against the glowing expectations of its founders and supporters. It could never be a deus ex machina, a worker of miracles, which would find and impose solutions to all international rivalries and conflicts. The League was weak because of the effort to make it perform a task beyond the power and willingness of its members. Amendment of the Covenant was neither wise nor necessary.[52]

On 11 September, Skelton departed Ottawa for the League. He took the train to Montreal and Quebec City, where the *Empress of Britain* was docked. Ernest Lapointe and his wife were there to see off the prime minister and his Geneva team, which included Mackenzie King, Norman Rogers, Vincent Massey, and the League perennial, Senator Raoul Dandurand. Skelton never tired of the trip along the St Lawrence, doubting that there was a more impressive approach to a country anywhere in the world. Built at the end of the 1920s by Canadian Pacific Steamship Lines to win customers away from the more southern run to Europe out of New York, the *Empress* was large, fast, and luxurious. Skelton had travelled in it with Bennett when they had gone together to Geneva two years before. The ship got the Canadians to Cherbourg in five days, a voyage that was too brief for OD's taste. The ride on the St Lawrence was very smooth, but a huge swell struck the ship in the Atlantic, not slowing progress but sending the prime minister and Massey below deck to their staterooms for a day or more.[53]

That was fine with Skelton. He resented the pretentious Massey, who aspired to be more aristocratic than the aristocracy, and he was quite content with the leisurely pace of life he quickly carved out in the sumptuously decorated mansion on the sea. He went nowhere near the punching bags and electric horses of the athletic room, confining himself to some reading and walking to accompany the fancy food and infrequent business meetings. Each night in first class, there were drinks and a multi-course dinner, followed by a movie or concert, late nights made later by the turning of the clock forward one hour to ready passengers for European time. Skelton felt the worries of his professional life ebb away. In mid-ocean, "we don't feel responsible for either Europe or America, though press cables or wireless messages indicate there's the usual daily grist of troubles in both continents."[54]

They reached Cherbourg early in the afternoon on 17 September and arrived by train in a rainy Paris just before nine in the evening. Oscar wrote home the next morning: "Behold us installed very pleasantly in the George V, a quite swanky hotel just off the Champs Elysées, and not very far from the Canadian Legation." Skelton, his worries back, hurried to the Legation and work. King bought francs and was headed, Skelton thought, to the shops. That night OD went to the home of Jean Désy and his wife, recently posted from Ottawa to the Paris Legation, where Skelton viewed their new baby in her fine pink satin bassinette. Not comfortable when enthusiasm was in order, he regarded the youngster as simply "a normal bit of protoplasm." The evening was half conducted in French, and he was not fully at ease with that either. From there, Désy drove him to the hotel to pay his bill and to the station to catch the overnight train to Geneva and the League. Another grand hotel was waiting. Walter Riddell transported Skelton from the station to the Hôtel de la Paix, where the government had rented a suite of rooms for the three weeks they would be there. He was given a room overlooking the street out front and the lake, with Mont Blanc on the horizon; a bathroom was shared with Georges Vanier, who had been imported from the Paris Legation to assist the delegation. It was at first difficult to sleep with the noise in the street below, but he became used to the bustle.[55]

At the League, which had begun to move into its handsome Palais des Nations building, Skelton found not much to do at the beginning. There was more marking time than he could ever remember in Geneva. He wrote to Mike Pearson at Canada House in London that it "does not look as if anything desirable will be done in any direction but even to hold the status quo is something of an achievement these days." Skelton watched from a safe distance as the question of the seating of the Ethiopian delegation dominated the initial proceedings and made everything else impossible apart from the most routine business of constituting committees and selecting their members. Ethiopia, in effect, was no more;

Mussolini had seen to that. He insisted, as a precondition of his participation in the fall meetings in Geneva, that the Ethiopians be excluded: "The Italian delegation," in the words of one disgusted observer, "must not be exposed to finding itself sitting in the same hall with a delegation representing Ethiopia." Or as Skelton put it, the issue was "to determine whether Haile Selassie or Mussolini is to speak for Ethiopia." The British and French were desperate to recapture the affections of the Italian dictator so that they could keep him out of Hitler's grip. Thus, they sided with the Italians, claiming that the government of Ethiopia no longer could claim actual authority over its territory, a reasonable enough argument if the method by which that authority had been destroyed was put aside.[56]

Skelton was in the delicate position of someone who felt the injustice of it all but himself had been unprepared to stand up for Ethiopia. He admitted that it was "sacrificing substance for shadow when we refuse to save Ethiopia from being conquered but boggle at the formality of admitting she is," but he sympathized with the dilemma that the British and French were in. If Italy opted out of the effort to reconstruct the Locarno process that was in tatters after Hitler's recent takeover of the Rhineland, it might mean that Germany would also refuse to cooperate, "and the peace of Europe will be still more precarious." Nevertheless, he could not bring himself to give Italy the satisfaction of ousting the Ethiopians. That was King's instinct too – Skelton noted that the prime minister had struck up "quite a friendship with a little Ethiopian delegate" – and in the end it was the League Assembly's instinct. Ethiopia was seated. Italy, its foreign minister waiting in Rome with his bags packed, refused to come to Geneva.[57]

Efforts to cozy up to Hitler were just as repellent to Skelton as the campaign to please the Italians. He observed and admired an inspiring pro-League speech by Britain's foreign secretary, Anthony Eden, the glamour boy of international politics, but OD thought that Eden and his colleagues were "much friendlier to Hitler than I like to see." The British were just like everyone else, "thinking of their own interest first." When King wanted to take advantage of their proximity to Germany to make a pilgrimage to Hitler in Berlin, Skelton firmly discouraged the idea. He told King that that he felt "very strongly that it would be resented in Canada; that it would only be flattering Hitler by having him feel that some more persons were coming to him." Nothing could influence him, and King should not try. The führer's speech three months before, in which he had spoken of his destiny as a somnambulist who walked in his sleep, demonstrated that he was a mystic, beyond control and impossible to sway.[58]

Skelton had no illusions about Canada's position or popularity at the League. Canadians were simply a "middle of the road harmless people." Their leaders, however, were not ruthlessly repressing their people, as was happening in Germany, Italy, and the Soviet Union. Canada was an experiment in democracy, and Skelton intuited that this was still valued in Geneva. That was the reason, he felt sure, that at the beginning of the Assembly meetings, League members elected King as vice-president rather than a delegate from the dictatorships.[59]

The Canadian preoccupation in Geneva for the first ten days at the League was King's speech to the Assembly, slated for 29 September. Little had been prepared beforehand. Skelton spent a day on a draft in his hotel room, using pieces of his summer memorandum on League reform, and the prime minister produced a version of his own. Rogers and Dandurand preferred Skelton's attempt, and he did not like King's at all, "but it's for him to decide and I'm not pressing my draft ... It's Mr. King who has to take the responsibility so it's up to him to decide how to put what he has to say."[60]

In the end, Skelton was less huffy and King more accepting of his deputy's help. They met closer to OD's wording than to King's. All the staple Skeltonisms were in the final address, as was OD's familiar rhetoric of cadence and repetition. The phrase from the 18 June speech about Canada's good fortune in its neighbours and lack of neighbours was prominent, a happy state of affairs that King compared with Europe's predicament, characterized by "the violent nature of the propaganda and recriminations hurled incessantly across the frontiers, the endeavours to draw all countries into one or other extremist camp, the feverish race for rearmament, the hurrying to and fro of diplomats, the ceaseless weaving and unravelling of understandings and alliances, and the consequent fear and uncertainty of the peoples." The comparative safety of the disarmed nations of North America, contrasted against the armed nations of Europe, was an argument made so often by Canadian speakers at Geneva in the past that it had raised widespread resentment. Skelton knew that, and he had warned King against the practice, but he could not help himself.[61]

At the core of the King speech was the insistence on Canada's standing as a free North American state, making it different from Europe in the obligations it could and was willing to take on. What was more, the prime minister claimed, its unwillingness to intervene in complicated international disputes automatically, with the threat of force, was now widely shared throughout the world. The shaken authority of the League could be restored only through a painstaking rebuilding of confidence and the spirit of conciliation, brutal realism about the limitations of the League after a decade and a half of hard experience, and a move back in the direction of universal membership. "Every vacant seat in this assembly is a broken link in the chain of collective security," Skelton reasoned through King. A punitive international organization was not practical politics. What was left, and what was possible, was "a League to further ideals of peace and goodwill among all nations, and between all classes." That was and had always been Canada's version of the League.[62]

Skelton was well pleased by the speech, which seemed to him much the best delivered of the Assembly addresses to that point. He noted a varied reaction from the other delegations. The "ultra-sanctionists," led by France and Russia, were perturbed by King's contention that collective coercion was impossible in the international circumstances of the time; the Scandinavians, along with the Dutch and the Swiss, were pleased by the blunt statement of views that were authentic for Canada and right for them. The British, continuing to send mixed signals, congratulated the Canadians warmly, though they did not approve of King's public reference to a dominion's freedom to stay out of empire wars. Following the Canadian speech, the Australian delegate, former prime minister Stanley Bruce, spoke to the Assembly in similar terms, and New Zealand, firmly in the sanctionist camp, annoyed Skelton with "a childishly amateur & unreal speech." So, OD told Isabel, "the dear old Empire was much to the fore."[63]

From Monday to Saturday over the three jammed weeks in Geneva, Skelton got up at 7:30 and had a breakfast in his room of hot chocolate, toast, and jam. He reviewed League documents for an hour, skimmed the Geneva and Paris newspapers, and searched for someone to whom he could dictate business letters, perhaps to London or Paris or back to headquarters. There was a morning walk, taking about half an hour, from the hotel to the Assembly to listen to speeches. Lunch was usually with a Canadian, Vanier and his wife, Pauline, being favourite companions, or someone from Norway, Sweden, Denmark, Finland, or Holland; he thought that Canada had more in common with these countries than any others on the continent. From three until just after six, OD was in the League's shiny new buildings for committee work. A meeting with the prime minister might follow, and a walk back to the hotel with him. For dinner Skelton often talked over general League questions with representatives from like-minded countries. After eating he worked most nights, conferring with Canadian staff and foreign and Commonwealth officials, reviewing documentation, and finishing up by writing personal letters. He felt well most of the time, catching a cold but fighting it off with a bedtime dose of brown Guinness and scotch. On Sundays, if the weather was good, he abandoned stuffy Geneva for a meal or a drive in the countryside nearby and to watch the sun bounce off the white peaks of Mont Blanc.[64]

Once his big speech was out of the way, King could almost always be counted on to leave his deputy alone during the evening. The prime minister was busily mopping up every available opportunity for gossip and a free meal, completely in his element, Skelton smiled, "so long as he's not sitting beside someone talking French." The shy official, by contrast, ventured out into society as seldom as possible. A Verdi opera took him out of himself and "the European mess" for a few hours. He "pulled through" a Walter Riddell reception. The fine garden and trees of his representative at the League were a consolation, and Skelton did not begrudge him his large house. He tried an Irish party, but only because it was given by his favourite country. It was a disaster. He "met everyone in Geneva I don't care about, and practically no Irish: I never felt more the truth of Walter Raleigh's lines – 'I do not like the human race. I do not like its silly face, etc.'"[65]

Skelton sat on the First Committee, dealing with legal and constitutional questions, and the Fourth, reviewing the League's budget. He enjoyed watching the machinery of the organization tick, but the issues were only intermittently interesting. The discussion tended to be dominated by half a dozen old timers who attended every Assembly, always sitting on the same committee. In both committees he made a point of working together with the northwest block of Swedes, Danes, Dutch, Finns, and Norwegians. He enjoyed getting reacquainted with Nikolaos Politis of Greece, Štefan Osuský of Czechoslovakia, and Alberto Guani of Uruguay, and saw a good deal of Maxim Litvinoff and Vladimir Potemkin of the USSR, Wellington Koo of China, Henri Rolin of Belgium, and René Cassin of France. Sir William Malkin of the British Foreign Office, with whom he had worked at the ODL conference in London in 1929, was very agreeable, but he thought the Commonwealth representatives on the committees were unimpressive, including those from the Irish Free State. Many did not even turn up for the meetings.[66]

Skelton seldom spoke at committee. When he did, he was quick about it, simply putting the Canadian position on the record or in one case objecting to a reactionary suggestion from a Balkan delegate. He was opposed to the subject of League reform coming to the First Committee, partly because the discussion in the General Assembly had shown such extreme differences of opinion that it was clear no immediate agreement could be reached, and partly because it seemed likely that any discussion in committee would simply repeat the General Assembly debate. Partly, too, he admitted, he did not like the idea of having "to get up a lot of stuff for the discussion."[67]

King had more travelling in mind as they made their way home. Skelton at least had managed finally to convince the prime minister to abandon his desire to try out his skills at conciliation on Hitler. King had suggested they proceed to Sweden via Berlin after the League session wound down, but OD cheerfully sacrificed the Swedes as a means of sidetracking a visit to the German leader. Instead the two Canadians went on to Paris and London. Thoroughly tired out, Skelton envied Dandurand and the Désys, who were off to Tunis and beyond into the desert for a month.[68]

Paris was nevertheless a relief after Geneva's "gloom and the dull provincial Calvinist bourgeois air of the place." He wrote home from the stately Crillon hotel, a fine old mansion facing the Place de la Concorde, with the Assemblée nationale, the Quai d'Orsay, and the Eiffel Tower all within sight across the Seine River. It had been a month since he left home: "It seems in another age; certainly it is another age over here – whether 25th or 15th century is another question." He put in two afternoons at the Legation, visited with Canadian bankers and businessmen, and had a lunch "in the best traditions" at the Foreign Ministry in the Quai d'Orsay, followed by a long discussion with the French prime minister, the minister of foreign affairs, and other officials and ministers. King was greatly taken with the Foreign Ministry building, but to OD's eye it was "too rococo Napoleon the Third, all gilt & gingerbread, to be impressive."[69]

The Sunday after arriving in Paris, the two Canadians travelled to the recently unveiled Vimy Memorial, at the scene of the country's signal military victory of the First World War. The visitors surveyed the powerful monument, with its towers of gleaming Croatian stone that leapt from the uninspiring landscape, and walked quietly through some of the wartime trenches and dugouts from the seven-mile Canadian front. The underground catacombs had been preserved as monuments themselves, and were more impressive to the visitors than the striking memorial because they had been built by the men themselves.[70]

Skelton and King arranged just enough work in Paris to justify a stay that was mainly busy days of pleasure. In glorious weather, Skelton strolled along the boulevards and up and down the Seine, shopping, sampling good restaurants, and watching his cash slip away. A modern staging of Flaubert's *Madame Bovary* and a production of Molière's *L'Ecole des Femmes* were not too taxing because of the clearly enunciated French of the actors. Aware that some of the members of King's entourage had been left out of the social mix, OD took them to the spectacle of motion, colour, and song at the Casino de Paris music hall: "I haven't laughed as much in years as at two skits, one on Hitler's followers in love & one a scene at a sub-prefect's evening reception, both somewhat vulgar but extremely funny." The next night he and Norman Rogers treated the entire Canadian League delegation and Legation staff to a doubleheader evening: two boxes at the ABC music hall, "artistic to the last word," followed by ringside tables at the Bol Talsarin in Montmartre, where a dancer came very close to kicking Skelton in the face; it was "somewhat more risqué than a Prime Minister, Senator & Diplomatic representative usually attend … but extremely well done, and Mr. King said that after the summer bathing costumes it was quite tame."[71]

In the middle of October, the Canadian caravan moved from Paris to London on the first public trip of the new overnight train-boat service, which ran the train on to an English Channel ferry at Dunkirk and disgorged it at Dover the next morning. "It's supposed to be a very fine item in the march of progress," Skelton surmised. He would have preferred to approach England by day so that he could view the Norman towns and the chalk cliffs of Dover. Nor was he impressed by the sleeping arrangements or the poor ventilation, made worse by his decision to take one of King's assistants into his compartment because the train had been overbooked.[72] He hardly slept, but the word quickly got around of his generosity, reinforcing his reputation as the most thoughtful of colleagues and bosses.

In London, they added the Ritz to their collection of deluxe hotels. It was far more luxurious than Oscar wanted or needed, but it was a King favourite and a convenient location for getting almost anywhere that mattered in London. Canada House was in nearby Trafalgar Square, the theatres, rail stations, and shops were close, and Green Park was right under his hotel room window. After a production of *Pride and Prejudice* at the St James Theatre, he confessed "a dark secret" to his wife. She was a Jane Austen aficionado, but he admitted that he had never read a line of the book, or any of her other works, apart from a paragraph or two Isabel had once passed to him. He recalled the piece he had written about Austen when he was in his twenties, which he had tried unsuccessfully to publish, but that had been done on the basis of some books about her and nothing at all by her: "After thirty years with a Jane Austen devotee, that may be considered Prejudice against Pride or merely Nature's way of evening up." He had much more theatre in mind, but the work accumulated and life subsided into the one he lived in Ottawa: full of King and commitments.[73]

Vincent Massey was unavoidable. The wealthy high commissioner and his haughty wife, Alice, who told Skelton that she knew how to drive English servants, had just installed themselves at fashionable 12 Hyde Park Gardens, and they insisted on entertaining the prime minister in high style. They did so by mounting a major dinner party, with a gaggle of lords and ladies as well as Anthony Eden, Dominions Secretary Malcolm MacDonald, and Vincent's actor brother, Raymond, who had played Abraham Lincoln, OD's political hero, on stage and in film. Skelton sat beside Baroness Ravensdale, the "quite strongly Fascist" daughter of Lord Curzon and sister-in-law of Oswald Mosley, the leader of Britain's fascists. Massey struck again with "a little cocktail party" a few days later – "600 present; I was an hour late fortunately."[74]

As he moved around London, Skelton was confronted everywhere by gossip about King Edward VIII and his romance with Wallis Simpson, which OD relayed to Isabel as the "endless serial story of the King and his doings which is the main topic of conversation in all classes & circles."[75] Mrs Simpson was American, divorced (once, but with another on the way), and completely unacceptable to the Church of England and the choir of establishment press and politicians. Yet the king was determined to have her as his wife. A confrontation between the headstrong king and the government was certain.

The crisis broke in late November, after Skelton and King had returned home. Edward was Canada's monarch too, and under the Statute of Westminster the Parliament in Ottawa had to assent to changes in royal succession and the royal styles and titles. On 28 November a request came from the British government for Canada's views on whether the king should leave the throne if he insisted on having his way, or whether some arrangement could be found to allow him to marry Mrs Simpson. Isabel wrote in her diary that she was sure her husband wanted the king to keep his throne; she knew that she did, and she hoped for a deal that would permit Edward and Wallis to marry but prevent her from ever becoming queen. The king was the most popular person in the world, in large measure because he was seen as the peoples' champion, devoid of pretense. Isabel concluded that one of his great virtues, his dislike of sham, was doing Edward in.[76]

By 9 December the king had decided to abdicate. Skelton helped the prime minister prepare his public response. While Isabel's reading circle was discussing T.S. Eliot's *Murder in the Cathedral*, Oscar worked into the evening with John Read, the External Affairs legal adviser, not getting home until 10 p.m. After catching a quick supper, the two then met Mackenzie King at Laurier House, where they stayed until 2 a.m. The king spoke to his peoples three hours later, at 10 a.m. London time, dramatically (and self-indulgently) choosing "the woman I love" over duty.[77]

Skelton was not an anti-monarchist, rather the contrary. He urged that the government take the opportunity to remove legislative references to the king as "Supreme Lord in and over the whole of Canada," but he also wanted to express regret and sympathy for the king and "hope for unity of all parts of the Empire around the Crown." The prime minister and the cabinet accepted the first recommendation but not the second. When Isabel and Oscar listened to Mackenzie King's broadcast on the abdication, Skelton thought back to the negotiations leading to the Statute of Westminster. He had written nearly every word and phrase of the statute's preamble, and now it was being used to remove one king and put in place another. He felt "very awkward."[78]

The king's fall was a tragic ending to a disastrous year in international affairs. Canada was fortunate in its neighbour and in its lack of neighbours, but a chaotic world was unavoidable. Would-be Caesars and Napoleons strutted in Italy, Germany, and Japan, all of them open sores of unrest and aggression. The United Kingdom, France, Russia, and the United States rested on their achievements, determined to keep what they had but too complacent to deploy their power generously or judiciously. On his way home from the League in the fall, Skelton had walked through Paris on a soft and hazy day. "I never felt," he wrote to Isabel, "the charm of Paris so much as looking up & down the Seine, & never felt so deeply the tragedy of the shadow of national antagonisms & class conflicts that threatens all this fine civilisation."[79]

12
Pretty Well Used Up, 1937–8

Mackenzie King had a strong sense of Skelton's worth. The prime minister relied, he admitted, almost solely on his deputy. OD was everywhere: advising on all the questions that came before the government, domestic and international; hovering outside the cabinet room; whispering advice to ministers about their next manoeuvre; sitting on all the important interdepartmental committees; and carrying important social responsibilities as Canada's chief diplomat. His position was unassailable, his influence ubiquitous. Yet King realized that Skelton was increasingly fatigued. He had "none too great reserve of strength, and is getting pretty well used up." There was no obvious person to replace him if he retired or became ill.[1]

Even if Skelton could have altered his obsessive approach to work, King was too much its beneficiary to do much more than fret about his deputy's health. He did, however, want recognition for his indispensable man. At the end of 1936, the prime minister asked the cabinet to admit Skelton into the Privy Council of Canada, a status usually reserved for the most senior politicians, and to accompany this honour with a substantial raise of $2,000 to his $10,000 salary. The under-secretary had declined the principalship of Queen's University at $15,000 a year and had turned back R.B. Bennett's offer of a knighthood. He was the fulcrum around which Canada's international policy turned, King told his colleagues, requiring "fuller recognition of his important position" if he was to deal on an equal basis with his opposite numbers in other countries and at the League of Nations. Skelton also had "more to do in the way of entertaining guests from outside than any other man in the Public Service. They come to him from every side. He is most hospitable." No one in the cabinet dissented: "All felt that this recognition was as necessary as it was deserving." When confronted with the offer of a privy councillorship, Skelton was dumbfounded, asking King not to make fun of him. The prime minister replied that he was prepared to make the appointment official immediately, and announce it to the press, but OD begged him not to do anything until he had had a chance to think the matter through and examine the historical precedents.[2]

Skelton seriously considered the possibility of the privy councillorship, going so far as to consult with colleagues in the British government. He was a proud and ambitious man, not at all the grey one-dimensional figure who appeared from time to time in the press – a virtuous servant of the public and a paragon of non-partisanship, as the Ottawa *Journal* characterized him in February 1937. He sought public prominence, and had become accustomed to its pressures, as Isabel never did. She wrote beside a clipping of the *Journal's* editorial, which repeated compliments by the prime minister and the leader of the Opposition: "This is the sort of thing [that] makes me so happy & proud I tremble for fear some day some awfully inexplicable disgrace will blow up out of a clear sky & that the papers will howl the very opposite."[3]

Honours made Skelton feel uncomfortable. It embarrassed him, and went against his beliefs, to have a label marking him out as superior or special. His U.K. contacts told him that the privy councillorship would have been unusual in the British system for a public servant who was still active. So he grabbed the extra $2,000 a year, a raise that slid easily through Parliament and took effect on 1 April 1937,[4] but nothing further was done to bring him into the Privy Council.

Skelton liked being the person who mattered most in the public service. He took great satisfaction from the fact that he had moved up the ladder of deputy ministers. After twelve years in the government, he was outranked in public-service seniority by only two other department chiefs. He was a conscious pioneer in the founding of a professional bureaucracy: using External Affairs as a prototype for discovering men of "breadth and flexibility of view," bringing them into government by competitive examination, and putting leaders struck from his mould into other departments – the appointment of his friend, Clifford Clark, as deputy minister of finance was a notable case in point. In his recruits into government there was the outline of an emerging Ottawa mandarinate. Skelton's style of quiet loyalty, long hours, and public reticence became their style too. Even the way he wrote his memoranda, lining up the pros and cons of an argument but leaving no doubt where he stood, was catching on.[5]

In his own department, he was a model but not a mentor. He was too busy for that, too ramshackle, and too unwilling to share responsibility, all the defects he saw in the prime minister. Junior officers at External Affairs headquarters were given little to do, while the staff abroad were given no systematic feedback about their reporting or what was going on in Canada. L.B. Pearson, who had come into the department in 1928, claimed that Skelton had a stunning disregard for the practical. He had no interest in or aptitude for departmental management and lacked the ruthlessness to confront its tough problems. He refused, on the one hand, to hurt his subordinates, and on the other to go all out on their behalf. "I wish we had a chief who would add to Dr. Skelton's admirable personal qualities and remarkable brain, an interest in and aptitude for personnel & organization problems and a determination to fight for his men." His ambition showing, Pearson added that he thought that he was exactly the leader that External needed.[6]

Criticisms of Skelton were part of everyday departmental chitchat. "The Dep't of External Affairs is lousy," exclaimed Hume Wrong, Pearson's acerbic colleague, and "will remain so while Skelton is at its head." Scott Macdonald, who had joined External in the same year as Pearson, was more kindly in recollection years later, remembering that Skelton was enormously approachable, but also that he offered no criticism or detailed direction to his officers and was reluctant to champion their causes to the prime minister. Skelton's reputation as a poor manager was confirmed by outsiders. "He is not a good administrator and his office is badly organized," the British high commissioner, Sir Francis Floud, reported to the Dominions Office in London shortly after taking up his duties, adding that he was "very kind and friendly" if "not a very easy man to get on terms with."[7]

Pearson and his colleagues misjudged their boss in one important respect. Skelton did fight for his people. Although notoriously frugal and reluctant to spend public money, he successfully pressed King to raise departmental salaries and grant promotions from the ranks. He protected Walter Riddell after his infamous oil initiative, and met his hurt feelings with genuine understanding. There was particular irony in Pearson's complaints because Skelton went out of his way to respond to the diplomat's demands that he be paid more at the High Commission in London, despite his evident (in Pearson's words) "pain and surprise" when confronted with youthful purposefulness. After Pearson's departure for England, Skelton affectionately let him know how much he was valued and how much he was missed. Through 1937 and into

1938 Pearson seriously considered an employment opportunity at the Canadian Broadcasting Corporation, while not being reluctant to use the opportunity to squeeze yet more money and a promise of advancement out of the department. With the under-secretary's help and support, he succeeded in getting the position he wanted in External Affairs at a considerably better salary. Skelton accommodated this exercise in naked self-advancement, even while not entirely approving of it. A little later on, when Pearson wrote from London to say how surprised he was that he had lost his car and chauffeur in a cost-cutting measure, OD responded sardonically: "I am surprised that you are surprised."[8]

The deputy minister's domination of the Department of External Affairs was so complete that Mackenzie King had to instruct Canada's diplomatic representative in Washington to pay attention to the political head of the department. The prime minister, King said heatedly, was "the responsible Minister, and had some say as well as Skelton in the affairs of the Department." As they prepared for the 1937 Imperial Conference, King was irritated that Skelton held all the arrangements, right down to the smallest details, in his own hands. "I know he tries to do the fair & just thing, but in many things his outlook is difficult, and he is most persistent in holding to his own point of view." Skelton was reluctant to hire personnel or spend money on the prime minister's behalf, and "yet," King complained, "he has a great staff of his own," featuring respected specialists like Loring Christie and Norman Robertson.[9]

Occasionally the resentment bubbled over. King had let Skelton talk him out of an excursion to see Adolf Hitler the previous autumn, but, desperately wanting to promote peaceful relations between the British Empire and Germany, he quickly had second thoughts. Skelton remained sceptical. When the boss brought the matter up again soon after the two men arrived home from their 1936 European trip, Skelton did not demur. However, King picked up the disapproval in Skelton's tone of voice, which was "critical of Germany." Skelton's judgment was frequently excellent, King complained to his diary, but he failed "wholly to see the wisdom of a course where his own feelings are strongly dominant." The under-secretary had "extreme radical sympathies" that spoiled his judgment; "there is a certain inferiority complex of a class akin to that of many of those who have Irish blood in their veins, which keeps unconsciously asserting itself." Skelton's outlook was an example of "the so-called scientific mind which during the last century has been a materialist mind"; it obscured "the finer truths which find their expression only in spiritual interpretation of history."[10]

Too much should not be made of this. Given to self-pity, King tended to carp about Skelton when they disagreed and hardly to take note when they were on the same tack, so that their disagreements bulk larger in the prime minister's diary than they did in their life together. Their relationship resembled a marriage, with both sides sure of their rectitude and needing to let off steam – a good marriage, though, with enough respect and goodwill to get them over the rough patches.

King's outburst was revealing nevertheless. He and Skelton both had controlling personalities. They were in that one sense a bad combination, apt to clash when each insisted on his own way. As the world edged closer to another great war, their differing views about Canada's international future were exposed. King thought that he was on the side of the angels in the titanic struggle taking shape between good and evil: God would triumph over the blind material forces that had been set loose in Europe and Asia. He fancied that he was not an observer, an academic thinker like Skelton, but a practical politician. Skelton might know what needed to be said most of the time. King knew that he knew how and when to say it. He had the judgment and sensitivity to guide international events in the proper direction.

Far more knowledgeable about international politics and relationships, and far less likely to rely on instinct, Skelton was inclined to the belief that the world was full of carnivorous animals. Although anxious to maintain a tight civilian control over the armed forces, he had a stronger belief in the military and in military force. There was still, as King observed, some of the radical and the outsider left in him, lending a hard critical edge to Skelton's thinking, which had at its base a hatred of tyranny, oppression, and class distinction. Part of that edge was anger, though, and that could be a weakness in his assessments of the deteriorating international situation – when it led him to conclude, for example, that Britons and Europeans could scarcely do anything right, or moral.[11] His anger only grew as his health problems increased, the world skidded ever closer to war, and so many Canadians seemed unwilling to put Canada first.

From time to time, an insecure prime minister needed to assert his independence from Skelton, with his vigorous array of core convictions. King would listen to advice, he insisted, but he would make his decisions by himself. He meanwhile never stopped thinking that Skelton was the wisest and best adviser a leader could have. A few days after his little explosion over the visit to Germany, which took place only in the privacy of his study, King was writing to his deputy to say that "there is no association which has been quite so valuable or helpful to me as that which I have been privileged to share with yourself."[12]

King imposed limits of his own on the development of the Department of External Affairs, and on that of its people. Since he was both the departmental minister and prime minister, he had a conflict of interest. He was more apt to champion the growth of his leader's office than that of External Affairs, poaching on the department to grab resources and people for his immediate needs. He was also determined to prevent his representatives abroad from expressing any kind of separate personality. Pearson wrote to Skelton conveying Wrong's 1937 plan for the representation of King's Canada at international conferences. "Our delegate would have a name, even a photograph; a distinguished record, even an actual secretary – but he would have no corporeal existence – and no one would even notice that he wasn't there." As Pearson put it from his post in London, but not to Skelton directly, "our foreign policy is to 'do nothing.'"[13]

King's post-1935-election diplomatic appointments to Washington, London, and Tokyo were all drawn from his political gang. Skelton understood that, but he warned King that there was "no hope of securing united national confidence in our diplomatic experiment if appointments to the Service continue to be confined to party figures." Gradually there had to be plums for the men of the department, "and it would also be helpful if an occasional appointment could be made of some man ... with no political leanings or even with leanings against the Government of the day." A network of diplomatic missions, serving direct Canadian interests, lay close to the heart of Skelton's conception of an independent country. He was worried that the Depression was having a terrible impact on working conditions in the posts abroad, all of which, he knew, had been severely affected by the decade's straightened budgets.[14]

A constant theme of the later 1930s was Skelton's plea for a dramatic expansion in the diplomatic service in order to deal with the disturbed condition of the world and pursue Canadian economic and political goals. Most important, he argued, was an exchange of high commissioners with Australia, New Zealand, South Africa, and Ireland, this to make the point that Canada and its Commonwealth partners had arrived independently on the international scene and were fully capable of direct contact by themselves and between themselves. The South Africans and the Irish were already well ahead of Canada in the establishment of a diplomatic service. Canada had pioneered the idea but had not moved beyond its initial legations in Washington, Tokyo, and Paris, decisions taken a decade before. Mother Britain, which continued to do most of Canada's diplomacy, had its own interests to put forward, as was proper; it could not be expected to have Canada always at the top of its priorities. There was also commercial potential in relationships with the other dominions, as there was in stronger links with countries such as Argentina and Denmark, where diplomats could help Canadian business cope with governments that held their economies in tight check. As King was about to increase military spending for 1937–8, Skelton advised that he could deflect criticism by balancing expenditure for defence with expenditure for peaceful development: 1 per cent of what the government was going to spend on defence would buy at least two legations.[15]

King turned these ideas down flat. Diplomats could get him into trouble, as Riddell had done at the League. Skelton tried a different argument, suggesting that posts in the dominions could be added together with new legations in Latin America, "a balanced ratio likely to appeal to the country as a whole." This proposal, like all the others, generated no political support. When Wrong pressed him to get External Affairs out from under the British diplomatic thumb, OD replied: "I entirely agree with what you say. Not a month has passed for some years without this argument being urged ... but I am not optimistic in making any forecast as to when the next steps will be." The only new mission opened before the Second World War was in Belgium, the result of an unwelcome initiative from that country.[16]

Skelton had a little more success with the recruitment of new officers. He was authorized by King to hold a competition for third secretaries in late 1936, and as a result three External Affairs officers were hired in 1937: Jean Chapdelaine, J.W. Pickersgill, and Max Wershof. Chapdelaine became one of the few francophones at an exclusively English-speaking External Affairs headquarters, and Wershof the department's first Jewish member. Like the other two, Pickersgill was consigned to the attic of the East Block, where the leisurely days included a thorough reading of the New York *Times* and the decoding of a couple of telegrams. Within a matter of weeks, he was shuffled off to work for the prime minister. Most young officers hated the duty, but "Pick" found a happy home at King's side and never returned to Skelton.[17]

The Chapdelaine appointment was important because Skelton was determined to have French-language officers in the department in order to counter the widespread Ottawa impression that francophones were admirable clerks but no better than that, and certainly not the material of leadership. To ensure fairness for French applicants, he had their exams reviewed by Laurent Beaudry, External's senior francophone. He also instructed Georges Vanier in Paris to send the odd dispatch back to headquarters in the French language. Vanier agreed to conform "à votre désir." "Merci bien," Skelton retorted with a twinkle, "mais pas trop souvent." Yet, as Chapdelaine recalled, not a word of French was spoken in the External Affairs offices in the East Block under Skelton, whose own French was no better than serviceable.[18]

Herbert Norman, a graduate student in Asian languages and history at Harvard University, wrote directly to Skelton to inquire about entering the competition for the 1937 intake of officers. External Affairs discouraged Norman from diverting himself from his studies to prepare for the exams: the department wanted to appoint him as a language officer in Tokyo, rather than bringing him in by examination. This was done in 1939. Norman had a distinguished career as an adviser to General Douglas MacArthur in Japan after the Second World War and then as a Canadian diplomat, but in the 1950s he was accused by a United States Senate subcommittee of having communist associations. Under a cloud of suspicion, he committed suicide in 1957. There is much still not known about Norman, but it is clear that he was a member of the Communist Party in the 1930s, as were many of the decade's committed and disillusioned. Skelton had no knowledge of this, and he did not go particularly out of his way to recruit Norman into the department. If there is a criticism to be made of the under-secretary, it is that he did not carefully scrutinize the backgrounds of any his appointees.[19]

During the Cold War, after both of them were dead, Norman and Skelton were the first two names that found their way into a communist-hunting Royal Canadian Mounted Police file named Featherbed. It contained, apparently, a document alleging that Skelton had some contact with the Communist Party of Canada in the 1920s, and this was doubtless viewed in the context of the suggestion that Norman was a Skelton appointment who acted as a communist agent in the department. No evidence was found, or has been found, of any Skelton wrongdoing in either respect. The idea that he was filling the department up with fellow communists is preposterous, as the RCMP itself seems to have concluded after an examination of his recruitment record as under-secretary.[20]

The gruelling recruiting process that Skelton dominated reflected his interests and goals, and was calculated to draw in candidates with kindred views about an independent Canadian policy abroad and a strong federal government at home. He was even willing sometimes to bring in promising officers without an examination, as he had done with Wrong and Loring Christie, and as he would do in 1939 with Escott Reid, with whom Skelton carried on a correspondence in the late 1930s. Reid impressed him as a lively and lucid thinker, qualities highly prized in Skelton's External.[21]

The result was that the department resembled the man who shaped it. The growing little cadre of Externalites had a professorial air, admiring the debate and analysis of international issues. They were flexible, versatile, and adaptable pragmatists. They were widely read generalists with a talent for written communication. They were anti-imperialists, suspicious of the worst excesses of both British and American power. They were resolute Canadians, with a commitment to a wider world. There is no line to be drawn between Skelton's External Affairs and the one that emerged under his successors. They were all internationalists. Any differences in departmental thinking before and after the Second World War can be attributed to the circumstances of the times, not a difference of philosophy or perspective.[22]

The liberal internationalist bent in Skelton's thinking was to the fore in his March 1937 Green Foundation lectures at Westminster College in Fulton, Missouri. John Findley Green was the father of Sandy Skelton's wife, Kathleen; OD had been an honorary pallbearer at his funeral in the summer of 1932. When Green's family established a lecture series in his memory, Skelton was their candidate to be the inaugural speaker. He was reluctant at first, because of the heavy pressures of his work and because public servants were meant to be private folk, seen occasionally, heard from never. Changing his mind late in the day, he threw himself into the preparation of the lectures and the book that grew out of them, *Our Generation: Its Gains and Losses*, which was published by the University of Chicago Press the next year.[23]

The Green Foundation's trustees feted Skelton in St Louis, and dispatched him to call on the governor of Missouri, before he reached Fulton. The crowd was big for the first lecture on Thursday, 18 March, and the occasion was complete with an academic procession and plenty of ceremony, speeches, and flashbulbs. Then, Oscar told the family, "the fatted calf advanced to the altar." About halfway through his speech, he began to "cough a good deal … I hadn't my cough drops along & the boy who went out for the water evidently went to the Mississippi." He made it to the end, though, and "all spoke warmly & the audience seemed interested." He gave the second lecture on the Friday morning, and the third early on Saturday to allow him to catch a noon train for Chicago and home. Skelton, paid $500 for his trouble, shied away from giving

more lectures – "I think three would be all the audience could stand" –
and refused a request from the college to have the lectures broadcast on
the radio. The St Louis newspapers took note of his presence but did not
give it prominence.[24]

In his Fulton lectures, Skelton's balance sheet of "the third of a century that has already gone by"[25] was full of paradox. International cooperation had never been so conscious, diversified, and extensive as it had
over the past generation, but at the same time political and economic
nationalism had never been so aggressive and pervasive. The movement
for world peace had never been as well organized, and widely and passionately supported, and yet there had just been the most universal war
in all history, followed by an uneasy peace, fresh explosions of violence,
and a recrudescence of armaments. The war had given nationalism a
new impetus and new tools, but it also demonstrated the necessity and
the possibility of internationalism. Science offered for the first time mas-
tery over nature and fate. Nevertheless, it had been turned by the state
and class rivalries into the devil's weapon, a Frankenstein monster using
radio to disseminate prejudice and propaganda, the airplane to kill
women and children and threaten civilization's suicide, and the chem-
ist's skill to manufacture the instruments of blind destruction. The ideas
and inventions that had the capacity to lessen the differences between
peoples and nations often operated in the first instance to do the opposite, intensifying localism and particularism as they were taken up by
those determined to exalt the power and glory of the state.

With these contradictions as context, Skelton discerned three competing national policy options, corresponding to the broad trends in
the international affairs of his generation: domination, isolation, and
cooperation. The first, life as an overlord or underling of empire, was
anathema. The second, the determination to cultivate one's own garden and no one else's, established distance and a space to grow; it was a
marked advance on domination and perhaps even a forerunner of measured cooperation. Both domination and isolation, however, ignored the
implications of a shrinking and troubled world. Only cooperation faced
the facts and set in motion institutions and methodologies to deal with
accelerating interdependence.

The unedifying push for domination had been the most striking feature of international life in Skelton's youth. "The smaller became the
visible supply of backward peoples to be saved," he told his Fulton audience on 19 March, "the more feverish was the race." Now a novel imperialism was on the scene, wearing the label with a twist. "To the motives

of prestige and profit and the desire to prove virtue and virility, it adds, or revives, the motive of a quasi-religious zeal." The ancient fervour to carry true religion to the backward was being repackaged in "the passion of political propaganda – the urge of the hot gospellers of communism or fascism to force upon other peoples the only true doctrine of social or economic organization." Out of that came a clash of state-generated ideologies. Skelton's listeners could find it in the vicious Spanish Civil War, "a tragic laboratory for the world's doctrinaires."

Isolation, a word he preferred to isolationism, turned away from muscular solutions, rejecting imperial sway on the one hand and the enforcement of international justice on the other. Putting it in its best light, isolation was the good neighbourliness of people minding their own business and avoiding injury to others; more realistically, it was the hard-headedness of refusing to be deluded into serving the interests of others and insisting on saving some part of the world for sanity and civilization. Skelton saw the mood everywhere in the two Americas and throughout the smaller countries of northern and western Europe. To have a disposition take the form of concrete policy, however, geographical distance from the centre of disturbance was needed, along with the capacity for self-sufficiency and self-defence. Even then, it was "not every people that can develop and maintain the ability to resist the calls of prestige, the urge of profit, the fear of economic collapse, the chance of a ship or a citizen bombed, the pull of racial or political sympathies, the honey of flattering propaganda, the vinegar of stinging epithets." Isolation could be only a stopgap. It might be feasible, or necessary, for a time. It might keep the wolf of war outside the door, but it could never tame or destroy it, a comment the press interpreted as casting doubt on the staying power of America's dash away from the world.[26]

Skelton put his emphasis on cooperation, but on cooperation of a particular kind. The movement for international collaboration and world peace had followed two main lines. One was the path of collective sanctions and collective coercion, and the other was that of consultation, conference, and conciliation. The League of Nations was the best expression and embodiment of each of these approaches. As he did in his policy memoranda, Skelton rejected a League of enforcement out of hand and concentrated his fire on the patient and persistent building up of peaceful forces to deter aggressors. The establishment of economic stability and prosperity was especially important because it would drive out the insecurity and fear that lay at the bottom of political tension and military arrogance.

Implicit in Skelton's hierarchy of state order was the Canadian experience as he saw it, a steady progress towards independence and international cooperation. Canada had been a colony, the lowest category of
national life. Emerging from the cocoon of empire into an incomplete
country with divided loyalties and powerful ties to the world, it could
find refuge in isolation, a higher calling than colonial status. That was
buying time for a stocktaking of interests, but it could never be a permanent or fully satisfactory way of existence. He spent the entire first
lecture at Fulton making the point that the world could not be avoided.
Progress was ever upward to a better world. Cooperation was the future.
Skelton used the transformation of the British Empire into the British
Commonwealth of Nations as a prime example of the growth of a more
collaborative international community. Under mainly Canadian leadership, the empire had terminated central control while working out a
relationship ensuring peace without compulsion and "co-operation by
consultation and harmony of outlook within one-fourth of the area of
the world." The Commonwealth was "a League of Nations without sanctions." What Skelton did not say was that this description fit the theory
better than the practice. Come another war, there would be compulsion again. The Commonwealth had worked out a relationship based on
members' equality of status that served for the good times, for a period
of peace, but (he left this out of his Fulton analysis) Canada's leaders
had not faced the problem of what to do in wartime.[27] Because they had
not, nothing would be different from 1914. The British connection still
contained, he feared, the seeds of his country's destruction.

Skelton arranged for the lectures to end early on a Saturday morning so that he could return to his preparations for the Imperial Conference in London and the coronation of George VI that was to accompany
it. This would be his third Imperial Conference at Mackenzie King's
elbow, and the nature of the challenge had not changed. The British
were manipulators, skilled in the art of drawing prey into their web and
convincing them that imperial interests were their interests. In the days
before the conference opened, Norman Armour, the United States
minister in Ottawa, reported on the process for Washington's benefit,
making reference to Skelton's *Life and Letters of Sir Wilfrid Laurier*, which
described the heady mixture of military power and social seduction to
which colonial statesmen were exposed in the mother country. "Such
displays and attentions, in the past," Armour wrote, "have done much to
disprove the general assumption that Canadians are 'poor Empire men.'
In this atmosphere, it has not always been easy for Canadian leaders to

maintain that detached attitude in the consideration of Imperial problems, demanded of them by their supporters in the Dominion." The
American had his doubts about whether King could withstand the barrage of charm. He was less a fighter than a peacemaker.[28]

Susceptible though the prime minister was to British displays and
attentions, Skelton knew better than to underestimate King's toughness.
The threat of imperial centralization was the greater, however, because
Germany, Italy, and Japan were dominated by dictators or military cliques
and committed to policies of ambition and force. He was anxious to have
Mackenzie King understand that Britain and France were not without
responsibility for the mess that Europe was in. They had held the fate of
the continent in the hollow of their hands for a dozen years. Italy might
have engaged in faithless and ruthless aggression in Ethiopia, but Britain
had designs of its own in the area, France gave Mussolini carte blanche
to do what he would with the tiny African country, and there had been
an Anglo-French pact to abandon League efforts to stop Italy and not
to use military force against it. Hitlerism might be terrible, but France
had resisted German pleas for a gradual approach to military equality,
and Britain had not effectively supported the movement for abolishing
all the aggressive weapons denied to Germany by the Versailles Treaty,
putting paid to efforts at disarmament. It would not occur to British officials and soldiers that "the present position" might have been averted by
more far-sighted policies and a willingness to consider and confront the
underlying economic causes of unrest.[29]

The dominating issue at the Imperial Conference would be foreign
affairs and defence, which Skelton saw as more intimately related, and
more nearly a single topic, than had been the case in the pacific 1920s.
The British agenda, he warned his prime minister, would be simple
and straightforward: "The United Kingdom and the Empire are facing
a troubled and dangerous world, what are you going to do in the way
of helping in defence?" Not that asking was enough. The London government was attempting to lead the Commonwealth along the path of
righteousness with a series of secret military memoranda, dispatched in
advance, identifying possible enemies, points of danger, and the contributions that each dominion might make to meet certain contingencies.
The under-secretary found it anomalous to have documents "sent to the
Dominion Governments without any request from them or any comment
or expression of view by the political heads of the United Kingdom." If
anomalous, however, it was convenient, because it exposed possible lines
of approach at the conference. In the event of a world war or a German

war, the British raised the possibility that Canada would mount an expeditionary force to fight in Europe, and that it would be provided sooner rather than later. In the case of a war with Japan, Canada's aid could take the form of facilities for the Royal Navy in Pacific ports and naval and air cooperation against Japanese trans-Pacific trade.[30]

The proposal for an expeditionary force to Europe, evoking the memory of the First World War and the crisis over conscription, particularly caught the adviser's eye. It was put forward calmly, Skelton fumed, "as if Canadians were prepared, without question or division, once every generation, whenever the button is pressed, to rush in tens of thousands to fight Europe's battles, in the name of peace or democracy or a war to end wars." The British seemed "entirely oblivious of the change in Canadian opinion, the feeling that we have more than squared any account with the Empire, the disillusionment over the results of the last war in Europe itself, the shifting of interest and loyalty to our own country, the memory of debt and death, the influence of the 'never again' movement in the United States, the realization of the need and the great difficulty of preserving unity in Canada itself."[31]

Skelton asked a series of rhetorical questions. Was intervention in European affairs automatic? Was Canada directly and inescapably tied to the European political process, and particularly to the orbit of the ancient, unresolved feud between Western and Eastern Europe? Was that link so embedded in the normal logic of events that Canada must deliberately prepare in advance for European wars, in a way that it had not done even before the First World War? Was the stance that an anti-war United States might take in another war entirely irrelevant? Was it possible to maintain a united Canadian country on the basis of an inevitable commitment to British wars? Was a Canadian return to Europe contributing to European or world stability, or to "civilization"?[32]

In his rage, Skelton was aiming his fire at the wrong target. The British had simply asked whether Canada "might" dispatch an expeditionary force in the event of war. In their predicament, with a huge empire to defend and vulnerable to attack from many points, they were anxious for any hint of support from their dominion colleagues. A decision about Canadian participation in a future war would be made in Ottawa, not London, by a King government, not by the British. It might be the wrong choice, from Skelton's standpoint, for the wrong reasons, but it would be a Canadian choice. He implicitly acknowledged as much when he admitted that a combination of national motives and impulses might combine to propel his country in the direction of "old memories and old loyalties." His one consolation was that the actual day of reckoning could be put off until a crisis intruded. Indeed, given the divided state of national politics, it had to be put off.[33]

For now, therefore, Canada could clearly underline its autonomy at the Imperial Conference. No commitments for military aid to Britain or any part of the Commonwealth would be made in advance, or any commitment not to give any assistance. Canada's direct and immediate responsibility was for its own defence, an obligation it would carry out to preserve its self-respect and proclaim its independence, not because it was in peril. Skelton took pleasure in pointing out that the British Chiefs of Staff Committee's review of danger spots made not the slightest suggestion of any direct menace to Canada from any source, emphasizing instead threats to the United Kingdom, Australia, New Zealand, South Africa, and India – almost everywhere else in the Commonwealth.[34] Canada was asked for help it did not need or would not receive if the position were reversed and Canadians were in trouble.

In mid-April, King read Skelton's Imperial Conference memoranda to the cabinet, where their angry tone found "general acceptance." The prime minister was outraged by British documents based on the idea of the Commonwealth as a single unit requiring a single policy. He pointed out to his colleagues "that this was the battle that every Liberal government had had to fight at every small conference in Great Britain, and not Liberal governments only, and that we would have a very unpleasant and difficult time in dealing with that aspect of the situation." King was anxious, however, to assist the British by bringing them closer to the United States. While Skelton was preparing to give his American lectures at Fulton, King had been with President Franklin Roosevelt in Washington, plotting vague schemes for world peace and searching for common ground they could share with the British. The prime minister was pleased, and quite surprised, that Skelton and Ernest Lapointe seemed to endorse these efforts. King wrote in his diary that his deputy "was more appreciative of them than I thought he would be – raised fewer objections, and seemed to feel they might bear practical fruits – he felt that what was said was along the right lines."[35]

At the same time, Skelton cautioned his prime minister against paying too high a price for good relations between the United States and Great Britain. Roosevelt and the British were talking about a trade agreement, and asking King to make it possible through a surrender of some of Canada's advantages in the British market, in order to open up room for American timber and farm products. King liked the idea of an agreement between the country's two best friends and contemplated a "big" and "generous" response to facilitate an Anglo-American deal. Skelton filled his speeches for King with references to the need for a less discriminatory economic system as a means towards a more peaceful world, but he thought it absurd and indefensible to offer up major economic concessions on "the altar of Anglo-American friendship" unless there was a substantial payoff for Canada. Public opinion would simply not stand for it otherwise. It was not long before King came around to Skelton's view on the matter and took up his suggestion that triangular negotiations, with Canada as a full partner with the United States and the United Kingdom, were the only way to protect the national interest.[36]

On the grounds that it was the chance of a lifetime, OD convinced Isabel to come to the coronation and to bring with them sixteen-year-old Sheila, who had just won scholarships to Queen's University in history and English. Isabel recollected that her "coronation trip happiness" began when she examined the family finances and found that they were much better off after her husband's raise than she had anticipated. It did distress her to leave her sister Edith – Edo, as she was known – who was fighting breast cancer.[37]

Isabel pushed Oscar out the door on 23 April as he rushed to get to Quebec City for the midnight departure for England of the *Empress of Austria*. She closed up their big house and shopped for the right clothes, paying attention to the exacting standards for women's dress at the coronation issued by the British Lord Chamberlain's Office. Once aboard ship, a week after Oscar's departure, she found that he had arranged flowers to greet her, and he was in Liverpool on 8 May, having sat up all night on the train to get there for her arrival. Isabel thought it "grand having Oscar to take charge & awfully dear of him to come after such a hard trip." With Sheila, they made it to London on a Sunday, and so he did further duty by taking his family to a church service at St James in Piccadilly. Their home for the next six weeks was Arlington House, a new apartment building just behind the Ritz hotel, the habitual home of Canadian government delegations in the British capital. Scattered and behind schedule as always, but insisting on controlling everything related to the coronation right down to the seating arrangements in Westminster Abbey, Skelton had been slow in letting Mike Pearson at Canada House know what the accommodation requirements were. The result was that only the prime minister ended up at the Ritz. Isabel now got her first glimpse of her husband's busy life when he was abroad, with the blur of activity and a staff to cope with of more than thirty people. She found it "bewildering & terrifying at first."[38]

Coronation day was 12 May. The three Skeltons awoke at five and were greeted by the grey weather and dampness that enveloped London, according to the *Globe and Mail*'s reporter, in an "anchovy paste of a mist." In drizzling rain and fog, along greasy streets and past soggy bunting and banners, they moved to Westminster Abbey, where the galleries were crowded by 8:00 and closed to ordinary ticket holders by 8:30. They waited hours in the central upper gallery of the south transept of the clammy old abbey, where the time was passed observing the great and near-great and nibbling on thin sandwiches fortified with sticky chocolate coffee. At 11:00, the king and queen arrived and made their way with the archbishop of Canterbury up the nave and to the royal chairs of estate. The two-hour ceremony, with its nearly eight thousand onlookers, could begin.[39]

The Toronto *Star*'s Matthew Halton, tough-minded in the face of Hitler and the dictators, melted at "the most fantastically gorgeous spectacle I ever saw. Wherever my vision moved I saw these people in their splendid crimson and ermine and purple robes and their flashing gems. They started in banked tiers of seats at the floor in front of the altar and throne of Scone, and rose up between pillars into the misty carving and lovely tracery of the abbey's roof ... Violins raved and trumpets trumped til the rafters shook, and the organ drowned the world in sound."[40]

Isabel was unmoved: the "solemnity for me was killed by the costume pageantry of it all." When the archbishop of Canterbury fumbled in trying to get the crown to sit properly on the king's head, she almost laughed out loud. Admiring hard work and knowledge and disdaining dilettantish pretension, she had tired of the social requirements of her husband's work: "The sooner any party breaks up the better." Sheila shared her mother's discomfort for the high life of protocol and prerogatives. A picture of the two women standing stiffly in their white silk coronation gowns, with the mandatory long gloves and white ostrich feather headdress, was published in the Montreal *Gazette* in July 1937, after the outfits had been recycled for the women's presentation to the king and queen at Buckingham Palace. It was a world they "hated," in Sheila's description.[41]

OD's own predilections led him to refuse, point-blank, to wear court dress to the coronation, as was the custom. Mackenzie King proudly stuffed himself into a military-style Windsor uniform for the occasion. Lester Pearson decked himself out in knee-britches, silk stockings, buckled shoes, and a black cutaway coat with buttons up to his neck – enough gold braid for an ambassador, he recalled, and sufficient military regalia, a sword and cocked hat included, to give him the appearance of an admiral. But not Skelton. "Some of our Canadian party," sniffed the high commissioner to the United Kingdom, Vincent Massey, "held views that savoured of Jacksonian democracy rather than the tradition we are supposed to have inherited." The Skeltons received no invitations to Massey's Canada House during their long 1937 visit to London.[42]

For Skelton, the solid substance of the coronation overcame its showy style. He was alive to the importance of the monarchy's old rituals and symbols and, superimposed upon them, the new political facts and constitutional arrangements of the Commonwealth. To him, the most memorable moment in the coronation ceremony came with the royal oath. For the first time, the king made his pledge of office not simply to the people of the United Kingdom alone, and the domains "thereunto belonging," as had been the case in the ancient oath used as late as the coronation of George V, but to the peoples of each of the member states of the Commonwealth. Amending the text of his Fulton lectures for publication, Skelton added an elaborate reference to the oath in order to drive home what could be done in international life when there was free cooperation between nation-states.[43]

The Imperial Conference opened on a Friday, two days after the coronation, with Skelton in his accustomed role as the prime minister's senior adviser on security questions. He attended almost all of the conference's major meetings at King's side. The *Financial Post* ran a large and complimentary article as the conference got under way on Ottawa's "distinguished corps of governmental and economic experts" who were behind the scenes, with OD at their head and Loring Christie "second in the group only to Dr. Skelton."[44] Skelton and Christie worked closely with King on foreign-policy and defence matters and, along with legal adviser J.E. Read, assisted Justice Minister Lapointe on constitutional issues.

Leo Amery, an MP still but no longer in the cabinet, watched Skelton from a distance, judging him to be "less unreasonable and pernickety" than on previous imperial occasions. British observers closer to the scene saw only the old Skelton: sharp of elbow in meeting rooms, although amiable enough in the corridors outside. Malcolm MacDonald, presiding over the Dominions Office as Amery had done in the 1920s, found the Canadian under-secretary a still-formidable adversary. "If I had expected some mellowing of his ferocious nationalism," MacDonald remembered, "how mistaken I was."[45]

Skelton coordinated efforts to root out any British attempt to inveigle the Canadians into commitments to assist the Mother Country should a great crisis come, right down to giving strict instructions to the delegation's military officers about what could and could not be discussed with their Commonwealth counterparts. The battleground was the conference report, which Skelton scrutinized carefully as it progressed through several drafts. The foreign-policy paragraphs went through a week of revisions; "resolutions" were watered down into "a statement," and a reference to the preservation of Commonwealth interests was removed. After a week of hard negotiation, King was satisfied.[46]

OD was prepared to give the final phrasing a passing grade: "On the whole it's not a bad document." Still, he had reservations. There was a reference to "the cause of peace" and the willingness of the dominions "to consult and co-operate with one another in this vital interest and all other matters of common concern." Skelton cautioned the prime minister that it was a familiar British stratagem, drawing the colonials subtly into their net: "Still a good bit of common policy here, disguised under peace label; every Foreign Office says its foreign policy is directed to peace – on its own terms." The tactic was a smokescreen for a much wider intent: "Don't like this – it covers all foreign policy really."[47]

The defence section of the report was even more worrying. When the preliminary defence document first arrived in his room at the Arlington late in the evening of 9 June, Skelton immediately complained to the prime minister that the bulk of it was written "in the manner of the Committee of Imperial Defence who have prepared it." That meant that it was full of implications, deliberately fostered by its British drafters, that the Commonwealth was an institution controlled from the centre and gearing up for war. In another epic battle of the communiqué, King put up a stubborn resistance to offensive words, phrases, clauses, sentences, and paragraphs until, he wrote in his diary, he had given "the whole emphasis at the close to the Canadian position." The final text heaped one anodyne generalization on another, but Skelton insisted that the thrust remained towards preparation for collaboration in an empire war. He wrote home to the prime minister's office to tell the officials there to play up Canadian autonomy in their publicity about the conference.[48]

Skelton composed King's key conference speeches. For the prime minister's major salvo on foreign policy, his deputy used as a unifying theme the awakening of a colonial people, now beginning to place national interests to the fore.[49] When Canada had been first pushed into the world, Skelton wrote, its attitude had been that of a spectator with little recognition of the importance of having distinctive positions on the big international questions of the day. Canadians were accustomed to take their views at second hand, frequently based on circumstances that were defined by others. Even in participation in League affairs, there was a tendency to regard Geneva as an automatic force that worked mysteriously and ideally. Recently, however, a more responsible and direct interest had developed, with some greater realistic appreciation of the forces and benefits that characterized more experienced and mature countries.

As the fifth-largest country in the total of international trade, Skelton's speech reasoned, Canada could not detach itself from the world. Yet it was protected and insulated by thousands of miles of ocean to the east and west. To the north were only polar bears, while to the south there was as friendly and sympathetic a neighbour as "human nature permits." Canada-United States relations, however, were not uncomplicated, and the burden of the speech's message lay there. Foreign policy must begin, and very nearly end, on the North American continent. Canadians were a border people, most of them living very close to the American frontier and vulnerable to the political and economic influences of the south, notably the isolationist tide in public opinion. The United States had made it clear through its neutrality legislation that it wanted no part of foreign wars, but also that it would intervene in the event of an unprovoked attack on Canada. That placed an added obligation on the King government to protect its sovereignty or, if the United States went to war, its neutrality. Canada must do enough for its own defences to maintain American respect.

Through his speechwriter, Mackenzie King warned the conference that antagonism in his country to war, any war, was growing. There was "outspoken rejection of the theory that whenever and wherever conflict arises in Europe Canada can be expected to send armed forces overseas to help solve the quarrels of continental countries about which Canadians know little, and which, they feel, know and care less about Canada's difficulties – and particularly so if a powerful country like the United States assumes no similar obligations." The recent increases in military spending had occasioned widespread opposition, even though they had been earmarked entirely for national defence; not one of the political parties had proposed preparations for overseas operations. Canada was not in any direct danger, and the economic burdens left by the last war continued to weigh down the country's finances. The prime minister admitted that there were many forces that would promote support of Britain in a great crisis, but he could make no prediction about what his diversified, regionalized, and easily divided country would decide "in the event of other parts of the Commonwealth actually being at war. Much would depend on circumstances of the hour, both abroad and at home – upon the measure of conviction as to the unavoidability of the struggle and the seriousness of the struggle, and upon the measure of unity that has been attained in Canada."

The address was a reflection of Skelton's hopes and biases, but it met the prime minister's purposes well. Cogently and firmly, it made the case that his government could provide none of the public assurances sought by London that Canada would support Britain no matter what. In the pressure-cooker atmosphere of the Imperial Conference, where dire warnings about the international situation were the daily fare, the speech expressed the frustration that King felt as he watched the world drift into war. He agreed with his deputy that the country's fragile unity was on the line when Britain pushed Canada to make a public statement of support, and he shared Skelton's bitterness that Canadians would again have to die because of the failures of European diplomacy. That, however, was only a part of the King calculus, and the less important part. In private discussions at the conference he made it clear that, if the United Kingdom was threatened, its enemies would have to reckon with Canada.[50] What he and Skelton really wanted, though, was to avoid war, so that divisive decisions would not have to be made.

Picturing himself as a missionary for international goodwill, King was determined to visit Hitler after the conference. This he did, without his deputy, who vigorously opposed the trip, as he had done ever since the prime minister had broached the subject. The German führer made a considerable impression on King, who concluded that Hitler was focused on the needs of his country, not on world domination. Nevertheless, there was the warning that the prime minister had promised the British he would deliver: if one part of the empire was threatened by foreign aggression, all its parts would join together to protect the freedom that lay at the basis of their association. Afterwards, in Paris but still out of Skelton's grasp, King gave a much-noticed speech in which he conveyed exactly the same message.[51]

Skelton gently rebuked his leader for the controversial Paris remarks, which were seized on by critics as a significant reversal of Canadian policy. He rehearsed the arguments he had put in King's mouth at the Imperial Conference and reminded him that the moderate middle ground

King had staked out before the conference "has been widely discussed in Canada and widely approved." The government had refused to make or recognize any commitment, formal or informal, to participate in a League or British war; at the same time, it had refused to accept the contention of neutralists that war was out of the question. This was the accepted Canadian view, Skelton pleaded – "a commonsense position, logical without being doctrinaire, realistic, and the one policy which can keep Canada united in days of peace: and if war comes, will leave the government free to propose whatever course seems best in the light of all the facts of that day, which will not be the facts of today." It would be a calamity if reports of a changed position damaged all the work they had done together; equally, there was nothing to be gained by drawing further attention to the matter by issuing a direct denial.[52] King needed little encouragement to rediscover caution. He and Skelton collaborated in writing an address to the Canadian people which placed the Imperial Conference in the context of the historic necessity to maintain national unity at all costs. That had been Wilfrid Laurier's aim and achievement, and it was likely to remain "the business of statesmanship in our country for some time."[53]

The unity of Canada was threatened not simply by its international or imperial connections but by centrifugal forces inside the country itself. Throughout the year, Skelton had been repeatedly counselling the prime minister that the country's chief problem over the next few years might well turn out to be domestic, not external. Canada was tough to govern: four or five fairly homogeneous geographical areas, politically united, but each differing from the others in preoccupation and outlook, and tied together by the shoestring of a creaky federal system that the Depression was sorely testing. There never was a time when the provinces as a whole were more dependent on the assistance of Ottawa, or had received more help. Yet there was no gratitude, only bitterness and recklessness. The provinces were stretching old powers and asserting new ones, demanding federal aid while rejecting federal control. Ontario and Quebec were in the hands of "reckless demagogues"; tendencies there and elsewhere were towards "an arbitrary and semi-fascist attitude"; west and east were at loggerheads; and the uneven return of prosperity across the land was causing anger and resentment. The disintegration of Canada was proceeding fast.[54]

The federal government had to take control of the chaos that was developing throughout the country. Good administration and sane policy were not enough. Skelton had welcomed the naming of a royal commission in the spring of 1937 to examine federal-provincial relations, but he told King that the people needed a definite lead that could not be given until there was a report from the new body. He pushed the prime minister to get strong members on the team and the work quickly under way. In promoting the cause, he was promoting his son Sandy, a recognized authority on provincial finances, who was appointed the commission's secretary and director of research and became the driving force behind what became known as the Rowell-Sirois Commission. The two Skeltons – the father steady, the son mercurial – had a loving yet adversarial relationship, but they were talking frequently about the country's plight now and drawing closer because of it. The eventual Rowell-Sirois report, heavily based on the research of Sandy's team, captured the belief of both Skeltons in a strong federal government as the instrument of social justice and economic efficiency.[55]

While King travelled to Germany, France, and Belgium, the Skeltons went on a European vacation, continuing the enjoyment that had begun in England during the conference with frequent visits to the theatre, meals at restaurants such as Oxford's swanky Mitre, and a prowl for books on socialism and architecture on London's Charing Cross Road. After the obligatory Paris, where OD's walks of the year before could be repeated with his family, they travelled to southern France and then to Switzerland, flying from Lucerne to Basel and then back to England at the end of June for the return home. With Isabel at his side for almost two months in Britain and Europe, recreating "old honeymoon days," Skelton was in an expansive mood. He arranged for fine food and accommodation, tipped "without help," and lost all his francs betting for her at the Paris horse races. After he gave her six five-pound English banknotes, his wife wrote tenderly in her diary: "Dear generous Oscar, must be more like him – more generous, more patient, hang on to my temper inwardly & voice outwardly better."[56]

Skelton was thoroughly worn-out, and Europe had not changed that. He had felt "tough" during the Imperial Conference, and he returned as soon as he got home to his recent pattern of hard work on top of debilitating fatigue. On 13 July, as they settled in after their time away, Oscar and Isabel had the family to dinner at home in Rockliffe to celebrate his fifty-ninth birthday. He was unusually quiet, even for him, and very tired, causing Isabel to scold him afterwards for not holding up his end of the conversation. King regretted later on that his adviser had not taken another month off in Europe, but the problem went deeper than that. For years he had worked seven-day weeks, seldom vacationed or exercised, and eaten quickly and badly. The job took an emotional toll too, as he worried himself into an uncertain future. He was a medical mess, unable to sleep and suffering from a variety of ailments from leg pains to headaches and eye strain.[57]

All through August, OD remained unwell. Before leaving for Washington for high-level trade talks with U.S. Secretary of State Cordell Hull, he visited his doctor, Robert Stevens, who vaguely diagnosed artery trouble. In mid-September, he was with Stevens again, where a cardiogram revealed that he had had a heart attack – just when, no one knew. Skelton was ordered to rest in bed for eight weeks. Isabel was furious that Stevens had not picked up on her husband's heart condition during the earlier visit, but she was reluctant to change doctors at a crucial time.[58]

It took three weeks for the prime minister to visit 459 Buena Vista. He was surprised and distressed by what he saw, and mightily worried by what it meant for him and his government. "This is very serious. What would happen to the External Affairs without Skelton I hardly know. I am hoping a rest may bring him back as I believe it will but he will have to go carefully from now on." Skelton was the head of a government department and, at the same time, the prime minister's chief of staff. The work was beyond what any one man could do. "He has attempted far far too much, is over conscientious in all things."[59]

Yet King would not leave Skelton alone. Having waited a good long time before visiting his closest professional confidant at a time of great difficulty, he returned to the house three more times that month, insisting on talking business and involving OD in his perpetual search for someone to take charge of the prime minister's office. King had his eye on External's Norman Robertson, and Skelton agreed that he was a young public servant of exceptional intelligence and judgment. They turned the primary responsibility for the Canada-United States trade agreement over to Robertson and arranged, King wrote, to have "him come more immediately into association with my office to take a position there corresponding, in some respects, with that which Skelton, himself, has with regard to External Affairs. Skelton has tried to keep both roles in one, and broken down as a consequence."[60]

Friends and colleagues, knowing Oscar's work routine, admonished him to follow his doctor's advice strictly. "For God's sake, the Gov't's and the country's," said Bill Herridge, "don't abridge this most needed period of rest. It's been coming to you, for a long, long time. *Please* take it." To Georges Vanier, Skelton promised that he was putting in the "magic" eight weeks as instructed. "It's a new experience for me, but you get used to anything." Mike Pearson's jaunty get-well note wondered if Skelton was avoiding the complete break from work that Stevens had prescribed. The under-secretary's legendary "habits of industry" and departmental gossip suggested otherwise.[61]

The gossip had it right. Marjorie McKenzie, Skelton's External Affairs clerk who was very close to both Oscar and Isabel, regularly visited with packages of departmental chores. He sat up in bed, reviewing news clippings, dispatches, and memoranda and scribbling out detailed and precise handwritten responses. "I have gone pretty carefully through these documents," was a typical opening remark, or "I am returning your draft herewith, with some suggested revisions." He relied heavily on Loring Christie, as did King, during this period. The experienced Christie took the lead on international issues, particularly the latest crisis in Asia, where an undeclared war had erupted the previous summer between Japan and China. Despite pressure at home to take a stand against Japan, Skelton, Christie, and King were united in their determination to stay out of the Far East's troubles. OD admitted to Canadian "inaction" but suggested that critics note the "inaction" of just about every other country, "and for the same reason."[62]

Christie wondered if King would have "shot the department all to hell" before Skelton returned. The prime minister was monopolizing Robertson and stealing one or two of the new recruits to do his prime-ministerial bidding. He had developed the nasty habit of dragging Christie into Canada's domestic affairs as well. "I am fed up with it," he wrote Pearson.[63]

During the long days of exile at home, Skelton raced through detective fiction for entertainment. His favourite mystery writer was the American Rex Stout, creator of Nero Wolfe, the gargantuan detective who solved crimes without leaving his brownstone house on New York's West 35th Street. Archie Goodwin was Wolfe's Skelton, the assistant who was really a partner. Wolfe was a certifiable genius at his craft, but he was eccentric, demanding, and exasperating, requiring handling with the utmost skill. Archie was the resourceful and not always quiet facilitator, without whom Wolfe's achievements would not have been possible. Part of the appeal for OD must have been the fun of watching the wise-cracking aide get the upper hand, as he frequently did. After all, Archie was the narrator of the Wolfe stories. He controlled the agenda.[64]

At the end of the stipulated eight weeks, Oscar got out of bed for the first time. He made his way to a nearby chair but "felt he lifted a lead of weight getting there." Three days later, on 19 November, Dr Stevens helped him to walk into the upstairs hallway of the Skelton's darkly lit home. The prime minister visited the next day, thinking that his under-secretary looked much better but still very frail. He made it down to the first floor after another week and out for a drive with his daughter-in-law, Kathleen, at the end of November. His muscles weakened by inactivity, he was exhausted by any movement at all.[65]

Skelton contemplated a cruise of a few weeks but not before he caught up on all the important files and sent them on their way. King had another plan. Since he was worn out himself, he suggested that they share a Flor-ida trip, where they could mix business with relaxation. Skelton arrived in the American south on a cool and windy morning in early December, with a secretary, typewriter, and dispatch boxes in tow. King met him at the train and was shocked to find him still looking so feeble. The prime minister was glad that Skelton had come – "it is for the best I know" – but he could see that his adviser would be unable to be very active, which "will make it more difficult for me to get out of the week which I hoped it might bring." Their conversation immediately took a contro-versial turn when they sat down to lunch, reflecting their increasingly divergent views of Canada's international future. After dinner, there was more disagreement when King spoke feelingly of his belief in life beyond the grave. Skelton would agree that impressions could be conveyed from one person to another by telepathy, but nothing more. He was too much the scientist, King concluded, too much the rationalist.[66]

Skelton continued his push for more representation in foreign coun-tries, and King pushed back. Diplomats spelled trouble: they were "almost certain to draw us into situations involving religious or other questions, from which it would be well to keep free at present." Instead of expanding the scope of the Department of External Affairs, the gov-ernment should give its attention to domestic affairs and to the proper organization of the prime minister's work. There was a victory for OD on that front, and not an unimportant one. Skelton was able to convince the boss that Norman Robertson, who had been migrating between External Affairs and the prime minister's office, ought to return to External on a full-time basis. With serious trade talks with the United States looming, he was too valuable as a trade negotiator. Robertson had been miserable as a prime-ministerial assistant, and his faith that Skelton would deliver him from this penance was justified.[67]

After several days in Lake Wales, where King had cadged a house from one of his supporters, they moved on to Palm Beach. As OD travelled on his own to Miami after a night's stay at the Breakers Hotel and a walk along the beach, the prime minister wrote a warm letter to Isabel assuring her that all was well with her husband. He was "as natural and cheerful as ever" and each day there had been a remarkable improvement in his strength. He was now able to walk a considerable distance and "his step had that quick, alert and natural movement which we all know to be so characteristic of him." Despite the wooly Ottawa business suits that he insisted on wearing even on vacation, Skelton wanted the heat of the sun and was enormously disappointed not to find it in Miami or farther south in Key West. Just as he was about to pack up and go home, the sunshine returned. He decided to stay on at the Miami Colonial Hotel into January.[68]

Early in 1938, Skelton returned to the office. On 14 January he met with Mackenzie King in his East Block office at the Parliament Buildings, where they spent a couple of hours on the estimates for the coming year's expenditures and other External Affairs business. "This is the first time I have seen Skelton in the New Year," the prime minister wrote that night. "I noticed, as we proceeded with work, that his face got a little flushed which would indicate a heart condition. I feel he cannot guard with too much care. It had been the first time he had spent all day at the Office. I advised against continuing that effort."[69] The Florida trip had demonstrated, however, that King was no more capable of letting Skelton get fully fit than OD was of extracting himself from the affairs of state. The two men were immediately back in the well-worn grooves of long-established routines.

13

Together and Apart, 1938–9

As Nazi Germany became more bellicose, Britain and France wavered, and a European conflict over Czechoslovakia threatened, the tensions between King and Skelton increased. Mackenzie King was certain that, if Britain were at war and the Mother Country's destiny was in the balance, Canada's ancient obligations and national interests made its course clear. Skelton wanted none of that. He was a nationalist and a neutralist, believing that an independent Canada should take care of its own immediate interests – to build a country, to stay united, to remain aloof from Europe's complications, and to declare neutrality if those complications turned into war.

"We look out upon a disturbed and seemingly chaotic world," Skelton wrote in a draft address he prepared for the prime minister at the end of March 1938, two weeks after Germany had incorporated Austria into the Nazi Reich and with Japan continuing its attacks on hapless China. "Bitter and destructive wars are being waged in two continents. Force is openly glorified. Solemn pledges are disregarded. Armaments are mounting to fantastic heights. A war of propaganda is filling the air." Surveying this "dark outlook," Skelton managed to dig out some optimism for his leader, and for himself. The present wars were not yet the "great war" that every Canadian feared. No one knew the future. What seemed inevitable often did not happen. The opponents of one day might be the friends of the next: "It is impossible to forecast what the issues abroad, the alignments abroad, the situation at home, may be in a year or five years from now."[1]

Wishful thinking was overrun by events in Europe. After his seizure of Austria, Hitler eyed Czechoslovakia. On 20 May 1938 reports came to Skelton through the British Foreign Office that German forces were

massing on the Czech border, preparing for an attack. Czechoslovakia mobilized for war, and Mackenzie King's Canadian government
girded itself to do the same. The prime minister informed his deputy
minister that the cabinet was almost unanimous in deciding that Canada would go to war against Germany if the British decided to do so.
Skelton was disgusted. So much for his dream of an independent foreign policy made in Ottawa and based on strictly Canadian principles
and interests. "My fourteen years effort here wasted," he spat out in
his diary.[2]

The emergency quickly passed because the Germans had no intention,
just then, of crossing the frontier into Czechoslovakia. King, however,
did not know that, nor did the British and French. Skelton met King at
the office on Saturday, 21 May, and gave sleeping pills to a highly agi-
tated prime minister, who was "blue over last Czech reports." On Sunday,
it seemed that Paris and London would fight to preserve Czechoslovakia.
The tension had eased by the next day: "No guns off – yet," OD observed.
"I think pressure & blackmail rather than force will be Hitler's present
game." Skelton was correct in his assessment, but at noon on the 24th
King's closest friend, Joan Patteson, telephoned him at Laurier House to
say that she had heard on the radio that German and Czech troops "were
marching across the border in both directions." OD checked the story
out with the Canadian Press and found there was nothing to it, but he
saw that the rumour was making an already jittery prime minister even
more unsure of himself.[3]

By coincidence, the prime minister had scheduled a debate for that
afternoon in the House of Commons on the Department of External
Affairs budget for the coming year. As the minister in charge of the
department, Mackenzie King led the discussion by resurrecting the
speech Skelton had prepared two months before. Deprived of sleep and
worried that Europe was tumbling towards war, King could do no better than to read out what his deputy had written about the need for
the utmost caution in world affairs, especially when Canada had more
than enough domestic problems with which to deal. The message was
clear. The government would decide upon the great questions of international relations when, and only when, circumstances demanded it. In
the meantime, Canada would stick to "peace and friendliness, a policy
of trying to look after our own interests and to understand the position
of other governments with which we have dealings." "Speech went pretty
well," OD wrote in his diary, "aside from the reading of it, which made it
doubly obvious it was mine. Fair applause at end." King thanked Skelton

"very warmly and profusely for the speech," although he worried that it "had overemphasized the isolationist case."[4]

"Isolationism" was exactly what Skelton had in mind. King, however, was only too aware of the contradiction between his address to Parliament and the cabinet's decision to go to war for Czechoslovakia if Britain did. He was enduring "all the feelings that a Prime Minister of Canada would necessarily experience upon the actual outbreak of war in which it was probable the whole world would be drawn." It had been a "frightful experience" to be visited by a war scare moments before having to give a major foreign-policy address, but he was comforted that he had Skelton's careful text to rely on.[5]

Throughout the spring and summer of 1938, Skelton observed the steady drumbeat of Nazi Germany's propaganda machine, led by Joseph Goebbels and directed against Czechoslovakia's treatment of its German citizens in the Sudetenland. Hours after the May weekend crisis that had surprised Hitler more than it had his adversaries, he had told his generals that he would take Czechoslovakia by force no later than 1 October. The Czech government in Prague negotiated with the country's German minority, offering concessions that were never enough, and especially not enough for Hitler's marionette in Sudetenland politics, Konrad Henlein. The Soviet Union and France, Czechoslovakia's allies, stepped delicately through the thicket of European diplomacy, hoping that there would not be war but making occasionally encouraging noises to the Czechs that they would help if Germany attacked them.[6]

The British also mixed their messages. They warned Germany that they would not be indifferent to a military move against the Czechs while insisting to Prague that they must make a settlement with their German population. Britain's Prime Minister Neville Chamberlain declared that he would not offer a guarantee to the Czechs because to do so meant that "the decision as to whether or not this country should find itself involved in war ... [would be] automatically removed from the discretion of His Majesty's Government." Skelton noted Chamberlain's comment approvingly in late June. He was advising King to follow the same course. To answer hypothetical questions about Canada's stance in the event of a European war would put a strain upon the unity of a country already divided by economic depression, regionalism, and divergent views about where Canada's international destiny lay.[7] Counselling King on political caution was like giving painting lessons to an old master. Skelton, however, did not fear the practical King but the emotional one, capable of being carried away on a flight of "doing the right thing" in a world crisis.

Skelton had visited Czechoslovakia in 1922, three years after its creation as part of the peace settlements that ended the First World War. His "casual impression of the Czechs as a race," gleaned from that brief trip and observations at the League of Nations, "was of a pretty hardboiled tough lot." They seemed to have learned "little or nothing" from their centuries of experience prior to 1919 as an underdog. Their treatment of their three-million-strong German minority "had been in many ways arbitrary and with a touch of 'beggars on horseback' behaviour in it." Nevertheless, he told the German consul general to Canada in August 1938 that "the Sudeten minority was immensely better treated individually and politically than members of minorities in any other country in Central or Eastern Europe." He could see nothing in the complaints of the Sudeten Germans that afforded "the slightest justification for any country plunging Europe again into war."[8]

While the European crisis simmered, the United States moved to shore up its position in the Western Hemisphere. In January 1938 U.S. President Franklin Roosevelt had taken the initiative in encouraging the Canadian prime minister to send the chief of the general staff and the chief of naval staff to Washington for discussions with their American counterparts. The visit took place with no measurable results, but a tentative beginning was made towards a defence relationship where there had effectively been none since the Great War. Skelton liked the idea of "getting our defence programme on a realistic North American basis," but he was wary about what the military could get up to without adult supervision and alive to the political dangers. He insisted that the talks take place with no "possibility of the slightest publicity."[9]

In the late summer of 1938, Roosevelt came to Canada to accept an honorary degree from Queen's University and to open the Ivy Lea bridge linking Canada and the United States across the St Lawrence River – heaven-sent occasions to boast about a peaceful North American continent and the implicit contrast between it and warlike Europe. At Queen's on 18 August under a sunny sky, his powerful hands fixed firmly on the podium to hold up his paralysed lower body, Roosevelt seized the opportunity to declare, in words that he had written on the train as he travelled from Washington to Kingston, that Canada was "part of the sisterhood of the British Empire. I give to you assurance that the people of the United States will not stand idly by if domination of Canadian soil is threatened by any other empire." Mackenzie King, who was on the platform with the president, had not asked for the American pledge, nor had he known it would be offered. He told Roosevelt that he had "dropped a bomb."[10]

King and Skelton were in similar minds about Roosevelt's guarantee. A very public Canadian response was imperative. "Warm appreciation," Skelton told King, was certainly in order, an expression of gratitude to a president who was giving "fresh evidence of the special neighbourly relations between Canada and the United States." No reciprocal assurance needed to be offered to the Americans – neither country was in the military-alliance business – but it was vital to point out that "we have always made great efforts to prevent any domination of Canada, and will continue to do so." The president must not be allowed to think that Canadians were going to let the United States do the work of defending their country. Nor, on the other hand, could the government permit Roosevelt's remarks to become an excuse "for shirking our own responsibility for our own defence."[11]

Skelton and King were apart in the aftermath of the Roosevelt speech, the prime minister in his private car on a train to southern Ontario and OD working his habitually long days in the East Block of the Parliament Buildings. By the time that King's train reached Toronto, he had concluded that he would respond to Roosevelt immediately, at a Saturday picnic in nearby Woodbridge on 20 August. That morning King fussed for hours over a Skelton package of speech ideas, which arrived by courier overnight. However, the address he delivered in the afternoon looked very much the way Skelton and his senior assistant, Loring Christie, imagined it. King thanked the United States, but said no thanks: Canada would take full responsibility for its own defence and see to it that enemy forces could not operate from Canadian territory against the United States. "Skelton had given me excellent material," King recorded in his diary. "It was really an answer to prayer to have had this come at the time."[12]

For his colleagues in External Affairs, OD sketched out the implications of Roosevelt's speech in a parable featuring America's Uncle Sam and the British John Bull, with Canada in the role of Little Nell, squeezed between two brawny men. Sam reassured John that they understood one another very well "as family men," and so John would surely not mind if Sam spoke "like a Dutch uncle to Little Nell as one of your girls." "Hitler & Co." needed to be cleaned up. That was John's work, with Little Nell alongside to help out. Sam would be staying home, looking after Nell's farm while she was away and selling John Bull "all the stuff you want from my farm."[13]

The tone was playful, but his paraphrase of the meaning of the Kingston declaration reflected Skelton's fears. Canada was a "little girl." If she could not protect herself, the United States would have no compunction about moving in to do the job for her. Skelton knew full well that Roosevelt's guarantee, however amiably put, was grounded in raw self-interest: the unwillingness of the United States to allow an aggressive enemy power to secure a foothold on the North American continent, and thus to use Canada as a backdoor for an attack on the United States. The Americans, moreover, were not about to become involved in a European war, except to profit from it. OD had written to Mike Pearson in London three months before that he foresaw no "possibility of the United States placing herself in advance on the side of Great Britain and France; she might a year after the war began."[14]

Skelton welcomed the Kingston-Woodbridge pledge of mutual obligations and its implicit promise of closer continental defence collaboration. Whatever his reservations about or criticisms of the United States, he was convinced that Sam was "a good neighbour – a neighbour that any free country in the Continent of Europe or elsewhere would thank its stars to have."[15] America's friendliness, its healthy devotion to its own safety, and its reluctance to become involved in Europe's quarrels were facts of life, and helpful ones, he hoped, in countering the too-common belief of Canadians that all their country could be was one of John Bull's girls. Skelton knew, but did not let it preoccupy him, that most Americans, when they considered Canada at all, thought the same thing. They would change their minds, he thought, when Little Nell finally grew up and took her rightful place in the world.

If the newspapers of the week during Roosevelt's visit were to be believed, it was a good thing that Skelton had not travelled with the prime minister. He was needed at home. The always unconventional Sandy Skelton, living near his parents in Ottawa's Rockcliffe Village and working long hours as the driving force behind the Royal Commission on Dominion-Provincial Relations, was keeping a bear cub as a pet. One evening he was out, and so was the bear. The Grahams, acquaintances of the Skeltons, were startled to encounter the cub in Rockcliffe Park, and more startled when it followed them home. The police (Rockcliffe had one policeman) were called, and Sandy's father was summoned. OD coaxed the bear from the Graham's tree, in which it had taken up residence, and managed to wrestle it back to Sandy's house on Acacia Drive.

The Rockcliffe Council quickly convened to ban bears from the village precinct. Undeterred, Sandy convinced the authorities that the rules did not apply to him – he was good at that – since his pet was the size of a small dog and quite harmless. There were regular sightings of Sandy and his bear cub in Rockcliffe and Ottawa over the months to come.[16]

The story was widely reported across the country, but the Ottawa *Journal* had the most fun with it. Sandy Skelton, it seemed to the *Journal*, was too busy saving the country to save Rockcliffe from his bear. The job therefore fell to the under-secretary of state for external affairs, "who rose manfully to the occasion." The bear was "borne triumphantly back to captivity in Dr. Skelton's car and custody; the eminent author-diplomatist holding him in the rear seat as a measure of most thoughtful but wholly valorous precaution. Our foreign policy, we may rest assured, is in good hands." Oscar and Isabel felt no embarrassment. They gathered up the accounts of Sandy's bear on the loose and preserved them among their papers. It had all been "hot-weather hilarity," the *Journal* said, and in the summer of 1938 that was in short supply.[17]

The Czech issue was set for an explosion in September. Efforts at mediation, negotiation, and compromise were at their fag end. Skelton nevertheless thought, or hoped, at the beginning of the month that "sufficient concessions will be shaken out of Czechoslovakia in the course of the next week or two to avert the likelihood of an armed invasion of Czechoslovakia by Germany." No one could be sure of this, of course, since the ringmaster of events was Hitler, "a paranoiac mystic." Yet, if Germany did decide to smash the Czechs, it seemed to Skelton very unlikely that the British would wage war against Hitler. Their hints of military intervention in German-Czech affairs were a "constructive game of bluff." Skelton had the evidence of that in front of him, he claimed, in a cable from Britain's foreign secretary, Lord Halifax, indicating that even a British-French-Soviet grouping could not prevent the Czechs from being overrun and that "from this point of view we could not think a European war would be justifiable if by any means this could be avoided." On that basis Skelton informed King that he need not "worry unduly at the present moment."[18]

Skelton was attempting to reassure a prime minister who had hidden himself away at his Kingsmere estate, thirty kilometres outside Ottawa. But King was not consolable. He was suffering from a painful sciatica that combined with the depressing events in Europe to drive him to despair. Czechoslovakia, King felt sure, was bringing war to Britain and by extension to Canada, where it would break apart his country, his Liberal Party, and the work of a lifetime spent keeping people together. Catastrophe had a way of exposing the best in him, sharpening his instincts and focusing his resources, but not this time. As the great international crisis of September 1938 unfolded, King was very nearly immobilized. For three weeks, he stayed away from the office. One of his few visitors was Skelton, who found the prime minister weak, lacking sleep, and "panicky." King's determination to stand with the British had not diminished. The meeting did not go well. "I'm still quite sure he won't get into war – before Britain does," OD wrote facetiously to Isabel. In a memorandum that was sent out to Kingsmere, Skelton again tried to tell King that he had nothing to worry about. Canada was "the safest country in the world – as long as we mind our own business."[19]

From his sickbed, and in the privacy of his diary, King unleashed a torrent of abuse at Skelton for his narrow vision of the national interest, "leading to a sort of isolationist attitude so far as Canada is concerned." Self-interest, as King interpreted it, ought not to be only about the self. He saw "our real self-interest" resting in the strength of the British Empire as a whole: "Cooperation between all parts of the Empire and the democracies is in Canada's interests in the long run and in her own immediate self respect." That, not Skelton's, was the "only possible attitude to be assumed."[20]

The British Empire was a force for peace, but the prime minister was for war if it came to that. With the distasteful Skelton encounter still on his mind, King talked to Norman Rogers, the labour minister, who was much admired by both the prime minister and the under-secretary. King and Rogers agreed that "it was a self-evident national duty, if Britain entered the war, that Canada should regard herself as part of the British Empire, one of the nations of the sisterhood of nations, which should cooperate lending every assistance possible, in no way asserting neutrality, but carefully defining in what ways and how far she would participate."[21]

The British had no idea that King was thinking such thoughts. What they saw was a prime minister, abetted by his deeply suspicious lieutenant, who was so intent on "carefully defining" the Anglo-Canadian relationship that worthwhile collaboration was very nearly impossible. A member of the Royal Air Force (RAF), Group Captain J.M. Robb, was in Ottawa over the summer of 1938 peddling a scheme for the establishment of aviation schools in Canada that would funnel trained Canadian airmen into the RAF. Skelton expertly judged such plans to be transparent British efforts to reduce Canada's aloofness to imperial-defence cooperation. He denounced the Robb idea as "purely and simply" an RAF recruiting scheme involving "a continuous use of Canada in peace and in war as a basis of training for United Kingdom military forces." King was of the same view. Robb was sent packing.[22]

If only there could be peace, any kind of peace. King and Skelton jumped at any report or rumour in the news or diplomatic cables that suggested a settlement of the Czech Sudetenland problem was in the air. They were thrilled by Prime Minister Neville Chamberlain's dramatic announcement that he would fly to Germany on 15 September to meet with Hitler in his mountain lair at Berchtesgaden. Skelton had been denouncing Britain's foreign policy under Chamberlain as "smug," "jingoistic," and not meriting "any unqualified approval." Yet Chamberlain had been cautious and realistic in avoiding definite commitments to the security of central Europe, and the Berchtesgaden initiative was a plea for peace rather than a summons to war. Full of gratitude to Chamberlain, Skelton wrote with relief to his wife in Peterborough, where she was visiting her mother, and to King at his Quebec estate. With the world's fate in the balance, the British prime minister's mission to Hitler was "a splendid stroke. Whatever the outcome, the mere proposal ensures Chamberlain an honoured place in history."[23]

The Chamberlain-Hitler talks at Berchtesgaden went well for them, but not for the Czechs. Hitler had been campaigning for Sudetenland autonomy, but he told the British leader that he expected more, the ceding of the region to the German Reich. Chamberlain readily concurred, receiving in return an assurance that Hitler's territorial aims had reached their limit. British-French discussions came in the days following Berchtesgaden, and the Czechs were told what they would have to concede. Chamberlain travelled to Bad Godesberg on 22 September to tell Hitler that he could have the Sudetenland, with certain qualifications and safeguards. To Chamberlain's astonishment, Hitler rejected the orderly transfer of territory under international supervision outlined by London and Paris and agreed to by the Czechs. Instead, he demanded immediate military occupation of the Sudeten lands. The dismal news from Godesberg came to Skelton from the British Dominions Office and the High Commission in London. Hitler seemed impossible to satisfy, while Chamberlain was on the verge of breaking off the negotiation against the background of stiffening opinion in his cabinet and party back home. "War shadows looming thicker," OD scribbled in a tiny leather notebook, taking up his diary again after weeks away from it.[24]

At noon on the 23rd, the day Chamberlain left Godesberg, Skelton received a Reuters news agency report of a German invasion of Czecho-slovakia. He telephoned Mackenzie King, who had returned from Kings-mere to his Ottawa residence at Laurier House. King immediately called the cabinet into session for 4:00 in the afternoon. Before that took place, Reuters had killed its war bulletin, but the damage was done from Skel-ton's standpoint. When they talked before the cabinet met, he noted with disgust King's "exalted imperial cum democracy and freedom mood, very belligerent." The world "had come to the crossroads" and "must decide whether men were to be ruled by reason or force, might or right, blood or persuasion, brute or God, matter or spirit, Paganism or Christianity." King expected opinion in Canada and around the world to rally against Germany and wanted to take the lead with a public dec-laration that "Canada will not stand idly by and see modern civilization ruthlessly destroyed if anything we can do would help save mankind."[25]

Knowing King well, and which buttons to push, Skelton marched an army of arguments to battle the prime minister's enthusiasms. The negotiation in Europe had not yet failed. Neither Britain nor France had indicated privately or publicly that they were willing to go to war to keep Czechoslovakia intact. After giving Hitler 95 per cent of what he wanted, they would surely hesitate to plunge the world into a great con-flict for the other 5 per cent. Was the prime minister asking Canadians, living thousands of miles from the trouble, to stick their necks out when others would not? Was he allowing the imperialists of the Toronto *Globe* and the Montreal *Gazette* to stampede him into precipitate action? War was a blunt instrument, replete with lies, propaganda, repression, and horrible modern weapons; moreover, it was not clear that a war fought now could even be won, since so many countries, the United States in particular, would not support it. These appeals to pragmatism and pride and against war were custom-made for King, or usually so. Skelton, how-ever, saw no sign that he was making any headway.[26]

Perhaps the cabinet would slow King down. The prime minister emerged from a two-hour meeting in the late afternoon of the 23rd to tell Skelton that there was reluctance among his colleagues about an immediate public statement but unanimity on the larger issue: a war for "reason and freedom" was coming and "Canada would have to go in." Even in Quebec, cabinet members were assured, feeling was run-ning against Germany. Things went more Skelton's way when "Good old Ernest" Lapointe weighed in with a telegram to King from Geneva counselling caution and "no irrevocable steps." Chamberlain meanwhile had managed to keep the prospects of peace alive at Godesberg. Skelton concluded from the diplomatic cables that were coming into the East Block that Hitler was "even more cunning, more ruthless, more arrogant than might have been anticipated," and very nearly a lunatic to boot. With his "extraordinary persistence and patience," Chamberlain had the right temperament to act as a mediator between the Germans and the Czechs.[27]

There might be peace, Skelton urged, if only the Czechs would "swallow the other 5%" of Germany's demands. But if he really believed that Godesberg was asking only a few more percentage points of concession than Berchtesgaden had, he was misleading himself – and his prime minister. Skelton wanted peace so fervently, or had so little sympathy for or understanding of the Czechs' predicament, that he reacted with sarcasm to their refusal to become "a nation of slaves" and accused them of heaping responsibility for their security on other powers. In the fourth week of September he watched uneasily as resistance provoked by Hitler's demands grew in Britain and France; as Sir Horace Wilson, a colleague from the 1933 Skelton Committee, travelled to Berlin on a mission to find common ground but also to caution that Britain would support the French if they became involved in a German-Czech war; and as Hitler ranted against the Czechs and their leadership in front of more than fifteen thousand of his fellow fanatics. OD listened briefly to the dictator's ravings on the radio in German, anxious to unearth whatever optimism he could from it: "the bits I heard less blatant, the applause more artificial than usual, a bad speech, but perhaps less bad than some."[28]

As Skelton wrote in his diary about Hitler's speech, he also took note of two telegrams and a telephone message from Vincent Massey, Canada's high commissioner in the British capital, who was "himself ready for further compromise rather than an incalculable war but says war spirit & hysteria are rising fast." The great fear in the United Kingdom was the imminent arrival of German airplanes in the skies above, with their payloads of bombs and poison gas. Beginning on 26 September, the British government issued a forty-page instruction booklet on the protection of households against air raids, a prospect that was not made to sound promising, and began the distribution of gas masks. Londoners, who were expected to bear the brunt of the coming onslaught, dug a million feet of trenches to serve as bomb shelters. Like many others, Arnold Toynbee, a political analyst and historian close to the government, braced for the destruction of their world: "In a few minutes the clock was going to stop, and life, as we had known it, was coming to an end."[29]

Skelton called in his senior staff to prepare for the "probable entry of Canada into the war." He gave his difficult-to-handle assistant under-secretary, Laurent Beaudry, the number two person in the department in name only, the perfunctory task of coordinating with Canada's missions and offices abroad. John Read, the legal adviser, returned from a game at the Larrimac Golf Club in the Gatineau Hills outside Ottawa to be asked to have the appropriate statutes, documents, and orders-in-council at the ready. The most important work was delegated to Loring Christie, who was to make suggestions for "a limited Canada first" war effort, an expansion on his earlier memorandum that made the case that Canada ought not be a participant in the war "in the same sense or on the same kind of unlimited scale as the European Allies," but only on the basis of "what for short may be called an 'Associate' – a North American associate." Christie was the colleague Skelton valued most. When Christie asked for a posting to one of Canada's foreign missions, Skelton told him that he could not spare him. He relied too much on his "moral & intellectual support." They thought the same way about attempts to ensnare Canada in imperial and international commitments and the need to respond to them with "out & out" Canadian independence. The only difference between the two, as Read recalled it, was that Skelton was an isolationist while Christie was an extreme isolationist.[30]

Skelton was in the East Block of the Parliament Buildings and Macken-zie King in the cabinet room not far away when they listened to Neville Chamberlain's radio broadcast in the middle of the afternoon of 27 September. Chamberlain appealed for peace but said that the United Kingdom would resist any nation seeking to dominate the world by force. Unlike many listeners, Skelton and King heard both parts of Chamberlain's message, yet they heard them differently. For Skelton, it was a "bad day": a European war was nearer than ever. King, on the other hand, was inspired by Chamberlain's leadership, telling Skelton that no one with a "spark of chivalry or red blood" could fail to back the British prime minister. A public declaration of Canada's support for Britain had been delayed for too long. King excitedly worked out a statement, rejecting two Skelton attempts and allowing his deputy to inject only "a sentence or two" of his own. The brief document, endorsing Chamberlain's radio speech, was handed out to the newspapermen milling about outside the prime minister's office. They took it for what it was, as a move of the cautious King government towards intervention in European affairs.[31]

Skelton expected Britain's diplomatic efforts to collapse imminently and Germany to march against Czechoslovakia. He preferred to hold off on any public announcement until then. As the prime minister fussed over his statement, OD tried unsuccessfully to convince him to allow it to be recast as a press release to be distributed when war broke out. Skelton produced a text regretting that, in spite of far-reaching concessions, the rulers of Germany had made demands that Czechoslovakia was unable to accept. France had gone to the aid of the Czechs and Britain was making it clear that it would support the French. Skelton did not say what Canada would do, instead reiterating the staple themes of Mackenzie King's foreign policy – national unity as the national imperative and Parliament as the arbiter of all great matters of state. At first he toyed with writing what the prime minister believed: the future of civilization had been put in jeopardy by German ruthlessness.[32] To say that, however, implied that the saving of the world was Canada's business.

Skelton and King reviewed the day's events over dinner at Laurier House. The prime minister feared that he had bent too far towards the "imperialists," and Skelton jumped at the opening to maintain that the country's empire-minded minority did not represent the mainstream of sensible and self-interested Canadians. The wary attitude of French Canadians like Ernest Lapointe and Raoul Dandurand, the Liberal leader in the Senate, was the "really Canadian" view. If there must be war, it ought to be a limited one, along the lines of what Skelton had been contemplating. He laid out for King a formula for keeping the war effort as close to home as possible: the government should make strictly Canadian interests the paramount consideration in all of its decisions and actions; the emphasis needed to be on the provision to the country's allies of the raw material of war, such as food and munitions, rather than the sending of men to battlefields far away; and the divisive mistakes of the First World War, the imposition of compulsory military service in particular, could not be repeated. King listened intently and took notes. Later in the evening, returning to the office, Skelton ran into Dandurand, who told him that his ideas for a limited war were a blueprint for the survival of the Liberal Party in Quebec.[33]

"No war yet," Skelton observed when he arrived at the East Block on the morning of 28 September. He sent home the telegram decoders who had been on duty for twenty-five consecutive hours and put others on the job to cover the cable traffic that was coming in at a heart-pounding pace from the British government, which was threatening Hitler and at the same time asking him why he would use force against Czechoslovakia when he could have all that he wanted without it and without delay. Then, suddenly, came the report that the German chancellor had stepped back from the brink. As Neville Chamberlain neared the end of his review of recent events in the House of Commons, he announced that Hitler had agreed to meet in Munich the next day with the prime ministers of the United Kingdom and France and Italy's Benito Mussolini. The shouts of relief and praise for Chamberlain poured out of the British Parliament on to the streets. Stephen Holmes of the British High Commission in Ottawa told Skelton that the cheering coming over the radio from the London area made him afraid that foreigners would think that the English were ready for peace at any price. Skelton replied that they were willing to pay "practically any price." So was he. He went to bed "much earlier & easier" than he had the night before.[34]

The summit at Munich produced the peace that Skelton, King, and Chamberlain so desperately sought. The cost was the Czech Sudetenland, delivered to Hitler on terms not very different from his Godesberg demands. Skelton did not doubt that "a great price" had been paid, but a bad peace might pave the way for a good peace, and Munich was better than a preventive war, the horrors and suffering of which "would begin where the last war left off." Time had been won for reason, and for every country and ruler, democrat or dictator, to realize how close they had come to disaster. Perhaps the universal outburst of relief after Munich was revealing of how little heart there was for war. Perhaps Hitler and Germany had achieved enough to banish their inferiority complex or obsession for revenge for the wrongs of Versailles. Skelton was gratified "that Chamberlain strove for peace so pertinaciously, that he never lost his temper or his head, and that he was man enough to continue working for peace when many in England were shouting war and it would have been easy and popular (for the moment) to have taken up that cry himself. He has done a good job."[35]

Having praised him, Skelton proceeded to bury Chamberlain and the "fumbling" foreign policies that he personified. The U.K. leadership had not stood up to Germany in any way that might have made a difference, in part out of a fear that they "might plunge Hitler's disordered mind over the edge, but chiefly because neither the government nor the British people were prepared to take up Czechoslovakia's quarrel if that meant German planes over London." Chamberlain had browbeaten Prague into accepting Hitler's demands, which amounted to the destruction of Czechoslovakia, with "no argument permitted." Peace was saved by retreat, Skelton's review of the Munich settlement ("if it can be called a settlement") for the prime minister concluded. No one "in civilized countries" could feel any pride or satisfaction. "We cannot deny that force and bluff have triumphed; that Hitler has won by threats and a show of force more than many rulers have won by war, that his position in his own country has been strengthened and his megalomania nourished by this last proof of his irresistible will."[36]

Skelton accepted that Britain's craven behaviour was not unique. The international community had failed Czechoslovakia. France, though bound by a solemn treaty with the Czechs, threw its ally to the wolves. Canny Russia laid back, looking to profit from war or from chaos. The Poles exploited the crisis to seize the Teschen territory of Czechoslovakia, proving themselves even more contemptible than the Germans. The smaller countries of Europe took to the storm cellar. The League of Nations adjourned. Munich and the months that preceded it had been striking for a "complete absence of any knight-errantry, any idealism, any readiness to risk a bit of one's skin in assisting another." Skelton said nothing of any responsibility Canada might bear, or of his own inclination to toss Czechoslovakia overboard for the sake of peace. Nor did he give any credit to the prime minister for his willingness to risk himself and his country for the Anglo-Canadian and Commonwealth values of freedom and democracy in which he deeply believed and for which he was ready to fight.[37]

Skelton blew off steam by turning the recent crisis into a fable, which he read out at a dinner party for Joseph Sirois, Sandy's boss at the royal commission. The tale's central character was Ben (Edvard Beneš, the Czech president), an ambitious young sheep farmer who had worked hard and made his farm into a model of the community, "though some people did say he was a bit cocky over his success." Ben had a muscular neighbour, Adolph, who was intent on stealing every farm to the east of his own. He spied some of Ben's sheep, who bleated like his own. Adolph declared that his heart bled for the sheep and announced that he would beat up Ben if he didn't surrender his sheep forthwith. Ben had friends, Nev (Neville Chamberlain) and Ed (France's Édouard Daladier). They shook their fingers at the ungentlemanly Adolph, but they meekly handed the sheep over to him, so long as he promised to keep the neighbourhood a respectable and orderly place. Nev and Ed kept Ben out of the way, tying him up so that he couldn't cause any unseemly trouble. The moral of the fable, duly absorbed by the farmers down the line, was that all of them were ultimately on their own.[38] Skelton believed that to be the naked truth, in life as in international affairs.

On 11 October King sailed south for a holiday with Skelton on the Fur-
ness Withy luxury liner *Queen of Bermuda* out of New York. "We both need
a rest," the prime minister told the press, making it clear that he leaned
heavily on his teammate. "No words can express what this country owes
to Dr. Skelton. His work during the recent crisis and in the months leading up to it put a tremendous load upon him and upon us all." King told
reporters that their destination and timetable were undecided – they
would go where the warm weather took them – but they had already
decided to stop in Bermuda and Jamaica. Accommodation on board the
English-owned ship was complimentary, the princely Sandringham Suite
for King and something a little less grand for "Dr. S."[39]

Skelton and King relaxed, toured, and overate for three weeks on Bermuda and down into the Caribbean, as comfortable together, it seemed,
as a pair of old shoes. They argued only once, inadvertently. King casually
mentioned that the visit to Bermuda made him think of the "richness of
the inheritance of partnership" in the British Empire "and what it meant
to its parts to have the good-will which existed throughout the whole." In
King's telling, Skelton angrily responded in a way that was new to him:
the British connection meant nothing to him, or to Canada's younger
generation, "except the possibility of being drawn into European wars."
He was "a Canadian, pure and simple," and a North American too, since
Canadians relied on the United States. King scorned dependence on the
United States. A "change of leaders there might lead to a vassalage so far
as our Dominion was concerned. There was more real freedom in the
British Commonwealth of Nations." Canada was strengthened "by being
part of a greater whole, with kindred aims, ideals and institutions."[40]

King brooded after their encounter about Skelton's republicanism
and his antagonism towards Britain, and his attempt to dominate the
intellectual agenda. "I felt his negative viewpoint & inferiority complex
in so many things," King wrote in his diary, his comments spilling over
into a complaint about the social Skelton, who condemned privilege and
belittled hospitality and yet who seemed hurt when he was left out of
things. But King never grumbled about Skelton for long. It was not easy
to travel with a head of government, and his deputy had been "mar-
velously considerate & self-effacing," qualities that the prime minister
found appealing. King took their time away as a reminder that he would
have "to lead and not be controlled," even while Skelton was in many
ways "the best of Counsellors and guides."[41]

Bermuda, where King and Skelton "felt like lords," was a deliberately
Anglo-Saxon paradise. The vacationers stayed in one of the cottages at

Cambridge-Beaches, an exclusive twenty-acre enclave of tidy beaches and gardens on the ocean a few minutes outside Somerset. The resort's brochure, which Skelton kept as a memento, contained the words that many island hotels put in their advertising to discourage Jewish visitors: Cambridge-Beaches "caters only to Gentile guests" and "it is desired, wherever possible, to have information before the arrival of guests as to their social or business standing." At the same time that Canada was pushing Jewish refugees away from its ports, the prime minister and his most senior official blissfully sunned themselves in a place that specialized in the same exclusionist sentiment.[42]

Skelton probably didn't notice. He acknowledged that Canadian anti-Semitism was pervasive (he occasionally fell into its stereotypes himself, calling Jews loud, pushy, and clannish) and was saddened when young Jewish men found their way to advancement in their professions barred because of their ethnicity. The "only white man I know," he told his old colleague W.L. Grant, "who has to struggle against a greater prejudice is the Mormon." He detested what the Nazis were doing to the Jews of Germany. In earlier times he had chided the King government for immigration laws that excluded potential new Canadians on the basis of their colour or race. Yet he did not champion the admission of Jewish refugees to Canada; only 748 of them were able to make their way to the country in 1938, and 1,763 in 1939. Skelton seldom raised the issue as a matter of policy and, when he did, he was too inclined to treat the issue with the cold logic of an international lawyer or a pragmatic Canadian politician. Why should Germany and other countries with unwanted minorities be allowed to throw on Canadians the responsibility of solving their internal difficulties? How could substantial numbers of Jews be brought to Canada when domestic opinion, led by his ally Ernest Lapointe, was so firmly opposed to the idea? On one of the great moral issues of his day, Skelton was missing in action.[43]

King and Skelton returned from their trip by way of New York. They met at the Harvard Club with Norman Robertson, who reported that the lengthy and difficult three-way negotiations between Canada, the United States, and Great Britain were coming to a satisfactory close. The thirty-four-year-old Robertson, Skelton's trade expert, had been virtually living in Washington for more than a year. He talked and wrote from there to Skelton, who talked and wrote to Mackenzie King; that was what passed for Canada's machinery and organization on trade questions. Robertson was often on his own, inventing policy and praying that his superiors would back him up. Skelton did. When the hard bargaining had seemed likely to lead to a collapse of the bargaining earlier in 1938, his first instinct was to protect Robertson from any blame that might fall on him. Robertson loved Skelton for the way he supported his troops. On 17 November, Skelton and King were back in the United States to sign off on the Canadian-American part of the triangular trade agreement, which asked relatively few concessions from Ottawa and generated major gains in accessing the U.S. market. OD dug out his tall black silk hat for the occasion.[44]

In the aftermath of Munich, Skelton claimed that the public no longer needed to be convinced of the need for a stronger military, making him more insistent that defence policy and expenditure must concentrate on the defence of Canada. As he had King tell Parliament the previous May, Canadians were fortunate in their neighbour and their lack of neighbours. Faraway Germany, Japan, and Italy were not about to seize and colonize "our vast areas" and, even if they had such ambitions, the United States would not allow aggressor states to overrun Canada. Attacks on Canada were thus unlikely, but they were "a possibility against which we must insure, in appropriate measure, and in self-respecting co-operation with the United States." The people in the final analysis would expect the government to protect them, not to rally to Britain's causes. Skelton all but ruled out the sending of a great army across the Atlantic Ocean, as Canada had done in 1914. So did the prime minister, whose government was directing small but important resources towards the navy and the air force and away from the army, which conjured up unhappy thoughts of battles in Europe, heavy casualties, and the imposition of compulsory military service.[45]

King privately did not suppose that Canada was safe from attack. He had an exaggerated idea of Canada as "a prize" in the forthcoming war, "the one land capable of colonization by large numbers of persons of other lands." When they were in Bermuda, the prime minister told Skelton that "Canada by itself would be a prey to aggressor nations in a world such as we have today, and would develop more than ever through the years to come." He counted on Britain for assistance, King explained to his sceptical assistant.[46] Girding for war, he saw danger everywhere, even where it did not exist. Skelton, wishing to keep Canada away from the world, minimized the threats, even outside Canada, where they did exist.

Skelton worried about what the military might be doing behind the government's back. He believed that their network of cooperation with Britain on matters of organization, training, and equipment was a serious impediment to Canadian independence. Canada's senior military officers, good men though they might be as individuals, seemed to him so tightly tied to Mother Britain's apron strings that they could do nothing other than snap a salute and do her bidding. It never occurred to him that they might have a different view of what was good and necessary for Canada. Aided by Loring Christie, and using his position at the top of the public service, Skelton systematically obstructed the military's attempts to encourage planning on a government-wide basis. A more subtle and skilled administrator might have kept the military close to him, so that he would know what they were thinking, but he shunned them. The army and the defence minister, Ian Mackenzie, silently went ahead on their own with preparations to send an expeditionary force abroad in a major war. Neither Skelton nor Mackenzie King was aware of their plan.[47]

In Europe the fears and rumblings of war returned very soon after Munich. Early in January 1939 reports began to come to the British government, and through London to Ottawa, about an imminent Hitler strike towards the west. Before the month was out, there were predictions of an air attack on England, "making," said Skelton, "our flesh creep." King's reaction was immediate and dramatic, even if he took his usual roundabout route to get there. Defending his foreign and defence policies in the House of Commons, the prime minister made an apparent detour to quote Sir Wilfrid Laurier's words during the debate on the Canadian navy three decades before. Laurier had described his "conviction that under British institutions my native land has found a measure of security and freedom it could not have found under any other regime," adding that when England was at war "we are at war and liable to attack." King stipulated at the same time that Parliament was in charge of Canada's fate, but that's not what people heard. He had tied the country to Britain and to a British war. The current prime minister was letting a revered predecessor speak for him.[48]

Skelton was upset by King's instinctive public response to the latest European crisis, which he reported had "provoked profound alarm & anger not only in Quebec but among all nationalists." But he regarded the prime minister's private reaction as more serious. King called the cabinet into emergency session on 27 January, where its members decided, "unanimously" he told Skelton, that Canada could not keep out of a European war involving Britain and that a statement to that effect ought to be made in advance "to prevent it being alleged that the Government had been dragged in or kicked in." Skelton was instructed to find the right words for the occasion.[49]

King was not telling the whole truth. The prime minister did inform Skelton that Ernest Lapointe had reservations about the "when England is at war" address, but not that he had deprecated a public statement and hinted that he might have to resign from the cabinet in the event of war, "knowing what the feeling would be in his province." King focused the discussion in cabinet on the defence of the Canadian homeland rather than the defence of the British homeland. He scarcely mentioned the "threat to freedom the world over," explaining away his Laurier speech by claiming that he was merely reflecting reality. No one could deny that, if a war began the next day, Canada's shipping and, if possible its harbours, would be immediately attacked by aggressor states – "not because we were at war with them or because they were at war with us, but because they were at war with Britain and regarded us as part of the British Empire."[50]

The prime minister used emotional blackmail, an art in which he was skilled, to deflect his cabinet colleagues away from a divisive discussion of the international situation and make them sympathetic to their beleaguered leader. He warned that any dissension would imperil the Liberal Party and throw the country into the arms of the hated Tories. He moaned that his health was fragile and gave the names of his doctors in case his associates wanted to check up on him. And he maintained that "almost my entire staff was against me," so that the cabinet could "see how much help I could expect to get from that source in dealing with the most baffling of our political situations." Notable was a story about one particularly obstructive aide, who went unnamed. King perhaps wanted the cabinet to think of Skelton, whose contrary views were well known.[51]

Having shamelessly manipulated the cabinet, King went to work on Skelton. They had not spoken about the Laurier speech, because the prime minister surmised that he would get a frosty reception. After a two-hour cabinet meeting, however, King had his justifications well rehearsed. He explained that he lived in the world of practical politics, an argument that always worked well with Skelton, and he underscored their shared stake in the success of the Liberal Party. A prime minister's job, King stated, was to "see far ahead and anticipate situations in advance." If "the blow came" and he had said nothing to Canadians about their vulnerability in an empire war, "the Party would never be forgiven for having remained silent for so long."[52]

Skelton tried to remind King of the dangers of saying "anything until we had to" and worked "to curve him back to his old position of not deciding prematurely." Drawing on his biography of Laurier, OD said that King's predecessor had been driven by "the imperialists on one side, and the nationalists on the other, and sought to take a middle position." Why shouldn't King do the same? The prime minister countered that he was doing exactly that. Over the past months he had been shoved into an "extreme nationalist position which was not my own position nor that of my party, and which would cause me no end of injury politically." He was restoring balance by ending his public silence and travelling to "the *reality* side of things," which would placate the imperialists and be tolerated by the nationalists. Skelton repeated a favourite theme. King would be surprised how many young people were unwilling to go to war "just because of our British connection." "I told him that I was all of that view myself," the prime minister replied.[53]

Each thought that he had moved the other in his direction. King recalled that Skelton had "evidently been prepared to take issue with me," but he listened "very intently" and "saw the force and truth of what I had said." He came around, "in the light of the actualities, to a readiness to state the position as I had." In Skelton's version, it was the prime minister who was backtracking, in part because the tension had eased in Europe after a Hitler speech that was less provocative than London and Ottawa expected. As King prepared for the weekly gathering of his Liberal caucus, Skelton buttressed the advice he had given verbally with a note designed to prevent the prime minister from responding to MPs' questions with another rash pledge to stand with Britain.[54]

Ernest Lapointe also feared another King outburst. He came to see Skelton on 2 February, before a meeting of the cabinet, "asking me to try to prevent the P.M. making any more breaks." Skelton said that was hard for him to do, if fifteen cabinet colleagues could not hold King back. Lapointe replied that "unfortunately some of the fifteen were worse" than the prime minister. However, King was fooling himself if he thought that that he could win Lapointe and his Quebec colleague Arthur Cardin over to the view that a British war was by definition a Canadian war. Mackenzie King did not know that the justice minister had provided OD with another avenue into the cabinet room.[55]

Skelton informed King and Lapointe that he and his departmental colleagues were giving thought to "whether Canada is automatically at war whenever Great Britain is, and if so, whether something should or should not be done about it." The question of Canada's legal and constitutional position in the event of a British war was being aired in the intellectual community and in Parliament, where the Liberal Progressive MP J.T. Thorson had introduced a bill stipulating that the country could become a belligerent only by a separate Canadian declaration of war executed by King George VI acting on the advice of the Ottawa government. For King, this route was favoured only by academics and hairsplitters divorced from the real world, and would inevitably dredge up controversy: he saw to it that the Thorson bill went nowhere. Skelton believed, along with most of the expert lawyers, that the outside world was "entitled to assume that we are automatically belligerent" in the absence of any clarifying action. He favoured Thorson's bill as a means of making it explicit that British politicians did not have the right indefinitely "to send tens of thousands of Canadian youth to war and death by pressing a button in London." In a lengthy memorandum to Mackenzie King and the cabinet, Skelton made his argument while conceding that the Canadian people were too deeply divided to allow for "any immediate logical solution, free of inconsistency and compromise." The best he could hope for was that, in practice, Canada would in future declare war entirely in and through its own institutions.[56]

The scare of January 1939 was followed by a period of relative calm in European affairs, reinforcing Skelton's belief that there had never been any valid ground for the "extreme forecasts" of an Anglo-German war. On 9 March a telegram from London that viewed no immediate crisis on the horizon buoyed his confidence that, as he wrote to King, "every month gained now puts the danger off several months further." Only six days later, that expectation was shattered. Hitler's troops strutted into Prague and occupied most of what was left of the Czechoslovak republic. Skelton's shock and surprise were shared across the foreign ministries of Europe's democracies. Canadian opinion meanwhile, to judge from newspapers across the country, was moving towards the grim realization that Germany would have to be stopped.[57]

Skelton's selfish concern was to keep Mackenzie King and Canada out of trouble. He urged the prime minister to do or say nothing precipitate and turned his fire on Neville Chamberlain, who might choose to react to Prague by confronting Germany and sweeping Canada along with him. The British leader was "self-confident to the point of arrogance, intolerant of criticism, and at the moment sore because he thinks in the eyes of the world Hitler has made a fool of him." He was also an imperialist, born and bred, "and cannot imagine that any part of the British Empire has any choice but to halt when he says halt and march when he says march." Men like that could not be trusted and must not be encouraged to think that Canada was standing nearby at attention, ready to carry out their will.[58]

Of necessity Skelton adopted a different tone when he sketched out the prime minister's statement on the Czech coup. He regretted "the overrunning of a gallant and vigorous small nation" and still more the evidence that Germany had given "that it does not consider itself bound by pledges freely exchanged a few short months before, and that it looks to force as the sole basis of relations with its neighbors." Knowing King's mind, Skelton larded his comments about the country's international future with the rhetoric of peace and restraint while also warning that Canadians would not tolerate "an aggressor launching an attack on Britain, with bombers raining death on London." The prime minister deployed his deputy's reluctant threat in the House of Commons on 20 March, amplifying it (over Skelton's objections) with a promise that the Canadian government would regard a direct attack on the United Kingdom "as an act of aggression menacing freedom in all parts of the British Commonwealth."[59]

The three crises over Czechoslovakia in 1938–9 convinced OD that Mackenzie King was determined to speed to Britain's defence in a European war, no matter what. Gone, unless a fragile peace could continue long enough to take Canada into a new time, were Skelton's hopes that Canada would make its own independent decisions about its place in the world, shouldering "clean-cut, adult responsibility for our policies and our destinies."[60] Yet he and the prime minister respected and needed each other so completely that they were able to paper over the deepening cracks in their relationship. They remained close, even as they came apart.

14
Half-Day's Work
Nearly Done, 1939–41

Skelton never fully recovered from the heart attack he had suffered in the summer of 1937. He arrived home late at night from the office "all in," slept badly, and became breathless with exertion. His daughter Sheila, when she could, brought the car to the East Block to pick him up after work, gently scolding him when he kept her waiting hour after hour, as he almost always did. Isabel had long ago given up any hope of slowing him down; she simply sighed that they both felt like "old crocks." When he allowed himself to think about it, OD sensed that he was gradually killing himself. He wrote in his diary how struck he had been by a remark Edith Murphy, his sister-in-law, made just before she died: "My half-day's work is nearly done." That brief sentence, summoning up work still undone and little time to do it, haunted him.[1]

Without knowing quite why, Sheila saw that Oscar drew his family and his home closer to him. He did not give them more time. There was even less of that as the telegrams from London grew more frequent and their reports about the prospect of war in Europe more dire. Yet, his daughter noticed, there was something about him that was different. Sympathizing with her problems and dreams, bursting with pride at Sandy's work at the royal commission, tending to Isabel's mother, taking the 1938 Packard out into the country with Isabel for long drives, buying plants and puttering in his prize garden – these were not extraordinary things, but they were done with more intensity. At External Affairs his colleagues observed a better, more caring boss, and, if possible, a more driven one. His emotions were more at the surface than before. A fierce anger had emerged after the heart attack, directed at the British, whose fault it was, he insisted, that Canada was having to go to the brink, and, sometimes, at the prime minister, who was taking them there. Independence's work was only half done, and a European war would threaten even what had already been achieved.[2]

"Shock and alarm" was how Skelton described the reaction to Hitler's march into the Czech capital of Prague on 15 March 1939, "contrary to firm pledges and contrary to assertions that it was only men of German blood in the neighbouring countries whom it sought to incorporate in the German Reich." OD had hoped that Munich, craven though it was, had set the conditions for a more stable Europe, rather than simply postponing war. He still insisted that conflict was not inevitable. Isabel was less sanguine, imagining that the last chance of European peace was gone. Oscar absorbed the seizure of Prague at External Affairs in the person of the Czech consul general, who had had no inkling of the German invasion. Skelton vowed to do what he could to arrange for the Czech diplomat to stay in Canada. On the 18th, the under-secretary's assistant, Agnes McCloskey, told Isabel that OD wished "he was in bed – the Germans have now taken the last of Czech Slovakia!" The bottom had been knocked out of Prime Minister Neville Chamberlain's foreign policy of accommodation and appeasement, Skelton told the prime minister, rightly predicting that what was next for the British leader and his country was more vigorous rearmament, the introduction of compulsory military service, and stronger efforts to support and get the support of other countries. Within two months of Prague, the Chamberlain government had issued security guarantees to Poland, Romania, Greece, and Turkey.[3]

Over the winter Skelton had been preparing a major address for the prime minister to deliver in the House of Commons. His speech draft was a massive document, written at different times and much revised. It reviewed the situation up to and after Munich, was harsh in its criticism of Hitler, and covered British and dominion opinion at length, emphasizing that Canada's cautious approach to international affairs and fear of war were commonplace – not exceptional at all. He was disdainful of those Canadians, "more innocent than informed," who "think the League of Nations or the British Commonwealth or even Canada alone should play the policeman and the arbiter." Canada should stay aloof from the affairs of others "thousands of miles away."[4]

Skelton trod well-worn ground, looking at contradictory "national feelings," the vital United States of America and the less vital states of the Americas to the south, the stew of European rivalries and feuds, the hapless but still worthwhile League, and Canada's "affection" for Britain. The long memorandum argued that no hard-and-fast course of action could be offered in advance of events. If there was war, the first task was the defence of Canada, the second to cooperate with allies. What should be clear, Skelton insisted, not for the first time, was that "the days of great expeditionary forces of infantry crossing the ocean are not likely to recur," although he did acknowledge that the changing strategic situation after the destruction of the Czech state made this conclusion less certain than it had been a few months before.[5]

King spent the morning of 25 March reviewing his counsellor's speech notes. He worried that Britain was moving towards a security guarantee of the "wretched little States" to the east of Germany, and even more that the deteriorating international situation was causing – or could cause if he was not careful – a national-unity crisis in Canada. Two days before, his great enemy (even though a fellow Liberal) Mitch Hepburn, the Ontario premier, had led his Parliament in a bellicose pro-conscription and anti-Mackenzie King resolution, and there were indications that the Quebec legislature would retaliate with a neutralist message. King pronounced Skelton's draft "admirable" and "well worked out," but it lacked "the kind of concrete statement which will be demanded by the H. of C. and the country." King told his diary that he needed to say something "that will keep this country together, and enable us to do most effectively in the end whatever may be decided upon." That translated into caution, a King specialty.[6]

The prime minister's address to the House of Commons, ponderously delivered over two hours on the afternoon of 30 March, fell short of the concrete in all but one respect. "Absolute statements of policy," he stated, "absolute undertakings to follow other governments, whatever the situation, are out of the question." King did edge his government towards support for Great Britain. Canada's security and Britain's security, he suggested, were indivisible; an attack on Britain was a menace to the freedom of all British countries. Yet, sandwiched in between his references to Britain as "a deep-felt and powerful factor in the shaping of Canadian policy," King put himself in the guise of a Skelton-style isolationist, having to choose and having no difficulty in choosing between "keeping our own house in order, and trying to save Europe and Asia." As Co-operative Commonwealth Federation (CCF) leader J.S. Woodsworth told the House, King managed to ride off in every direction: "The Canadian nationalist, the imperialist, the League of Nations collectivist, the North American, the belligerent militarist – all will find some crumbs of comfort." About conscription for service overseas, however, King was clear. He would have none of it; large armies sailing to foreign lands were a thing of the past. In this he used Skelton's words but he was not following Skelton. The federal Conservative leader, Dr R.J. Manion, had addressed the issue with a statement to the press on the 27th that he did not support the conscription of Canadian youth "to fight outside the borders of Canada." The Liberal chief, who had privately been moving in that direction since January, had no choice but instantly to make the same promise.[7]

Isabel Skelton noted on her copy of King's 30 March address that it was "all ... O.D.S.'s." It wasn't, not entirely. King, often with Skelton at his side, pored over the draft in the period leading up to the speech, revising the text and massaging its message so that there was an ambiguous something for everyone's taste.[8] All that said, the great bulk of the text came from Skelton and from his original memorandum, complete with the flourishes and cadences that characterized his writing – how striking it must have been to King-watchers to see such colourful words coming from the colourless prime minister. Everyone knew who the real scribe was.

The speech was replete with unmistakable Skelton themes: the vital importance of "a positive and distinctive Canadian patriotism" and of accepting "adult responsibility" to make national choices; democracy as an active, not a passive, way of life, calling for the hard work of self-discipline and free cooperation; the "great and enduring common interests" of Canadians and Americans; the failure of the League of Nations to control international relations, but its potential as a centre of cooperation and focus of goodwill; the disproportion between the resources available for military preparations and those for bettering peoples' standards of living; the way that the modern inventions of film and radio were shrinking the world and bringing it and its danger to Canadian doorsteps ("it is perhaps fortunate that television has not yet come to take popular hold"); and the futility of war, which settled nothing, proved nothing, helped nothing.[9]

Most important of all was the need to complete an unfinished country and to stay out of the trouble that was brewing abroad. "The idea," went the speech's most memorable and remembered lines, "that every twenty years this country should automatically and as a matter of course take part in a war overseas for democracy or self-determination of other small nations, that a country which has all it can do to run itself should feel called upon to save, periodically, a continent that cannot run itself, and to these ends risk the lives of its people, risk bankruptcy and political disunion, seems to many a nightmare and sheer madness."[10] Skelton wrote that sentence and King read it out to the House of Commons. Both believed it. In the crunch, however, King believed other things more.

King regretted that his speech had not been "as immediately helpful to Britain as I should like." He blamed the isolationists and neutralists around him, led by Skelton, who had "too strongly influenced" him. A month later, he wrote that it had been "fortunate I did not go as far as External Affairs in urging neutrality, etc," given the hay that Hitler was making with the uncooperativeness of the Irish prime minister, Éamon de Valéra. "Hitler would have quoted me as another representing another part of the Empire, not to be counted upon. I feel more and more that I have at this time made a mistake in letting myself be too controlled by the isolationist attitude of External Affairs." This was nonsense, a flimsy excuse for King's own restraint. His speech had said what he wanted it to say. Neutrality had never been "urged" and never considered. Although he regularly complained about yielding "too much to the academic and purely official type mind which has little in the way of political understanding," King was in full control of Skelton and his department. And the under-secretary, despite his tenacious views, knew his place. As King acknowledged, Skelton's "fidelity to duty and seeing things through" was unsurpassed in the public service. He did too much and too much of the business of government was channelled through him, to the annoyance of other departments and their ministers, but Skelton "never fails."[11]

In the aftermath of Prague, Skelton had testy exchanges with Germany's representatives in Canada about the policies of Hitler's Reich. When the German consul, Hans Granow, expressed his surprise "at the sudden rise of anti-German feeling in Canada," Skelton replied that most Canadians had been quite prepared to recognize the mistakes in the Treaty of Versailles. That, however, had been a "mild and statesmanlike document" compared to the terms that Germany had imposed on Russia in the punitive 1918 Treaty of Brest-Litovsk. Canadians also could see some strength in the plea of self-determination for the Sudeten Germans, but it was an entirely different matter when Germany grabbed neighbouring states with no racial affinity and no desire for union with it. Granow justified Germany's desire for expansion by referring to British, French, and American imperialism. He wondered why Germany was not supposed to act as a policeman in Czechoslovakia if Britain's similar role in India was acceptable. Skelton thought that a particularly unfortunate parallel. India was steadily tossing off its policeman-empire, and he did not know of any people who required a guardian less than the progressive, disciplined, and democratic Czechs. When he saw the German consul general, Erich Windels, in April, Skelton said that the strategy of the United Kingdom and France was "wholly defensive, and that if war started, it would not be from any attack on the part of the Western powers." Windels told Skelton that "Germany knew quite well that Canada would go into the fight if Germany were in any way an aggressor."[12]

Skelton found merit in the sharp and sudden turn that British strategy had taken after Prague – "the most momentous change in British foreign policy in generations," he called it, a complete reversal of the traditional policy "of avoiding commitments in the distant and shifting areas of Eastern Europe." There was a strong case, he told the prime minister, for ceasing to appease Hitler and for increasing defensive preparations against possible Axis aggression. More than that, in demonstrating that they were determined to resist force by force, the British were winning back prestige abroad and regaining confidence at home, "to the point of jingo cockiness in some cases, but a quiet assurance in most." Their dogged courage and capacity for working together in free cooperation had returned.[13]

But Skelton wondered whether an active policy of security guarantees to Poland, Romania, Greece, and Turkey was within the capacity of the United Kingdom. These were countries located where the danger was assumed to be the greatest, but also where it was most difficult to bring Britain's (and its ally, France's) military and economic power to bear. Poland had courage and martial ability, but no industrial staying power, and it was surrounded by Germany and its satellites. Romania, Greece, and Turkey were all liabilities, not assets. To challenge Germany at her strongest point and at Britain's weakest was sheer madness. "It's not a case," as Skelton put it, "of swopping horses when crossing a stream, but of jumping off the Appeasement horse and finding the Eastern Alliance horse isn't there." Citing a former British prime minister, Lloyd George, Skelton argued that the only way to achieve a temporary balance of forces in Eastern Europe was to secure the immediate assistance of Russia. The British government set out to seek that assistance, but with a continuing suspicion of the Soviets (the chief sceptic being Neville Chamberlain himself) that diminished the urgency of the mission.[14]

The British were forming a battlefront against Germany and its allies. The strategy's advantages, OD advised King, lay in stealing the initiative from the Germans and Italians and creating some breathing space that might turn into an opportunity for constructive dialogue. Yet Hitler and his subordinate Mussolini, both of them arrogant, neurotic, and unpredictable, might think that they had been issued a challenge from which they could not back away. In a world of two antagonistic armed camps, every issue was bound to become one of prestige and no surrender. There would be "no more little wars in Europe, only world wars."[15]

Skelton understood well that the tougher British line posed problems for Canada. Even before Prague, the U.K. secretary of state for war had announced the formation of an army field force of nineteen divisions for service on the European continent in the event of war. "Obviously this development has repercussions on the Canadian situation," the prime minister was informed. The pressure for developing a Canadian expeditionary force would grow: "It will make it more difficult to persuade the people who examine our militia defences carefully that our defence measures are really designed for the defence of Canada; it will make it more difficult to contend that if we did take part in an overseas war, any overseas participation by Canadians would be confined to a few thousand airmen; it will make it more difficult to give an assurance against conscription."[16]

British emissaries were buzzing around Canada in search of possibilities for defence production. The under-secretary wanted the government to exert control to ensure the country's defence and other needs were met in wartime, offering the view that it should be for Ottawa, "not for any private interest, to determine the destination and regulation of supplies from Canada to the United Kingdom or other countries over and above the needs of Canada itself." This sounded to the British like the habitual Skelton, standing in the way of Anglo-Canadian cooperation, and his influence was sufficient to slow the process to a crawl. When, however, the Canadian Manufacturers' Association did some buzzing of its own, the prime minister rejected Skelton's advice and gave permission for direct negotiations between Britain and the firms concerned, with the government "glad to collect and furnish such information as might be helpful." The CMA soon sent a delegation to Britain to seek out orders.[17]

King George VI and Queen Elizabeth toured Canada in May-June 1939, the first such visit in the country's history. Everywhere that the royals went, Mackenzie King was sure to go, crammed into his gold-braided diplomatic uniform and basking in the monarchial glow. Skelton was a member of the interdepartmental committee in charge of arrangements for the royal visit, but he was too busy with External Affairs business to attend all of its meetings and had little to do with the tour's day-to-day details. He wrote to Arnold Heeney of the prime minister's office, who was aboard the royal train, that the king and queen were driving Europe's troubles out of the headlines and the minds of Canadians, and he told D'Arcy McGreer at the Canadian Legation in Tokyo that the tour, then just nicely under way, "has been a remarkable success from the point of view both of the King and Queen and of the several hundred thousand Canadians who have thus far managed to see them from fairly close range." Privately, however, Skelton's reactions were likely closer to those of one of his diplomats in London, Charles Ritchie, who remarked in his diary that the royal tour was "an overwhelming manifestation" of the power that the British connection wielded in Canada and a demonstration of the British elite's genius at manipulation. There was little doubt that the enthusiasm that swept the country drew Canadians closer to Britain and a British war, and it seemed conceivable that the London government had arranged the royal visit with precisely that in mind.[18]

King thought that Skelton was a republican, but he was not. OD admired the monarchy and considered it an instrument of Canadian self-government. Apologizing for the homely metaphor, he had once written that the crown acted as "a siphon which transferred power from His Majesty's Government in the old land to His Majesty's Governments in the Dominions." Skelton was ahead of his time, and of constitutional practice, in thinking that the monarchy could be divided up into parts. The royal couple were for him the king and queen of Canada – "our own King," OD called George VI.[19]

While Mackenzie King travelled, monopolized by the royal visit, Skelton coordinated the government's response to a plea from George Wrong from the University of Toronto, *Saturday Night* magazine's B.K. Sandwell, and a group of eminent Canadians on behalf of the 907 German Jewish exiles on the Hamburg-American ship, the *St. Louis*. The refugees, hounded out of Germany and looking for a home, were turned away from Cuba and the United States. The Canadian government did the same. The exiles were sent back to Germany, and to persecution and death at the hands of the Nazis.[20]

Skelton communicated Ottawa's decision about the *St. Louis* to Wrong, the father of one of OD's most gifted External Affairs officers, in icy bureaucratic prose. Canada, he concluded, was already making a substantial contribution to a problem that presented "great difficulties, particularly perhaps in the case of admission of those who wish to settle in Canadian cities where our own unemployed are mainly congregated." Wrong replied that the refugee problem "haunts my mind. The only solution is either to let these people die off gradually, or for the nations to take up the problem on an adequate scale, commensurate with the magnitude of the problem." Skelton regretted Hitler's attacks on his Jewish citizens and sympathized with the goal of a national home for Jews in Palestine. But he did not champion Jewish causes within the government, in part because he knew that it was not a fight that could be won but also because the emotions he felt were an abstraction, not deeply experienced. He had none of Wrong's haunted mind or "unhappy hours."[21] He reserved those for the war that he still hoped would not come.

Skelton was pessimistic about Britain's attempts to reach an anti-Hitler agreement with the Soviet Union. An understanding with the Soviet ruler Stalin was essential if British commitments to Poland and Romania were to be implemented, and yet London had traded away its bargaining power by giving security guarantees to those countries before Soviet support had been lined up. Britain was at the mercy of the Soviets, who could name the price for their cooperation. Receiving regular bulletins from the U.K. Dominions Office and Vincent Massey, the Canadian high commissioner in London, Skelton reported to the prime minister that Moscow was demanding a "full-blooded" Anglo-Soviet alliance. The Chamberlain government was holding out for something a good deal less: an assurance that the Russians would "assist any of its European neighbours which was a victim of aggression and which was resisting that aggression." The British, Skelton concluded, feared getting too close to the Soviets and alarming anti-communist sentiment at home and abroad. Nor did they want to tie themselves "to the Russian chariot on unknown adventures."[22]

Mackenzie King's view of the Soviet Union had been locked in long ago. It was a godless communist country, malignant, dangerous, and capable of anything. Soviet ideology, on the other hand, was unimportant to Skelton, or rather he judged it as relatively unimportant to the men who ruled the USSR. Noting that Peter the Great had been restored to favour in Russian films, he saw (and had been seeing at least since 1935) the Soviet Union as "definitely more nationalist and less communist save where communism serves the needs of a central autocracy." Stalin was a despot but also an old-fashioned national-interest diplomat. He had the British where he wanted them, and intended to make them pay for his aid, "not only in rebuffs and snubs but by making it plain that in any alliance they were to serve Russia's ends at least as fully as he would serve theirs." King warned against an alliance with the Soviets, but, in the world according to OD, if a British pact with the "indispensable but irritating" Soviet Union was necessary to achieve even a temporary balance of forces and thus of stability in Europe, so be it. More than King, much more than King, Skelton wanted peace, almost at any price.[23]

Most of the intelligence that Canada received about the international situation came from British sources. For that reason Skelton argued regularly for more Canadian diplomatic representation abroad. He complained that information came from Britain after the fact, and that there was no effort made to consult Canada before or after action was taken. The grumble was yet another way of saying that the British were in the wrong and that Skelton's Canadians were on the side of the righteous. He did not wish to be asked to approve British policy or associate Canada with it. That would imply a commitment to follow dutifully on after Prime Minister Chamberlain, which was the last thing on OD's mind. As the Dominions Office delicately and correctly put it in an internal document, formal consultation was "distasteful" to Canada. Sir Gerald Campbell, the British high commissioner to Canada since October 1938, discovered how difficult it was to promote a give and take with a balky prime minister and under-secretary of state for external affairs. Campbell's chiefs in London insisted that they consulted Canada to the extent that Mackenzie King would allow, and they were not above telling the world that they were acting on behalf of the entire empire – "British Ministers calmly announcing what 'our' Dominions will do," in Skelton's acrid words.[24]

The latest of Europe's hot spots, because Hitler wanted it to be so, was Danzig, which had been established as an international city in 1919 by the Treaty of Versailles. The German-speaking port city stood on the Baltic Sea at the top of the Polish corridor, another of the innovations of Versailles, separating eastern Germany from the rest of the Reich. Danzig was Poland's crucial outlet to the sea. Hitler claimed it on the basis of the self-determination of an ancient German community, but he used the issue pre-eminently as a method of putting pressure on Poland, which the German leader wanted to dominate as part of his grand scheme, he told his generals, of "expanding our living space to the east." In early July 1939, with Berlin pumping up tensions along the Polish-Danzig border, Skelton considered whether the city was worth an Anglo-French war with Germany. He listed the pros and cons at almost equal length, but his opinion was not in doubt. Hitler had to be halted, but Danzig was not the place to do it and Poland was not the country to back.[25]

Skelton acknowledged that concessions made to Hitler over Danzig would only lead to further demands. If, however, positions hardened to the point that no bargaining was possible, "there is nothing but disaster ahead." OD wrote to Vincent Massey in London that Europeans had become accustomed to thinking of themselves as "the centre and essential part of the world." They were probably unaware of how extraordinary the spectacle they were presenting to the world must seem to an outsider. Canadians had close and continuing links with Europe, but their attitude to what was going on there "must be different in kind and not merely in degree from that of the actual members of the region" and, moreover, "the differences must have significant practical consequences." Those responsible for safeguarding Canada's national life must stand objectively back from Europe; neither duty nor necessity required them to do otherwise. Massey, believing that British policy no matter its changes of course should be endorsed by Canada, could not have welcomed Skelton's not-so-thinly-veiled lecture on the importance of an independent Canadian point of view in matters imperial and international.[26]

The talks aimed at a British agreement with the Soviet Union had ground down to nothing. Basing his report on intelligence from a secret agent close to Nazi groups in Canada, the commissioner of the RCMP informed Skelton in August 1939 that the Soviets were talking to the Germans. The news that came over the radio on the evening of the 21st was nevertheless shocking to Skelton, King, and all of official Ottawa – indeed, to all of the Western democracies. The Soviet Union and Germany had agreed to conclude a non-aggression pact, each new partner promising not to attack the other. Germany's path to Poland was unimpeded, and Hitler readied his attack. Skelton moaned that the Nazi-Soviet deal spelled "the collapse of the Anglo-French house of cards in Eastern Europe" and brought the continent to "the brink of war." He added, in a conversation with the British high commissioner, that "the Russo-German agreement would ... disgust the United States with European politics and appreciably confirm many circles in that country in their determination not to be drawn into developments themselves."[27]

Any balance that there had been in Skelton's assessments of Britain's foreign policy disappeared. The bumbling effort to bring the Soviets into the fold was "the greatest fiasco in British history." The Soviet Union, instead of joining a "Stop Hitler" alliance, had all but joined the German camp. Since the German occupation of Prague, the United Kingdom's international record had been a string of "failures and follies." The only result of the "panic pledge" to Poland was that the British had acquired an ally that they could not protect. Germany was not deterred; instead it was "strengthened and hardened." Britain having failed to bring it onside, Italy too was hostile and now riveted to Hitler. As for the

British prime minister, too much of his motivation arose from personal pride and domestic political factors. Skelton claimed that Chamberlain had departed from appeasement because of attacks from his political enemies on the left and out of pique at Hitler's betrayal of his Munich pledges.[28]

Skelton's analysis was skewed. The chief responsibility for Europe's predicament lay with Hitler, who was always a more likely partner for the Soviets than the British. London had taken a number of concrete steps to meet the threat of the dictators in the aftermath of Munich, including yet another increase in the already enormous program of rearmament and the decision to regard an invasion of the Low Countries as a casus belli. These cannot be treated as examples of Chamberlain's wounded vanity after the seizure of Prague. What is more, the drawbacks of the guarantees in central and Eastern Europe were widely acknowledged, and by no one more than Chamberlain. If, however, as seemed certain, Hitler was fixed upon expansion, and if the British had in effect already guaranteed the frontiers in the west, the guarantees in the east might have some deterrent effect. At the least, they serve to show that there was no truth in the allegation, freely made then and ever since, that the British (and French) were deliberately encouraging a rampant Germany to move east and overwhelm Russia.[29]

Skelton prepared for the "stampede over the edge" into a "Polish war." The British might throw their ally overboard, but it was conceivable that they would go to war with Germany if Poland resisted a Nazi invasion – "One reason for believing this is possible is that it is the only possible mistake that has not yet been made." If war there must be, and Canada must participate in it, Skelton argued for an involvement that kept the country as far away from the fighting as possible. Economic contributions, in the form of munitions, raw materials, and food, would be "most effective to our war allies and most consistent with Canadian interests." A high priority would have to be given to the "big job" of defending Canada's coasts, British Columbia included because of the threat from Japan, even though he conceded that any attack on the country would be "on a minor scale." Military action overseas should be confined, at least in the first instance, to the building of airplanes and the training of airmen for service in the Canadian Air Force, which he expected would produce few casualties. On 24 August the prime minister read Skelton's recommendations for a war of limited liability to the cabinet, which signalled its approval at the same time as deciding once and for all that Canada would go to war if Britain did.[30]

The first shots of the Second World War were fired close to Danzig from the German ship *Schleswig-Holstein* on 1 September 1939. A full-scale invasion of Poland began at the same time, and the progress of Hitler's Wehrmacht was rapid. The Chamberlain government momentarily seemed to flinch from its Polish commitment, exactly as Skelton wished would happen, but after an ultimatum that his aggression must stop went unheeded by Hitler, the United Kingdom declared war on Germany on the 3rd. Mackenzie King summoned Parliament into an immediate special session which, in Skelton's bitter words, trotted behind Britain, "blindly and dumbly, to chaos." He stayed away from the House of Commons in silent protest and, unusually, few of his words found their way into the prime minister's rambling war speech.[31]

British High Commissioner Campbell reported to his home government on the six-day session's "moments of great poignancy and other moments that fell little short of bathos": Ernest Lapointe's speech, in which he "took his political life in his hands and declared that it was impossible for Canada to stay out of the war"; J.S. Woodsworth's declaration "that he could not abandon his personal conviction that war was wrong"; the "lengthy and frequently eloquent" address of the prime minister, dissolving in the end into fourteen lines of badly read poetry, causing a buzz of conversation to break out around him; and the vote on the Speech from the Throne, "which, though it marked the actual assent of Parliament to Canada's entry into the war, was taken almost without any one realizing what was happening and with a large number of members, including the Prime Minister himself, absent from their seats." Campbell wrote also about the government's little band of senior officials, fatigued and overworked over the many weeks leading up to the war and often hostile to him, now moving cooperatively to meet the challenges of a great war.[32]

Skelton was not in a cooperative mood. Even though he had seen it coming, and predicted that it would happen, he was devastated by what he interpreted as the easy, casual, automatic way that Canada was going to war. Over twenty-five years, the country had carefully built up a claim to an independent control of its destiny. That worked well enough in peacetime, but nothing had ever been done, despite his steady reminders, to clarify what self-government would mean when Britain went to war. Now Canadians had their answer. It meant nothing. In September 1939 the prime minister of the United Kingdom had taken over as the prime minister of Canada. The button had been pressed in London, and thousands of Canadians were to be sent to war and death. After all that he had done, said, advised, and dreamed, Canada had slipped back to being a colony again.[33]

Wilfrid Eggleston, who had worked for Sandy Skelton at the Rowell-Sirois commission, was one of the group of reporters – "the largest crowd of newsmen I could remember" – who were summoned to a prime-ministerial press conference on the day of Germany's invasion of Poland. Just outside Mackenzie King's office, Eggleston encountered Skelton, the "great public servant" and "great patriot of Canada," who was "slumped down in his chair, looking more exhausted and more strained than I had ever seen him." The journalist knew of Skelton's opposition to active participation in another European war; his attitudes and the advice he was giving King were an open secret in Ottawa circles. Observing OD's "courageous despair," Eggleston felt "a swift stab of compassion."[34]

Since he was a writer and not a talker, Skelton poured out his frustrations onto paper, in a memorandum composed on 10 September, immediately after the proclamation of King George VI that Canada was at war. The British claimed that they were fighting to defend liberty and democracy, but to Skelton that was as much rhetoric as it was a genuine impulse. Their primary motive was "the attempt, after years of humiliation, to revive the prestige of Britain, to compel Europe again to heed her decisive voice." This was their war, not Canada's, and "the British Government which blundered into it, should have been allowed to blunder out." How "fantastic and insane" it was "for Canadians to allow themselves to be maneuvered and cajoled every quarter century into bleeding and bankrupting this young country because of the age-long quarrels of European hotheads and the futility of British statesmen." Canada was merely "the prize exhibit" in the latest of the British Empire's adventures.[35]

Skelton did not confine his criticism to the British. Mackenzie King had done some manoeuvring of his own. The prime minister was masterly in his parliamentary strategy, and he had brought a united Canada into the war. The unity, however, was superficial and misleading. The all-but-unanimous backing that Parliament had given to Britain's war did not represent the feeling of the country. In Quebec there was rampant scepticism; the province would certainly oppose unlimited sacrifice. Young Canada and rural Canada felt no connection to the war. Even war supporters had no enthusiasm for the task ahead. The old, the conservative, and the empire-minded – among them, of course, the prime minister – were shaping events. It was "very doubtful if a majority of the people of Canada would in a free plebiscite have voted for war." A three-year war, the time the British thought it would take to achieve victory, if there was to be victory, would strain the national fabric and threaten Confederation.[36]

Skelton shared in the widespread Canadian hatred of Hitler and all his works. He understood that the Germans were out to dominate Europe, but he could not help minimizing the extent of what was at stake by writing that they wanted "to make themselves as much the masters of the Continent as the British once were of the sea." To Britain's avowed objective of defeating Nazism, he replied: "possible, with complete victory, but what next? We overthrew the Kaiser and got Hitler." It was the same old Europe, in other words: "our overlords in Britain" competing with "dictator thugs" to rearrange the map of the continent. He insisted that the war did not touch core Canadian interests, but then, as he had written sarcastically in an earlier note to the prime minister, "Canada is supposed never to think of her own interests in foreign policy."[37]

Mackenzie King had a different, and superior, grasp of the national interest. He understood the tight economic, military, and psychological links that bound Britain to Canada: the United Kingdom was a vital trading partner, the Royal Navy protected Canada, and the British connection helped immunize Canadians from the temptations and dangers coming from the United States. King also, and with the surest of touch, recognized the requirements of Canadian unity. Just as his careful peacetime balancing act had taken into account all shades of opinion, so his declaration of war, together with the promise that there would be no conscription, respected both the English-speaking Canadian majority and the substantial francophone minority population. King, moreover, brought Canadian interests and values together in standing with Britain in an all-out fight for liberty and democracy. The furthest Skelton would go was to say that "sentiment as well as reason" led him "to wish to see Britain retain as strong and secure a place in the world as actual realities make conceivable."[38]

Skelton had his jeremiad of 10 September typed, and he put it away in a filing cabinet, where it was not discovered until a decade after his death. He discussed it with no one – not Loring Christie, his like-minded associate in External Affairs, who was named the Canadian minister to the United States the day before Canada's declaration of war on Germany; not Marjorie McKenzie, his assistant at External Affairs from the first days and his closest office confidante; and not Mackenzie King, a prime target of Skelton's criticism. Nor did he confide the darkest of his thoughts to Isabel, whose diary of the period concentrated on her husband's uninterrupted seven-day weeks and late nights at work and

on "Oscar's love and Oscar's self always here to rely on." She found in
him consideration, sensitiveness, courage, and dependability, the same
characteristics that the officials in his department valued and admired.[39]

Skelton's virtues masked his bad health and fatigue, but the people
around him knew how badly he was struggling. Agnes McCloskey, close
to the family and another key woman in the under-secretary's office,
told Isabel of her complaints to Mackenzie King "about O.D.S. and how
ill he was." In the summer of 1939 he was worn out enough, despite a
favourable report from his doctor, to contemplate retirement and possible successors. The Winnipeg *Free Press* man in Ottawa, Grant Dexter,
basing his comments on "two or three sources in the external affairs
branch," privately recorded that Loring Christie and John Read, "the two
next in line," could not hope for Skelton's job, and he "can't bring himself to choose as between the others." OD preferred as his replacement
Norman Rogers, the minister of labour in the King cabinet, "beaten,"
according to Dexter, by continuing high unemployment and apparently
ready for a change. Said the journalist, Skelton "is very fond of Norman and thinks he is exactly the right man. When you come to think
of it, there is a great resemblance between the two men." They were
both former Queen's University teachers, smart, quiet, and scholarly, but
politically adept and skilful in the ways of the prime minister. Along with
Ernest Lapointe, Skelton and Rogers were the colleagues in whom King
had the most confidence.[40]

The war put any thoughts of leaving External Affairs out of Skelton's
mind, although Mackenzie King, years later, remembered it differently.
Near the end of his life, King told his biographer, Bruce Hutchison, that
Skelton was "so broken by frustration and despair" in early September
1939 that he was on the verge of resigning from the department that he
had built because of his antagonism to the war. For two days, Hutchison wrote, "with only Lapointe privy to their secret, King and Skelton
wrestled with their consciences, in perfect amity and insoluble disagreement," until finally the under-secretary was persuaded to stay. Old men
forget, the saying goes. King's story, dramatic and almost plausible, is
inaccurate. Skelton was heartbroken by a decision to go to war that he
thought was disastrous for his country, but he kept on an even keel. As
he wrote, and believed, "we must all in our several ways do our utmost to
ensure victory and what lies beyond victory."[41]

Opposed to the war, Skelton took a leading role in organizing Ottawa
for war. He was at the prime minister's elbow in the Emergency Council, a subcommittee of the cabinet on government policy that became

the Cabinet War Committee at the end of 1939, and in the cabinet's Defence Committee, which carried out military planning for a government that had done very little of it. War aims, economic planning, foreign-exchange controls, British purchasing in Canada, defence procurement in the United States, internal security, alien propaganda – all came before Skelton for his comments, and all called for his advice.[42] Gone, though, almost without exception, were the lengthy memoranda that he had regularly prepared for the prime minister in peacetime. He was too taken up by the day-to-day to reflect on, analyse, and write about the large movements of international affairs.

He had his own war aims. Unlike Mackenzie King, who held out a faint hope that peace might be salvaged after Hitler had invaded Poland, Skelton knew that there could be no turning back after September 1939 – though he remained committed to a strictly limited war on Canada's part. Still intent on fighting the war as much as possible by emphasizing home defence and economic contributions to Britain, and still bitterly distrustful of the motives of the British and French, he insisted that there were clear limits to what a small country and small economy could do. "If we accept all the schemes put forward by the United Kingdom and certain Canadian advisers, in addition to what has already been undertaken, it is clear that the Canadian Government would be taking out of the people a much larger proportion of their annual resources than Hitler is taking out of the German people." In order to maximize Canada's war contribution and keep it within the range of the country's power and resources, there had to be "a planned and concerted national effort." A robust and well-coordinated machinery of war followed, painstakingly built up; among its architects were men Skelton had recruited to government, Clifford Clark in the lead.[43]

Skelton also knew what he did not want the war to become: a fight for democracy in Europe that compromised democracy in Canada. He steadfastly opposed the erosion of the civil liberties of ethnic minorities, democratic socialists, and Canadian fascists and communists – so long as they stayed within the law and did not become the tools of foreign and unfriendly governments. Sedition was one thing, as he put it, criticism entirely another: "A good many people in Canada are prone to think that anyone who differs from their convictions or prejudices should be suppressed." The line of distinction ought to be to "prosecute anyone guilty of espionage, sabotage or similar action, but suppress the propaganda or criticism only of those who can be shown to be acting as agents of alien governments." Yet the Defence of Canada Regulations (DOCR), part of the framework of national security set out at the war's beginning, were progressively tightened. Ernest Lapointe, Skelton's political friend, was on the other side of the debate, and the justice minister prevailed. After Japan came into the war, the DOCR were used to segregate twenty-three thousand Canadian Japanese into camps. Skelton undoubtedly would have opposed that measure, since he had written in the early autumn of 1940 that the vast proportion of Japanese born in Canada "regard this as their country and with careful handling could be made an asset rather than a liability."[44]

The pressures were crushing, the need for decision and action immediate. OD liked it that way. He had to be at the centre of the drama and to be in control; if he was, he could run the Department of External Affairs on his own terms. Because he was unwilling to delegate responsibility, and because he had no instinct for administration, he managed through the first months of the war with only five officers assisting him at headquarters. None of them had anything like his workload. The sole part of the department that he reorganized was the code room, which was busier than ever as the telegrams and messages flowed in and out of Ottawa. The room was on the third floor and, when he decided to visit it one day, the climb left him exhausted, his mouth wide open as he gasped for breath. He should have known better, Isabel admonished. He needed to know the difference between what was important and what was not.[45]

Skelton's thinking about a limited war fit in with Mackenzie King's plans less than it appeared. Compulsory military service was unthinkable to both, but the prime minister and cabinet agreed to prepare the dispatch of an army division to England and contemplated the immediate sending of pilots overseas, moves that Skelton did not support. The British proposal at the end of September 1939 for a large-scale air-training program based in Canada offered the prospect of keeping the war very close to home, but even here Skelton and King differed. King effused that there could be no "finer thing for ourselves or for the Empire than to become the great air training centre." He conceded that "the British are very selfish," but his deputy failed to understand "the larger significance of the fight for freedom that is being waged." Greeting the beginning of negotiations to establish a British Commonwealth Air Training Plan (BCATP), Skelton deposited his rage on the doorstep of the prime minister in the form of a mocking statement of gratitude to the "British statesmen whose sublime and effortless assurance, coupled with a gentlemanly vagueness on the sordid questions of finance and a unique eminence in diplomacy, which if in some slight measure not so completely successful as usual in the European field, has retained its full potency among the native tribes."[46]

As the often contentious BCATP discussions unfolded in Ottawa, "the sordid questions of finance" were at the front of Skelton's mind. What of the "money factor," he asked, underlining the words. "What would be the total training cost? Cost of providing aerodromes and ground equipment? Cost of training planes? Cost of maintenance and instruction?" There were other costs too. He maintained that the agreement would result in a "colossal" number of Canadians fighting and dying in the air war that was to come. He further pointed out the inconsistency of the government's insistence on its right to organize Canadian trainees into national air units while allowing the United Kingdom to meet the expenses of those units overseas and so have them under British control. The prime minister, inebriated by the size, scale, and political utility of the plan, paid little attention. He grandly signed the BCATP agreement just after midnight on 17 December 1939, his sixty-fifth birthday. The BCATP was a major Canadian contribution to the Allied war effort, but Skelton's warnings proved shrewdly drawn.[47]

Hostility to the Mackenzie King government came from the central provinces of Canada. Quebec Premier Maurice Duplessis' challenge to the federal government and what he claimed was its domineering way of war had been turned back in October 1939. The Quebec Liberals, led by Adélard Godbout, won the provincial election of that month, with a considerable assist from Ernest Lapointe and other Quebec ministers, who had promised to resign from the federal cabinet if Duplessis was not defeated. Now it was Ontario's turn to challenge Ottawa, but from the opposite direction. In the Ontario legislature on 18 January 1940, Premier Mitch Hepburn moved a resolution denouncing Ottawa's sluggish conduct of the war. He carried with him the majority of his MPPs and the Opposition Conservatives, led by George Drew. Skelton derisively called Hepburn and Drew the "Ontario twins."[48]

The prime minister was quick to seize the opportunity that Hepburn's foolish words offered, deciding within hours that the government would fight an election on the Ontario premier's challenge. When King told Skelton what he had done, he reported that his deputy minister "seemed more or less struck dumb but later when we were together, he told me he thought that the public would appreciate the bold course and he agreed with me that the thing which was most important was that it would probably get the elections over before the worst came in Europe. That he said had been causing him some real concern." Skelton, like King, had decided that the coming of spring in Europe would bring on large-scale enemy action: an election campaign fought while battles raged overseas could put a good Liberal result in jeopardy. King won the election overwhelmingly on 26 March, capturing a majority of the popular vote (the first time that had been done since 1911) and taking 181 seats to 40 for the Conservatives, with Social Credit, the CCF, and assorted stragglers dividing up the remaining 24 seats.[49]

OD had returned from two weeks of holiday on the eve of the election. "I'm feeling in first rate shape," he assured his leader.[50] Afterwards, he sent the prime minister a handwritten note of congratulations that went through two drafts, so that he could get the message just right. He began by saying that the victory belonged to King. "In no other free country in our time has there been such overwhelming and continuing evidence of public confidence and support, and this in spite of depression difficulties, war demands, pendulum swings, and bitter and unscrupulous attacks. It is emphatically a personal triumph." There were regrets. Skelton was sad to see the defeat of Agnes Macphail, a progressive force in Parliament for the past two decades. The Opposition indeed would be "too weak for their essential work; we have come pretty close to a National Government and a one party system." Yet, and without saying how, Skelton tossed that problem off as "curable." The country had escaped great political danger; everything else, by comparison, was "a minor point."

The Skelton-King concern in January 1940 at the direction the war would take was borne out by post-election events. In April, Hitler seized Denmark in a day, without a shot being fired, and simultaneously sent troops into Norway. Within three weeks, almost all of Norway's populated areas, ports, railways, and industrial establishments were in German hands. The Anglo-French campaign to expel the Germans from Norway was a disaster, driving Neville Chamberlain from office, to be replaced as British prime minister by Winston Churchill. Germany's greedy friends, the Russians, had grabbed part of Poland and then Finland and the Baltic states of Latvia, Lithuania, and Estonia. Italy's Mussolini jealously watched the conquest of Europe and was poised to plunge into the war before the spoils of victory had all disappeared. "His hands fairly itch," his foreign minister said of Il Duce. Skelton noted the buying power of the Allied side, its naval power and increasing strength in the air, and the tacit support of the neutral United States, but admitted that "we can no longer shut our eyes to the fact that the war has steadily gone against us." Nor was there certainty or even the likelihood that the tide would soon turn. More and more, Skelton was fighting the war on Mackenzie King's terms, as a crusade against the cabal of evil men who were terrorizing the world.[51]

On 10 May, Hitler launched his armies through the Ardennes Forest and into the Low Countries of Belgium and Holland. Within ten days they had reached the Atlantic coast, effectively slicing France into two parts. Anglo-French forces were pushed back to the English Channel, where the only means of escape was the port of Dunkirk. In a stroke of luck, the German tanks laid back for three days, allowing an armada of ships and boats of every imaginable variety to cross the Channel from England and rescue 335,000 Anglo-French troops. The legend of Dunkirk was born: the unimaginable had happened; the escape had been a miracle, perhaps even a victory. Yet Dunkirk masked defeat. From his office Skelton wrote to his wife and her mother in Peterborough lamenting the failures of Allied leaders and generals and the dire prospects that lay ahead. France was defeated and democratic Europe eclipsed. The United Kingdom lay wide open to attack. The "dogged determination of the Britisher" and the effectiveness of the new Churchill government were among the few gleams of sunshine that the deputy minister could discern.[52]

With the fall of France, Skelton told King that he "did not want me to suggest any help for Canada, but rather the need for Britain." The prime minister noted that his under-secretary had reversed what he had been advocating until a short time before, and that was true, but Skelton was recalibrating the national interest. He could be wrong, as he had been in September 1939, but he aimed to make his judgments on the basis of what he believed was of most benefit to Canada and Canadians. "He now sees," said King, "that the real place to defend our land is from across the seas." But Britain's peril also struck a raw emotional chord in Skelton. When he helped the prime minister prepare a message of sympathy and support to Churchill at the end of May, OD's choice of words was more vivid and heartfelt than King's. The life of the British people was in the balance, Skelton wrote; they were facing "the greatest trial that has beset them in all their history." He and Canada would stand with them, "no matter what." The limited-liability war went into the dustbin, and the expenditure of outlandish (by pre-war standards) sums of money ceased to matter, even to the parsimonious Skelton.[53]

The immediate challenge was to encourage Franklin Roosevelt's United States to do more for the faltering Allied cause. "True," Skelton wrote at the end of April 1940, "the United States is already giving in many respects as much help as if it were in the war, but its further

diplomatic and financial and naval and perhaps air support are powerful potentialities. Our task is two-fold: to make effective our own share
and to speed in every practical and discreet way the co-operation of the
United States." Canadian political, official, and military exchanges with
the United States proliferated, while informed public opinion, watching the Dunkirk evacuation and the surrender of France, was absorbing
the need to confront directly the problems of continental defence. In
mid-July a group of twenty prominent Canadians issued a report stating
bluntly that cooperation with Washington "is going to be either volun-
tary on Canada's part, or else compulsory; in any event it is inevitable."
Skelton received the document with enthusiasm, in line with his long-
held desire to tie the two countries more tightly together. Suggestions
for a new relationship were heard in Washington too, and in mid-August
Roosevelt invited King to meet him at Ogdensburg, New York, a few kilometres from the Canada-United States border.[54]

The two leaders rapidly devised the first Canada-U.S. defence alliance.
The Ogdensburg Declaration of 18 August 1940 established a bilateral
Permanent Joint Board on Defence (PJBD) that immediately, efficiently,
and sometimes contentiously planned for the defence of North America. Canada had guaranteed its safety no matter the result of the war in
Europe. Skelton was exhilarated: "The best day's work done for many
a year," he told King. The new American alliance had "not come by
chance, but as the inevitable sequence of public policies and personal
relationships." Those policies and relationships were precisely, he was
bound to be thinking, what he had been advocating and promoting for
decades. But North America was not everything, especially not now. The
agreement at Ogdensburg, for Skelton, was also based "upon the realization of the imperative necessity of close understanding between the
English-speaking peoples." Canada-United States military cooperation
meant that Canada could offer maximum support to the British, sure
that its own defence was secure.[55]

The defence of Newfoundland was at the top of the agenda at the
first meeting of the PJBD, an institution into which Skelton injected a
key member of his staff, Hugh Keenleyside, as the Canadian secretary.
There were a number of factors in play: Newfoundland, reaching out
into the Atlantic Ocean, was crucial to the defence of Canada and North
America; the island was a poor cousin of the British Empire, all but
defenceless against the new Nazi surge and unlikely to get much help
from London; the Canadian government was energetically moving men
and resources into Newfoundland, and the still-neutral United States was

about to establish bases there; Canada welcomed the help of the United States but at the same time was concerned about American influence in what was regarded in Ottawa as part of Canada's sphere of interest. Skelton urged King to ensure that Canada would be involved in any U.S.-Newfoundland military agreements. And when the army chief, Major-General H.D.G. Crerar, said that he assumed the U.S. military presence in Newfoundland meant that Canada would retire from its defence commitments there, Skelton was quick to demur. He was planning ahead, looking to "the definite possibility" that Newfoundland would one day soon become part of Canada.[56]

Like Mackenzie King, Skelton had harboured deep suspicions of Winston Churchill, and like King, he changed his mind. On his prime minister's birthday in late December 1940, OD wrote King that he and Churchill were the British Commonwealth's "most irreplaceable" men. Skelton had a propensity to dash off over-flattering letters, but he meant what he said this time and his judgment was correct. He pressed King "for your own sake and the country's ... to avoid being overtired or over-driven."[57] The advice was not needed. King paced himself impeccably. Skelton, of course, did not: the concept was foreign territory to him.

Skelton began the new year as he left the old, swamped by paperwork, meetings, committees, and an ever-bigger department's administration, the part of his work that he did not like and did indifferently. He was carrying, his assistant Agnes McCloskey noted, "a heavier load than it could be expected any human person could shoulder." A "dreary year ahead," he predicted for 1941, although (probably thinking of Ogdensburg's good news) "less so than might have been expected six months ago." An added complication accompanied all the others. He spent 31 December and New Year's Day in bed with an infection and a high fever: "After trying to ignore the flu for a few days, it declined to ignore me," he wrote the prime minister from home.[58]

He was at work first thing the next week, preoccupied by the upcoming Ottawa meeting of the Dominion-Provincial Conference, in which Sandy was immersed, and the final stages of negotiations with the United States for a St Lawrence Seaway. "I am the one man who has pushed this," he claimed of his recent involvement in the slowly unfolding drama of the St Lawrence Seaway and Power Project. On 25 January, Oscar and Isabel took their car over icy roads to Cornwall, so that he could look over what seaway development might mean for the St Lawrence River and the people who lived nearby. That weekend he travelled momentarily back to his teenage years, pointing out to Isabel the family's first apartment in the city, modest rooms over a store, and reminiscing about the boat that he had rowed on the mighty St Lawrence – without a map, he now admitted. He recalled an introspective boy, not yet alive to his surroundings and the world outside.[59]

The 27th of January was a Monday. Skelton worked a long day at the Parliament Buildings that included a four-hour Cabinet War Committee meeting and advice afterwards to the prime minister that action was needed to strengthen Canada's home defences. Over a late dinner, he and Isabel opened letters and mulled over family business. The next morning, Skelton woke up his wife to say that busy days and nights lay ahead for the rest of the week. He ate breakfast, told the housekeeper that he had purchased a $50 war bond in her name, and took an unusual fifteen-minute nap before heading downtown. He arrived at the office at 9 a.m., as he routinely did. One meeting after another followed, although he found time to talk to Isabel on the telephone. At 1 p.m., as he was putting on his overshoes to leave for lunch, Agnes McCloskey came into his room to have him to sign a dispatch. They exchanged some good-natured comments that included a McCloskey scolding about his habit of mislaying important papers and his pleasure at seeing an article on Norman Robertson in the Montreal *Standard*. A splendid picture of Robertson had accompanied the piece, OD remarked with a smile.[60]

He took his car to the unpretentious Venetian Sweets, where he liked to eat lunch and be served by Pauline. She told him that he didn't look well. "Bad heart," he replied, and rushed through his meal. Driving back to the office along O'Connor Avenue, as he neared Sparks Street, he felt a sharp and sudden pain. Then he felt nothing. The Packard slid slowly into a streetcar. A police car was quickly on the scene to take him to Water Street Hospital, but the heart attack this time had been fatal. A little after 2 p.m., Isabel received a call from the police that there had been an accident involving a man named Skelton. Thinking that perhaps it was Sandy, who was always getting into scrapes, she discovered instead her "darling Oscar on hospital carrier with coat & tie & shirt open. Face did not look like suffering. I just wanted to keep my cheek right to his."[61]

The next day he was taken to 459 Buena Vista, back to Edgehill and the garden that were his anchor. The funeral was held there on the 30th, Mackenzie King and hundreds of mourners crowding into the house. The family asked that no flowers be sent, but no one listened. Skelton was buried alongside his wife's family at Pakenham, in the Ottawa valley close to the capital – a quiet place for a quiet man. "Pretty cold and bleak at the cemetery," Mackenzie King recalled that night. "Nothing in the way of attractiveness about the little place itself. Even this, however, was not out of keeping with S.'s sense of values. He disliked the artificial and rather glorified the common place which was one of his many attributes of true greatness."[62]

The prime minister did and said all the right things. As soon as he heard the "bad news, very bad news," in the words of the aide who delivered the message, King went straight to the Skelton house and then to the hospital. He carefully reworked tributes that he released to the press and gave in Parliament. He replied graciously to the dozens of letters of sympathy that he received, claiming Skelton as "one of my dearest and closest friends." He had condolence messages sent to Marjorie McKenzie and Agnes McCloskey, the people at External Affairs on whom Skelton relied most. But King's private reactions were less generous. "I was quite unmoved," he wrote of his immediate response to the calamity. He talked in his diary about Skelton's death as an event he had anticipated "at any time," and how he knew there to be "a great purpose" at work – he was being shown that he would have to rely on himself. This "most serious loss thus far sustained" was seen entirely in the context of "my public life and work." King's were characteristically self-centred responses, and doubtless understandable in the circumstances, but they were not the thoughts of someone who had lost a cherished friend.[63]

Skelton's death shocked official Ottawa. He had been at the centre of the public service for so long that it was hard to believe he was gone. Clifford Clark, his counterpart at the Department of Finance, was heartbroken. He had begged his friend to slow down but Skelton had sacrificed himself for his country, "just as truly as any member of the armed forces." At External Affairs, Norman Robertson, replacing Skelton as under-secretary, wrote to Mike Pearson at the High Commission in London: "This has been a bleak & miserable week – Dr. Skelton's death has just flattened out everybody. It's only when you start taking an inventory that you begin to realize what a range of responsibilities he took – and how we all lived & worked secure in the shadow of a great rock." "Seldom, I suppose," Pearson responded, "in any organization has the loss of one man meant so much."[64] As early recruits to a Department of External Affairs that Skelton sought to fashion into the instrument and expression of an autonomous foreign policy grounded in the national interest, Pearson and Robertson were crucial to their chief's vision of an independent Canada.

Skelton had despaired as he watched Canada follow along meekly after Britain into battle. His health and his dreams were in ruins. He committed himself nevertheless to the war, and the war in turn contributed to the greater sense of national spirit and cohesiveness that he had made it his mission to promote.[65] The post–Second World War generations of Canadians accepted their freedoms almost nonchalantly, scarcely realizing that there was a time not long before when the country's independence could not be taken for granted.

Conclusion

Grant Dexter, the Ottawa correspondent of the Winnipeg *Free Press*, described his visits with Oscar Skelton as the 1930s crashed to an end and the Second World War took its ugly shape. The Skelton office, in the East Block of the Parliament Buildings next door to Mackenzie King's room, was in casual disarray, the desk and chairs stacked with papers and documents. A lonely fern struggled to get at the light streaming into the window that overlooked Parliament Hill's immense lawn. Skelton's thinning hair sat uneasily on his head, and his ample eyebrows trailed down over his glasses, which he pushed up in conversation. He was unhurried, friendly, in control. His influence, and the confidence that ministers, members of Parliament, and public servants had in him and his judgment, were staples of Canadian government life, unquestioned and unquestionable. Such, the reporter wrote, "was the magic of the man that at Ottawa one needed only to indicate that Dr. Skelton had been consulted to dispose of opposition."[1]

Writing only hours after Skelton's death, Dexter revealed how sad and ill his friend had been. They had discussed OD's hope in earlier days that there would be international cooperation on a grand scale after the First World War. He believed that the League of Nations was the noblest of experiments, but Geneva had crumbled, and he despaired as the world wrecked itself all over again. Nor had he eased off after his heart attack in 1937. Dexter disclosed the warnings of Skelton's doctors that "unless he worked less hard, his life would be forfeit. He knew this advice was sound – knew it full well. But he deliberately refused to act upon it."[2]

Dexter accepted the widely held notion that Skelton was a selfless and timid paragon, with a power and authority that were unsought and "a source of annoyance" to him. That missed the essential Skelton. Mackenzie King was a better judge of his deputy, understanding his driving ambition and the zeal to refashion Canada that had thrust him into the public arena. King considered the self-assured way that his associate conducted himself in public policy and the energy with which he connected himself to the concerns of Canadians. "He was always," the prime minister said of Skelton, "very independent, self reliant, liked to direct things himself, and to be in the thick of the tide, to share the life of the active and busy world and of the men on the street."[3] He had to fight the insecurities of the introvert, but Skelton never had any uncertainty about his future or the country's.

Self-doubt came readily to a colonial people. An ambitious Canadian, or ambition for Canada, would have aroused suspicion and discomfort among Skelton's contemporaries had they known the extent of his appetites. But he did not put them on display. His grey exterior and natural reticence covered a vast range of ambitions – for an extraordinary life, for power and influence, for social standing and prosperity, and for an important place in the remaking of Canada as an independent and progressive country. He said that he loathed fashion and privilege, and he heaped condescension on pretension and human vanity, yet he wanted and expected to live well, to have fine possessions and a position of distinction, and never to repeat the ups and downs of his father's business career. He had once played with the idea of getting into politics, but he didn't have a politician's ooze. He would never be prime minister, but there was no question in his mind that he would have been a better one than Mackenzie King. Skelton was made more for influence than power, but power came from his influence. Sensitive to the unpopularity of his cause, he was particularly careful to hide his campaign for Canadian independence. At the Imperial Conference of 1923, General Smuts had complimented King on doing nationalist good by stealth. Skelton learned from the master, advancing his agenda of ambitions quietly, as he did at the 1929 ODL conference and in the Skelton Committee of 1933.[4]

Skelton and King were an odd couple. Their relationship was grounded in the business of advancing their mutual liberal (and Liberal) causes as they each interpreted them, not in any deep personal connection. In the many years that they spent together, the almost friendless King never called Skelton by his first name, while the prime minister was always, for OD, Mr King. Neither man was expert at intimacy. Yet they were the perfect partners, each giving the other what he most wanted. King placed Skelton at the centre of the public service and public life of Ottawa, where he had a clout unrivalled by any official in the Canadian experience. In return he provided King with utter reliability. Skelton would never fail to do what was needed.

The international-affairs perspectives of the prime minister and his foreign-policy chief proceeded from many of the same assumptions – that foreign policy had to originate at home; that the country must above all remain unified; that Europe was a cesspool of militarism and imperialism; that the British government and its haughty politicians and officials had to be watched carefully; that the Canadian-American relationship was an example to the world of a peaceable neighbourhood; and that the last thing Canada needed was a repeat of the First World War. Skelton was committed to the League of Nations as an indispensable agency for the promotion of peace and international goodwill. King thought quite otherwise, seeing it as a trap and delusion. Like his leader, however, Skelton refused to entertain League-inspired collective security, which after all had been the principal reason why that institution had been brought into existence. At Geneva in 1924, when Senator Raoul Dandurand compared Canada to a fireproof house far removed from any possible danger, he did so with Skelton at his side. OD probably supplied those memorable and telling words.

The strength of the Skelton-King relationship was demonstrated by the way that they worked through their differences. In the late 1930s, the prime minister moved away from Skelton, letting him (but almost no one else) know that Mackenzie King's Canada would stand by Britain in a war pitting totalitarianism against democratic values. Skelton should not have been surprised. He had been in the London meeting room at the Imperial Conference of 1923 when King pledged Canadians' support if another great call of duty arrived, as it had at the start of the First World War. But Skelton was surprised – and angry. Month after month, as Europe disintegrated into two armed camps, he let loose broadsides at the incompetence and worse of British statecraft, sometimes widening the attack to include his own prime minister. King held his temper and kept his criticisms of his deputy minister to himself. He knew that, in his Ottawa at least, politicians ruled, not public servants. Skelton knew that too. When war came in September 1939, Skelton exploded at Britain's overlords and a manipulative Canadian leader, but he did so privately and remained faithfully at King's side. Thoroughly worn out, OD had hinted at retirement that summer. The war persuaded him otherwise, if he needed persuading.

As Skelton interpreted it, Canada's entry into the Second World War was automatic, the result of the dredging up of old loyalties that ought to

have been discarded a long time before. It was the behaviour of a subordinate. He had spent a lifetime contradicting the assumption that Canada was an eternal child, incomplete without Mother Britain to imitate
and lean on. In his professor days, Skelton extensively explored methods
of untethering Canada from its British anchor. When he moved on to
the Department of External Affairs, he advanced on the basis that the
control of foreign policy was sovereignty's acid test. Although a partisan appointed to his position because of his Liberal Party connections,
he built a merit-based and non-partisan government department as a
vehicle of systematic and autonomous policy making. He was an important part of the Imperial Conference negotiations that extracted Canada
from the embrace of the British Empire, and he wrote crucial parts of
the Statute of Westminster, giving his country its legal liberty. Skelton
campaigned for more diplomatic missions, so that Canadians would
have their own source of support, advice, and intelligence in the world's
capitals. He sought closer ties with the United States not to cozy up to
the Americans but to diminish the pressure that the British connection
could exert on Canadians. He promoted a common Canadianism but
was convinced, particularly after the divisions of the First World War, that
it must be achieved with francophone Canada, not against it: his closest
partner in the independence wars was Ernest Lapointe.[5]

Skelton saw an independent future more clearly, and prepared for it
more thoroughly, than any of his contemporaries. It was therefore little
wonder that, broken in health, he reacted so bitterly when Canada's ruling classes seemed to go off to a world war reflexively, without serious
discussion, debate, or independent thought. He had wanted Canadians
to take "clean-cut, adult responsibility for our policies and destinies, in
friendly co-operation with other countries of like-minded ideals, but with
full freedom to make our own decisions in light of our own knowledge
and aims and interests."[6] September 1939 turned that dream into dust.

He set himself to winning the war. When Germany attacked France in
May 1940, with Great Britain surely to be next, he saw the urgency of British survival and declared that he would stand with them no matter what.
Mackenzie King concluded that Skelton was repenting his Canada First
views, and the historian C.P. Stacey later agreed, commenting sharply on
"the education of O.D. Skelton." But events had changed, not the man.
Skelton saw that Britain was now Canada's front line of defence. The
arrangements at Ogdensburg in August of that year to coordinate Canadian and American defences were welcomed by Skelton as a means to
prop up the British and bring the neutral United States closer to the war.

In the bargain Ogdensburg furthered Skelton's desire to bring North Americans together in constructive ways. Such thinking was not a rejection of Canada's British heritage. "We have many a lesson to learn from England and from the United States," he had written in one of his first articles as the Macdonald professor at Queen's University.[7]

Skelton's dream of Canadian independence from Great Britain was a beginning, not an end. There is a temptation to draw a distinct line between blinkered Skeltonism and its parochial preoccupations and the sunny foreign policy of a generation later, when the country and its diplomats took a firm hold on their global responsibilities and projected a cosmopolitan outlook.[8] Yet Skelton saw that international day coming and wanted it to come. His Canada was young and fragile and in so many ways still a colony. It was only sensible, he reasoned, to concentrate for the time being on Canada's problems and possibilities, but he left no doubt that the next stage in national development was measured international cooperation. Canadians had the work of the world to do. They would take it up once they were free.

Notes

The biographer of O.D. Skelton has a distinguished body of literature with which to begin. Terry Crowley, *Marriage of Minds: Isabel and Oscar Skelton Reinventing Canada* (Toronto: University of Toronto Press 2003), is the study of an extraordinary early-twentieth-century marriage. Barry Ferguson, *Remaking Liberalism: The Intellectual Legacy of Adam Shortt, O.D. Skelton, W.C. Clark, and W.A. Mackintosh, 1890–1925* (Montreal and Kingston, Ont.: McGill-Queen's University Press 1993), examines Skelton's formative ideas and those of his Queen's University colleagues, while Doug Owram describes the intellectual activism of Skelton and his circle in *The Government Generation: Canadian Intellectuals and the State, 1900–1945* (Toronto: University of Toronto Press 1986). Skelton is a central figure in John F. Hilliker, *Canada's Department of External Affairs,* vol. 1: *The Early Years, 1909–1946* (Montreal and Kingston, Ont.: McGill-Queen's University Press 1990); in J.L. Granatstein's *The Ottawa Men: The Civil Service Mandarins, 1935–1957* (Toronto: Oxford University Press 1982); and in John English, *Shadow of Heaven: The Life of Lester Pearson,* vol. 1: *1897–1948* (Toronto: Lester and Orpen Dennys 1989). The biographers of Skelton's prime ministers are H.B. Neatby, *William Lyon Mackenzie King,* vol. 2: *1924–1932, The Lonely Heights,* and vol. 3: *1932–1939, The Prism of Unity* (Toronto: University of Toronto Press 1963 and 1976); Roger Graham, *Arthur Meighen: A Biography,* vol. 2: *And Fortune Fled* (Toronto: Clarke, Irwin 1963); and P.B. Waite, *In Search of R.B. Bennett* (Montreal and Kingston, Ont.: McGill-Queen's University Press 2011).

Major treatments of foreign policies in the Skelton period are C.P. Stacey's *Canada and the Age of Conflict,* vol. 2: *1921–1948, The Mackenzie King Era* (Toronto: University of Toronto Press 1981), and Zara Steiner, *The Triumph of the Dark: European International History 1933–1939* (New York: Oxford University Press 2011). Specialized studies of Canadian policies based on extensive archival research include Richard Veatch, *Canada and the League of Nations* (Toronto: University of Toronto Press 1975); Philip G. Wigley, *Canada and the Transition to Commonwealth: British-Canadian Relations 1917–1926* (Cambridge: Cambridge University Press 1977); John MacFarlane, *Ernest Lapointe and Quebec's Influence on Canadian Foreign Policy* (Toronto: University of Toronto Press 1999); and John D. Meehan, *The Dominion and the Rising Sun: Canada Encounters Japan, 1929–41* (Vancouver: University of British Columbia Press 2004). Norman Hillmer, ed., *O.D. Skelton: The Work of the World, 1923–1941* (Montreal and Kingston, Ont.: McGill-Queen's University Press; and Toronto: Champlain Society; both editions 2013), collects and comments upon Skelton's letters, diaries, and memoranda as they relate to international policy.

Notable among Skelton's own voluminous writings are his frequent articles in *Queen's Quarterly* between 1907 and 1921 and his *Socialism: A Critical Analysis* (Boston and New York: Houghton Mifflin 1911); *Life and Letters of Sir Wilfrid Laurier*, 2 vols. (New York: Century 1922); and *Our Generation: Its Gains and Losses* (Chicago: University of Chicago Press 1938). His diary, a crucial document despite relatively few entries, can be found in the O.D. Skelton Papers at Library and Archives Canada, vols. 11–13. Isabel Skelton's diary and scrapbook are in her papers at the Queen's University Archives.

Abbreviations

AO	Archives of Ontario
CAB	Cabinet Office (U.K.)
DEA	Department of External Affairs
DO	Dominions Office (U.K.)
FO	Foreign Office (U.K.)
IS	Isabel Skelton
ISS	Isabel Skelton Scrapbook
KD	William Lyon Mackenzie King Diary (King Papers)
KP	William Lyon Mackenzie King Papers
LAC	Library and Archives Canada
NAUK	National Archives of the United Kingdom
ODS	O.D. Skelton
PC	Privy Council (Canada)
QQ	*Queen's Quarterly*
QUA	Queen's University Archives
SD	O.D. Skelton Diary
SP	O.D. Skelton Papers

Introduction

1 On the making of modern Ottawa, see Jeff Keshen and Nicole St-Onge, eds., *Ottawa: Construire une capital/Making a Capital* (Ottawa: Les Presses de l'Université d'Ottawa 2001): essays by John C. Walsh, John Taylor, Jeff Keshen, and Rhoda Bellamy.

2 QUA, W.A. Mackintosh Papers, box 9, Skelton file, R.B. Taylor to Mackintosh, 16 June 1941.

3 LAC, SP, vol. 1, file 16, ODS to IS, 14 May [1907].

4 Ibid.

5 The Roosevelt speech, "Citizenship in a Republic," was delivered in Paris, 23 April 1910. I have discussed Skelton's attachment to "in the arena" in exchanges with James Gibson and Arthur Menzies. See also W.A. Mackintosh, "O.D. Skelton," in Robert L. McDougall, ed., *Canada's Past and Present: A Dialogue. Our Living Tradition, Fifth Series* (Toronto: University of Toronto Press 1965), 59 and 63–4.

6 ODS, "Adam Shortt," Royal Society of Canada, *Proceedings and Transactions*, 3rd Series, 25 (1931): vii; Barry Ferguson, *Remaking Liberalism: The Intellectual Legacy of Adam Shortt, O.D. Skelton, W.C. Clark, and W.A. Mackintosh, 1890–1925* (Montreal and Kingston, Ont.: McGill-Queen's University Press 1993), 27–9. In *Atlantic Crossings: Social Politics in a Progressive Age* (Cambridge, Mass.: Belknap Press of Harvard University 1998), Daniel Rodgers defines the period from 1870 to 1945 as "the Atlantic era in social politics" (4).

7 The quotations in this paragraph are from, respectively, ODS, "Current Events," *QQ*, 24, 1 (July-September 1916): 136–7; and LAC, W.L. Grant Papers, vol. 9, Skelton file, ODS to Grant, 19 March 1917.

8 This paragraph is in part taken from the author's "O.D. Skelton: Innovating for Independence," in Greg Donaghy and Kim Richard Nossal, eds., *Architects and Innovators: Building the Department of External Affairs and International Trade, 1909–2009* (Montreal and Kingston, Ont.: School of Policy Studies, Queen's University / McGill-Queen's University Press 2009), 59–60. "Out and out independence" is in SP, vol. 13, SD, 3 June 1938. See also QUA, Norman Rogers Papers, box 1, General Correspondence 1931, ODS to Rogers, 28 October 1931.

9 Vincent Massey, *What's Past Is Prologue: The Memoirs of the Right Honourable Vincent Massey* (Toronto: Macmillan 1963), 135; J.S. Willison, "Canada in the Empire," *The Nineteenth Century and After*, 92 (July-December 1922): 25.

10 David Twiston Davies, "Mackenzie King's Anglophobe-in-Chief," *Dorchester Review*, 3, 2 (autumn-winter 2013): 65–8; Donald Creighton, "Presidential Address," Canadian Historical Association, 1957, printed in his *Towards the Discovery of Canada* (Toronto: Macmillan 1972), 41–2 (and the introduction

to that volume, especially 7); J.M.S. Careless, "Frontierism, Metropolitanism, and Canadian History," *Canadian Historical Review*, 35, 1 (March 1954): 4–5. For further examples of the characterization of Skelton as anti-British and anti-empire, see R.N. Kottman, *Reciprocity and the North Atlantic Triangle, 1932–1938* (Ithaca, N.Y.: Cornell University Press 1968), 106; D.G. Creighton, *Canada's First Century* (Toronto: Macmillan 1970), 185–6; H. Duncan Hall, *Commonwealth: A History of the British Commonwealth of Nations* (London: Van Nostrand Reinhold 1971), 300–1; Correlli Barnett, *The Collapse of British Power* (London: Eyre Methuen 1972), 181; Ian M. Drummond, *Imperial Economic Policy 1917–1939: Studies in Expansion and Protection* (London: Allen and Unwin 1974), 93; C.P. Stacey, *Mackenzie King and the Atlantic Triangle* (Toronto: Macmillan 1976), 25–7 and 65; Roy MacLaren, *Commissions High: Canada in London, 1870–1971* (Montreal and Kingston, Ont.: McGill-Queen's University Press 2006), 242–54. C.P. Champion rejects the notion that anti-imperialist nationalists were necessarily "anti-British." Skelton, he rightly asserts, represented "a spectrum of hybrid Britishness" within his Canadianism. *The Strange Demise of British Canada: The Liberals and Canadian Nationalism, 1964–1968* (Montreal and Kingston, Ont.: McGill-Queen's University Press 2010), 77 and 81–2. Simon J. Potter discusses imperial and national identities in a British Empire context, as played out in the first quarter of the twentieth century and later interpreted by scholars. He makes the case that the two identities were frequently at work in a single ideology, an assertion that would apply to Skelton. "Richard Jebb, John S. Ewart, and the Round Table, 1898–1926," *English Historical Review*, 72, 495 (February 2007): 105–32.

11 ODS, "Current Events," *QQ*, 27, 1 (July-September 1919): 108–9, 113; 27, 3 (January-March 1920): 322–3; 28, 1 (July-September 1920): 95. See also ODS, "Canada, the Empire, the League," pt. 1, *Grain Growers' Guide*, 25 February 1920, 7. On the meanings of empire and imperialism, see Barbara Bush, *Imperialism and Postcolonialism* (Harlow, U.K.: Pearson Education 2006).

12 QUA, Isabel Skelton Papers, ISS, *Picton Times*, 15 December 1921, ODS to P.C. Macnee. For Skelton's post-First World War views about Ireland, see his "Current Events," *QQ*, 27, 1 (July-September 1919): 110–13; 27, 3 (January-March 1920): 324–6; 28, 1 (July-September 1920): 96–8; 29, 2 (October-December 1921): 205–8. Maurice Pope, an ODS colleague, told the author that Skelton wore his allegiance to the south of Ireland conspicuously: "He was a red-hot home ruler." For the Irish Canadian debate over the island's destiny, see Robert McLaughlin, *Irish Canadian Conflict and the Struggle for Irish Independence, 1912–1925* (Toronto: University of Toronto Press 2013).

13 The "ultimate independence" incident took place in 1923: LAC, SP, vol. 11, SD, [2 November] 1923. "Britain of the West" comes from William Lyon Mackenzie King, *The Message of the Carillon* (Toronto: Macmillan 1927), 22. On the distinction between "British" and "English," see historian W.L. Morton's reminiscence of growing up in 1920s Manitoba, *Globe Magazine*, 24 September 1964, 10, and Fintan O'Toole, "The Real Men of England," *New York Review of Books*, 6 June 2013, 18.

14 Robert Kelley, *The Transatlantic Persuasion: The Liberal-Democratic Mind in the Age of Gladstone* (New York: Knopf 1969), chs. 5–6 and especially 145–6, 195–6, and 235–7. The lust to dominate, a Kelley theme, is a phrase from St Augustine. On principle versus practice in Gladstone's empire policies, see Roy Jenkins, *Gladstone: A Biography* (New York: Random House 1997), 500–1.

15 Norman Hillmer, "O.D. Skelton and the North American Mind," *International Journal*, 60, 1 (winter 2004–5): 93–110. Those identifying ODS as a "pro-American" include Stacey, *Mackenzie King and the Atlantic Triangle*, 27 and 65; Allan Smith, "Doing the Continental: Conceptualizations of the Canadian-American Relationship in the Long Twentieth Century," *Canadian-American Public Policy*, Occasional Paper Number 44 (Orono: University of Maine, December 2000), 5; Damien-Claude Bélanger, *Prejudice and Pride: Canadian Intellectuals Confront the United States, 1891–1945* (Toronto: University of Toronto Press 2011), 36; Nicholas Tracy, *A Two-Edged Sword: The Navy as an Instrument of Canadian Foreign Policy* (Montreal and Kingston, Ont.: McGill-Queen's University Press 2012), 42 and 94; Neville Thompson, *Canada and the End of the Imperial Dream* (Don Mills, Ont.: Oxford University Press 2013), 11.

16 QUA, Adam Shortt Papers, 2147, box 3, file 15, ODS to Shortt, 2 March 1909; IS annotation, undated, beside a clipping from the Ottawa *Citizen*, 23 January 1922, in ISS. The "religion" comment is in SP, vol. 11, SD, 1923, 11.

17 Isabel Skelton Papers, IS Diary, 9 June 1924. The author is grateful to Professor Terry Crowley for his indispensable assistance with the Isabel Skelton Diary.

18 London *Free Press*, 29 May 1925; SP, vol. 9, file 21, ODS, "Western," notes for University of Western Ontario convocation address of 29 May 1925, and London *Free Press*, 29 May 1925; ODS, "Current Events," *QQ*, 25, 2 (October-December 1917): 226–9.

1. Going Away and Coming Home, 1878–1908

1 British Library, London, India Office Records, Judicial and Public Department Papers, L/P and J/6/577/1677 and L/P and J/6/579/1808, Civil

Service Commission results table and documents, September-October 1901. I was greatly assisted in the writing of this chapter by Theresa LeBane, whose paper, "When Skelton Was Young," was prepared as part of her research for the book.

2 Civil Service Commission results table. On Skelton as likely the first Canadian to pass the ICS entrance examination, see "Dr. O.D. Skelton," *The Times* (London), 30 January 1941. The information on the ICS is derived from A. Lawrence Lowell, *Colonial Civil Service: The Selection and Training of Colonial Officials in England, Holland, and France* (New York: Macmillan 1900); Sir Edward Blunt, *The I.C.S.: The Indian Civil Service* (London: Faber and Faber 1937); L.S.S. O'Malley, *The Indian Civil Service: 1601–1930* (London: Frank Cass 1965).

3 L.C.B. Seaman, *Victorian England: Aspects of English and Imperial History, 1837–1901* (London: Routledge 1973), 347. Lord Dufferin is quoted in O'Malley, *The Indian Civil Service*, 173. See also Robert H. MacDonald, *The Language of Empire: Myths and Metaphors of Popular Imperialism, 1880–1918* (Manchester, U.K.: Manchester University Press; New York: St Martin's Press 1994), especially ch. 5; Jeffrey Richards, ed., *Imperialism and Juvenile Literature* (Manchester, U.K.: Manchester University Press 1989).

4 SP, vol. 11, SD, list of expenditures, 12 March [1900], and vol. 1, file 3, "Writing Book of Oscar Skelton: Synopsis & Review of Reading from Aug. 98," 46; LeBane, "When Skelton Was Young," 22–7. The Agnes Laiter quotation is from "Yoked with an Unbeliever," in Kipling's *Plain Tales from the Hills* (London: Macmillan, 1965 ed.), 35. A sepoy was an Indian soldier serving with the British Army in India. *Soldiers Three* was published in 1888 and went through many editions in the 1890s. On Kipling's messages and ambivalences, see John Gross, ed., *The Age of Kipling* (New York: Simon and Schuster 1972), and Caroline Rooney and Kaori Nagai, eds., *Kipling and Beyond: Patriotism, Globalisation and Postcolonialism* (New York and London: Palgrave Macmillan 2010), essays by Rashna B. Singh and Donna Landry and Caroline Rooney.

5 SP, vol. 1, file 5, Dr H.H. DePew to ODS, 7 July 1901, Civil Service Commission to ODS, 3 October 1901, and G.M. Grant to ODS, 2 December 1901; Department of Foreign Affairs, Trade and Development, Historical Section Records, undated memorandum of Marjorie McKenzie, recalling a conversation with ODS and establishing the importance of "reading Kipling" and the fact that the ICS was the only British civil-service destination that interested him. The diagnosis in the DePew letter was analysed for the author by Drs Michael A.J. Alexander, Ronald Gerridzen, Edward Rawling, and Hugh Robertson. The Skelton version of the story, repeated frequently by others,

was that he did not qualify for the ICS because of his poor eyesight. See *The Times* (London), 30 January 1941, and the McKenzie memorandum.

6 H.B. Neatby Papers, David R. Keane, "The Education of O.D. Skelton, 1878–1910," unpublished manuscript, 21; LeBane, "When Skelton Was Young," 5.

7 The information in this and the next paragraph is derived from an examination, for the periods that Jeremiah Skelton lived or worked in these centres, of the Orangeville *Sun*, the Shelburne *Economist* and *Free Press*, the Pembroke *Observer*, and the Cornwall *Freeholder* and *Standard*. Also helpful were the censuses of 1851–1901; family information in the SP, vol. 1, file 1 and vol. 3, file 18; and Keane, "Education."

8 Cornwall *Freeholder*, 12 January and 23 December 1900; Cornwall *Standard*, 23 October 1903.

9 SP, vol. 3, file 4, Jeremiah Skelton to ODS, 24 March 1925, and vol. 2, file 23, Jeremiah Skelton to ODS, 28 September 1924. See also Terry Crowley, *Marriage of Minds: Isabel and Oscar Skelton Reinventing Canada* (Toronto: University of Toronto Press 2003), 13–14; and QUA, Isabel Skelton Papers, IS Diary, 22 February 1941. The Shelburne testimonial of 23 December 1889 is in SP, vol. 1, file 2. "Kitty" comes from the Shelburne *Economist*, 8 September 1927.

10 QUA, Queen's Student Registry, vol. 6, #2905–3456, 1895–1899/1900, Oscar Skelton, Student no. 2963, 518; IS Diary, 22 February 1941; Cornwall *Freeholder*, 11 May 1900; Cornwall *Standard*, 8 June 1900; Keane, "Education," 22–3. The "system" quotation is in SP, vol. 11, SD, 18 June 1899.

11 "Writing Book of Oscar Skelton." See Crowley, *Marriage of Minds*, 23–4, for a further discussion of Skelton's reading, and Orangeville *Sun*, 12 May 1898, for the trip to Europe.

12 SP, vol. 11, SD, 21 and 31 May and 2 June 1899.

13 SP, vol. 11, SD, 9 May and 1 June 1899. The Imperial Federation debate is reported in *Queen's University Journal*, 26 (1898–9), 114, and described, unconvincingly, in W.A. Mackintosh, "O.D. Skelton," in Robert L. McDougall, ed., *Canada's Past and Present: A Dialogue. Our Living Tradition, Fifth Series* (Toronto: University of Toronto Press 1965), 61.

14 This paragraph and the next two are based on LeBane, "When Skelton Was Young," 6–8. The quotations are from SP, vol. 11, SD, 9, 20, 22, 26, and 28 May, and 7 and 13 June 1899; and "Writing Book of O.D. Skelton."

15 SP, vol. 11, SD, May–July 1899 and lists of expenditures, June–July 1899.

16 Cornwall *Freeholder*, 28 September 1900; SP, vol. 11, SD, 6 and 18 June 1899; Crowley, *Marriage of Minds*, 17.

17 Keane, "Education," 58–9.

18 Stanley C. Hollander and Kathleen M. Rassuli, "Revolving, Not Revolution-
   ary Books: The History of Rental Libraries until 1960," *Journal of Macromar-
   keting*, 21, 2 (December 2001): 125. See also Edith Anderson Rights, "The
   Cover," *Libraries & Culture*, 41, 2 (spring 2006): 259; Dal Hitchcock, "The
   Booklover's Library," *Publishers' Weekly*, 116 (6 July 1929): 44–7; Philip B. Eppard, "The Rental Library in Twentieth-Century America," *Journal of Library
   History*, 21, 1 (winter 1986): 242; Frank Luther Mott, *A History of American
   Magazines*, vol. 5: *Sketches of 21 Magazines 1905 –1930* (Cambridge, Mass.:
   Harvard University Press 1968), 27–9.There is a photograph of Eaton in
   Hitchcock, "Booklover's," 45.
19 SP, vol. 1, file 4, Shortt to ODS, 26 February 1902; QUA, Adam Shortt Papers, 2147, box 1, file 7, ODS to Shortt, 22 February 1902.
20 SP, vol. 1, file 4, Shortt and Grant letters of recommendation, both of 26
   February 1902, and Shortt to ODS, 26 February 1902; and Shortt Papers,
   2147, box 1, file 7, ODS to Shortt, 1 March 1902.
21 ODS to Shortt, 1 March 1902; Norman Hillmer, "O.D. Skelton and the
   North American Mind," *International Journal*, 60, 1 (winter 2004–5): 96.
22 ODS to Shortt, 1 March 1902. On Shortt, see Barry Ferguson, *Remaking
   Liberalism: The Intellectual Legacy of Adam Shortt, O.D. Skelton, W.C. Clark, and
   W.A. Mackintosh, 1890–1925* (Montreal and Kingston, Ont.: McGill-Queen's
   University Press 1993), 72; S.E.D. Shortt, *The Search for an Ideal: Six Canadian
   Intellectuals and Their Convictions in an Age of Transition, 1890–1930* (Toronto:
   University of Toronto Press 1976), 98.
23 The examples of magazine contents are taken from *Booklovers Magazine*
   (January-June 1904). The New York *Times* published its review on
   10 January 1903.
24 LAC, W.L. Grant Papers, vol. 9, Skelton file, ODS to Grant, 29 January and
   12 February 1904.
25 SP, vol. 1, file 6, certificate dated 9 May 1904.
26 ODS to Grant, 12 February 1904.
27 SP, vol. 1, file 6, Elizabeth Skelton to ODS, [June-July 1904], and vol. 1, file
   4, ODS to IS, 28 June 1904.
28 Cornwall *Standard*, 13 January 1905; and LeBane, "When Skelton Was
   Young," 38.
29 SP, vol. 1, file 6, ODS to IS, 26 March 1905; Mott, *American Magazines*, 29, 31;
   Eppard, "The Rental Library," 242; Hitchcock, "Booklover's Library," 46.
30 SP, ODS to IS, 26 March 1905, and vol. 1, file 7, H.P. Chandler (University
   of Chicago) to ODS, 4 September 1905; Shortt Papers, 2147, box 2, file 11,
   ODS to Shortt, 9 January 1906; Keane, "Education," 29; Cornwall *Standard*,
   18 August 1905.

31 Crowley, *Marriage of Minds*, 32. "Independent" and "hemmed-in" are from Douglas Hall (O.D. Skelton), "Jane Austen's Heroines: A Study of Woman's Horizon in 1806," submitted to *The Reader* for publication in 1906 and rejected in 1907. SP, vol. 11, file 4.

32 Shortt Papers, 2147, box 2, files 11 and 12, ODS to Shortt, 9 January and 4 June 1906, and 16 April and 8 June 1907; SP, vol. 1, file 14, ODS to IS, 2 July 1908; Keane, "Education," 31–3 and 38–9; Ferguson, *Remaking Liberalism*, 23, 102–3, 237, and 270. On Veblen, see Irving Louis Horowitz, ed., *Veblen's Century: A Collective Portrait* (New Brunswick, N.J.: Transaction Pub. 2002). Crowley, *Marriage of Minds*, 28–9, describes Laughlin and the political economy department. "Never a follower of Veblen" was found in W.A. Mackintosh to R.F. Neill, 8 December 1965 (copy courtesy of Professor J.L. Granatstein). The "steel-trap" portrait of Laughlin is from Shortt Papers, 2147, box 1, file 8, J.A. Donnell to Shortt, 29 March 1903.

33 ODS, "Current Events," *QQ*, 15, 1 (July-September 1907): 75–8; 18, 2 (October-December 1910): 168–71; 20, 1 (July-September 1912): 113–16; 20, 2 (October-December 1912): 238–9; 24, 1 (July-September 1916): 142–3.

34 Shortt Papers, 2147, box 2, file 12, ODS to Shortt, 16 July 1907; SP, vol. 1, file 8, Laughlin to ODS, 19 December 1907, and file 14, ODS to IS, 19 April 1908; Crowley, *Marriage of Minds*, 32–3. Edward Peacock, not Skelton, was Shortt's first choice for the Macdonald chair.

35 SP, vol. 1, file 14, ODS to IS, 13 July and 1 August 1908, and vol. 9, file 24, Laughlin to ODS, 8 October 1908, with enclosure from thesis examiner Frank Arnold. "Hasty summer's effort" is in Shortt Papers, 2147, box 3, file 15, ODS to Shortt, 14 January 1909.

36 Shortt Papers, 2147, box 2, file 14, ODS to Shortt, 25 August 1908; SP, vol. 1, file 14, IS to ODS, 2 August 1908.

2. Citizen Entrepreneur, 1908–14

1 QUA, Adam Shortt Papers, 2147, box 2, file 12, ODS to Shortt, 16 July 1907. Skelton's salary is given in QUA, Queen's University Board of Trustees Minutes, vol. 3, 286, 14 October 1908.

2 E-mail from Alexandra Skelton, 17 December 2008; Sheila Skelton Menzies–David Fransen interview, 10 November 1981 (courtesy of Dr Fransen); Terry Crowley, *Marriage of Minds: Isabel and Oscar Skelton Reinventing Canada* (Toronto: University of Toronto Press 2003), 34–5.

3 SP, vol. 1, file 14, Jeremiah Skelton to ODS, 1 and 4 November 1908. See also ODS, *Life and Letters of Sir Wilfrid Laurier*, vol. 2 (New York: Century 1922), 280–3.

4 W.A. Mackintosh, "O.D. Skelton, 1878–1941," *Canadian Journal of Economics and Political Science*, 7, 2 (May 1941): 273.

5 Ibid., 273–4; W.A. Mackintosh, "O.D. Skelton," in Robert L. McDougall, *Canada's Past and Present: A Dialogue. Our Living Tradition, Fifth Series* (Toronto: University of Toronto Press 1965), 70–1; information given to the author by J.B Stirling. See also Robert A. Wardhaugh, with Douglas MacEwan and William Johnston, *Behind the Scenes: The Life and Work of William Clifford Clark* (Toronto: University of Toronto Press 2010), 11.

6 Mackintosh, "Skelton," in McDougall, *Canada's Past and Present*, 59; Gerald S. Graham, "Skelton of Queen's," *Queen's Review*, February 1941, 43.

7 Mackintosh, "Skelton, 1878–1941," 274–5; Graham, "Skelton of Queen's," 42–3; J.L. Granatstein, *The Ottawa Men: The Civil Service Mandarins, 1935–1957* (Toronto: Oxford University Press 1982), 33; H.B. Neatby Papers, David R. Keane, "The Education of O.D. Skelton, 1878–1910," unpublished manuscript, 40.

8 Barry Ferguson, *Remaking Liberalism: The Intellectual Legacy of Adam Shortt, O.D. Skelton, W.C. Clark, and W.A. Mackintosh, 1890–1925* (Montreal and Kingston, Ont.: McGill-Queen's University Press 1993), 16–17; F.W. Gibson, *Queen's University*, vol. 2: *1917–1961* (Montreal and Kingston, Ont.: McGill-Queen's University Press 1983), 6.

9 SP, vol. 9, file 24, Laughlin to ODS, 8 October 1908.

10 Ibid., Laughlin to ODS, 7 January 1909, and Hart Schaffner and Marx to ODS, 13 January 1909; Crowley, *Marriage of Minds*, 37. Skelton's salary as a lecturer may be found in QUA, Queen's University Board of Trustees Minutes, vol. 3, 283, 29 April 1908.

11 SP, vol. 1, file 17, ODS to IS, 17 May 1910, and vol. 9, file 24, Acland to ODS, 9 February 1909, and Laughlin to ODS, 6 and 12 March 1909. See also Crowley, *Marriage of Minds*, 37.

12 SP, vol. 1, file 17, ODS to IS, 31 May 1910.

13 Ibid., ODS to IS, 5 June 1910. On the sites commission, see Harry T. Logan, *Tuum Est: A History of the University of British Columbia* (Vancouver: University of British Columbia 1958), 40–1.

14 ODS, "Current Events," *QQ*, 16, 3 (January-March 1909): 296; 17, 3 (January-March 1910): 262–3.

15 ODS et al., "Ultimate Politics," *QQ*, 17, 1 (July-September 1909): 79–82.

16 AO, Whitney Papers, MU 3128, Whitney to Ross, 12 November 1909, and Ross to Whitney, 20 November 1909.

17 ODS et al., "Ultimate Politics," *QQ*, 17, 1 (July-September 1909): 79; ODS, "Current Events," *QQ*, 17, 3 (January-March 1910): 263.

18 ODS et al., "Ultimate Politics," 80. The historian of the Round Table is J.E. Kendle, *The Round Table Movement and Imperial Union* (Toronto: University of Toronto Press 1975).

19 ODS, "Reciprocity: The Canadian Attitude," *Journal of Political Economy*, 19, 2 (February 1911): 77–97.

20 ODS, "Current Events," *QQ*, 18, 4 (April-June 1911): 329–36; ODS, *General Economic History of the Dominion 1867–1912* (Toronto: Publishers' Association of Canada 1913; repr. from Adam Shortt and Arthur G. Doughty, eds., *Canada and Its Provinces*), 231–2.

21 SP, vol. 1, file 18, ODS to Isabel, 28 June 1911 and [July 1911]; Thomas Fisher Rare Book Room, University of Toronto, James Mavor Papers, box 16, Skelton file, ODS to Mavor, 8 February 1910; Crowley, *Marriage of Minds*, 58.

22 KP, J1, vol. 19, reel C-1916, 16963–4, ODS to King, 20 August 1911. See also SP, vol. 1, file 18, ODS to IS, [July 1911], and L.E. Ellis, *Reciprocity 1911* (New Haven, Conn.: Yale University Press 1939), ch. 10.

23 KP, J1, vol. 19, reel C-1916, 16959–64, ODS to King, 9 and 20 August 1911, and King to ODS, 11 August 1911; SP, vol. 1, file 18, ODS to IS, 4 August 1911.

24 ODS, "Canada's Rejection of Reciprocity," *Journal of Political Economy*, 19, 9 (November 1911): 726–31.

25 KP, J1, vol. 19, reel C-1916, 16965–6, ODS to King, 24 September 1911; ODS, "Canada's Rejection of Reciprocity," 726, 730–1.

26 ODS, "Canada's Rejection of Reciprocity," 730–1. See also ODS, "Current Events," *QQ*, 18, 4 (April-June 1911): 329.

27 ODS, "Current Events," *QQ*, 16, 4 (April-June 1909): 376–7. "Quits" is from ODS, "Canada's Rejection of Reciprocity," 726.

28 ODS, *Socialism: A Critical Analysis* (Boston and New York: Houghton Mifflin 1911), 17. "Husbandly" is in SP, vol. 1, file 18, ODS to IS, 4 August 1911.

29 SP, vol. 11, file 1, review of Edward R. Pease, in *Archiv für die Geschichte des Sozialismus* (translated for the author by Boris Stipernitz). For other reviews, see ibid.; on university courses, see Keane, "The Education of O.D. Skelton," 2.

30 Lenin read the socialism book in Switzerland in late 1915 or 1916: V.I. Lenin, *Polnoe sobranie sochinenii* (Complete Collected Works, vol. 28; Moscow, 1962), 740. Lenin's letter to ODS was apparently destroyed in a fire at Sandy Skelton's farm in October 1948; H.S. Ferns reconstructs the letter in *Reading from Left to Right: One Man's Political History* (Toronto: University of Toronto Press 1983), 176. On the author's behalf, Ambassador Robert Ford put the tale of Lenin's tomb to Soviet authorities, who debunked it. There is no copy of *Socialism: A Critical Analysis*, or any reference to it, in the extensive holdings of the Institute of Marxism-Leninism in Moscow or the Lenin Apartment Museum in the Kremlin. For an example of the repetition of the Lenin tomb myth, see D.A. Farquharson's obituary of ODS, *Globe and Mail* (Toronto), 29 January 1941.

31 Ferguson, *Remaking Liberalism*, 96–7; ODS, "Current Events," *QQ,* 17, 3
(January-March 1910): 264; ODS, "Reciprocity: The Canadian Attitude," 89.

32 ODS, *Socialism,* 11, 15; ODS, "Current Events," *QQ,* 17, 3 (January-March
1910): 258; 15, 2 (October-December 1907): 158–9; Ferguson, *Remaking
Liberalism,* 103, 108, and 116.

33 ODS, *Socialism,* ch. 3.

34 Ibid., 59–61.

35 Crowley, *Marriage of Minds,* 59–60; *Kingston City Directory, August 1916 to
August 1917* (Kingston, Ont.: Leman A. Guild and George Hanson 1917), 3.

36 ODS, "Current Events," *QQ,* 16, 3 (January-March 1909): 292–3; 17, 3
(January-March 1910): 258–9, 267; 18, 2 (October-December 1910): 172; 20,
1 (July-September 1912): 105–6; 20, 4 (April-June 1913): 474; 21, 4 (April-
June 1914): 515–16; ODS, "Reciprocity: The Canadian Attitude," 93.

37 ODS, "Current Events," *QQ,* 17, 3 (January-March 1910): 264–6; Ferguson,
Remaking Liberalism, 116.

38 ODS, "Current Events," *QQ,* 15, 2 (October-December 1907): 156. Skelton
and his ilk also excluded Canada's aboriginal populations from the benefits
of liberal democracy. See Adele Perry, "Women, Racialized People, and
the Making of the Liberal Order in Northern North America," and Robin
Jarvis Brownlie, "A Persistent Antagonism: First Nations and the Liberal
Order," in Jean-François Constant and Michel Ducharme, eds., *Liberalism
and Hegemony: Debating the Canadian Liberal Revolution* (Toronto: University
of Toronto Press 2009).

39 ODS, "Current Events," *QQ,* 22, 1 (July-September 1914): 100. A negative
view of East Indians was common in colonial discourses. Studying racialized
and gendered ideas in the Indian Civil Service, Mrinalini Sinha traces how
Indian men were portrayed as effeminate, dependent, and degenerate –
antithetical to the type of men needed for modern, democratic societies. *Colonial Masculinity: The 'Manly Englishman' and the 'Effeminate Bengali' in the Late
Nineteenth Century* (Manchester, U.K.: Manchester University Press 1995), 20.

40 ODS, "Current Events," *QQ,* 20, 1 (July-September 1912): 107.

41 Ibid., 111.

42 Ibid. "True Skeltonism" is in SP, vol. 1, file 19, IS to ODS, 19 January 1912.
Ideas about Quebec's passivity and provincialism have been questioned in
histories of the province's business and intellectual communities. Fernande
Roy's *Progrès, harmonie, liberté: le libéralisme des milieux d'affaires francophones
à Montréal au tournant du siècle* (Montreal: Boréal 1988) explores French
business councils and the business press in turn-of-the-century Montreal,
suggesting that they were united by the belief in economic development
and progress (9, 112).

43 SP, vol. 1, file 20, Hawkes to ODS, 28 July 1912–17 October 1913, Cooper
    to ODS, 6 October 1913, and "Objects" and "Memorial" of the Canadian
    League, [1913]; North York Central Library, Toronto, John A. Cooper
    Papers, box 4, file 14, ODS to Cooper, 2 September 1913; Damien-Claude
    Bélanger, *Prejudice and Pride: Canadian Intellectuals Confront the United States,
    1891–1945* (Toronto: University of Toronto Press 2011), 184–5. Cooper,
    Hawkes, and the League are discussed in Simon J. Potter, "Richard Jebb,
    John S. Ewart, and the Round Table, 1898–1926," *English Historical Review*,
    72, 495 (February 2007): 111–13. The Canadian League was a revival of the
    organization that had fought reciprocity in the 1911 election campaign.
    More on the League can be found in the Cooper Papers, boxes 4 and 5, es-
    pecially a Cooper-Hawkes exchange in the Toronto *Sunday World*, 17 August
    1913 (box 5, file 44).
44 ODS, "Current Events," *QQ*, 20, 4 (April-June 1913): 472–4. Note also ibid.,
    17, 3 (January-March 1910): 258.
45 ODS, "Current Events," *QQ*, 20, 4 (April-June 1913): 470–1.
46 Ibid., 471–2; 21, 4 (April-June 1914): 508.
47 ODS, "Current Events," *QQ*, 16, 4 (April-June 1909): 378–9; 18, 2 (October-
    December 1910): 167; 20, 1 (July-September 1912): 108; LAC, Adam Shortt
    Papers, vol. 58, ODS to Shortt, 14 December 1913.
48 ODS, "Current Events," *QQ*, 17, 1 (July-September 1909): 81; 18, 2 (Octo-
    ber-December 1910): 167; 20, 1 (July-September 1912): 108; 20, 4 (April-
    June 1913): 473. Christopher Clark, *The Sleepwalkers: How Europe Went to War
    in 1914* (New York: HarperCollins 2012), counters the argument that the
    First World War was inevitable.

3. War and Sir Wilfrid, 1914–19

1 ODS, *Life and Letters of Sir Wilfrid Laurier*, vol. 2 (New York: Century 1922),
   427–35. See also Elizabeth H. Armstrong, *The Crisis of Quebec, 1914–1918*
   (Toronto: McClelland and Stewart 1974), 55–6; J.L. Granatstein and J.M.
   Hitsman, *Broken Promises: A History of Conscription in Canada* (Toronto: Oxford University Press 1977), 25 (but see 24 as well).
2 ODS, "Canada in Wartime," *Political Quarterly*, 6 (May 1915): 58–9. "Vision"
   is from ODS, "Current Events," *QQ*, 24, 1 (July-September 1916): 137.
3 ODS, "Current Events," *QQ*, 23, 1 (July-September 1915): 105–6.
4 Ibid., 100, and ODS, "The European War and the Peace Movement,"
   QQ, 22, 2 (October-December 1914): 213.
5 ODS, "Canada in Wartime," 58–9; ODS, "Current Events," *QQ*, 24, 1 (July-
   September 1916): 135.

6 ODS, "Current Events," *QQ*, 23, 1 (July-September 1915): 100–1; ODS, "Canada in Wartime," 58–9.

7 SP, vol. 1, file 19, ODS to IS, 23 September 1913; ODS, *The Day of Sir Wilfrid Laurier: A Chronicle of Our Own Times* (Toronto: Glasgow, Brook 1916), prefatory note and 323; Terry Crowley, *Marriage of Minds: Isabel and Oscar Skelton Reinventing Canada* (Toronto: University of Toronto Press 2003), 61.

8 SP, vol. 1, file 22, ODS to IS, [September 1914].

9 Ibid., ODS to family, 6, 7, 9, and 10 July 1914; ODS, *Life and Letters of Sir Wilfrid Laurier*, vol. 2, 426–7.

10 SP, vol. 1, file 22, ODS to family, and postcard to Sandy, 9 July 1914; ODS to IS, 19 December 1914. See also SP, vol. 1, file 19, ODS to IS, 23 September 1913.

11 ODS, *The Day of Sir Wilfrid Laurier*, 325; Vancouver *Sun*, 5 September 1916; SP, vol. 1, file 22, Laurier to ODS, 12 and 22 October and 1 November 1915; LAC, Sir Wilfrid Laurier Papers, reel C-908, vol. 696, 191155–6, ODS to Laurier, 18 February 1916.

12 ODS, "Current Events," *QQ*, 24, 1 (July-September 1916): 132–8.

13 Ibid., 135–6; ODS, *Life and Letters of Sir Wilfrid Laurier*, vol. 2, 457–8.

14 ODS, "Current Events," *QQ*, 24, 1 (July-September 1916): 136–7; ODS, *Life and Letters of Sir Wilfrid Laurier*, vol. 2, 461–2.

15 Robert Rumilly, *Henri Bourassa: La Vie publique d'un grand Canadien* (Montreal: Les Editions Chantecler 1953), 529; ODS, *Life and Letters of Sir Wilfrid Laurier*, vol. 2, 468–70.

16 ODS, "The Language Issue in Canada," *QQ*, 24, 4 (April-June 1917): 460–3; ODS, "Current Events," *QQ*, 24, 1 (July-September 1916): 137.

17 Brian Cameron, "The Bonne Entente Movement, 1916–1917: From Cooperation to Conscription," *Journal of Canadian Studies*, 13, 2 (summer 1978): 42–6.

18 Ibid., 42, 47–8; LAC, W.L. Grant Papers, vol. 9, Skelton file, ODS to Grant, 19 March 1917.

19 ODS to Grant, 19 March 1917. See also Cameron, "The Bonne Entente Movement," 49–50; Granatstein and Hitsman, *Broken Promises*, 42; Crowley, *Marriage of Minds*, 62–3; Robert Rutherdale, *Hometown Horizons: Local Responses to Canada's Great War* (Vancouver: University of British Columbia Press 2004), 158–9; Dale C. Thomson, *Louis St. Laurent: Canadian* (Toronto: Macmillan of Canada 1967), 80–1.

20 Cameron, "The Bonne Entente Movement," 52–4; Grant Papers, vol. 9, Skelton file, ODS to Grant, 13 August 1917. See also Granatstein and Hitsman, *Broken Promises*, 46n., 70–1, and Tim Cook, *Shock Troops: Canadians Fighting the Great War, 1917–1918*, vol. 2 (Toronto: Viking Canada 2008), 6. "The

going became harder" is from ODS, *Life and Letters of Sir Wilfrid Laurier*, vol. 2, 450.

21 ODS, "Current Events," *QQ*, 24, 1 (July-September 1916): 132–9; ODS, *Life and Letters of Sir Wilfrid Laurier*, vol. 2, 449, 508, and, generally, 506–50.

22 ODS to Grant, 19 March 1917; ODS, "Current Events," *QQ*, 25, 2 (October-December 1917): 221.

23 ODS to Grant, 13 August 1917; Laurier Papers, reel C-913, vol. 709, 195815–6, ODS to Laurier, 30 May 1917, and vol. 711, 196547–9, ODS to Laurier, 7 August 1917.

24 This paragraph and the next are based on ODS to Grant, 13 August 1917, and ODS, "Current Events," *QQ*, 25, 2 (October-December 1917): 223–5 and 229.

25 ODS, "Current Events," *QQ*, 25, 2 (October-December 1917): 226–9; ODS to Grant, 13 August 1917; ODS, *Life and Letters of Sir Wilfrid Laurier*, vol. 2, 508–9, 545–7. The scholarship on conscription has evolved: the impact of the conscripts on the final battles of the First World War is now better understood. Compare Granatstein and Hitsman, *Broken Promises*, 98–9, with J.L Granatstein, *The Greatest Victory: Canada's One Hundred Days, 1918* (Don Mills, Ont.: Oxford University Press 2014), 141.

26 ODS, *Life and Letters of Sir Wilfrid Laurier*, vol. 2, 529–30; ODS, "Current Events," *QQ*, 25, 2 (October-December 1917): 230–2. See also Robert Craig Brown, *Robert Laird Borden: A Biography*, vol. 2: *1914–1937* (Toronto: Macmillan 1980), 100–1.

27 Laurier Papers, reel C-913, vol. 711, 196547–9, ODS to Laurier, 7 August 1917.

28 For this paragraph and the next, see Laurier Papers, reel C-914, vol. 714, 197648–51, ODS to Laurier, 18 October 1917, and reel C-914, vol. 715, 197833–5, ODS to Laurier, 29 October 1917; "Laurier's Manifesto to the People of Canada," 6 November 1917, in D. Owen Carrigan, ed., *Canadian Party Platforms 1867–1968* (Toronto: Copp Clark 1968), 69–74.

29 ODS to Laurier, 18 and 29 October 1917; Laurier Papers, reel C-915, vol. 716, 198247, ODS to Laurier, 12 November 1917.

30 SP, vol. 1, file 24, Jeremiah Skelton to ODS, 12 December 1917.

31 ODS, *Life and Letters of Sir Wilfrid Laurier*, vol. 2, 537–8n.1; Jeremiah Skelton to ODS, 12 December 1917; Réal Bélanger, "Sir Wilfrid Laurier," in Ramsay Cook and Réal Bélanger, eds., *Canada's Prime Ministers: Macdonald to Trudeau* (Toronto: University of Toronto Press 2007), 188–9.

32 Laurier Papers, reel C-916, vol. 718, 198974–5, ODS to Laurier, 18 December 1917, and reel C-916, vol. 720, 199261–2, ODS to Laurier, I January 1918.

33 SP, vol. 1, file 24, Taylor to John MacNaughton, 14 January 1918, and "Notes of Interview with Mr. Walter Douglas," 11 January 1918 (ODS transcriptions); Crowley, *Marriage of Minds*, 65–7; diary of Queen's professor George D. Ferguson (courtesy of his daughter, Catherine Ferguson), 7 January 1918. See also SP, vol. 1, file 24, G.Y. Chown to ODS, 8 January [1918] and reply of 9 January [1918]. Chown erred in dating his letter, as did Skelton, both writing 1917 instead of 1918. Professor Crowley repeats the error.

34 ODS to Chown, 9 January [1918]; Barry Ferguson, *Remaking Liberalism: The Intellectual Legacy of Adam Shortt, O.D. Skelton, W.C. Clark, and W.A. Mackintosh, 1890–1925* (Montreal and Kingston, Ont.: McGill-Queen's University Press 1993), 27–36; F.W. Gibson, *Queen's University*, II: *1917–1961* (Montreal and Kingston, Ont.: McGill-Queen's University Press 1983), 15.

35 The following four paragraphs are derived from ODS to Chown, 9 January [1918].

36 Laurier Papers, reel C-916, vol. 722, 200135–6, ODS to Laurier, 23 March 1918, and reel C-917, vol. 723, 200727–8, ODS to Laurier, 7 June 1918. See also ODS to Chown, 9 January [1918], and John Keegan, *The First World War* (London: Hutchinson 2001), 364–78.

37 Laurier Papers, reel C-916, vol. 722, 200057–8 and 200135–6, ODS to Laurier, 15 and 23 March 1918, and ODS to Laurier, 7 June 1918; ODS, "Current Events," *QQ*, 26, 1 (July-September 1918): 112–5, 121–2.

38 Laurier Papers, reel C-918, vol. 727, 201865–6, ODS to Laurier, 15 November 1918.

39 Ibid., 201865–75, ODS to Laurier, 15 November 1918, and attached "Suggestions for Farmers' Platform."

40 "Progressive Platform of 1921," in Carrigan, *Canadian Party Platforms*, 90–3; ODS to Laurier, 15 November 1918. See also ODS, review of W.C. Good, *Production and Taxation in Canada from the Farmers' Standpoint*, *QQ*, 27, 2 (October-December 1919): 221, and Ferguson, *Remaking Liberalism*, 145–6 and 188–90.

41 ODS, "Canadian Federal Finance – II," *QQ*, 26, 2 (October-December 1918): 228; ODS to Laurier, 15 November 1918.

42 ODS, "Current Events," *QQ*, 27, 1 (July-September 1919): 127; 27, 3 (January-March 1920): 319, 321–2, 326–8; 28, 1 (July-September 1920): 99–100, 104; 29, 2 (October-December 1921): 202–3; ODS, "Canada, the Empire, the League," pt. 2, *Grain Growers' Guide*, 3 March 1920, 14.

43 LAC, W.C. Good Papers, vol. 4, 2829–32, ODS to Good, 10 January 1919; ODS, "Current Events," *QQ*, 27, 1 (July-September 1919): 121–2; 27, 3 (January-March 1920): 326–7; 29, 2 (October-December 1921): 204–5.

44 ODS, "Current Events," *QQ*, 27, 1 (July-September 1919): 113–18; 27, 3 (January-March 1920): 319.

45 For this and the next paragraph, ODS, "Current Events," *QQ,* 27, 1 (July-September 1919): 121–8; 27, 3 (January-March 1920): 319–21, 329; 28, 1 (July-September 1920): 92.

46 ODS, "Canada, the Empire, the League," pt. 1, *Grain Growers' Guide,* 25 February 1920, 7; "Current Events," *QQ,* 27, 1 (July-September 1919): 108; ODS, "Current Events," *QQ,* 27, 3 (January-March 1920): 319–21, 329. "100% Americanism," accompanied by a demand for patriotic conformity, was a cry frequently heard in the United States during the First World War.

47 ODS, "Canadian Federal Finance – II," 228; ODS, "Canada, the Empire, the League," pt. 1, 7, 71–2; ODS, "Current Events," *QQ,* 27, 1 (July-September 1919): 108.

48 SP, vol. 1, file 24, ODS to IS, 13 October [1917]. "Common houses" is in SP, vol. 1, file 19, ODS to IS, 10 October 1913.

49 University of Toronto, Thomas Fisher Rare Book Room, James Mavor Papers, box 16, Skelton file, ODS to Mavor, 26 February 1919; H.B. Neatby Papers, Laurier to ODS, 3 February 1919, and reply, 7 February 1919.

50 Bélanger, "Sir Wilfrid Laurier," 190.

51 ODS, "Current Events," *QQ,* 28, 1 (July-September 1920): 91, and "The Canadian Elections," *New Republic,* 23 November 1921, 367; W.A. Mackintosh, "O.D. Skelton," in Robert L. McDougall, ed., *Canada's Past and Present: A Dialogue. Our Living Tradition, Fifth Series* (Toronto: University of Toronto Press 1965), 67. For "sorrowing pilgrims," see ODS, *Life and Letters of Sir Wilfrid Laurier,* vol. 2, 555, and information from J.W. Pickersgill.

4. Courting Mr King, 1919–22

1 ODS, "Current Events," *QQ,* 27, 1 (July-September 1919): 121 and 128; ODS, "The New Partnership in Industry," *Canadian Author and Bookman,* 1 April 1919, 62; Barry Ferguson, *Remaking Liberalism: The Intellectual Legacy of Adam Shortt, O.D. Skelton, W.C. Clark, and W.A. Mackintosh, 1890–1925* (Montreal and Kingston, Ont.: McGill-Queen's University Press 1993), 220–1.

2 LAC, KP, reel C-1939, J1, vol. 51, 43986, ODS to King, 8 August 1919; ODS, "Current Events," *QQ,* 28, 1 (July-September 1920): 89.

3 KP, reel C-1939, J1, vol. 51, 43987, King to ODS, 22 August 1919; ODS to King, 8 August 1919; LAC, Charles Sissons Papers, vol. 4, "S" file, ODS to Sissons, 16 October 1920.

4 KP, reel C-1939, J1, vol. 51, 43989–90, ODS to King, 24 November 1919 and reply of 28 November 1919; Ferguson, *Remaking Liberalism,* 145, 189–91; ODS, "Current Events," *QQ,* 27, 3 (January-March 1920): 326.

5 ODS, "Current Events," *QQ,* 28, 1 (July-September 1920): 89–90, and "The Canadian Elections," *New Republic,* 23 November 1921, 367. See also Robert Craig Brown, *Robert Laird Borden: A Biography,* vol. 2: *1914–1937* (Toronto: Macmillan 1980), ch. 14.

6 Roger Graham, *Arthur Meighen: A Biography,* vol. 2: *And Fortune Fled* (Toronto: Clarke, Irwin 1963), 121; J. Castell Hopkins, ed., *The Canadian Annual Review of Public Affairs, 1921* (Toronto: Canadian Review Company 1922), 460; ODS, "Current Events," *QQ,* 27, 1 (July-September 1919): 117; 28, 1 (July-September 1920): 92.

7 LAC, Charles Murphy Papers, vol. 27, Skelton file, 11525–6, ODS to Murphy, 7 June 1921. See also ODS, "The Canadian Elections," 369.

8 ODS, "The Canadian Elections," 367–9; ODS, "Current Events," *QQ,* 29, 2 (October-December 1921): 199–200.

9 KP, reel C-1951, J1, vol. 67, 57579–80, ODS to King, 25 November 1921; ODS, "Current Events," *QQ,* 27, 1 (July-September 1919): 121. See also R. MacGregor Dawson, *William Lyon Mackenzie King,* vol. 1: *1874–1923* (Toronto: University of Toronto Press 1958), 355; J.E. Rea, *T.A. Crerar: A Political Life* (Montreal and Kingston, Ont.: McGill-Queen's University Press 1997), 80.

10 ODS to King, 25 November 1921; ODS, "The Canadian Elections," 369; Terry Crowley, *Marriage of Minds: Isabel and Oscar Skelton Reinventing Canada* (Toronto: University of Toronto Press 2003), 49.

11 KP, reel C-1951, J1, vol. 67, 57576–8 and 57581, King to ODS, 10 September and 29 November 1921; 57579–80 and 57582–3, ODS to King, 25 November and 8 December 1921. See also Graham, *Arthur Meighen,* 170–4, and Dawson, *William Lyon Mackenzie King,* 374–6.

12 ODS, "Current Events," *QQ,* 29, 2 (October-December 1921): 202–4.

13 ODS, "Canada and Foreign Policy," in *The Canadian Club Year Book, 1921–1922* (Ottawa: Canadian Club 1922), 58–69 and particularly 58–63; "Sir Robt. Borden's Washington Status," Ottawa *Citizen,* 23 January 1922.

14 ODS, "Canada and Foreign Policy," 59–60, 65–6.

15 Ibid., 66. See also ODS, "Current Events," *QQ,* 29, 2 (October-December 1921): 201–2.

16 ODS, "Canada and Foreign Policy," 60, 65–6.

17 Ibid., 62, 68–9.

18 LAC, R.L. Borden Papers, vol. 122, file 626, "Extract from an Address Delivered by Prof. OD Skelton, at the Ottawa Canadian Club, January 21, 1922." The "aberrations" remark was deleted from the printed version of the speech, in ODS, "Canada and Foreign Policy," 64. See also Philip G. Wigley, *Canada and the Transition to Commonwealth: British-Canadian Relations 1917–1926* (Cambridge: Cambridge University Press 1977), 144–8 and

153. The Isabel Skelton Scrapbook at QUA collected pieces on Skelton's Canadian Club speeches from the Ottawa *Citizen*, 23 January 1922 (misidentified as 13 January); Toronto *Star*, 23 and 30 January 1922; Ottawa *Journal*, 25 January 1922; Toronto *Mail and Empire*, 30 January 1922; *British Whig* (Kingston, Ont.), 31 January 1922; and *Globe* (Toronto), 31 January 1922.

19 "Shall We Balkanize the Empire?" Ottawa *Journal*, 25 January 1922; "Sir Robt. Borden's Washington Status"; "Canada at Armament Conference," Ottawa *Citizen*, 23 January 1922.

20 ISS, annotation below clipping of "Shall We Balkanize the Empire?" See also Grattan O'Leary, *Recollections of People, Press, and Politics* (Toronto: Macmillan 1977), 36–45.

21 KD, 21 January 1922.

22 "Queen's Theological Alumni Association," and "Conference Concludes," *British Whig* (Kingston, Ont.), 31 October and 3 November 1922. See also LAC, Papers of the Canadian Political Science Association, vol. 1, Minutes of the CPSA, 18 May 1922; Victor Ross et al., *The History of the Canadian Bank of Commerce*, vol. 1 (Toronto: Oxford University Press 1920); *Fifty Years of Banking Service 1871–1921: The Dominion Bank* (Toronto: Dominion Bank 1922).

23 QUA, Queen's University Board of Trustees Records, minutes of meetings of 28 April 1915, 30 April and 15 October 1919, and 20 October 1920; LAC, Sir Wilfrid Laurier Papers, vol. 683, reel C-905, 186929, Merchants Bank of Canada note, due 10 June 1921.

24 Guy MacLean, introduction to his edited Carleton Library edition of *The Life and Times of Sir Alexander Tilloch Galt* (Toronto: McClelland and Stewart 1966), xvi–xvii.

25 ODS, *The Life and Times of Sir Alexander Tilloch Galt* (Toronto: Oxford University Press 1920), 548; ODS, "Canada and Foreign Policy," 61, 67–8. Maclean, *Galt*, xiv–xv; Carl Berger, *The Sense of Power: Studies in the Ideas of Canadian Imperialism, 1867–1914* (Toronto: University of Toronto Press 1970), 50–1. The "personal touch" quotation is in Crowley, *Marriage of Minds*, 88. For a contemporary academic review of the Galt book, see L.J. Burpee, in *Canadian Historical Review*, 1, 3 (September 1920): 325–8.

26 ODS, *Life and Letters of Sir Wilfrid Laurier*, vol. 1 (New York: Century 1922), preface; Grant Dexter, "Oscar Douglas Skelton," *QQ*, 48, 1 (spring 1941): 6.

27 ODS, *Life and Letters of Sir Wilfrid Laurier*, vol. 2, 62–3, 98, 100.

28 The ODS Papers, vol. 6, files 28–9, and the ISS preserve articles and reviews of the Laurier biography, drawn from Canadian, American, and British publications. This paragraph employs *Times Literary Supplement*, 23 March 1922; *Spectator*, 1 April 1922; *Westminster Gazette*, 6 April 1922; and Manchester *Guardian*, 10 April 1922, all from ISS.

29 ISS; Beard, quoted in Berger, *The Sense of Power*, 50; V.L.O. Chittick, *The Nation*, 9 August 1922, 151–2.

30 J.W. Dafoe, *Laurier: A Study in Canadian Politics* (Toronto: McClelland and Stewart 1963), 78, 98. See also Fredericton *Gleaner*, 4 April 1922; Montreal *Witness and Canadian Homestead*, 20 December; Montreal *Gazette*, 4 February 1922; Toronto *Daily Star*, 30 November, 3 and 15 December 1921; book advertisement for R. Uglow and Company, all in ISS.

31 Arthur Hawkes, "The Spotlight: Oscar Skelton," Toronto *Daily Star*, 3 February 1922.

32 KP, reel C-2249, J1, vol. 82, 69050, ODS to King, 26 May 1922; Crowley, *Marriage of Minds*, 126.

33 QUA, Queen's University Personnel Records, Skelton file, ODS to Taylor, 27 July 1922; ODS, "The Remaking of Europe, VI: Britain – The Highway of Education," *Globe* (Toronto), 2 October 1922; ODS to King, 26 May 1922; Crowley, *Marriage of Minds*, 126.

34 Queen's University Personnel Records, Skelton file, ODS to Taylor, 27 May and 27 July 1922.

35 ODS, "The Remaking of Europe, I: Britain – A Patient People," and "The Remaking of Europe, III: The Press of London," *Globe* (Toronto), 5 and 19 September 1922.

36 ODS, "The Press of London."

37 ODS, "A Patient People," and "VII: Britain – Other Ways Out," *Globe* (Toronto), 6 October 1922.

38 ODS to Taylor, 27 July 1922; Crowley, *Marriage of Minds*, 115, 127.

39 ODS to Taylor, 27 July 1922; ODS to King, 26 May 1922.

40 ODS, "The Remaking of Europe, VIII: Europe's Chinese Walls," *Globe* (Toronto), 24 October 1922. See also Crowley, *Marriage of Minds*, 127.

41 ODS, "Europe's Chinese Walls."

42 On ODS and journalism, see Dexter, "Oscar Douglas Skelton," 3–4.

43 Crowley, *Marriage of Minds*, 126, 127–8; SP, vol. 1, file 31, ODS to the Murphys, 4 June 1922, and file 32, PC 1679, 11 August 1922; KP, reel C-2249, J1, vol. 82, 69055–8, ODS to King, 28 July and 17 August 1922.

44 KP, reel C-2249, J1, vol. 82, 69059–60, ODS to King, 13 October 1922; Crowley, *Marriage of Minds*, 127–9; ODS, "Impressions of Brazil," *Journal of the Canadian Bankers' Association*, 30, 3 (April 1923): 337–45.

45 ODS to King, 13 October 1922. On Chanak, see C.P. Stacey, *Canada and the Age of Conflict*, vol. 2: *1921–1948, The Mackenzie King Era* (Toronto: University of Toronto Press 1981), 17–27; Richard Toye, *Churchill's Empire* (New York: St Martin's 2011), 158–60.

46 See Queen's University Personnel Records, Skelton file, ODS to Bruce Taylor, 17 March 1925.
47 SD, 1923, 21.

5. Amen, Downing Street, 1923

1 LAC, SP, vol. 11, SD, 27 June 1923, 3–9.
2 Ibid.
3 Ibid.; Michael Dirda, "Mencken Roars Again," *Times Literary Supplement*, 26 (November 2010): 3–4.
4 SP, vol. 2, file 2, King to ODS, 7 July 1923; LAC, KP, reel C-2259, J1, vol. 95, 80364–5, ODS to King, 9 July 1923.
5 ODS, *Life and Letters of Sir Wilfrid Laurier*, vol. 1 (New York: Century 1922), 67, 294, 396.
6 QUA, Isabel Skelton Papers, IS Diary, 1 January 1940; SD, 1923, folios 21 and 23, "Kingston"; SP, vol. 2, file 2, ODS to IS, 8 July 1923; ODS to King, 9 July 1923.
7 SP, vol. 2, file 2, ODS to IS, 8 July 1923, and vol. 1, file 33, ODS to Taylor, 30 April 1923; SD, 1923, 11.
8 SP, vol. 1, file 31, ODS to IS and Sandy, 7 December 1922; "The Late Mrs. J. Skelton," *British Whig Standard*, 11 December 1922; Terry Crowley, *Marriage of Minds: Isabel and Oscar Skelton Reinventing Canada* (Toronto: University of Toronto Press 2003), 130.
9 SP, vol. 1, file 33, contract with Henry Holt publishers for a book "relative to the Government of Great Britain."
10 Robert A. Wardhaugh, with Douglas MacEwan and William Johnston, *Behind the Scenes: The Life and Work of William Clifford Clark* (Toronto: University of Toronto Press 2010), 33; SP, vol. 1, file 33, Clark to ODS, 1 March 1923.
11 SD, 27 June 1923, 3–9; Clark to ODS, 1 March 1923; Wardhaugh, *Behind the Scenes*, 14–15, 31–3.
12 SP, vol. 1, file 33, IS to Sandy, 29 January 1923; KP, reel C-2249, J1, vol. 82, 69061–2, King to ODS, 16 October 1922; 69040, ODS to King, 27 January 1922; 69043, 4 February 1922; and 69049, King to ODS, 1 May 1922; SD, 1923, 11.
13 SD, 1923, 11, 13, and 15.
14 SD, 1923, 13; John F. Hilliker, *Canada's Department of External Affairs*, vol. 1: *The Early Years, 1909–1946* (Montreal and Kingston, Ont.: McGill-Queen's University Press 1990), 89; Robert Bothwell, *Loring Christie: The Failure of Bureaucratic Imperialism* (New York and London: Garland 1988), 322–34.

15 SD, 1923, 11, 13, and 15; Philip G. Wigley, *Canada and the Transition to Commonwealth: British-Canadian Relations, 1917–1926* (Cambridge: Cambridge University Press 1977), 185–6.

16 PC 1529 and 1550, 14 August 1923; SD, 1923, 15; KP, reel C-2259, J1, vol. 95, 80372–3, ODS to King, 1 August 1923.

17 SD, 1923, 17, 19. See also Dafoe Diary, 22 September 1923, in Ramsay Cook, "J.W. Dafoe at the Imperial Conference of 1923," *Canadian Historical Review*, 41, 1 (March 1960): 23.

18 KP, reel C-2695, J4, vol. 81, file 641, C62300–24, memorandum of ODS, "Preliminary Notes," n.d.

19 Ibid., file 644, C63217–24, memorandum of ODS, "Naval Defence," n.d. See also ibid., file 641, C62327–33, memorandum of ODS, "As to Resolutions – re Imperial Defence," n.d.; and Roger Sarty, *The Maritime Defence of Canada* (Toronto: Canadian Institute of Strategic Studies 1996), 86.

20 Hilliker, *Canada's Department of External Affairs*, 95, 98; SD, 1923, 15, 17, 19; KP, reel C-2259, J1, vol. 95, 80374ff, ODS to King, 28 August 1923, and KP, reel C-2695, J4, vol. 81, C62298, "Data in Preparation," n.d., and, generally, J4, vols. 81, 82, and 85.

21 KP, reel C-2695, J4, vol. 81, file 641, C62245–69, memorandum of ODS, "Canada and the Control of Foreign Policy," n.d.; for Skelton's handwritten text, see SP, vol. 2, files 7–8.

22 KP, reel C-2695, J4, vol. 81, file 641, C62389–97, ODS, "Notes for Prime Minister re Opening Address, Imperial Conference," n.d.; ODS, "Canada and the Control of Foreign Policy."

23 KP, reel C-2695, J4, vol. 81, file 641, C62377–87, memorandum of ODS, "Preliminary Review," n.d.

24 ODS, "Canada and the Control of Foreign Policy."

25 KD, 11 September 1923.

26 ODS, "Canada and the Control of Foreign Policy."

27 Norman Hillmer, "Defence and Ideology: The Anglo-Canadian Military 'Alliance' in the Nineteen Thirties," *International Journal*, 33, 3 (summer 1978): 588–612. On Curzon, see NAUK, CAB 32/9, 1923 Imperial Conference minutes, plenary meeting 3, 5 October 1923. For the best of Skelton's historian critics, consult Wigley, *Canada and the Transition to Commonwealth*, 174 and 182–8.

28 SP, vol. 2, file 4, ODS to IS, 28 September 1923; KD, 21–28 September 1923.

29 LAC, Charles Sissons Papers, vol. 4, "S" file, ODS to Sissons, 6 February 1923; Ramsay Cook, *The Politics of John W. Dafoe and the Free Press* (Toronto: University of Toronto Press 1963), 138–9.

30 Dafoe Diary, 22 September 1923, in Cook, "J.W. Dafoe at the Imperial Conference of 1923," 23; SP, vol. 2, file 4, ODS to IS, 28 September 1923; SD, 1923, 25.

31 J.L. Granatstein, *A Man of Influence: Norman A. Robertson and Canadian Statecraft, 1929–68* ([Toronto]: Deneau 1981), 10, and conversation with Professor Granatstein.

32 J.S. Willison, "Canada in the Empire," *The Nineteenth Century and After*, 92 (July–December 1922): 25; Willison to Beer, a letter generously supplied by Professor John English; ODS to IS, 28 September 1923. See also Richard Clippingdale, *The Power of the Pen: The Politics, Nationalism, and Influence of Sir John Willison* (Toronto: Dundurn 2011), 359.

33 SP, vol. 2, file 4, ODS to IS, 1 and 2 October 1923; SD, 29 September 1923; LAC, Doughty Papers, vol. 8, Diary, 29 September 1923.

34 ODS to IS, 1 October 1923, and SP, vol. 2, file 6, ODS to IS, 18 November 1923.

35 SD, 29 September and 12 November 1923; ODS to IS, 2 October and 18 November 1923.

36 ODS to IS, 1 October 1923; SD, 29 September 1923.

37 ODS to IS, 1 and 2 October 1923; SD, 1, 4 October 1923.

38 Ibid.

39 SD, 3, 4, 9, and 31 October 1923.

40 "The Imperial Conference" and "Canada – The Sensitiveness of Canadian Nationalism," *Round Table*, 52 (September 1923): 683–700 and 824–6; Bodleian Library, Oxford University, Round Table Papers, Glazebrook to Dove, 24 August 1923; SP, vol. 2, file 4, ODS to IS, 5 October 1923.

41 SP, vol. 2, file 6, ODS to IS, 18 November 1923. On Coats, see Dafoe Diary, 11 October 1923, in Cook, "J.W. Dafoe and the Imperial Conference of 1923," 27; on the Skelton-Irish alliance, see David Harkness, *The Restless Dominion: The Irish Free State and the British Commonwealth of Nations, 1921–31* (London: Macmillan 1969), 51–5.

42 ODS to IS, 18 November 1923; SD, 23 October and 8 November 1923.

43 ODS to IS, 5 October 1923; SD, 22 October and 7 November 1923.

44 SD, 5 October 1923; Bothwell, *Loring Christie*, 269–70 and 319.

45 SD, 6–7 October 1923; ODS, "Notes for Prime Minister re Opening Address."

46 C.P. Stacey, *Canada and the Age of Conflict*, vol. 2: *1921–1948, The Mackenzie King Era* (Toronto: University of Toronto Press 1981), 72; SD, [8] October 1923; SP, vol. 2, file 5, ODS to IS, 14 October 1923; KD, 7–8 October 1923.

47 See SD, 8 and 9 October 1923.

48 SD, [2 November] 1923, 141. The L.S. Amery quotation is from his diary, 2 October 1923. I am indebted to the Rt. Hon. Julian Amery for allowing me to examine his father's papers, which I did at the Amery home in Eaton Square, London. The Leo Amery Papers are now housed at Churchill College, Cambridge.

49 ODS, *Canada, the Empire, the League* (Canadian Council of Agriculture [1920]; copy in North York Central Library, Toronto, John A. Cooper Papers, box 5, file 46), 4–5 and 13–14.

50 SD, 13 and 31 October 1923; SP, vol. 2, file 5, ODS to IS, 19 and 28 October 1923. See, as an example of Skelton's work, LAC, DEA Records, RG 25, vol. 3416, file 1–1923/11, 1923 Imperial Conference, minutes of Committee on India's Contribution to the League of Nations.

51 SD, 13 October 1923; SP, vol. 2, file 5, ODS to IS, 14 October 1923.

52 SD, 15 and 22 October, and 2 [November] 1923; LAC, Lomer Gouin Papers, vol. 58, file 114, ODS to Gouin, 12 November 1923. For the treaty committee, see SD, 25 October 1923; Imperial Conference of 1923, *Summary of Proceedings*, Cmd 1987 (London: His Majesty's Stationery Office 1923), 13–15.

53 Cmd 1987, 16; SD, 2 [November] 1923. See also Norman Hillmer, "Mackenzie King, Canadian Air Policy and the Imperial Conference of 1923," *High Flight*, 1, 5 (1981): 189–193 and 196.

54 SD, 5 November 1923; SP, vol. 2, file 6, ODS to IS, 8 November 1923; KP, reel C-2695, J4, vol. 81, file 641, C62474–8 and C62480–84; DEA Records, RG 25, vol. 3416, 1–1923/6, "Resolution on Foreign Policy."

55 Dafoe Diary, 27 October, 6 November 1923, and his "General Notes on the Conference," in Cook, "J.W. Dafoe and the Imperial Conference of 1923," 32 and 39; SD, 5–6 November 1923; KD, 6 November 1923.

56 SD, 5–6 November 1923; KD, 6 November 1923; Dafoe Diary, 6 November 1923, in Cook, "J.W. Dafoe and the Imperial Conference of 1923," 37.

57 SD, 6–7 November 1923; KD, 7 November 1923; Churchill College, Cambridge, England, Maurice Hankey Papers, Diary, 11 November 1923; Cmd 1987, 13; Dafoe Diary, 6 November 1923; KP, reel C-2695, J4, vol. 81, file 641, C62495–6, memorandum of ODS, "Foreign Relations," 7 November 1923.

58 KP, J4, vol. 85, reel C-2698, file 653, C66044–62, memorandum of ODS, "Imperial Economic Conference: Preliminary Notes," [1923], and ibid., file 654, C66197–201, memorandum of ODS, "Imperial Economic Conference: State-Aided Settlement," [1923]; Ian M. Drummond, *Imperial Economic Policy 1917–1939: Studies in Expansion and Protection* (London: Allen and Unwin 1974), 23–40 and 90–4.

59 Gouin Papers, vol. 58, file 114, ODS to Gouin, November 1923; SD, 6 and 8 November 1923; KP, reel C-2698, J4, vol. 85, file 653, C65935, memorandum of ODS, "Economic Conference," 2 October 1923; Wigley, *Canada and the Transition to Commonwealth*, 202; DEA Records, RG 25, vol. 3432, file 1–1933/8A, [L.B. Pearson], "Proposals for an Imperial Secretariat [1933], 28–30.

60 Crowley, *Marriage of Minds*, 115; ODS to IS, 14, 19, 28 October, and 16 November 1923.
61 ODS to IS, 18 November 1923; SD, 23 October and 8 November 1923.
62 SD, 13, 15, [17], 18, 19, 20, and 22 November 1923; SP, vol. 2, file 6, ODS to IS, 18 and 28 November 1923.
63 SD, 24–29 November 1923; Halifax *Chronicle* and Halifax *Herald*, 1 December 1923; Merv Daub, *Gael Force: A Century of Football at Queen's* (Montreal and Kingston, Ont.: McGill-Queen's University Press 1996), 48–9.
64 SD, 8 November 1923; ODS to IS, 8 November 1923; LAC, Dafoe Papers, reel M-74, ODS to Dafoe, 24 March 1925. Curzon's biographer, David Gilmour, portrays the Imperial Conference as a triumph, the great man's last, in *Curzon* (London: John Murray 1994), 592. Curzon had fallen off a horse when he was fifteen, sustaining a serious back injury that was with him all of his life: hence Skelton's mention of "physical difficulties."
65 University of Toronto Archives, J. Burgon Bickersteth Papers, box 2001–0018/00, Bickersteth to his parents, 25 December 1923.
66 SD, 8 November 1923.

6. The Decision, 1924–5

1 LAC, SP, vol. 11, SD, 24–28 November 1923; KD, 18 January 1924.
2 LAC, Dafoe Papers, reel M-74, Ewart to ODS, 30 January 1922.
3 Douglas L. Cole, "The Better Patriot: John S. Ewart and the Canadian Nation," PhD thesis, University of Washington, 1968, especially 355 and 371a. The author remembers warmly Doug Cole and our stimulating conversations about this and so many other subjects. See also SD, 14 May 1925.
4 LAC, Charles Sissons Papers, vol. 4, "S" file, ODS to Sissons, 22 July 1924; KP, J1, reel C-2271, vol. 109, 92955, ODS to King, 8 April 1924, and 92958, ODS to King, 14 April 1924. See also C.P. Stacey, *Canada and the Age of Conflict*, vol. 2: *1921–1948, The Mackenzie King Era* (Toronto: University of Toronto Press 1981), 40; Philip G. Wigley, *Canada and the Transition to Commonwealth: British-Canadian Relations 1917–1926* (Cambridge: Cambridge University Press 1977), 209–20.
5 ODS to King, 8 April 1924; House of Commons, *Debates*, 20 March 1924.
6 ODS to King, 8 April 1924; KP, J1, vol. 109, reel C-2271, 92962–3, ODS to King, 18 April 1924; QUA, Isabel Skelton Papers, IS Diary, 4–5 April 1924.
7 IS Diary, 4–5 April and 11 May 1924; see also ibid., 8 and 25 January 1924.
8 ODS to King, 18 April 1924; KP, J1, vol. 109, reel C-2271, 92965, ODS to King, 22 April 1924; LAC, Sir Joseph Pope Papers, Diary, 26 February and 25 April 1924.

9 IS Diary, 20 May and 9 June 1924; SP, vol. 2, file 22, ODS to IS, 20 May 1924. See also House of Commons, *Debates*, 9 June 1924.

10 KP, J1, vol. 101, reel C-2265, 85691, Haydon to King, 11 June 1924.

11 SP, vol. 11, SD, 17–20 July 1924.

12 Ibid.

13 QUA, Queen's University Personnel Records, Skelton file, ODS to Taylor, 11 and 17 July 1924; QUA, Queen's Board of Trustees Records, principal's report of 18 October 1924, and Taylor to ODS, 12 March 1925; SD, 17–20 July 1924; SP, vol. 2, file 22, ODS to Sandy Skelton, 21 July 1924.

14 KP, J1, vol. 104, reel C-2267, 88456, Skelton to F.A. McGregor, 18 June 1924.

15 PC 1181, 10 July 1924; Queen's University Board of Trustees Records, "Estimated Expenditures," April 1924–May 1925.

16 PC 1347, 5 August 1924.

17 *Globe* (Toronto), 15 July 1924; Kingston *Whig*, quoting Ottawa *Citizen*, 12 July 1924.

18 SP, vol 2, file 22, Wrong to ODS, 4 August 1924.

19 Ibid.; *Globe* (Toronto), 15 July 1924; Kingston *Whig*, quoting Ottawa *Citizen*, 12 July 1924; PC 1347, 5 August 1924; PC 1181, 10 July 1924; Queen's University Board of Trustees Records, "Estimated Expenditures," April 1924–May 1925; ODS to F.A. McGregor, 18 June 1924. The author's copy of Skelton's *Life and Letters of Sir Wilfrid Laurier* belonged to Hume Wrong, who purchased it in December 1926.

20 ODS to Sandy Skelton, 21 July 1924. See also SD, 20 August 1924.

21 SD, 17–20 July and 20 August 1924.

22 Grant Dexter, "Oscar Douglas Skelton," *QQ*, 48, 1 (spring 1941): 3–4; SD, 20 August 1924. On Bassett, see SP, vol. 2, file 4, ODS to IS, 28 September 1923.

23 SD, 19 July and 20 August 1924; Pope Diary, 30 July 1923, 27 November 1924, 6 October 1925; John F. Hilliker, *Canada's Department of External Affairs*, vol. 1: *The Early Years, 1909–1946* (Montreal and Kingston, Ont.: McGill-Queen's University Press 1990), 102–3.

24 KD, 27 August 1924; SD, 20 August 1924; KP, J1, vol. 99, reel C-2264, 83967–71, Dandurand to King, 22 July 1924, and reply of 23 July 1924.

25 SD, 20 August 1924.

26 SD, 21–27 August 1924.

27 Ibid.

28 SP, vol. 2, file 25, ODS to IS, 31 August 1924; SD, 1924, 15–16; F.P. Walters, *A History of the League of Nations* (London: Oxford University Press 1969), 268–9.

29 SP, vol. 2, file 25, ODS to IS, 4, 16, and 21 September 1924.

30 ODS to IS, 9 September 1924; SP, vol. 2, file 25, ODS to IS, 16 September 1924; SD, 12 September 1924. See also Hilliker, *Canada's Department of External Affairs*, 99.
31 ODS to IS, 9 September 1924.
32 SD, 4 September 1924; ODS to IS, 4 September 1924.
33 SD, 4 September 1924; ODS to IS, 4 and 9 September 1924. See also Marcel Hamelin, ed., *Les Mémoires du Sénateur Raoul Dandurand (1861–1942)* (Québec: Les Presses de l'Université Laval 1967), 269–71.
34 LAC, DEA Records, RG 25, G1, vol. 1411, file 95, pt. 1, section 1, memorandum of ODS, "Notes on the Protocol of Geneva," 8 January 1925; SD, 12 September 1924; ODS to IS, 16 September 1924. See also Tavis Harris, "Wind Words and Fury: Canada and the Geneva Protocol, 1925–26," *War & Society*, 30, 3 (October 2011): 189–206.
35 SP, vol. 2, file 25, ODS to IS, 16 September 1924. The Dandurand speech is reproduced in "Report of the Canadian Delegates to the Fifth Assembly of the League of Nations, 1 September to 2 October 1924" (Ottawa: F.A. Acland 1925), 5–7. See also ODS to IS, 16 September 1924; Hamelin, ed., *Les Mémoires du Sénateur Raoul Dandurand*, 273; Walters, *A History of the League of Nations*, 275–6.
36 SP, vol. 2, file 25, ODS to IS, 2 and 6 October 1924.
37 ODS to IS, 2 October 1924; SP, vol. 2, file 25, ODS to IS, 21 September and 9 October 1924.
38 Lovell C. Clark, ed. *Documents on Canadian External Relations*, vol. 3: *1919–1925* (Ottawa: Information Canada 1970), Document 389, ODS to Pope, 13 December 1924, with memorandum, and Document 508; ODS, "Notes on the Protocol of Geneva"; QUA, ISS, ODS address to the University Club of Ottawa, December 1924, unidentified clipping; SP, vol. 11, file 14, 1924 expenditure book; SP, vol. 2, file 22, Walshe to ODS, 20 October 1924. See also Stacey, *Canada and the Age of Conflict*, 60–4; Wigley, *Canada and the Transition to Commonwealth*, 235, 238–9.
39 KP, J1, vol. 125, reel C-2284, 106485, ODS to King, 11 March 1925; Queen's University Personnel Records, Skelton file, ODS to Taylor, 10 March 1925; University of Toronto Archives, B87–0082, Massey Papers, box 385, file 006, ODS to Vincent Massey, 18 April 1928.
40 SP, vol. 3, file 4, ODS to IS, 19 March 1925.
41 SP, vol. 3, file 4, Jeremiah Skelton to ODS, 24 March 1925. See also SP, vol. 2, file 23, Jeremiah Skelton to ODS, 28 September 1924.
42 SP, vol. 3, file 4, ODS to IS, 31 March 1925; PC 448, 31 March 1925.
43 ODS to IS, 31 March 1925; SD, 20 August 1924. Isabel Skelton, *The Life of Thomas D'Arcy McGee* (Gardenvale, Que.: Garden City Press 1925). For a

slashing assessment of the book's methodology and "adulatory" conclusions, see David A. Wilson, *Thomas D'Arcy McGee*, vol. 1: *Passion, Reason, and Politics, 1825–1857* (Montreal and Kingston, Ont.: McGill-Queen's University Press 2008), 35 and 37–8.

44 SP, vol. 3, file 4, ODS to IS, 18 March and 1 April 1925. See also David A. Wilson, *Thomas D'Arcy McGee*, vol. 2: *The Extreme Moderate, 1857–1968* (Montreal and Kingston, Ont.: McGill-Queen's University Press 2011), 397.

45 SP, vol. 3, file 4, ODS to IS, 1, 7, and 8 April 1925.

46 Ottawa *Journal* and London *Free Press*, both of 8 April 1925; *Manitoba Free Press*, 9 April 1925.

47 The previous two paragraphs are derived from Janice Cavell and Jeff Noakes, *Acts of Occupation: Canada and Arctic Sovereignty, 1918–25* (Vancouver: University of British Columbia Press 2010), 220–2, 226–31, 234–7, and 244–6.

48 SP, vol. 3, file 4, ODS to IS, 20 and 26 May and 3 June 1925. See also Hilliker, *Canada's Department of External Affairs*, 103–4.

49 SP, vol. 11, SD, 14 and 27 May 1925. See also *Report of the Under-Secretary of State for External Affairs for the Year 1926* (Ottawa: King's Printer 1927).

50 Hilliker, *Canada's Department of External Affairs*, 121; SD, 22 May 1925.

51 ODS to IS, 7 April and 20 May 1925.

52 SP, vol. 3, file 4, ODS to IS, 17 May 1925; SD, 16–17 May 1925. On disreputable Hull in the inter-war years, see André Cellard, "Le petit Chicago: la 'criminalité' à Hull depuis le début du XXe siècle," *Revue d'histoire de l'Amérique française*, 45, 4 (1992): 526–33.

53 Ibid.

54 SD, 14 May 1925; Hilliker, *Canada's Department of External Affairs*, 103.

55 SP, vol. 3, file 4, ODS to IS, 3 June 1925.

56 Ibid., ODS to IS, 3 and 15 June 1925; SD, 14 May 1925; H.B. Neatby, *William Lyon Mackenzie King*, vol. 2: *1924–1932, The Lonely Heights* (Toronto: University of Toronto Press 1963), 63.

57 KD, 1 April 1925; ODS to IS, 26 May 1925.

58 Hilliker, *Canada's Department of External Affairs*, 102–6.

59 Ibid., 103–4; SP, vol. 3, file 4, ODS to IS, 2 April 1925.

60 ODS to IS, 15 June 1925; SD, 27 May 1925.

61 SP, vol. 3, file 4, ODS to IS, 3 June 1925.

7. You Ought to be Prime Minister, 1925–6

1 Montreal *Standard*, 21 March and 4 July 1925.

2 LAC, SP, vol. 11, SD, 13–17 November 1925; Arthur Hawkes, "The Spotlight: Oscar Skelton," Toronto *Daily Star*, 3 February 1922.

3 QUA, Isabel Skelton Papers, IS Diary, 14, 16, and 20 August 1925; SP, vol. 3, file 4, IS to ODS, 31 March 1925.

4 IS Diary, 14 August 1925; Terry Crowley, *Marriage of Minds: Isabel and Oscar Skelton Reinventing Canada* (Toronto: University of Toronto Press 2003), 156–7.

5 IS Diary, 25 August 1925; Crowley, *Marriage of Minds*, 157; information from Arthur Menzies, 15 May 2008.

6 SP, vol. 11, SD, 27 January and 2, 23, 25, and 27 February 1926.

7 SD, 30 October 1925 and 3, 23, and 31 January 1926.

8 SD, 29 January 1926; *The Canadian Annual Review of Public Affairs, 1925–26* (Toronto: Canadian Review Company 1926), 362.

9 SD, 28 October 1925, and SP, vol. 3, file 4, memorandum of ODS, 31 October 1925; H.B. Neatby, *William Lyon Mackenzie King*, vol. 2: *1924–1932, The Lonely Heights* (Toronto: University of Toronto Press 1963), 78.

10 SD, 29 October 1925.

11 SD, 30 October and 1 November 1925.

12 SD, 1 November 1925; SP, vol. 3, file 4, memorandum of ODS, "Notes on the Political Situation," 31 October 1925.

13 ODS, "Notes on the Political Situation"; SP, vol. 3, file 4, memorandum of ODS, "The Customs Tariff," n.d.

14 SD, 2 November 1925.

15 Neatby, *The Lonely Heights*, 79–84; KD, 2–4 November 1925.

16 SD, 3 November 1925; KD, 2 November 1925.

17 SP, vol. 3, file 4, memorandum of ODS, "Notes," and ODS to King, both of 3 November 1925.

18 KD, 8 November 1925; SD, 5–6 and 10 November 1925; SP, vol. 3, file 4, memoranda of ODS, ["Prime Ministers of Canada: Electoral Vicissitudes"] and "Practice in Great Britain as to Action of Government following a General Election," both n.d. See also SD, 4 November 1925; KD, 4 November 1925.

19 SD, 6–7 and 10 November 1925.

20 SD, 13–17 November 1925 and 10 January 1926; KD, 17 November 1925.

21 KP, J1, vol. 139, reel C-2293, 118226–59, memorandum of ODS, "The Locarno Treaties / Proposed Imperial Conference," 1 January 1926. See also SD, 7 January 1926; C.P. Stacey, *Canada and the Age of Conflict*, vol. 2: *1921–1948, The Mackenzie King Era* (Toronto: University of Toronto Press 1981), 79–80; and KP, reel C-2284, J1, vol. 125, 106601, ODS to King, 30 December 1925.

22 ODS, "The Locarno Treaties"; SD, 1 January 1926.

23 SD, 6–7 January 1926; KP, J1, vol. 139, 118226, ODS to King, 1 January 1926. See also Stacey, *Canada and the Age of Conflict*, 79–80.

24 SD, 1, 2, 7, and 29 January 1926 and 1 February 1926. On Isabel's dislike of public life, see QUA, Isabel Skelton Papers, box 3, "Daily Journals 1926," entry of 1 March 1926.

25 SD, 6 January 1926; SP, vol. 3, file 9, King to ODS, 24 and 25 November 1925.

26 SD, 6, 8, and 12 January 1926; House of Commons, *Debates*, 8 January 1926.

27 SD, 28 January 1926; SP, vol. 3, file 4, King to Woodsworth, ODS handwritten draft, 20 January 1926, and ODS memorandum to King, n.d.; Neatby, *The Lonely Heights*, 110–11.

28 SD, 27 January and 1–2 February 1926. See also ibid., 17 September and 16 December 1925 and 23 June 1926; Neatby, *The Lonely Heights*, 112–14.

29 SD, 26–27 June 1926; KD, 26 June 1926.

30 SD, 28 June 1926; KD, 27 June 1926. Neatby, *The Lonely Heights*, 147–8, reviews the constitutionality of Lord Byng's decision making.

31 SD, 1 and 5 July 1926; Roger Graham, *Arthur Meighen*, vol. 2: *And Fortune Fled* (Toronto: Clarke, Irwin and Company 1963), ch. 16.

32 SD, 2, 22, and 26–27 July 1926. Allan Levine, sharing Skelton's horror at King's relationship with Mrs Bleaney, discusses the prime minister's meetings with the soothsayer in 1925 and 1929–30 but does not mention the 1926 encounter. *King: William Lyon Mackenzie King. A Life Guided by the Hand of Destiny* (Vancouver/Toronto: Douglas and McIntyre 2011), 1–2, 139–40, 143–5, 187–8, and 196–7.

33 SD, 9 and 13 July 1926. See also ibid., 10–11 and 15 July 1926.

34 LAC, J.W. Dafoe Papers, reel M-74, ODS to Dafoe, 6 October 1926; KD, 24 September 1926. See also SD, 10 July 1926.

35 Ottawa *Journal*, 16 February 1926; LAC, DEA Records, RG 25, vol. 3423, file 1926–93, ODS to J. Reid Hyde, 5 October 1926. See also SP, vol. 3, file 16, ODS to IS, 9 October 1926, and KD, 24 September 1926.

36 DEA Records, RG 25, vol. 3422, file 1-1926/80, memorandum of ODS, "Notes on the Imperial Conference, 1926," n.d.

37 SP, vol. 3, file 16, ODS to IS, 14 October 1926: KD, 11 October 1926. On Hose and Skelton, see SD, 26 January and 19 July 1926.

38 ODS to IS, 14 October 1926.

39 SP, vol. 3, file 16, ODS to IS, 19 October 1926. On Doughty, see SD, 10 January 1926.

40 ODS to IS, 19 October 1926; SP, vol. 3, file 16, ODS to IS, 4 November 1926.

41 Ramsay Cook, ed., "A Canadian Account of the 1926 Imperial Conference," *Journal of Commonwealth Political Studies*, 3, 1 (March, 1965): 55.

42 SP, vol. 3, file 16, ODS to IS, 28 October 1926; Dafoe Papers, reel M-74, ODS to J.W. Dafoe, 8 January 1927; Philip Wigley and Norman Hillmer, "Defining

the First British Commonwealth: The Hankey Memoranda on the 1926 Imperial Conference," in Norman Hillmer and Philip Wigley, eds., *The First British Commonwealth: Essays in Honour of Nicholas Mansergh* (London: Frank Cass 1980), 105–16. The most detailed study of the drafting of the Balfour Report is in H. Duncan Hall, *Commonwealth: A History of the British Commonwealth of Nations* (London: Van Nostrand Reinhold 1971), ch. 20.

43 ODS to Dafoe, 8 January 1927. On Skelton's small role in the drafting of the Balfour "equal in status" formula, see DEA Records, RG 25, vol. 3418, file 1–1926/12, memorandum and notations of Marjorie McKenzie (various dates) and attached documents from the 1926 Imperial Conference.

44 Wigley and Hillmer, "Defining the First British Commonwealth," 106.

45 Cook, "A Canadian Account of the 1926 Imperial Conference," 61; SP, vol. 3, file 16, ODS to IS, 19 and 28 October and 4 and 10 November 1926.

46 ODS to IS, 19 and 28 October 1926.

47 ODS to IS, 4 and 10 November 1926.

48 ODS to IS, 10 November 1926; SP, vol. 3, file 16, ODS to IS, 19 November 1926.

49 ODS, "Notes on the Imperial Conference." See also SP, vol. 3, file 16, IS to her family, 21 November 1926.

50 Norman Hillmer, "A British High Commissioner for Canada, 1927–28," *Journal of Imperial and Commonwealth History*, 1, 3 (May 1973): 339–56; ODS, "Notes on the Imperial Conference."

51 Norman Hillmer, "The Foreign Office, the Dominions and the Diplomatic Unity of the Empire, 1925–29," in David N. Dilks, ed., *Retreat from Power: Studies in Britain's Foreign Policy of the Twentieth Century*, vol. 1: *1906–1939* (London: Macmillan 1981), 66 and, generally, 65–6. See also SP, vol. 3, file 16, ODS to IS, 12 November 1926; Neatby Papers, unpublished manuscript of James Eayrs, "The Imperial Conference of 1926, II," 158–9. On ODS and Hurst, see SP, vol. 2, file 25, ODS to IS, 21 September 1924.

52 NAUK, CAB 32/57, Committee on Inter-Imperial Relations, Treaty Procedure Sub-Committee, Minutes, Meeting 1, 28 October; Meeting 4, 5 November; Meeting 6, 8 November 1926.

53 Treaty Procedure Sub-Committee, 5 November 1926.

54 ODS to Dafoe, 8 January 1927; Dafoe Papers, reel M-74, Dafoe to ODS, 9 December 1926; Imperial Conference 1926, *Summary of Proceedings* (Ottawa: F.A. Acland 1926), 14–16.

55 SP, vol. 3, file 16, ODS to IS, 23 November 1926.

56 Ibid.; SP, vol. 3, file 16, ODS to IS, 19 November 1926.

57 SP, vol. 3, file 18, ODS to Lord Willingdon, 13 December 1926 (draft). See also SP, vol. 2, file 25, ODS to IS, 16 September 1924, and SD, 2 July 1926. On the deterioration of the health of Skelton's father, compare the

handwriting in SP, vol. 3, file 18, Jeremiah to ODS and IS, 9 October and 23 and 30 November 1926. The Kingston *Whig-Standard* published an obituary of Jeremiah Skelton on 8 December 1926.

58 Isabel Skelton Papers, IS Diary, 2 November 1939.

8. Inching towards Independence, 1927–9

1 QUA, Isabel Skelton Papers, ISS, clipping from Montreal *Standard*, 17 March 1928.

2 LAC, SP, vol. 11, SD, 4 January 1926, and Claude Bissell, *The Young Vincent Massey* (Toronto: University of Toronto Press 1981), 123–4.

3 University of Toronto Archives, Vincent Massey Papers, B87–0082/012 (13), ODS to Massey, 8 February 1927.

4 LAC, KP, J4, vol. 59, file 380, reel C-2478, C45711–14, ODS, "Notes on the Washington Legation Appropriations," [March 1927]; ODS to Massey, 8 February 1927.

5 ODS, "Notes on the Washington Legation Appropriations"; Vincent Massey, *What's Past Is Prologue: The Memoirs of the Right Honourable Vincent Massey* (Toronto: Macmillan 1963), 129–34; information from Claude Bissell and H.L. Keenleyside.

6 ODS, "Notes on the Washington Legation Appropriations."

7 Massey Papers, B87–0082/012 (07), ODS, "Memorandum to the Prime Minister in Council," with prime minister's minute, attached to ODS to Massey, 19 March 1927, and External Affairs to Massey, 21 March 1927; ODS to Massey, 16 April 1927, in Massey, *What's Past Is Prologue*, 132–4.

8 Massey to King, 21 May 1927, and ODS to Massey, 23 May 1927, in Massey, *What's Past Is Prologue*, 135–7.

9 Massey Papers, B87–0082/385 (006), ODS to Massey, 13 August 1928, and reply of 15 August 1928. On Skelton's sartorial preferences, see Massey, *What's Past Is Prologue*, 251–2.

10 Massey Papers, Diary, 20 May 1929. Professor Claude Bissell generously guided me through the Massey Diary. Glimpses into the Skelton-Massey relationship can be found in the Massey Papers, B87–0082/385 (006), ODS to Massey, 8 April 1929, and B87–0082/181 (03), ODS to Massey, 21 January 1939. See also Massey, *What's Past Is Prologue*, 130 and 134–5.

11 Department of Foreign Affairs, Trade and Development, Records of the Historical Section, transcript of J.D. Hickerson-Robert Bothwell interview, 12 December 1978; John F. Hilliker, *Canada's Department of External Affairs*, vol. 1: *The Early Years, 1909–1946* (Montreal and Kingston, Ont.: McGill-Queen's University Press 1990), 118–19.

12 See Martin Weil, *A Pretty Good Club: The Founding Fathers of the U.S. Foreign Service* (New York: Norton 1978), chs. 1 and 3; Keith Hamilton and Richard Langhorne, *The Practice of Diplomacy: Its Evolution, Theory and Administration* (London and New York: Routledge 1995), 169–72.

13 Hilliker, *Canada's Department of External Affairs*, 119–20. The job-poster extract is in J.L. Granatstein, *A Man of Influence: Norman A. Robertson and Canadian Statecraft, 1929–68* ([Toronto]: Deneau 1981), 25. A copy of Skelton's foreign-service examination, as it had evolved by 1933, is printed in *bout de papier*, 2, 2 (June 1984).

14 Hilliker, *Canada's Department of External Affairs*, 120.

15 LAC, Norman Robertson Papers, vol. 15, Robertson to his mother, 18 July 1927.

16 Massey Papers, B87–0082/387 (07), ODS to Massey, 27 July 1928; John English, *Shadow of Heaven: The Life of Lester Pearson*, vol. 1: *1897–1948* (Toronto: Lester and Orpen Dennys 1989), 137–40; L.B. Pearson, *Mike: The Memoirs of the Right Honourable Lester B. Pearson*, vol. 1: *1897–1948* (Toronto: University of Toronto Press 1972), 59.

17 Gilles Lalande, *The Department of External Affairs and Biculturalism* (Ottawa: Queen's Printer 1969), 77, 81; Hilliker, *Canada's Department of External Affairs*, 123.

18 NAUK, FO 627/11/U291, Whiskard to Hadow, 30 April 1929; information from Jean Chapdelaine and Charles Ritchie; Hilliker, *Canada's Department of External Affairs*, 121–2; *Le Devoir*, 12 April 1929.

19 H.L. Keenleyside, *Memoirs of Hugh L. Keenleyside*, vol. 1: *Hammer the Golden Day* (Toronto: McClelland and Stewart 1981), 229–31; Hilliker, *Canada's Department of External Affairs*, 83, 103–4, 124, 142, and 243–4; Margaret K. Weiers, *Envoys Extraordinary: Women of the Canadian Foreign Service* (Toronto: Dundurn 1994), 13–34.

20 Keenleyside, *Memoirs of Hugh L. Keenleyside*, 217–18 and 233; English, *Shadow of Heaven*, 140 and 150; Pearson, *Mike*, 71.

21 Massey Papers, B87–0082/182 (07), ODS to Massey, 13 April 1939.

22 SP, vol. 11, SD, 4 March 1926.

23 Hilliker, *Canada's Department of External Affairs*, 119, 122–3, and 127; Pearson, *Mike*, 70–71; Keenleyside, *Memoirs of Hugh L. Keenleyside*, 215–18 and 231–44; information from J.W. Pickersgill.

24 Keenleyside, *Memoirs of Hugh L. Keenleyside*, 241–4.

25 KP, J4, vol. 112, file 799, C84216–24, memorandum of ODS, "Notes on Legations," n.d.

26 W.L.M. King, "Canada's Legations Abroad," *Canadian Nation*, 2, 1 (March–April 1929): 5–7, 24–6. The article was beyond any doubt written by Skelton;

it was widely publicized in the British press and parts were printed in the
Ottawa *Citizen*, 22 October 1929; see FO 627/12/U229 and NAUK, DO
114/22/25.

27 ODS, "Notes on Legations." On Coolidge, see SD, 19 March 1926.
28 ODS, "Notes on Legations."
29 Ibid.; House of Commons, *Debates*, 31 January and 11 June 1928; Patricia
   E. Roy, *The Oriental Question: Consolidating a White Man's Province, 1914–41*
   (Vancouver: University of British Columbia Press 2003), 83–8; Tou Chu Dou
   Lynhiavu, "Canada's Window on Asia: The Establishment of the Tokyo Lega-
   tion in 1928–1931," *Journal of Canadian Studies*, 31 (1996–7): 97–123. On
   Canadian representation in Japan as a hobby of the prime minister's, see
   Massey Papers, B87–0082/387 (07), ODS to Massey, 31 December 1927.
30 H.B. Neatby Papers, memorandum of ODS, 2 January 1929.
31 FO 627/2/U205, Clark to L.S. Amery, 20 March 1929; FO 627/6/U174,
   Hadow to British Embassy in Tokyo, 12 March 1929; FO 627/6/U390,
   Hadow to H.F. Batterbee, 10 June 1929.
32 FO 627/2/U158, telegram: Clark to secretary of state for dominion affairs,
   19 March 1929; KD, 18 March 1929.
33 Neatby Papers, ODS working file, "Basis of Diplomatic Appointments," for
   example, memorandum of ODS, 8 March 1929.
34 FO 627/2/U205, minutes of P.A. Koppel, Chamberlain, and Montgomery,
   11 April 1929; FO 627/2 /U229, minutes of Maxse, 18 April 1929. For a full
   account of this little crisis in Anglo-Canadian relations, see Norman Hillmer, "The Foreign Office, the Dominions and the Diplomatic Unity of the
   Empire, 1925–29," in David N. Dilks, ed., *Retreat from Power: Studies in Britain's
   Foreign Policy of the Twentieth Century*, vol. 1: *1906–1939* (London: Macmillan
   1981), 64–77. Note also, on how resistance shaped the manner in which
   empires worked, Danielle Kinsey, "Assessing Imperialism," in John McNeill
   and Kenneth Pomeranz, eds., *The Cambridge History of the World*, vol. 7
   (Cambridge: Cambridge University Press 2015), 347–50.
35 SP, vol. 11, SD, 31 May 1927. "Disagreeable" is in ibid., SD, 18 May 1925.
36 KD, 1 March 1928. See also ibid., 5 and 10 January and 1 March 1927, 3–4
   July and 29 December 1928, 22 January, 26 February, 15 and 17 March 1929,
   and 21 January 1930; SD, 3 November 1927; SP, vol. 3, file 25, memoranda
   of ODS, "Budget Speech," 9 April 1929, "Note to Prime Minister," n.d., and
   "Proposed United States Tariff Changes," n.d.
37 LAC, DEA Records, RG 25, vol. 1436, file 1163-A-25, ODS, "Memorandum for the Prime Minister," 8 January 1927; KP, J4, vol. 113, file 802, reel
   C-2711, C83260–2, memorandum of ODS, "Canada and the Council of the
   League of Nations," [early June 1927]; KP, J4, vol. 113, file 806, reel C-2712,

C83930–1, memorandum of ODS, "Seat on Council of League of Nations," 13 July 1927.

38 SD, 7 June 1927; ODS, "Canada and the Council of the League of Nations" and "Seat on Council of League of Nations."

39 SD, 19 June 1927, ODS, "Seat on Council of League of Nations," and Cecil Hurst et al., *Great Britain and the Dominions* (Chicago, 1928). On O'Higgins, see SD, 10–11 June 1927; compare KD, 11 June 1927.

40 Lorna Lloyd, "'Another National Milestone': Canada's 1927 Election to the Council of the League of Nations," *Diplomacy & Statecraft*, 21 (2010): 656–8; H.B. Neatby, *William Lyon Mackenzie King*, vol. 2: *1924–1932, The Lonely Heights* (Toronto: University of Toronto Press 1963), 194–5; KP, J1, vol. 149, reel C-2301, 127129–30, ODS to King, 19 August 1927. See also John MacFarlane, *Ernest Lapointe and Quebec's Influence on Canadian Foreign Policy* (Toronto: University of Toronto Press 1999), 69–72. MacFarlane vigorously promotes his subject's importance, but the claim that Mackenzie King "contributed to the advancement of Canadian autonomy in the 1920s largely because of pressure from Lapointe" (73) is not credible. There was a complex of factors bearing down on the making of external policy, the prime minister's own cautious nationalism not the least.

41 KP, vol. 149, reel C-2301, 127132–5, ODS to King, 19 September 1927; FO 800/261/316–19, Chamberlain to Tyrrell, 15 September 1927; Lorna Lloyd, "Council," 659–63, and her "Le Sénateur Dandurand, pionnier du règlement pacifique des differends," *Revue Études Internationales*, 23, 3 (September 1992): 593; R. Speaight, *Vanier: Soldier, Diplomat and Governor General* (Bungay, U.K.: Collins 1970), 134.

42 ODS to King, 19 September 1927; KP, vol. 149, reel C-2301, 127136–8, ODS to King, 27 September 1927. LAC, Ernest Lapointe Papers, vol. 10, file 52, has an ODS note on the letter of 19 September 1927. On ODS and Dandurand, see SD, 13 March 1926; SP, vol. 3, file 20, ODS to IS, 10 September 1927. See also Dominion of Canada, *Report of the Canadian Delegates to the Eighth Assembly of the League of Nations, September 5 to 27, 1927* (Ottawa: F.A. Acland 1928), 5–6, and on ODS, 3–4, 7, and 12–13.

43 SP, vol. 3, file 16, ODS to IS, 4 November 1926, and file 20, ODS to IS, 10 September 1927; Escott Reid, *Radical Mandarin: The Memoirs of Escott Reid* (Toronto: University of Toronto Press 1989), 41; "Snag Skelton of Athletic and Academic Fame at Queen's Wins a Rhodes Scholarship to Oxford," *Queen's Journal*, 26 September 1926; KP, J1, vol. 149, reel C-2301, 127129–30, ODS to King, 19 August 1927.

44 QUA, Isabel Skelton Papers, IS Diary, 6 and 14 October 1927, and October generally. See also ODS to IS, 10 September 1927; ODS to King, 27

September 1927; and DO 35/29/D10160, "Extract from a Note of a Discussion with Dr. Skelton," 14 October 1927.

45 SP, vol. 3, file 22, ODS to IS, 22 August 1928.

46 Ibid.

47 SP, vol. 3, file 22, ODS to IS, 28 August 1928. See also Stephen Roskill, *Hankey: Man of Secrets*, vol. 2: *1919–1931* (London: Collins 1972), 469, and, on the Kellogg-Briand ceremony, Gérard Unger, *Aristide Briand: le ferme conciliateur* (Paris: Fayard 2005), 534–6.

48 The three paragraphs that follow are based on KP, J4, vol. 140, file 1140, reel C-2727, C101966–73 and C102030–5, memoranda of ODS, "Multilateral Pact against the War," [June] 1928, and "The General Treaty for the Renunciation of War," 16 February 1929. King's speech to the House of Commons, 19 February 1929, on the Kellogg-Briand treaty made liberal use of Skelton's words and reasoning.

49 SP, vol. 3, file 22, IS to ODS, 27 August 1928.

50 ODS to IS, 28 August 1928; SP, vol. 3, file 22, ODS to IS, 25 August 1928.

51 SP, vol. 3, file 22, ODS to IS, 30 August and 4 and 10 September 1928. Canada, *Report of the Canadian Delegates to the Ninth Assembly of the League of Nations, September 3 to 26, 1928* (Ottawa: F.A. Acland 1929), 4, and, on ODS specifically, 8–10, 19–21. Skelton's handwritten draft for the prime minister's Assembly address was found in SP, vol. 2, file 24, incorrectly catalogued.

52 ODS to IS, 30 August 1928; H.S. Ferns, *Reading from Left to Right: One Man's Political History* (Toronto: University of Toronto Press 1983), 174; Rhodes House Library, Oxford, Rhodes Scholars' Files, Douglas Alexander Skelton file, Skelton to F.J. Wylie, 23 December 1927, and 1928 Skelton activities report.

53 DEA Records, RG 25, vol. 3425, file 1–1929/21, ODS to Lapointe, 17 November 1928; memorandum of ODS, 17 November 1928, and ODS to Ewart, 29 June 1929; National Archives of the Republic of Ireland, Records of the Department of External Affairs, D5340 (DFA), ODS to Sean Murphy, 22 November 1928, and reply of 23 January 1929; DEA Records, RG 25, vol. 3425, files 1–1929/13–14, containing Ewart memoranda.

54 Archives of the University College Dublin, Blythe Papers, P24/546(3), J.M. Costello to J.M. O'Sullivan, 7 October 1929; SP, vol. 3, file 26, ODS to IS, 4 and 6 October 1929; D.W. Harkness, *The Restless Dominion: The Irish Free State and the British Commonwealth of Nations, 1921–31* (London: Macmillan 1969), 148n1.

55 SP, vol. 3, file 26, ODS to IS, 9 October 1929; KP, reel C-2314, J1, vol. 169, 143821–5, ODS to King, 12 October 1929; KP, J4, vol. 134, file 1059, reel C-2723, C97519–49, memorandum of ODS, "Notes on Conference on

Operation of Dominion Legislation and Merchant Shipping," December 1929. See also W.N. Medlicott, *Contemporary England* (London: Longman 1967), 294.

56 NAUK, CAB 32/69, Conference on the Operation of Dominion Legislation and Merchant Shipping Legislation, DL, minutes, meetings of 1 and 8 October 1929.

57 ODS, "Notes on Conference on Operation of Dominion Legislation and Merchant Shipping"; SP, vol. 3, file 27, ODS to IS, 10 November 1929; Archives of the University College Dublin, P.J. McGilligan Papers P35/161, "Secession," meeting of Gwyer Committee, ODL, 14 November 1929.

58 SP, vol. 3, file 26, ODS to IS, 19 October 1929; file 27, ODS to IS, 25 October 1929; and, generally, files 26–27, ODS to IS, 2 October–1 December 1929.

59 SP, vol. 3, file 27, ODS to IS, 20 October 1929; ibid., file 26, ODS to IS, 2 and 16 October 1929.

60 SP, vol. 3, file 27, ODS to IS, 22 October 1929; SP, vol. 12, SD, 10 April 1929.

61 ODS to IS, 16 October 1929.

62 Norman Hillmer, "The ODL, 1929: A Neglected Imperial Conference," *Bulletin of Canadian Studies*, 6, 2–7, 1 (autumn 1983; Philip Wigley Memorial Issue): 15–24; Great Britain, Secretary of State for Dominion Affairs, *Report of the Conference on the Operation of Dominion Legislation and Merchant Shipping Legislation, 1929* (London: His Majesty's Stationery Office 1930). On the ODL as "less a gathering of legal experts" than a "specialist imperial conference," where "deliberations were often highly political," see W. David McIntyre, *The Britannic Vision: Historians and the Making of the British Commonwealth of Nations, 1907–48* (Basingstoke, U.K.: Palgrave Macmillan 2009), 178–84.

63 House of Commons, *Debates*, 31 March and 9 September 1939. Lapointe added that Canadians could change that state of affairs if they wished, but they did not wish it.

64 See SP, vol. 12, file 2, SD, 6 April 1929.

9. Life with RB, 1930–3

1 F.W. Gibson, *Queen's University*, vol. 2: *1917–1961, To Serve and Yet Be Free* (Montreal and Kingston, Ont.: McGill-Queen's University Press 1983), 85–6.

2 *Queen's Review*, 2, 8 (December 1928): 266; D.D. Calvin, *Queen's University at Kingston* (Kingston, Ont.: Queen's University 1941), 162.

3 Gibson, *To Serve and Yet Be Free*, 15 and 51–9.

4 LAC, SP, vol. 3, file 21, Clark to ODS, 22 June 1929.

5 Ibid., ODS to Clark, 17 July 1929. See also SP, vol. 3, file 16, ODS to IS, 4 November 1926.

6 ODS to Clark, 17 July 1929; Gibson, *To Serve and Yet Be Free*, 85.
7 KD, 6 and 10 February 1930; KP, J1, vol. 182, reel C-2323, 155121–2, ODS to King, 8 February 1930; Gibson, *To Serve and Yet Be Free*, 86.
8 ODS to King, 8 February 1930.
9 SP, vol. 12, SD, 5 March 1929.
10 Gibson, *To Serve and Yet Be Free*, 88–9.
11 John Hilliker, *Canada's Department of External Affairs*, vol. 1: *The Early Years, 1909–1946* (Montreal and Kingston, Ont.: McGill-Queen's University Press 1990), 137. On the election of 1930, see Larry Glassford, *Reaction and Reform: The Politics of the Conservative Party under R. B. Bennett, 1927–1938* (Toronto: University of Toronto Press 1992), ch. 4.
12 University of Toronto Archives, Vincent Massey Papers, B87–0082/192 (05), Bassett to Massey, 19 July 1938; National Archives of Scotland, Lothian Papers, GD 40/17, J.A. Stevenson to Lothian, [1933]. On Skelton's liking for Bennett, see SD, 15 and 29 April 1929.
13 LAC, R.B. Bennett Papers, M-3172, 593759, Bennett to Grote Stirling, 15 April 1941. "Cheerfully" comes from the transcript of an interview with J.E. Read, who in 1930 was the External Affairs legal adviser; the document lacks a date and the name of the interviewer. LAC, J.E. Read Papers, vol. 10. See Hilliker, *Canada's Department of External Affairs*, 137, for a balanced discussion of the implications of Bennett's election victory for Skelton and his department.
14 SP, vol. 12, SD, 13 August and 1 September 1930 and, generally, 13 August–2 September 1930.
15 Ibid., 18 August 1930.
16 Read interview.
17 Bennett to Stirling, 15 April 1941; SD, 13 August–2 September 1930; Hilliker, *Canada's Department of External Affairs*, 137.
18 Norman Hillmer, "Anglo-Canadian Relations 1926–1937: A Study of Canada's Role in the Shaping of Commonwealth Policies," PhD thesis, University of Cambridge, 1974, 163–70. See also SP, vol. 12, SD, 3 January 1931; DEA Records, RG 25, vol. 3428, file 1–1930/32, Department of External Affairs, "Imperial Conference, 1930," 8 August 1930. France's representatives in Canada, never well connected, seldom engaged ODS or mentioned him in dispatches, but the chargé d'affaires at the Legation in Ottawa did go out of his way to inform Paris that Skelton would not be part of the Canadian delegation to the Imperial Conference of 1930 because of his Liberal ties. Archives du Ministère des Affaires Étrangères, Fonds de la Correspondence Politique et Commerciale, reel P12783, H. Coursier to Quai d'Orsay, 24 September 1930.

19 H.B. Neatby Papers, memorandum of ODS, "Canadian Representation Abroad," 27 December 1930. "I am Minister of External Affairs," Bennett told the League of Nations Society in 1934, "by a statute, not by choice." *Interdependence*, 2, 2 (1934): 59.

20 SD, 18 August 1930 and 26 February and 19 May 1931.

21 SD, 22 August 1930, 1–2 and 29 January, and 24 February 1931; SP, vol. 4, file 14, ODS to IS, 27 February 1933. The Arch Dale cartoon was published on 19 January 1931 and reproduced in *Five Years of R.B. Bennett with Arch Dale of the Winnipeg Free Press* (1935).

22 SP, vol. 4, file 10, IS to her mother, 20 February 1931. "Long-haired professors" is from Bennett to Stevens, 31 January and 18 May 1931, in Richard Wilbur, *H.H. Stevens, 1878–1973* (Toronto: University of Toronto Press 1977), 93.

23 SD, 29 January, 5 February (both typed and handwritten versions), 14 February, and 10 October 1931.

24 SD, 26 February 1931; SP, vol. 4, file 10, IS to her mother, 10 April 1931; Christopher Armstrong, *The Politics of Federalism: Ontario's Relations with the Federal Government, 1867–1942* (Toronto: University of Toronto Press 1981), 147–9.

25 SD, 9 January 1931.

26 Ibid., 21, 23, and 26 September and 14, 15, and 18 October 1931; Robert B. Bryce, *Maturing in Hard Times: Canada's Department of Finance through the Great Depression* (Montreal and Kingston, Ont.: McGill-Queen's University Press 1986), 124–30.

27 LAC, Canadian Political Science Association (CPSA) Papers, vol. 1, minutes of the Annual Business Meeting of the CPSA, Chateau Laurier Hotel, Ottawa, 20 May 1930; QUA, Isabel Skelton Papers, ISS, unidentified clippings of 21 May 1930. On Leacock, see SD, 30 August 1930, and Margaret MacMillan, *Stephen Leacock* (Toronto: Penguin Canada 2009), 89–90 and 138. Leacock's social criticism is examined by Ramsay Cook in "Stephen Leacock and the Age of Plutocracy, 1903–1921," in John S. Moir, ed., *Character and Circumstance: Essays in Honour of Donald Grant Creighton* (Toronto: Macmillan 1970), 163–81. Like ODS, Leacock had his doctorate from the University of Chicago and had been a student of Thorstein Veblen. Veblen's influence seems to have run deeper in Leacock than it did in Skelton.

28 SP, vol. 4, file 10, W.H. Fyfe to Skelton, 25 April 1931, with attached eulogy of 6 May 1931. CPSA Papers, vol. 1, minutes of meetings of the CPSA, Ottawa, 18 May 1922, 25 May 1923, and 23 May 1929; SD, 1 and 10 January 1931; S.E.D. Shortt, *The Search for an Ideal: Six Canadian Intellectuals and Their Convictions in an Age of Transition 1890–1930* (Toronto: University of Toronto Press 1976), 116.

29 ODS, "Is Our Economic System Bankrupt?" *Papers and Proceedings of the Annual Meeting of the CPSA*, 3 (Ottawa, 1931): 67–87.
30 SD, 11, 14, and 15 February, 11 and 29 March, 17, 28, and 29 May, 17 September and 11 and 31 October 1931.
31 SD, 4 February, 17 and 19 September and 12 and 25 October 1931; SP, vol. 12, SD, February 1932.
32 SD, 7 January, 25 February, 3 March, 11–13 June, and 9, 17, and 23 October 1931.
33 SD, 8 April 1929, 14 June, 19 September 1931, 1 January 1932, and 2 February 1933; ISS, Montreal *Star*, 30 December 1930, and Ottawa *Citizen*, 6 February 1933.
34 SD, 17 April 1929 and 18 January 1934; SP, vol. 3, files 26–7, ODS to IS, 9 October and 12 November 1929; Rhodes House Library, Oxford, Rhodes Scholars' Files, Douglas Alexander Skelton file, "Report to the Selection Committee, 1927–1928." Sandy Skelton, then a senior official at the Department of Trade and Commerce, died in the waters off Lagos, Nigeria, in July 1950. The warden of Rhodes House wrote that Skelton "was an interesting example of a man who somehow did not seem to take to Oxford, but most certainly justified himself in later life." Rhodes Scholars' Files, Skelton file, warden to D.R. Michener, 16 August 1950. See also A.W. Currie to J.L. Granatstein, 31 August 1982 (copy kindly provided by Professor Granatstein).
35 SD, 16–18 July 1931; *The Canadian Who's Who*, 4 (Toronto, 1948): 866. T.D. Regehr's *The Beauharnois Scandal: A Story of Canadian Entrepreneurship and Politics* (Toronto: University of Toronto Press 1989) does not mention Sandy Skelton.
36 SD, 11 October, 2 and 11 November 1931, and 3 February 1932; SP, vol. 12, SD, 5 January 1934; *Queen's Journal*, 11 October 1931.
37 SP, vol. 4, file 11, ODS to William Herridge, 10 December 1931.
38 Ibid., IS to her mother, n.d.
39 NAUK, Board of Trade Records (BT) 11/58, F.W. Field to Sir William Clark, 11 March 1932; J.L. Granatstein, *The Ottawa Men: The Civil Service Mandarins, 1935–1957* (Toronto: Oxford University Press 1982), 28, 43–4, and 289n.86; I.M. Drummond, *Imperial Economic Policy 1917–1939: Studies in Expansion and Protection* (London: Allen and Unwin 1974), 192, 464; Bryce, *Maturing in Hard Times*, 80–1; Robert A. Wardhaugh, with Douglas MacEwan and William Johnston, *Behind the Scenes: The Life and Work of William Clifford Clark* (Toronto: University of Toronto Press 2010), 61–72.
40 IS to her mother, n.d; NAUK, DO 114/42/136–7, telegram: U.K. high commissioner in Canada to Dominions Office, 19 May 1932; Drummond, *Imperial Economic Policy*, 94–5, 192, and 194.

41 Norman Hillmer and J.L. Granatstein, *Empire to Umpire: Canada and the World into the Twentieth Century* (Toronto: Thomson Nelson 2008), 106–7; Hillmer, "Anglo-Canadian Relations," 199–200.

42 SP, vol. 4, file 11, IS to her mother, 21 August 1932; see also Imperial Economic Conference, 1932, *Report of the Conference* (Ottawa: F.A. Acland 1932), 63; Imperial Economic Conference, Ottawa, 1932, *General Directory* and *Report of the Conference* (Ottawa: F.A. Acland 1932). The closing conference speeches (*Report*, 147–58) praised ODS, but not so generously as Isabel advertised to her mother.

43 SP, files 6–7, SD, 2–3 January 1933 and 1 January 1934. See also P.B. Waite, *The Loner: Three Sketches of the Personal Life and Ideas of R.B. Bennett 1870–1947* (Toronto: University of Toronto Press 1992), 65–6.

44 SD, 26 February and 2 March 1931.

45 SP, vol. 4, file 14, IS to her mother, 1 February 1933; NAUK, FO 627/48/U59, telegram: Bennett to dominions secretary, 2 February 1933.

46 IS to her mother, 1 February 1933.

47 SP, vol. 4, file 14, ODS to IS, 21 February 1933.

48 SP, vol. 4, file 14, ODS to IS, 13 February 1933; DEA Records, RG 25, vol. 3432, file 1–1933/7, telegram: ODS to Bennett, 14 February 1933.

49 NAUK, CAB 32/118, Imperial Economic Conference, Committee on Economic Consultation and Co-operation, 1933, stenographic notes of 1st Meeting, 14 February 1933; SP, vol. 2, file 24 (misfiled under Geneva Conference, 1924), handwritten notes for opening address, Committee on Economic Consultation and Co-operation, 1933.

50 SP, vol. 4, file 15, ODS to IS, 10 March 1933; University of London, Institute of Commonwealth Studies Archives, Tallents Papers, ICS 79/7/3, UK Cabinet Paper (CP) 141 (33), dominions secretary's "Report of the Committee on Economic Consultation and Co-operation," 27 May 1933; see also the Canadian government's sceptical "Draft Report of Inter-Departmental Committee on the Existing Machinery for Inter-Imperial Co-operation," [1933], in DEA Records, RG 25, vol. 3432, file 1–1933/8A.

51 SP, vol. 4, file 14, ODS to IS, 21, 23, and 27 February 1933.

52 SP, vol. 4, file 15, ODS to IS, 21 March 1933; Committee on Economic Consultation and Co-operation, 1933, stenographic notes of 13th Meeting, 20 March 1933.

53 SP, vol. 4, file 15, ODS to IS, 26 and 30 March and 4 April 1933; DEA Records, RG 25, vol. 3432, file 1–1933/7, telegram: ODS to Bennett, 29 March 1933.

54 SP, vol. 4, file 15, ODS to IS, 4 April 1933; LAC, R.B. Bennett Papers, vol. 240, 160199–200, telegram: ODS to Bennett, 6 April 1933; London *Times*, 8

June 1933; Drummond, *Imperial Economic Policy*, 227–8. The Skelton Committee's findings were published as Cmd 4335, Imperial Committee on Economic Consultation and Co-operation, 1933, *Report* (London: His Majesty's Stationery Office 1933).

55 Skelton described his progress through the committee's meetings in SP, vol. 4, files 14–15, ODS to IS, 13 February–7 April 1933. See also DEA Records, RG 25, vol. 3432, file 1–1933/7, telegram: ODS to Bennett, 7 April 1933.

56 ODS to Bennett, 6 April 1933; Tallents Papers, ICS 79/8/1, 12 and 28, notes of Tallents, 11 April and 4 and 28 July 1933; DO 35/232/8671/73, "Monetary and Economic Conference, 1933, British Commonwealth Delegations," 13th Meeting, 28 July 1933.

57 DEA Records, RG 25, vol. 3432, file 1–1933/7, Bennett to ODS, 16 March 1933.

10. The Moderate Leaguer, 1933–5

1 LAC, DEA Records, RG 25, vol. 3432, file 1–1933/7, Bennett to Skelton, 16 March 1933. See also LAC, SP, vol. 4, file 15, ODS to IS, 15 and 19 March 1933; F.P. Walters, *A History of the League of Nations* (London: Oxford University Press 1969), 541.

2 SP, vol. 4, file 14, ODS to IS, 10 March 1933; ODS, "Is Our Economic System Bankrupt?" *Papers and Proceedings of the Annual Meeting of the CPSA*, 3 (Ottawa, 1931): 80, 86.

3 DEA Records, RG 25, vol. 1607, file 786–31C, ODS to Herbert Marler, 23 January 1932. The best study of the Manchurian crisis remains Christopher Thorne, *The Limits of Foreign Policy: The West, The League and the Far Eastern Crisis of 1931–1933* (New York: Putnam's 1973).

4 Alan Mason, "Canada and the Far Eastern Crisis, 1931–1933," a paper presented at the Canadian Historical Association Annual Meeting, 6 June 1974, 4–9; SD, 22–23 September 1931. On Marler's "ivory neck," see Charles Ritchie, *The Siren Years: A Canadian Diplomat Abroad 1937–1945* (Toronto: Macmillan 1974), 13.

5 SD, 2 March 1932; ODS to Marler, 23 January 1932.

6 SD, 13 October 1931; LAC, Norman Robertson Papers, vol. 10, file 100, ODS to Agnes Macphail, 4 March 1932; ODS to Marler, 23 January 1932.

7 SP, vol. 12, SD, 7 and 16 February 1932; LAC, N.W. Rowell Papers, vol. 8, 6063–6, ODS to Rowell, 1 March 1932.

8 ODS to Rowell, 1 March 1932; ODS to Macphail, 4 March 1932.

9 DEA Records, RG 25 D1, vol. 723, file 64, pt. 1–2, 1931–9, reel T-1748, memorandum of ODS, "Manchurian Question," 29 November 1932; ODS to Rowell, 1 March 1932; SD, 7 February 1932.

10 SD, 30 January and 16 and 19 February 1932.

11 Alan Mason, "Canada and the Manchurian Crisis," in Robert Bothwell and Norman Hillmer, eds., *The In-Between Time: Canadian External Policy in the 1930s* (Toronto: Copp Clark 1975), 114–16. See also ODS, "Manchurian Question," 29 November 1932; DEA Records, RG 25, D1, vol. 1607, file 786, pt. VII, telegram: Bennett to Canadian minister, Paris, 2 December 1932, which contained the Canadian League delegate's instructions.

12 DEA Records, RG 25, D1, vol. 1607, file 786, pt. VII, ODS to Chinese consul general in Canada, 13 December 1932; DEA Records, RG 25, D1, vol. 723, file 64, pt. 1–2 (1931–9), ODS to Herridge, 12 December 1932; Clara Thomas Archives and Special Collections, York University, W.A. Riddell Papers, vol. 1, Correspondence 1932–1934, ODS to Riddell, 7 January 1932.

13 See SP, vol. 12, SD, 4 January 1934, and John D. Meehan, *The Dominion and the Rising Sun: Canada Encounters Japan, 1929–41* (Vancouver: University of British Columbia Press 2004), 88; Riddell Papers, vol. 1, Correspondence, 1932–1934, ODS to Riddell, 24 December 1932.

14 Riddell Papers, vol. 4, Riddell Diary, 7 February 1932; Mason, "Canada and the Far Eastern Crisis," 31–2; Norman Hillmer, "Anglo-Canadian Relations 1926–1937: A Study of Canada's Role in the Shaping of Commonwealth Policies," PhD thesis, University of Cambridge, 1974, 241–2. Compare the accounts in Donald C. Story, "Canada, the League of Nations and the Far East, 1931–3: The Cahan Incident," *International History Review*, 3, 2 (April 1981): 251–3, and Meehan, *The Dominion and the Rising Sun*, 86–91.

15 Meehan, *The Dominion and the Rising Sun*, 93–4. On Bennett's view of the League, the authority is Donald Story. See his "Canada's Covenant: The Bennett Government, the League of Nations and Collective Security, 1930–1935," PhD thesis, University of Toronto, 1976.

16 SP, vol. 4, file 15, ODS to IS, 15 March 1933; Walters, *A History of the League of Nations*, 541–4; New York *Times*, 16 March 1933.

17 SP, vol. 4, file 15, ODS to IS, 19 March 1933; Donald Story, "Canada's Covenant," 136–8; David Marquand, *Ramsay MacDonald* (London: Jonathan Cape 1977), 754–5.

18 ODS to IS, 15 and 19 March 1933; SP, vol. 4, file 15, ODS to IS, 10 March 1933. See also DEA Records, RG 25, D1, vol. 766, file 311, "Note of a Meeting of the Delegations of the Members of the British Commonwealth of

Nations Held at the Hotel Beau Rivage, Geneva, at 5 p.m. on Wednesday 15th March, 1933," and Peter Oliver, *G. Howard Ferguson: Ontario Tory* (Toronto: University of Toronto Press 1977), 403.

19 Story, "Canada's Covenant," 138–9; LAC, KP, J1, vol. 198, 168954–7, reel C-3674, ODS to Bennett, telegrams of 31 March and 1 April 1933; SP, vol. 4, file 15, ODS to IS, 30 March 1933; SP, vol. 12, SD, 6 March 1933. The Ottawa *Citizen*, 24 March 1933, reported that ODS publicly called the MacDonald plan "very promising."

20 Riddell Diary, 15–16 March 1933; ODS to IS, 19 March 1933.

21 SD, 12 January 1934; see also ibid., 16 March 1932, 1 and 8 January and 19–20 February 1934; John F. Hilliker, *Canada's Department of External Affairs*, vol. 1: *The Early Years, 1909–1946* (Montreal and Kingston, Ont.: McGill-Queen's University Press 1990), 174; information from Charles Ritchie and L.B. Pearson.

22 Hilliker, *Canada's Department of External Affairs*, ch. 6, and ODS to Keenleyside, 27 April 1934, in E.M. Andrews, *The Writing on the Wall: The British Commonwealth and Aggression in the East 1931–1935* (Sydney, Australia: Allen and Unwin 1987), 20.

23 SD, 4 and 20 January 1934; information from Charles Ritchie. On Bennett and the DEA job competition in 1933–4, see P.B. Waite, *In Search of R.B. Bennett* (Montreal and Kingston, Ont.: McGill-Queen's University Press 2011), 192–3.

24 SD, 8 January 1934; DEA Records, RG 25, D1, vol. 793, file 454, ODS to Herridge, 2 February 1934.

25 SP, vol. 12, SD, 12 January 1935.

26 SP, vol. 4, file 18, ODS to IS, 1, 5, and 6 September 1934.

27 Ibid., ODS to IS, 14 and 16 September 1934.

28 SD, 8–9 February 1934; QUA, Isabel Skelton Papers, ISS, unidentified clipping of ODS Address to University Club, 3 May 1933; SP, vol. 4, file 21, memorandum of ODS, "Foreign Policy Discussions in London, 1935," [April] 1935.

29 ODS Address to University Club.

30 ODS to IS, 16 September 1934; Norman Hillmer, "Canada and the 'Godless Country,' 1930–1939," in David Davies, ed., *Canada and the Soviet Experiment: Essays on Canadian Encounters with Russia and the Soviet Union, 1900–1991* (Toronto: Canadian Scholars' Press 1994), 57–63. See also SP, vol. 12, SD, 26 February and 2 March 1931 and 6 January 1932; DEA Records, RG 25, D1, vol. 732, file 107, memorandum of ODS, "Admission of Russia into the League of Nations," 5 September 1936.

31 ODS to IS, 16 September 1934; SP, vol. 4, file 18, ODS to IS, 18 September 1934.

32 Ibid.; Hillmer, "Canada and the 'Godless Country,'" 57–8; ISS, clipping from Toronto *Star*, 18 September 1934. The ODS speech is in *Report of the Canadian Delegates to the Fifteenth Assembly of the League of Nations* (Ottawa: King's Printer 1935), 21–2.

33 ODS to IS, 18 September 1934; SP, vol. 4, file 18, ODS to IS, 25 September 1934.

34 ODS to IS, 21 September 1934; SP, vol. 4, file 18, ODS to IS, 14 September 1934. See *Report of the Canadian Delegates to the Fifteenth Assembly*, 22–3.

35 ODS to IS, 21 September 1934; SP, vol. 4, file 18, ODS to IS, 14 September 1934. See also SD, 19 February 1932.

36 ODS to IS, 14, 16, 18, and 21 September 1934; SP, vol. 4, file 18, 20 October 1934.

37 ODS, "Foreign Policy Discussions in London, 1935."

38 Ibid.

39 Ibid. See also Nicholas Mansergh, *Nationalism and Independence* (Cork, Ireland: Cork University Press 1997), 109.

40 ODS, "Foreign Policy Discussions in London, 1935."

41 Ibid. In the summer of 1931, Skelton had convinced Bennett to establish a Canadian Legation in China, but the prime minister quickly changed his mind. NAUK, DO 35/165/6210/22, Sir William Clark to Dominions Office, 9 July 1931; Norman Hillmer, ed., *O.D. Skelton: The Work of the World, 1923–1941* (Montreal and Kingston, Ont.: McGill-Queen's University Press; and Toronto: Champlain Society; both editions 2013), 225–32.

42 Story, "Canada's Covenant," 288; ODS, "Foreign Policy Discussions in London, 1935."

43 DEA Records, RG 25, G1, vol. 1718, file 927, pt. 1, ODS to W.D. Herridge, 23 August 1935; ODS, "Foreign Policy Discussions in London, 1935." For a survey of Quebec newspaper opinion, see Gwendolen M. Carter, *The British Commonwealth and International Security: The Role of the Dominions, 1919–1939* (Toronto: Ryerson Press 1947), 209.

44 Robert Bothwell and John English, "'Dirty Work at the Crossroads': New Perspectives on the Riddell Incident," Canadian Historical Association, *Historical Papers*, 1972, 266–7; Hillmer, "Anglo-Canadian Relations," 246–7.

45 KP, J4, vol. 164, file 1507, reel C-4260, 117300–5, memorandum of ODS, 24 August 1935.

46 LAC, Loring Christie Papers, 26/24126–59, memorandum of Christie, "Notes on the European Crisis," 5 October 1935; Bothwell and English, "'Dirty Work at the Crossroads,'" 264. On Christie's return to External Affairs, see National Archives of Scotland, Lothian Papers, GD 40/17/233, John Stevenson to Philip Kerr (later Lord Lothian), 14 May 1928, and

GD 40/17/305, Stevenson to Lothian, 2 September 1935; SD, 4 February 1932 and 10 January 1934. Robert Holland erroneously states, because that is what the British documents indicate, that Skelton brought the now-nationalist Christie back into the Department of External Affairs to prove to Mackenzie King that ODS had not become a British Empire enthusiast during the Bennett regime. *Britain and the Commonwealth Alliance, 1918–1939* (London: Macmillan 1981), 185. Hilliker, *Canada's Department of External Affairs*, 151, suggests that Prime Minister Bennett, with Skelton's support, invited Christie to return to government service.

47 Montreal *Gazette*, 7 September 1935, in C.P. Stacey, ed., *Historical Documents of Canada*, vol. 5: *The Arts of War and Peace 1914–1945* (Toronto: Macmillan 1972), 110; SD, 2, 7, and 22 January 1935. The definition of the New Deal comes from L.M. Grayson and Michael Bliss, eds., *The Wretched of Canada: Letters to R.B. Bennett, 1930–1935* (Toronto: University of Toronto Press 1973), xviii–xix.

48 Hillmer, "Anglo-Canadian Relations," 250–4; Bothwell and English, "'Dirty Work at the Crossroads,'" 268–72.

49 Richard Veatch, *Canada and the League of Nations* (Toronto: University of Toronto Press 1975), 146–7 and especially 191–2. See also telegram: Bennett to Geneva, 13 September 1935, in Alex I. Inglis, ed., *Documents on Canadian External Relations (DCER)*, vol. 5: *1931–1935* (Ottawa: Information Canada 1973), 383. An alternative explanation of Ferguson's actions is provided in Oliver, *G. Howard Ferguson*, 416–28.

50 "Note by Under-Secretary of State for External Affairs on a Telephone Conversation with Prime Minister," 10 October 1935, in A.I. Inglis, ed., *DCER*, 5: 391–2. See also Riddell Papers, vol. 1, Correspondence, Notes, 1935–1936, Riddell to External Affairs, 2 October 1935, and also memorandum of Riddell, and Bennett to Riddell, both 9 October 1935. For another Bennett-Skelton tussle over the League, during which the prime minister accused ODS of "welshing" on Canada's League commitments in September 1935, see Veatch, *Canada and the League of Nations*, 146–7 and 191–2.

51 See Bothwell and English, "'Dirty Work at the Crossroads,'" 269–70.

52 Larry A. Glassford, *Reaction and Reform: The Politics of the Conservative Party under R.B. Bennett, 1927–1938* (Toronto: University of Toronto Press 1992), ch. 7; SD, 2, 7, and 22 January 1935.

53 SP, vol. 4, file 18, ODS to IS, 1 September 1934.

54 SP, vol. 4, file 16, IS to ODS, 4 March 1934, and vol. 4, file 17, handwritten note of IS; ISS note on page 135, with unidentified clipping, 2 March 1934; SD, 1 January and 9 May 1934; Kingston *Whig-Standard*, 9 May 1934.

55 SP, vol. 4, file 23, IS to mother, 26 September 1935; SD, 10 January 1935; ISS, unidentified clippings of 13 April 1934 and 25 September 1935, with Isabel Skelton's notations; Hilliker, *Canada's Department of External Affairs*, 170.
56 For example, SP, vol. 4, file 24, ODS to IS, 23 July 1937.

11. Fortunate in Our Neighbours, 1935–6

1 F.W. Gibson, *Queen's University*, vol. 2: *1917–1961* (Montreal and Kingston, Ont.: McGill-Queen's University Press 1983), 139–40.
2 Ottawa *Citizen*, 9 October and 6 November 1935, Toronto *Star*, November 1935, and Ottawa *Journal*, 19 October 1935, all in QUA, Isabel Skelton Papers, ISS.
3 KD, 17 April 1936; John F. Hilliker, *Canada's Department of External Affairs*, vol. 1: *The Early Years, 1909–1946* (Montreal and Kingston, Ont.: McGill-Queen's University Press 1990), 178.
4 QUA, Norman Rogers Papers, box 2, General Correspondence 1935, ODS to Rogers, 16 October 1935. See also KD, 25 October 1935; H.B. Neatby, *William Lyon Mackenzie King*, vol. 3: *1932–1939, The Prism of Unity* (Toronto: University of Toronto Press 1976), 136; Hilliker, *Canada's Department of External Affairs*, 178.
5 LAC, KP, reel C-3684, J1, vol. 211, 182276, memorandum of ODS, "Outstanding External Questions," 24 October 1935; LAC, DEA Records, RG 25, G1, vol. 1718, file 927, pt. 1, memorandum of ODS, "Application of Sanctions in Italo-Ethiopian Dispute," 26 August 1935.
6 The cabinet meeting of 25 October 1935 is described in King's diary of that date and in C.P. Stacey, *Canada and the Age of Conflict*, vol. 2: *1921–1948, The Mackenzie King Era* (Toronto: University of Toronto Press 1981), 189. The ODS document read by King to his colleagues was a recycled version of "Application of Sanctions in Italo-Ethiopian Dispute."
7 LAC, SP, vol. 4, file 20, note of IS on 29 October 1935 press release, a document printed in Secretary of State for External Affairs, *Documents Relating to the Italo-Ethiopian Conflict* (Ottawa: King's Printer 1936), 165–6. See also KD, 29 October 1935.
8 W.A. Riddell, *World Security by Conference* (Toronto: Ryerson Press 1947), ch. 15. The "hall of fame" comment is in Clara Thomas Archives and Special Collections, York University, W.A. Riddell Papers, vol. 1, Correspondence 1937, ODS to Riddell, 18 April 1937.
9 KP, reel C-3683, J1, vol. 210, 181147–55, Riddell to ODS, 22 October 1935.
10 Hilliker, *Canada's Department of External Affairs*, 179; Robert Bothwell and John English, "'Dirty Work at the Crossroads': New Perspectives on the

Riddell Incident," Canadian Historical Association, *Historical Papers,* 1972, 274–7; KD, 4 November 1935. See also KP, reel C-3683, J1, vol. 210, 181201–2, Riddell to King, 5 November 1935; Riddell Papers, vol. 1, Correspondence 1935, ODS to Riddell, 27 March 1935.

11 National Archives of the United States, Washington, Department of State Records, 611.4231/826, HSC to file, 8 July 1933, and letter of introduction from Canadian high commissioner to U.K. to U.S. secretary of state, 29 January 1933.

12 Ibid., 611.4251/805½, Elliott to Phillips, 12 May 1933, with letter and memoranda by D.A. Skelton, April 1933, and Phillips to Hickerson, 15 May 1933. On Elliott, and for an account of the discussions culminating in the Canada-U.S. trade agreement of 1935, see Marc T. Boucher, "The Politics of Economic Depression: Canadian-American Relations in the Mid-1930s," *International Journal,* 41, 1 (winter 1985–6): 3–36.

13 Department of State Records, 611.4231/1264, Armour to U.S. secretary of state, 4 October 1935. See also ibid., 611.4231/1257, chargé d'affaires to U.S. secretary of state, 23 September 1935; QUA, Isabel Skelton Papers, IS Diary, early October 1935.

14 Franklin Delano Roosevelt Library, Hyde Park, New York, F.D. Roosevelt Papers, PSF, Canada, 1933–1941, Armour to Phillips, 22 October 1935; Department of State Records, 611.4231/1273, Armour to U.S. secretary of state, 17 October 1935, with memorandum of same date and Phillips to Roosevelt, 7 November 1935.

15 Ibid.

16 Department of State Records, 611.4231/1286, Armour to U.S. secretary of state, 25 October 1935, with memorandum of 24 October 1935.

17 KD, 5 November (see also 29 October) 1935; Department of State Records, 611.4231/1318, Armour to U.S. secretary of state, 8 November 1935, with memorandum of 31 October 1935; Boucher, "The Politics of Economic Depression," 31.

18 SP, vol. 4, file 23, IS to her mother, 6 November 1935.

19 KD, 7 November 1935.

20 SP, vol. 4, file 23, ODS to IS, 8 November 1935.

21 Ibid.; KD, 8 November 1935.

22 SP, ODS to IS, 10 November 1935; KD, 29 October and 9 November 1935; Boucher, "The Politics of Economic Depression," 33.

23 ODS to IS, 10 November 1935. See also KD, 12 and 13 November 1935.

24 SP, vol. 4, file 23, ODS to IS, 12, 13, and 16 November 1935; KD, 15 November 1935.

25 ODS to IS, 10 and 16 November 1935.

26 ODS to IS, 10 November 1935.
27 Boucher, "The Politics of Economic Depression," 31 and 35.
28 ODS to IS, 10 and 12 November 1935.
29 SP, vol. 4, file 23, ODS to IS, 25 November 1935; KD, 18, 21, 24, and 28 November 1935.
30 ODS to IS, 25 November 1935; SP, vol. 4, file 23, ODS to IS, 2 December 1935.
31 ODS to Laurent Beaudry, 26 November 1935, in A.I. Inglis, ed., *Documents on Canadian External Relations*, vol. 5: *1931–1935* (Ottawa: Information Canada 1973), 410; See also DEA Records, RG 25, D1, vol. 715, file 1, reel T-1745, memorandum of ODS, "Canada and the Italo-Ethiopian Conflict," [1936]; Bothwell and English, "'Dirty Work at the Crossroads,'" 277; H.B. Neatby Papers, memorandum of ODS, "Hoare's statement of Dec. 5," [December 1935]; ODS to IS, 2 December 1935.
32 Neatby Papers, memorandum of ODS, "Italo-Ethiopian Situation," 11 December 1935; KD, 28 November 1935.
33 KD, 2 December 1935 and 3 August 1936; Hilliker, *Canada's Department of External Affairs*, 180.
34 ODS to IS, 2 December 1935; ODS to Beaudry, 26 November 1935; ODS, "Canada and the Italo-Ethiopian Conflict." On British policy, see David Carleton, *Anthony Eden* (London: Allen Lane 1981), 64–70.
35 SP, vol. 4, file 23, King to ODS, 24 December 1935; KD, 27 and 31 December 1935; ODS to Rogers, 16 October 1935.
36 SP, vol. 13, SD, 1 and 4 January 1936.
37 Ibid., January 1936, passim.
38 SD, 2–10 January 1936; KD, 31 December 1935. See also H.L. Keenleyside, *Memoirs of H.L. Keenleyside*, vol. 1: *Hammer the Golden Day* (Toronto: McClelland and Stewart 1981), 439–52.
39 Roosevelt, "State of the Union Address," 3 January 1936, widely available online.
40 SD, 3 January 1936; Neatby Papers, ODS to Wrong, 7 January 1936.
41 DEA Records, RG 25, D1, vol. 763, file 284, pt. 1–4, reel T-1767 (1936), memorandum of ODS, "Seventeenth Assembly of the League of Nations, Sept. 1936, Part II, Notes on the Proposal, Reconsideration of the Covenant and League Policy," [August] 1936.
42 KP, reels C-4260–1, J4, vol. 165, file 1509, C118006–35, memorandum of ODS, 17 May 1936: Neatby Papers, ODS to Marler, 2 January 1937.
43 KP, reel C-4262, J4, vol. 167, file 1540, C119403, memorandum of ODS, "Re: International Affairs," 29 May 1936; KP, reel C-3694, J1, vol. 228, 196193–6, ODS to Massey, 5 March 1936.

44 KP, reel 4279, J4, vol. 205, file 1964, C141850, memorandum of ODS, "Canada and the Rhineland," [March 1936]; ODS, "Re: International Affairs."

45 KP, reel C-4260, J4, vol. 165, file 1508, C117603, ODS, "Canada and the Italian-Ethiopian Conflict," January 1936.

46 House of Commons, *Debates*, 11 February 1936.

47 This and the three following paragraphs are taken from King's speech in House of Commons, *Debates*, 18 June 1936.

48 SP, vol. 4, file 20, Isabel Skelton note on her proof copy of King's 18 June 1936 address to Parliament. See also Bennett's statement of praise in House of Commons, *Debates*, 18 June 1936.

49 Vincent Massey, *What's Past Is Prologue: The Memoirs of the Right Honourable Vincent Massey* (Toronto: Macmillan 1963), 232–3; F.P. Walters. *A History of the League of Nations* (London: Oxford University Press 1969), 684–8.

50 ODS, "Seventeenth Assembly of the League of Nations, Sept. 1936, Part II, Notes on the Proposal." This paragraph and the four that follow are based on this document.

51 IS Diary, 8 July 1936; KD, 1 July 1936; KP, reel C-4274, J4, vol. 192, file 1745, C134859–64, undated memorandum of ODS, and reel C-3685, J1, 184200, King to Maurice Brasset, 7 July 1936.

52 ODS, "Seventeenth Assembly of the League of Nations, Sept. 1936, Part II, Notes on the Proposal."

53 SP, vol. 4, file 22, ODS to IS, 17 September 1936.

54 Ibid., and undated letter in the same file.

55 SP, vol. 4, file 22, ODS to IS, 18 and 23 September 1936.

56 Walters, *A History of the League of Nations*, 689; LAC, L.B. Pearson Papers, vol. 14, ODS to Pearson, 21 September 1936.

57 ODS to IS, 23 September 1936; Walters, *A History of the League of Nations*, 690.

58 KD, 1 October 1936. See also Walters, *A History of the League of Nations*, 713.

59 SP, vol. 4, file 22, ODS to IS, 28 and 30 September 1936.

60 ODS to IS, 23 September 1936.

61 DEA Records, RG 25, vol. 1779, file 208, memorandum of ODS, 1 September 1936.

62 The King-Skelton speech was printed as *League of Nations Policies: Address at the Seventeenth Session of the Assembly of the League of Nations, 29 September 1936* (Ottawa: King's Printer 1936).

63 SP, vol. 4, file 22, ODS to IS, 30 September and 6 October 1936.

64 SP, vol. 4, file 22, ODS to IS, 12 October 1936.

65 ODS to IS, 6 October 1936.

66 Ibid.

67 Ibid., and SP, vol. 4, file 22, ODS to IS, 8 October 1936.
68 ODS to IS, 30 September, and 8 and 12 October 1936.
69 ODS to IS, 12 October 1936; SP, vol. 4, file 22, ODS to IS, 16 October 1936.
70 ODS to IS, 12 October 1936.
71 ODS to IS, 12 and 16 October 1936.
72 ODS to IS, 16 October 1936.
73 SP, vol. 4, file 22, ODS to IS, 20, 23, and 27 October 1936. See also Douglas Hall (O.D. Skelton), "Jane Austen's Heroines: A Study of Woman's Horizon in 1806," and SP, vol. 11, file 4.
74 ODS to IS, 23 and 27 October 1936.
75 ODS to IS, 23 October 1936.
76 IS Diary, 10 December 1936; KD, 28 November 1936; Neatby, *Prism of Unity*, 183–4.
77 IS Diary, 10 December 1936.
78 Ibid.; KD, 10–11 December 1936.
79 ODS to IS, 16 October 1936.

12. Pretty Well Used Up, 1937–8

1 KD, 5 December 1936 and 28 January and 23 April 1937.
2 KD, 5 December 1936.
3 LAC, SP, vol. 12, SD, 8 December 1936. QUA, Isabel Skelton Papers, ISS, Ottawa *Journal* clipping of 11 February 1937, and undated annotation.
4 PC 17/447, 5 March 1937.
5 SP, vol. 12, SD, 1 January 1937; J.L. Granatstein, *The Ottawa Men: The Civil Service Mandarins, 1935–1957* (Toronto: Oxford University Press 1982), 43–4; H.B. Neatby, *William Lyon Mackenzie King*, vol. 3: *1932–1939, The Prism of Unity* (Toronto: University of Toronto Press 1976), 134.
6 LAC, L.B. Pearson Papers, vol. 1, Diary, 1 January 1936.
7 Churchill College, Cambridge, P.J. Grigg Papers, 2/7/1 (a), Floud to Batterbee, 16 January 1936; Granatstein, *The Ottawa Men*, 120; Granatstein–J. Scott Macdonald interview, 8 September 1978 (transcript provided by Professor Granatstein).
8 Granatstein, *The Ottawa Men*, 81–4; John F. Hilliker, *Canada's Department of External Affairs*, vol. 1: *The Early Years* (Montreal and Kingston, Ont.: McGill-Queen's University Press 1990), 188; Clara Thomas Archives and Special Collections, York University, Walter Riddell Papers, Diary, 6 April 1936; information from L.B. Pearson.
9 KD, 4 February 1937; Hilliker, *Canada's Department of External Affairs*, 182–204.
10 KD, 26 December 1936.

11 See, for example, the final paragraph of LAC, DEA Records, RG 25, D1, vol. 745, file 167, pt. 1–3, memorandum of ODS, "United Kingdom-United States Trade Agreement," 15 April 1937. The "carnivorous animals" comment is with apologies to Frank H. Underhill. See his "Was King Innocent or Statesman?" *Globe and Mail* (Toronto) *Magazine*, 1 January 1966.
12 SP, vol. 4, file 22, King to ODS, 22 December 1936; see also KD, 16 and 26 December 1936.
13 Granatstein, *The Ottawa Men*, 81; SP, vol. 4, file 24, Pearson to ODS, 11 November 1937.
14 Hilliker, *Canada's Department of External Affairs*, 177–9, 182, and 188; LAC, KP, reel C-4255, J4, vol. 154, file 1340, C11118–9, memorandum of ODS, "Canadian External Affairs Service," 16 January 1936.
15 KP, J4, vol. 159, file 1427, memorandum of ODS, 19 December 1936.
16 Hilliker, *Canada's Department of External Affairs*, 188–90; E.A. Kelly, "Diffident Diplomacy: The Expansion of Canadian Diplomatic Representation Abroad, 1930–1939," paper presented at the Annual Meeting of the Canadian Historical Association, Winnipeg, Manitoba, June 1986. See also DEA Records, RG 25, vol. 1843, file 690, memorandum of ODS, "Establishment of Legations in Belgium and Holland," 25 May 1938.
17 Hilliker, *Canada's Department of External Affairs*, 191 and 194; information from J.W. Pickersgill; LAC, MG 30 E151, vol. 6A, file 38, Civil Service of Canada, Third Secretaries (External Affairs Service), competition listing, 21 September 1936, and examinations in essay writing, economics, international affairs, Canadian constitutional law, international law, political science, and modern history.
18 Information from Jean Chapdelaine; LAC, Georges Vanier Papers, vol. 10, folder 1939 XA, ODS to Vanier, 14 February 1939; LAC, J.E. Read Papers, vol. 10, undated Read interview transcript.
19 Roger Bowen's *Innocence Is Not Enough: The Life and Death of Herbert Norman* (Vancouver: Douglas and McIntyre 1986) asserts that Skelton actively recruited Norman. James Barros, in *No Sense of Evil. Espionage: The Case of Herbert Norman* (Toronto: Deneau 1986), contends that Skelton may have been led by his own "youthful" interest in socialism to overlook Norman's communism, and that External Affairs examinations put an emphasis on a knowledge of socialism. None of these arguments is correct. See Norman Hillmer's review of these two books in the *Canadian Historical Review*, 69, 4 (December 1988): 563–5. See also DEA Records, RG 25, vol. 1797, file 1936–1942, Norman to ODS, 1 October 1936, Norman to Keenleyside, 8 October 1936, and Keenleyside to Norman, 13 October 1936.

20 The author made an access request to the Canadian Security Intelligence
   Service for the Featherbed file or other documents relating to Skelton, but
   the response was that "we were unable to locate any record relevant to your
   request" (letter of 5 November 1998). A brief investigation of the Soviet
   Union archives in Moscow by the author failed to turn up anything but perfunctory references to Skelton's position in the government and his famous
   book on socialism. The Featherbed caper is examined in John Sawatsky, *For
   Services Rendered: Leslie James Bennett and the RCMP Security Service* (Toronto
   and Garden City, N.Y.: Doubleday 1982), 253–9; and Reg Whitaker, Gregory
   S. Kealey, and Andrew Parnaby, *Secret Service: Political Policing in Canada from
   the Fenians to Fortress America* (Toronto: University of Toronto Press 2013),
   223–4. The latter book also delivers the best short account of the Herbert
   Norman affair (211–17).
21 Escott Reid, *Radical Mandarin: The Memoirs of Escott Reid* (Toronto: University
   of Toronto Press 1989), 94.
22 On the continuities between Canada's international policies of the inter-
   war years and those of the post-1945 period, see John English, "'A Fine
   Romance': Canada and the United Nations, 1943–1957," in Greg Donaghy,
   ed., *Canada and the Early Cold War, 1943–1957* (Ottawa: Minister of Public
   Works and Government Services Canada 1998), 80–6, and Norman Hillmer,
   "The Foreign Policy That Never Was," in Serge Bernier and John MacFarlane, eds., *Canada, 1900–1950: Un pays prend sa place / A Country Comes of Age*
   (Ottawa: Organization for the History of Canada 2003), 146–7, 151–3.
23 SP, vol. 11, file 8, ODS to F.L. McCluer, 3 April 1937; St Louis *Post-Dispatch*,
   24 August 1932, and unidentified clippings, ISS. Skelton's liberal inter-
   nationalism was not complicated: it was another of his inheritances from
   William Ewart Gladstone. See Robert Kelley, *The Transatlantic Persuasion: The
   Liberal-Democratic Mind in the Age of Gladstone* (New York: Knopf 1969), 235–7.
24 SP, vol. 4, file 24, ODS to "Everybody," 18 March 1937; and vol. 11, file 8,
   ODS to McCluer, 18 February and 12 March 1937, and McCluer to ODS, 12
   March 1937. Also, St Louis *Daily Globe-Democrat*, 19–20 March 1937, and St
   Louis *Post-Dispatch*, 18 March 1937, ISS.
25 ODS to McCluer, 18 February 1937. The quotations in the following sum-
   mary of the Fulton lectures are from the published version: ODS, *Our
   Generation: Its Gains and Losses* (Chicago: University of Chicago Press 1938).
26 St Louis *Daily Globe-Democrat* and Montreal *Star*, 20 March 1937, ISS. Stephen
   Azzi argues against "isolationism" as a description of American and Canadian perspectives and policies in the inter-war years: *Reconcilable Differences:
   A History of Canada-US Relations* (Don Mills, Ont.: Oxford University Press
   2015), 101–2. Historians of the United States have exploded the mythology

of American isolationism in the 1920s, but many readily attach that label to the 1930s. Adam Tooze is an example: *The Deluge: The Great War, America and the Remaking of the Global Order, 1916–1931* (New York: Viking 2014), 348 and 505.

27 KP, reel C-4262, J4, vol. 167, file 1540, memorandum of ODS, 20 March 1936, recycling SP, vol. 4, file 21, memorandum of ODS, "Foreign Policy Discussions in London, 1935," [April] 1935.

28 National Archives of the United States, State Department Records, 841.0, Imperial Conference, 1937–38, Armour to secretary of state, 5 May 1937.

29 KP, reel C-4264, J4, vol. 174, C123278–85, memorandum of ODS, "Imperial Conference 1937," [April] 1937.

30 Ibid.

31 Norman Hillmer, "The Pursuit of Peace: Mackenzie King and the 1937 Imperial Conference," in John English and J.O. Stubbs, eds., *Mackenzie King: Widening the Debate* (Toronto: Macmillan 1978), 153.

32 Memorandum of ODS, 29 March 1937, in James Eayrs, *In Defence of Canada*, vol. 2: *Appeasement and Rearmament* (Toronto: University of Toronto Press 1965), 54.

33 Hillmer, "The Pursuit of Peace," 153; NAUK, CAB 32/127, Imperial Conference 1937, Review of Imperial Defence by the Chiefs of Staff Sub-Committee, 22 February 1937.

34 Memorandum of ODS, "Imperial Conference 1937."

35 KD, 27 March and 15–16 April 1937; Hillmer, "The Pursuit of Peace," 151–2.

36 Ian M. Drummond and Norman Hillmer, *Negotiating Freer Trade: The United Kingdom, the United States, and the Trade Agreements of 1938* (Waterloo, Ont.: Wilfrid Laurier University Press 1989), ch. 3. The key document is DEA Records, RG 25, D1, vol. 745, file 167, pt. 1–3, memorandum of ODS, "United Kingdom-United States Trade Agreement," 15 April 1937.

37 QUA, Isabel Skelton Papers, IS Diary, 15 April 1937; Terry Crowley, *Marriage of Minds: Isabel and Oscar Skelton Reinventing Canada* (Toronto: University of Toronto Press 2003), 220.

38 IS Diary, April and 15 June 1937; KD, 3 and 27 March 1937; L.B. Pearson, *Mike: The Memoirs of the Right Honourable Lester B. Pearson*, vol. 1: *1897–1948* (Toronto: University of Toronto Press 1972), 119–20.

39 IS Diary, May-June 1937; accounts in *Globe and Mail* (Toronto), 12–13 May 1937. The Skeltons' bright red coronation tickets are in SP, vol. 4, file 24.

40 M.H. Halton, "Most Gorgeous Spectacle Ever Known to Man," Toronto *Star*, 13 May 1937.

41 IS Diary, May-June 1937; Montreal *Gazette*, 22 July 1937.

42 University of Toronto Archives, Vincent Massey Papers, B87–0082/326/03, 1937 Guest Lists; Hilliker, *Canada's Department of External Affairs*, 200; Pearson, *Mike*, 116.

43 ODS, *Our Generation*, 52–3; see also "Imperial Conference, 1937: Summary of Proceedings," in Maurice Ollivier, ed. *The Colonial and Imperial Conferences from 1887 to 1937*, 3 vols. (Ottawa: Queen's Printer 1954), 3: 433.

44 ISS, *Financial Post*, 22 May 1937.

45 QUA, John Buchan Papers, box 8, Amery to Buchan (Lord Tweedsmuir, governor general of Canada), 29 May 1937; author's interview with Malcolm MacDonald, University of Canterbury, 12 July 1976.

46 Hilliker, *Canada's Department of External Affairs*, 201; C.P. Stacey, *Canada and the Age of Conflict*, vol. 2: *1921–1948, The Mackenzie King Era* (Toronto: University of Toronto Press 1981), 207–8; Neatby, *Prism of Unity*, 214–15 and 345n.9.

47 H.B. Neatby Papers, ODS to Pickering, 24 June 1937; Eayrs, *In Defence of Canada*, 57–60.

48 ODS to Pickering, 24 June 1937; Eayrs, *In Defence of Canada*, 87–91; Ollivier, *Colonial and Imperial Conferences*, 437–40.

49 King's address on foreign policy is in NAUK, CAB 32/128, Imperial Conference 1937, minutes, mtg. 3 of principal delegates, 21 May 1937. The three-paragraph summary that follows is based on that document.

50 Hilllmer, "The Pursuit of Peace," 163; Stacey, *Canada and the Age of Conflict*, 211.

51 Stacey, *Canada and the Age of Conflict*, 211–13; Neatby, *Prism of Unity*, 222–4.

52 DEA Records, RG 25, D1, vol. 722, file 59, memorandum of ODS, 17 July 1937.

53 W.L.M. King, "Crown and Commonwealth: An Address on the Coronation, the Imperial Conference, and Visit to the Continent of Europe," Canadian Broadcasting Corporation National Network, 19 July 1937; KP, reel C-4262, J4, vol. 167, file 1541, C119666–70, memorandum of ODS, 17 July 1937.

54 DEA Records, RG 25, G1, vol. 1808, file 859-A-36, memorandum of ODS, 28 December 1936; ibid., D1, vol. 718, file 31, pt. 1–2, 1937–1938, memorandum of ODS, 20 April 1937; KP, reel C-3730, J1, vol. 243, 208827–9, ODS to King, 22 December 1937; KD, 20 April 1937; ODS imperial conference speech for King, 21 May 1937.

55 David Fransen, "'Unscrewing the Unscrutable': The Rowell-Sirois Commission, the Ottawa Bureaucracy, and Public Finance Reform, 1935–1941," PhD thesis, University of Toronto, 1984, 12–14, 66–7, 74–6, 87–8, 102–3, 459–60; Doug Owram, *The Government Generation: Canadian Intellectuals and the State*,

1900–1945 (Toronto: University of Toronto Press 1986), 233–52; Crowley, *Marriage of Minds*, 222–3. See also DEA Records, RG 25, D1, vol. 718, file 31, pt. 1–2, 1937–1938, memorandum of ODS, 20 April 1937; IS Diary, 17 January 1937.

56 IS Diary, June-July 1937.
57 Ibid., late May, 13 July 1937; KD, 9 October 1937.
58 IS Diary, 17 September 1937. Compare Crowley, *Marriage of Minds*, 223. On the Hull talks, see SP, vol. 4, file 24, ODS, notes of 27 August 1937, and DEA Records, RG 25, D1, vol. 747, file 167, pt. 8–11, memorandum of ODS, "Visit to Washington re Procedure in Trade Discussions," 30 August 1937.
59 KD, 9 October 1937.
60 KD, 28 October 1937; see also ibid., 16, 21, and 31 October 1937.
61 SP, vol. 4, file 24, Herridge to ODS, 20 October 1937, and Pearson to ODS, 11 November 1937; Vanier Papers, vol. 9, 1937 miscellaneous folder, ODS to Vanier, 22 October 1937.
62 LAC, Escott Reid Papers, vol. 36, file "Skelton," notes by ODS, "Canada and the Commonwealth," December 1937; John D. Meehan, *The Dominion and the Rising Sun: Canada Encounters Japan, 1929–41* (Vancouver: University of British Columbia Press 2004), chs. 6–7; KD, 19 October 1937. See also DEA Records, RG 25, G1, vol. 1819, file 72M, memorandum of ODS for Christie, 17 November 1937; ibid., vol. 1820, file 77D, memorandum of ODS for Read, 22 November 1937.
63 Pearson Papers, vol. 1, Christie to Pearson, 1 December 1937.
64 See, for example, Rex Stout, *The Red Box* (New York, 1937); on Skelton's interest in Wolfe, information from Sheila Skelton Menzies and Arthur Menzies.
65 IS Diary, 16, 19, 25, and 29 November 1937; KD, 20 and 29 November 1937.
66 KD, 6 December 1937.
67 J.L. Granatstein, *A Man of Influence: Norman A. Robertson and Canadian Statecraft, 1929–68* ([Toronto]: Deneau 1981), 53–4; information from James Gibson; KD, 9 December 1937.
68 KP, reel C-3730, J1, vol. 243, 208827–9, ODS to King, 22 December 1937; SP, vol. 4, file 24, King to IS, 11 December 1937. On the Lake Wales house, see KP, J1, vol. 234, 201309–10, King to Mrs G.T. Fulford, 26 November 1937.
69 KD, 14 January 1938.

13. Together and Apart, 1938–9

1 LAC, KP, reel C-4264, J4, vol. 167, file 1541, C119691–704, memorandum of ODS, "Note re Canada's Foreign Policy, Particularly in Relation to the UK,"

[March 1938]; LAC, DEA Records, RG 25, Dl, vol. 715, file 4, part 1–5, ODS draft speech for the prime minister, "Canada and Foreign Policy," 30 March 1938. The first of these documents is a draft of the second.

2 LAC, SP, vol. 13, SD, 20 May 1938.

3 Ibid., 20–24 May 1938. On the Czech crisis of May 1938, see Zara Steiner, *The Triumph of the Dark: European International History 1933–1939* (New York: Oxford University Press 2011), 571–2. See also SP, vol. 5, file 5, ODS to "everybody" in Peterborough, 22 May 1938.

4 SD, 24 May 1938; KD, 24 May 1938. With minor alterations, King's speech was as set out in Skelton's "Canada and Foreign Policy" of 30 March 1938. House of Commons, *Debates*, 24 May 1938.

5 KD, 24 May 1938.

6 Steiner, *The Triumph of the Dark*, 572 and ch. 10.

7 KP, reel C-3736, J1, vol. 255, 217377–84, ODS to Canadian high commissioner in the U.K., 28 June 1938. See also ODS, "Canada and Foreign Policy," and Steiner, *The Triumph of the Dark*, 589.

8 DEA Records, RG 25, D1, vol. 724, file 66 (I-C-215), memorandum of ODS for the prime minister, 12 August 1938; ibid., vol. 1781, file 254, pt. II, memorandum of ODS, 30 November 1937. For a more balanced portrait of inter-war Czechoslovakia and its German minority, see Richard J. Evans, *The Third Reich in Power, 1933–1939* (New York: Penguin 2005), 665–7.

9 Galen Roger Perras, "'Behaving as Adults': External Affairs and North American Security in the 1930s," in Greg Donaghy and Michael K. Carroll, eds., *In the National Interest: Canadian Foreign Policy and the Department of Foreign Affairs and International Trade, 1909–2009* (Calgary, Alta: University of Calgary Press 2011), 39–40; Norman Hillmer and J.L. Granatstein, *For Better or for Worse: Canada and the United States into the Twenty-First Century* (Toronto: Thomson Nelson 2007), 133.

10 KD, 18 August 1938, appending notes of King-Roosevelt conversations of that day; Hillmer and Granatstein, *For Better or for Worse*, 115–16.

11 DEA Records, RG 25, vol. 1873, file 359, memorandum of ODS, "Points to Be Considered re President Roosevelt's Kingston Speech," 19 August 1938.

12 KD, 20 August 1938. The Skelton speech package, in DEA Records, RG 25, vol. 1873, file 359, included his "Points to be Considered" and a L.C. Christie draft speech, "Re President Roosevelt's Kingston Speech," 19 August 1938 (misdated as 1935); the latter document appears to have been based on the former. King had the Woodbridge speech printed alongside Roosevelt's Kingston address in *The United States and Canada: Reciprocity in Defence* (Ottawa: King's Printer 1939); copies of the publication are in KP, reel H-1529, J4, vol. 348, file 3772, C240039–45, and SP, vol. 5, file 5.

13 John A. Munro, ed., *Documents on Canadian External Relations (DCER)*, vol. 6: *1936–1939* (Ottawa: Information Canada 1972), 606–7, "F.D.R. – Kingston – August 18, 1938." This document, like "Points to Be Considered," is unsigned. Both, however, bear Skelton's stamp, and his Roosevelt parable resembles ODS, "A Fable (1938 Model)," [3 October 1938], in DEA Records, RG 25, D1, vol. 726, file 74, pt. 5–7, reel T1750.

14 LAC, L.B. Pearson Papers, vol. 14, Skelton file, 1935–1938, ODS to Pearson, 16 May 1938. See also DEA Records, RG 25, D1, vol. 744, file 163, memorandum of ODS for the prime minister, 13 September 1938.

15 ODS, "Canada and Foreign Policy."

16 QUA, Isabel Skelton Papers, ISS, with stories from the Ottawa *Journal*, Montreal *Gazette*, Vancouver *Province*, and Toronto *Star*, 17–19 August 1938; information from Sheila Skelton Menzies.

17 ISS, August 1938; SP, vol. 5, file 6, clipping from Ottawa *Journal*, 19 August 1938.

18 DEA Records, RG 25, D1, vol. 724, file 66, vol. 1 (I-C-210), memorandum of ODS, "European Situation," 3 September 1938.

19 SP, vol. 5, file 6, ODS to IS, 16 September 1938, and H.B. Neatby, *William Lyon Mackenzie King*, vol. 3: *1932–1939, The Prism of Unity* (Toronto: University of Toronto Press 1976), 287–9. "For the first time in his life," Neatby writes, King "lost hope." The prime minister had a different version of events: see QUA, John Buchan Papers, box 10, King to Buchan (Tweedsmuir), 25 August and 20 September 1938.

20 KD, 12 September 1938.

21 Ibid., 13 September 1938; J.L. Granatstein and Robert Bothwell, "'A Self-Evident National Duty': Canadian Foreign Policy, 1935–1939," *Journal of Imperial and Commonwealth History*, 3, 2 (1975): 221–2. For a King-Rogers clash earlier that year over federal government unemployment policy, with Skelton on the side of the labour minister and an activist state, see James Struthers, *No Fault of Their Own: Unemployment and the Canadian Welfare State, 1914–1941* (Toronto: University of Toronto Press 1983), 175–84.

22 W.A.B. Douglas, *The Official History of the Royal Canadian Air Force*, vol. 2: *The Creation of a National Air Force* (Toronto and Ottawa: University of Toronto Press 1986), 197–202. In 1939 the King government agreed to train a handful of British pilots in Canada.

23 KP, reel C-3736, J1, vol. 255, 217161, note of ODS, 14 September 1938; SP, vol. 5, file 6, ODS to IS, 14 September 1938, and, on "smug," DEA Records, RG 25, D1, vol. 715, file 4, pt. 1–5, memorandum of ODS, "Re Chamberlain's Policy," 14 April 1938.

24 David Reynolds, *Summits: Six Meetings That Shaped the Twentieth Century* (New York: Basic Books 2007), 57–74; SD, 23 September 1938. See also Ian Kershaw, *Hitler, 1936–1945: Nemesis* (London: Penguin 2001), 114.

25 SD, 23 September 1938.

26 Ibid.

27 Ibid., 23–25 September 1938; SP, vol. 5, file 7, memorandum of ODS, 24 September 1938. The Lapointe telegram is in SP, vol. 5, file 7.

28 SD, 26–27 September 1938. The "slaves" comment, delivered by the Czech ambassador in London on 26 September, may be found in Reynolds, *Summits*, 79.

29 SD, 26 September 1938; Reynolds, *Summits*, 83–4. The German air force did not have the capacity to inflict the damage feared by so many Londoners in 1938, but that fact was not known at the time.

30 SD, 3 June and 26 September 1938; H.B. Neatby Papers, memorandum of Christie, "Note on the Canadian Position in the Event of a German-Czech Conflict Involving Great Britain," 8 September 1938; LAC, J.E. Read Papers, vol. 10, undated interview transcript; information from James Gibson.

31 SD, 27 September 1938; Munro, ed., *DCER*, 6: 1097, "Statement by the Prime Minister," 27 September 1938. Chamberlain's warning to Germany in his 27 September speech is in David Dilks, "'We Must Hope for the Best and Prepare for the Worst': The Prime Minister, the Cabinet and Hitler's Germany, 1937–1939," *Proceedings of the British Academy*, 73 (1987): 342. The accounts of the speech in Reynolds, *Summits*, 82–3, and Steiner, *The Triumph of the Dark*, 631, characterize it only as "a plea for peace."

32 SP, vol. 5, file 7, ODS memorandum and draft statement, [27 September 1938].

33 SD, 27 September 1938.

34 Ibid., 28 September 1938.

35 Ibid., 30 September 1938; DEA Records, RG 25, G1, vol. 1782, file 254, pt. VI, memorandum of ODS, "After the Munich Agreement," 3 October 1938. For the terms of the Munich settlement, see Steiner, *The Triumph of the Dark*, 639–40.

36 ODS, "After the Munich Agreement"; SD, 30 September 1938; ODS to Vincent Massey, 8 October 1938, in Terry Crowley, *Marriage of Minds: Isabel and Oscar Skelton Reinventing Canada* (Toronto: University of Toronto Press 2003), 239.

37 ODS, "After the Munich Agreement."

38 ODS, "A Fable (1938 Model)"; QUA, Isabel Skelton Papers, IS Diary, 3–4 October 1938.

39 ISS, Ottawa *Journal*, 10 October 1938, and unidentified Canadian Press report of 11 October 1938; KD, 11 October 1938.

40 KD, 24 October 1938, and, for the King-Skelton trip south, ibid., 11 October–7 November 1938.

41 Ibid., 14 November 1938.

42 The Cambridge-Beaches brochure is in SP, vol. 5, file 5. The "lords" comment is from KD, 17 October 1938. On anti-Semitism in Bermuda, see Duncan McDowall, *Another World: Bermuda and the Rise of Modern Tourism* (London and Basingstoke, U.K.: Macmillan 1999), 128–9.

43 Irving Abella and Harold Troper, *None Is Too Many: Canada and the Jews of Europe, 1933–1948* (Toronto: Lester and Orpen Dennys 1982), 15, 22, and 27; LAC, W.L. Grant Papers, vol. 9, Skelton file, ODS to Grant, 3 February 1934.

44 J.L. Granatstein, *A Man of Influence: Norman A. Robertson and Canadian Statecraft, 1929–68* ([Toronto]: Deneau 1981), ch. 3; Ian M. Drummond and Norman Hillmer, *Negotiating Freer Trade: The United Kingdom, the United States, Canada, and the Trade Agreements of 1938* (Waterloo, Ont.: Wilfrid Laurier University Press 1989), especially 124, 162, and, for Skelton's top hat, Plate 7.

45 DEA Records, RG 25, D1, vol. 754, file 235 (II-B-76), memorandum of ODS, "Canadian Defence," 14 November 1938. See also ODS, "Canada and Foreign Policy," and, on defence policy in the late 1930s, Roger Sarty, "Mr. King and the Armed Forces," in Norman Hillmer, Robert Bothwell, Roger Sarty, and Claude Beauregard, eds., *A Country of Limitations: Canada and the World in 1939* (Ottawa: Canadian Committee for the History of the Second World War 1996), 217–46.

46 KD, 18 January and 24 October 1938.

47 Stephen J. Harris, *Canadian Brass: The Making of a Professional Army, 1860–1939* (Toronto: University of Toronto Press 1988), 160–6 and 183–6; Paul Douglas Dickson, *A Thoroughly Canadian General: A Biography of General H.D.G. Crerar* (Toronto: University of Toronto Press 2007), 81, 102–3, and 106–8; Norman Hillmer, "Defence and Ideology: The Anglo-Canadian Military 'Alliance' in the Nineteen Thirties," *International Journal*, 33, 3 (summer 1978): 588–612.

48 House of Commons, *Debates*, 16 January 1939; KD, 26 January 1939; H.B. Neatby Papers, memorandum of ODS, 30 January 1939; Steiner, *The Triumph of the Dark*, 671 and 721–4. Professor Neatby's *Prism of Unity*, 296–7, makes plain the intent of King's speech.

49 SP, vol. 13, SD, 2 February 1939.

50 Ibid.; KD, 27 January 1939.

51 KD, 27 January 1939.

52 Ibid.
53 Ibid; SD, 2 February 1939.
54 Ibid. For Skelton's nuanced view of the Hitler speech of 30 January 1938, sce DEA Records, RG 25, vol. 1832, file 277, pt. A, ODS to chargé d'affaires, Canadian Legation in France, 8 February 1939.
55 SD, 2 February 1939.
56 LAC, H.H. Wrong Papers, vol. 3, file 17, ODS to Wrong, 2 and 4 March 1939, the latter letter enclosing memorandum of ODS, "Automatic Belligerency," [February 1939]. Further details, and information on the supporters of Skelton's position on this issue, may be found in Norman Hillmer, ed., *O.D. Skelton: The Work of the World, 1923–1941* (Montreal and Kingston, Ont.: McGill-Queen's University Press; and Toronto: Champlain Society; both editions 2013), ch. 21. See also KD, 27 January 1939, and Neatby, *Prism of Unity*, 297.
57 DEA Records, RG 25, vol. 726, file 74, pt. 5–7, reel T-1750, 87–8, pp. 1–2, memorandum of ODS, "European Situation," 9 March 1939; Steiner, *The Triumph of the Dark*, 725–7 and 733; Pearson Papers, vol. 14, Skelton file, 1939–1941, ODS to Pearson, 6 February and 9 March 1939. For Canadian newspaper opinion, see Nicole Marion, "Evaluating an 'Unspeakable Horror': The Discourse on War in Canadian Newspapers in the Face of the 1938–1939 Czechoslovakian Crises" (MA thesis, University of Ottawa, 2011), 34 and 47–8, and Terry Copp, "Ontario 1939: The Decision for War," in Hillmer, Bothwell, Sarty, and Beauregard, eds., *A Country of Limitations*, 113–16.
58 DEA Records, RG 25, D1, vol. 715, file 4, pt. 1–5, reel T-1745, memorandum of ODS, "As to a Statement on the International Position," 20 March 1939.
59 Ibid., attachments; Neatby, *Prism of Unity*, 298–9; House of Commons, *Debates*, 20 March 1939; Hillmer, *Work of the World*, 392–400.
60 ODS, "Automatic Belligerency."

14. Half-Day's Work Nearly Done, 1939–41

1 LAC, SP, vol. 13, SD, 30 May 1938; QUA, Isabel Skelton Papers, IS Diary, February-March 1939; information from Sheila Skelton Menzies; Terry Crowley, *Marriage of Minds: Isabel and Oscar Skelton Reinventing Canada* (Toronto: University of Toronto Press 2003), 226.
2 Information from Sheila Skelton Menzies and J.W. Pickersgill.
3 IS Diary, 15 and 18 March 1939; ODS speech for King, House of Commons, *Debates*, 30 March 1939; LAC, KP, reel C-4263, J4, vol. 170, file 1561, C120881–6, memorandum of ODS, 22 March 1939.
4 LAC, DEA Records, RG 25, Dl, vol. 715, file 4, pt. 1–5, memorandum of ODS, "Notes for a Statement on Foreign Affairs," 18 March 1939.

5 Ibid.

6 KD, 22, 25, and 28–29 March 1939; H.B Neatby, *William Lyon Mackenzie King,
   1932–1939: The Prism of Unity* (Toronto: University of Toronto Press 1976),
   299–300; John T. Saywell, *'Just Call Me Mitch': The Life of Mitchell F. Hepburn*
   (Toronto: University of Toronto Press 1991), 419–20.

7 House of Commons, *Debates*, 30 March 1939; Neatby, *Prism of Unity*, 300–2;
   C.P. Stacey, *Canada and the Age of Conflict*, vol. 2: *1921–1948, The Mackenzie
   King Era* (Toronto: University of Toronto Press 1981), 242–3; J.L. Granat-
   stein and J.M. Hitsman, *Broken Promises: A History of Conscription in Canada*
   (Toronto: Oxford University Press 1977), 127.

8 KD, 26–30 March 1939; IS Diary, 30 March 1939. Isabel Skelton's copy of the
   30 March Mackenzie King speech is in SP, vol. 5, file 13.

9 House of Commons, *Debates*, 30 March 1939.

10 Ibid.

11 KD, 29 March, 14, 15, 27, and 28 April and 23 June 1939.

12 KD, 25 April 1939; memorandum of ODS, 22 March 1939; DEA Records,
   RG 25, vol. 726, file 74, pt. 5–7, reel T-1750, rp.108–114, memorandum of
   ODS, 14 April 1939.

13 SP, vol. 5, file 12, memorandum of ODS, "Developments in the European
   Situation since March 31st," 10 May 1939; DEA Records, RG 25, vol. 726,
   file 74, pt. 5–7, reel T-1750, rp.123–64, memorandum of ODS, 19 July
   1939.

14 ODS, "Developments in the European Situation since March 31st," and DEA
   Records, RG 25, vol. 726, file 74, pt. 5–7, reel T-1750, memorandum of ODS,
   "The New British Policy in Europe," 12 April 1939 (identified in John A.
   Munro, ed. *Documents on Canadian External Relations* [*DCER*], vol. 6: *1936–
   1939* [Ottawa: Information Canada 1972], 1155–64, as written by Loring
   Christie but bearing Skelton's turns of phrase, handwriting, and initials).
   See also Zara Steiner, *The Triumph of the Dark: European International History
   1933–1939* (New York: Oxford University Press 2011), ch. 16.

15 ODS, "Developments in the European Situation since March 31st."

16 DEA Records, RG 25, D1, vol. 721, file 47, ODS to King, 10 March 1939;
   Munro, ed., *DCER*, 6: 1137–8, memorandum of ODS, "British Expeditionary
   Force," 10 March 1939.

17 H.B. Neatby Papers, memorandum of ODS, "Defence," 15 April 1939; DEA
   Records, RG 25, D1, vol. 755, file 241, memorandum of ODS, "British Munitions Orders," 16 August 39.

18 DEA Records, RG 25, vol. 1880, file 1938, 767-B-38, ODS to D'Arcy Mc-
   Greer, 23 May 1939; ibid., vol. 726, file 74, pt. 5–7, reel T-1750, rp. 335, p.
   1, ODS to Arnold Heeney, 23 May 1939; SP, vol. 5, file 13, King to ODS, 3

July and reply of 12 July 1939. See also Neatby, *Prism of Unity*, 310–14, and
Stacey, *Canada and the Age of Conflict*, 243–8. For Charles Ritchie's memory
of the royal tour, see Thomas Fisher Rare Book Library, University of Toronto, Ritchie Diaries, 18 March 1941. Cited with the permission of Judith
Robinson.

19 DEA Records, RG 25, D1, vol. 726, file 74, reel T-1750, 561–73, memorandum of ODS, "Confidential," [10 September 1939]. The "siphon" reference
is in ODS, *The Day of Sir Wilfrid Laurier: A Chronicle of Our Own Times* (Toronto: Glasgow, Brook 1916), 288–9.

20 Irving Abella and Harold Troper, *None Is Too Many: Canada and the Jews of
Europe, 1933–1948* (Toronto: Lester and Orpen Dennys 1982), 63–4.

21 Thomas Fisher Rare Book Library, George Wrong Papers, box 3, ODS file,
ODS to Wrong, 23 June 1939. Wrong's reply of 28 June 1939 and other doc-
uments relating to the *St. Louis* can be found in KP, J1, vol. 280, 237087ff.
On Palestine, see KP, reel C-4277, J4, vol. 199, C138735–6, memorandum of
ODS, 12 May 1939.

22 DEA Records, RG 25, reel T-1750, vol. 726, file 74, pt. 5–7, rp. 123–64,
memorandum of ODS, "The European Situation: Developments from Mid-
May to Mid-July," 19 July 1939.

23 Norman Hillmer, "Canada and the 'Godless Country,' 1930–1939," in David
Davies, ed., *Canada and the Soviet Experiment: Essays on Canadian Encounters
with Russia and the Soviet Union, 1900–1991* (Toronto: Canadian Scholars'
Press 1994), 64 and 67; ODS, "The European Situation: Developments
from Mid-May to Mid-July"; DEA Records, RG 25, vol. 1782, file 254, pt. IX,
ODS to Arnold Heeney, 3 June 1939; ibid., vol. 1909, file 643, ODS to Nick
Ignatieff, 28 July 1939; NAUK, DO 114/98, "International Situation Leading
to the Outbreak of War, Correspondence, March-September, 1939," British
high commissioner in Canada to Dominions Office, 28 March and 27 April
1939.

24 "International Situation Leading to the Outbreak of War," introduction and
documents on 5–7, 9–10, and 12; ODS, "The New British Policy in Europe";
Kent Fedorowich, "Sir Gerald Campbell and the British High Commission
in Wartime Ottawa, 1938–1940," *War in History*, 18, 3 (2011): 361–5; J.L.
Granatstein and Robert Bothwell, "'A Self-Evident National Duty': Canadian
Foreign Policy, 1935–1939," *Journal of Imperial and Commonwealth History*, 3, 2
(1975): 226–8.

25 DEA Records, RG 25, vol. 726, file 74, pt. 5–7, reel T-1750, memorandum of
ODS, "Danzig Coup," 5 July 1939. On Danzig, see Richard Overy, *The Road
to War* (with Andrew Wheatcroft; Toronto: Stoddart 1989), 1–20 (the "living
space" quotation is on 16), and Steiner, *The Triumph of the Dark*, 838–44.

26 DEA Records, RG 25, vol. 1783, file 1936–254, pt. X, ODS draft letter, 5 July
    1939, and ODS to Massey, 26 July 1939. "Massey saw international develop-
    ments through English eyes": Claude Bissell, *The Imperial Canadian: Vincent
    Massey in Office* (Toronto: University of Toronto Press 1986), 80.
27 KP, reel H-1554, J4, vol. 393, file 42, C276609–10, memorandum of ODS,
    22 August 1939; SP, vol. 5, file 12, memorandum of ODS, "Canada and the
    Polish War," 25 August 1939; Hillmer, "Canada and the 'Godless Country,'"
    69; DO 114/98, British high commissioner in Canada to Dominions Office,
    23 August 1939.
28 ODS, memorandum of 22 August 1939 and "Canada and the Polish War."
29 This paragraph owes much to David Dilks, "'We Must Hope for the Best
    and Prepare for the Worst': The Prime Minister, the Cabinet and Hitler's
    Germany, 1937–1939," *Proceedings of the British Academy*, 73 (1987): 337–47.
    In this and other works, Professor Dilks eloquently defends Chamberlain
    and his policies. R.A.C. Parker provides quite another view in *Chamberlain
    and Appeasement: British Policy and the Coming of the Second World War* (London
    and Basingstoke, U.K.: Macmillan 1993).
30 KP, reel H-1555, J4, vol. 395, file 52, C27830–5, memorandum of ODS, "Ca-
    nadian War Policy," with handwritten note of the prime minister, 24 August
    1939; KD, 24 August 1939; memorandum of ODS, 22 August 1939; DEA
    Records, RG 25, reel T-1750, vol. 726, file 74, pt. 5–7, 166–7, memorandum
    of ODS, "European Situation. Aug. 22, 1939."
31 ODS, "Canada and the Polish War"; information from J.W. Pickersgill. See
    also Overy, *The Road to War*, 17–20, and, on King's speech of 8 September
    1939, Bruce Hutchison, *The Incredible Canadian: A Candid Portrait of Mack-
    enzie King, His Works, His Times, and His Nation* (Toronto: Longmans 1953),
    251–5.
32 DO 114/98, Campbell to Dominions Office, 20 September 1939.
33 ODS, "Canada and the Polish War." See also LAC, H.H. Wrong Papers, vol.
    3, file 17, ODS to Wrong, 2 and 4 March 1939, the latter letter enclosing
    memorandum of ODS, "Automatic Belligerency," [February 1939].
34 Wilfrid Eggleston, *While I Still Remember: A Personal Record* (Toronto: Ryerson
    Press 1968), 253–4.
35 ODS, "Confidential."
36 Ibid.
37 Ibid. See also KP, reel C-4281, J4, vol. 211, file 2011, C144802, memoran-
    dum of ODS, "Recent Developments in Sino-Japanese Conflict," 7 January
    1939.
38 ODS, "Canada and the Polish War," and Norman Hillmer, "O.D. Skelton:
    Innovating for Independence," in Greg Donaghy and Kim Richard Nossal,

eds. *Architects and Innovators: Building the Department of External Affairs and International Trade, 1909–2009* (Montreal and Kingston, Ont.: School of Policy Studies, Queen's University / McGill-Queen's University Press 2009), 69.

39 IS Diary, 26 March and 1–16 September 1939. On 12 April 1951 McKenzie noted at the top of Skelton's "Confidential" memorandum: "There is no indication that this went to anybody." Information from Pickersgill and James Gibson also contributed to the author's assessment.

40 KD, 6 January 1942; QUA, Grant Dexter Papers, box 2, file 16, memorandum of 12 July 1939; IS Diary, 7 May and 1 August 1939. On Rogers' longstanding interest in External Affairs, see Rhodes House Library, Oxford, Rhodes Scholars' Files, Norman Rogers file, Rogers to F.J. Wylie, 7 August 1927.

41 ODS, "Canada and the Polish War"; Hutchison, *The Incredible Canadian*, 250–1. King told the same story to another journalist, Max Freedman: Dexter Papers, box 5, July-December 1949 Correspondence, memorandum of Freedman, July 1949.

42 John F. Hilliker, *Canada's Department of External Affairs*, vol. 1: *The Early Years, 1909–1946* (Montreal and Kingston, Ont.: McGill-Queen's University Press 1990), 218.

43 LAC, J.W. Pickersgill Papers, vol. 3, "Canada's War Effort, Part 1," memorandum of ODS, 23 October 1939; Stacey, *Canada and the Age of Conflict*, 276–7, and, generally, Norman Hillmer, ed., *O.D. Skelton: The Work of the World, 1923–1941* (Montreal and Kingston, Ont.: McGill-Queen's University Press; and Toronto: Champlain Society; both editions 2013), ch. 24.

44 DEA Records, reel T-1809, RG 25, D1, vol. 805, file 573, memorandum of ODS, 30 September 1940; William Kaplan, *State and Salvation: The Jehovah's Witnesses and Their Fight for Civil Rights* (Toronto: University of Toronto Press 1989), 31–44; KP, reel C-4249, J4, vol. 230, file 2218, C155901–3, memorandum of ODS, "Subversive Activities," 13 December 1939.

45 IS Diary, 3 December 1939. See also Hilliker, *Canada's Department of External Affairs*, 218–19 and 221.

46 KP, reel H-1548, J4, vol. 382, file 1, C267906, ODS mock communiqué on air training, 1 October 1939; KD, 28 September 1939; Stacey, *Canada and the Age of Conflict*, 271–3; ODS, "Canadian War Policy."

47 W.A.B. Douglas, *The Official History of the Royal Canadian Air Force*, vol. 2: *The Creation of a National Air Force* (Toronto and Ottawa: University of Toronto Press 1986), 206 and ch. 5; Stacey, *Canada and the Age of Conflict*, 296.

48 SP, vol. 5, file 14, ODS to King, 27 March 1940; Saywell, *'Just Call Me Mitch,'* 435–8; John MacFarlane, *Ernest Lapointe and Quebec's Influence on Canadian Foreign Policy* (Toronto: University of Toronto Press 1999), 152–8.

49 KD, 19 January and 27 March 1940; J.L. Granatstein, *Canada's War: The Politics of the Mackenzie King Government, 1939–1945* (Toronto: Oxford University Press 1975), 76–92.

50 KP, reel C-4575, J1, vol. 297, 252108–9, ODS to King, 27 March 1940 (draft in SP, vol. 5, file 14).

51 DEA Records, reel T-1791, RG 25, D1, vol. 774, file 353, memorandum of ODS, "The Present Outlook," 30 April 1940. The reference to Mussolini's itchy hands is taken from Ian Kershaw, *Fateful Choices: Ten Decisions That Changed the World, 1940–1941* (New York: Penguin 2007), 150.

52 SP, vol. 5, file 14, ODS to IS and her mother, 30 May 1940. On the rationale of the German decision not to attack the Anglo-French armies at Dunkirk immediately, see P.M.H. Bell, *Twelve Turning Points of the Second World War* (New Haven, Conn., and London: Yale University Press 2011), 7; David Dilks, *"The Great Dominion": Winston Churchill in Canada, 1900–1954* (Toronto: Thomas Allen 2005), 138, comments on the legend of Dunkirk.

53 ODS draft telegram of 29 May 1940, in "Drafts of Messages to Mr. Churchill," 28–30 May 1940, KP, reel H-1558, J4, vol. 400, file 75, C281990–282026; KD, 24 May 1940. On Ottawa's transformation after the fall of France, see Hector Mackenzie, "Sinews of War and Peace: The Politics of Economic Aid to Britain, 1939–1945," *International Journal*, 54, 4 (1999): 648–70.

54 Granatstein, *Canada's War*, 117–28; ODS, "The Present Outlook." The report of the Group of Twenty Canadians, "A Programme of Immediate Canadian Action," along with other information in this paragraph, was supplied to the author by J.W. Pickersgill, one of the Group of Twenty.

55 Note of ODS to King, in David R. Murray, ed. *Documents on Canadian External Relations*, vol. 8: *1939–1941*, pt. II (Ottawa: Minister of Supply and Services Canada 1976), 134. For the establishment and early period of the PJBD, see C.P. Stacey, *Arms, Men, and Governments: The War Policies of Canada, 1939–1945* (Ottawa: Queen's Printer 1970), 336–54.

56 KP, reel H-1549, J4, vol. 384, file 9, C269593 and C269595, and vol. 410, file 7, C282287: memoranda of ODS, 22 August 1940, and British high commissioner to Canada to ODS, 2 September 1940; David MacKenzie, *Inside the Atlantic Triangle: Canada and the Entrance of Newfoundland into Confederation, 1939–1949* (Toronto: University of Toronto Press 1986), ch. 3; Peter Neary, *Newfoundland in the North Atlantic World, 1929–1949* (Montreal and Kingston, Ont.: McGill-Queen's University Press 1988), ch. 5. See also H.L. Keenleyside, *Memoirs of H.L. Keenleyside*, vol. 2: *On the Bridge of Time* (Toronto: McClelland and Stewart 1982), 54.

57 KP, reel C-4575, J1, vol. 297, 252163, ODS to Mackenzie King, 17 December 1940. For King's moveable attitudes towards Churchill, see C.P. Stacey, *Mackenzie King and the Atlantic Triangle* (Toronto: Macmillan 1976), 52–3.

58 KP, reel H-1522, J4, vol. 332, file 3544, C229398, memorandum of ODS, 2 January 1941; LAC, RG 32, vol. 327, file 1227, J.H. Kelly personnel file, McCloskey to Kelly, 6 February 1941; Crowley, *Marriage of Minds*, 255; IS Diary, 1, 3, and 4 January 1941.

59 IS Diary, 3, 6, 12, 14, 16, 18, 25–26 January and 22 February 1941; Crowley, *Marriage of Minds*, 254–5; Doug Owram, *The Government Generation: Canadian Intellectuals and the State, 1900–1945* (Toronto: University of Toronto Press 1986), 277–8; McCloskey to Kelly, 6 February 1941. ODS was involved in two St Lawrence agreements: the 1932 treaty and the 1941 executive accord that would come shortly after his death. Both failed to gain the approval of the U.S. Congress. Although a proponent of the integration represented by the St Lawrence megaproject, Skelton at times advocated an all-Canadian seaway rather than a bilateral waterway. Daniel Macfarlane, *Negotiating a River: Canada, the U.S., and the Creation of the St. Lawrence Seaway* (Vancouver: University of British Columbia Press 2014), ch. 1.

60 McCloskey to Kelly, 6 February 1941; Montreal *Standard*, 25 January 1941; IS Diary, 28 January 1941; KD, 28 January 1941.

61 Crowley, *Marriage of Minds*, 255–6; IS Diary, 28 January 1941; Ottawa *Journal*, 28 January 1941.

62 KD, 30 January 1941; Ottawa *Citizen*, 31 January 1941.

63 KD, 28 January 1941. Sympathy letters to and responses from the prime minister are in KP, J4, vol. 332, file 3544; condolence messages to Isabel Skelton are contained in SP, vol. 5, files 16–20, and vol. 6, files 1–3. The "friend" remark is in DO 35/591/G162/1, King to W.C. Hankinson, 29 January 1941.

64 LAC, L.B. Pearson Papers, vol. 13, N.A. Robertson, 1936–1941 file, Robertson to Pearson, 30 January 1941, and reply, 4 March 1941; Robert A. Wardhaugh, with Douglas MacEwan and William Johnston, *Behind the Scenes: The Life and Work of William Clifford Clark* (Toronto: University of Toronto Press 2010), 195–6; information from J.W. Pickersgill.

65 Granatstein, *Canada's War*, 419–24.

Conclusion

1 Grant Dexter, "Oscar Douglas Skelton," *QQ*, 48, 1 (1941): 1–6, and "Irreparable Loss," Winnipeg *Free Press*, 29 January 1941.

2 Ibid.
3 KD, 28 January 1941.
4 Elizabeth Hay was very helpful in the writing of this paragraph. Smuts's comment about "doing good by stealth" is in NAUK, CAB 32/9, 1923 Imperial Conference minutes, plenary meeting 15, 6 November 1923; for the context, see Norman Hillmer "Mackenzie King, Canadian Air Policy and the Imperial Conference of 1923," *High Flight*, 1, 5 (1981): 189–93, 196.
5 On Skelton as "an English-Canadian example of French-Canadian perceptions," see P.B. Waite. "French-Canadian Isolationism and English Canada: An Elliptical Foreign Policy, 1935–1939," *Journal of Canadian Studies*, 18, 2 (1983): 145. The chargé d'affaires at the U.S. Legation characterized Skelton thus the week after his death: "An exponent of the North American as contrasted with the colonial point of view, he was a great patriot and staunch friend of the United States." National Archives of the United States, State Department Records, RG 59, box 4883, 842.00, PR/195, J.F. Simmons to secretary of state, 5 February 1941. In the early spring of 1941, Mackenzie King reflected on the widespread impression that Skelton had been anti-British, "which is not true. He was strongly pro-Canadian." KD, 5 April 1941.
6 LAC, H.H. Wrong Papers, vol. 3, file 17, memorandum of ODS, "Automatic Belligerency," [February 1939].
7 Norman Hillmer, "O.D. Skelton and the North American Mind," *International Journal*, 60, 1 (2004–5): 108–9. Stacey's comment is in his *Arms, Men, and Governments: The War Policies of Canada, 1939–1945* (Ottawa: Queen's Printer 1970), 37. Hillmer differs in "O.D. Skelton: Innovating for Independence," in Greg Donaghy and Kim Richard Nossal, eds., *Architects and Innovators: Building the Department of External Affairs and International Trade, 1909–2009* (Montreal and Kingston, Ont.: School of Policy Studies, Queen's University / McGill-Queen's University Press 2009), 68–71.
8 For an example of this tendency in the scholarship of Canadian foreign policy, see Michael Hart, *From Pride to Influence: Towards a New Canadian Foreign Policy* (Vancouver: University of British Columbia Press 2008), 78. Norman Hillmer makes the counter-argument in "O.D. Skelton: Innovating for Independence," 71–3.

Archival Sources

Library and Archives Canada, Ottawa
Oscar Douglas Skelton Papers
William Lyon Mackenzie King Papers
Canadian Political Science Association Records
Civil Service Commission Records
Department of External Affairs Records
Department of National Defence Records
Privy Council Records
R.B. Bennett Papers
Loring Christie Papers
J.W. Dafoe Papers
A.G. Doughty Papers
W.C. Good Papers
Lomer Gouin Papers
W.L. Grant Papers
H.L. Keenleyside Papers
Ernest Lapointe Papers
Wilfrid Laurier Papers
Agnes Macphail Papers
Charles Murphy Papers
L.B. Pearson Papers
J.W. Pickersgill Papers
Joseph Pope Papers
John Erskine Read Papers
Escott Reid Papers
Norman A. Robertson Papers
Newton Rowell Papers

Adam Shortt Papers
Charles Sissons Papers
Georges Vanier Papers
Hume H. Wrong Papers

Queen's University Archives, Kingston, Ontario
Board of Trustees Records of Queen's University
Personnel Records of Queen's University
Principal's Office Records, Queen's University
Student Register, Queen's University
John Buchan Papers
Grant Dexter Papers
W.A. Mackintosh Papers
Norman Rogers Papers
Adam Shortt Papers
Isabel Skelton Papers

National Archives of the United Kingdom, Kew
Board of Trade Records
Cabinet Office Records
Dominions Office Records
Foreign Office Records

University of Toronto Archives
J. Burgon Bickersteth Papers
Vincent Massey Papers

Thomas Fisher Rare Book Library, University of Toronto
James Mavor Papers
Charles Ritchie Diaries
George Wrong Papers

Clara Thomas Archives and Special Collections,
York University, Toronto
Walter Riddell Papers

Archives of Ontario, Toronto
James Whitney Papers

*Department of Foreign Affairs, Trade
and Development, Ottawa*
Historical Section Records

North York Central Library, Toronto
John A. Cooper Papers

National Archives of the United States, Washington, D.C.
Department of State Records

Franklin Delano Roosevelt Library, Hyde Park, New York
F.D. Roosevelt Papers

Cambridge University Library
Stanley Baldwin Papers

Churchill College, Cambridge
Leopold Amery Papers
P.J. Grigg Papers
Maurice Hankey Papers

Bodleian Library, Oxford
Round Table Papers

Rhodes House Library, Oxford
Rhodes Scholars' Files

British Library, London
India Office Records

Institute of Commonwealth Studies, University of London
Richard Jebb Papers
Stephen Tallents Papers

National Archives of Scotland, Edinburgh
Lothian Papers

National Archives of the Republic of Ireland, Dublin
Department of External Affairs Records

University College Dublin Archives
  Ernest Blythe Papers
  P.J. McGilligan Papers

Archives du Ministère des Affaires Étrangères, Paris
  Fonds de la Correspondence Politique et Commerciale

In Private Hands
  George D. Ferguson Papers
  H.B. Neatby Papers

Index

93, 99, 102, 182, 220, 289, 294, 302, 334;
relocation of Japanese Canadians, 322;
war-manufacturing industries, 56
Canada-France trade agreement, 217
Canada House, 246, 252, 270, 272. *See also*
Canadian High Commission (London)
Canada-U.S. relations: Canadian-American
smuggling conference, 166; continental defence, 285–7, 299, 326–7; King's
concern over dependence on U.S., 297,
319; Skelton's understanding of, 11,
13, 23, 39, 48, 96, 168, 238, 274, 333–4;
undefended border, 146, 177. *See also*
Canada-U.S. trade agreements; International Joint Commission; Ogdensburg
Declaration
Canada-U.S. trade agreement (1911),
36–8, 71, 232. *See also* Laurier, Wilfrid
Canada-U.S. trade agreement (1935):
American advantages, 233; Armistice
Day announcement, 231–2; King's election promise, 227–9; opposition to, 232;
Sandy Skelton on need for, 196; Skelton
as trade expert, 229–30, 278
Canada-U.S.-U.K. trade agreements
(1938), 269–70, 298–9
Canadian autonomy: autonomy vs independence, 7, 74; growth of, 78, 97, 114,
157; independent foreign policy, 12–13,
43, 73–5, 95–9, 104–5, 113–14, 118,
134, 158–9, 212, 218, 220, 260, 262, 266,
282–3, 304, 315, 317, 329, 332, 334;
national defence, 34, 238, 261, 269, 274,
286–7, 299–301, 311, 321; participation
in European wars, 268–9, 282, 291, 293,
302, 303–6, 335. *See also* Canadian diplomatic missions; North Americanism;
Statute of Westminster
Canadian Bank of Commerce, 77
Canadian Bankers' Association, 77, 85, 97
Canadian Broadcasting Corporation
(CBC), 258
Canadian citizenship, 182
Canadian Club: Skelton remarks about
Borden, 75–6, 112; Skelton speeches on
Canadian autonomy, 12, 73–4, 91–2
Canadian Council of Agriculture, 62, 105
Canadian diplomatic missions: calls for ex-
pansion, 13, 134, 159, 167–8, 189, 219;

democratization of, 162, 166, 272; need
for independent sources of intelligence,
314, 334; presentation of credentials,
169; uniforms, 161. *See also* Canadian
High Commission (London); Canadian
Legations; Riddell, Walter A.
Canadian High Commission (London),
81, 166, 200, 212, 260, 290,
312–13, 329
Canadian League, 44, 80, 349n43. *See also*
Canadian National League
Canadian Legation (Paris), 167–8, 177,
189, 212, 246, 251–2, 260
Canadian Legation (Tokyo), 167–9, 189,
206, 212, 260, 312
Canadian Legation (Washington), 160–2,
167–8, 189–90, 212, 224, 230, 260
Canadian Manufacturers' Association
(CMA), 197, 228, 232, 311
Canadian military: preparations for world
war, 299–300
Canadian National League, 38. *See also*
Canadian League
Canadian navy, 34, 43–6, 94, 300; opposi-
tion from Quebec, 38
Canadian Pacific Railway (CPR), 45, 139
Canadian Pacific Steamship Lines, 245
Canadian Political Science Association
(CPSA), 49, 67, 77, 99, 192–3
Cardin, Arthur, 302
Careless, J.M.S., 8
Cassin, René, 250
Chamberlain, Austen, 170, 173
Chamberlain, Neville: chancellor of the ex-
chequer, 197–8, 229; handling of Czech
crisis, 284, 290–3, 295, 306; resignation,
324; Skelton's opinion of, 295–6, 303,
314–16; suspicion of Soviets, 310, 313
Chanak crisis (1922), 86, 95. *See also*
Turkey
Chapdelaine, Jean, 261, 262
Chiang Kai-shek, 244
China: Canadian diplomatic representa-
tion in, 189, 219, 381n41; Japanese
aggression against, 239, 244, 279, 282.
See also Manchurian crisis
Chittick, V.L.O., 79
Chown, G.Y., 60
Christie, Agatha, 193